Organized Labor
and the Black Worker
1619–1981

Organized Labor
and the Black Worker
1619–1981

Philip S. Foner

Haymarket Books
Chicago, Illinois

Originally published in 1974 by Praeger Publishers
Second edition published in 1981 by International Publishers

This edition published in 2017 by
Haymarket Books
P.O. Box 180165
Chicago, IL 60618
www.haymarketbooks.org

ISBN: 978-1-60846-787-7

Distributed to the trade in the US through Consortium Book Sales and
Distribution (www.cbsd.com) and internationally through Ingram
Publisher Services International (www.ingramcontent.com).

This book was published with the generous support of Lannan
Foundation and Wallace Action Fund.

Special discounts are available for bulk purchases by organizations and
institutions. Please call 773-583-7884 or email info@haymarketbooks.org
for more information.

Cover design by Eric Kerl.

Printed in the United States.

Library of Congress Cataloging-in-Publication data is available.

10 9 8 7 6 5 4 3 2 1

To the Students and Faculty of Lincoln University

Errata

Page 108, line 12 should read: "An Injury to One is an Injury to All."

Pages 173, 179, Foner gives a misleading impression of the number of blacks in labor unions when he writes that the Brotherhood of Sleeping Car Porters (BSCP) had a membership of 35,000 in 1930. The BSCP would have had less than 3,500 porters in its ranks in 1930, and it's also untrue that porters made up half "the colored members of national unions" (as stated on page 173).*

Page 179, lines 14–15: 240-hour week should be 240~hour month.

Page 192, Clyde Johnson was not black.*

Page 194, 2nd paragraph, line 12: NMW should be NMU.

Page 196, 3rd line from bottom: Miners' National Union should be National Miners Union.

Page 223, It was in 1942, not 1941, that "Little Steel" gave "in to industrial unionism"—the contracts were signed during the summer of 1942.*

Page 237, 2nd paragraph, line 10: Monroe Strickland should be Monroe Sweetland.

Page 283, 3rd paragraph, line 6: 50,000-member should be 500,000-member.

Page 297, footnote: Communist should be Communists.

Page 321, 3rd paragraph, line 5: 1967 should be 1957.

Page 328, 2nd paragraph, line 14: raliroad should be railroad.

Page 345, line 3: "accomplished nothing" should read "accomplished little."

Page 355, 2nd paragraph, line 2: SNCC instead of SNNC.

Page 360, 4 lines from bottom: 1954 should read 1964.

Page 377, last paragraph, line 3: 1,200 should be 1,300.

Page 397, line 4: American Labor Alliance should be Alliance for Labor Action.

Page 400, 6 lines from the bottom: University of Alabama should be University of Mississippi.*

Page 412, 3rd paragraph, line 5: "hardly a half dozen" should read "relatively few."

Page 425, 2nd paragraph, line 17: 1.8% should be 18%.

Page 460, line 25: Galeson should be Galenson.

Page 470, 2nd column, line 7 from bottom: American Labor Alliance should be Alliance for Labor Action.

* Thank you to Robin D. G. Kelley for bringing these issues to our attention.

Contents

Foreword

Robin D. G. Kelley

Haymarket's reissue of Philip S. Foner's *Organized Labor and the Black Worker, 1619–1981* could not have been more serendipitous. Donald J. Trump, a reckless billionaire known for making racist comments, failing to pay his workers, and outsourcing his manufacturing firms, is the forty-fifth president of the United States. He presides over a cabinet made up of billionaires and extreme right-wing ideologues utterly hostile to environmental protections, civil rights, public education, any sort of social safety net, and labor. And yet, mainstream news outlets such as CNN, MSNBC, and the *New York Times* attribute Trump's success to his ability to speak to, and for, a disaffected white working class.

If Foner could come back from the grave, he would probably think this was all a bad science-fiction movie. But he would also detect a familiar theme to the story—one that is foundational to *Organized Labor and the Black Worker*. The book documents a very long history of trade union and white working-class intransigence to black working-class advancement alongside episodes of interracial class unity and the elusive promise of a radical future. It remains elusive because those precious moments of solidarity repeatedly crash on the shoals of white supremacy. Although Trump's victory owes much to the surprisingly solid backing from the Republican base, especially middle-class white folks with a median income of $72,000 a year, frustrated white workers who flocked to Trump tended to blame immigrants, black people, and anti-patriotic business moguls who hired foreign labor or sent jobs overseas for their misery. Pundits played down white racism and instead chalked it up to legitimate working-class populism driven by class anger. But if this were true, then why didn't Trump win over black and brown voters, since they make up the lowest rungs of the working class and suffered disproportionately more than whites during the financial crisis of 2008? Why did Trump's victory inspire a wave of racist attacks and emboldened white nationalists to flaunt their allegiance to the president-elect? Because 63 per cent of white men and 53 per cent of white women voted for a president who openly opposed regulating the financial sector, strengthening union power and labor protections, increasing the minimum wage, and restoring the social safety net. Instead, they voted for an essentially anti-labor platform dressed up in populist clothing, and ignored (or embraced) Trump's message of white supremacy, Islamophobia, misogyny, xenophobia, homophobia, militarism, anti-Semitism, and anti-science. The vast majority of people of color voted *against* Trump, with black women registering the highest voting percentage for Clinton of any other demographic (94 per cent).[1]

Foner had little patience for arguments that racism is merely a veneer for the true sentiments of white working people. It was a psychological wage, to use W. E. B. Du Bois's apt phrase, and a structure to ensure job security, higher wages, and the elimination of competition. "To many a white unionist, the black was not simply a rival who threatened his control of the job. He was also a racial and social inferior . . . . Hence, a union that refused to admit blacks not only eliminated a threat to its white members' monopoly of jobs but preserved their status and its own reputation in the white community."[2] His book is filled with anecdotes of working-class racism undermining genuine workers' power in favor of the paltry protections of white privilege—from the erection of occupational color bars by unions to the outbreak of wildcat strikes against the hiring of black workers. But it is also peppered with episodes of antiracism and interracial unity, from the New Orleans General Strike of 1892 to the sit-down strikes organized by the Congress of Industrial Organizations (CIO). Foner showed that white workers were not a monolithic bloc and that racism and opposition to it divided the working class, though not always by color. Anticommunism often masked racist ideologies, and both conspired to mobilize workers for capital and against each other. He tells the story of CIO organizers in Tampa, Florida, who in 1936 "were attacked by an incredible alliance of the Klan, Catholic followers of Father [Charles] Coughlin, leading state AF of L [American Federation of Labor] officials, and various criminal elements of the city. Hiram Evans, Imperial Wizard of the Klan, praised the AF of L for its anti-Communism." Klansmen joined the AF of L, distributed leaflets at its 1940 convention vowing to rid the country of "CIO Communists and nigger lovers" and even participated in assaults on CIO organizers.[3]

Black workers were not a monolithic bloc either, nor were they merely victims of racism or mute pawns in the machinations of white-led labor unions. Foner reminds us that African Americans provided leadership to white workers—or at least they tried. From the Colored National Labor Union to the Brotherhood of Sleeping Car Porters, from the League of Revolutionary Black Workers to the Coalition of Black Trade Unions, black labor militants appealed to whites and other workers of color for solidarity. Indeed, solidarity is the book's central message; when white workers attempt to go it alone or build exclusionary racist unions, they don't win. Foner drives home the point by looking at the 1866 campaign for an eight-hour day: in St. Louis, unionists built a biracial campaign and won, while in New Orleans a lily-white campaign went down in defeat. And yet, rather than place the blame entirely on the unions, Foner situates union history within a larger context of structural racism in which the most powerful agents are the capitalists. The book is replete with stories of capitalists using the coercive arm of the state to put down strikes or contract out convict labor, bribing conservative black leaders to oppose unions and break strikes, and fomenting mob violence in the name of protecting white womanhood or fighting communism.

Foner's three substantial chapters on the "Negro-Labor Alliance" anticipate recent scholarship "rediscovering" the civil rights movement's economic agenda.[4] He details the critical roles of figures such as A. Philip Randolph, Bayard Rustin, Cleveland Robinson, and Dr. Martin Luther King, Jr., in empowering black workers, recruiting major labor leaders to the cause of civil rights, and drawing the connection between economic and racial justice. He pays special attention to the Negro American Labor Council (NALC), a lead sponsor of the March on Washington, which provided the glue that held together the often tenuous alliance between organized labor and the black freedom movement. The NALC organized local marches under the slogan, "Freedom from Poverty through Fair and Full Employment," and threatened to hold a national one-day work stoppage to pressure Congress to pass the Civil Rights bill. It also fought to raise the federal minimum wage and extend its coverage to all workers, and backed efforts to organize domestic workers, abolish the House Un-American Activities Committee, and build up the American Labor Party as a third-party alternative. Shifting from the national to the local, Foner offers a detailed and riveting account of the Charleston hospital workers strike in 1969—an incredible example of the working-class character of the black freedom movement.

In light of over four decades of scholarship on race and labor in the United States, it may be difficult to appreciate the value of *Organized Labor and the Black Worker*.[5] Having first appeared in 1974, with the sweeping periodization ending in 1973 instead of 1981 as it does in the second edition, its institutional and organizational focus reflects what even then was called "old" labor history. Women scarcely appear in these pages; gender as an analytical category was entirely absent, and Foner seems unaware of the latest methodological advances of social history.[6] He has been accused of ideological rigidity, sloppy research, and even plagiarism by scholars who were generally sympathetic to his work.[7] Nevertheless, the book was a stunning achievement; it still stands as the most comprehensive treatment to date of African American workers and the labor movement. More importantly, it appeared at a decisive moment when the global restructuring of capital and the suppression of the black freedom movement portended an uncertain future for organized labor. When the first edition hit bookstores in 1974, the United States was experiencing a global slump on the heels of a major recession. President Richard Nixon's abandonment of the gold standard in 1971 and OPEC's (Organization of Petroleum Exporting Countries) oil embargo to protest support for Israel during the Yom Kippur War was followed by a 400 per cent increase in the price of oil. Gas and other consumer goods skyrocketed in price. The slump devastated U.S. stock values, triggered bank failures, and caused massive layoffs. Workers responded with one of the largest strike waves in history, but capital responded with an all-out assault on organized labor.[8]

The economic crisis and weakening of organized labor opened the door for neoliberal restructuring. New federal and state policies based on free market principles of free trade, deregulation, and privatization produced unprecedented inequality, colossal debt, capital flight, the dismantling of the welfare state, the weakening of anti-discrimination laws and policies, and a wave of police and vigilante killings. New developments in communications technology enabled corporations to move manufacturing operations virtually anywhere in the world in order to take advantage of cheaper labor, relatively lower taxes, and a deregulated environment hostile to trade unions. The decline of manufacturing jobs in steel, rubber, auto, and other heavy industries had a devastating impact on black workers. Although black joblessness had been about twice that of whites since the end of World War II, black unemployment rates increased even more rapidly, especially after 1971. While the number of unemployed white workers *declined* by 562,000 between 1975 and 1980, the number of black unemployed *increased* by 200,000 during this period. The loss of manufacturing positions was accompanied by an expansion of low-wage service jobs with little or no union representation and few health or retirement benefits.[9]

Unionized manufacturing jobs began to disappear and the service sector economy grew just as the black urban population reached its apex. These structural shifts were buttressed by an ideological war on the "social wage," or government expenditures and tax measures that ensure all working people and the poor a decent standard of living. This includes welfare programs, health care, public education, housing supports, a robust minimum wage, and the like. Increasingly, the social wage came to be seen as *racial entitlements*, handouts (or in current Republican lingo, "free stuff") for *black* people. The 1970s witnessed a middle- and upper-class revolt against rising property taxes, which fueled opposition to tax-financed, state-provided goods and services while extolling the private market as a source for delivering goods and services. The financial and budgetary crises brought on by the economic slump justified social cuts, but the shifting ideological grounds made them permanent. The word "public" itself became pejorative, as in "public hospitals" and "public housing." Social welfare was not about protecting the common good but encouraging laziness, turning black people into a nation of dependents.[10]

Foner concedes that black workers made a few genuine gains during the 1970s, particularly in the courts. Despite the weaknesses of the Equal Employment Opportunity Commission (EEOC), black workers made significant progress in the 1970s.[11] In 1973, the EEOC successfully sued the U.S. Steel Corporation and Detroit Edison for failing to promote black workers, opening the door for a robust—though short-lived—affirmative action policy intended to redress ongoing racial discrimination. Meanwhile, the struggle for full employment intensified just as International Publishers issued the paperback edition of the book. Two pieces of progressive legislation, the Humphrey-Hawkins Full Employment Act of 1976 and the significantly weaker Full Employment and Balanced Growth Act of 1978, ultimately went down in defeat in what had become a showdown between a civil rights/labor coalition and a state oriented to neoliberal reforms. Corporate interests, the Federal Reserve, and many members of both major political parties adopted the position that the biggest culprit in the economic crisis was "wage inflation." Curtailing wages in an inflationary economy meant quelling labor unrest, suppressing radical movements, criminalizing the poor through "law and order" policies, and enabling capital to seek cheaper workers anywhere.[12]

It could be said that Philip Foner spent three decades researching this book and a lifetime fighting to realize its aspirations. The son of Russian immigrants whose siblings also grew up to become scholars and activists, he attended City College of New York in the 1930s when it was a hotbed of left-wing radicalism. He earned his bachelor's and master's degrees from City and taught there while completing his doctorate at Columbia University under the direction of the distinguished historian Allan Nevins. His dissertation examined the city's financial ties to the slave-based cotton economy and the political implications of New York capitalists' unwavering defense of slave power. They even supported the sovereignty of states when it was in the South's interests. But once the political winds shifted with Abraham Lincoln's election, New York financiers closed ranks with the Republican Party.

Foner's dissertation was published as *Business and Slavery: The New York Merchants and the Irrepressible Conflict*, in 1941, the same year the New York State Rapp-Coudert Committee—a precursor to the House Un-American Activities Committee (HUAC)—identified Foner as a Communist. Consequently, City College fired Foner along with dozens of other employees, including his brothers Jack, also a member of the history department at City College, and Moe, who worked in the college registrar's office. Henry, a substitute teacher in the city's high schools also lost his job. Thus began what turned out to be Foner's twenty-six-year blacklist from academia. He made his living by writing and lecturing and as the publisher of Citadel Press. Although he and his family lived comfortably on the proceeds from his books and Citadel Press, he still had to endure FBI surveillance and state harassment for his political affiliations.[13]

With no teaching duties, a knack for archival research, and an enormous well of energy, Foner became one of the most prolific historians of the twentieth century, generating about 130 volumes of prose and edited documents—mainly in the fields of labor, radicalism, and African American history. During the Second World War, he published books on "morale education" in the U.S. military, the history of American Jews, and his edited volumes of selected writings by George Washington, Thomas Jefferson, Thomas Paine, and Abraham Lincoln. In 1947, he published the first in what would become his ten-volume *The History of the Labor Movement of the United States*. Three years later, he made his first foray into African American history with the publication of the five-volume *The Life and Writings of Frederick Douglass*, which significantly shaped the study of black history and allowed for a deeper interrogation of Douglass's thought and activism beyond abolition. Foner returned to academia in 1967, accepting a tenure-track position at Lincoln University, the historically black college in Pennsylvania—although it doesn't seem to have slowed his output. He spent the next decade writing and editing books on topics ranging from the Black Panther Party, the speeches of W. E. B. Du Bois, U.S. imperialism, Cuba, the Russian Revolution, the American Revolution, American labor songs, and, of course, African Americans and organized labor.[14] And it is worth noting that he followed the original edition of *Organized Labor and the Black Worker, 1619–1973* (which he later updated to 1981), with, among other works, *History of Black Americans* (1975), *Black Americans and American Socialism* (1977), the two-volume *Women and the American Labor Movement* (1979–80), and an eight-volume collection of documents coedited with Ronald Lewis under the title *The Black Worker: A Documentary History from Colonial Times to the Present* (1978–84). It is a collection of which I'm personally quite fond since it became the primary source for virtually all of my undergraduate research papers.

The *Black Worker* proved not only an indispensable source, but I suspect was Foner's answer to those critics of *Organized Labor and the Black Worker, 1619–1981* who questioned his research and biases. The reviews were generally positive. Writing for the *Review of Black Political Economy*, William K. Tabb called it "simply the best treatment of the history of the black worker yet to appear and is likely to be the standard work in the field for a long time to come."[15] However, the book was subject to relentless criticism, sometimes tainted by thinly veiled anticommunism. Herbert Northrup, conservative labor scholar and author of *Organized Labor and the Negro* (1944) dismissed the book as "warped by an ideological bent" and accused Foner of masking unsubstantiated assertions behind voluminous footnotes. His review veered dangerously close to red-baiting, attacking Foner's discussion of HUAC's attack on black workers as merely an apologia for the Soviet Union and Communist machinations in the labor movement.[16] Dan Leab's review described Foner as prolific but "idiosyncratic," someone who promotes "an extreme left-of-center view in variance with the facts." Leab especially took him to task for overstating the role of the Communist-led unemployed councils and ignoring the role the New Deal played in alleviating black workers' suffering.[17] Likewise James A. Gross found the book flawed by "careless documentation" and "a pronounced ideological bias." Foner's treatment of the unemployed councils, Gross asserts, was exaggerated, and his claim that black workers flocked to left unions simply "contradicts the whole body of scholarship indicating that left-wing and radical ideology had few takers among black workers."[18] Subsequent research—including my own—has proved Foner correct. Left unions such as the International Mine, Mill and Smelter Workers and the Food, Tobacco, Agricultural, and Allied Workers not only organized significant numbers of black workers but became vehicles for early civil rights organizing in the late 1940s and early 1950s. As the CIO leadership strengthened its alliance with the government, it joined the growing Red Scare and expelled the left unions.[19]

Of course, Foner was prone to exaggerate the impact of the Communist Party, especially the role of the Trade Union Unity League in setting the stage for the CIO's mass industrial organizing campaign. He also made errors—several errors have since been corrected in subsequent editions; others have been corrected in this edition. And there are also several places where new scholarship simply deepened or complicated his findings. But as a whole, the book still holds up nearly four decades later, and the lessons are as relevant today as they were when the second edition appeared in 1982. To the pundits and political scientists now chastising "Democrats" for not knowing how to talk to white workers and blaming the Movement for Black Lives and so-called identity politics for alienating the white working class and driving them into the arms of Donald Trump, Foner would have insisted that the labor movement prioritize the struggle against racism, which he consistently regarded as the primary obstacle to solidarity. Indeed, when Bayard Rustin—speaking at a convention of the International Association of Machinists in 1972—lectured disgruntled black workers to "stop griping always that nobody has problems but you black people" and that the privileges and positions of power white workers held in the union were not on account of race, Foner was quick to denounce the civil rights icon. "This was delivered at the convention of a union that for sixty years of its eighty-year history barred 'non-Caucasians'!" (p. 431)

Anyone serious about rebuilding the labor movement must recognize the fundamental role racism has played in undermining solidarity and internationalism, and concealing the structural relationship between the white middle class's standard of living and the exploitation of immigrant labor. And rebuild the labor movement we must, for it has been under attack on a global scale for at least half a century. Today labor unions are portrayed as corrupt, bloated, a drain on the economy, and modern-day cartels that threaten workers "liberty." Corporations and the CEOs who run them are portrayed as the most efficient and effective mode of organization. In our neoliberal age, emergency financial managers are sent in to replace elected governments during real or imagined economic crises; charter schools organized along corporate lines are replacing public schools; universities are adopting corporate strategies with presidents increasingly functioning like CEOs; a businessman with a checkered record, a history of improprieties and legal violations, and no experience whatsoever in government, is elected president of the United States. The once-powerful unions are doing little more than fighting to restore basic collective bargaining rights and deciding how much they are going to give back. Union leaders are struggling just to participate in crafting austerity measures.

Yet, when we shift our attention from the big industrial unions where we imagine the white working class resides to low-wage, marginalized workers in fast food, retail, home care, domestic work, and so on, the horizon looks radically different. Once powerful engines of racial and gender exclusion, often working with capital to impose glass ceilings and racially segmented wages, the twenty-first-century labor movement has largely embraced principles of social justice, antiracism, immigrant rights, and cross-border strategies. They have adopted new strategies, from passing minimum-wage laws at the municipal and state levels to using community benefits agreements to secure living-wage jobs, equitable working conditions, green building practices, and affordable housing, as well as childcare provisions. And in alliance with movements such as Occupy Wall Street, the Movement for Black Lives, the DREAMers, campaigns such as OUR Walmart, and the fast-food workers Fight for Fifteen, they are leading the way, building the most dynamic labor movement we have seen in generations.[20] They are writing the next chapter.

Los Angeles
March 14, 2017

1. Doug Sanders, "Economic Victims Didn't Elect Trump. The Well-Off and Segregated Did," *Globe and Mail*, November 9, 2016, http://www.theglobeandmail.com/news/world/us-politics/the-average-trump-supporter-is-not-an-economic-loser/article32746323/; Vanessa Williams, "Black Women – Hillary Clinton's Most Reliable Voting Bloc—Look Beyond Defeat," *Washington Post*, November 12, 2016.

2   Philip S. Foner, *Organized Labor and the Black Worker, 1619–1981*

(New York: International Publishers, 1982), 74.

3   Ibid., 230.

4   See, for example, William P. Jones, *March on Washington: Jobs, Freedom, and the Forgotten History of Civil Rights* (New York: W. W. Norton, 2013); Michael K. Honey, *Going Down Jericho Road: The Memphis Strike, Martin Luther King's Last Campaign* (New York: W. W. Norton, 2008); Robert Zeiger, *For Jobs and Freedom: Race and Labor in America since 1865* (Lexington: University Press of Kentucky, 2010). The reexamination of labor and the civil rights movement isn't entirely new. Some critical contributions to this scholarship include Alan Draper, *Conflict of Interest: Organized Labor and the Civil Rights Movement, 1954–1968* (Ithaca, NY: Cornell University Press, 1994); Michael K. Honey, *Southern Labor and Black Civil Rights: Organizing Memphis Workers* (Urbana: University of Illinois Press, 1993); Robert Korstad and Nelson Lichtenstein, "Opportunities Found and Lost: Labor, Radicals, and the Early Civil Rights Movement," *Journal of American History* 75 (December 1988): 786–811; Robert Korstad, *Civil Rights Unionism: Tobacco Workers and the Struggle for Democracy in the Mid-Twentieth-Century South* (Chapel Hill: University of North Carolina Press, 2003).

5. Philip Foner built on a long and established intellectual tradition of black labor studies. Some of the foundational works include Charles H. Wesley, *Negro Labor in the United States, 1850–1925: A Study in American Economic History* (New York: Vanguard Press, 1927); Sterling D. Spero and Abram L. Harris, Jr., *The Black Worker: The Negro and the Labor Movement* (New York: Columbia University Press, 1931); Horace Cayton and George Mitchell, *Black Workers and the New Unions* (Chapel Hill: University of North Carolina Press, 1939); Herbert R. Northup, *Organized Labor and the Negro* (New York: Harper & Brothers, 1944); Ray Marshall, *The Negro and Organized Labor* (New York: John Wiley & Sons, 1965). For a brilliant study of the early historiography of black labor, see Francille Rusan Wilson, *The Segregated Scholars: Black Social Scientists and the Creation of Black Labor Studies, 1890–1950* (Charlottesville and London: University Press of Virginia, 2006). There have been other attempts to update the history of black workers and the labor movement, notably William H. Harris, *The Harder We Run: Black Workers since the Civil War* (New York: Oxford University Press, 1982); Stephen A. Reich, *A Working People: A History of African American Workers since Emancipation* (Lanham, MD: Rowman and Littlefield, 2013); and Paul D. Moreno's fairly conservative *Black Americans and Organized Labor: A New History* (Baton Rouge: Louisiana State University Press, 2006). None of these books match Foner's in terms of scope or comprehensiveness,

and like virtually every other synthesis, they begin after the Civil War.

6. See Sally M. Miller, "Philip Foner and 'Integrating' Women into Labor History and African-American History," *Labor History* 33, no. 4 (1992): 456–69; Melvyn Dubofsky, "Give Us That Old-Time Labor History: Philip S. Foner and the American Worker," *Labor History* 26 (1985): 118–35.

7. "Was Philip Foner Guilty of Plagiarism?," History News Network, June 4, 2003, http://historynewsnetwork.org/article/1481.

8. David McNally, *Global Slump: The Economics and Politics of Crisis and Resistance* (Oakland, CA: PM Press, 2011); Thomas Borstelmann, *The 1970s: A New Global History from Civil Rights to Economic Inequality* (Princeton, NJ: Princeton University Press, 2012); Jefferson Cowie, *Stayin' Alive: The 1970s and the Last Days of the Working Class* (New York: New Press, 2010).

9. Barry Bluestone and Bennett Harrison, *The Deindustrialization of America: Plant Closings, Community Abandonment, and the Dismantling of Basic Industry* (New York: Basic Books, 1982), 42, 25–48; Robert B. Hill, "Economic Status of Black America," *New Directions* 8, no. 3, Article 6 (April 1981), http://dh.howard.edu/newdirections/vol8/iss3/6.

10. Nancy Fraser, "Clintonism, Welfare, and the Antisocial Wage: The Emergence of a Neoliberal Political Imaginary," *Rethinking Marxism* 6, no. 1 (1993): 9–23; Ange-Marie Hancock, *The Politics of Disgust: The Public Identity of the Welfare Queen* (New York: New York University Press, 2004).

11. Foner addresses this in the last chapter of this book, but he expands the discussion in an essay published a few years later: Philip S. Foner, "Organized Labor and the Black Worker in the 1970s," *Insurgent Sociologist* 8, nos. 2 and 4 (1978): 87–95.

12. David Stein tells this story in a brilliant forthcoming book, *Fearing Inflation, Inflating Fears: The Civil Rights Struggle for Full Employment and the Rise of the Carceral State, 1929–1986* (Chapel Hill: University of North Carolina Press, 2018).

13. Lawrence Van Gelder, "Philip S. Foner, Labor Historian and Professor, 84," *New York Times*, December 15, 1994; James R. Barrett, "Philip S. Foner," *Saothar: Irish Labour History Society* 20 (1995): 11.

14. Barrett, "Philip S. Foner," 11; Van Gelder, "Philip S. Foner, Labor Historian and Professor, 84"; Catherine Clinton, "Philip Foner's Fond Farewell," *New Yorker*, March 6, 1995, 38.

15. William K. Tabb, Review, *Review of Black Political Economy* 5, no. 3 (1975): 323.

16. Herbert R. Northrup, Review, *Labor History* 16, no. 1 (1975): 143–44.

17. Daniel J. Leab, Review, *Political Science Quarterly* 90, no. 1 (Spring 1975): 180–82. William H. Harris also takes Foner to task for accumulated errors and sloppy research. See his review in *Journal of American History* 61, no. 4 (March 1975): 1073–75.

18. James A. Gross, Review, *Industrial & Labor Relations Review* 29 (1975–1976): 145–46.

19. Korstad, *Civil Rights Unionism*; Honey, *Southern Labor and Black Civil Rights*; Robin D. G. Kelley, *Hammer and Hoe: Alabama Communists during the Great Depression* (Chapel Hill: University of North Carolina Press, 1990). Ironically, one of the few glowing reviews to support Foner's argument about the importance of the left-led unions in the Cold War period was published in *Business History Review*. See Joseph M. Gowaskie, Review, *Business History Review* 48, no. 4 (Winter 1974): 548–50.

20. See Sarah Jaffe, *Necessary Trouble: America's New Radicals* (New York: Nation Books, 2016); Bill Fletcher, Jr. and Fernando Gapasin, *Solidarity Divided: The Crisis in Organized Labor and a New Path toward Social Justice* (Berkeley and Los Angeles: University of California Press, 2009); Dorian T. Warren, "The American Labor Movement in the Age of Obama: The Challenges and Opportunities of a Racialized Political Economy," *Perspectives on Politics* 8, no. 3 (September 2010): 847–60; Robin D. G. Kelley, "Building a Progressive Movement in 2012," *Souls* 14, nos. 1 and 2 (2012): 10–18; Premilla Nadasen, *Household Workers Unite! The Untold Story of African-American Women Who Built a Movement* (Boston: Beacon Press, 2016).

Preface

In February, 1968, the Kerner Commission on Civil Disorders, a formally constituted government body, declared that the black violence and riots of the previous year had been caused chiefly by a profound racism on the part of the white majority. In its historical analysis of white racism, the Commission traced its origin to the beginnings of the American experience and described its manifestations in many of our institutions over time. One American institution, however, received no attention—organized labor.

As this study shows, from the formation of the first trade unions in the 1790's to the mid-1930's, the policy and practice of organized labor so far as black workers were concerned were largely those of outright exclusion or segregation. Yet, as this study also makes clear, there have been exceptions. Black-white unity was attempted at several periods in the history of the American labor movement before the mid-1930's, and, despite the bitter opposition of employers and sections of the trade-union leadership and rank-and-file, in some instances it achieved a lasting success. This study is thus an examination of both the exclusionary history of organized labor with respect to black workers until very recently and also—the minor theme—black-white unity. And it is the story of the continuing struggle of black workers to achieve equality as members of organized labor, once the barriers of exclusion and segregation were lowered.

Most labor historians today agree that craft unions created an aristocracy of skilled workers at the expense of the unskilled and semiskilled and, at the same time, retarded the further organization of American industry, thus, in the long run, adversely affecting all workers, skilled as well as unskilled. Yet not many are willing to acknowledge that the racist policies and practices of organized labor created a privileged group of white workers at the expense of black workers and thus strengthened the employers' ability to divide the working class and weaken efforts to unionize major industries. The crippling effects of racism on organized labor were recognized soon after slavery was abolished by the *Boston Daily Evening Voice*, one of the staunchest champions of black-white labor unity. An editorial on October 5, 1865, read:

The workingmen's success is simply impossible without united and harmonious action. If the machinist says to the wielder of the pick and shovel, I will not associate with you—if you want better wages you must get it on your own hook; if the clerk says to the coal-heaver, between you and I there is a gulf fixed; or if the white says to the black, I do not recognize you as a fellow workman; and these feelings prevail, there is the end of hope for the labor movement.

Look at it for a moment. There are now four million of the negro race about to enter the field of free labor. If we take them upon equal ground with ourselves in the contest for the elevation of labor, they become an ally; but if we reject them—say we will not work in the shop with them— what is the result? The black man's interests and ours are severed. He that might have been our co-operator becomes our enemy. This vast force of four million workers is in the field against us. We refuse their alliance; the enemy sees and seizes his opportunity, and the black man becomes our competitor. He will underwork us to get employment, and we have no choice but to underwork him in return, or at least to work as low as he, or starve. Shall we then be so blind and suicidal as to refuse to work with the black man? Here he is—a power to tell one side or the other in the contest for the elevation of labor. Shall this power be on our side, or on the side of our opponents? It is first offered to us. Shall we reject it? We hope there is more intelligence among workingmen than to persist in the indulgence of an old prejudice when that indulgence is the ruin of their cause.

Similarly, in a speech before the Central Labor Union of Brooklyn, in January, 1902, Robert Baker said:

The more organized labor champions the cause of all labor, unorganized as well as organized, black as well as white, the greater will be the victories; the more lasting, the more permanent, the more beneficial and the more far-reaching will be its successes. If it would extend and broaden its influence—aye, if it would accomplish most for itself—it must persistently and vigorously attack special privilege in every form; it must make the cause of humanity, regardless of race, color, or sex, its cause.

These words are as valid today as when they were uttered.

The present work is the product of research in a wide variety of sources. To cite them all would require a small book in itself. I have, therefore, cited in the main only sources for quoted material. For those who wish to pursue the subject further, I have furnished a selected bibliography.

I have many indebtednesses to acknowledge in the preparation of this volume. Numerous libraries and historical societies have made available to me their collections of manuscripts, newspapers, pamphlets, and published and unpublished monographic studies. I wish to thank especially the staffs of the Library of Congress, the National Archives, the Schomburg Collection of the New York Public Library, the Tamiment Institute Library of New York University, the State Historical Society of Wisconsin, the Chicago Historical Society, the Library of the U.S. Department of Labor, the Boston Public Library, the American Federation of Labor Library, and the libraries of Columbia University, Howard University, Princeton University, Atlanta University, Vanderbilt University, Washington University, the State College of Washington, the University of Georgia, Emory University, the University of Alabama, the University of Texas, Catholic University of America, the University of Michigan (Labadie Collection), the University of Pittsburgh, Radcliffe College, Temple University, Georgetown University, the New School for Social Research, Bryn Mawr College, Tulane University, and Indiana University. I wish also to thank the National Association for the Advancement of Colored People for permission to use its archives in the Manuscripts Division of the Library of Congress, and Local 1199 for permission to use the union's archives. I am grateful to Herbert Hill, labor secretary of the NAACP, for the opportunity to read his unpublished paper on the United Mine Workers and the black miners. I owe a special debt of gratitude to the staff of the Lincoln University Library for assistance in the use of the library's splendid collection of materials relating to black history, and to Jean Trombore for her help in obtaining, through interlibrary loan, materials from many institutions.

For the present edition Chapter 26 has been enlarged to enable the history of *Organized Labor and the Black Worker* to be brought to the year 1981.

Weld, Maine, November, 1981   PHILIP S. FONER
                                   Professor Emeritus of History
                                   Lincoln University, Pennsylvania

Organized Labor
and the
Black Worker
1619-1981

"The colored laborer in America has been the special victim of avarice and cupidity from the time he first set foot on the continent."

—Report on Capital and Labor submitted to the Second Convention of the Colored National Labor Union, Washington, D.C., January 11, 1871

"Their [the black workers'] cause is one with the labor class all over the world. The labor unions of the country should not throw away this colored element of strength. . . . It is a great mistake for any class of laborers to isolate itself and thus weaken the bonds of brotherhood between those on whom the burden and hardships of labor fall. The fortunate ones of the earth, who are abundant in land and money and know nothing of the anxious care and pinching poverty of the laboring classes, may be indifferent to the appeal for justice at this point, but the labor classes cannot afford to be indifferent."

—FREDERICK DOUGLASS, address to the Convention of Colored Men, Louisville, Kentucky, September, 1883

1 From Slavery to Freedom

Slavery was a system designed to provide a permanent labor supply to develop the New World. Efforts to enslave Indians were not successful, for they could not adjust to labor in captivity and often escaped into the familiar terrain of the forest. Free white laborers were scarce and were unwilling to work when cheap land was available. White indentured servitude was an important source of labor in some colonies, but with its limited term of bondage it could not meet the growing demand for workers. Negroes could be forced into slavery more easily than whites and, once enslaved, could not easily run away and mingle readily in strange surroundings. More important, slavery of blacks could be justified by the ideology of racism. A black skin connoted evil and inferiority; Negroes were said to be destined to be slaves by the "Curse of Ham." They were pictured as savages and infidels from a barbaric, dark continent without a civilization, and enslavement was adjudged an improvement in their way of life. As Winthrop Jordan points out: "Slavery could survive only if the Negro were a man set apart; he simply had to be different if slavery were to exist at all."[1]

The first group of twenty Africans brought to Jamestown, Virginia, in 1619 were not slaves but indentured servants. But between 1660 and 1682, court decisions, special laws, and codes in all the colonies transformed the black servant into a slave. The slave codes generally provided that black people were to be slaves for life, that children were to inherit their mothers' condition, and that Christian baptism would not automatically assure freedom. They also prohibited marriage between whites and blacks and forbade bondsmen to acquire or to inherit property, to hold secret gatherings, to be parties to contracts or suits, to marry legally, or to engage in certain trades. Those who violated the slave codes were punished by a variety of means from fines to imprisonment, from whipping to death.

The number of black slaves grew slowly in the seventeenth century. By 1700 there were probably no more than 25,000 in colonial America. Thereafter, growth was rapid owing to the expansion of tobacco, rice, and indigo plantations in the South. Slavery was suited to plantation agriculture and to the Southern economy generally. Slave labor could be maintained at a subsistence standard of living, and the offspring of black women added to the profits of the masters.

Many of the Africans carried to America as slaves brought with them skills in metallurgy, woodworking, and leather. Slaveowners were quick to use these skills and to teach their bondsmen other trades associated with the operation of farms and plantations.

Only one city developed in the South during the colonial period—Charleston, South Carolina—and here slaves were used to perform skilled and unskilled labor, and slave craftsmen were even hired out. But it was in the Northern colonies, where agrarian development was diversified and the farmers' need for slaves was limited, that the use of slaves as artisans and craftsmen grew. A large number of slaves were employed in Northern cities as house servants, sailors, sailmakers, and carpenters. New York had a higher proportion of skilled slaves than any other colony—coopers, tailors, bakers, tanners, goldsmiths, naval carpenters, blacksmiths, weavers, sailmakers, millers, masons, candlemakers, tobacconists, caulkers, cabinetmakers, shoemakers, and glaziers.

Throughout the colonial period free white craftsmen fought a losing battle to exclude blacks from most of the skilled trades; as early as 1707 free mechanics in Philadelphia complained of the "Want of employment, and Lowness of wages, occasioned by the Number of *Negroes* . . . hired out to work by the Day."[2] But they were challenging the right of slaveowners to use their property as they saw fit, opposing the men who dominated the colonial assemblies. Some restrictions were in fact imposed on the use of slave artisans, but they did not end the rivalry between slaves and white workers. In the North, where trade and manufacturing grew, slaves continued to move into the skilled trades in competition with white artisans, driving down wages. As a result, many white craftsmen and mechanics in the urban areas joined the movement to abolish slavery. The opposition of white workers to the continued competition of slave labor was an important factor in ending slavery in the North.

Many Americans, including some Southerners, believed that the spirit of the American Revolution, combined with the economic stagnation in tobacco, rice, and indigo planting, would force slavery to die out in the South, just as it was disappearing in the North. But in 1793 Eli Whitney invented the cotton gin, and planters began to take acreage out of other crops and enter the cotton market. The demand for slaves grew. By 1800, they were selling for twice the price of 1790. Not even the prohibition by Congress of the importation of slaves from Africa after 1807 could keep cotton from becoming king. With big money to be made from planting cotton with slave labor or from breeding slaves for sale to the planters, the plantation system spread westward and slavery became solidly rooted in fifteen Southern states. By 1860 there were 4 million slaves in these states.

"Free Negro wage earners were members of the labor force before the Civil War," writes Philip Taft in his *Organized Labor in American History.*[3] But from the time the first trade unions were formed by white workers in the 1790's to the Civil War—in which period the free black population grew from 59,000 to 488,000—no free Negro wage-earner was a member. To be sure, the trade unions of the 1850's were exclusively craft unions composed of skilled mechanics. Unskilled workers found it impossible to join most of these unions, and several, such as the printers, hotel waiters, shoemakers, and tailors, excluded women as well. But not one of the unions allowed a black worker, skilled or unskilled, male or female, to join its ranks.

The short-lived Industrial Congress—a national organization of reformers and workingmen—did admit Negro delegates to an 1851 convention, but the Mechanics' Assembly of Philadelphia so resented the admission of blacks that it voted to sever all ties with the Industrial Congress. The Communist Club of New York, formed in 1857, required all members to "recognize the complete equality of all men—no matter what color or sex."[4] But there is no evidence that this position had any effect on other labor societies.

Of nearly 500,000 free blacks in the United States in 1860, 238,268 were in the North and West. At one time they had occupied an important economic position; it is quite likely that in a number of Northern cities between 1790 and 1820 a large proportion, perhaps most, of the skilled craftsmen were blacks. Of course, most of them received less money than white artisans for the same work, but they at least found employment in their trades. The reason was that from 1776 to 1815 immigration from Europe had declined, leaving openings for free black artisans. But with the end of the Napoleonic Wars in 1815 immigration to the United States started to flow once again, and immigrants from Europe, many with skills acquired in their native lands, flocked to this country and settled in its Northern cities. Industrial development also attracted native Americans from the farms to the city, where they soon acquired the skills necessary to meet the demand for labor.

By 1817 the supply of skilled labor, for the first time in the country's history, exceeded the demand. In the face of competition from skilled workers with white skins, many black artisans found themselves unemployed, and to survive skilled black workers had to accept unskilled, semiskilled, and domestic work. Thus early in American history the black worker experienced being the first to be fired when the job market was tight.

By 1837 only about 350 of the 10,500 Negroes in Philadelphia, for example, pursued trades, or about one in every twenty adults. By 1849 the black population had increased substantially. but the number of black craftsmen had risen only to 481. By 1859, the number of black craftsmen had declined. On the eve of the Civil War Negro members of the labor force in Philadelphia were engaged in 400 different occupations, but eight out of every ten black male workers were unskilled laborers. Another 16 per cent worked as skilled artisans, but fully half of this group were barbers and shoemakers; the other skilled craftsmen were scattered among the construction, home-furnishing, leather goods, and metalwork trades. Less than half of 1 per cent found employment in Philadelphia's developing factory system. Finally, more than eight out of every ten black working women in Philadelphia were employed as domestic servants. The 14 per cent who worked as seamstresses accounted for all the skilled workers among the black female labor force.

Before the 1840's and 1850's, black workers in many Northern cities had monopolized the occupations of longshoremen, hod-carriers, white-washers, coachmen, stablemen, porters, bootblacks, barbers, and waiters in hotels and restaurants. A huge influx of white foreigners, particularly after the Irish famine in 1846, caused a radical change. The unskilled Irish, in particular, pushed the Negroes out of these occupations, depriving many blacks of employment. "Every hour," Frederick Douglass, the most influential black leader of the nineteenth century, lamented, "sees the black man elbowed out of employment by some newly arrived immigrant whose hunger and whose color are thought to give him a better title to the place."[5] In November, 1851, the *African Repository* noted that in New York (and in other Eastern cities) it was no longer possible to see the Negro "work upon buildings, and rarely is he allowed to drive a cart of public conveyance. White men will not work with him."

Carter G. Woodson and Lorenzo B. Greene, in their study of Negroes as wage-earners, state that "without a doubt many a Negro family in the free States would have been reduced to utter destitution had not it been for the labor of the mother as a washerwoman." Occasionally, according to John Hope Franklin, free Negroes found Northern society so opposed to their advancement that they voluntarily sold themselves back into slavery. "I . . . can't get work from no one," was the cry of one Cincinnati free Negro who could endure the "idleness and poverty" of his "freedom" no longer.[6]

"White boys won't work with me," the black youth cried in despair. "White men will not work with him," the reports on the conditions of colored people emphasized.

J. F. W. Johnston, an observant Englishman, wrote in the 1850's, following a tour of the Northern states: "Whenever the interests of the white man and the Black come into collision in the United States, the Black man goes to the wall. . . . It is certain that wherever labor is scarce, there he is steadily employed, when it becomes plentiful, he is the first to be discharged."[7] Friction between white and black laborers heightened during rivalry for jobs in years of depression. It was intensified further by the use of blacks in place of striking laborers. Struggling for economic survival, blacks were forced to become scabs. The white workers retaliated not only by attacking the strike-breakers but by invading Negro ghettos, assaulting and killing black people, and destroying homes and churches in an attempt to force blacks to leave the city. Unskilled Irish workmen, themselves victims of nativist riots and anti-foreign and anti-Catholic elements, could usually be counted upon to join an anti-Negro mob. While competition for jobs between the Irish and blacks, both poverty-stricken, was a major cause of many anti-Negro riots, the mobs were often organized—and sometimes even led—by "scions of old and socially prominent Northern families" who had close economic and social links with the South, and who exploited fear of black competition to combat the Abolitionists.[8]

Frederick Douglass appealed to white employers to give blacks an opportunity to become apprentices and to work at trades once they had acquired skills; he pleaded with the labor organizations and labor papers to educate white workers on the value of unity in the struggle for a decent livelihood, regardless of race or color. When his pleas fell on deaf ears, Douglass came out in support of Negroes who took the jobs of striking white workers, blaming the whites for forcing the blacks to act as scabs as the only way to earn a livelihood. He wrote bitterly, "Colored men can feel under no obligation to hold out in a 'strike' with the whites, as the latter have never recognized them."[9]

The general situation in the antebellum South also spawned bitter hatred of blacks among many white workers, who blamed the Negro for the institution of which he was the principal victim. The white artisan resented the threat to his livelihood from the slave mechanic, and white industrial workers increasingly found themselves required to compete with black bondsmen. (By the 1850's, 160,000 to 200,000 blacks—about 5 per cent of the total slave population—worked in industry.) Some Southern white workers understood that their economic future was linked to the destruction of slavery, but most raised their objection not to slavery but only to the use of slaves in industrial occupations, especially the skilled crafts. They petitioned Southern legislatures to forbid slave competition, but only in a few cases were they successful.* Southern capitalists were usually able to take advantage of the availability of slave labor in both skilled and unskilled trades to keep down wages and curb attempts to form unions.

While there are numerous instances of labor unrest and even labor organizations in the South before the Civil War, several factors retarded the growth of organized labor, the most important being the slave society which dominated the South. In 1842 Chief Justice Shaw of Massachusetts in *Commonwealth v. Hunt* upheld the legality of the strike weapon. This decision cut no ice in the South, where courts continued to declare strikes illegal. A South Carolina judge, when sentencing twenty-three Irish construction workers to two months in prison for conducting a strike in 1855 against the use of slave labor to reduce wage scales, admonished white workers not to "make war upon the Negroes . . . for slaves are, preeminently, our most valuable property—their rights center in the master, which he will vindicate to the bitter end." When white workers at the Tredegar Iron Works in Richmond, Virginia, went on strike to stop the increasing employment of slaves, they were prosecuted for "conspiracy" against their employer. They lost their battle and were never rehired. Thereafter, as Tredegar's chief executive noted, the company used "almost exclusively slave labor except as the

---

* As Robert Starobin notes: "White artisans did not seek to abolish slavery altogether, only to exclude Negroes from certain trades . . . the net effect of most protests by white artisans was thus not to weaken slavery but to entrench it more firmly in the southern city." Robert S. Starobin, *Industrial Slavery in the Old South* (New York and London: Oxford University Press, 1970), pp. 312–13.

Boss men. This enables me, of course, to compete with other manufacturers."

It also enabled him to keep unionism out of the Iron Works. Slave
competition was thus the most important deterrent to the formation of
effective trade unions in such slave states as Virginia, South Carolina,
and even Louisiana, even though it did not prevent the establishment of
some form of a labor movement and the spread of militant strikes. "With
the blacks," wrote a mill owner in North Carolina, "there is no turning
out for wages."[10]

Racism blinded the workers and diverted their enmity from the capitalists to the slaves, while at the same time the slaves were used to keep
them in subjugation. Frederick Douglass, writing from personal experience as a slave field hand and craftsman, exposed the technique used
by the slaveowners to maintain their dominance and pointed up the significance of racial prejudice:

> The slaveholders . . . by encouraging the enmity of the poor, laboring
> white man against the blacks, succeeded in making the said white man al-
> most as much a slave as the black man himself. . . . Both are plundered,
> and by the same plunderers. The slave is robbed by his master, of all his
> earnings above what is required for his physical necessities; and the white
> man is robbed by the slave system, of just results of his labor, because he
> is flung into competition with a class of laborers who work without wages.
> At present, the slaveholders blind them to this competition, by keeping
> alive their prejudices against the slaves as *men*—not against them as *slaves*.
> They appeal to their pride, often denouncing emancipation, as tending
> to place the white working man on an equality with Negroes, and, by this
> means, they succeed in drawing off the minds of the poor whites from the
> real fact, that by the rich slave-master, they are already regarded as but a
> single remove from equality with the slave.[11]

In 1860 there were more free blacks in the South than in the North—
250,787 as against 238,268—mainly because in most Southern cities free
Negro artisans were essential to supply the needs of the community. In
Charleston, there were free blacks in highly skilled occupations—carpenters, tailors, shoemakers, cabinetmakers, masons, and butchers. "There
are many callings in which the colored people have a decided preference," a Charleston Negro wrote in the *African Repository* of October,
1832, "and in some cases they have no competitors." Moreover, the children of free black craftsmen were able to learn a trade, usually through
apprenticeship. Free black artisans were so important to the economy of
many Southern cities that whites who valued their work resisted efforts
to force them out of the state.

After 1850, the fear that urban surroundings would weaken their hold
over slaves caused many slaveowners to restrict the use of bondsmen in
cities. As the black population dropped, whites took over crafts formerly
occupied by slaves and then turned to eliminating free black competition.
With or without official sanction, and usually with violence, they forced
blacks out of the better jobs, and in some cases out of cities altogether.
(Slaveowners reminded the free blacks who were assaulted by white

artisans that the assaults were no threat to the institution of slavery, hence they saw no reason to protect them.) Still, many free blacks were able in the South to work at their trades and to hand on their skills to their children. In this respect, they were economically better off than their brothers in the North.

Nevertheless, the free Negro occupied a wretched social position in the South. To prove that he was not a runaway slave, he had to carry identification papers at all times. He could not vote, and in courts of law his testimony was not admissible in cases where white persons were parties. Free Negro artisans, unlike white craftsmen, were subject to special taxes; they could not form trade unions and were excluded from all unions that did exist in the South. Not even in New Orleans, the most cosmopolitan of Southern cities, with a large proportion of free black workers and a relatively strong trade-union movement, could free Negroes organize their own unions or join those formed by white workers.

Because of the fear of slave rebellions, free blacks were prevented by law from entertaining or visiting slaves.* In 1822, after the Denmark Vesey slave conspiracy, South Carolina passed a law forbidding free black seamen to leave their vessels when in South Carolina ports. In 1829, after free Negro sailors had distributed a revolutionary pamphlet by David Walker, a free black tailor in Boston, calling upon the slaves to revolt, several slave states passed laws requiring that free Negro seamen be kept in jail until twenty-four hours before departure time.

In the North, racism was the basic reason for the black worker's deteriorating economic position. Whites, employers and workers alike, maintained a solid front against the black worker and successfully contained him within the menial job market. "To drive a carriage, carry a straw basket after the boss, and brush his boots, or saw wood and run errands, was as high as a colored man could aspire to," William Wells Brown, the black Abolitionist, noted.[12]

Alexis de Tocqueville observed on his visit to the United States in the 1830's that racial prejudice seemed to be stronger in the North than in the South and was most intense in the Western states, which had never known slavery. Only five states, all in New England, allowed the black man equal suffrage. In the West, Negroes were excluded from the public schools, and four states—Indiana, Illinois, Iowa, and Oregon—even

---

* A number of the leaders of the slave insurrections between 1790 and 1861 were artisans or industrial slaves. Gabriel Prosser, organizer of the conspiracy in Henrico County, Virginia, in 1800, was a blacksmith, while Nat Turner, leader of the great slave rebellion in Virginia of 1831, was a carpenter and millwright before he became a slave preacher. The great slave conspiracy organized in Charleston in 1821–22 was led by Denmark Vesey, a free black carpenter, and Vesey's recruits came mainly from the urban industrial slaves in Charleston. The slave conspiracy of 1856 involved hundreds of industrial slaves—sugar mill workers, lead miners, and ironworkers—in Louisiana, Arkansas, Missouri, Tennessee, and Kentucky.

The records of slave revolts reveal that, while these black workers could not organize and strike, they were eager to end their bondage by any means necessary and that they often received aid and cooperation from their free black brothers.

barred them from entering their territory. All over the North the blacks lived in a world segregated by both law and custom. Even in New England, the Negro was confined to menial occupations and subjected to constant discrimination. In the antebellum North there were Negro pews in the churches, Negro seats in the courtrooms, Negro balconies in the theaters, and separate and inferior schools for Negro children. Negroes were forced to live in the worst neighborhoods, were excluded from many public omnibuses, most streetcars, and the cabins of steamers (although they were permitted to travel on the exposed deck). They even had to be buried in separate graveyards. The American belief that "God himself separated the white from the black" was to be found, everywhere, "in the hospitals where humans suffer, in the churches where they pray, in the prisons where they repent, in the cemeteries where they sleep the eternal sleep."[13]

Thus, from the cradle to the grave, the white worker, whether native-born or foreign-born, was taught to regard the Negro as an inferior. In a society in which racial prejudice was all but universal, it is hardly surprising that he refused to work with a black craftsman or laborer, believed that no black should receive the same wages and conditions as a white worker, and excluded blacks from his union. To work with a Negro in the same shop, even to travel with him on the same streetcar, was to mean a loss of social status. John Campbell, a Philadelphia typesetter, spoke for many white workers in his book *Negromania*, (1851):

> Will the white race ever agree that the blacks should stand beside us on election day, upon the rostrum, in the ranks of the army, in our places of amusement, in places of public worship, ride in the same coaches, railway cars, or steamships? Never! never! nor is it natural or just that this kind of equality should exist. God never intended it.[14]

In at least one instance, however, white workers before the Civil War sought to improve relations with blacks in their trade. Negro waiters in New York were successful in 1853 in forcing their employers to pay $16 a month at the same time that white waiters received $12. In this exceptional situation the whites held a meeting to form the Waiters' Protective Union and to force equalization of their wages. While they did not open their ranks to blacks, the whites invited the leader of the Negro waiters to attend the meeting. The New York *Herald* of March 31, 1853, reported that "Mr. Hickman (colored) . . . said the colored men were the pioneers of the movement, and would not work for less than eighteen dollars a month." The paper quoted the black waiter as saying, to the cheers of the whites: "I advise you to strike upon the 15th of April for $18 a month; and if the landlords do not give it, then you turn-out, and be assured that we will never turn in your places."

Denied the right to vote in most states, black workers could not exert political pressure to redress their grievances. Still, there is evidence that they tried to unite for protection and alleviation of their conditions. But such societies as the New York African Society for Mutual Relief, founded in 1808; the Coachmen's Benevolent Society and the Humane Mechanics, organized in Philadelphia in the 1820's; and the Stewards' and Cooks' Marine Benevolent Society, established in New York in the 1830's, resembled fraternal lodges more than trade unions, emphasizing "the need to relieve the distressed, and soften the forms of poverty, by timely aid to the afflicted."[15]

Another type of organization in existence before the Civil War is exemplified by the American League of Colored Laborers, organized in New York City in July, 1850, with Frederick Douglass as a vice-president. Its main object was to promote unity among mechanics, foster training in agriculture, industrial arts, and commerce, and assist member mechanics in setting up in business for themselves. Clearly, the league was interested in industrial education rather than trade-union activity; moreover, its orientation was toward the self-employed artisan.

Still another type was the Association of Black Caulkers in Baltimore, formed in July, 1858. Caulking was of great importance in shipbuilding, because a ship was not fit for service unless it was insured against leakage. Before 1858, Negroes had completely monopolized the trade. But Baltimore, even though it was a slave city in a slave state, was a major industrial and commercial center and, unlike most other Southern cities before the Civil War, attracted immigrants. Beginning in 1858 Irish and German immigrants began a concerted effort to drive the blacks out of the caulking trade. When petitions to legislative bodies failed to achieve this objective, the whites resorted to violence. Riots between Negro and white caulkers began to occur in the early summer of 1858. To defend themselves and protect an occupation that had always belonged to them but was now in danger of being taken away, the blacks formed the Association of Black Caulkers. Their white rivals then formed their own society of caulkers. We do not know much about the black association, for it went out of existence when a local court ordered both societies of caulkers to dissolve. The white society refused to dissolve and even forced the owner of the leading shipyard to hire whites in place of blacks, conceding a few Negroes the right to work only after obtaining a permit from the president of the white society. Negroes continued to constitute a majority of the caulkers in Baltimore but were often attacked and beaten by whites, and a number moved to other seaboard cities in search of employment.

In the first volume of *Capital*, published in 1867, Karl Marx insisted that the self-interest of the working class as a whole required the liberation of the black slaves. He wrote: "In the United States of America, any sort of independent labor movement was paralyzed as long as slavery disfigured a part of the republic. Labor with a white skin cannot emancipate itself where labor with a black skin is branded."[16] Twenty-one years earlier, the New England Workingmen's Association had used almost the same language when it resolved that "American slavery must be uprooted before the elevation sought by the laboring class can be effected."[17] But not many white workers understood the truth of their principle as the nation moved to Civil War. Most believed that their own struggles took priority over the emancipation of the slaves and feared the competition of freed slaves who might come North. Their employers, not the slaveholders, were their chief enemies.

To be sure, many workers were influenced by the Republican Party's stand against further extension of slavery in the territories and by its argument that only in a free economy, without slavery, could every man have an equal chance to succeed. The Party appealed to workers to understand that only through its program of free soil, free men, and free labor could they achieve economic independence. Workers who wanted free land for themselves realized that slave power was the chief obstacle to the realization of their dream, and they joined forces with others to resist the aggressions of the slavocracy by supporting the Republican Party. This trend accelerated in the late 1850's as fear developed in labor circles that the movement to extend slavery into the territories was only a prelude to the extension of slavery into the free states, leading finally to the reduction of the laboring class in the North to actual slavery. Republicans took pains to distribute among Northern workers literature quoting Southern designs to replace free labor in the North with slavery, such as the following editorial from a South Carolina paper: "Master and slave is a relation as necessary as that of parent and child; and the Northern States will yet have to introduce it. Slavery is the natural and normal condition of laboring men whether *white* or *black*."[18]

On the eve of the presidential election of 1860, the pro-Southern New York *Herald* appealed to Irish and German laborers: "If Lincoln is elected to-day, you will have to compete with the labor of four million emancipated negroes. . . . The North will be flooded with free Negroes, and the labor of the white man will be depreciated and degraded."[19] Most workers, however, supported Lincoln because he promised a Homestead Act (free land) and a free economy where every man would have an equal chance to succeed. But the votes contributed by workers in the urban centers to Lincoln's victory in 1860 did not signify that they endorsed immediate emancipation. Following Lincoln's election, twenty-six trades with national organizations met in convention. Not one of them even mentioned slavery or abolition. To be sure, the German-American workers under the leadership of Joseph Weydemeyer, a pioneer American Marxist, protested "most emphatically against both black and white slavery," and the Communist Club of New York not only denounced human bondage but expelled any member who manifested the slightest sympathy for the Southern point of view. But they were the exceptions. The Workingmen of Massachusetts, meeting in Faneuil Hall in Boston in December, 1860, summed up the prevailing attitude of Northern workers:

We are weary of the question of slavery; it is a matter which does not concern us; and we wish only to attend to our business, and leave the South to attend to their own affairs without any interference from the North. The Workingmen of the United States have other duties.[20]

Once the Civil War started, workers united in support of the Union. But as the war objective became increasingly to free the slaves in order to enable the North to win, the fear of Negro competition mounted in Northern white working-class circles, despite the shortage of labor in many Northern cities due to army enlistments and the reduction of foreign competition. Pro-slavery, pro-Southern Democratic and Copperhead newspapers incited white workers against the war and against blacks, exploiting not only economic fears but also racial antagonisms through vicious charges of Negro inferiority and accusations that the party of Lincoln was plotting to raise the black workers to the status of whites. On July 4, 1862, the Democratic Party of Pennsylvania denounced the Republicans as

> the party of fanaticism or crime, whichever it may be called, that seeks to turn the slaves of the Southern States loose to overrun the North and enter into competition with the white laboring masses, thus degrading and insulting to our race and merit[ing] our emphatic and unqualified condemnation.[21]

At the time this statement was adopted, there were already strikes and labor riots in a number of Northern cities involving the Negro question. Opposition to the presence of black workers, who were accused of accepting lower wages than were paid to white workers, expressed itself in strikes against employers who used Negroes, and often in violence against blacks. In a number of instances, strikes and riots broke out over the hiring of Negroes at the same rates as whites, but usually the spark that provoked the outbursts was the fear that blacks, especially escaped slaves, by working for less, were displacing white workers.

Anti-Negro sentiment in Northern working-class circles grew even more bitter with the Emancipation Proclamation of January 1, 1863. Lincoln's proclamation stirred fears of Negro competition to a new peak, stimulated by flaming editorials in the Copperhead newspapers predicting an influx of hordes of freed slaves into the factories and shops. Then came news of the proposed draft law, which would allow the rich to buy their way out of military service, and discontent among the workers soared. With new calls for volunteers producing fewer responses as the war progressed, Congress on March 3, 1863, passed legislation authorizing the first federal draft in United States history. The Conscription Act contained a clause that made it legal to evade service by providing a substitute or paying a $300 commutation fee. Many capitalists, already prosperous from wartime profits, availed themselves of this provision.

The unfair provisions of the draft law, coming on top of inflation, profiteering, and speculation by capitalists, the breaking of strikes by the Union Army, hostile state legislation, and the competitive employment of Negroes, aroused the anger of many workers to the highest pitch. The Copperheads quickly took advantage of these conditions. They denounced through their press the provision that permitted all who "possess $300 in 'greenbacks' filched from the *people*" to escape military service.

What would the workers fight for? the Copperheads asked. And they replied: "to enable 'abolition capitalists' to transport Negroes into Northern cities in order to replace Irish workers who were striking for higher wages." It was true that, during strikes for higher wages since the Emancipation Proclamation, the use of Negro strikebreakers by employers became more frequent, particularly in the longshoremen's field dominated by the Irish. In 1863 a strike of 3,000 white longshoremen in New York failed because Negroes were hired to replace the strikers. Similar failures took place in Albany, Boston, Buffalo, Chicago, Cleveland, and Detroit, and bloody rioting between Negro and Irish dock workers was quite frequent. The New York *Daily News*, a leading Copperhead paper, called it a strange perversion "to leave one's family destitute . . . while one goes to free the negro who being free will compete with him in labor."[22]

On July 13, 1863, a few days after the opening of recruiting, a mob wrecked the main recruiting station in New York City. For three whole days the mob, with the longshoremen in the vanguard, roamed through the city, destroyed shipyards, railroads and street car lines, closed factories and machine shops, attacked the homes and offices of leading Republicans, and killed and wounded an undetermined number of Negroes. (For weeks after the draft riots, bodies of Negro dock workers floated in the East and Hudson rivers.) Before the riot was quelled, more than 400 had been killed and wounded, and property estimated at $5 million in value had been destroyed.

The rioting spread to other cities—Newark, New Jersey; Troy, New York; Hartford, Indiana; Port Washington, Wisconsin—and into the mining districts of Pennsylvania. Everywhere Negroes were attacked, their homes sacked and burned, and thousands made homeless. Many blacks were driven out of jobs, despite years of service in a number of cases, and employers, fearing attacks by mobs, simply refused to employ Negroes in any kind of work.

Actually, those involved in the riots represented only a small part of the working class. But this was small comfort to the black workers who found that employers, even those who asserted that they would uphold the principle of the right of men to labor "without distinction of color," proved to be too timid to hire Negroes lest their shops be attacked or their entire working force quit. Commenting on this experience, William J. Watkins, a black lawyer, wrote in the *Christian Recorder*, official organ of the African Methodist-Episcopal Church: "Since the commencement of the rebellion, the spirit of caste has become tenfold more virulent and powerful than before. Colored men and women are being driven out of vocation after vocation. The determination of the white man is to starve us out."[23]

During the draft riots in New York, white mobs attacked the Colored Seamen's Home, partly damaged the building, and forced black seamen and others in the home "to escape over the roof for their lives."[24] The home was the headquarters of the American Seamen's Protective Association (ASPA), a pioneer organization of Negro labor and the first seamen's organization of any kind or color in the United States. That it was formed by Negro seamen is hardly surprising, since at least one-half of the 25,000 native American seamen who manned American vessels in 1850 were blacks. Many seamen were victimized by loan sharks and rent-gouging landlords while in port, and the ASPA was formed mainly to counteract these evils. It used the home as a shipping hall for black seamen, thereby eliminating some of the malpractices they were subjected to in port, but it does not appear to have functioned as an agent for dealing with their economic grievances on the job. Nevertheless, its founder, William M. Powell (born in New York City of slave parents), reported in the *New Era* on April 28, 1870, that the association had improved conditions for 3,500 colored seamen then in New York City who were earning aggregate wages of $1,269,000 annually.

The ASPA was organized during the wave of unionization that began in the summer of 1862. While wages rose during the Civil War as a result of the labor shortage, prices rose more rapidly. (Between 1860 and 1865 wages rose 43 per cent, and prices 116 per cent.) Facing ever increasing prices and seeking to prepare for the expected contraction in employment in the postwar period, the labor force moved into unions. In December, 1863, the trade union directory of *Fincher's Trades' Review*, one of the leading labor papers of the day, listed only 79 local unions, representing 20 trades; by the end of 1864 the number of locals had grown to 207, and the number of trades had increased to 53; by November, 1865, approximately 300 locals representing 61 different trades were listed. Citywide trades' assemblies (into which local unions merged) also sprang up rapidly in the war period, and before the conflict was over there were more than thirty trades' assemblies established in every important industrial city in the country. The 1860's also saw the first large-scale development of national trade unions. In the ten years from 1860 to 1870 twenty-one new national unions were formed, with the largest number appearing during the 1863–65 period. At least 120 daily, weekly, and monthly labor papers were founded in those years, another indication of the revival of the labor movement.

As the war drew to a close, labor could point with pride to the fact that, despite Copperhead incitement, it had contributed immensely to victory over the Confederacy and to the ending of slavery. At the end of the war, the Senate estimated that between 500,000 and 750,000 men had left Northern industries to enlist in the Northern army. It is likely that more than 50 per cent of the North's labor supply served in the Union Army, but whatever the exact figure, more workers wore the blue uniform than members of other economic groups. Among them, though fighting in separate regiments and under white officers, were black workers. More than 186,000 Negro soldiers fought in the Northern armies, many of them escaped slaves, and their troops suffered 35 per cent more casualties than any other group.

When the war ended, labor served notice that in the future it would expect more of the wealth it had produced, "and a more equal participation in the privileges and blessings of those free institutions defended by their manhood on many a bloody field of battle."[25] In the name of the

workingmen of Europe, the General Council of the International Work
ingmen's Association (the First International) sent an address, penned
by Karl Marx, urging the white workers in the United States to make
certain, out of basic self-interest, to include black workers in their plans
for the future. Congratulating them that "slavery is no more," the address added the following "word of counsel for the future":

> An injustice to a section of your people has produced such direful results,
> let that cease. Let your citizens of to-day be declared free and equal, with-
> out reserve.
> If you fail to give them citizens' rights, while you demand citizens'
> duties, there will yet remain a struggle for the future which may again
> stain your country with your people's blood.
> The eyes of Europe and of the world are fixed upon your efforts at re-
> construction and enemies are ever ready to sound the knell of the downfall
> of republican institutions when the slightest chance is given.
> We warn you then, as brothers in the common cause, to remove every
> shackle from freedom's limb, and your victory will be complete.[26]

Would labor, as it entered the era of Reconstruction, heed these
words of wisdom?

2 The Reconstruction Period

At the conclusion of the Civil War, organized labor faced a number of serious problems. Unemployment arising from demobilization, the sudden cessation of war contracts, the renewal of large-scale immigration, and the postwar depression, which began late in 1865 and lasted well into 1867, created unpromising conditions for strengthening the trade unions and advancing the movement for an eight-hour day without a decrease in pay. To these questions, the *Boston Daily Evening Voice* of May 2, 1866, added another, which it declared was of the utmost importance: "Can white workingmen ignore colored ones?"

This question could no longer be avoided. Slavery as a labor system had been eliminated, and several million blacks had been added, nominally at least, to the nation's labor supply. How were these ex-slaves to earn a living? Would they be used to strengthen the employers or the labor movement?

One issue was immediate and paramount: the use of Negro strikebreakers. Employers were refusing the demands of unskilled workers, confident that they could replace strikers with blacks, and at lower pay. In the spring of 1866, the labor press reported that an emigration company was being organized for the purpose of shipping 200,000 to 300,000 Negro workers from the South to the manufacturing centers of New England, enabling employers there to lower their labor costs and defeat any move to raise wages or reduce working hours.

Negro competition was a threat for skilled white workers as well. Before the Civil War, free blacks in the South, as we have seen, had pursued many occupations requiring a high degree of skill. Many ex-slaves who had gained experience in the army, freedmen's camps, and relief associations were added to the reservoir of skilled black workers. On an inspection tour of the South in 1868, John M. Langston, an agent for the Freedman's Bureau, reported that there were at least two Negro craftsmen for every white one in Mississippi, and six Negro mechanics for every white mechanic in North Carolina.

In a number of Southern cities, white workers joined with Negroes in strikes, but not even they would open their unions to blacks. As an illustration, in 1865 white and black laborers on the levee in New Orleans struck together for higher wages. "They marched up the levee in a long procession, white and black together," one observer wrote.[1] The New

Orleans *Tribune,* the first daily Negro newspaper in the United States, supported the joint action and also championed the eight-hour day. But the Workingmen's Central Committee of New Orleans, representing eleven trades that excluded Negroes, demanded that the *Tribune* pledge to limit the eight-hour demand to white workers only. The newspaper refused, of course, and asked the central committee: "How will you get justice, if you yourselves are unjust to your fellow-laborers?" Shortly thereafter, the white bricklayers of New Orleans went on strike for higher wages, and the Negro bricklayers, excluded from the union, continued to work. When the strikers realized that the employers intended to dispense with them entirely, they issued a call for a general meeting of all bricklayers, without regard to color. The *Tribune* eloquently summed up the basic issue facing black workers in its words of advice to the bricklayers:

> We hope that the colored bricklayers, before entering into any movement with their white companions, will demand as a preliminary measure, to be admitted into the benevolent and other societies which are in existence among white bricklayers. As peers, they may all come to an understanding and act in common.
>
> But should the white bricklayers intend to use their colored comrades as tools, and simply to remove the stumbling block they now find in their way, without guaranty for the future, we would say to our colored brethren: Keep aloof, go back to your work, and insist upon being recognized as men and equals before you do anything.
>
> Labor equalizes all men; the handicraft of the worker has no color and belongs to no race. The best worker—not the whitest—is the honor and pride of his trade.[2]

The white bricklayers refused to open their ranks to the blacks and lost the strike when the Negroes voted not to join the walkout.

Even this experience did not teach the white workers of New Orleans a lesson. When the Eight-Hour League was organized in the city, it rigidly excluded Negroes from membership. When white laborers went out for an eight-hour day in the spring of 1866 under the sponsorship of the league, Negroes did not hesitate to act as scabs and break the strike.

Nationally, organized labor's attention that year was riveted on Baltimore, where a National Labor Congress was to meet in August. The Industrial Assembly of North America, projected at a convention at Louisville in 1864, had failed to materialize, but the need for a national federation of labor continued to be emphasized by labor leaders. The struggle for the eight-hour day turned discussion into action. Under the direction of Ira Steward, a Boston machinist, eight-hour leagues sprang up everywhere, combining organized and unorganized workers in a mass movement. By unifying workers all over the country around a single issue, the struggle for the eight-hour day provided the stimulus for the formation of a national labor federation.

As local and national labor groups, trades' assemblies, eight-hour leagues, and farm and reform interests prepared to elect delegates to the Baltimore congress, a few labor leaders and labor papers hammered away at the theme that the convention must deal with the all-important issue of the relationship between labor and the Negro. William H. Sylvis, President of the Iron Molders' International Union, and A. C. Cameron, editor of the Chicago *Workingman's Advocate*, emphasized that self-interest dictated cooperation between white and black labor. The *Boston Daily Evening Voice*, advocating "universal liberty and equal suffrage" and recognizing "no distinction or preference based upon Race or Color," warned in numerous editorials that indifference to the Negro worker would be a course fraught with peril for the labor movement. It contrasted the successful Saint Louis strike, where white and black workers joined together and won their demands, with the unsuccessful attempt of the New Orleans Eight-Hour League to win the eight-hour day for the white worker alone. "How many kicks like that which the working-men of New Orleans have received," asked the *Voice* on May 21, 1866, "will be required to give them the hint that the colored labor of the country is henceforth in competition with the white; and if the white will not lift the colored up, the colored will drag the white down?"

The *Voice* shared with Sylvis and Cameron the perception of the danger to organized labor of excluding blacks, but it stood alone in the post-war labor movement in understanding the special problems facing the Negro people during Reconstruction. The *Voice* saw early that the Reconstruction policies of Andrew Johnson threatened the newly acquired freedom of the Negro and thus endangered the entire labor movement. Through the operation of the "black codes" adopted by the Southern state governments elected during Johnsonian Reconstruction, the freedmen were being restored to a situation of quasi-slavery, tied to the land by law, and forced to accept whatever wages were offered them or to work under share arrangements that forced them into long-term indebtedness. The *Voice* argued that without land, citizenship, and the right to vote, all of which Johnson opposed, black labor in the South would be degraded, which would "consequently cheapen white labor." It urged labor, meeting in convention in Baltimore, to ally itself with the Negro people in fighting Johnson's policies and to demand a radical program of reconstruction that would include full citizenship and suffrage for the ex-slaves.

But most Northern workers, including more advanced labor leaders and papers, were largely indifferent to the special problems of the Negro during Reconstruction and applauded Johnson for supporting a number of labor demands. When Johnson ordered the adoption of the eight-hour day in the Government Printing Office (GPO), the labor press, with the exception of the *Voice*, proclaimed that he was helping "to free the white slaves of the North." The *Voice* insisted that no man could be called "labor's champion" when he was assisting in the re-enslavement of the black workers in the South.

Neither the *Voice*'s position on Reconstruction nor its stand on the necessity of accepting Negroes into the labor movement won approval at the founding convention of the National Labor Union. The Negro question was not even mentioned. Sylvis termed the congress "a great success," but he deplored the fact that not even a recommendation was made for the inclusion of blacks in existing trade unions. The *Voice* charged the delegates with "colorphobia."[3] Similar criticism was expressed by Alexander Troup, vice-president of the National Labor Union for Massachusetts. But General Patrick F. Guiney, candidate of the Workingmen's Party for the Third Congressional District, won more applause on the same occasion when he advised workingmen to "insist that the negroes should have a right to vote, for that will be an inducement for them *to stay where they are.*"[4]

As its final act, the Labor Congress had appointed a committee to prepare and issue *The Address of the National Labor Congress to the Workingmen of the United States.* Although there was no instruction that the address concern itself with the issue of Negro labor, when it appeared in June, 1867, just before the second NLU convention, the document did deal with the question in a forthright manner—probably because A. C. Cameron, the committee chairman, was the main author. "Unpalatable as the truth may be to many," it declared, the Negroes were now in a new position in America, and the actions of the white workingmen would determine whether the ex-slaves became "an element of strength or an element of weakness" in the labor movement. It continued:

> They number four million strong, and a greater proportion of them labor with their hands than can be counted from among the same number of any other people on earth. Their moral influence, and their strength at the ballot-box, would be of incalculable value to the cause of labor. Can we afford to reject their proferred co-operation and make them enemies? By committing such an act of folly we would inflict greater injury upon the cause of Labor Reform than the combined efforts of capital could accomplish. . . .
> [The] interests of the labor cause demand that all workingmen be included within its ranks, without regard to race or nationality; and . . . the interests of the workingmen of America especially require that the formation of . . . labor organizations should be encouraged among the colored race and that they be invited to cooperate with us in the general labor undertaking.[5]

In presenting the address to the 1867 convention, Cameron urged speedy action, noting that the vast majority of blacks were now free to compete with white workers for jobs. But the convention refused to meet the problem. The question was referred to a Committee on Colored Labor, chaired by A. W. Phelps of the Carpenters and Joiners Union of New Haven, an organization whose constitution excluded Negroes. The committee's report acknowledged the "danger in the future of competition in mechanical negro labor" but proposed, since the problem was "involved in so much mystery," and opinions on it among the membership were so diverse, that the subject of Negro labor be referred to the next convention.[6]

In the heated debate that followed submission of the report, Sylvis voiced the viewpoint of those who favored admission of the Negro to the unions to strengthen the labor movement. He insisted that there was no time for further delay: The use of white scabs against blacks and black scabs against whites had already created an antagonism that would "kill off the Trades Unions" unless the two groups were consolidated. "The time will come when the negro will take possession of the shops if we have not taken possession of the negro. If the workingmen of the white race do not conciliate the blacks, the black vote will be cast against them."[7] (This last remark was a reminder to the delegates that under the Congressional plan of Reconstruction, adopted in March, 1867, over Johnson's veto, Negroes were soon to become citizens, and black males in the South were to gain the vote.)

But not even this warning carried the day. Only one union, the Carpenters and Joiners Union No. 1 of Boston, admitted blacks, and even those opposed to the report that precipitated the debate came from organizations that excluded Negroes.

A new report evaded the issue by stating that the "constitution already adopted prevented the necessity of reporting on the subject of negro labor." The Boston Daily Evening Voice called it a "disgrace to the Labor Congress that several members of that body were so much under the influence of the silliest and wickedest of all prejudices as to hesitate to recognize the Negro. . . . We shall never succeed till wiser counsels prevail and these prejudices are ripped up and thrown to the wind."[8]

At the 1868 NLU convention the delegates adopted a resolution, introduced by Cameron, expressing gratification at the downfall of slavery and asserting that "it is expedient that the whole force of labor in this country—agricultural, mining, mechanical, intellectual, and moral—be organized and united with us in order to secure justice to all laborers."[9] But neither Cameron nor Sylvis spoke up for the admission of blacks, and the convention once again ignored the issue. Moreover, the severe economic depression of the winter of 1867–68, featured by widespread layoffs and wage cuts throughout the country, pushed the issue of black-white unity farther into the background.

But a new factor was emerging to make further evasion impossible. Black workers, spearheaded by the caulkers of Baltimore, were forming their own associations. Even before the war, whites had resorted to violence to eliminate blacks from the caulking trade. In October, 1865, the white caulkers of Baltimore, joined by the ship carpenters, went on strike, insisting that blacks be discharged as caulkers and longshoremen. Supported by the city government and by the police, the strikers succeeded in driving the blacks from the shipyards.

Thrown suddenly out of employment, the black workers held a meeting to decide what to do next. Isaac Myers proposed that they form a union to sponsor a cooperative company that would purchase a shipyard and railway and carry on business cooperatively. Myers, who became the first important black labor leader in America, was born a free Negro of poor parents in Baltimore in 1835. He grew up in a slave state that afforded no public school education for black children, but he received a common school education in a private school and at sixteen was apprenticed to a prominent black ship caulker. By 1860 the young Myers was a skilled caulker, superintending the caulking of clean-line clipper ships. But in 1865 a strike of white workers against the presence of black mechanics and longshoremen resulted in the dismissal of more than 100 Negroes from their jobs in the Baltimore shipyards.

Myers's proposal to purchase a shipyard cooperatively caught fire. The caulkers issued stock and quickly raised $10,000 among blacks in Baltimore and other cities. (Among the first stockholders was Frederick Douglass.) They borrowed $30,000 more from a ship captain, secured a six-year mortgage, purchased an extensive shipyard and railway, and took possession on February 12, 1866.

Within six months after beginning operations, the Chesapeake Marine Railway and Dry Dock Company employed 300 blacks at an average wage of three dollars a day. It obtained a number of government contracts and paid off its debt within five years. As it expanded, it employed white mechanics as well as blacks. There were now two caulkers' unions in Baltimore: the Colored Caulkers' Trade Union Society of Baltimore with Isaac Myers as president, and the white caulkers' union. The unions now cooperated and even met to discuss common problems.

The successful Baltimore venture was often pointed to as a way to solve the employment problem for black workers in the North, but most blacks found it difficult to raise the funds necessary to follow the Baltimore example. In the South, however, where employment was not the major problem, blacks began to organize and strike to improve their conditions. Early in 1867 a strike on the levee in Mobile spread to other industries, resulting in some of the most stirring mass demonstrations in Southern history. About the same time black longshoremen in Charleston formed the Longshoremen's Protective Union Association and won a strike for higher wages. In February the dock workers of Savannah, Georgia, nearly all black, went on strike against the city council's poll tax of $19 on all persons employed on the wharves and won repeal.

Some of the strikes did not end in victory, but they nonetheless marked the entry of the black working class into the labor movement. In Philadelphia, the black brickmakers jointly struck with whites in July, 1868, for higher wages. While the strike was largely a failure, it stimulated organization of black workers in the city. By the fall of 1868, there was not only an active Colored Brickmakers' Association, but a large Hod Carriers' and Laborers' Association and a Workingmen's Union built by Negroes in Philadelphia. By then, too, Negro labor organizations had grown to the point where Isaac Myers was encouraged to devote his efforts to starting a black movement for nationwide suffrage, civil rights, and the elimination of all aspects of discrimination. "We want every boy to have a trade, to be master of some profession," he wrote in November, 1868. "It is unfortunate as it is unjust, that the colored boy is not permitted to enter the workshops of the Northern cities to learn a trade."[10] Myers recommended the formation of cooperative workshops in the North and trade unions in the South.

Meanwhile a labor-Negro alliance was being discussed in the labor press, prominently supported by Sylvis and Cameron. Sylvis identified a new slave power in the country—the "money power"—which, "under the cloak of philanthropy for the Negro," had forged a wage slavery more oppressive than chattel slavery. "Capital," he wrote, "blights and withers all it touches. It is a new aristocracy, proud, imperious, dishonest, seeking only profit and exploitation of the workers." Moreover, the money power made no sexual, racial, or color distinctions in exploiting its victims. "The working people of our nation, white and black, male and female, are now sinking to a condition of serfdom oppressed by the center of slave power in Wall Street."

Sylvis warned those unions that ordered strikes when Negro workers were employed that their "fanatical bigotry" jeopardized the future of the labor reform movement, for it was "impossible to degrade one group of workers without degrading all." Besides, he said, labor must realize that the Negro now had suffrage in the South, would gain the ballot in the North, and would even hold the balance of political power in the nation. "If we can succeed in convincing these people to make common cause with us . . . we will have a power . . . that will shake Wall Street out of its boots."[11] But it was too much to expect the Negro to use his ballot in the cause of labor reform when the unions denied him membership, and even the opportunity to earn an honest living.

To Sylvis, defeating the money power and ending its control over the national government meant defeating the dominant Republican Party. In the presidential election of 1868, Sylvis had aided the Democrats in Pennsylvania in their attempt to win the labor vote, announcing publicly that there was "no hope for laboring men in the Republican Party because Wall Street runs the whole concern." But he made it clear at the same time that his faith lay only in the organization of an independent political party comprising labor, the Negro people, and the farmers.

A victory for the Democratic Party meant to Sylvis a defeat of the party controlled by Wall Street. But to the Negro people, who looked upon the Republican Party as the party of emancipation and the safeguard for their further social, economic, and political elevation, it would have meant the loss of all they had gained. Nor would they abandon the Republican Party for a new political movement dominated by labor leaders whose unions excluded them from membership.

Sylvis's insight into labor problems (marred though it was by racist attitudes*) and his organizing genius were lost to the American labor movement when he died suddenly on July 26, 1869. Yet before his death Sylvis, as President of the National Labor Union, provided the organization's forthcoming session with a magnificent opportunity for labor unity. In December, 1868, he and the Executive Committee of the NLU

---

* When Sylvis was on an organizing tour for the NLU in 1869, he sent letters to the Chicago *Workingman's Advocate* in which he sneered at the new Reconstruction governments, which were introducing public education and developing social legislation of great significance to poor people, white as well as black. He was particularly offended by the social intermingling of black and white under the new regime in the South. (*See* issues of March-April 1869, especially March 27, 1869.)

met in Washington, D.C., and, in a precedent-shattering action, made the organization's first official overture to the Negro by extending a formal invitation to all persons interested in the labor movement, regardless of color or sex, to attend the annual convention in Philadelphia on August 16, 1869.

On July 20, 1869, the Baltimore *Sun* carried the news of a "Meeting of Colored Persons"—approximately thirty Negroes—at Douglass Institute for the purpose "of effecting an organization into trades unions and societies." Isaac Myers, who convened the meeting, stated that its aim was to organize the colored mechanics of Maryland, where white mechanics had refused to permit black mechanics to work with them or join their unions. He pointed out that the extension of the franchise to the Negro would not guarantee him economic benefits if he did not organize to protect himself and his family. He referred to the plan "now afoot" to import Chinese laborers into the South to take the place of Negroes. Were that to occur, black workers would be further threatened. George Myers, a Baltimore caulker and a member of the cooperative shipbuilding company organized by blacks, pointed out that without organization black workers could accomplish nothing, "but with it everything. It is the duty of colored men to look after their rights in the labor market."[12] He urged the colored workers to associate themselves with the National Labor Union.

Three significant actions were taken at the July 20 meeting. A permanent organization for the state of Maryland was created, with Isaac Myers as president and representatives from each trade present constituting an executive board. This new state labor body was to become the dynamic center of organization for black workers throughout the nation. The second action v.as the election of delegates to the NLU convention. The third was the initiation of plans for a national Negro labor convention the following December to consider ways of protecting the interests of black workers.

These actions marked a significant development in the history of the black working class in the United States. The delegates had considered whether to continue the struggle for admission to existing unions on equal terms or to organize separate trade unions. They had decided to do both.

Chosen to represent the black workers of Maryland at the NLU convention were Isaac Myers of the Colored Caulkers' Trade Union Society, Ignatius Gross of the Colored Moulders' Union Society, Robert H. Butler of the Colored Engineers' Association, and James W. W. Hare of the Colored Painters' Society. About the same time five delegates were selected to represent the black workers of Pennsylvania: Robert M. Adger and Peter P. Brown of the United Hod Carriers' and Laborers' Association of Pennsylvania, John H. Thomas and James Roane of the United Carriers Union No. 2 of Philadelphia, and Isaiah Weir of the Workingmen's Union of Philadelphia. It is difficult to determine whether there was communication between the Maryland and Pennsylvania delegates before the convention opened, but once they arrived in Philadelphia the black delegates acted as a united group.

The highlight of the convention was Isaac Myers's magnificent address, in which he voiced the sentiments and aspirations of black workers. He opened by paying tribute to the delegates for their awareness of the need for unity between Negro and white workers. "Silent, but powerful and far-reaching is the revolution inaugurated by your act in taking the colored laborer by the hand and telling him that his interest is common with yours." He then gave a brilliant analysis of the need for unity, pointing out that Negro workers desired above all equal opportunity to labor under conditions similar to those enjoyed by white workers and to earn wages that would "secure them a comfortable living for their families, educate their children, and leave a dollar for a rainy day in old age." White workers, he assured the delegates, had nothing to fear from black laborers, for they desired just what the whites wanted, and they were ready to join in a common struggle to achieve it.

Cooperation had not always been evident in the past, because the workshops and trade unions had been barred to the Negro, hence he had been compelled to put his labor on the market for whatever he could get. Myers warned against the continuation of such rivalry; he stressed the desire of the Negro to cooperate in the future, but he made it clear that cooperation was a two-way street. His words have lost none of their significance since they were uttered more than a century ago:

> American citizenship is a complete failure, if [the Negro] is proscribed from the workshops of this country—if any man cannot employ him who chooses, and if he cannot work for any man whom he will. If citizenship means anything at all, it means the freedom of labor, as broad and as universal as the freedom of the ballot.

Then Myers asked pointedly whether "the minor organizations throughout the country" would be influenced by the convention's example in admitting black delegates. As for the blacks, "We carry no prejudices. We are willing to forget the wrongs of yesterday and let the dead past bury its dead." As an illustration, he told of the black shipyard workers in Baltimore who, forced out of their jobs by a strike of white shipyard workers, organized a cooperative, raised $40,000, bought a shipyard, and gave employment to many blacks who otherwise would have been unemployed. "And is that all? No. We gave employment to a large number of the men of your race, without regard to their political creed, and to the very men who once sought to do us injury. So you see, gentlemen, we have no prejudice."

Myers announced that Negro labor leaders had issued a call for a National Labor Convention to meet in Washington in December. Delegates were to be admitted without regard to color, and he would be happy to have the cooperation of the NLU at that meeting "as you have ours now." He then touched on political issues on which he differed with key positions of his hosts. The NLU, along with many labor reformers of the period, advocated effective repudiation of the national debt by paying holders of government bonds in greenbacks rather than in gold, as called for, and generally favored the issuance of greenbacks, "the People's Money." Furthermore, the NLU consistently condemned the Republican Party as the agent of Wall Street and President Ulysses S. Grant as the spokesman for industrial and financial capitalists.

Myers told why the Negro opposed repudiation of the national debt. Had not slavery been abolished, he reminded the delegates, it would have spread over the entire country, "and you white laboring men . . . would have been forced to work for what a man chose to give you, and that very often under the lash." The money borrowed by the government had financed emancipation, and labor was an important beneficiary. As for President Grant, Myers said, labor should feel fortunate to have in the White House a man who had ordered the eight-hour day for government workers without a reduction in pay.* "The colored men of the country thoroughly indorse him."

"Gentlemen," Myers said in conclusion, "again thanking you for what you have done, and hoping you may finish the good work of uniting the colored and white workingmen of the country by some positive declaration of this Convention, I wish you a complete success."[13] The convention did make a "declaration" by adopting a resolution encouraging the organization of separate Negro unions to be affiliated with the NLU. "The National Labor Union knows no north, no south, no east, no west, neither color nor sex, on the question of rights of labor, and urges our colored fellow members to form organizations in all legitimate ways, and send their delegates from every state in the union to the next Congress." In addition, a special committee of five black delegates was appointed to "organize the colored men of Pennsylvania into labor unions" and report their progress to the president of the NLU.[14]

The NLU did not, however, adopt a policy of racial integration, which its leaders evidently considered too advanced a position to endorse at the first convention attended by blacks. Still, the 1869 NLU convention was the first occasion in American history when a national gathering of white workingmen advocated the formation of labor unions by Negroes and authorized the admission of blacks to the annual sessions. The black delegates did not object to the policy of separate unionism. Robert H. Butler of the Colored Engineers Association of Maryland emphasized that black workers were looking not for "parlor sociabilities, but for the rights of mankind."[15]

Isaac Myers said that the convention had marked the beginning of a "revolution" so far as the Negro was concerned. But how far the "revolution" would go in bringing equality of opportunity without distinction of race or color would depend upon the response of the national and local unions, and in this respect prospects were not promising. The *Christian Recorder*, published in the very city where the NLU convention

---

* On July 25, 1868, Congress passed, and a few days later President Grant signed, a law providing for an eight-hour day for laborers, mechanics, and all other workmen in federal employ. About a year later, after many government departments had reduced wages of federal workers in proportion to the change in hours, President Grant issued an executive order that "no reduction should be made in wages by the day to such laborers . . . on account of such reduction in the hours of labor."

was held, warned that "the ineffable meanness as well as stupidity of the American Trades-Unions in regard to color" was too deeply ingrained to expect actions "consistent with common sense and the spirit of our American democracy."[16] After its survey of its city's black population in the summer of 1869, the *New York Times* had disclosed that all trade unions kept Negro mechanics from work by the double process of barring blacks from membership and refusing to work with them. White workers, especially the Irish, often combined to force their employers to discharge Negro workers, and quite often blacks were victims of physical violence while on the job. The "powerful effects of prejudice" were visible throughout the city's economic life.

> I was informed by highly respectable persons, who were by no means desirous of glossing over the faults of their people, that they did not know a single workshop in this city where a colored man could get employment as an artisan, however respectable or however clever at his trade he might be, or where a colored lad would be taken as an apprentice.[17]

There was some change in the New York picture following the 1869 NLU convention. One of the American sections of the International Workingmen's Association (First International), affiliated to the NLU as Labor Union No. 5, appointed a committee in October, 1869, to organize trade unions among Negro workers. Two weeks later a delegation of black workers reported that a union of fifty members had already been organized. The section provided a hall for the Negro union and in March, 1870, succeeded in having this and other Negro labor unions admitted to the Workingmen's Union, a central labor body of the city.

In the opening address to a convention of the New York Workingmen's Assembly early in 1870, with the American Marxists present as delegates, President William J. Jessup called upon the affiliated unions to organize colored workmen. "The negro," he said, "will no longer submit to occupy positions of a degraded nature, but will seek an equality with the whites in the trades and profession. . . . If we discard this element of labor and refuse to recognize it, capital will recognize it and use it to our great disadvantage." In a letter published subsequently, Jessup wrote that black labor was "seeking organization and recognition; we are disposed to treat it fairly as we believe it is necessary for the well-being of our own labor in the future that it should receive attention."[18]

Few labor bodies were willing to follow the example of the American Marxists, the New York Workingmen's Union, and the New York State Workingmen's Assembly. More typical was the action at the fifth annual session of the Carpenters and Joiners National Union in September, 1869. The Committee on Colored Labor reported the following resolution, which was adopted by the whole convention: "Resolved that we are ever willing to extend the hand of fellowship to every laboring man, more especially to those of our own craft; we believe that the prejudices of our members against the colored people are of such a nature that it is not expedient at present to admit them as members or to organize them under the National Union."[19] Another instance was the widely pub-

licized stand of the International Typographical Union in the case of
Lewis H. Douglass.

In May, 1869, the son of Frederick Douglass obtained employment at
the Government Printing Office. At the same time he applied for membership in the Columbia Typographical Union, the Washington branch
of the ITU—only union members could work in the GPO—and obtained
from the financial secretary a permit to work until his case could be
acted upon. News of the decision spread rapidly among the GPO employees. At the May meeting of the union, many members took a stand
in favor of "the right of colored men to earn an honest livelihood on
equal terms with whites," but the opponents of this principle, deciding
it was impolitic to object to Douglass as a member on the ground of
color, resorted to the subterfuge of denouncing him as a "rat" (scab). A
resolution was introduced censuring the financial secretary and ordering
that Douglass's work permit be revoked. But so heated was the debate
that the meeting was adjourned without any action being taken.

Before the Columbia Union could meet again, the International Typographical Union held its annual convention. Without any discussion, the
convention adopted a resolution introduced by a delegate from the Columbia Union censuring the GPO for employing Douglass, an *"avowed
rat,"* calling upon the Washington branch to rescind his application, and
pledging the International Union to see that this resolution would be
enforced.[20] The action of the international infuriated Douglass's supporters, who appealed to the international president to nullify the convention's decision. But their appeal for justice was ignored; Douglass was
denied membership in the Columbia Union, with the full approval of
the international, and forced out of the GPO. Frederick Douglass
pointed out that his son had been "denounced for not being a member of the Printers' Union by the very men who would not permit him to
join such a union . . . There is no disguising the fact—his crime was his
color. . . . Some men have shown an interest in saving my soul; but of
what avail are such manifestations where one sees himself ostracized, degraded and denied the means of obtaining his daily bread?"[21]

The *Printers' Circular*, organ of the ITU, defended the action of both
the local and the international: "That there are deep-seated prejudices
against the colored race no one will deny; and that these prejudices are
so strong in many local unions that any attempt to disregard or override
them will almost inevitably lead to anarchy and disintegration . . . and
surely no one who has the welfare of the craft at heart will seriously contend that the union of thousands of white printers should be destroyed
for the purpose of granting a barren honor of membership to a few Negroes."[22] The fact that this "barren honor of membership" brought with
it the right to work did not appear to concern the union paper.

This capitulation set the pattern for other unions. The New York *Herald* reported in the summer of 1869:

> Some of the workingmen's associations here, warned by the troubles of the
> Printers' Union, are taking measures to keep the negro out of their mem-
> bership. The house carpenters held a meeting last evening, at which a con-

stitution was adopted, wherein the word "white" was inserted in all places where the character of the members of the association is described. Some objection was made that the word was unnecessary, because if the name of a negro was presented for membership he could be rejected by a vote of the association. A majority of the members, however, thought that it was better to make doubly sure, by providing that negroes would be ineligible for membership, and this was finally agreed to. It is said that other workingmen's associations will take similar action.[23]

Small wonder that black workers were more than ever determined to build an independent movement of their own. In the summer and fall of 1869 the black press prominently featured the official call for a National Labor Convention to be held on the first Monday in December at Union League Hall, Washington, D.C. "Fellow-Citizens," the call declared, "you cannot place too great an estimate upon the important subjects this convention is called to consider, viz.: your Industrial Interests." In the greater portion of the United States, "Colored Men are excluded from the workshops on account of their color." In the South, the black worker was "unjustly deprived of the price of his labor" and, in areas far from courts of justice, "forced to endure wrongs and oppression worse than Slavery." These and many other problems of black workers could "only be effectually remedied by the meeting in National Council of the Mechanics and Laborers of this country."

> We . . . appeal to the white tradesmen and artisans of this country to conquer their prejudices so far as to enable Colored Men to have a fair field for the display of competitive industry; and with this in view to do away with all pledges and obligations that forbid the taking of Colored Boys as Apprentices to trades, or the employment of Colored Journeymen therein.

Delegates were to be admitted to the National Convention "without regard to race or color." State or city conventions would be entitled to send one delegate for each department of trade or labor represented in these bodies, and every mechanical or labor organization throughout the country would also be entitled to one delegate. "It is hoped that all who feel an interest in the welfare and elevation of our race will take an active part in making this Convention a grand success."[24]

The call was widely circulated in the black press and through the Negro churches. Blacks in various parts of the country, North and South, held meetings and conventions to elect delegates to the Washington gathering and to discuss labor conditions in general. Some were small events, such as the meeting held at Avery College, a black institution near Pittsburgh, while others were citywide and statewide in scope. But all were imbued with the feeling that they were dealing with the most important issue facing black Americans.

3 The Colored National Labor Union

On December 6, 1869, 214 officially accredited delegates assembled in Union League Hall in Washington, D.C. The eighteen states represented were Alabama, California, Connecticut, Delaware, Florida, Georgia, Louisiana, Massachusetts, Maryland, Mississippi, Missouri, North Carolina, Nevada, New Jersey, New York, Ohio, Pennsylvania, Rhode Island, South Carolina, Tennessee, and Virginia. Fifty-four of the delegates came from the Deep South. Black workers were too poor to come to Washington, so many of the delegates were lawyers, preachers, teachers, or merchants.* There were a few white delegates in attendance, including Richard F. Trevellick, president of the National Labor Union, and female delegates were admitted without dispute.

The Colored National Labor Union convention was called to order by Isaac Myers, but before the delegates could proceed further a clash developed over the admission of two white delegates, Samuel P. Cummings and Charles MacLean, both of the Massachusetts Labor Reform Party. John M. Langston of Howard University, a prominent black lawyer and Republican Party leader, contended that their admission would encourage the convention to desert the Republican Party, which had shown such goodwill to the Negro. Isaac Myers criticized Langston for narrow-mindedness, and J. Sella Martin bitterly rebuked him for "denouncing white delegates because of color." Martin emphasized the identity of interests between black and white labor and argued that the blacks could not afford to reject the support of sympathetic whites. George T. Downing of Rhode Island agreed with Langston that the party of Lincoln had earned respect for its part in overthrowing slavery

* In the official proceedings of the list of delegates, there are many whose occupations are not listed. But those who are listed break down as follows: Minister, 10; Attorney-at-Law, 6; Government employees, 11; Merchant, 9; Merchant and farmer, 1; Farmer, 8; Teacher, 2; Professor, 1; Carpenter, 5; Caulker, 3; Dressmaker, 1; Showman, 2; Printer, 1; Engineer, 1; Tailor, 3; Jailor, 1; Cabinetmaker, 1; Glazier, 1; Constable, 1; Fireman, 3; Plumber, 1; Brickmaker, 1; Plasterer, 3; Builder, 1; Barber, 1; Policeman, 1; Constable, 1; Hotel keeper, 1; Stevedore, 1; Paper and paperhanger, 2; Laborer, 1. (*Proceedings of the Colored National Labor Convention Held in Washington D.C., on December 6, 7, 8, 9, 10, 1869*, Washington, D.C., 1870, pp. 37-40.

but said it was by no means above reproach because of its failure to provide in its Reconstruction program for distribution of land among freemen. "We think it should have been more consistent," he continued, "more positive in its dealings with our and the country's enemies. . . . We should be secured in the soil, which we have enriched in our toil and blood, and to which we have a double entitlement."

Cummings and MacLean were finally admitted, but by no means did the delegates endorse their views on independent political action for labor, particularly after a speech by Richard F. Trevellick, the president of the National Labor Union. After greeting the delegates in the name of the NLU, Trevellick conceded that white workers monopolized the trades "to the entire exclusion in some instances of the colored man," that the plight of the black worker as a consequence was dismal, and that in the South he was being forced into peonage, subject to the caprices of the landowners. The speaker's only remedy, apparently, was a change in the monetary system, which had produced an unequal distribution of wealth and had dragged the white worker down to the dismal level of the blacks. Trevellick denounced both the Republican and Democratic parties and spoke eloquently of the need to unite all working people without regard to race, color, or sex. Only through such unity, he said, could the freedom and progress of the toiling millions be guaranteed.

The delegates welcomed the NLU president's call for unity but were disappointed to hear that "carrying on factories and workshops or taking apprentices to learn trades are not political questions that legislation can interfere with," and that, these issues being "matters of taste and being local, different rules may be established depending on local considerations." To the black worker these were issues of economic life or death, since local union membership and apprenticeship policies were barring Negroes from the right to work and strangling their children's economic opportunities. Yet Trevellick, a skillful labor agitator, saw nothing inconsistent in asking the Negro to abandon the Republican Party while offering nothing meaningful in return. On the contrary, he in effect promised to do nothing himself about restrictive union practices, since he regarded them as local matters.

The basic principles of the organization to be launched by the convention were enunciated by the Platform Committee, chaired by Isaac Myers: "Labor has its privileges no less than its duties, one of which is to organize." Specifically, the committee asserted that (1) every man and woman should "receive employment according to his ability to perform the labor required" and that this right should be restricted only "by the laws of political economy," not by "exclusion of colored men and apprentices from the right to labor"; (2) capital and labor were complementary and necessary to each other, harmony between the two should be cultivated so that " 'strikes' may be avoided and the workingman convinced that justice is done him," and, to promote better understanding between labor and capital, "political economy" should be made a mandatory subject for study "in all our labor organizations"; (3) intemperance was the "natural foe and curse of the American family, especially the working classes"; (4) educated labor was "less dependent upon capital" and commanded higher wages, and, therefore, "there should be a liberal free school system enacted by the legislature of the several states for the benefit of all the inhabitants"; (5) no laws should be enacted by any legislative body to the advantage of one class and against the interest of another, but all legislation should be for the benefit of all the people; and (6) the learning of trades and professions by colored youth should be encouraged so as to impress them with the fact that "all labor is honorable and a sure road to wealth; that habits of economy and temperance, combined with industry and education, are the great safeguard of free republican institutions."

Finally, the Platform Committee appealed to colored workingmen to "form organizations throughout every state and territory" in order that their rights might be more adequately protected. In addition, the committee recommended the establishment of a Bureau of Labor through which the grievances of black workers could be presented to the proper legal authorities and "justice . . . meted out" to colored workingmen who resided in districts far removed from courts of justice, "as though they lived in the large cities" where courts were maintained.[1]

The principles enunciated by the Platform Committee reveal how differently the spokesmen for black workers and the leaders of the NLU viewed issues. The right to work without regard to race, a just and equitable system of apprenticeship, education, temperance, fair and full remuneration for a day's work—these were the cardinal principles of Negro labor's program. The key to the black American's future was not a change in the monetary system but the chance to work and rise in American society through industry, temperance, frugality, and education. (It was a future in the United States, moreover: The Platform Committee made no mention of emigration to Africa or Central America, and the convention adopted a resolution opposing such plans.) Seeing no reason, with such an outlook, for antagonism between capital and labor, the Platform Committee rejected the idea that capital was inimical to labor, and the convention rejected resolutions that spelled out such a principle.

But nothing was said about the Southern Negro's need for land and the refusal of landowners to sell land to blacks on reasonable terms. Calling attention to this omission, James H. Harris, described by W. E. B. Du Bois as "an astute and courageous Reconstruction leader,"[2] reminded the delegates that the South, having passed through a political reconstruction, needed "another reconstruction in the affairs of the laboring class." Other delegates bluntly told the convention that the sessions would accomplish little if no attention was paid to the special needs of Southern agricultural laborers.

In response the convention drew up a petition to Congress. It painted a frightening picture of the status of black agricultural labor and explained the difficulties the black labor movement would face in building effective unions among rural Southern Negroes. The average annual wage of agricultural labor in the South was only sixty dollars. While employers made huge profits, the laborers who produced their wealth "have not only been left penniless, but are nearly two millions of dollars in debt, despite the utmost thrift and economy on their part." The workers were practically powerless to change these conditions; the landowners were able to combine against the laborer, but there was no opportunity for black workers to unite against their exploiters. Indeed, "resistance by organized effort is impossible for the earnings of the laborer leave him no surplus, and when he ceases to labor he begins to starve." His right to vote and his other civil rights not only offered little protection but actually invited "aggression which he cannot repel, and his political privileges become to him the source of personal peril." If the black agricultural laborer cast his vote against the political wishes and interests of the landlords—there was no secret ballot—he could easily be deprived of what meager livelihood he had and became a target for marauding bands like the Ku Klux Klan, the Knights of the White Camelia, or the White Leagues.

The petition made it clear that the "condition of the colored laborers of the southern States appeals forcibly to Congress to intervene in their behalf."[3] The legislation Congress was asked to pass would subdivide the public lands of the South into forty-acre farms. A resident who settled on a site for one year would automatically gain title to the land. In addition, a sum not to exceed 2 million dollars would be placed in the control of a commission to aid the settlers. The commission would purchase land in states where public land was unavailable. Five-year interest-free loans would be offered to blacks. The petition argued that if more blacks owned land there would be fewer farm laborers, and the scarcity of labor would force employers to be more "mindful of the treatment of their employees."

Although the labor convention concentrated on national problems, it also displayed a high degree of internationalism, as reflected in its passage of a resolution of sympathy for the Cubans struggling for independence from Spanish rule. J. Stella Martin was designated as a delegate to the World Labor Congress scheduled to meet in Paris in September, 1870.

The new national organization of black workers was officially designated the National Labor Union, and its purpose was the "amelioration and advancement of the condition of those who labor for a living."[4] Membership was open to all workers, not as individual members but through organized local affiliates. Locals having the prescribed minimum of seven workers of the same occupation could be organized on the basis of trades; others would be composed of workers of varied occupations. Each local organization was entitled to send one delegate to national conventions, and each state labor union could send three. The constitution provided for the offices of president, vice-president, secretary, assistant secretary, and treasurer and for an Executive Committee. The national officers constituted the Bureau of Labor, which, among other functions, was to promote state and federal legislation for protection of the civil, political, and economic rights of workers. More specifically, the duties of the Bureau of Labor were (1) to grant charters to locally organized unions; (2) to encourage the establishment of land, loan, and cooperative associations; (3) to make annual reports to the NLU; (4) to regulate the salaries of the national officers; and (5) to serve as an employment agency by keeping a register of jobs available throughout the United States, informing various locals of employment opportunities, and assisting workers to move where jobs were available. This last function was considered the most important. The bureau was to be not only an agency for distributing information and an organizer of cooperative associations but also a counseling and employment agency.

The officers of the Colored National Labor Union for the years 1869–79 were Isaac Myers, president; George T. Downing, vice-president; William U. Saunders, secretary; Lewis H. Douglass, assistant secretary; and Colin Crusor, treasurer. The members of the Executive Committee were Isaiah C. Weir, Anthony Bowen, John H. Butler, Mrs. Mary A. S. Carey,* George W. Mabson, C. H. Hamilton, J. Sella Martin, and George Myers. Although the constitution did not spell out the duties of the Executive Committee, it probably was meant to act as a policy-making body for the union.

And so in 1869 black leaders, North and South, had reached the conclusion that, if Negro workers were to obtain equal employment opportunities and receive better pay for their labor, they would have to organize. What began in July in Baltimore as a local colored workers' union soon expanded into a statewide and then a national movement, culminating in the Colored National Labor Union convention in December. Here, for the first time in American history, blacks representing a wide variety of trades, occupations, and professions discussed the conditions of Negro labor in the United States and made recommendations on how to improve them. More important, a national labor organization was established to mobilize the united power of the black working class to secure improvements in those conditions.

The Colored National Labor Union, like its white counterpart, was to be a confederation of autonomous local and state unions. Unlike the NLU, which concentrated on skilled artisans and mechanics, the black union would include all workers—industrial, agricultural, skilled craftsmen, common laborers—men and women alike. Primarily concerned with the needs of blacks, it nonetheless invited membership from all sections of the working class, including even the Chinese, thus becoming the only labor organization of the period to open its ranks to the Chinese immigrant. Yet, for all its advocacy of labor unity, the Colored National Labor Union made clear that it would never yield an inch in its

---

* Mrs. Carey was one of several female delegates admitted to the convention without dispute. The convention also upheld the equal rights of women in industry and unions. The Committee on Women's Labor recommended, "profiting by the mistakes heretofore made by our white fellow citizens in omitting women . . . that women be cordially included in the invitation to further and organize cooperative societies." The proposal was unanimously approved. *Proceedings of the Colored National Labor Convention Held in Washington, D.C., on December 6, 7, 8, 9, 10, 1869,* Washington, D.C., 1870.

opposition to the restrictive policies of the white unions. It would be up to the white unions to prove that they were truly interested in unity by abandoning these policies.

Under the auspices of the officers and Executive Committee of the Colored National Labor Union, a large interracial meeting was held on February 21, 1870, in Washington, D.C., to consider sending an agent to organize Negro workers. Isaac Myers was officially named agent, and so, as Sylvis had done for the NLU, the black labor leader undertook an organizing trip for the colored labor federation.

Myers spoke in Richmond and Norfolk, Virginia, to racially mixed audiences. He castigated white artisans for being "organized for the extermination of colored labor," but he emphasized that white and black workers must come together for mutual benefit. For the time being separate organization was necessary as a safeguard for Negro labor. "The watchword of the colored men must be Organize!" he told the Virginia workers. "Labor organization is the safeguard of the colored man. But for real success separate organization is not the real answer. The white and colored mechanics must come together and work together. . . . The day has passed for the establishment of organizations based upon color." Myers urged labor organizations everywhere to affirm publicly that they were organized for the benefit of all workingmen, black and white, and to prove it by choosing officers from both races. Blacks, he said, should take the lead in this direction and set the example.

The Richmond meeting passed resolutions supporting the Colored National Labor Union, urging the black workers of the city immediately to form unions, and asserting that only through organization could labor "secure its rights and the respect due it . . . and that all men of whatever color, who oppose the systematized organization of labor, are enemies of the best interests of the working people." D. Collins, a white speaker at the Norfolk meeting, voiced approval of the CNLU and asserted that, given closer cooperation between white and black workers, "wages would be much better for both white and colored." The Norfolk assembly adopted a resolution endorsing the Colored National Labor Union and pledging the "support of the workingmen of Norfolk in aid of working out the principles laid down in its platform."[5]

Encouraged, Myers returned to Washington to address a meeting of 1,000 at Bell Church. He now predicted that for the workers of both races to triumph the "black race must be so intermingled with the white man that they cannot be told apart." Before that could happen, blacks still had to unite among themselves. If they failed to do so, he warned, they would find themselves pushed out of the trades to become "the servants, the sweepers of shavings, the scrapers of pitch, and carriers of mortar."[6]

Myers's speeches, reported in the *New National Era*, official organ of the CNLU, stimulated black workers to move forward aggressively in organizing local unions and affiliating them with the national labor federation. In New York City black workers, under the leadership of William F. Butler, were making such progress that a call went out for a New

York State Colored Labor Convention. At this convention, which met
on August 24 at Saratoga, committees were set up to form unions and
cooperative associations throughout the state, and a permanent state organization was established. Butler noted in his speech to the delegates
that, "owing to the prejudices of trade unions, many colored tradesmen
and mechanics were obligated to become servants and waiters in hotels
and such places." He and other speakers expressed the hope that, if the
CLNU and its New York state affiliate did their duty, these restrictions
would be done away with. A resolution was adopted recommending the
formation under the State Labor Union of city and county organizations,
membership in which would be open to all regardless of race, color, or
sex.[7] A State Bureau of Labor was also set up to function as a free employment agency for black workers.

The National Labor Bureau of Colored Men met in Washington to
choose representatives to the 1870 convention of the NLU. Aware that
the issue of imported contract coolie labor was assuming increasing importance among the white unions and was bound to be a leading issue at
the NLU convention, the bureau instructed its delegates to oppose such
importation; at the same time, they were to make clear their opposition
to any restrictions imposed upon Chinese who entered the country as
free immigrants.

The fourth annual convention of the National Labor Union opened
in Cincinnati on August 15, 1870. On its eve, the *Workingman's Advocate* heralded the "grand inaugural movement . . . to consolidate the
colored element of the Southern states," which, it predicted, would "ultimately have but one result—a clear alliance with, and an endorsement of
the principles of the National Labor Union."[8] This was wishful thinking. A bitter dispute arose early in the proceedings between the white
and black delegates. After Samuel F. Cary, ex-labor Congressman from
Ohio, had been granted the privileges of the floor, the blacks moved that
John W. Langston be accorded the same rights. Immediately the objection was raised that Langston had sought to tie the black worker to the
Republican Party and that no politician should be given the opportunity
to influence the proceedings of the NLU. The black labor press quoted
Samuel Cummings, the white delegate whose admittance Langston had
opposed at the founding convention of the CLNU, as saying he had no
doubts that Langston was "here in the interests of the Republican
Party." He pleaded for withdrawal of the motion for seating Langston
on the grounds that Langston was not a man of the labor movement but
a politician and that he had done all he could to estrange the black laborer from the white worker at the Washington convention. But the
black delegates stood firm: If the objection to Langston was that he was
a member of the Republican Party, they asked, why were men identified
with the Democrats admitted? After a lengthy debate, Langston was excluded by a vote of 49 to 23. The vote marked the beginning of the end
of cooperation between the NLU and the CNLU. To the black delegates it symbolized the unwillingness of white labor spokesmen to treat
blacks on the basis of equality and their utter failure to recognize the

Negro's special problems, including his reasons for adherence to the Republican Party.

The split widened as the convention proceeded. The delegates adopted a resolution demanding the same wage scales for women as for men and the opening to them of many of the closed avenues of industry, a move applauded and supported by the black delegates. But the convention saw no need for a similar resolution for the Negro. The blacks endorsed the prohibition of Chinese contract labor but attacked the report of the Committee on Coolie Labor recommending that the Convention demand "the abrogation of the treaty between the United States and China whereby Chinese are allowed to be imported to our shores." The black delegates made a distinction between importation of contract labor and immigration, but the convention brushed aside the distinction and adopted the committee's proposal.

But the real conflict between white and black delegates arose over the political resolution. The resolution declared that the major political parties were dominated by nonproducers, specifically the financial capitalists, who drew their wealth from public plunder and their control of the monetary system and were interested in the workers only where their own pecuniary or political gain was concerned. Noting that blacks constituted an important segment of the working class and were armed with the ballot, the resolution appealed to "our colored fellow citizens" to abandon the existing political parties and unite with white workers in a Labor Reform Party. It assured blacks that their "highest interests" would be served by supporting a party of labor reform, since both Negroes and whites were slaves of capital and could never achieve liberation through the existing parties.

Cameron added his voice to the resolution's plea for black support. He asked the Negroes "whether the men who oppressed their race would be more likely to do them justice than their fellow workingmen" and, reminding them of the admission of black delegates to the NLU convention in 1869 on terms of equality, he argued that they could put their faith in a political movement sponsored by the Labor Congress. The labor press reported Cameron's warning to the blacks: "If they preferred to cast their lot with their oppressors, the responsibility would lay heavy on their own hands."

But the black delegates had little confidence that the white workers would reward them for political support by doing them "justice" on the economic front, and they were more interested in eliminating barriers against the right to work than in reforming the monetary system. While not uncritical of the Republicans, they were scarcely ready to abandon the party they credited with ending slavery and enfranchising the Negro in favor of a movement launched by an organization of unions that excluded blacks from work and apprenticeship opportunities. "While the Republican Party is not the *beau idéal* of our notion of a party," said Isaac Myers, "the interests of workingmen demand that they shall not hazard its success either by the organization of a new party or by an affiliation with the Democratic Party."

Delegate Ewing delivered a long oration inveighing against the Republican Party as representative of a moneyed aristocracy. On the other hand, the Democratic Party was pictured as making "a new departure in favor of the principles of the NLU." Ewing extolled the Southern leaders of the Democratic Party for their veneration of the Constitution and dismissed the notion that the Ku Klux Klan represented a threat to the black workers of the South. He termed reports about Klan atrocities nothing more than a "red herring" with which the "radicals" were attempting to justify the "rule of the carpetbaggers."[9]

It was hardly a speech that would endear the NLU to the black delegates, who knew the Klan from bitter experience.

It is curious that men like Cameron and Cummings, both sympathetic to the black workers' problems, showed no understanding of their special needs in that crucial period of American history. It is also incredible that F. A. Sorge, the leading Marxist in the United States, said nothing at the convention to enlighten the delegates on the special needs of black workers. To be sure, Sorge joined the blacks in opposing the proposition that monetary reform was the cure-all for the workers' problems—although for reasons different from the blacks'—but at no time during the convention did he join the Negroes in their call for the removal of restrictions imposed upon black workers by nearly every affiliate of the NLU.

The resolution in favor of a Labor Reform Party was overwhelmingly passed, 60 to 5, with all of the black delegates opposed. The action signified that the two labor movements would go in separate directions. The 1870 NLU Convention was the last one the black delegates attended.

The leaders of the NLU were soon to discover that their success with the political resolution was an empty victory. Not only did it guarantee the irrevocable separation of the Negro and white labor movements, but it hastened the demise of the NLU. The trade unions lost interest in the organization as it became almost entirely a political institution, offering middle-class panaceas like monetary reform for the problems of the working class. Gradually one after another of the important national affiliates withdrew, declaring that the NLU was actually a political party and no longer served the needs of the unions. At the final National Labor Congress, in September, 1872, only seven delegates were present. Only one represented a national trade union (Morocco Dressers), whereas in 1867 ten national unions had sent delegates.

In November, 1870, the call went out for the second annual meeting of the Colored National Labor Union, to be convened in Washington, D.C., on January 9, 1871. Delegates were again to be admitted "without regard to race, color, or sex." In response conventions were held in a number of states, and delegates were elected to the Washington convention from the same eighteen states represented the year before, joined by Texas.

Isaac Myers delivered the keynote address, his swan song as president of the union. As in the past, he stressed that the interests of capital and labor were mutual, but this time he went on at great length to accuse capital of "cupidity" and of being "often destitute of brains." Lack of planning and slipshod organization of industry, he charged, had had the result that "thousands of laborers are robbed of their wages." Competition among manufacturers often produced a lowering of wages, but there was no corresponding reduction in prices; on the contrary, workers were often forced to pay more for the goods they needed just as their wages were being reduced. "It is but natural," he continued, "that labor should ask . . . to relieve itself from the rapid fluctuations of capital and put itself in a safe position that it may be able to demand and command a compensation that will afford it an independent living." Myers said that trade unions were necessary "for advancing the claims and protecting the interests of the workmen" but criticized the tendency of "brainless" labor leaders to resort to strikes as the first remedy. Since capital was better organized and more powerful financially, strikes could be effective only if the trade were first thoroughly organized and the workers "provided with a fund sufficient to pay the rate of wages demanded during the continuance of the strike, otherwise it is folly to attempt the experiment."

Even more disastrous, Myers continued, was the proposal for a Labor Reform Party, "a grand farcical clap-trap, cunningly worked upon the unwary workingman by intriguing politicians." He called legislation to change the monetary system "deceptive and preposterous." While he recognized labor's interest in such legislation as a national education law, land grants to actual settlers, and a tariff to protect American industries, its major concern was wages, which could not be regulated "by any legislative body that can be created." Wages were the responsibility of the trade unions, hence labor organization was the real answer to labor's needs, and it was "the duty of the laboring man to adopt that form of organization separate and distinct from politics, that will readily meet capital in a fair and equitable race." Myers argued strongly for the establishment by unions of cooperative associations as a means of combating employers who would "not concede living wages to the laborer."

Myers was able to report progress in the work of the CNLU for the year 1870. Unions established by the National Labor Bureau were "in a flourishing condition," labor bureaus were functioning in several states, and the New York City bureau had "succeeded in obtaining employment for several hundred workmen." However, Myers conceded that the union, hampered by financial difficulties, had not been "as successful as many friends of our race and cause anticipated" in reaching black workers. In the South, where trade unions had always encountered opposition, "great prejudices" confronted any attempts by workers to unite to improve their conditions. "Besides, in some localities, it is impossible to reach the colored laborers except you are steel-plated against the Ku-Klux bullets." The delegates from the Southern states could testify, he said, to the difficulty of organizing blacks in the midst of the "fearful reign of terror" existing throughout the South. "There is little or no value placed upon human life, if it be a negro." Myers suggested that emigration might be the only solution for Southern labor, for it would "produce a spirit of independence and enterprise that is absolutely necessary to elevate the condition of labor, both black and white." Meanwhile, conventions should be held in every state, North and South, to form more labor unions. "Politics," Myers stressed, "should be left entirely out of these conventions, and the business interests of the people considered." In conclusion, he said the conventions should be open to all workers regardless of color or race: "There is no desire, upon our part, to have separate organization based upon color. We believe the condition of the white laborers will be materially advanced by cooperation with the colored laborers."

Myers was implying, then, that cooperation was still possible between the blacks and the National Labor Union as long as politics was excluded. But most of the delegates were in no mood to conciliate the white labor movement. Delegate Belcher of Georgia introduced a resolution condemning the National Labor Union and its platform for "illogically, violently, and unfairly" attacking the financial policy of the Republican Party. A "spirited debate" followed in which, according to the official report, "some unkind words were said." Finally, George T. Downing moved that the convention endorse Myers's condemnation of the NLU's financial program and of its appeal to the colored voters to support a Labor Reform Party, as well as his adherence to the "principles and policy of the Republican Party."[10] The resolution was approved by acclamation.

This action has often been interpreted as the Colored National Labor Union's reduction to a mere appendage of the Republican Party, and the election of Frederick Douglass to replace Isaac Myers as president has been taken as further proof of the politicalization of the black labor movement. But this is an oversimplification. Douglass had clearly demonstrated his understanding that suffrage alone was no solution to the black American's problems. In a letter to the *Christian Recorder*, printed on August 7, 1869, he had urged the paper: "Let it defend the black man's equal rights to work as well as his equal rights to vote. We have been doomed for ages to menial employments, and shall never be much better off than slaves, till we stand upon a common footing with other men in the right to work as well as to vote." Douglass stressed that the key issue confronting his people was "that the gates of every form of industry shall be opened to us—and kept open." "Give them employments by which they can obtain something like a respectable living," he had told the delegates to the American Anti-Slavery Society meeting on May 11, 1869.[11]

At the 1871 CNLU convention, the report of the Committee on Capital and Labor, submitted by Downing, was a masterful analysis of the economic problems of the black working class, and in no way did it reflect purely political thinking. It opened with a brief historical survey:

> The colored laborer in America has been the special victim of avarice and cupidity from the time he first set foot on the continent. He has been held in abject slavery, despoiled of all rights, consequently is, as must be

the case, extremely poor. He was freed from the claim of an individual master and became more completely a slave to the impoverished circumstances that environed him; he became a subject of murderous hate now cherished toward him because of his emancipation and loyalty.

His first two imperative needs—bread and shelter—he had not when he was declared free; the want, without money or land, makes him poor indeed; but without them, and added thereto the lack of a *material* friend, makes his situation most deplorable. The colored man is struggling against all this.

For the black laborer of the South, freedom had turned out to be a cruel hoax. He could protest neither economically nor politically; indeed, it was a common occurrence for the black tenant of his former slave-master "to be set on the roadside with his family, if he is not murdered, for disregarding as a voter the pleasure of the lord of the soil." The only possible escape for the oppressed black was to move into industry either as a worker or, by obtaining some capital, as an independent producer. Since the latter was not a likely prospect, most blacks could hope to escape only as workers. But here they faced an almost insuperable obstacle, the white trade unions:

> Your committee would simply refer to the unkind, estranging policy of the labor organizations of white men, who, while they make loud proclaims as to the injustice (as they allege) to which they are subjected, justify injustice so far as giving an example to do so may, by excluding from their benches and their workshops worthy craftsmen and apprentices only because of their color, for no just cause. We say to such, so long as you persist therein we cannot fellowship with you in your struggle, and look for failure and mortification on your part.[12]

It was clear that the obstacle to cooperation between the black and white labor movements was basically economic and that cooperation was not possible so long as the white trade unions refused to remove the economic barriers against black workers.

The activities of the organization after the convention were further proof that the movement had not lost its interest in economic problems. Several unions were formed in the South, and there were struggles for wage increases. In March, 1871, state officers of the CNLU called a convention to form a Laborers Union Association of the State of Texas. The call went, in part: "All are alike interested in this great work—the white man as well as the black. Ours is a common interest, and the sickly sentimentality which induces distinctions by reason of color, in this great work is entirely ignored. There is labor sufficient for all, and all are invited to attend."[13] Workers of both races met in convention at Houston on June 8. Similar state conventions were held in Tennessee, Alabama, Georgia, and Missouri, but none of them led to the forming of permanent labor organization.

In several communities the CNLU stimulated black and white workers to form local unions, which then won strikes. It helped to organize black dock workers into the Longshoremen's Association No. 1 of Baltimore in 1871 and led their successful struggle to secure a wage increase from twenty to twenty-five cents an hour—"the present rates being insufficient to support ourselves and families"—and improvements in working conditions.

But the vast majority of the blacks were former slaves living in the South under conditions that were growing rapidly more intolerable. Their low standard of living as tenant-farmhands, their bondage to those who supplied them with food and other necessities at outrageously high prices, and the meagerness of their economic and educational opportunities were scandalous. When they sought to change their conditions, they were set upon by the Klan and similar terrorist organizations.

The freedmen were defenseless. Federal troops, inadequate in number from the beginning of Reconstruction, were being withdrawn from state after state in the South, and the Negro militias were being disarmed by governors fearful of the white supremacists, leaving the blacks at the mercy of the Klan. (During the period 1868–71 in Georgia alone, the estimate of Negroes killed exceeded 1,500.) The Colored National Labor Union was in no position to make strides in the South in the face of Klan opposition. Jacob Montgomery, a South Carolina Negro sharecropper, told a Congressional investigating committee that he had been visited by masked Klansmen and told that if he attended a union meeting "we'll kill you, but if you stick to [the landlord] we will stick to you." W. Jones, a Georgia sharecropper, replied when the committee asked him, "What was [the planter] going to take your life for?":

> He said I should not leave him; he wanted me to work with him and make 30 bags of cotton, and he promised to give me half. I went to him after I made the crop and asked for some pay to support my family. He said I should stay there and work for nothing. I said I could not stand it and was going to leave and join a union. He said if I undertook to leave he would Ku-Klux me.[14]

Frederick Douglass saw some hope in a bill presented to Congress by George F. Hoar, Republican of Massachusetts, calling for the President to appoint a commission to investigate "the social, educational, and sanitary condition of the laboring classes of the United States." Douglass anticipated that such an investigation would be "of especial advantage to colored labor. The country generally does not understand the degrading conditions in which it too largely remains, and therefore fails to see the means which might legitimately be enacted and set in motion to effect the changes so imperatively demanded." Douglass urged the "two important National Colored Conventions about to assemble at Columbia, South Carolina," to endorse the bill and campaign for its passage.[15]

Douglass referred to "two conventions" because the sessions of the convention of the Colored National Labor Union on October 18, 1871, at Columbia were to be held jointly with the Southern States Convention of Colored Men. In issuing the call, Douglass, as President of the CNLU, specifically stated that "by orders of the National Bureau of Labor, the annual meeting of the National Labor Union is called to meet in the city of Columbia, South Carolina, during the sessions of the

Southern Convention which commences October 18, 1871."[16] It is impossible at this date to distinguish between the delegates of the Southern Convention and those of the Colored National Labor Union, but most of the prominent black Reconstruction political leaders were present at Columbia, along with such prominent black labor leaders as Isaac Myers.

The Southern States Convention of Colored Men had been called primarily to consider the political and civil rights of Negroes. But the joint convention adopted the constitution and bylaws of the CNLU, and the speeches at the joint convention emphasized that the economic problems of the Negro people could not be divorced from their political and civil rights, and that a single organization to promote the economic welfare of black workers and establish labor unions, while at the same time campaigning to uphold political and civil equality, was the only answer for the plight of the black working class. John T. Quarles, speaking for the Southern Negro, declared that there were only two possible ways to achieve a truly free labor class: "Either the Southern people must protect and foster free labor by giving it the means of developing itself . . . or the restless and discontented laborer will involve the protection of the National Government."[17] Since there was little likelihood that the first would be realized, every ounce of energy had to be devoted to obtaining the protection of the government for the oppressed Southern laborers.

As the CNLU turned more and more to political action as its hope for the economic advance of black labor it was inevitable that it would become more and more a political organization linked to the Republican Party.* In a letter to the state presidents of the union in answer to inquiries regarding support for the Labor Reform Party, Isaac Myers and Frederick Barbadoes pointed out that "the Colored National Labor Union is not a political organization. The object for which it is organized is to develop the intellectual and improve the material condition of its members." However, while "no political test" was applied as a qualification for membership, the CNLU felt "morally bound" to give its support to the Republican Party. Nothing could be "more disastrous" than a victory for the Democratic Party, which support for the Labor Reform political movement might make possible.[18]

Although some of the local black labor organizations brought into being by the influence of the Colored National Labor Union continued their existence, the CNLU itself never met again after 1871.† While

---

* Du Bois notes that about this time Douglass wrote an editorial that concluded: "The Republican Party is the true workingmen's party of the country." Du Bois adds: "This sounded strange for the North, but it was at the time true of the South." W. E. B. Du Bois, *Black Reconstruction in America, 1869–1880* (New York, 1935), p. 367.
† The Labor League of Jacksonville, Florida, formed by black mill workers in the early 1870's under CNLU influence, called a strike in May, 1873, when its demands for a minimum wage of $1.50 a day and a ten-hour working day for unskilled labor was rejected by the mill owners. Although seventeen mills were shut down by the walkout, the employers broke the strike by importing white scabs.

The Alabama Labor Union was still active in the spring of 1874, as evidenced by

political influence undoubtedly hastened its decline, it is too simple to attribute its demise to political forces. It is difficult to see how the CNLU's failure could have been avoided. It was operating against insurmountable obstacles. Most Negroes lived in the South during that era and gained their livelihood as agricultural laborers, tenant farmers, domestics, or skilled craftsmen. The low income and isolation of the laborers and tenant farmers retarded effective organization. Moreover, foes of unionization resorted to all sorts of intimidation, and even murder, to prevent the establishment of a black labor movement in the South. For a brief period during Reconstruction the state legislatures in which Negroes and poor whites had an influence passed laws benefiting the urban black workers in the South and facilitating their organization. But even while the CNLU was emerging, the Reconstruction governments were being undermined and overthrown. No stable black labor movement could be built in the South in the face of such obstacles.

In the North the skilled Negro workers who were able to find employment were still too few in numbers and too poor to create a viable labor movement by themselves. Perceptive black leaders understood that if Negroes were to receive equal pay for their work and equal employment opportunities they would have to organize, but they also realized that the only real solution was not a separate labor movement but a unified one of black and white workers, which was impossible to achieve. Some leaders of the National Labor Union and of the American sections of the First International understood the importance of an alliance between black and white labor, but the white trade union members of the period were not in step with such a position. Even the more advanced labor leaders were not willing to wage a consistent struggle against discrimination in unions on behalf of the Negroes and for equality of treatment for blacks within the labor organizations. Black members of a waiters' union and Negro plasterers marched with the IWA sections in an eight-hour parade in New York City on September 13, 1871,* which was certainly a great advance in the metropolis that had been the scene of draft riots eight years before. "Such is progress," the *Workingman's Advocate* noted correctly. But at the conventions of the National Labor Union neither the delegates from the IWA nor the editor of the *Advocate* raised the

---

the fact that it instructed its state agent to respond to an editorial by Lewis H. Douglass in the *New National Era* of May 7, 1874, entitled, "The Folly, Tyranny, and Wickedness of Labor Unions." William V. Turner, the state agent, sharply rebuked Douglass and noted that in Alabama the Labor Union was "supplying a want that has long been felt by our people." Douglass quickly changed his position, observing that unions like those described by the Alabama state agent "cannot be objectionable," and were to be welcomed by black workers. *New National Era*, May 28, 1874.

* However, when it became clear in April, 1872, that Section 44 of the International Workingmen's Association at Galveston, Texas, would invite Negro laborers to affiliate, most of the 200 white members quit. As one put it, if "the colored man is to be taken into full fellowship in this society, socially and politically, I must decline to become a member." By June, 1872, Section 44 was all but dead. James V. Reese, "The Early History of Labor Organization in Texas, 1838–1876," *Southwestern Historical Quarterly* 81 (1968): 13.

question of exclusion of blacks from unions. The *Workingman's Advocate* did castigate several national unions for failing to remove bans against Negroes, calling such actions "a libel on the intelligence of the nineteenth century," but its strictures produced no results.[19]

By the 1870's the failure of the national government to distribute lands to the ex-slaves guaranteed that the end of slavery would not bring real freedom. Blacks were reduced to peonage, powerless to resist complete domination by the landlord class. By then, too, the rise of craft unionism with its apprenticeship system was effectively barring the Negro from the more remunerative trades at a time when industry, relying mainly on foreign-born labor, was shutting its doors to blacks. "The foundry, the factory, the workshop of every kind are closed against us, whether they are public or private," Isaiah Weir wrote in the *Christian Recorder* of May 1, 1871.

Negro labor had no reliable allies in its efforts to retard, much less reverse, the worsening of the black man's economic condition. The Republican Party did nothing meaningful to halt the expansion of peonage or to protect the agricultural laborer from the violence of the Klan. Still, if the Negro quit the Republican Party and allied himself with the independent political movement of labor, he risked assuring victory to the Democrats, the allies of his former masters. And he would still come up against the restrictions of the white trade unions. Even when a few national trade unions acted to remove restrictions against blacks, the action proved to be of value only on paper. At the 1870 convention of the Carpenters and Joiners National Union, the Committee on Colored Labor advised instructing the secretary "to invite all carpenters and joiners, no matter what may be the color of their skin," and urged that each local union should have the power "to admit such colored members as in their judgment they deem best." This was hailed by the *Workingman's Advocate* as an important advance, but the national union by that time had practically "ceased to exist as an organization," and the fact that the resolution left to local unions the decision on the entrance of blacks ensured that no Negro members would be admitted. When the Cigar Makers' International Union in 1871 eliminated from its constitution the clause allowing no person to belong to any local union "unless said person is a white practical cigar maker," it specified that the "definition of a practical cigar maker shall be left to the local unions to determine"—a phrase, it soon became clear, that enabled the local union to continue its restrictive policy against blacks. Typical too was the stand taken by the sixth annual convention of the Bricklayers National Union in 1871. Although a delegate favored the Negro's admission on the ground that "if we don't organize him he will work for anyone at any price," the convention passed a resolution leaving the decision to local unions.[20]

So it went from union to union. Most of them simply ignored the blacks, others left discretion to their locals, and still others openly excluded Negroes by constitutional provision. In the last group were the unions of railroad workers; the Sons of Vulcan, the pioneer union of iron workers; and the National Order of United American Mechanics, which barred not only Negroes but also foreign-born whites.

On May 7, 1870, the *Workingman's Advocate* expressed a noble sentiment: "We firmly and honestly believe that the success of the labor movement for years to come depends on the cooperation and success of the colored race. . . . Their interests are our interests; our interests are theirs." But trade union practice went in the opposite direction. The pattern was one of exclusion, and this pattern, established by organized labor in the post–Civil War period, became, with some important exceptions, a characteristic tradition of the American labor movement for years to come. But it is now time to look at one of the exceptions.

4 The Knights of Labor and the Black Worker

In 1869, the year the Colored National Labor Union issued its first appeal for the unity of American workers "without regard to race or color," nine Philadelphia garment-cutters, whose union had been shattered and its members blacklisted, formed a secret society that ultimately was to transform this sentiment into reality. They named it the Noble Order of the Knights of Labor. The Knights of Labor at first admitted only garment-cutters but later took in workers of other trades (called "sojourners"), who were expected to form branches in their own industries. Soon it opened its membership to anyone eighteen or older who worked for a living, except for lawyers, doctors, bankers, and those engaged in selling liquor. Women were not eligible for membership until 1881, but from the outset the Knights of Labor did not exclude any male worker because of color or race, political or religious belief, or place of birth.* It was founded and grew on the rock of labor solidarity, expressed in its slogan: "An injury to one is the concern of all."

In 1879, when Terence V. Powderly became Grand Master Workman, the title for president in the Knights, the order's membership was 20,151, and four years later it had grown to 51,914. Its explosive growth during the next four years is unparalleled in the history of the labor movement. Estimates of the membership of the Knights of Labor at its peak in 1886 vary from 700,000 to more than 1 million. Whatever the specific figure, the fact is that the Knights achieved what no labor body before it had accomplished—the organization and unification of the American working class. The Knights did not wage a constant, determined campaign to eliminate racism from its ranks, but it brought large numbers of skilled and unskilled black workers into the predominantly white labor movement for the first time.

Replying to a member's query, the *Journal of United Labor*, the official newspaper, explained on August 15, 1880, that black workers were wel-

---

* Unless he was Chinese. When efforts were made to organize local assemblies of Chinese in New York and Philadelphia, the General Executive Board of the Knights refused to grant them charters. Black workers were prominent in the fight to include Chinese: Frank J. Ferrell, an outstanding Negro leader of the Knights and a Socialist, made a special effort to get the GEB to reverse its stand.

comed in the Order. No man earning his living by honest labor was to be excluded. "Why," the statement concluded, "should workingmen keep out of our organization anyone who might be used as a tool to aid the employer in grinding down wages?" In 1884 the Knights reaffirmed this policy. The constitution promulgated for all local assemblies declared that the order made no distinction of "nationality, sex, creed, or color."

Available records do not reveal the actual number of black workers in the Knights of Labor, but a man who had been its general secretary estimated that in a total membership exceeding 700,000 in 1886 no fewer than 60,000 were black.

The Knights of Labor included both all-Negro assemblies (the first formed in Ottuma, Iowa, in 1881) and assemblies of mixed black and white membership. Although segregated locals were predominant, especially in the South, some locals even below the Mason-Dixon line were mixed. The Knights began organizing in the South in 1878, assigning fifteen organizers to the area, and Negroes as well as whites were asked to join. The blacks formed or joined locals of longshoremen, miners, iron and steel workers, and farm workers. After the ban on women membership was rescinded in 1881 Negro women joined assemblies with men or formed their own locals, most of which were made up of domestic workers—laundresses, chambermaids, and housekeepers—and a few comprised women agricultural laborers.

Bitter opposition made it necessary for the Southern organizers to conceal their purposes by using names like "Franklin Lodge," "Washington Lodge," and "Protective Lodge"; to post sentries at meetings as a defense against sudden raids; and to take extensive precautions to insure secrecy. Everywhere the organizers were accused by landlords, industrialists, and the press of seeking to stir up racial insurrection. In 1885 a white organizer wrote to Powderly from Raleigh, North Carolina:

> You have no idea of what I have to contend with [in] the way of prejudice down here. There is a continual cry of "nigger," "nigger!!" . . . I believe that our Order is intended to protect all people who work, the poor ignorant underpaid and overworked as well as the skilled mechanic, and have tried to act up on that principle. And for this alone I have incurred abuse and social ostracism.[1]

But he also reported that blacks were flocking into the Order, paying their dues regularly even when it meant a severe hardship, and often walking miles to attend meetings.

On April 12, 1885, *John Swinton's Paper*, the leading labor journal of the decade, reported the existence of "hundreds of colored assemblies in the South." At the Knights' convention in that year a resolution calling for the appointment of a Negro organizer for each of the old slave states was referred to the executive board and approved. In June, 1886, a labor paper observed that "colored Knights of Labor assemblies are springing up all over the South since Negroes realize that they were not set free from the new slavery* by Lincoln's proclamation." At the 1886 conven-

---

* "New slavery" in the argot of the labor press meant wage slavery.

tion the general secretary-treasurer reported, "Rapid strides have been made in the South, especially in Virginia, the Carolinas, Georgia, and Alabama. The colored people of the South are *flocking* to us, being eager for organization and education; and when thoroughly imbued with our principles are unswerving in their fidelity."[2]

Black Knights were best organized in Richmond, where there were said to be 3,125 members in twenty-one local assemblies and a separate black district assembly. But every major Southern city—Atlanta, Memphis, New Orleans, Louisville, Charleston, Houston, Birmingham—had black assemblies. Black assemblies were even reported in small towns like Paducah, Kentucky; Henseley, Alabama; Plainsville, Georgia; and many others.*

In 1886 black workers constituted half of Virginia's 10,000 to 15,000 members; half of the 3,000 Arkansas and 4,000 North Carolina Knights, and a high percentage of the membership in Alabama, Florida, Georgia, Kentucky, Tennessee, and Louisiana. Even South Carolina and Mississippi, with fewer than 2,000 Knights, included blacks in the order. It has been estimated that black workers constituted between one-third and one-half of the Southern membership.

While most of the Negro assemblies were in Southern and border states, almost every industrial section of the nation contained at least one, usually an organization of miners, hod carriers, coke burners, or waiters.† The Knights' active enlistment of unskilled labor gave them a powerful appeal among black workers, who were almost completely relegated to menial occupations.

Even the trade union element within the Knights of Labor, which had long excluded Negroes from locals, became somewhat imbued with the idea of labor solidarity. The cigar makers, bricklayers, and carpenters lowered the barriers against Negro craftsmen in several locals or, where the hostility of the white membership made this impossible, organized them in separate locals. By 1886 the Brotherhood of Carpenters and Joiners had fourteen unions of Negro carpenters scattered throughout the South. Negro and white longshoremen, draymen, yardmen, and other dock workers were admitted on equal terms to the Federation of Dock Workers in the ports of Savannah, New Orleans, and Galveston. In an address entitled "Plain Talk to Workingmen," in July, 1884, the central committee of the trade unions of Austin, Texas, urged all workers, skilled and unskilled, black and white, to join the order.

Faced with the choice between losing strikes and acknowledging the community of interests of all miners, members of the Knights in the mines recruited blacks. Segregated locals in the mines were impractical, hence the blacks joined the existing locals. National Trade Assembly No. 135 of the Knights of Labor was an integrated organization of miners.

* The *Journal of United Labor* of July 2, 1887, carried the following dispatch from Alabama: "Knightsville is a village composed of nothing but colored people, who now number thirty-three. They own about two hundred and eighty acres of land. Knightsville is solid for the Knights of Labor."

† The only all-Negro local in New York City, the "Rossmore Association," founded in 1884, was composed of waiters.

Although the Knights of Labor leadership frowned upon strikes, Negro members were involved in struggles to increase wages and reduce the work week soon after they joined the order. Black and white Knights went on strike together in some cases, and cooperation existed between the races in the order apart from strikes as well. In Richmond, Virginia, they worked together harmoniously in the same factories. The Cleveland *Gazette,* a black weekly, reported that half the Knights in Norfolk, Virginia, were Negroes and that "harmony prevails between white and black workmen."[3] In New Orleans the Central Trades and Labor Assembly, composed of all labor organizations in the city, held a parade in which 10,000 workers, black and white, took part. It met with such success that it was repeated in the following year. After a parade and picnic in which whites, blacks, and Mexican-Americans marched and ate together, District Assembly 78 of Fort Worth, Texas, heard speeches by D. H. Black, the Negro leader of the Assembly; Manuel Lopez, Master Workman of the first Mexican-American local; and several whites.* "This is the first time such a thing happened in Texas," a contemporary paper observed.[4] As evidence mounted of harmonious relations between black and white workers in the South, *John Swinton's Paper* editorialized on May 16, 1886: "This is a grand stride. The organization of the Knights of Labor has done much for the South. When everything else had failed, the bond of poverty united the white and colored mechanic."

Interracial solidarity reached a high point on May 1, 1886, when 340,000 workers demonstrated for the eight-hour day on the first May Day in labor history, and 200,000 actually went on strike. (Of these, approximately 42,000 won the eight-hour day; 150,000 others obtained a shorter working day than they had had before.) Although the leadership of the Knights of Labor discouraged the eight-hour demonstrations and strikes and did everything possible to keep members from joining, rank-and-file Knights, black and white, participated with other workers. In Louisville, more than 6,000 blacks and whites marched in the eight-hour demonstration. Louisville parks had been closed to Negroes before, but after marching through the streets, the parade entered National Park, and black newspapers in many parts of the country reported the news that "thus have the Knights of Labor broken the walls of prejudice." In Baltimore, more than 20,000 workers "of all colors and nationalities" participated in the May Day parade. The Negro workers, cheered along the way, carried signs reading: "Shall We Send Our Boys to Prison to Learn a Trade?" "Eight Hours Pay for Eight Hours Work," "Live and Let Live," and "All We Ask Is Justice and Our Old Wages."[5]

The following September, 25,000 workers, black and white, marched in Baltimore in a Labor Day parade reviewed by Powderly. *John Swinton's Paper* reported on September 19, 1886:

---

* At a gathering of District Assembly No. 87 held in San Antonio in July, 1886, black and white Knights paraded together, spoke from the same platform, and dined at the same tables. "The only evidence of segregation was separate dances, yet they were held in the same building." Lawrence D. Rice, *The Negro in Texas, 1874–1900* (Baton Rouge, 1971), p. 192.

At the great parade here on Labor's Holiday, colored men were well mixed in and through the procession. In some instances, you would see an assembly composed entirely of colored Knights; another assembly would be perhaps half colored, and in some instances one solitary colored individual would be marching with any number of his white tradesbrothers. The procession was a very orderly one, the colored and white fraternizing as if it had been a common thing all their lives.

But the existence of segregated locals in the Knights of Labor did not sit well with many black spokesmen, and they urged Negroes to reject affiliation with the order for that reason. According to a black contributor to the *Labor Leaf*, a labor paper published in Detroit, Negroes were staying away from the order because they lacked knowledge "of the true objects and benefits" to be derived from membership. He asked: "Cannot something be done to arouse my brethren in this city?" The Detroit *Plain Dealer*, a Negro weekly, advised "the race to have nothing to do with separate assemblies," which "will foster and encourage the idea of inferiority and thus delay their emancipation as workmen."[6]

Then there was the complaint of black workers that membership in the order did not solve the age-old problem of exclusion of blacks from the skilled trades. A Durham, North Carolina, black mason told the state labor commission: "The white Knights of Labor prevent me from getting employment because I am a colored man, although I belong to the same organization." The black Hod Carriers' Union in Louisville refused to join the order until the city's Knights reversed their role in excluding blacks from skilled labor. "There is an agreement of all colored unions in this city," the Hod Carriers' president told a correspondent, "to stand aloof from all white organizations that refuse to recognize us as their brother. These white labor organizations must concede all rights to the colored men themselves. When they do this the Hod Carriers unions will be with them."[7]

Some black leaders argued that if Negroes joined the Knights they would no longer be able to work for lower wages than whites, would therefore be discharged by employers, and would ultimately find themselves deserted by the white Knights. Others urged blacks to fill the places of striking white workers on the ground that blacks were usually denied the opportunity to work under any conditions and could thus gain entrance to some formerly closed occupations. They pointed out that in Springfield, Ohio, Negroes were employed as molders for the first time as the result of a strike and that blacks used as strikebreakers in a railroad strike in Saint Louis made their first appearance as mechanics. Such sentiments were not universal among black leaders. The Cleveland *Gazette*, though critical of segregated assemblies as a practice, insisted that Negroes, particularly in the South, stood to benefit by their identification with hundreds of thousands of workers in organized labor. T. Thomas Fortune, whose New York *Freeman* was critical of the failure of the Knights to suppress anti-Negro elements, firmly opposed the idea that black workers should undercut whites by accepting lower wages and assist employers by strikebreaking. "If the inequality in the relative wages paid black and white laborers is to be rectified," he wrote, "it is to be accomplished by an understanding with white laborers and a union of forces to compel the equalization. The colored laborer stands on the same footing with the white laborer in point of interest, and to better secure their just rights the two must combine and work together. The colored laborer cannot antagonize the white laborer without jeopardizing his own interest." The *Freeman* pointed out that Negroes usually resisted being used as strikebreakers and were often unaware that a strike was on when they were brought in from outside. It featured an item from *John Swinton's Paper* telling of a New York restaurant that had imported several black waiters from Boston to take the places of striking whites. When a committee of the waiters' union met with the blacks and informed them of their grievances and demands, the Boston waiters immediately announced, "Though we are black, we have hearts that beat for justice for all, whether black or white," and left for home. The *Freeman* came out frequently against Negro strikebreaking as "opposed to the common interest of laboring men and yielding only a temporary benefit to the colored man."[8] Fortune compared the Negro who took the side of capital against labor with the black before the Civil War who took a proslavery stand. "Nothing short of potentiality like the Knights of Labor," he wrote in the *Freeman* on May 1, 1886, "can ever force Southern capitalists to give their wage workers a fair percentage of the results of their labor. If there is any power on earth which can make the white Southern employers of labor face the music, it is organized white and black labor, with the labor power of the nation to sustain it."

Many black Knights applauded Fortune and defended the Knights against the charge of failing to champion the rights of Negro workers. A Brooklyn Knight wrote to John Swinton:

> I am connected with an Assembly of the Knights of Labor which contains 450 members, 25 of whom are colored, and there has not been a single outburst of feeling on account of color. I am a colored man myself, and am Worthy Treasurer, an office which was forced upon me for the third time.

Another Brooklyn Knight wrote: "In view of the prejudice that existed a few years ago against the negro race, who would have thought that negroes could ever be admitted into a labor organization on an equal footing with white men?"[9] His local had 32 black members, one of whom was an officer. When one of the black members died, the pall-bearers chosen for his funeral by the assembly were four whites and two Negroes.

Two tendencies were apparent in the attitude of the Knights of Labor toward the Negro. One was reflected in the widespread evidence of unity in strikes, labor demonstrations, picnics, assembly halls, and the election of blacks to office in predominantly white locals. Nothing like this had ever occurred before in the American labor movement. The other tendency was the reluctance of the leadership to antagonize Knights who were not prepared to grant equality to black members and its unwillingness to take steps to eliminate restrictions barring Negroes from entrance to industry and apprenticeships.

To many blacks it seemed that the Knights of Labor in 1886, at the peak of its numerical strength and influence, stood at the crossroads so far as the Negro people were concerned. Would it wage an active battle for real equality, or would it make a token fight while seeking compromise with white supremacists within and without the order? This issue came to a climax at the convention in Richmond, Virginia, in October, 1886, and it centered upon one man. He was Frank J. Ferrell, an engineer from New York City and the only black in the sixty-man New York delegation to the convention. Active in trade union, Socialist, and labor party affairs, Ferrell was a leading figure in the Central Labor Union and was chosen Captain of Police in its 1884 labor parade. He lectured in the union school of District 49 of New York City on economic issues. Even before the Richmond convention, Ferrell was described in the black press as the "ablest exponent of the race in Knights of Labor circles."

A few months before the convention, an officer of District 49 went to Richmond to see which hotels would be available for the delegates, including Ferrell. Arrangements were made for all the delegates to stay at a hotel owned by Colonel Murphy, a Confederate veteran. When Murphy discovered that one of his guests would be a Negro, he refused to honor the contract, arguing that "customs here must be respected."[10] He offered to accommodate Ferrell at a Negro hotel.

When the members of District 49 learned that they could stay at the hotel only if Ferrell were excluded, they resolved unanimously to accept no hotel accommodations that excluded any delegates because of "color, creed or nationality." The delegates, most of whom were Socialists, came to Richmond carrying tents. Several boarded with Negro families, and a dozen Irish delegates worshiped at the only Negro Catholic Church in Richmond. "The delegates," wrote the *New York Times* correspondent from Richmond, "are determined to fight the battle on the color line right in the midst of that part of the country where race prejudice is the strongest, and they will insist on carrying on what they claim is a fundamental principle of their order—that the black man is the equal of the white socially as well as politically, and that all races stand upon an equal footing in all respects."[11]

The New York delegation was not alone in dealing with the problem of segregated quarters for blacks. When the proprietor of the St. Charles Hotel informed the Baltimore delegates that he would not accommodate Joseph W. Edmonds, a Negro delegate, the white delegates resolved that the entire delegation would take lodgings together.

However, most of the delegates stayed at hotels that excluded blacks. White delegates from the South condemned District 49's action and vowed to oppose any practice that threatened the fabric of social institutions in their section. Their stand did not go unnoticed. "Will white delegates consent to live in hotels from which colored delegates are excluded?" the *New York Times* asked on September 28. *John Swinton's*

Paper on October 10, 1886, noted the paradox that "the Knights as a body stand up for the equal rights of their colored brethren according to the principles of the Order, but most of the colored delegates from the Southern states are quartered with colored families."

Before the convention opened, Master Workman Thomas Quinn of District 49 approached Powderly, explained what had happened to Ferrell at Colonel Murphy's hotel, and proposed that the black delegate be permitted to introduce Virginia's Governor, Fitzhugh Lee, to the assemblage. "I do not believe that it would be an act of courtesy on our part to violate any recognized rule of this community," Powderly answered. "It would not be pleasant for either the Governor or the convention to attempt to set at defiance a long-established usage." Many District 49 delegates were of the opinion that it was precisely the duty of the Knights to defy a "long-established usage" based on racism. It was finally agreed that Ferrell would introduce Powderly after the Governor had spoken.

Delegate Ferrell introduced the Grand Master Workman to the more than 800 delegates assembled in the Armory Hall of the First Virginia Regiment: "It is with extreme pleasure that we, the representatives from every section of our country, receive the welcome of congratulations for our efforts to improve the condition of humanity. One of the objects of our order is the abolition of those distinctions which are maintained by creed or color. . . . We have worked so far successfully toward the extinction of those regrettable distinctions."

Powderly praised the New York delegation for standing by "the principle of our organization, which recognizes no color or creed in the division of men."[12] In an assertion of this principle, the New York contingent and twenty other delegates attended a performance of *Hamlet* at the Mozart Academy of Music in Richmond. Ferrell sat in the orchestra between two of his white brothers, causing complaints from several white members of the audience. He was the first Negro in Richmond's history to occupy an orchestra seat in any theater.

The events at the convention and at the theater created a sensation all over the nation. Southern newspapers heaped abuse on the Knights. "If the offense is repeated, it is to be hoped that the guilty ones will be pitched headlong into the street," the Atlanta *Constitution* raged. "It is better to settle this issue at the start than to wait until it becomes serious."[13] It called upon Southern members of the order to secede immediately.

The Negro press and many labor and Northern newspapers applauded the actions of the delegates. The *Freeman* proclaimed:

> The Bourbons of the South may rage to their hearts' content but the fact remains that here is one great organization in the land which recognizes the brotherhood of all man and has the courage to practice what it teaches . . . and Southern prejudice and intolerance will yet be made to eat grass like an ox.[14]

Powderly was dismayed by the attacks on the order in the Southern press, its interpretation of the events at Richmond as attempts to force "social equality" upon the South, and its advice that whites should secede and form an Order made up of white Southern labor. To mollify the Southern critics, he wrote a letter to the Richmond *Dispatch*, which printed it during the convention:

> I have no wish to interfere with the social relations which exist between the races of the South. . . . There need be no further cause for alarm. The colored representatives to this convention will not intrude where they are not wanted, and the time-honored laws of social equality will be allowed to slumber undisturbed."[15]

A group of delegates proposed a resolution endorsing Powderly's letter, but it was tabled and a substitute adopted, "recognizing the civil and political equality of all men" but upholding "the social relations which may exist between different races." Three other resolutions affecting Negroes were passed. One, introduced by District 41 of Maryland, urged that Negroes be admitted to apprenticeship; the second proposed that organizers be sent to the South "to organize all classes of labor"; and the third proposed the formation of a union bureau to collect statistics on relations between black and white workers and to learn whether Negroes were receiving full liberties and rights.[16]

The convention closed with a parade and a picnic. The parade to the picnic grounds was headed by a squad of police, followed by Grand Master Lynch, with mounted Negro and white marshals riding at his side. A band followed, then the delegates from District 49, with Ferrell in the front rank. The rest of the delegates came next, and behind them the officers of the order. Negro and white women in carriages brought up the rear of the procession. Almost the entire Negro population of Richmond turned out to watch, and several thousand joined the delegates at the picnic. It was the largest black-white affair in Richmond's history.

For many white delegates the convention was a significant lesson, a firsthand glimpse of the conditions confronting black workers in the South. "It opened their eyes to the true condition of affairs in the South as nothing else could have done," wrote a white member of the Knights from Virginia. They realized as never before that "appeals to race prejudice" were part of the conspiracy against all workingmen, and that in the interest of all members of the order, "a colored Knight of Labor must be placed on equal terms with a Knight of Labor who is white, so far as wages and political rights are concerned."[17]

The black press continued to praise the Knights of Labor after Powderly's letter to the Richmond *Dispatch* and the adoption of the resolution upholding "the social relations which may exist between different races," but the praise was mixed with disappointment and some distrust. The New York *Freeman*, in an editorial entitled "Powderly's Straddling," criticized the Grand Master Workman for "craven deference to the yell of the Southern white press and the demands of white Southern Knights of Labor." Its editorial on the resolution, headed "The Knights of Labor Show the White Feather," noted that the organization had sacrificed labor solidarity in the face of opposition from Southern white members. But then, "the Southern dog always wags his Northern tail. We are not surprised that the Knights of Labor backed down at the command of the Southern delegates." The Knights had merely demonstrated that they were no exception to the American way of life.[18]

The dominant opinion in the black press was that expressed by the Cleveland *Gazette,* which considered the events at Richmond full justification for blacks to join the Knights of Labor. "Taking all things into consideration, time, place, surroundings, it is the most remarkable thing since emancipation. The race's cause has secured a needed ally in the Knights of Labor organization."[19] It urged all black newspapers to encourage their readers to join the Knights, "a grand organization that will do more for them than any other agency in existence." The Louisville *Labor Record* exhorted: "Organize, organize, and still organize. Every laborer, black or white, man or woman, in the United States, should be a member of some trade or labor union. Thus, and thus only can we protect each other and protect ourselves."[20]

At that particular time, however, workers were being driven out of unions. A tremendous employers' counteroffensive had been launched with the ruthless victimization of eight anarcho-syndicalist leaders of the eight-hour movement in Chicago. In a travesty of justice, without the slightest evidence, they were convicted on charges of exploding a bomb at a meeting in Chicago's Haymarket Square on May, 4, 1886, called to protest the shooting of four workers near the struck McCormick Harvester plant. The employers were determined to use the Haymarket incident to attack organized labor, especially the Knights of Labor. In several cities, entire district executive boards of the order were arrested and charged with conspiracy. Lockouts, blacklists, arrests, and imprisonments were used to drive workers out of the Knights. The order began to lose members as rapidly as it once had gained them. Between 1886 and 1888, its membership declined from 702,924 to 221,618.

At the same time, however, blacks were joining in increasing numbers, especially in the South. On June 26, 1887, the New York *Sun* estimated that 90,000 to 95,000 Negroes belonged to the order and that "they are growing at rate out of proportion to the increase of white members." The New Orleans *Weekly Pelican* a month later gave the figure as 90,000 black members in 400 all-Negro locals. The total membership at the time was 511,351, so blacks accounted for almost 20 per cent.

Why was the order more attractive to black workers than to whites after 1886? The reform program of the Knights stressed land reform, increased education, and workers' cooperatives, matters of minor interest to the national trade unions, which concentrated on higher wages, shorter hours, and improved working conditions. But the program appealed to blacks, especially in the South, for it buoyed their hopes of escaping oppression and domination by landlord-merchant power. Lack of capital among the poverty-stricken Negroes in the South generally prevented the successful operation of cooperatives, but black members of the Knights were able to establish a number of them. Usually the first floor of the union hall was the site of a cooperative store. The Knights, moreover, provided blacks with the mutual-benefit and social functions —picnics, banquets, socials, and the like—associated with churches and fraternal societies and usually neglected by trade unions. It also offered blacks the opportunity to rise to leadership status.

Finally, for many months after the Richmond convention, the Knights of Labor remained faithful to its principles of labor solidarity and interracial unity. In Labor Day parades in Newark and Boston in 1887, more than 20,000 black and white Knights marched together. The Boston Knights invited the Wendell Phillips Club, a Negro organization, to join them in decorating the grave of the great abolitionist and labor reformer. A Negro carpenter in Boston carried a sign reading "Equal Rights for All" on one side and "We Make No Distinction" on the other. Negro coal handlers, shovels on their shoulders, were enthusiastically cheered as they marched.[21]

Such adherence to the order's principle was not limited to the North. In 1887 the Knights of Labor recommended to the Maryland legislature that the word "white" be struck out wherever it occurred in the constitution and laws of the state. Ida B. Wells, a black journalist and teacher, soon to become internationally famous as an anti-lynch-law crusader, wrote in the Memphis *Watchman* in 1887:

> I was fortunate enough to attend a meeting of the Knights of Labor. . . . I noticed that everyone who came was welcomed and every woman from black to white was seated with the courtesy usually extended to white ladies alone in this town. It was the first assembly of the sort in this town where color was not the criterion to recognition as ladies and gentlemen. Seeing this I could listen to their enunciation of the principles of truth and accept them with a better grace than all the sounding brass and tinkling cymbal of a Moody or Sam Jones, even expounded in a consecrative house over the word of God.[22]

Six Negro delegates attended the 1887 convention of the order in Minneapolis and drew almost as much comment as Ferrell had in Richmond the year before. The *Journal of United Labor* commented in October, 1887:

> These colored members possess every recommendation of the white members. At this moment the representative leaders of the race are placing themselves on record as fully abreast of the time and wide awake to its issues. The Knights have a strong following in the colored people. They are good Knights and thus far have occasioned no troubles to the Order. We extend to them our hearty cooperation.

The comment that the black Knights were causing "no trouble" was undoubtedly meant to stigmatize the many white delegates who were vehemently objecting to Powderly's stand on the Haymarket incident. They had presented a resolution requesting clemency for the condemned Haymarket defendants, but Powderly demanded the resolution's rejection. He denounced its supporters as "anarchists" who were continually stirring up strife with employers and antagonizing the public by their radical activities, and he even blamed them for the employers' offensive against labor. The black delegates remained silent during this dispute, but they soon had ample opportunity to observe that the policies of the leadership would adversely affect black members of the order.

When the employers' offensive began, the Richmond *Planet*, a black weekly, had commented: "The laboring white men, who are now being so vigorously ostracized and assaulted on every hand, can now only slightly realize the position of the colored man for the last twenty years." It had predicted that before long the blacks would feel the full impact of the offensive.[23]

To defeat efforts to organize workers, Northern employers used the blacklist, the lockout, the Pinkertons, the "iron-clad" oath, antilabor laws, intimidation of organizers, and discharge of men, black and white, known to be members of the Knights of Labor. In the South, employers added some special sectional weapons to the arsenal: vigilante terrorists, lynchings or the threat of lynchings, the militia, and, of course, blatant, hysterical appeals to racist feelings. After his organizing trips to Virginia, Georgia, Mississippi, and the Carolinas, in the course of which he was nearly lynched twice, Thomas B. Barry, a member of the GEB, told the 1888 General Assembly: "It is as much . . . as a person's life is worth to be known as a member of the Knights of Labor there."[24]

A. W. Jackson of Milton, Florida, a prominent member of the Knights, conducted a successful business, helped by patronage from members of the order's local assembly. As his success became evident, he was ordered by local Klansmen to leave town. "Thinking that he was a free man and had a right to live where he chose, he disobeyed the order, and was shot dead in his own establishment," the New York *Freeman* reported bitterly on October 8, 1887.

South Carolina displayed special fury toward Negro Knights and the men who organized them. In December, 1886, the state legislature, which the white planters controlled, appropriated funds for the maintenance of a militia specifically to "suppress riots." The Senate passed, by a large majority, a bill to prevent Negroes from organizing into local assemblies; it extended the provisions of the conspiracy statute, adopted during slavery, to make interference between employer and employee in any contract, verbal or written, an offense punishable by fine and imprisonment. The New York *Freeman* noted that the measure "virtually reduces the laborers of South Carolina to the condition of slaves." The Reverend J. Wofford White, a Negro, declared that the object of the bill was to "grind down and drive to the wall" the black laborer simply because he sought to join an organization to better his condition; he warned that, if it became law, huge migrations of Negroes would ensue. Because of widespread pressure by members of the order throughout the country, the bill was killed, but its mere proposal had led to the migration of Negroes from South Carolina to "seek freedom elsewhere."[25]

Such conditions forced the Knights to recruit blacks secretly. H. F. Hoover, a white organizer in South Carolina, recruited Negroes into the "Co-operative Workers of America." Its stated goals were to "dignify and elevate labor," to repeal all laws not bearing equally on capital and labor to support the weekly payment of wages, a reduction in the hours of labor, repeal of the poll tax, a free cooperative school system, the use of public lands only by settlers, a graduated income tax, an inheritance tax, direct election of Senators, a "free ballot," and opposition to war. Hoover described the organization as independent, mentioning only that it sought cooperation with the Knights of Labor and "all similar organization," and emphasized that its objectives were to be achieved by "lawful peaceful means," but mere publication of the goals sufficed to convince Southern whites that the "Co-operative Workers of America" was a secret branch of the "anarchist Knights of Labor." Forewarned, the organization held its meetings between midnight and daylight and posted black sentries outside to protect members from raids. Men known to be associated with the organization were rounded up by local deputies and threatened with long terms in prison, to say nothing of lynching, if they continued to serve as members or officers.

After establishing the South Carolina organization, Hoover went to Georgia to continue his organizational efforts. He was shot and killed in Warrenton, Georgia, on May 20, 1887, as he was addressing an audience composed predominantly of Negro workers. The local Knights of Labor assembly promptly denounced the shooting as a "case of capitalistic conspiracy against Labor" and appealed to the General Executive Board "to consider the matter and take proper action." At the Minneapolis convention, the black delegates requested, and the convention passed, a similar resolution. But Powderly and his henchmen were too busy raging against the "radical anarchist" elements in the Knights to concern themselves with the murder of an organizer. The GEB simply sent the request to the district assembly in Georgia to investigate and report.

Infuriated by the inactivity of the Knights of Labor leadership, an editorial writer of the *Advance and Labor Leaf* of Detroit raged that the "Knights of Labor organizer Hoover was shot like a dog by the 'best citizens of South Carolina'* because he was organizing the laborers, Negroes as well as whites, in that labor-hating country, and yet our general officers have had nothing to say about it." The paper urged the Knights to marshal all the resources of the order to bring the murderers to justice. If the officers of the Knights "are to stand by with folded arms, see their organizers butchered in cold blood, and make no protest, it is time the rank and file of the Order took means to defend their noble and self-sacrificing organizers even in the South." It further insisted that the general officers immediately send as many organizers as possible to South Carolina, demanding protection from the governor and the federal government, and, if that failed, "ask the Order at large for protection." The right to organize blacks as well as whites "must be maintained at all costs" if the Knights' motto, "an injury to one is the concern of all," was to mean anything. But the newspaper's strong plea was ignored by a leadership bent upon proving that the Knights of Labor was not an organization dominated by "radical anarchists."[26]

---

* It was felt that Hoover's murder in Georgia had been engineered by South Carolina employers.

The greatest strike of the decade in which Negroes were involved oc-curred in the sugar districts of Louisiana in November, 1887. Prior to the appearance there of the Knights of Labor, several strikes had broken out over low wages—fifty cents a day in 1884—but they were invariably smashed by the state militia, sometimes (as in 1880) supplemented by the state field artillery. In 1886, the black and white sugar workers began to organize in the Knights of Labor, and in November, under the union's sponsorship, 1,000 laborers walked off the Fairview Plantation, near New Orleans, demanding a 50 per cent increase in wages. Faced now with a union-backed strike, the planters formed the Sugar Planters' Association, drove the Negro Knights from their homes on the plantations (owned by the planters), and imported strike-breakers. Once again the strikers were defeated.

Conditions made another strike inevitable. The average wage set by the association was eighty-five cents a day for men, but women and children working for forty to fifty cents a day were displacing many of the male laborers. With twenty working days in the month, the average monthly wage of a male laborer was $13, paid not in legal tender but in pasteboard tickets redeemable only at company stores controlled by the planters, where prices were often marked up 100 per cent over the whole-sale cost. The planters made a double profit, while the laborers were lucky if they had enough to provide for their families. "At the end of the year," a reporter wrote in the *Weekly Pelican* of November 19, 1887, "the laborer is 'poor as a church mouse,' and the demands of his stom-ach are such that he is compelled to enter into a new contract for an-other year." Since the association determined wage rate and working conditions for all its members, there was little point in looking for better terms elsewhere.

On October 24, 1887, District Assembly 194, representing the sugar workers of four parishes, circularized the planters with demands for $1.25 a day without board or $1 a day with board, 60 cents for six hours' "watch" at night, day wages to be paid every two weeks and "watch" wages every week, and payment of wages in money. The district offered to submit the demands to arbitration if they were thought to be exces-sive, but the majority of the planters rejected them totally. Some 9,000 Negroes and 1,000 other sugar workers thereupon walked off the plantations.

Immediately the planters called upon Governor McEnery to send in the militia, and he readily complied. The governor was enraged at the spectacle of black and white workers acting in concert, which he declared violated the precept that "God Almighty has himself drawn the color line."[27] When 50 to 100 Negroes refused to disperse at the order of the sheriff, the militiamen opened fire, killing four blacks and wounding five. Strikers all over the sugar-raising areas were arrested or evicted from their cabins and forced to camp on public grounds and highways. Strike-breakers were promptly imported to take their places, and the governor suggested that they might be enrolled into the militia if necessary. In Thibodaux, 300 of the "most prominent residents" formed themselves into a military unit to supplement the militia.[28]

The planters finally agreed to pay $1 a day with board and 50 cents for night watch. The strikers rejected the terms because the planters refused to recognize the Knights as a bargaining agent for the sugar workers. As the strike continued, George and Henry Cox, black strike leaders, were arrested and imprisoned. Then armed whites, headed by the "Clay Knobloch Guards," a local military unit numbering 100 to 200 men, attacked the Negro settlement in Thibodaux, where evicted strikers with their families were crowded into churches and empty buildings. The vigilantes went from building to building firing at all blacks who appeared. An old blind woman ran out of her cabin and was mortally wounded. Many Negroes escaped to the fields and woods, but it was reported that more than twenty were massacred; the pro-planter New Orleans *Times-Democrat* conceded, in fact, that the number of Negroes slain might reach thirty when all the corpses were found. The terrorism reached its climax when George and Henry Cox were taken from their cells by a mob of whites and lynched.

The lynching, intimidation, violence, and massacres undermined the morale of the strikers. With no assistance from the national leadership of the Knights of Labor, most were forced to return to work on the old terms. Only on a few plantations was the strike successful. Some white Knights in Louisiana had rallied to the support of the strikers and condemned the massacres as "inhuman and too dark a deed for such a civilized country as America," but others had helped to break the strike.[29] Afraid of unemployment and mindful of the threats in the pro-planter press, they had regarded the strikers as more dangerous than the employers. About twenty members of the Berwick, Louisiana, Knights had been members of the militia that helped suppress the strikers. The secretary of the local wrote to ask Powderly if there was any way the militiamen could be expelled without breaking up the 250-member local. Powderly replied that, while he disapproved of Knights' joining a military organization used against labor, it was a matter for the local assembly to decide.[30]

That was typical of the national leadership's conduct throughout the bitter struggle. When black newspapers called upon Powderly to rally the entire order against the terrorist tactics used against the hard-pressed strikers and to demand prosecution of those responsible for the massacres and lynchings, he remained silent. Instead, he lectured the black editors about the evils of strikes, assured them that he never would endorse a walkout, and urged them to tell black Knights that "cooperation is the true remedy for the ills of industry." When District 194 of Berwick petitioned the GEB to take protest action against the terror, the request was referred to a board member in the South with instructions that he investigate. The following year, when District 102 of New Orleans asked the national leadership what action had been taken as a result of the investigation, it learned that there had not even been an investigation. Moreover, the report of District 102's own investigating committee, which named the men responsible for the murders and lynchings, had simply been referred to the national Legislative Committee.[31]

As the Knights of Labor declined, all efforts by the national officers to enforce the principle of brotherhood of labor halted. As the more radical white Knights left the order or were expelled by Powderly, the anti-Negro members assumed greater influence. After 1886, letters to Powderly from black Knights in the South complained that white Knights were not eager to organize blacks. When an attempt was made to begin a Negro women's assembly in Savannah, Georgia, several white locals in the city protested. White members were now objecting to the formation of black assemblies in Norfolk, Virginia. The 1887 convention received a complaint from black members in Harrisburg, Texas, charging white members with blatant discrimination. The GEB directed local assemblies to treat black speakers with respect and courtesy, but it did nothing to enforce the ruling.

As such incidents multiplied, black workers showed great reluctance to become involved with the Knights of Labor. Richard Thompson, a Richmond tobacco-roller representing the all-Negro District 92, was the only black delegate at the 1888 convention at Indianapolis. The district was also represented by one delegate at the 1889 convention in Atlanta, but it sent no more delegates after that. Blacks continued to serve as delegates to state conventions and district assemblies, but for all practical purposes by 1891 the majority of black Knights had left the organization. In Chicago, where black waiters had been an important element in the Knights and where they, together with white waiters, had won a strike for higher wages in 1887, the departure was evident. In 1890 most of the black waiters left the Knights and formed the independent Culinary Alliance of Chicago, an interracial organization of waiters and hotel employees. A small Negro local of the Knights, the Charles Sumner Waiters' Union, remained, but most black waiters were no longer associated with the order.

The response to the Knights of Labor in the black press of the 1890's was a far cry from the enthusiastic praise of a few years before. The Knights were declining even more rapidly than before, and the opportunistic attitude of the leadership on the Negro question became ever more obvious. Powderly, once the idol of the black papers, came under sharp criticism for a speech at the Saint Louis convention in 1890 in which he stated that Southern whites were capable of managing the Negro. In 1893 the organization's General Assembly refused to take a stand on a petition submitted "on behalf of the Afro-American members of the Order in Chicago," which had appealed to the General Assembly "to speak out in thundering tones against the discriminations against our race throughout this country, against Jim Crow cars, race prejudice from every section and source, also Judge Lynch."[32] When the assembly voted to insert the petition in its minutes, the *Christian Recorder* termed its inaction "indeed an indication of how meaningless were our hopes in the Knights of Labor a few years before."[33]

In 1894 the Knights of Labor announced that the only solution for the Negro problem in the United States was to raise federal funds and deport blacks to the Congo Basin, Liberia, "or some other parts of Africa."[34] A poll of white locals had revealed overwhelming sentiment in favor of the idea. Grand Master Workman James R. Sovereign of Iowa,

Powderly's successor, was instructed by the GEB to mobilize support for an appropriation of funds to deport Negroes to Africa. Black workers were outraged. "Who came to this country first, the negro or the Knights?" the *Northwestern Christian Advocate* asked.[35] "Negroes have been residents of this country for two hundred and fifty years and are as much American citizens as anybody," the Chicago Colored Women's Club announced. "If this country is too small for the Knights of Labor and the Negro, then let the Knights leave."[36]

A former black Knight, addressing Grand Master Workman Sovereign, wrote in the Chicago *Interocean*: "There was a day when you preached the universal brotherhood of man. Why not once again accept the Negro into the Order on the basis of equality and prove yourself faithful to the fundamental principles of your organization?"[37]

The "fool notion" of deporting Negroes, one critic declared, "could only emanate from men ignorant of economic laws and bankrupt in morals." So far as the majority of the Negroes were concerned, it was final proof that the once great Knights of Labor, the one organization in American life to have challenged the pattern of discrimination and segregation, had joined all other institutions in relegating black Americans to an inferior status.

By 1893 the Knights membership had dropped to 200,000. Two years later it had plummeted to 20,000. Although it continued to exist thereafter—the last local of the Knights, Local 3030 in Boston, consisting of fifty motion picture projectionists, went out of existence in October, 1949—the Knights of Labor ceased to be a viable labor organization after 1895.

The decline and disappearance of the Knights of Labor was a tragedy for all American workers, but especially for the black workers. For a brief period, a national labor body had actually challenged the racist structure of American society. "Perhaps one of the noblest acts of the Knights of Labor," a member wrote in 1886 in his book, *The Great Labor Question, or the Noble Mission of the Knights of Labor*, "is that of rising above the prejudices of thousands and millions of people that were engendered against the negro race when they were in bondage." The *Globe and Lance*, a black paper, said about the same time: "It is not organized as the special champion of the negro, but it has done more to abolish the color line, south and north . . . than all politicians and special friends of freedom."[38]

At its height and at its best, the Knights had acted upon the words of Frederick Douglass in 1883: "The labor unions of the country should not throw away this colored element of strength. . . . It is a great mistake for any class of laborers to isolate itself and thus weaken the bond of brotherhood between those on whom the burden and hardships of labor fall."[39] By applying this principle, the Knights contributed immensely toward a brief era of good feeling between black and white workingmen, even in the South. From those heights the Knights of Labor steadily declined, year after year weakening the fraternal bonds it had built, until at the end it became an apologist for white supremacy.

5 The AF of L and the
Black Worker, 1881–1915

Even while the Knights of Labor was achieving its greatest successes, an organization was emerging that soon was to supplant it as the leader of the American labor movement. In the first few years after it was founded, the American Federation of Labor and its leadership pursued a policy toward black workers that had many features in common with the Knights' policy. At the founding convention in 1881, Samuel Gompers, chairman of the Committee on Organization, declared, "We do not want to exclude any workingman who believes in and belongs to organized labor."[1] Although the precise number of Negro delegates at the founding session is not known, the fact that four specifically designated colored organizations were represented was indicative of the federation's early policy not to discriminate.

Moral reasons aside, there was a fairly clear understanding that exclusion based on race was inimical to the interests of the white workers, in that it would make it easier for employers to use blacks to break strikes. Jeremiah Grandison, a Negro delegate from a Pittsburgh Knights of Labor assembly, warned the delegates:

> Our object, as I understand it, is to federate the whole laboring element of America. I speak more particularly with a knowledge of my own people and declare to you that it would be dangerous to exclude from this organization the common laborers, who might, in an emergency, be employed in positions they could readily qualify themselves to fill.

The delegates resolved in response that the new federation would take in "the whole laboring element of this country, no matter of what calling." Candidates for affiliation were required to pledge "never to discriminate against a fellow worker on account of color, creed or nationality."[2]

The first significant challenge to the federation's commitment to labor equality came in 1890 at its tenth annual convention, held in Detroit. A resolution was introduced requesting that an organizer be furnished for the National Association of Machinists, a predominantly

Southern organization whose constitution limited membership to whites. The AF of L Executive Council, by a vote of 51 to 5, refused to authorize an organizer for the machinists unless the discriminatory clause was removed from the constitution, declaring that it looked with disfavor upon trade unions that excluded members on the basis of race. President Gompers himself visited the machinists' association's convention that year and made a formal request to officials that they lift the color bar, which they agreed to do the following year. When the machinists failed to honor their agreement, the AF of L called a convention of unaffiliated machinists' unions with the aim of uniting the machinists in an organization "based upon the principles which recognize the equality of all men working at our trade regardless of religion, race or color." Out of that convention emerged the International Machinists Union of America, which drew up a constitution extending membership to blacks and whites. The federation quickly issued a charter to the new union. It was understood that the IMU had as its purpose to compel a change in the national association's membership policy. Once that end was achieved, the new union would amalgamate with the older one, provided that the latter was willing to do so "on an honorable basis."[3]

The AF of L adopted a similar policy toward the Brotherhood of Boiler Makers and the Iron Ship Builders of America. When those two organizations consolidated in 1893, their constitution contained a clause limiting membership to whites. The AF of L not only refused to charter the new union but also helped organize an independent union of boilermakers, which opened its ranks to Negroes and promptly received a charter from the federation.

The actions of the AF of L toward unions that barred Negro workers are the more interesting because, from the start, it was committed to a principle of autonomy. Affiliated national and international organizations had the right to regulate their internal affairs without interference from the federation. The AF of L exercised authority within its organizational framework only through the force of suggestion and moral suasion. But when suggestion and suasion failed to persuade the machinists and boilermakers to strike the color bar from their constitutions, the AF of L denied them affiliation. And it did so at a time when the AF of L was still engaged in a struggle for survival with the Knights of Labor, when its membership was growing slowly, and when it had a biased press, a hostile government, and powerful business opposition to contend with. In that early period of his long career, Samuel Gompers, the first president of the federation, repeatedly emphasized that exclusion based on race was against the interests of the labor movement as a whole and that employers would continue to exploit all workers so long as they remained divided. "Wage workers," he wrote, "like many others, may not care to socially meet colored people, but as working men we are not justified in refusing them the right or the opportunity to organize for their common protection. . . . We will only make enemies of them and of necessity they will be antagonistic to our interests." In a letter to a friend, Gompers amplified this position:

If the colored man is not permitted to organize, if he is not given the opportunity to protect and defend his interests, if a chance is not given him by which he could uplift his condition, the inevitable result must follow, that he will sink down lower and lower in his economic scale. . . .

If our fellow white wage worker will not allow the colored worker to cooperate with him, he will necessarily cling to the other hand (that of the employer) who also smites him, but at least recognizes his right to work. If we do not make friends of the colored men they will of necessity be justified in proving themselves our enemies. . . . I wish the slogan would come forth among the toilers of the South, working men organize regardless of color.

Throughout the late 1880's and early 1890's Gompers frequently asserted that AF of L representatives should make special efforts to organize Negro workers; that city and state AF of L bodies must not bar Negro delegates; that, wherever local unions barred Negroes, efforts should be made to eliminate such barriers; that, meanwhile, the Negro workers should be organized into separate locals "but attached to the same national organizations with the same rights, duties and privileges" as all other locals. "In other words, have the Union of white men organized and have the Union of colored men organize also, both unions to work in unison and harmony to accomplish the desired end."

The policy of organizing separate locals was thus part of the AF of L's early approach toward Negro workers, but it was only one feature of the approach; separate locals were to be organized only when there was no other way to bring Negro workers into the federation, and then only as temporary locals. The main point in Gompers's replies to all inquiries was that the Negro worker *must* be organized. Not only did humanity demand it, but so did the practical needs of the trade union, for the AF of L could not succeed unless it waged a relentless struggle "to eliminate the consideration of a color line in the country."[4]

Gompers's opinion did not sit well with many AF of L representatives in the South. They bluntly informed him that in no circumstances would they heed his advice to organize the Negro workers, that to do so would be fatal to the federation. But the ability existed to build a viable labor movement in the South, based on the solidarity of black and white, skilled and unskilled, in the teeth of employer-sponsored racist assaults. The New Orleans General Strike of 1892 was proof. At the call of forty-nine unions affiliated with the AF of L, about 25,000 workers in New Orleans stopped work for four days. The unions, many of them organized during the summer of 1892, were united in the Workingmen's Amalgamated Council, to which each union sent two delegates.

Among the recently organized unions in New Orleans was the Teamsters, Scalesmen, and Packers, the so-called Triple Alliance. Many of its members were Negroes. On October 24, 1892, between 2,000 and 3,000 members of the Triple Alliance left their jobs because the Board of Trade had refused to grant them a ten-hour day, overtime pay, and a preferential union shop.

The strikers relied upon the support of the Workingmen's Amalgamated Council to win out against the merchants and their allies—the four railway systems entering New Orleans; the cotton, sugar, and rice exchanges; the clearing house; and the mechanics' and dealers' exchange. This support was immediately forthcoming; if necessary, the council's president announced, every AF of L union in New Orleans would walk out in sympathy with the strikers.

The employers tried a splitting maneuver. The Board of Trade announced that it would sign an agreement with the scalesmen's and packers' unions but not with the largest component in the Triple Alliance—the teamsters—for under no circumstances would it enter into any agreement with "niggers." To sign an agreement with the Triple Alliance including the teamsters, the board declared, would be to place the employers under the control of Negroes, for soon the man who would control the Alliance "would be a Big Black Negro."[5]

The press attempted to stampede the white strikers into returning to work by publishing fabrications about assaults on whites. "Negroes Attack White Man," a New Orleans *Times-Democrat* headline shrieked on November 2. "Assaulted by Negroes" was its headline two days later. But, surprisingly to the employers and the press, the labor ranks held firm, and the scalesmen and packers publicly declared that they would never return to work until the employers signed up with all three members of the Triple Alliance. The other AF of L unions began holding meetings to voice their solidarity with the strikers, black and white, and the unions proceeded to poll their members on the question of a general strike. They found uniform enthusiasm for the proposal, and the unions went on record threatening a general strike if the employers did not come to terms with all three members of the Triple Alliance.

The *Times-Democrat* accused the white trade unionists of lunacy for considering a general strike to assist the Negro trade union of the Triple Alliance. It charged that the threat of a general strike proved that the blacks had gained a dominant position in the New Orleans labor movement. "The very worst feature, indeed, in the whole case seems to be that the white elements of the labor organizations appear to be under the dominance of Senegambian influence, or that they are at least lending themselves as willing tools to carry out Senegambian schemes."[6] Senegambia was a region of West Africa, and this was a way of raising the hoary cry of "Negro domination," so effectively used in the South to overthrow Radical Republican Reconstruction.

But this time it did not work. On November 8, after two postponements, the general strike went into effect. Each of the forty-nine unions that called out their members demanded union recognition, the closed shop, and in some cases wage increases and shorter hours. Several of the unions, including those of the streetcar drivers and printers, broke their contracts to join the general strike in violation of a principle that was already becoming fixed for most craft unions.

The general strike was under the leadership of a committee of five, one of whom was a black, James E. Porter, assistant state organizer of the Car Drivers' Union, who had recently been commissioned as an assistant organizer for the AF of L. J. Madison Vance, a black lawyer, also played a prominent part in the strike. John M. Callahan, AF of L general organizer and representative of the Cotton Yardmen on the committee of five, wrote excitedly to Gompers on November 7: "There are fully 25,000 men idle. There is no newspaper to be printed, no gas or electric light in the city, no wagons, no carpenters, painters or in fact any business doing. . . . I am sorry you are not down here to take a hand in it. It is a strike that will go down in history."[7]

Antistrike leaflets distributed among the white strikers warned that blacks would use the strike situation to seize control of the city and made much of "instances where ladies and school children have been insulted by the blacks." Once again the appeals to race prejudice were in vain; the strikers' ranks remained solid. B. Sherer, financial secretary of the New Orleans Marine and Stationary Firemen's Protective Union, assured Gompers that the black and white workers had resolved "to cement the Bonds of Brotherhood and Fraternal ties that will stand before the world as an everlasting monument of strength, and show to the world at large that in unionism there is strength, and that our order [the AF of L] stands preeminently at the head of the human Race."[8]

Governor Foster of Louisiana called out the militia, but the employers finally had to agree to arbitrate. Although the unions did not win the preferential union shop, there was to be "no discrimination against union men," and many of the other original demands of the strikers—a ten-hour day, overtime pay, and adjusted wage schedules—were achieved. The agreement was reached at conferences where employers sat down with black and white representatives of the strikers.

Existing unions of black and white workers increased their membership, and new unions of both groups were formed during the strike. "Yesterday," the New Orleans *Times-Democrat* reported on October 30, 1892, "there were three new unions formed and admitted to membership. The names of the unions were not given to the press, but it was intimated that every man in the Federation of Labor was actively engaged in furthering the interests of the order, and in getting together as many bodies of organized labor as possible." It also reported that several of the new unions were integrated.

The New Orleans General Strike was one of the most important in AF of L history and in the history of American labor. The outstanding feature of the strike was its great demonstration of interracial labor solidarity in action. Thousands of workers in the Deep South had shown that they could unite in a common struggle, black and white, skilled and unskilled, and that they could stay united despite the efforts of employers and their agents to divide them by appeals to anti-Negro prejudice. Gompers noted this in a letter to Callahan:

> To me the movement in New Orleans was a very bright ray of hope for the future of organized labor and convinces me that the advantage which every other element fails to succeed in falls to the mission of organized labor. Never in the history of the world was such an exhibition, where with all the prejudices existing against the black man, when the white wage-

workers of New Orleans would sacrifice their means of livelihood to defend and protect their colored fellow workers. With one fell swoop the economic barrier of color was broken down. Under the circumstances I regard the movement as a very healthy sign of the times and one which speaks well for the future of organized labor in the "New South" about which the politicians prate so much and mean so little.[9]

Had the AF of L adhered to the principles set forth in this statement, Gompers's optimism might have been fully warranted. It is clear that the early AF of L, especially in the South, made important contributions toward building the unity of workers regardless of color. It laid down as a cardinal principle the policy of organizing and uniting black and white workers "for the purpose of elevating the condition of both black and white"; it could take pride in the fact that international unions that barred Negroes as members were in turn barred from affiliation with the federation; it boasted that within the federation's ranks "the colored man and his white brother are joined by the fraternal wand of fellowship."[10]

But by 1893 affiliated unions were balking under the "fraternal wand." Gompers's position was that competition with black workers could be eliminated only by bringing Negroes into labor unions. White skilled workers in the organized trades and their leaders, on the other hand, contended that the competition had to be ended by excluding blacks from their unions and from the labor market. Their determination to continue that practice, already well established by the time the AF of L was founded, was strengthened by the panic of 1893 and the ensuing serious economic depression, which lasted until 1898. With 50 to 75 per cent of their members unemployed by the fall of 1894, the idea of removing barriers against blacks seemed utopian even to more liberal union leaders. Negroes were in dire economic straits—some were "found actually dying of want," the Colored Mission in New York City reported as early as 1893[11]—and racial clashes intensified as blacks sought work desperately, undercutting the white unionists. In New Orleans the interracial solidarity built during the General Strike of 1892 weakened in the face of economic stress. When cotton shippers attempted to replace white screwmen with unemployed Negro screwmen at lower wages, upsetting a division of work between the two groups that had been in operation for decades, white screwmen boarded vessels and threw the tools of the Negroes overboard. Several blacks drowned when they jumped into the river to avoid being beaten. Shipping firms continued to hire Negro screwmen at low wages, and the starving blacks accepted the work even though they knew it would bring violence and perhaps even death at the hands of the white screwmen. In March, 1895, Governor Foster had to call out the militia to protect Negro screwmen hired by an English shipping firm.[12]

As employers stepped up the use of black workers and manipulated racial antagonisms to drive down labor costs in the economic crisis, most unions affiliated with the AF of L continued to refuse to accept Negroes as equal members and instead increased their efforts to drive black workers off the job. The AF of L continued to stress the need to organize workers regardless of race, color, or nationality, but it added the qualification that the worker must be skilled, despite Gompers's exhortations to organize all workers. The craft orientation of the AF of L and the policy of limiting union organization to skilled craft workers nullified the lofty principle of racial equality and led inevitably to the abandonment of the black worker even during the AF of L's early years.

In the spring of 1895, James Duncan, acting president of the AF of L, told the National Association of Machinists in a letter:

> [As] long as you have the word "white" establishing a color line as part of your constitution either your action must be changed or your lodges and your national body must stand debarred from all affiliation with us. . . . I believe yours is the only national union that at present has the color line as distinctly formed, while at the same time many crafts refused to admit a colored man without having any such provision in their constitution, the matter being left absolutely with the local unions as to whether or not they admit colored applicants.[13]

The association, now the International Association of Machinists (IAM), having amalgamated with the National Machinists Union in late 1894, responded to Duncan's counsel by transferring the color clause from its constitution to the initiation ritual. Affiliation with the AF of L followed shortly, at the federation's annual convention in December, 1895. The AF of L–sponsored rival of the IAM, the International Machinists Union (IMU), was ordered to join the new affiliate, but the IAM refused to accept the IMU as a body and reserved the right to accept members on an individual basis. The IMU protested because the procedure resulted in the exclusion of its Negro members, and the federation responded by revoking its charter.

Acting President James Duncan cannot be fairly charged with responsibility for the subterfuge by which the IAM gained entry to the AF of L. As he had pointed out to the machinists' union, unions desiring to discriminate against blacks had already hit upon the method. James O'Connell, head of the IAM, disclosed that he had discussed the constitutional ban against Negroes with Gompers "and many other leading lights" in the AF of L, and that the suggestion to remove the color ban from the constitution, transfer it to the ritual, and then apply for membership in the federation had come from them, along with assurances that "rejection would not stare us in the face." Thus did the highest-ranking officials of the AF of L show themselves ready to break with the federation's early policy of racial equality.[14]

For the next fifty-three years, the IAM effectively excluded Negro machinists from its ranks. In 1902, when W. E. B. Du Bois was writing a study of the Negro artisan at Atlanta University, the Secretary of the IAM's Washington lodge wrote to him that "the Negro is not admitted to the International Association of Machinists." Although the excluded

Negro had no choice but to undercut the white union member, and although warnings were repeatedly voiced at machinists' conventions that the union was suffering economically because of its stand, discrimination remained the rule. A member of the union, asked if he had ever worked with a Negro machinist, answered: "No, sir, I never worked in a shop with a Negro as a machinist. . . . I would not."[15]

In 1896 Gompers, once again AF of L president, sought to bring the Brotherhood of Locomotive Firemen into the organization. W. S. Carter, editor of the *Locomotive Firemen's Magazine*, told him the Brotherhood was reluctant to join the AF of L because it wanted to keep Negroes out of the union. Gompers suggested doing what the machinists had done, that is, remove the lily-white clause from its constitution and accomplish the same purpose by allowing each lodge to regulate its own membership. The Brotherhood rejected such a course and told Gompers that the membership would "not care to belong to an organization that is not honest enough to make public its qualification of membership."[16]

Other unions were not so sensitive. One year after the IAM, the Boiler Makers and Iron Ship Builders of America, previously excluded because of a color ban in its constitution, was welcomed into the AF of L after exchanging the constitutional restriction for a less formal one. A year later the International Brotherhood of Blacksmiths did likewise and was admitted to the federation.

Thus ended the short-lived AF of L policy of refusing affiliation to any union that barred blacks. The federation still insisted publicly that no charter would be granted to a union with a color clause in its constitution, but it welcomed unions that excluded blacks in some less obvious way. By the turn of the century, federation officials were no longer bothering to insist that discriminatory unions conceal the practice to gain admittance. In 1899 and 1900 the Order of Railroad Telegraphers and the Brotherhood of Railway Trackmen—both with explicit constitutional provisions barring blacks from membership—had no difficulty obtaining charters from the AF of L. Gompers not only reported their affiliation "with much pleasure" but expressed the hope that the other railway brotherhoods would follow suit.[17] (In 1909 and 1910 the Brotherhood of Railway Carmen and the Brotherhood of Railway Steam Clerks and Freight Handlers also joined the Federation without altering their constitutional ban against blacks.) In 1902 the Stationary Engineers, a national union already affiliated with the AF of L, amended its constitution to restrict membership to whites, and not a single word of rebuke was forthcoming from Gompers and the federation.

Gompers's surrender on the color bar was accompanied by changes in the AF of L procedure for organizing black workers. In the past his insistence that the Negro be organized had led him to encourage the establishment of separate black unions wherever local prejudice made integrated unions impossible. The separate black locals were to be attached to the national organizations with the same rights, duties, and privileges as all other unions. Eventually they would disappear when more favorable circumstances permitted their members to enter integrated locals.

In any event, they represented only a part of the AF of L's general effort to "organize and re-organize" the black workingman.

In the Southern organizing drive launched in 1898–99 by the AF of L, the Negro painters, barbers, carpenters, quarrymen, wheelwrights, and others who were brought into unions were organized almost exclusively into separate locals. The new locals were not permitted to send delegates to the AF of L central labor bodies. The black workers protested, but Gompers maintained that a central body was "the sole judge of the eligibility of a Delegate being seated therein." Gompers was informed that the application of this rule in the South was hampering attempts to organize Negro workers, but he did nothing to change the situation. The Negro locals set up their own central labor bodies and applied for AF of L charters. A charter was granted only with the consent of the white central labor body in the area. Consent was frequently withheld because the black central labor unions, if chartered, "would be entitled to seats in the State Federation [of Labor]."

In March, 1900, the Central Trades and Labor Council of New Orleans, set up by seven AF of L black unions when permission to send delegates to the official central labor body in the city was denied them, applied to the federation for a charter, promising to work in harmony with the council of white unions. The AF of L Executive Council turned the application over to Gompers, who told the black unionists that the charter would require the consent of the white central body. James Leonard, AF of L general organizer in New Orleans, informed Gompers that, "in the matter of organizing a CLU of colored workers, the feeling against a project of this kind is so great that it would cause a great deal of trouble at this particular time," whereupon Gompers refused to grant the charter. He added insult to injury by telling the blacks "there is no use kicking against the pricks" and "we cannot overcome prejudice in a day." James E. Porter, secretary of the Central Trades and Labor Council of New Orleans, replied: "I did not understand that there is a prejudice when the wages and interest are the same and can only be upheld by concert[ed] action." Porter was paraphrasing some of Gompers's own earlier statements, with understandable bitterness.

Gompers referred the matter of the New Orleans Central Council to the 1900 AF of L convention. He conceded that the federation had earlier revoked the charters of some central labor bodies for refusing to accept delegates from the black unions, but to insist on a Negro union's representation in a white central labor body, he said, would cause the latter to disaffiliate. He therefore proposed giving the federation the authority to charter directly the councils composed exclusively of black union representatives.

The convention adopted a constitutional amendment empowering the Executive Council to issue charters to separate central bodies and also authorizing the organization of blacks into separate local trade and federal labor unions, unaffiliated with an international union but operating under a charter issued directly by the AF of L. The section of the AF of L constitution sanctioning Jim Crow unionism was worded: "Separate charters may be issued to central labor unions, local unions or federated labor unions composed exclusively of colored workers where in the judgment of the Executive Council it appears advisable."

Segregated locals, originally conceived by the AF of L as a temporary alternative to racial exclusion, had become the preferred method of organizing black workers. The AF of L had let it be known that affiliated national and local unions could continue to refuse admission to workers because of color. Thus the federation had abandoned even the formal endorsement of equal status for Negro workers. Segregation, Gompers declared, was the best solution for both black and white workers and for the entire labor movement, for it would avoid "arousing bitterness."[18]

The AF of L did not make it a condition that black as well as white workers should desire separate organizations; it did not urge the white unions to accept black workers before acceding to the establishment of separate unions; indeed, it specifically refused to make such requests of central labor unions. The federation decided in December, 1901, that, even where there were not enough Negro locals to form separate central councils, the white central labor bodies did not have to admit black delegates.

Jim Crow unionism was successful in appeasing the racial prejudices of federation affiliates, but as a means of furthering the organization of black workers it was a failure. When the federation chartered a local of Negroes barred from the white union of their craft, the international union generally objected, forcing the Executive Council to retreat and cancel the charter. When the international did not object, conflict immediately arose regarding jurisdiction over the black local. In theory, it was the Executive Council's responsibility to protect the interest of black locals. But the council never had the right to represent such bodies at wage negotiations and therefore had no authority to see that they received the wages agreed upon. In practice, the task of protecting the federation's directly chartered black locals fell to the national union that regulated the wage scale for the craft. Since the very existence of the black local attested to the racism of the national union, this was no protection at all. Nor did black craftsmen organized in separate locals receive assistance from the city central labor bodies, composed of white men representing white locals. Hence it is not surprising that members of Negro locals worked longer hours and at lower wages than their white counterparts.

By 1910 there were eight AF of L national affiliates that denied membership to blacks by ritual or constitutional provision: the Wire Weavers' Protective Association, the Order of Switchmen's Union in North America, the Brotherhood of Maintenance of Way Employees, the Order of Railway Telegraphers, the Brotherhood of Railway and Steamship Clerks, the Commercial Telegraphers Union, the International Brotherhood of Boiler Makers and Iron Ship Builders, and the IAM. The fact that the remaining fifty-odd AF of L national unions had no rules forbidding admission to black workers did not necessarily mean that they admitted blacks upon application. Some unions proclaimed the equality of all workers in their constitutions but set such stringent skill requirements for applicants that blacks, with their meager industrial experience, were automatically excluded. This explained the absence of Negroes in unions of engravers, lithographers, jewelry workers, molders, piano and organ workers, printers, and stone cutters. Other national organizations requiring less sophisticated skills charged high initiation fees (sometimes higher for black applicants than for whites), barred blacks from apprenticeship programs, refused to honor their travel cards from sister locals,* and allowed local unions to disregard admission policies of the national bodies.

In his masterly study of the Negro artisan in 1902, W. E. B. Du Bois investigated the racial practices of many unions throughout the country and found forty-three national unions operating in both Northern and Southern states, including the railroad brotherhoods, without a single black member. Twenty-seven others had very few black members, in many cases because they barred Negro apprentices. Du Bois found, too, that in some AF of L affiliates Negro membership had declined from 1890 to 1900, the decade in which the policy of Negro-white unity had retrogressed.

It was during this era, which the black historian Rayford W. Logan calls the nadir of American concern for the rights and welfare of its black citizens, that the AF of L developed, and some historians argue that it was clearly in no position to buck the rising tide of racism and uphold the rights of black workers in their quest for economic freedom. The failure of the federation and its leadership to maintain the earlier policy of black-white labor solidarity was, in this view, a national failure rather than solely a failure of the white labor movement.

In Gompers's defense, it is pointed out that he tried but was not able to convince unions in Southern communities that their self-interest required acceptance of the black worker. Even in the North, his exhortations failed to alter the unions' hostility to any increase in the number of workers in their trades, with the consequent decrease in wages. Unionists persisted in showing concern not for labor solidarity but for preserving job security in a limited labor market through a monopoly of the trade. Racial prejudice, of course, strengthened this attitude. To many a white unionist, the black was not simply a rival who threatened his control of the job. He was also a racial and social inferior seeking to compel whites to associate with him, a spreader of "infectious diseases" that made any close contact with him on the job a real danger.† Hence a union that refused to admit blacks not only eliminated a threat to its white members' monopoly of jobs but preserved their status and its own reputation in the white community.

---

* A travel card enabled a member of one local to become a member of another local of the international when he moved from one city to another.

† The myth that blacks harbored contagious diseases received endorsement by the government of the United States during the Wilson Administration, when it was used to justify the establishment of segregated facilities for workers in federal departments, particularly the Treasury and Post Office departments.

Gompers, according to his defenders, recognized that it was in labor's best interest to unite regardless of color, but as the years went by he found his position increasingly difficult to maintain. He was faced with a choice: Uphold the principle of black-white labor equality and doom the possibility of organizing the white workers, especially in the South, or sacrifice the interests of the Negro and preserve the AF of L. As a realistic, pragmatic trade union leader, the argument goes, he made the only logical decision. He may well have had misgivings about his retreat, but he perceived that the development of a strong, stable labor movement could not be achieved by placing the AF of L in open conflict with racially prejudiced white workers.

Many contemporary studies offer ample evidence that racist thinking was rife even in ostensibly enlightened white union circles. Gompers and other AF of L leaders urged blacks to be patient, promising that the federation's program of education and "moral suasion" would gradually whittle down the influence of racism in the labor movement. But the men who were supposed to do the educating not only accommodated themselves to racism but contributed to it. Many organizers publicly and privately expressed contempt for blacks and defended Jim Crow practices. They justified the exclusion of blacks from machine jobs with the slanderous argument that they were "clumsy and would be lulled to sleep by the whirring of the wheels" and that they spread "contagious diseases." Blacks did not want "to work steady," they said. Being "natural strike-breakers," they sought jobs only when they were assured special treatment by employers, as during strikes of white unionists. Such organizers insisted that blacks were unfit to be members of a trade union and told AF of L national officers not to count on them in any attempt to unite blacks and whites in the same locals.[19]

Gompers, for all his eloquent pleas for unity of all workers regardless of race, color, or national origin, was basically a bigot. He referred repeatedly to white workers as superior to blacks. In the *American Federationist* and in his speeches and letters, he used the common, demeaning epithets of the day in referring to blacks. He was a master also at fanning race hatred against Chinese and other Oriental workers. He advocated the exclusion of immigrants from Southeastern Europe, calling them "cheap labor that cannot be Americanized and cannot be taught to render the same intelligent service as is supplied by American workers."

Gompers never spoke out on the disfranchisement of Negroes in the South. Many AF of L bodies urged him to do so, pointing out that the devices employed to keep blacks from the ballot box were depriving white workers of the vote as well. He also resisted appeals that he speak out in protest against "those horrible 'lynchings' that are now disgracing the nation"—a conservative estimate placed the number of Negroes lynched between 1900 and 1914 at 1,079—on the ground that neither he nor the AF of L had any desire to interfere with the "internal affairs" of the South: "I regard the race problem as one with which you people of the Southland will have to deal; without the interference, too, of meddlers from the outside." To blacks who were calling for full equality he offered only a familiar piece of advice: "You must hold and hope for a time."[20]

As we have noted, Gompers did not take long to retreat from his early strictures against anti-Negro policies in the unions. At the turn of the century, he told the U.S. Industrial Commission that if organized labor discriminated against blacks, it was not because of prejudice against their color, but because they have "so conducted themselves as to be a continuous convenient whip placed in the hands of the employers to cow the white men and to compel them to accept abject conditions of labor." In April, 1901, the AF of L Executive Council issued a statement, signed by Gompers on behalf of the Council, asserting that the absence of black members in most of the trade unions affiliated to the AF of L was no indication of their reluctance to organize blacks. The real blame rested on the black workers themselves, who "have allowed themselves to be used with too frequent telling effect by their employers as to injure the cause and interests of themselves, as well as of white workers." The statement concluded by warning black workers not to frustrate the efforts of the AF of L and its affiliates to organize them by scabbing and otherwise serving the interests of the employers. In the same month, in an article in the *American Federationist* entitled "Trade Union Attitude Toward Colored Workers," Gompers charged that black workers did not possess the skill required to become members of the craft unions. He did not mention that most of these unions prevented blacks from acquiring that skill by refusing to accept them as apprentices. By taking the places of white workers on strike, blacks were helping the employers to destroy the unions, he said, and so it was hardly surprising that the unions should regard them as enemies rather than allies.[21]

Many other articles and speeches by Gompers used the words "Negro" and "scab" as synonyms. In all his public statements, he fixed the blame for the blacks' exclusion on the blacks themselves. But privately he admitted that the fault really lay with most of the affiliates of the AF of L. In a letter to Henry Randall, the federation's Birmingham organizer, on March 19, 1903, he wrote: "The Negro workers must be organized in order that they may be in a position to protect themselves and in some way feel an interest with our organized white workmen, or we shall unquestionably have their undying enmity."

Gompers had reason to know whereof he spoke. As early as 1896, he was receiving complaints from blacks who charged that they were kept out of AF of L unions "simply because they are colored" and were consequently losing faith in organized labor. White correspondents reported to Gompers that black workers in their region were complaining bitterly that unions affiliated to the AF of L "had Barred the Door of their Unions against colored men" and were openly threatening to "tell the unions to go to the devil and play along with the bosses."[22]

At the same time, leading black newspapers and prominent black spokesmen were advocating a policy of planned strike-breaking to gain entry for black workers into industries that had previously barred them.

This attitude, of course, had existed even before the Civil War and had found expression throughout the post–Civil War period. But its popularity had declined in the 1880's because of the direct appeal for black members and the widespread organization of black workers by the Knights of Labor, which did much to win over black leaders and newspapers to the labor movement. Now, as the AF of L abandoned its early progressive emphasis in the organization of black workers, the old hostility to the trade unions and the endorsement of strike-breaking were revived.

On July 19, 1894, the *Christian Recorder*, formerly a sturdy champion of organized labor, especially the Knights, called upon "the leaders of the race to spell out the danger of co-operating with labor malcontents in their fight against capital." As long as the unions barred black workers from membership and access to trades, it reasoned, the only alternative was to prove to employers the Negro's "trustworthiness," even if this meant continuing on the job when white unions went on strike. Booker T. Washington, head of the Tuskegee Institute and the most important black leader of the period, had belonged to the Knights of Labor in West Virginia and had once believed that unions would become an important agency for eliminating racial prejudice. But in 1897, after completing an investigation of union policies, Washington charged that the unions were seriously hindering the economic advancement of black workers by refusing to organize them and by keeping them out of many desirable crafts and trades. He singled out the AF of L for special criticism and warned that unless it abandoned its discriminatory practices, black workers would have no choice but to join the employers against the unions.

The AF of L angrily refuted Washington's views at its 1897 convention. It reaffirmed that it "welcomes to its ranks all labor without regard to creed, color, sex, race or nationality" and that it favored organization "of those most needing its protection, whether they be in the North or the South, the East or the West, white or black."²³ But the pattern of exclusion and segregation by many important AF of L affiliates actually gained in scope after these lofty sentiments were voiced. Unsupported by actions, the words failed to impress the black community. On the contrary, Washington's indictment of the trade unions gained influence, especially after the importation of black strike-breakers to work in the bituminous coal fields of Pana and Virden, Illinois, led to bloody battles in 1898.

The Afro-American Labor and Protective Association of Birmingham opposed the recruiting of Negro strike-breakers for the Chicago-Virden Company in its struggle with the United Mine Workers, but labor agents began to recruit the blacks over its opposition. When the recruited miners arrived and learned that a strike was in effect, they "complained that they had been deceived by the operators, and most of them refused to work. Deputies stationed on the grounds are charged with threatening to shoot Negroes who attempted to leave," *The Public*, a liberal Chicago weekly, reported on August 27, 1898. The white miners of Pana and Virden were determined to keep out all black scabs, whether willing or unwilling. Armed with shotguns, revolvers, and rifles, they waited for a train carrying blacks to arrive at Virden. When it did they opened up a steady fire. Deputies guarding the blacks on the train returned the fire. Fourteen white miners lost their lives and twenty-four were wounded. A few blacks were also wounded. Illinois Governor John R. Tanner, a Republican, called out the National Guard, promising the white miners that he would not tolerate the importation of blacks into Pana and Virden.*

The white miners applauded the governor for his stand, as did the AF of L at its convention, but to most black spokesmen, Tanner's action was further proof of the unions' hostility to their people. "Tannerism" symbolized a conspiracy between politicians and white trade unionists. "They bar the Negro from the benefits that unions are designed to confer," *The Colored American* raged, "and then proceed to terrify capitalists and politicians into connivance with their indefensible schemes. Governor Tanner can best subserve the ends of justice as well as his own political future by protecting poor Negro miners in their efforts to earn an honest living, and rely upon the good sense and moral courage of the more intelligent and Christian workingmen to sustain them." The *Christian Recorder* expressed sympathy for the striking miners, "for we all know that labor does not receive its rightful compensation," but added that not even they had the right to tell black miners not to attempt "to seek employment by which they can earn bread," when so many white trade unionists deprived blacks of any opportunity to do so.[24]

Not even the fact that the strikers included black miners lessened the bitterness voiced in the black press. No trade union could be trusted, went the argument, not even those that did not bar blacks, for "as soon as unionism was strong enough in these United States, it joined forces with the colored man's enemy and cried 'no quarter.'"[25] The Indianapolis *Freeman* and the *Recorder* were the only two black papers to take a different view of the events in Illinois. The *Freeman* condemned the mine operators "for the introduction of Negro workmen for the express purpose of defeating white workmen" and caustically suggested that, if employers who imported black strike-breakers were so concerned about the need of blacks for work, "let them employ Negro workmen in times of peace; put them in wherever they can and as many as they can until the faces of black men excite no curiosity."† At the same time, it urged the trade unions to contribute toward "the relaxation of the high-tensioned relations between the races" by proving that "they are for the

---

* On April 10, after the National Guard was removed by Governor Tanner, a riot broke out between white and black miners (many of the latter strike-breakers). Six persons were killed and fourteen wounded. Five of the six dead and seven of the fourteen wounded were blacks.

† In his article, "Black Strikebreakers and Racism in Illinois, 1865-1900," John H. Keiser accuses the employers of having "deliberately attempted to increase and exploit racial tension and division by employing black strikebreakers." He concludes that "employers must accept the greater share of the blame for the growing racism." *Journal of the Illinois State Historical Society* 65 (Autumn, 1972): 326.

Negro workmen."* The *Recorder* concurred and added its own plea: "It is now in order for the Indianapolis Federation of Labor to lower the bars and allow Negro labor to enter. Give us a chance."[26]

When the *Recorder*'s appeal met with no response from the white trade unions of the city, the Indianapolis *News* (white) pondered the dilemma of the black workers who, when skilled, were denied access to employment and, when unskilled, were prevented from learning a trade. It concluded with the query: "If non-union men are not permitted to work and colored men are not permitted to join the union, where does the colored man come in? Or does he stay out?" The *Recorder*, bitter over the rejection of its plea, answered, "Most assuredly he stays out."[27]

When the Phyllis Wheatley Literary Society in Indianapolis debated the question "Resolved that Labor Unions Are a Detriment to the Negro Race," the overwhelming vote of the black audience, not surprisingly, was in the affirmative. Increasingly this view was voiced in the black press. *The American*, published in Coffeyville, Kansas, put it succinctly early in 1899: "They hang the negro in the South, but they are not so bad in the North; they just simply starve him to death by labor unions."[28]

A remedy proposed by some Negro leaders was the establishment of a system of schools specifically designed to enable black youths to learn trades. But it soon became clear to most of them that this was no solution. At a conference held at the Hampton (Virginia) Industrial School in 1898, black educators decided that "it was quite impossible to rise as long as the trade unions so generally excluded colored workmen. Some of the graduates at Hampton who had learned there complained that they had not been able to work at their trades because [they are] excluded from the union."[29]

But Booker T. Washington, the leading exponent of industrial education, refused to concede defeat. He insisted that the barriers imposed by the trade unions could be overcome by appealing to employers to use black labor, if only they could be convinced that the black worker was preferable to the white. Negro labor's great advantage was that it was "not inclined to trade unionism"; the black worker "is almost a stranger to strife, lock-outs and labor wars; [he is] labor that is law-abiding, peaceable, teachable . . . labor that has never been tempted to follow the red flag of anarchy."[30] This note was struck again and again by Washington and his followers, and the black press, largely dominated by Washington, carried the message in countless editorials: "The Negro is the most reliable laborer this nation has ever had. He is a hard worker, he does not join unions and he seldom ever strikes, and if he does, he never uses violence to compel his employer to come to terms."[31]

---

* Reverdy C. Ransom, Chicago black clergyman and founder of the Institutional Church and Social Settlement, presented a similar analysis. He told the white workers that there was much to learn from Virden and Pana since "the degradation, by industrial and political serfdom of the millions of black toilers in this land," menaced "their own industrial independence and prosperity, as well as their political liberty." The *Public*, Chicago, October 22, 1898.

Washington was sharply criticized by the AF of L Executive Council in 1901 for saying that "the economic, social, and moral progress and advancement of the negro is dependent upon the philanthropic and humane consideration of . . . employers." The Executive Council warned that the Tuskegee principal, by encouraging Negro strike-breaking, was injuring black workers as well as whites.[32] But there was little the AF of L could say in 1901 that would carry weight with the Negro people, and the influence of Washington's philosophy continued to grow, endorsed, of course, by leading capitalists as well as by the black press.

By the turn of the century, however, opposition to Washington's position was developing among blacks themselves, which in turn helped to create a more friendly attitude toward the trade unions. The leadership of the anti-Washington ideology was assumed by W. E. B. Du Bois, who pointed out that industrial education was no solution for the blacks' economic problems at a time when skilled artisans and mechanics in many industries were being displaced by machines. Washington's attack on trade unionism was inappropriate when Negroes were turning from the field to the factory and had a stake in the development of a powerful labor movement; his doctrine was to place trust in white employers, who shared responsibility with reactionary craft unions for barring Negroes from work and who would hire blacks only to prevent unionization or only because they accepted lower wages than whites for the same work. Du Bois argued that the antiunion attitudes of men like Washington were ammunition to justify the anti-Negro policies of the AF of L.

To the unionists, Du Bois acknowledged that strike-breaking and the competition of black "cheap labor" had kept down the rate of wages for white unionists. But, he pointed out, blacks "are not working for low wages because they prefer to, but because they have to," and "if Negroes had been received into the unions and trained into the philosophy of the labor cause [which for obvious reasons most of them did not know], they would have made as staunch union men as any." Du Bois advocated a dual position: Negroes should work unceasingly to build black-white unity in the labor movement, but at the same time they should challenge and unrelentingly attack segregation and discrimination in the trade unions.[33]

Du Bois's proposal was set forth at the Atlanta Conference on Negro Americans in 1902, which recommended that blacks support the labor movement where it pursued a fair policy but denounced the unjust proscription against black membership practiced by many unions. There were unions, even in the South, that pursued "a fair policy" and deserved the support of black workers, a fact made clear that same year in Du Bois's pioneering study *The Negro Artisan*. In a lecture delivered in Atlanta in 1907, Du Bois noted:

> It is only a question of time when white working men and black working men will see their common cause against the aggressions of exploiting capitalists. Already there are signs of this: white and black miners are working as a unit in Alabama; white and black masons are in one union in Atlanta.

The economic strength of the Negro cannot be beaten into weakness, and therefore it must be taken into partnership, and this the Southern white working man, befuddled by prejudice as he is, begins dimly to realize.[34]

Although events were to prove Du Bois unduly optimistic, black-white unity in unions affiliated with the AF of L at the time was not a figment of his imagination. True, most national unions and labor leaders were ignoring black workers or equivocating about organizing them, and most craft unions were pursuing racially restrictive membership policies. Still, Negro-white unity in the labor movement was part of the experience of many unions affiliated with the AF of L.

6 The AF of L and the
Black Worker, 1881–1915 (Cont.)

From its inception the AF of L had to deal with the accusation that it was interested solely in the organization of skilled craftsmen and actually objected to organizing the unskilled. The federation was often characterized in labor circles as a "business organization of the skilled mechanics of the country."

Gompers vigorously challenged the accusation. The federation always maintained that an affiliated union could be organized "from all classes of wage workers of any particular trade or calling, whether skilled or unskilled," he said. He consistently warned unions affiliated with the AF of L against neglecting the welfare of the unskilled lest they permit themselves to be utilized as strike-breakers.[1]

But the fixed policy of most AF of L affiliates was to limit union organization to skilled craft workers. This had the effect of excluding women and foreign-born workers, the vast majority of whom were unskilled, but it was especially tragic for black workers. At the end of the nineteenth century, those few Negro workers in the North who were employed in industry were mostly unskilled factory hands. Advancement into the skilled trades, if not denied them by employers, was blocked by the craft unions. By then, too, the process of displacement of black workers in the South from the skilled trades had begun. As we shall see, this trend increased by leaps and bounds in the next decade.

Hence, the early AF of L refusal to admit national affiliates that barred Negroes was of no benefit to the majority of the black working class. Significantly, the only AF of L affiliate to include a substantial number of blacks soon after its formation, the United Mine Workers, was also the only genuine industrial union in the federation.

When the United Mine Workers of America was founded in 1890, about a thousand black Knights came into the new organization. Not only did the UMW inherit a black membership but, as was stated at its founding convention, the union itself was the product of persistent attempts, dating from the founding of the American Miners' Association in 1861, "to unite in one organization, regardless of creed, color or na-

tionality, all workmen . . . employed in and around the coal mines."*
The constitution of the new miners' union declared: "No member in
good standing shall be barred or hindered from obtaining work on account of race, creed or nationality."[2] At the founding session in Columbus, an Ohio Negro was made a member of the UMW National Executive Board (NEB).

Richard L. Davis, a black miner who was one of the founders of the
UMW and a delegate at its first convention, held many leading positions in the union and served two terms as an NEB member. He drew
the top convention vote for the NEB in 1896 and the second highest in
1897. In the early years of the UMW, black men were also elected to
district and local office. William Riley was secretary-treasurer of District
19, Tennessee, in the 1890's; F. A. Bannister was vice-president of West
Virginia's district; in Illinois, where only one-fourth of the miners were
black, Henry Rector was vice-president. Thomas Rollins was unanimously elected vice-president of the predominantly white Saginaw,
Michigan, district. Negroes headed many locals, some of which had only
a tiny minority of black members. This is partly explained by the fact
that a large foreign-born element in the mines of western Pennsylvania,
Ohio, and upper West Virginia was not able to speak, read, and write
English, as Negroes could. The foreign-born miners needed the blacks to
help draw up wage agreements and otherwise represent them.

The fact that the UMW was from the outset an industrial union also
had much to do with the status it offered blacks. Craft unionism was impossible to apply in organizing coal mines, for their occupations could
be learned with brief training. Moreover, any attempt to organize on an
all-white basis would have been suicidal for the union. Blacks had
worked in Southern coal mines since the days of slavery, and by the
time the UMW was formed there was already a substantial number of
experienced blacks in the industry. Their numbers increased in the next
decade in the bituminous fields of Pennsylvania, the Southwest, and especially in Illinois. To white miners reluctant to let blacks into the
union, Richard L. Davis pointed out, in a letter published in the *United
Mine Workers Journal* of November 24, 1891: "Take the Negro out of
the organization and you have a vast army against you, one that is strong
enough to be felt and feared." The possibility that Negroes from Alabama and West Virginia might serve as strike-breakers in Illinois, Ohio,
Kansas, and Colorado mines lent weight to Davis's argument. The organization of black miners was a matter of life and death for the UMW.

The UMW's structure as an industrial union worked in the favor of
black miners in Alabama. Many of the 6,000 Negroes who worked in
Alabama's coal mines at the beginning of the twentieth century were

---

* The American Miners' Association was the first union of miners organized in the
United States. Its constitution provided for an all-inclusive union that would embrace
all miners without distinction. When the miners met in a national convention in
Ohio on October 14, 1873, to form the Miners' National Association, John Siney,
head of the organization, stressed the necessity of unity of black and white. Responding to this appeal, the convention called upon all miners to join, including "our
colored brethren." *Workingman's Advocate*, October 25, 1873.

common laborers of the type neglected by craft unions. The UMW, because it organized industries and not occupations, brought them into one union with whites. It has been estimated that by 1904 more than half of the 13,000 UMW members in Alabama were blacks. A number of the UMW locals in the state were all black, but several, including the one at Pratt City, the largest UMW local in the country in the early twentieth century, were integrated. In all locals with black members, moreover, black miners served as officers and as delegates to the district and national conventions. "Some camps whose living conditions were almost completely segregated," one student of the Alabama labor movement during this period writes, "met at integrated union halls, heard reports from black officers, and elected black men as local committeemen and as convention delegates. Even at camps with racially separate locals, black and white representatives served on grievance committees and as checkweighmen together."[3]

In 1902 the United Mine Workers, with 20,000 black members, had more than half the total black membership of the AF of L. The International Longshoremen's Union (ILU), made up of semiskilled workers, was second highest in black membership, with 6,000 Negroes among its 20,000 members. The secretary of the ILU wrote to Du Bois from the Great Lakes: "We have many colored members in our Association, and some of them are among our leading officials of our local branches. In one of our locals . . . there are over 300 members of which [sic] five are colored; of these two hold the office of President and Secretary." From the New Orleans ILU came the report: "I believe that we are the only craft in that city who [sic] have succeeded in wiping out the color question. Our members meet jointly in the same hall and are the highest paid workmen in New Orleans."[4]

Like the miner, the Negro longshoreman was an element in the labor supply that could not be ignored if the union was to survive. Negroes had been employed in dock work since the days of slavery, and by the time of the Civil War they had achieved an important foothold in Southern ports. Their employment in the North ended when the Irish forced blacks off the docks, usually by violence, but blacks returned during and after the Civil War as strike-breakers. As a result of the 1895 strike on the Ward Line in New York City, when the company employed Negroes to break a strike, blacks were able to enter the longshore industry from which the union had excluded them. Eventually even the Irish learned that exclusion of blacks only helped the employers; the Irish longshoremen in New York, noting that the Negro outside the union was "a perpetual menace as a scab," decided to organize blacks as members of their union with equal status with the white workers. In some ports, Negroes demanded half the work "in consideration for supporting the strike and refusing to take the white man's place."[5] When the International Longshoremen's Association was organized in 1894, it included Negroes already organized in local unions in ports along the coast. In fact, the first ILA charter to be granted to a local west of the Mississippi was given in 1898 to Local No. 51 of Sabine Pass, Texas, which was composed of Negro longshoremen.

Du Bois counted only the miners and the longshoremen as national unions that "welcome Negroes in nearly all cases." In several cities, however, local unions and federations of labor welcomed blacks even when their national organizations were hostile or indifferent to Negro membership.

In the summer of 1900, the Chicago Building Trades Council, the central labor body for most of the construction workers in that city, rejected a contractors' plan to introduce labor-saving machinery and increase the number of apprentices. The Chicago contractors insisted on proceeding with their plan, to which the Building Trades Council responded with a strike. The secretary of the employers' association told the press: "When all the machinery devised to break the strike is set in motion nothing can withstand it." A chief strike-breaking weapon was the use of Negro scabs, largely imported from the South.

Shortly after the arrival of the strike-breakers, the Chicago Federation of Labor, representing all of the organized labor bodies in the city, addressed an eloquent appeal to the blacks. Conceding that the building trades unions had been guilty of systematically rejecting blacks when they applied for membership, the federation insisted that this policy was not in keeping with the real aims of the labor movement:

> The trades-union movement knows no race or color. Its aims are the bettering of the condition of the wage earner, whatever his color or creed. In this spirit we appeal to the colored workingman to join us in our work. Come into our trade unions, give us your assistance and in return, receive our support, so that race hatred may be forever buried, and the workingman of the country united in a solid phalanx to demand what we are entitled to—a fair share of the fruits of our industry.[6]

The Indianapolis *Record*, the black weekly, hailed the appeal: "Such a radical departure from past custom—if not law, portends much for the Negro."[7] Many blacks left the ranks of the strike-breakers to join the unions and became noted for their zeal in the cause of unionism. By 1905 there were a half-dozen black delegates from unions in the Chicago Federation of Labor, as well as several Negro local officers.

Blacks had first appeared in the Chicago stockyards as strike-breakers in 1885, but most left after that strike was broken, management having no further use for them. Only 500 Negroes were in the Chicago packing plants in 1904, many of them members of the Amalgamated Meat Cutters and Butcher Workmen. Mary E. McDowell, head resident of the University of Chicago Settlement, situated "back of the yards," noted that "black men sat with their white comrades" at union meetings. The union held a funeral for "Bro. Wm. Sims (colored), tail sawyer at Swift's East House, with sixty-eight whites and seven blacks attending." Miss McDowell described the initiation of a black candidate in the women's union organized by the girls in the stockyards:

> It was a dramatic occasion on that evening, when an Irish girl at the door called out—"A Colored sister asks admission. What shall I do with her?" And the answer came from the Irish young woman in the chair—"Admit her, of course, and let all of you give her a hearty welcome!" And a tall,

dignified, but frightened colored girl walked up the aisle between a crowd of girls, Irish, German, American, Polish, Bohemian, some well dressed, others with a shawl or handkerchief over the head. One felt that there was here a law stronger than that of Robert's Rules of Order.[8]

Stronger, too, she might have added, than lofty pronouncements by the AF of L leadership.

Jim Crow unionism enabled white workers to earn more than blacks, but it drove the wages of black workers so far down, especially in the South, that the wages of white workers were kept low as well. The Industrial Commission on Relations and Conditions of Capital and Labor, set up by Congress in 1898, heard abundant testimony that the unorganized state of the Negro working class was "a drag on the white laboring class in the South, and tends to cut down their wages." "The white journeyman bricklayer in our section," a Southern employer testified, "gets $2.50 a day, and we are able to employ a colored bricklayer for $1.75." Asked how this affected the wages of the white bricklayer, the employer replied frankly: "If a white bricklayer . . . asks for employment and makes known his rate of wages, which is $2.50 a day . . . the employer may say to him in return, I can employ a Negro bricklayer who has as much skill as you, and will do as good service for $1.75. Now, I will put you on at $2.25."

After a careful investigation of conditions in all Southern trades, C. C. Houston, editor of the *Atlanta Journal of Labor*, told the Industrial Commission:

> My observation of colored labor in the South, so far as it relates to the trades where skilled labor is required, is that it is held over the head of white labor to the extent of holding down wages. . . . In the building trades, for instance . . . the wages paid to white labor are based primarily on the wages paid to colored labor; and in every instance in which an increased wage scale has been secured, with one or two exceptions, it has been reached only after the colored man was organized and a combined effort of the two was made.

Houston urged white workers in the AF of L to understand that "the white man, in order to retain his wages and in the hope of increasing his wage scale, has not only to recognize but to assist the black man, and unless you do assist him, and raise him up, he is going to pull you down to his standard." He vehemently took issue with certain trade union officials who justified discriminatory practices on the ground that black workers were not really interested in bettering themselves: "They have an ambition to receive a wage equal to that of the white man and to live on a plane relatively equal to that of the white man."[9]

There is no doubt that many white workers in the South believed the white-supremacist propaganda that being white and "superior" gave them a status that would be threatened by equal rights for blacks, and so opposed any efforts to unite Negro and white workers. White cotton-mill workers in the South deliberately sacrificed their own living standards to keep blacks out of the mills. When the president of the Fulton

Bag and Cotton Mills in Atlanta, with 1,400 employees, hired twenty Negro women to work in the folding department of one of the mills on August 4, 1897, the entire white work force struck. The company agreed to discharge the blacks and rehire the strikers on condition that they work overtime without extra pay, and on these terms the strike was settled. This was only one example of how, as Melton A. McLaurin points out, "mill officials skillfully encouraged the mill hands' hatred of the Negro and manipulated that hatred to their own ends."[10]

Yet there were also white workers in the South who understood that to discriminate on the basis of color was to play into the hands of the employers. A white business agent for the Carpenters and Joiners in Savannah put it best: "The mere fact that all of the boss builders in the South are advocating leaving the negroes out of the union is a good reason why we should organize them."[11]

The same kind of understanding led to the acceptance by Southern white members of the Carpenters and Joiners of the appointment of a South Carolina–born Negro, then head of a Savannah local, as a Southern organizer. The white President of Atlanta's District Council answered those carpenters who saw the appointment as a "threat" of social equality: "Let us lay aside all our prejudice (I have as much as any Southern-born white man) and look the question fair and square in the face." He was convinced that a black organizer who would recruit black carpenters into the union was the only alternative to disastrous wage competition. "We want that organizer here in Atlanta for about three months. I believe he can do us more good than anything else." The black organizer's appointment was not rescinded.[12]

Alabama, too, was witness to black-white labor solidarity. "In spite of mounting hysteria by Alabama's white supremacists," Paul B. Worthman writes, "there were white workingmen in Birmingham at the beginning of the twentieth century who not only supported the organization of black laborers, but also encouraged such organization." A Birmingham *Labor Advocate* editorial headed "Obliterate the Color Line" urged the city's unions to recognize that "the common cause of labor is more important than racial difference." The paper cautioned against the rejection of integrated unionism, arguing that "it is a response to conditions to which there is no other solution." The editor urged white workers to "accept the inevitable with ready grace and strive to better the conditions of the Negro by every means, knowing that doing this is the only way to better [your] own conditions."[13]

Few unions in Birmingham or in Alabama as a whole, apart from some UMW locals, were integrated. Most blacks were in segregated locals but were not isolated from the white labor movement. The Birmingham Trades Council accepted delegates from black locals and remained integrated until 1903, after which a Colored Central Labor Council was established with twenty affiliated unions. An alliance between the two councils prevented the use of members of either organization as strikebreakers. The blacks marched under their union banners in the city's annual Labor Day parades, sponsored by the white Trades Council.

In Charleston the Bricklayers Union No. 1 of South Carolina, affiliated with the AF of L's International Bricklayers Union, included both
white and Negro members. When they paraded together the Charleston
Recorder, the local black paper, commented that it presented "quite a
curiosity, especially when we take into consideration the mixture of the
Union, being white and black. It is a fact that black and white men can
dwell together in peace, even in South Carolina. The order presented a
very fine appearance, and the sight will not be soon forgotten."[14]

The Alabama State Federation of Labor, formed in 1900, included
delegates from black unions and central labor councils during the first
five years of its existence, and each year two or three Negroes were
among the five vice-presidents elected. The State Federation of Labor
held its 1902 convention in Selma, where the city officials refused to supply a decent hall because of the presence of black delegates. "Rather
than see one accredited delegate, black or white, thrown out of this convention," a delegate from Birmingham's typographical union declared,
"I would go to the woods and hold this meeting."[15] After the convention
officials threatened to leave Selma rather than draw the color line, the
United States Confederate Veterans offered its hall, where the convention proceeded on an interracial basis.

In 1902 Du Bois estimated that blacks in Florida unions included
2,000 cigarmakers, 1,200 building-trades laborers, 1,000 carpenters, 800
longshoremen, 200 bricklayers, and 300 plasterers. A black unionist,
probably in Jacksonville, wrote to the Atlanta University scholar: "The
Negroes in this city have no need to complain, as the white men work,
smoke, eat and drink together with them, meet in the Central Union
and hold office together. I organized and installed the Central Union as
General Secretary and I am a Negro, and have held the same for two
elections and was elected by the whites who are in majority. I have presided over the same body, but do not visit their daughters and have no
wish. The white painters do in a way draw a line, but not openly; the
boiler makers also, but none others."[16]

The AF of L national leaders often excused their discrimination on
the grounds that the docility and antiunion attitudes of black labor
made organization of the Negro practically impossible. They stigmatized
blacks as a scab race for their part in the great teamsters' strike in Chi
cago in 1905. Little mention was made of the estimated 5,000 of the
5,800 strike-breakers used who were white. To the contrary, the AF of L
leaders singled out the Negroes for special abuse. Writing in *Charities* of
October 7, 1905, R. R. White, black pastor of Chicago's Trinity Mission,
observed:

> The bulk of Negro workmen never consisted of strikebreakers. Nor are Ne-
> groes opposed to unions. Many struck with the unions and remained loyal
> to them at the stockyards. In the teamsters' strike, while there were 800
> Negro strikebreakers, the unions held a membership of nearly 2,000 Negro
> teamsters, and one of their number represented the coal drivers at the
> Philadelphia convention of the Brotherhood of Teamsters in August. . .
> Yet it still remains that in times of industrial peace the more desirable

places are closed against Negroes, either because the employers will not hire them or the men will not work with them.

In the opening decade of the twentieth century, Southern black workers, far from being "opposed to unions," were often among the most militant unionists in the region. Black UMW members in Alabama and West Virginia made desperate sacrifices to ensure the success of their union. In 1903, three militant black miners in West Virginia were shot to death in their sleep by deputy sheriffs. Chris Evans, who investigated the slayings for the UMW, said, "this slaughtering of miners, simply because they are forced to struggle for a just cause [is] a sad commentary on our boasted Republic."[17] In the spring of 1903 a local of black women in Jacksonville, Florida, the city's largest union, invited the editor of the *Florida Labor Journal*, the state AF of L's weekly newspaper, to a meeting. The editor found the black local "well regulated" and urged all unions to emulate it. "It is to the shame of some unions in Jacksonville," he wrote in the *Journal* on January 30, "that they sit back and knock their brethren while these women, who on an average draw less than $3 per week, attend their meetings, keep in good standing and pay a sick benefit of $2 per week. Too much credit cannot be given to these good women."

The Socialist and labor editor Oscar Ameringer offers convincing evidence of the union-consciousness of the black worker. In describing his experience as an organizer for the Brewery Workers' Union in New Orleans in 1906–7, he wrote:

> As strikers, there could be no better. I saw some of those boys lose the shine of their skins, grow thinner as weeks went on, but they stuck. Their women, too, proved themselves staunch helpmates. Many of them worked in white men's kitchens, and the supplies they carried home at night under their aprons contributed greatly toward holding out. . . . There was, let me say, considerably less danger of the Negroes deserting the whites than of the whites deserting the blacks.

To the blacks, Ameringer concluded, the union "was far more than a matter of hours and wages. It was a religion, and their only hope of rising from the depths of a slavery more cruel in many respects than that of the chattel slave." Not only were the blacks as faithful to the union as the whites, but "mentally they were the equal of the white strikers. . . . In some respects the blacks even surpassed the whites on their own economic level. Rules of the union required recipients of strike benefits to sign their names beside the amount stated on the books. And on those books I found a smaller percentage of 'his mark' among the black strikers than among the whites."[18]

At the time Ameringer was in New Orleans organizing for the brewery workers, white and black unionists were engaged in a great levee strike. Friction deliberately fostered by the employers had long kept white and black waterfront workers in New Orleans battling each other, and racial violence pushed the memory of the unity during the general strike of 1892 far into the background.

To end this self-defeating cycle of racial antagonisms, the white and black screwmen in New Orleans reached an agreement in 1902 by which all jobs would be divided equally between whites and blacks. The two unions, white and black, both affiliated with the AF of L, also joined forces to demand regulation of the number of bales the workers were supposed to load each day, despite the fact that the Negro organization had still two years to go on a three-year contract. "In a gang of four men working in a hold," the New Orleans *Daily Picayune* reported on October 22, 1902, "two of them must be black. If the man at a forward hatch is white, the one aft must be black. . . . If the whites and blacks stand together . . . then all will be serene again on the levee." There were to be equal wages and working conditions as well as equal division of jobs. But the white and black unions still met separately, and it was felt that to avoid misunderstandings and friction, often inspired and stimulated by the employers, a unifying central body should be organized. This led to the formation of the Dock and Cotton Council, a representative body composed of white and black delegates. The seventy-two delegates, thirty-six white and thirty-six black, represented 36 unions of dock workers, and the officers of the council were divided equally between white and black: a white president, a Negro vice-president, a white financial secretary, a Negro corresponding secretary, and so forth. At each annual election, the rotation of officers was reversed. Delegates addressed each member and officer as "brother."

The big question was whether such black-white labor solidarity in the Deep South—at a time when segregation and disfranchisement of blacks were becoming the way of life—would hold up in the face of employer opposition. The test came when the employers refused to renew the 1906 contract. On October 4, 1907, a strike began, involving 10,000 workers on the levee in the following unions: white and black screwmen, white and black longshoremen, white and black yardmen, coal wheelers (all black), teamsters and loaders (all black), white and black freight handlers, cotton inspectors and markers (all white), and scale hands (all black). The strike lasted twenty days without a single break in the ranks. President E. S. Swan, evidently unaware or forgetful of the 1892 general strike, declared: "The whites and Negroes were never before so strongly cemented in a common bond and in my 39 years of experience of the levee, I never saw such solidarity. In all the previous strikes the Negro was used against the white man, but that condition is now past and both races are standing together for their common interests. . . . If the two would combine everywhere as they have combined here, they would have better conditions."[19]

They continued to "stand together" until the end. The New Orleans *Times-Picayune* tried to break the unity of black and white by noting the "simple fact that a number of negroes have been anarchists and fanatical denouncers of authority." But the strikers answered by solidifying their ranks even more. On October 24, the employers gave in and consented to arbitration. The arbitration committee was to consist of two or four representatives from each side with an impartial umpire to be selected by Mayor Behrman and the president of the Cotton Exchange. The screwmen named two whites and two blacks as their representatives. The employers' representatives refused to meet with the Negroes, and the mayor, in an attempt to intimidate the black secretary of the strike committee, told him: "Take these names back to your association and let the members know their interests demand that there will be no colored men on the committee." His ultimatum was rejected, and the mayor appeared before the Dock and Cotton Council to urge the screwmen to appoint only white men. "The Mayor sagely pointed out," reported the *Daily Picayune*, "the feelings and conditions in this section, but despite the logical contentions, the negro stood firm and the Council backed him up. . . . A well-known white longshoreman and a mulatto, whose reputation as an agitator and a leader of the disturbing element among the screwmen is wide, were the committee who came downstairs to inform the Mayor that his mission had borne no fruit."

The mayor then sadly told the shipowners: "For your information I would state that the screwmen have selected as their representatives: Edward Nestor, James Jemison, Edward Gay and John D. Grandeson. I regret to say that the last two named are colored men appointed against my earnest appeal to the organization." The shipowners' representatives still refused to meet. "Mr. George," the *Daily Picayune* reported, "who is a Kentuckian, with all the instincts and traditions of the true Southern gentleman, stated last evening without reservations that he would not serve on the committee with negroes." Another employers' representative, the manager of the Texas Transport & Terminal Co., described as a "Virginia gentleman, a former major in the Confederate army," stated publicly "that he would not serve with darkeys."

The issue was then brought to the New Orleans Central Labor Union with the plea that it use its influence to eliminate the Negroes from the committee. But this, too, failed. President T. R. LeBlanc of the CLU declared in a public statement:

> There being a controversy relative to the acceptance of negro representatives on the Port Investigating Committee, and as debarring them would only be an injustice to the thousands of negroes who constitute a majority of the laboring organizations of New Orleans, and would tend to make a settlement of the present trouble more difficult, it is to be hoped that the objections will be withdrawn. The negro has always been a strong bulwark in the labor union movement, and as he forms the greater number of the laborers in general it would be unjust and untimely to debar him.

The New Orleans press charged the blacks with seeking representation on the committee to achieve social equality. They warned the white labor leaders that the blacks were simply using the strike settlement as a means of "trying to further pull down the barriers which bar them from equity in all things with the superior race." But the white unionists of New Orleans stood firm. In the end, the employers had to yield. They chose representatives who, however reluctantly, would meet with the Negroes to settle the strike.

During the meetings of the arbitration committee, the employers tried to split the ranks of the strikers by warning the white trade unionists that they were undermining the sacred honor of the State of Louisiana. But this attempt failed utterly. As a Negro union representative declared: "We are not here to save the honor and prosperity of the great State of Louisiana. We are here to settle the strike."[20] The strike settlement brought the white and black workers all of their original demands.

The unity of black and white workers so manifest during the strike continued after the struggle was over. The New Orleans *Daily Picayune* of March 28, 1908, carried the following dialogue from a session of the Port Investigating Commission:

> "Do I understand you to say that twelve white men, and twelve negroes dominate the commerce of this port?" Senator Cordill asked.
> William J. Kearney, stevedore for the Harrison Line, answered, "Yes, sir."
> "Well, sir, we are practically under negro government," was Senator Cordill's comment.

The New Orleans strike was one of the most stirring manifestations of black-white labor solidarity in American history, and its significance is the greater for its having occurred during the depression of 1907–8, which was otherwise marked by intense racial conflicts arising from increased competition for work. Samuel Gompers, who had nailed the example of black-white labor solidarity in the New Orleans general strike of 1892 as a "very bright ray of hope for the future of organized labor," this time was silent. As far as New Orleans was concerned, his attention was focused on a jurisdictional dispute between the AF of L unions in New Orleans breweries and the United Brewery Workers.

The Brewery Workers had infuriated the AF of L craft-union leaders as far back as 1900 by attempting to organize all workers in the breweries, skilled and unskilled, black and white, into one union under the slogan: "Solidarity, man for man, from roof to cellar, all for each and each for all. This alone can secure our future."[21] The champions of craft unionism insisted upon the jurisdictional rights of every craft union in the breweries, some of which excluded unskilled workers, especially blacks. The Brewery Workers refused to submit to the restrictive AF of L policies, insisting that to do so would reduce the union to the same helpless condition as most craft organizations in the mass production industries. The 1906 AF of L convention ordered the Executive Council to expel the brewers, and on May 30, 1907, the AF of L revoked the charter of the United Brewery Workers.

The AF of L's insistence on preserving the vested interests of the craft-union bureaucracies and the craft-minded mechanics in the face of technological changes doomed its efforts to organize black workers. For a brief period at the beginning of the twentieth century in a number of cities and states, North and South, in the face of the rising tide of white racism and the constant efforts of employers to stir racial hostility and prevent labor unity, thousands of black workers were brought into the

AF of L. The vast majority of them were unskilled. The federation's craft-unionists were committed to preserving union autonomy and protecting the interests of the skilled minority, so the craft unions were not obligated to accept semiskilled or unskilled workers. Consequently, most of the black workers were organized into locals, called Federal Labor Unions, directly affiliated with the AF of L. These locals were the neglected stepchildren of the American labor movement. Without a national union to bargain for them, without funds to sustain them when on strike, and subject to raids by craft unions, the Federal Labor Unions could not protect their members' interests. Their life span was generally brief; they disappeared because they were incapable of protecting their members, and the members abandoned them.

After 1904 the AF of L gave up even the feeble attempt to organize the unskilled, especially the blacks, into Federal Labor Unions. In 1904 the employers' counteroffensive was well under way, and the AF of L, its treasury depleted by a drop in membership and by the costs of defending itself in court battles, had little to spend on organizing the unskilled. The Federal Labor Unions throughout the country collapsed, carrying along with them organizations of black laborers. By 1913 most of the locals of black workers in Birmingham, Jacksonville, Atlanta, Houston, Chicago, and other cities had disappeared. The experience of the all-black Federal Labor Union of Port Arthur, Texas, was typical. In 1913, in a plea to the State Federation of Labor, it cited the AF of L claim that it "does not discriminate against a fellow worker on account of creed, color, or nationality." Black members of the federation in Port Arthur, the plea said, had "been greatly discriminated against, and we as members of organized labor ask that some steps be taken to stop the discrimination of the colored laborers of this city." The State Federation of Labor declined to act on the appeal, judging it "a purely local affair." Directly afterward the Federal Labor Union of Port Arthur went out of existence.[22]

What unionism still existed among black workers after 1904 was due primarily to the numerical strength of blacks in certain occupations, which would make them a threat to the whites if left unorganized. In general, the less the skill required for a trade, the more likely it was that there were blacks in large numbers and that they would be taken into the local unions already in existence—and into mixed, as opposed to segregated, locals. The black hod carriers had little trouble securing admittance to the Hod Carriers' Union in the North and the Border States, and they were usually taken into mixed locals. According to the black historians Lorenzo J. Greene and Carter G. Woodson, the admission of blacks into mixed locals was "principally because of the menace they constituted to the whites in these pursuits as a result of their numerical strength."[23] They were writing mainly with reference to the hod carriers, but the same principle applied to many other unions that permitted blacks to join. The purpose was not to promote labor solidarity but to regulate the competition of black workers and to prevent their use against white labor.

The few skilled black members of unions affiliated with the AF of L often learned to their sorrow that for them union membership meant second-class status. Du Bois detailed in 1902 how skilled black workers with traveling cards were denied access to union jobs throughout the United States. One of his correspondents reported from Cincinnati that, when black bricklayers came from Chicago with white union members, the white worker received a union card and immediate work while the black "was kept dancing attendance on the master of the local union and delayed upon one pretext and the other until he was driven from the city without being permitted to follow his trade because the local union did not give him his card." One employer who was remodeling a building gave a Negro a job as a plasterer, but "the hod carrier would not carry for him, and the Negro worker was compelled to work as a scab to get money enough to get out of town."[24] Du Bois cited case after case where union membership failed to protect blacks from racial hostility and where national labor leaders, by ignoring complaints of racial discrimination, nullified their union's antidiscrimination position.

The correspondence in 1903 between Robert Rhodes, a black Indianapolis bricklayer and local union official, and national officers of the Bricklayers' and Masons' International Union offers further evidence on this score. The bricklayers' constitution prohibited racial discrimination. The national organization required its locals to accept traveling cards from black members, and the 1903 national convention set a fine of $100 for any individual member or local found guilty of discriminating against black union bricklayers. When Rhodes tried to obtain work on a union job, his white union brothers refused to work with him and conspired with the contractor not to employ him. Rhodes's persistent efforts to obtain redress within the union, local and national, failed. He was compelled to accept a nonunion job to stay alive, whereupon the Indianapolis local first fined and then suspended him for "scabbing." His appeals to officials of the national union for protection of his rights as a union member were ignored for two years. Finally the national convention, at the insistence of a black delegate from Georgia, declared the Indianapolis local guilty of racial discrimination and fined it $100 (only part of which was paid). By then, Rhodes had renounced his union membership and no longer worked as a bricklayer. His last letter to the national union speaks volumes about what it meant to be a black member of an AF of L affiliate:

I beg to say to you that I acted under the advice of our secretary, Mr. Dobson, and filed a complaint against certain members of Union No. 3. The charges were made. The Union refused to take any steps at all. . . . If I attempt further proceedings I will be stopped because of my suspension for working with non-Union men, after a repeated offer to get work with my rights on legal technicalities, while in fact it is simply because of my color, as they fairly said so, and wanted me to leave the city and get work elsewhere. If I can't get a proper understanding I will pursue some other course, and I beg of you to take the matter up, as I want no further unpleasantness.[25]

Even in the two national unions Du Bois listed as the only ones to "welcome Negroes in nearly all cases"—the longshoremen and the miners—black members did not enjoy equality. Equal division of work in Southern ports, under which work was shared by white and black members of the International Longshoremen's Association on a fifty-fifty basis, often brought peace but not justice. The number of black longshoremen so exceeded whites in Southern ports that the white workers got steadier and better work, while hundreds of blacks got no work at all. In some ports discrimination against black longshoremen was so keen and the segregation of black ILA members so deep-seated that many blacks openly voiced disgust with the union and, as we shall see, welcomed opportunities to join any organization that promised to give them equal rights as members.

At the beginning of the twentieth century, Richard E. Wright, Jr., observed that the mass of the black workers were unorganized and had little contact with unions, but "the United Mine Workers is one of the few unions in which Negroes agree that they receive fair treatment."[26] Yet the evidence, even in the *United Mine Workers Journal*, reveals that black miners in the UMW did not believe they received "fair treatment." For one thing, there were many complaints that blacks were not represented in the union leadership—national, state, and local—in proportion to the large percentage of Negro membership. For another, black miners frequently complained that racist practices in the union kept them out of the better-paid jobs in the mines. "We are not good enough to have a good job if we are capable of fulfilling its duties," R. A. Scott wrote to the union *Journal*, which labeled his letter "A Pathetic Appeal by a Colored Man of Hackett, Pa."

Richard L. Davis found that "possibly [in] Ohio and a few other of the Western states," the black miner worked for the same wages and under the same conditions as the white, "but this only applies to his work in and around the mines. Promotion is a slow process with him; it seems hard for him to get above the pick and shovel no matter how competent he may be. . . . This we believe to be unfair."

Although so strongly pro-union that he proclaimed that labor unions "have done more to eliminate the color line than all other organizations, the church even included," and although he praised examples of black-white solidarity in the UMW, Davis minced no words in his letters to the *Journal* criticizing the union's failure to live up to its principles in the treatment of its black membership:

> Will you admit that you need us in your unions? If so, why should we not hold offices, also? Are we not men? Have we not the same ambitions as you people have? Are we not in many instances as competent as you? Then why should we not hold office? Not office in name, but office in deed; something there is money in that we may cope with our white brothers as an equal.

Davis also observed that the separation of black and white at work and in housing was a tactic of the employers to extract higher profits, hence the union should not condone it.

He was particularly disturbed by what he found during a visit to Alabama. Organized on the eve of the "great strike" of 1894, the union was established on the basis of segregated locals. Despite their contributions in the 1894 strike, the black miners were still not accepted as equals. In 1898 the UMW negotiated a contract in Alabama that covered black as well as white miners. But a year later Davis found that

> while white and colored miners work in the same mines, and maybe in adjoining rooms, they will not ride even on a worktrain with their dirty mining clothes on together; nor will they meet in a miners' meeting together in a hall without the whites going to one side of the hall, while the colored occupy the other side.

Several years later, Davis wrote that "even in the North, no matter how good a union man he may be, [the black miner] cannot get work only as a blackleg. And in the South he can work almost anywhere provided he is willing to be the other fellow's dog, and I don't mean the employer's alone, but the white laborer as well." Many such findings led Davis to write of the blacks in the UMW: "I say now that when it comes to a fair shake we are not in it. Do you catch on? If not, say so and I will be more plain, as I am confident I can sustain my argument with strong and sufficient proof." He warned the white miners that if they continued to treat the black miner as a second-class worker and refused to work beside blacks, the blacks would be forced to work as strike-breakers:

> It is just such treatment as this that has caused the negro to take your places when you were striking. Now, if there is anything that I do despise it is a blackleg, but in places in this country that they will not allow the negro to work simply because of his black skin, then I say boldly that he is *not* a blackleg in taking your places. He is only doing his plain duty in taking chances with the world.

Davis helped to build the UMW in its crucial early years. When he was blacklisted by Ohio coal operators for his many years of union activity, the UMW turned its back on him. His friend, "Old Dog," pleaded: "I think he should be provided for in some way. . . . You do not often meet up with colored men like Dick. . . . He has a family to keep and I think we owe him something. He nor his children cannot live on wind, and further, *if he was a white man he would not be where he is*—mark that, but being a negro he does not get the recognition he should have." The plea fell on deaf ears, and Davis died a pauper in 1900, a victim of "lung fever" and poverty, at the age of thirty-five.

In his last letter, Davis wrote: "That which is good for a white man is good for me, provided, however, it is administered the right way." The grievances presented by black miners indicated a frequent belief that the UMW was not "administered the right way" for its black membership. At the Illinois State Miners' Convention of 1900, a grievance was presented by black miners in the Springfield district, "charging discrimination against them on account of color." Cal Robinson, a black miner from Spring Valley, told the delegates:

There are five shafts in and around Springfield, all supposed to be managed by good union men, and in these shafts no colored men work, simply
on account of their color. Because their faces are a little dark they cannot
work in these shafts. I claim that when that man [pointing to the painting of Abraham Lincoln] emancipated the black race he gave them all
privileges and equal rights. I think when a colored man pays his money
into the union and conducts himself as a good union man should, he is
discriminated against when he has to walk two or three miles to his own
work when there is a shaft at his door. . . . When a man takes an oath
to make no discrimination against another man on account of race, creed
or color he should keep that oath. At the two east shafts, the New North
and the Two Citizens, my people are discriminated against. Even the cooperative shaft here that is run by labor itself, where all men are supposed
to be laboring men who run it, the negroes can not enter that shaft. We
want to abolish all of these evils [and] I hope you will help to abolish this
there here and now.

After further discussion, the grievance was referred to the district officers,
where it was buried without action.

The question of fairer black representation in the union governing
bodies and leadership was also sidetracked at convention after convention. At the 1906 convention, Local 298 of Richmond, Missouri, recommended an amendment to the union constitution that would give large
local unions "where there are 100 or more colored members" the right
"to send one colored delegate" to district and national conventions. The
Committee on the Constitution opposed the motion, and the delegates
voted it down. At the same convention, three delegates introduced a resolution that summed up a widespread feeling among the black miners:

> *Whereas,* Our race of people will easily be estimated to constitute at least
> one-fourth of the entire membership of the organization; and
>   *Whereas,* It is a long-established fact that taxation without representa-
> tion will not content any people, and in view of the fact that . . . we feel
> that we should be more encouraged if we were more recognized along the
> official line of the organization; therefore be it
>   *Resolved,* That the State and International Constitutions be so
> amended that the colored brothers be represented on the official staff in
> the state and districts along with the white brethren as far as their per-
> centage will warrant and prove practicable.

The percentage of black membership in the union stated in the resolution was exaggerated. The UMW in 1905, according to the official report, had 267,351 members, which would have made the black membership, if one-fourth, about 67,000, or 27,000 more black miners than
could be found in the entire country in 1910. Nevertheless, the proposal
for fairer representation for the black miners reflected a deep-seated and
long-standing grievance of the Negro UMW members. But the resolution was quickly buried. The same fate met a resolution presented at the
1909 convention by a black delegate from Oklahoma, urging that "the
colored brothers shall have a part of the official work of each district of
the United Mine Workers of America, such as Vice-President or Assist-

ant Secretary-Treasurer and part of the District Executive Board, Auditors or Tellers."

In fact, most of the grievances of black union members, when brought to the attention of the union leadership and white delegates at state and national conventions, were buried or voted down. As Herbert Hill points out in an unpublished study of the black miner and the UMW: "Black miners might protest and supplicate to their dying day, but there was little chance of moving the main white union leaders to their point of view."

Black miners warned, in letters to the *Journal* and in convention speeches, that failure to launch a campaign against the second-class status of Negro members and against the racism of the white membership would encourage black strike-breaking, reduce the union's appeal for black miners, and lend substance to the operators' argument that they, not the union, were protecting the rights of black miners. A Brazil, Indiana, black miner, writing under the sobriquet "Willing Hands," told the *Journal* that blacks, even black union members, helped in breaking strikes "simply because you refuse to allow the colored man to work among you in times of peace. If such be true, then, is it any wonder that in times of trouble these men retaliate for the treatment that they received at your hands?" His conclusion might well have been posted in every union hall in the country, including the lodges of the UMW: "Do away with the system and allow him the privilege of working with you, and I dare say that instead of the colored man taking your place he will be at all times to the front, doing all that he can for the upbuilding of the craft."

At the 1900 Illinois State Miners' Convention, Cal Robinson told the delegates: "If you do what is right in this matter, gentlemen, you will have none of your Virden* and Carterville riots,† and no blood will be spilled. If this discrimination is blotted out you will never hear of such riots as we have had in this State. . . . We want to abolish all these evils, and then we shall not have to get out our Gatling guns, we will have no fights along these lines, and we will have no riots."‡

Davis expressed the same view in a letter to the editor of the *Journal*: "I dare say that you seldom or never hear of negroes being brought into

---

* For the Virden riots, see above pp. 77–78.

† A battle in Carterville, Illinois, on September 17, 1899, between armed white miners and black strike-breakers ended with six Negroes dead.

‡ While blacks were used as strike-breakers by the coal operators, they were just one of many groups used, and as more and more blacks joined the miners' unions the operators began to favor immigrants and white "mountaineers" who, they felt, were less likely to join the union. As Spero and Harris point out, "when all is said and done, the number of strikes broken by black labor, have been few as compared with the number broken by white labor." They note further that white miners were always more hostile to blacks who worked during strikes than they were to whites who walked through the picket lines. They quote a Negro union miner's bitter remark: "You hear . . . honest-to-goodness white miners say: 'I don't mind the white scab, but I be damned if I will stand for a 'Negro scab.' " Sterling D. Spero and Abram L. Harris, *The Black Worker: The Negro and the Labor Movement* (New York, 1931), pp. 265–66.

a locality to break a strike in which both white and black worked together, and even if they were you always found the negro on the side of
the right." Lewis Coleman, another black member, wrote to the *Journal*
that, "if the white man would only be true to [the] organization, [blacks]
would not have to take their places when they come out on strike."[27]

John Mitchell, president of the UMW, declared in 1899 that the
main problem facing the union was that "colored labor has been and is
being used for the purpose of reducing wages of workingmen." Mitchell
lost all credibility with black UMW members after he appeared at the
convention of Alabama's UMW District 20 in 1900. The Birmingham
Trades Council of the AF of L had asked the miners at the convention
to pledge in a resolution to give their business only to union workmen.
When the black vice-president, Silas Brooks, strongly urged mine workers to vote against the resolution because the Trades Council and some
of its affiliates discriminated against blacks, Mitchell, who favored such
a pledge, announced that as a member of the Executive Council he
could assure black delegates that no AF of L affiliate barred Negroes.
The delegates would not buy this gross distortion of truth, and the resolution was tabled.[28]

The UMW did not move effectively to eliminate white racism within
its ranks, and, as black miners had warned, blacks lost interest in the organization. The United Mine Workers grew tremendously after 1900,
especially following the anthracite coal strike of 1902, increasing from
fewer than 100,000 to more than 250,000 members in 1910, but its black
membership actually declined. The number of black members in 1910 is
difficult to determine accurately, but it certainly was nowhere near the
40,000 reported by a union official. The total number of Negroes in the
whole industry was about 40,000 at the time. Most black miners, moreover, were located in Alabama and West Virginia, and in both states the
UMW suffered serious setbacks between 1900 and 1910.

The UMW in Alabama declined from some 12,000 members in 1902
—including at least 6,000 black miners—to fewer than 600 by 1910. A
smashing defeat of the union in 1908 was the turning point. Undoubtedly
racism among the white miners and the failure of the UMW leadership
to deal with it contributed to the great setback. Herbert R. Northrup
puts it this way: "The white miners, themselves divided between native
'mountaineers' and recent immigrants from southeastern Europe, were
loath to make common cause with the Negroes. The employers were
quick to capitalize upon the situation by spreading rumors that should
the United Mine Workers be successful, the black miners would lose
their jobs."[29]

The same situation, Northrup makes clear, prevailed in West Virginia, where, moreover, Negro ministers helped the operators to convince the black miners that the companies, not white miners, would protect their interests best. The 1902 strike in the previously unorganized
bituminous coal fields of West Virginia had ended in total failure, and
thereafter for many years, even after the bitter strikes of 1912–13, the
mines in West Virginia were mainly unorganized. In 1912, at the begin-

ning of the strike, the UMW strength represented 3 per cent of the miners of West Virginia. By 1915 it was only 5 per cent. Black miners were working mainly in the almost totally nonunion fields of the southern half of the state. The union leadership showed little interest in organizing this section, which would have meant mounting a huge campaign to eliminate racism among the white miners.

Whether the exact number of black members of the UMW in 1910 was 4,000, as Spero and Harris estimate, or between 8,000 and 9,000, as Herbert Hill says, it clearly had dwindled considerably from the 20,000 figure in 1900. A partial explanation for the decline might be gathered from remarks of the president of an Alabama coal company, who testified before the Industrial Commission in 1901 that he had dealings with a grievance committee composed of "two white men and a colored brother. He [the Negro] is not expected to say much, but he is on the committee." It was such situations that Richard Davis had in mind when he stated in the UMW *Journal* that black members wanted and deserved office in the union—"not office in name, but office in deed."

Yet the UMW, though hardly committed to thoroughgoing racial integration, was still far superior to most white trade unions in the period between 1890 and World War I so far as the black worker was concerned. It was one of the very few unions affiliated with the AF of L that admitted blacks (although in segregated locals in some areas), did not prevent them from working at the trade (although keeping them out of better-paid jobs), and imposed a fine on any local that discriminated on the basis of color. In an address to the National Association for the Advancement of Colored People on April 30, 1912, John H. Walker, president of the Illinois UMW, boasted with justification that, in writing a new contract affecting 175,000 coal miners in Illinois, Indiana, Ohio, and Pennsylvania, the Illinois union had insisted on a clause "that no workers shall be discriminated against in any way on account of race, creed, nationality or color."[30]*

Some delegates to the NAACP convention, themselves members of the UMW, noted all too often a wide gap existed between clauses on paper and performance. Still, very few unions affiliated with the AF of L in that year even had such a clause to point to.

From its inception in 1909, the NAACP urged Negroes to make common cause with the working class but blamed discrimination in the trade unions for keeping most black workers in a state resembling peonage. In 1913, it put forward a "Minimum Program of Negro Advancement." A major point was "the Right to Work: the End to Peonage; Equal Service and Equal Pay for the Negro." On behalf of the association, Dr. Du Bois wrote: "Whatever the tactics, the result is the same

---

* During the anti-Negro riots in Springfield, Illinois, in August, 1908, a number of white miners demanded that blacks be discharged and threatened to close down the mines if this was not accomplished by UMW Illinois officials. Walker, who was then president of the Illinois UMW, let it be known that "the local that took such action would first be fined, and, if still obstinate, would be expelled from the organization." Chicago *Daily Socialist*, August 19, 1908.

for the mass of white workingmen in America; beat or starve the Negro out of his job if you can by keeping him out of the union; or, if you must admit him, do the same thing inside union lines." "So long as union labor fights for humanity, its mission is divine," Du Bois emphasized; when unionists fought only for white skilled workers, practiced segregation and discrimination, and forced competent Negro workers into starvation, "they deserve themselves the starvation which they plan for their darker and poorer fellows."[31]

In 1910, the year following the founding of the NAACP, Samuel Gompers was said by the Saint Louis press to have "read the negro out of the labor movement." The report was picked up by papers throughout the country and resulted in a flood of protests from Negro spokesmen. Gompers said that he had been misquoted and that the alleged remark in no way represented his attitude toward the Negroes. What he had said, he explained, was that Negro workers were difficult to organize because they did not have the same conception of their rights and duties as did white workers. He had alluded to the "present unpreparedness of the colored people as a whole for fully exercising and enjoying the possibilities existing in trade unionism." Once again Gompers placed the blame for their lack of organization on the Negroes themselves. In short, he had not read the Negroes out of the labor movement; the Negro workers had read themselves out of it.[32]

In the same year, the AF of L admitted the Brotherhood of Railway Carmen (BRC), a union that openly discriminated against Negro workers. This action was accompanied by the departure from the AF of L of the International Association of Car Workers (IACW), which refused to amalgamate with the BRC because of its discrimination against Negroes. The BRC had insisted that, before becoming affiliated, the IACW had to accept the clause in the BRC constitution denying membership to Negroes. The IACW refused, despite the urging of the AF of L leaders. In August, 1910, the AF of L Executive Council canceled the car workers' charter and named the BRC, with its anti-Negro clause intact, as the "regular" union of car workers. The IACW appealed the decision at the 1910 AF of L convention, accusing the Executive Council of violating its "sacred principle of trade autonomy" and of conspiring with the enemies of labor solidarity, but to no avail. At the 1911 convention, the International Association of Car Workers dramatically surrendered its charter.[33]

Philip Taft, a leading apologist for the AF of L's retreat from the organizing of Negro workers, defends the retreat this way: "Whatever its own view, the Federation could not determine the admittance policies of the autonomous unions; as long as they met the other formal requirements of the A.F. of L., the latter could not inquire into the conduct of its affiliates."[34] But, as we have just seen, the AF of L did not hesitate to force the discriminatory practices of the BRC upon an affiliate, the International Association of Car Workers, which it then punished for upholding the principle of labor solidarity. The very same men who punished the car workers publicly continued to proclaim the AF of L's desire to unionize "all the men and women of labor without regard to creed, color or nationality."

In 1912, as in 1902, the vast majority of black workers were excluded from the AF of L. Most of its affiliates had few if any Negro members. The largest black membership, whatever the exact figure, was still in the United Mine Workers. The Teamsters had 6,000 Negro members; the Cigar Makers, 5,000; the Hotel and Restaurant Employees, 2,500; and the Carpenters, 2,500. But the Printers had only 250, the Pressmen fewer than six, the Lithographers one, the Photo-Engravers fewer than six, the Iron, Steel and Tin Workers two or three, the Potters none, the Glass Bottle Blowers none, the Hatters none, the Molders twelve, the Pattern Makers one, the Glass Workers "a few," the Boot and Shoe Workers five, and the Wood Workers "a few."[35]

7 The Railroad Brotherhoods and the IWW, 1890–1915

The two main federations of labor unions not affiliated with the AF of L in the period from 1890 to 1915 were the railroad brotherhoods and the Industrial Workers of the World. For the black worker, the difference between the two organizations was as between night and day.

During the great railroad strike of 1877, black and white railroad workers struck together on a number of lines. Peter H. Clark, principal of the Colored High School of Cincinnati, Ohio, and probably the first American Negro Socialist, hailed this unity in a speech in which he defended the strikers and called for socialism as the solution for labor's grievances. But black and white unity on the railroads did not continue after the smashing of the strike by federal troops, and it vanished almost completely as a result of the racist policies of the railroad brotherhoods.

Before the formation of the railroad brotherhoods—the Brotherhood of Locomotive Engineers (founded in 1863), the Order of Railway Conductors (1868), the Brotherhood of Locomotive Firemen (1873), the Brotherhood of Railroad Brakemen (September, 1883; renamed the Brotherhood of Railway Trainmen, 1890), and the Switchmen's Mutual Association (1886)—blacks held many of the higher-paying jobs, and many were firemen or brakemen. After the organization of the brotherhoods, blacks were forced gradually to relinquish these positions. Since the job of fireman was difficult and unpleasant, it tended to remain a Negro job, especially in the South; and, because many engineers learned their craft as firemen, it was not unusual to find black engineers. But, as the brotherhoods succeeded in securing agreements with the roads, all blacks employed by the railroads as other than porters and waiters found their jobs threatened.

From the outset, the railroad brotherhoods excluded blacks from membership by means of constitutional provisions defining as eligible "any white man," "any white male between the ages of 18 and 45 who is sober and industrious," or "any employee born of white parents, who is sober, moral and otherwise of good character." From the beginning, too, the brotherhoods tried to persuade operators to discharge blacks and replace them with members of the all-white organizations. In the South, where employers had long relied upon blacks as a cheap labor source, this campaign was unsuccessful for a number of years. The white Brotherhood of Locomotive Trainmen called a strike against the Houston and Texas Central Railroad in 1890 demanding the discharge of black employees. When the strike failed owing to the company's stubborn refusal to yield; the Brotherhood went into court demanding that Negroes be judged incompetent to work on the railroads. The court, however, refused to allow race to be used as a basis for judging competence.[1]

In the North, however, the brotherhoods' campaign was more successful. By the summer of 1894 the Philadelphia *Press* reported: "Negroes are tacitly but none the less completely excluded from railroad positions on most Northern lines. No Negro is ever seen in a position on a railroad. This industrial exclusion is a most serious injustice and, with other like exclusions, lies at the bottom of much of the industrial deficiencies of the Negro."[2]

When Eugene V. Debs, editor of *Locomotive Firemen's Magazine*, took the lead in forming the American Railway Union (ARU) in June, 1893, he sought to apply the principle of uniting all railroad workers in one union regardless of craft, race, creed, or nationality. Most railroad workers were fed up with the conservative craft approach of the brotherhoods, but they refused to abandon the policy of keeping blacks out of the union and driving them out of railroad jobs. Despite Debs's strong objections, membership in the new industrial union of railroad workers was limited to whites who served a railroad in any way except in a managerial capacity. Debs warned the ARU that this policy could lead to disaster. "I am not here," he told the delegates to the union's 1894 convention, "to advocate association with the Negro, but I am ready to stand side by side with him, to take his hand in mine and help him whenever it is in my power." But the ban against black membership in the ARU constitution was reaffirmed at the national convention in June, 1894, by a vote of 112 to 100. The delegates offered their "sympathy and support" to any effort to organize black railroaders—which represented progress from the brotherhoods' insistence that blacks be barred from jobs on the railroads—but Negroes saw no practical value in the offer.[3]

Not surprisingly, blacks felt no inclination to help the ARU when it challenged the General Managers Association in 1894. The strike, which started among Pullman workers, spread to the entire industry. "Do your duty," the Cleveland *Gazette*, a black weekly, exhorted Negroes who were replacing strikers in the yards and switch towers of the Rock Island line. Some blacks formed the Anti-strikers' Railroad Union to even the score with the ARU. The *Christian Recorder* reminded the ARU of its exclusion of blacks and pointed out that "the practical result of this great upheaval is to give a chance to men who had no chance or small chance before."[4]

The great strike was defeated, cutting short the ARU's career. In a speech in Harlem on October 30, 1923, Debs recalled how thirty years before he had fought at the founding of the ARU to persuade the delegates "to open the door to admit the colored as well as the white men upon equal terms." Actually, the Pullman strike was defeated largely by government intervention through a court injunction under the Sherman Anti-trust Act which meant the occupation of Chicago by 50,000 federal troops. But the error of banning blacks also contributed heavily. Had the ARU admitted Negroes, Debs noted, "there would have been a different story of the strike, for it would certainly have had a different result."[5]

After the ARU fell apart, most railroad workers returned to the brotherhoods, and the drive to oust blacks from railroad jobs was resumed. At the convention of the brotherhoods in Norfolk, Virginia, in November, 1898, Grand Master Frank P. Sargent of the firemen was quoted in the press as saying that "one of the chief purposes of the meeting . . . was to begin a campaign in advocacy of white supremacy in the railway service."[6] The campaign was accompanied by an unprecedented outburst in the brotherhood journals of racist polemics asserting that blacks were "immoral, untrustworthy, inherently vicious and indolent by nature," and a menace to the public, for not only did they go to sleep on the job but "their stupidity caused many accidents." Grand Chief Warren S. Stone of the engineers wrote that blacks made poor engineers because they could not keep awake and always lost their heads in an emergency. One brotherhood member addressed himself to the training of blacks: "I think it almost as well to educate a hog, for the animal can not accomplish any harm with his education, while the negro can."

A brotherhood member from the North pointed out that all the talk about blacks' being "too stupid" to make good firemen or engineers masked the fear that they did make capable railroad workers but, being forced to accept lower wages, were a threat to the pay scales of white engineers and firemen. The white railroad unions, he continued, dared not press for wages much higher than those paid to Negroes for fear that their members would be entirely replaced by black crews. Little wonder, then, that wages in the South for these occupations were considerably below those in other areas. There was really only one solution to the problem of wage competition, he concluded: to admit blacks into the union and with them present a solid front against the employer.

The *Locomotive Firemen's Magazine* offered the following reply:

> Now, my brother, I think if you would come South and get a glimpse of our typical Southern "coon" or "burr-head" and get one good sniff of the aroma he always carries with him, both winter and summer, but more especially when he is out on an excursion train, cooped up in a passenger coach when the thermometer registers about 104 in the shade, you would be in favor of sending him back to Africa, his original home, and never entertain so much as a thought of trying to organize him.[7]

Meanwhile, the engineers and firemen were cooperating to forbid the hiring of Negroes as firemen on any road where none were employed and to keep the percentage of black firemen already employed jointly with white firemen from increasing, in the hope that blacks would in time be entirely eliminated. (The engineers, of course, were anxious to prevent blacks from being trained as firemen, which would place them at one remove from qualifications as engineers.) In Pittsburgh and Cleveland the unions succeeded in forcing the carriers to exclude black firemen from service. A promise was obtained from Baltimore and Ohio officials that they would make no effort to hire other Negroes, and those already employed would be removed.

In the South, the railroads resisted the elimination of blacks, as in the case, already noted, of the Houston and Texas Central's refusal in September, 1890, to get rid of Negro switchmen. But the brotherhoods did not give up, and on June 16, 1909, the white firemen on the Georgia Railroad went on strike against the employment of black firemen. The railroad management, headed by E. A. Scott, termed the strike "the beginning of an effort to drive all the colored firemen from the southern roads" and resisted the demand. E. A. Ball, a vice-president of the brotherhood, asked the public not to use the railroad so long as blacks were employed as firemen and urged all who believed in white supremacy to rally behind the strikers:

> It will be up to you to determine whether the white fireman now employed on the Georgia Railroad shall be accorded rights and privileges over the negro, or whether he shall be placed on the same equality with the negro. I stand for white superiority, and Mr. Scott stands for Negro superiority; let the South judge between us.

Most businessmen along the line supported the strikers, a somewhat surprising development in an area noted for the fact that its "best citizens" had forced "many a union organizer to leave town in a hurry to avoid getting a coat of tar and feathers." But then, as some papers noted, a strike "actuated by race hatred" was quite in keeping with the "sacred principles of the institution of white supremacy."

The strike lasted two weeks, during which time black firemen were beaten and otherwise intimidated. It ended when a board of arbitration ruled that the Georgia Railroad was allowed to employ blacks as firemen wherever they were qualified to fill the job, but at the same wages as white firemen received. Technically the white firemen had lost the case, but, as the brotherhood leaders jubilantly told the Atlanta *Constitution*, they accepted the ruling because "white firemen would be preferred to a Negro fireman when the same wages were paid." The black press knew that, with the blacks' wage equal to that of the white firemen, and with the brotherhood determining who was "qualified to fill the job," blacks would be ousted as firemen, and all opportunity to become engineers would end. The only inducement for the railroads to hire blacks in the first place had been removed.[8]

Events bore out this interpretation. Black firemen were discharged from the Georgia Railroad, and other Southern roads soon followed suit. The trainmen and the conductors negotiated an agreement with the Mississippi Valley railroads in 1911 under which blacks were not to be employed as baggagemen, flagmen, or yard foremen. By 1915 there was not a single black engineer in the entire country. The Brotherhood of Locomotive Engineers, eager to enlarge its membership, considered extending its jurisdiction to Cuba but, after investigation, abandoned the plan. In May, 1910, at the ninth biennial convention of the engineers, F. A. Burgess, assistant grand chief, explained why:

> We did not organize any of the engineers in Cuba for what we considered the most excellent of reasons: that we were unable to distinguish the nigger from the white man. Our color perception was not sensitive enough to draw a line. I do not believe the condition will improve in a year from now or in 10 years from now or in any other time, unless you stock the island of Cuba with a new race, entirely getting rid of the old. . . . I hope the time will never come when this organization will have to join hands with the negro or a man with a fractional part of a negro in him.[9]

With whatever contrivance was necessary, including brutal murders of Negro railroad workers, the four brotherhoods—the firemen, trainmen, conductors, and engineers—persisted in their campaign to drive blacks from the railroads. It took decades to achieve their goal. As late as 1920 there were 6,595 Negro firemen and a total of 8,275 Negro brakemen, switchmen, flagmen, and yardmen. But there was virtually no hiring of Negro replacements as the older workers retired or died, and eventually the brotherhoods achieved their aim of keeping blacks not only out of the highly skilled, well-paid railroad jobs, but out of all job categories other than waiters and porters.

In 1913 Mary White Ovington, one of the founders of the NAACP, wrote: "There are two organizations in this country that have shown they do care about full rights for the Negro. The first is the National Association for the Advancement of Colored People. . . . The second organization that attacks Negro segregation is the Industrial Workers of the World. . . . The IWW has stood with the Negro."[10]

The IWW, popularly known as the "Wobblies," was founded in the summer of 1905 by progressive-minded elements in the American labor and Socialist movements. Its leaders, Eugene V. Debs, Daniel De Leon, and William D. (Big Bill) Haywood, were convinced of three basic propositions: (1) the superiority of industrial unionism over craft unionism in the struggle against the monopolistic, highly integrated organizations of employers; (2) the impossibility of converting the conservative American Federation of Labor to an organization willing and able to achieve real benefits for the majority of working men and women; and (3) the inability of existing industrial and radical organizations to unite the entire working class, regardless of skill, color, sex, or national origin. In their eyes, a new organization was clearly necessary, one that "would correspond to modern conditions, and through which the working people might finally secure complete emancipation from wage slavery for all wage workers."

On June 27, 1905, in Chicago's Brand Hall, "Big Bill" Haywood, militant secretary-treasurer of the Western Federation of Miners, called the 200 delegates representing 43 organizations to order and declared:

"This is the Continental Congress of the Working Class." He made it clear that the organization about to come into being would take a firm and clear stand against discrimination based on race or color. He then cited the well-known fact that "there are organizations that are affiliated with the AF of L. which in their constitution and by-laws prohibit the initiation of a colored man." Haywood pledged that the newly organized industrial union would strongly oppose such anti-working-class, racist practices, along with other restrictions on the right of black workers to join the labor movement.

At a later session the Industrial Workers of the World adopted the motto "An Injury to One Is the Concern of All" (a modification of the old Knights of Labor motto). The first section of the bylaws stated that "no working man or woman shall be excluded from membership because of creed or color." Haywood told reporters that, whereas unions affiliated with the AF of L discriminated against a worker who was a Negro, to the IWW it "did not make a bit of difference whether he is a Negro or a white man."[11]

Despite its pledge, the IWW appears to have accomplished little in the way of organizing black workers during its first four years of existence. Torn by internal ideological dissensions and by repeated resignations and expulsions, and seriously weakened by the impact of the depression following the Panic of 1907, the IWW hardly organized any workers at all. In 1909 its membership was down to 3,700, in contrast to the 1,488,872 affiliated in that year to the AF of L. Yet the IWW was far from dead. In the next few years, organizers would make the Wobblies known throughout the nation through their famous free-speech fights and their unionizing drives in the steel and textile industries of the East, the lumber camps of the Northwest and Southeast, the farmlands of the Pacific Coast and the Midwest, and the maritime and shipping industries throughout the country. The spectacular rise of the IWW would bring the principle of industrial unionism and the principle of labor solidarity to the attention of hundreds of thousands of unorganized American workers, including the black workers.

Beginning in 1910, the IWW made a determined effort to recruit black membership. Leaflets and pamphlets were distributed by the thousands to convince the black man that he "has no chance in the old-line trade unions. They do not want him. They admit him only under compulsion and treat him with contempt. There is only *one* labor organization in the United States that admits the colored worker on a footing of absolute equality with the white—the Industrial Workers of the World. . . . In the IWW the colored worker, man or woman, is on an equal footing with every other worker. He has the same voice in determining the policies of the organization, and his interests are protected as zealously as those of any other member." The Negro, IWW literature emphasized, was subject to discrimination, first because of his color, and second because "for the most part the Negro still belongs in the category of the 'unskilled.'" This state of affairs could be wiped out not by appeals to sentiment alone but only by a union that taught its members to recognize all workers as equal regardless of color and that organized the unskilled by the only method through which they could be organized—industrial unionism. Such a union was the IWW.

All IWW journals participated actively in this educational campaign, including *Voice of the People*, the Southern organ of the IWW, published in New Orleans under the editorship of Covington Hall. Mississippi-born and a one-time adjutant general in the United Sons of Confederate Veterans, Hall became a radical, a Socialist, and an active organizer for the IWW, especially among Negroes in the South. He regularly featured appeals in the *Voice* urging white workers in the South to remember how racism had always been used by the ruling class to divide black and white to the injury of both and predicting that no real improvement could be made in the conditions of either race unless they united. In issue after issue, Hall drove home the message: "The workers, when they organize, must be color blind. . . . We must aim for solidarity first, and revolutionary action afterwards."

In an article headed "Down with Race Prejudice," published in December, 1912, Phineas Eastman, an IWW organizer, asked his "fellow workers of the South, if they wish real good feelings to exist between the two races (and each is necessary to the other's success), to please stop calling the colored man 'Nigger'—the tone some use is an insult, much less the word. Call him Negro if you must refer to his race, but 'fellow worker' is the only form of salutation a rebel should use." IWW speakers and newspapers made a distinction by referring to black strike-breakers as "niggers" and to black union men as "Negro fellow workers." Further, black strike-breakers in strikes involving a craft union were viewed differently from those who scabbed against an industrial union like the IWW. When the firemen on the Cincinnati, New Orleans, and Texas Railroad went on strike to protest the promotion of Negroes, *Solidarity* saw nothing wrong in blacks' taking their places. "We have no sympathy for the striking firemen; they are reaping the folly of un-working class conduct. They are getting what they deserved. Unity, regardless of race, creed or color, is the only way out." The IWW's answer to the AF of L's lament that Negroes were "natural strike-breakers" and hence "unorganizable" was clear and concise:

> The whole trend of the white craft labor organization is to discriminate against the negro and to refuse to accord him equal economic rights. When, as a consequence, the negro is used to their own undoing, they have no one but themselves to blame.

Members of the IWW were constantly reminded that the organization of the Negro was an unavoidable fact of industrial life. "As the employer compels us to work in the shop on an equality of wage slavery with the Negro," an IWW booklet pointed out, "we fail to see why we shouldn't meet him on the basis of that same equality in our unions. The Negro is exploited precisely as we are. Why, then, shouldn't we organize him precisely as we organize ourselves, 'we whites'?" It was not so much a moral as an "economic bread-and-butter" issue. "Leaving the

Negro outside of your union makes him a potential, if not an actual
scab, dangerous to the organized worker, to say nothing of his own interests as a worker." Race prejudice on the job could have only one result
—"keeping the workers fighting each other, while the boss gets the benefits." The idea fostered by the capitalists that the white worker was
"superior" was part of the same game. "Actually he is only 'superior' if
he shows that he can produce more wealth for the boss than his colored
brother can." In an appeal directed especially to Southern workers, the
IWW asked:

> If one of you were to fall in a river and could not swim, and a Negro
> came along who could swim, would you drown rather than accept his
> offer of aid? Hardly!
> That is the I.W.W. position. Labor organized on race lines will drown.
> Only organized on *class* lines will it swim. . . .
> Don't let them sidetrack you from the main line which is, Shall we be
> freemen or slaves?

The IWW condemned all manifestations of Jim Crowism. It de-
nounced the lynching of Negroes as "savagery" usually resorted to when
Negroes were demanding more of their product. In a pamphlet entitled
"Justice for the Negro: How Can He Get It?" the IWW pointed out:

> Two lynchings a week—one every three or four days—that is the rate at
> which the people in this "land of the free and home of the brave" have
> been killing colored men and women for the past thirty years . . . put to
> death with every kind of torture that human fiends can invent.

The pamphlet made it clear that "the wrongs of the Negro in the
United States" went beyond lynchings:

> When allowed to live and work for the community, he is subjected to
> constant humiliation, injustice and discrimination. In the cities he is
> forced to live in the meanest districts, where his rent is doubled and
> tripled, while conditions of health and safety are neglected in favor of the
> white sections. In many states he is obliged to ride in special "Jim Crow"
> cars, hardly fit for cattle. Almost everywhere all semblance of political
> rights is denied him.
> When the Negro goes to ask for work he meets with the same sys-
> tematic discrimination. Thousands of jobs are closed to him solely on ac-
> count of his color. He is considered only fit for the most menial occupa-
> tion. In many cases he is forced to accept a lower wage than is paid the
> white men for the same work. *Everywhere the odds are against him in the
> struggle for existence.*
> Throughout this land of liberty, so-called, the Negro worker is treated
> as an inferior; he is cursed and spat upon; in short, he is treated not as a
> human being, but as an animal, a beast of burden for the ruling class.
> When he tries to improve his condition, he is shoved back into the mire
> of degradation and poverty and told to "keep his place."

A leaflet addressed "To Colored Workingmen and Women" promised, "If you are a wage worker you are welcome in the IWW halls, no
matter what your color. By this you may see that the IWW is not a
white man's union, not a black man's union, not a red man's union,

but a working man's union. All of the working class in one big union."
On September 19, 1912, the *Industrial Worker*, the Western organ of
the IWW, carried the following item:

> Fearing that the IWW will organize the steel mills in the Pittsburgh dis-
> trict the Carnegie Steel Company is importing Negroes so as to create ra-
> cial hatred and prevent solidarity. It won't work. The IWW organizes
> without regard to color. The only Negro we fight is he who employs labor.
> There is no color line in the furnace hells of the steel trust and there will
> be none in the *One Big Union*. White, black or yellow, the workers of the
> world must unite!

The IWW, unlike most unions of its time and since, practiced what
it preached, even in the deepest South, and on an international scale as
well. In 1910–11 the Industrial Workers' Union of South Africa, a
branch of the IWW founded by Wobbly seamen from the United
States, conducted a vigorous campaign to convince the rank and file of
the white workers of South Africa "that their real enemy is not the
colored laborer, and that it is only by combining and co-operating irrespective of color that the standard of life of the whites can be maintained and improved." The union led a strike of trainwaymen in Jo-
hannesburg in which Negro and white workers for the first time united
in struggle. The *Voice of Labor*, the IWW's South African organ, asserted that the strike, although not successful, had taught "the white
and black workers of South Africa some much needed lessons."

Clarence Darrow, the progressive lawyer and frequent champion of the
rights of Negroes, welcomed the IWW as a major solution for the basic
problem of black Americans. The blacks, being mainly workers, could
lift themselves to a higher standard of living only by organizing, he observed. "But most unions of the AF of L and the railroad brotherhoods
barred Negroes, and until the IWW came into existence there was little
the black workers could do to improve their lot. But now the situation
was different."[12]

The IWW opposed political action at the ballot box as a waste of
energy and put its faith primarily in industrial organization and "direct
action," leading ultimately to the general strike. Negro disfranchisement
in the South was not an obstacle for the IWW—as it was for election-
oriented unionists—in its plans for building black and white unity. For
their part, black workers, deprived of the right to vote, were drawn to
an organization that placed its main emphasis on economic struggle.
Then again, at no time in its history did the IWW ever establish segregated locals for black workers, even in the deepest South. Wherever it
organized, members were brought together in locals regardless of race
or color. In fact, the Industrial Workers of the World is the only federation in the history of the American labor movement that never chartered a single segregated local.

No statistics are available on Negro membership in the IWW. Spero
and Harris estimate that, of 1 million membership cards issued by the
IWW between 1909 and 1924, "100,000 cards were issued to Negroes."
But no IWW publication ever made such a claim, and it is likely that

the Wobblies never succeeded in recruiting so large a Negro membership.

Many of the great organizing drives of the IWW were in the textile
industry of the North, in which few black workers were employed prior
to World War I. Negroes were employed, but not in great numbers, in
the lumber camps of the West and in the Western agricultural fields,
where the IWW also made significant headway. Those black migratory
workers who did find a place in these industries also found a haven in
the IWW. In *The Messenger* of July, 1923, George S. Schuyler recalled that "there was no discrimination in the 'jungles' of the IWW.
The writer has seen a white hobo, despised by society, share his last loaf
with a black fellow-hobo."[13]

The IWW did recruit many Negro members among the waterfront
workers along the Atlantic Coast and the lumber workers in the South.
In 1913 it created the Marine Transport Workers' Industrial Union to
organize waterfront workers regardless of craft or race. A manifesto issued late that year to all workers in the industry announced the IWW's
plans to organize, criticized Jim Crow unionism in the International
Longshoremen's Association, and pledged that "no color line" would
exist wherever the Wobblies recruited members. It also declared:

> We shall compel the masters to pay us wages that will enable us to de-
> velop ourselves mentally and socially, support those depending upon us
> and eventually support a family of our own.
> We shall reduce our hours enough to make room for the unemployed,
> thereby solving the unemployed problem.
> We shall build a union that will be a real hope for all workers on the
> waterfront, black and white, a real support in the hour of our need, and
> compel the respect and recognition of all society. Generally speaking, we
> shall ourselves assume control of our industry and dictate the conditions
> of work.[14]

The IWW kicked off its campaign in Philadelphia. It was long overdue. The ILA had established a foothold on the waterfront in the
1890's but had lost it when it failed to support striking longshoremen in
1898. For fifteen years the Philadelphia longshoremen were unorganized.
During that time, the employers had frustrated all attempts at organization by pitting blacks and whites against each other, meeting each complaint about conditions from members of either group with the threat
that their jobs would be given to the other. The IWW entered the
picture by telling the dock workers that, whether whites and blacks
liked each other or not, their only hope was to organize in one union.
The man who led the organizing campaign was Philadelphia-born Benjamin Harrison Fletcher, the leading black in the IWW.*

---

* The first important black organizer for the IWW was R. T. Sims, who came
over to the Wobblies from the Socialist Trade and Labor Alliance. He attended the
1906 convention, was appointed to the "Good and Welfare Committee," and introduced a resolution protesting lynchings of Negroes and antiblack riots as "a blot
on the garment of civilization" and calling for the elimination of "such wanton and
atrocious acts." The resolution was adopted.

Within a few months Marine Transport Workers' Local 3 was organized in Philadelphia over the opposition of the ILA, the AF of L, and even the Philadelphia branch of the Socialist Party. On May 13, 1913, Local 3 struck for recognition, supported by the African Methodist Episcopal Church in Philadelphia. One minister declared: "The IWW at least protects the colored man, which is more than I can say for the laws of this country."

For weeks, to quote the *Public Ledger*, "upward of 3,000 Italians, Poles, Slavs and colored men, who are employed as stevedores, gangmen, and haulers, have tied up the shipping industry in this city." Under the leadership of the IWW, the strikers battled police and invaded the mayor's home to protest the police department's protection of scabs and brutality toward the workers. The shipping interests assured Philadelphia that under no circumstances would they yield to the "lawless IWW." The solidarity of white and black longshoremen, unprecedented in the history of the Philadelphia labor movement, forced the shipping owners to eat their words. The dock workers won all their demands except the thirty-five cent hourly wage. The final settlement included recognition of the union, the right to bargain collectively, and thirty cents an hour.

In October, 1913, the boatmen's branch of the IWW, Local 8 of Philadelphia, was organized and struck for higher wages and shorter hours. After two days most of the employers gave in.

Those IWW victories proved that labor solidarity could win out over bitter opposition from the shipowners. "Only after many unsuccessful attempts to use scabs, police, gunmen, bribery, race prejudice, etc., to break their ranks," Fletcher wrote in *Solidarity*, "the shipping trust was forced to surrender to the solidarity of labor."

On May 14, 1914, the longshoremen again went on strike, this time for a wage increase. The struggle ended two weeks later in victory. During the strike, the first anniversary of the longshoremen's branch of the National Industrial Union of Marine Transport Workers was celebrated in Philadelphia. The main speakers were "Big Bill" Haywood and Alanzo Richards, a black member of the Philadelphia local. Both whites and Negroes participated in a parade through the waterfront district and at a local park.

Strikes in 1915 and 1916 completed the union's control of the docks. In the spring of 1916, Local 3 gained job control on the waterfront for the longshoremen. By then the union's membership exceeded 3,000, and it had raised wages for black and white longshoremen from $1.25 to $4 a day, with time-and-a-half for overtime and double time for Sundays. In keeping with its belief in equality of black and white, the local had a rotating chairmanship; one month a Negro was chairman; the next month a white member.[15]

Other locals of the Marine Transport Workers, composed largely of black longshoremen, were established in Galveston, New Orleans, and Baltimore. All maintained the principle of full equality of black and white members. The AF of L Central Labor Council in New Orleans refused to admit delegates from the black unions of waterfront workers. In 1910 the IWW, under the leadership of Covington Hall and backed by the Dock and Cotton Council, established the United Labor Council, which admitted delegates from both white and black waterfront unions. Soon the council was an important force in the New Orleans labor scene. As in Philadelphia, the meetings of the Council were chaired alternately by black and white waterfront workers.[16]

One of the most inspiring chapters of the IWW's organizing activity relates to the lumber industry of the South. There were important differences between the labor forces of Southern and Western lumbering. The former was composed not of migrant workers but rather of men who lived the year round in the area. Also, the labor force in the Southern lumber industry was made up of both white and Negro workers; in 1910, more than half of the 262,000 workers were blacks. In the main, the blacks were unskilled workers in the lowest-paid jobs and had little opportunity to rise. They did most of the heavy manual work in the sawmills, on railroads, in the turpentine camps, at skidways, and in the swamps. In 1910, of 7,958 Negroes in the sawmills and planing mills of Texas, 7,216 were laborers; there was not a single black sawyer. *St. Louis Lumberman*, the official journal of the industry, justified this situation on the ground that "there is a limit to the amount of wages that can be paid with safety to colored laborers around sawmills and wood camps. Too much pay breeds discontent and idleness among them." For the black lumber worker, a student of the industry notes, "emancipation from slavery had not brought the fruits of freedom. He simply had exchanged his lot for a different system of economic bondage."

For average weekly wages of from $7 to $9, men were forced to labor ten to twelve hours a day. Wages were usually paid monthly, and then largely, if not entirely, in scrip or time checks. "Scrip" was simply some substitute for legal currency—paper, chits, cardboard coin, metal tags, or the like—which ordinarily bore the name of the issuing company, a valuation, and the words "good for merchandise only." It could be spent in the company store at face value or converted to cash at a discount of 5 to 30 per cent. Prices in the company stores ranged from 29 to as high as 50 per cent above prices in surrounding communities, so that in effect the wages used for merchandise were always considerably below face value.

The time check bore the condition that it was to be cashed at some specified future date. If the bearer, for whatever reason, cashed it prior to the specified date, he generally took a discount of 5 to 10 per cent. To obtain legal tender, workers were sometimes forced to borrow from the employer at usurious rates of interest. In other words, they were actually paying interest on wages being withheld from them.

The majority of lumber workers lived in communities owned and operated by the mill companies, where they were charged outrageous rents for primitive huts heated with open fires and forced to pay a compulsory medical-insurance fee, usually $1.00 to $1.50 a month, for doctors in whose selection they had no voice and who knew little or nothing of medicine. They were forced to pay 75 cents to $1 a month for "accident insurance," which the lumber company then secured for only 50 to 60 cents per man.[17]

The AF of L showed no interest in organizing the oppressed workers of the Southern lumber industry, so they had to unionize by themselves. On December 3, 1910, Arthur L. Emerson, Jay Smith, and a group of lumber workers in the De Ridder area of Louisiana, most of them sympathetic to the IWW and the Socialist Party, set up a local union. Emerson, Smith, and a few other Wobblies, disguised as book agents, insurance solicitors, evangelists, and even card sharps to avoid company gunmen, went from camp to camp and mill to mill, bringing the message of unionism to the lumber workers. By June, 1911, enough locals had been organized to set up the Brotherhood of Timber Workers (B of TW) as a national union with Emerson as president and Smith as general secretary.

Since blacks made up a large portion of the lumbering labor force, the leaders of the brotherhood saw that no union could be effective in the yellow pine region unless it opened its doors to blacks as well as whites. The constitution of the organization allowed blacks to join, but the Southern tradition of segregation was preserved by providing for "colored lodges," which were required to hand over their initiation fees and dues to the nearest white local "for safe-keeping." The B of TW spread rapidly over Texas, Louisiana, and Arkansas, recruiting Negro and white lumberjacks, mill workers, small farmers who worked in the lumber industry for parts of the year, and town craftsmen. The employers quickly struck back. More than 350 mills in the three states were closed down, and union men were locked out and blacklisted. During the summer and fall of 1911, between 5,000 and 7,000 of the most active members of the brotherhood, white and Negro, were blacklisted.

There were two ways in which the locked-out workers could return to their jobs. One was by individually signing the familiar "yellow dog" contract, an ironclad oath not to belong to the brotherhood as long as the signer remained in the company's employ. The other was for groups of workers to sign resolutions condemning the B of TW and pledging loyalty to the operators. The vast majority of lumber workers, black and white, refused to sign either yellow dog contract. One black worker expressed the common attitude: "Only a low-life lickskillet would do such a thing. . . . I would live on wild plants that grow in the hills before I would sign." The lumber operators tried a new strategy to destroy the brotherhood. The idea was to reopen the plants, invite black members of the brotherhood to return to work at higher wages, and recruit black scabs to keep the mills operating.

This plan also failed. No black members of the brotherhood went back to work, and few black scabs could be recruited. When the mills reopened—the lockout was officially ended in February, 1912—it was not with scab labor. By May, 1912, the brotherhood had a membership of 20,000 to 25,000 workers, about half of them Negroes.

The refusal of the black members to desert the union and of other

blacks to scab during the lockout gave the brotherhood a clearer perspective on what it called the "Negro Question." In *An Appeal to the
Timber and Lumber Workers*, published in April, 1912, the union declared:

> As far as the "Negro question" goes, it means simply this: Either the
> whites organize the Negroes, or the bosses will organize the Negroes
> against the whites, in which last case it is hardly up to the whites to damn
> the "niggers." Southern workers ought to realize that while there are two
> colors among the workers in the South there is actually only one class. It
> is the object of this organization . . . to teach that the only hope of the
> workers is through industrial organization, that while the colors in ques-
> tion are two, the class in question is only one; that the first thing for a
> real workingman to do is to learn by a little study that he belongs to the
> working class, line up with the Brotherhood of Timber Workers or the
> Industrial Workers of the World, and make a start for industrial freedom.[18]

Up to this point the brotherhood, although friendly to the Wobblies,
had not affiliated with the IWW. But as the AF of L continued to show
no interest in a movement in which the number of Negroes was substantial, the brotherhood turned to the IWW. The leaders of the B of TW
and the IWW agreed to affiliate, and Bill Haywood and Covington
Hall were sent to the brotherhood's convention at Alexandria, Louisiana,
in May, 1912, to present the case to the delegates.

At the convention, Haywood expressed surprise that no Negroes were
present. He was informed that the blacks were meeting separately in
another hall because it was against the law in Louisiana for whites and
Negroes to meet together. Haywood declared:

> You work in the same mills together. Sometimes a black man and a white
> man chop down the same tree together. You are meeting in convention to
> discuss the conditions under which you labor. This can't be done intelli-
> gently by passing resolutions here and then sending them out to another
> room for the black man to act upon. Why not be sensible about this and
> call the Negroes into this convention? If it is against the law, this is one
> time when the law should be broken.

Covington Hall told the delegates that he supported Haywood's suggestion completely. "Let the Negroes come together with us, and if any
arrests are made, all of us will go to jail, white and colored together."

The blacks were called into the session. The mixed gathering adopted
the proposal to affiliate with the IWW and elected black and white
delegates to the September convention of that organization in Chicago,
where the merger would be formally effected.

Haywood and Hall also addressed a mass meeting at the Alexandria
Opera House under the brotherhood's sponsorship. Here, too, for the
first time in the city's history, there was no segregation. (Not even the
Socialist Party in Louisiana had allowed Negroes and whites to meet
together.) "There was no interference by the management or the police," Haywood reported later, "and the meeting had a tremendous effect
on the workers who discovered that they could mingle in meetings as

they mingled at work." *Solidarity* featured the news from Alexandria under the heading: "Rebels of the New South No Longer Fighting to Uphold Slavery but to Abolish It." The *Industrial Worker* carried the news under the heading: "Miracle of the New South."[19]

The convention's vote to affiliate with the IWW was overwhelmingly confirmed by the brotherhood's rank-and-file membership in a general referendum in July. At the September convention of the IWW, the merger was consummated, and the Brotherhood of Timber Workers became the Southern District of the National Industrial Union of Forest and Lumber Workers.

Space does not permit a full account of the moving story of the Southern lumber workers after the decision to affiliate with the IWW. Suffice it to say that the feudal-minded lumber barons made intense efforts to destroy the unity of black and white workers and to smash the union. They resorted to every weapon in the arsenal of antiunionism: blacklisting of union members; arrest and trial of the president and sixty-four leading members, Negro and white; eviction of union members from company houses; and spreading the charge throughout the South that the union was a revolutionary organization that sought, through its policy of equality for black and white, to undermine the entire fabric of Southern society.

None of the measures succeeded. The men brought to trial were acquitted, after having been held in jail for four months. On November 11, 1913, nine days after the close of their trial, 1,300 union men—whites, Indians, and Negroes—went on strike at the American Lumber Company in Merryville, Louisiana, in the biggest strike in the brotherhood's history.

Soon after the strike began, the company began shipping in nonunion crews, mostly blacks from other parts of Louisiana and Texas. The Negro quarters were surrounded with a high barbed-wire fence charged with electricity to keep the strikers from talking to the scabs, but the strikers got to them nevertheless. The railroad track was lined with pickets for four miles on each side of town, and as the trains carrying the scabs slowed down to enter Merryville leaflets were thrown through the windows announcing that a strike was taking place and appealing "to you colored wage workers of Louisiana and Texas to do your duty by the lumberjacks of Merryville, white, Indian and Negro."

Many of the imported blacks refused to enter the mill and quite a few joined the strikers. Foreign-born workers and Mexicans who were brought in as scabs also showed their solidarity with the strikers. The union pointed out in a widely published statement:

> It is a glorious thing to see, the miracle that has happened here in Dixie. This is coming true of the "impossible"—this union of workers regardless of color, creed or nationality. To hear the Americans saying, "You can starve us, but you cannot whip us"; the Negroes saying, "You can fence us in, but you cannot make us scab!" Never did the Sante Fe Railroad, the Southern Lumber Operators' Association and the American Lumber Company expect to see such complete and defiant solidarity.

The black and white lumberjacks raised the battle cry "Don't be a Peon! Be a Man!" Daily meetings were held, addressed by both white and black speakers. Union solidarity defeated attempt after attempt by the company to create division among the workers. One IWW organizer said that the entire working class "may feel proud of the solidarity displayed by these fighting timbermen and their wives and daughters. . . . For be it known that many of the colored men belonging to Local 218 [of the brotherhood] are standing pat with their white fellow slaves; and also be it known that the writer has realized for years that all the colored workers needed was for the white workers 'to meet them half way,' and they will always respond eager and anxious to fight for to better their conditions." He noted that "our colored fellow-workers showed their solidarity by walking out with their white comrades," and no amount of terror could induce them to scab. "They were arrested and jailed on different absurd charges, such as 'unlawfully meeting in the same hall with white men,' but they laughingly lined up and marched to the town bastille, singing the rebel songs they had learned at their daily mass meetings in the Union Hall, and despite threats, after their release, they appeared in greater number the next day to hear speakers, and sing more songs to fan the flames of discontent."

The company recruited a gang of strong-arm men. A characteristic "public-spirited" committee named the "Good Citizens League" was formed by the community's principal businessmen, who sided with the company. The strong-arm men were taken into the "league" and were made deputy sheriffs.

The company, in conjunction with the "Good Citizens League" and the city authorities, launched its main attack on the union. The deputies molested Negro strikers and ransacked their homes. On January 9, 1913, Robert Allen, a black striker who had been one of the most faithful pickets, was arrested at a union meeting and taken to jail. No warrant was produced, nor was any reason given for the arrest. The same evening Allen was deported from Merryville. The following night several other strikers received the same treatment.

On February 16, 1913, the vigilante offensive against the union reached a climax as the lumber company, aided by many townspeople, unleashed a chain of mob violence aimed at driving out all union people. Five organizers were kidnapped, and four of them were terribly beaten and deported. F. W. Oliver, a Negro, was shot. The businessmen, gunmen, and company employees who were creating the riots had decided to make an example of Oliver so as to intimidate black strikers. On February 18, another mob of gunmen and citizens league members raided the union headquarters and carried all books and papers into the offices of the American Lumber Company. That same day, the mob deported the acting secretary of the union and tore down the tent in which the strikers' soup kitchen was housed. On February 19, all remaining union men in Merryville were deported under penalty of death if they returned. Union signs were torn from shops and houses. Citizens were searched without warrant, and anyone found with a union leaflet or circular on him was arrested. The town of Merryville was completely in the hands of the mob as company gunmen armed with rifles, many deputized as sheriffs, marched through the streets, terrorizing every family.

The union tried to get Governor Hall to halt the reign of terror. But the governor, charging that the union, by allowing Negroes to meet with whites in the same union halls, was seeking to destroy the Southern way of life, refused to act.[20]

The four-day wave of mob violence broke the back of the strike. Most of the strikers were blacklisted throughout the entire Southern lumber industry. Everywhere in the South the union met the same experience: mob violence, attacks by gunmen, arrests and deportation of union members. Appeals to governors, even to the Presidᵊnt of the United States, brought only silence. Everywhere, too, in the face of the terror, black and white timber workers continued to meet together to plan resistance. Mary White Ovington noted: "Only one familiar with the South can appreciate the courage of this position, and the bravery demanded of both races."[21]

But courage was not enough. By the spring of 1914, the Brotherhood of Timber Workers had been effectively destroyed. Yet, with the IWW, which influenced and inspired its stand, the brotherhood left a noble tradition of militant struggle and labor solidarity, uniting black and white workers as never before in a Southern industry. Selig Perlman and Philip Taft were plainly incorrect when they wrote in 1935: "The IWW was acutely aware of the danger of raising or even appearing to raise the issue of race equality in a Southern community where even the workers for whom it was leading this fight might have been completely alienated by that issue."[22] The IWW did raise the issue of race equality in the lumber communities of the South, and it was the lumber companies and their allies, not the workers, who were "completely alienated by that issue."

Despite its policy of integrated activity, the IWW never succeeded in recruiting the great masses of black workers. The vast majority of blacks in the South were sharecroppers and tenant farmers. They lived in communities where even the attempt to unionize would have brought wholesale arrests, imprisonments, and lynchings. By the time blacks began entering Northern industries in considerable numbers, after 1915, the IWW, as we shall see, was in the process of being savagely destroyed. Yet at the height of their influence and power, before World War I, the Wobblies united black and white workers as never before in American history and maintained solidarity and equality regardless of race or color such as most labor organizations have yet to equal.

8 The Black Worker on the Eve of World War I

In 1914 Negro labor was overwhelmingly concentrated in agriculture and personal and domestic services. According to the census of 1910, more than half of the 5,192,535 Negroes listed as gainfully employed—2,881,454—were engaged in agricultural pursuits. Another fourth—1,357,598—were employed in domestic and personal services. No other group in the American population showed such a vast preponderance of its workers in the two lowest-paid occupations.

The vast majority of the Negro people still lived in the South and were still the chief cultivators of the South's staple crops, enmeshed in a farm tenantry and sharecropping system that consigned them to a life of tilling the soil under conditions almost as restrictive and pernicious as chattel slavery, in rural isolation and a state of perpetual indebtedness. The lien laws required the tenant or sharecropper to liquidate his debts before he could escape from his share-tenant arrangement, hence he was bound to the soil and denied any opportunity for industrial training.

When the Industrial Revolution swept through the South after 1880, jobs in the new textile, iron, and steel factories fell to the poor whites. The black man's share of the South's industrial development was limited to the dirty, disagreeable tasks of unskilled labor. Of course, there were black miners, especially in Alabama, where 46.2 per cent of the coal miners in 1889 were Negroes. But many of them worked under the convict lease system. In January, 1888, the State of Alabama gave an exclusive contract to the Tennessee Coal, Iron and Railroad Company, the chief coal operator in the state, on condition that the company use all convicts who were able to work. Blacks were arrested for trivial reasons or for no reason at all and sentenced to work out their penalty in the mines. The contract gave the company cheap labor—it compensated the state at a rate ranging from $9.00 to $18.00 a month per convict, depending on his classification—and at the same time saved the state money. In other Southern states, especially Georgia, the convict-lease system supplied cheap black labor to companies building railroads or cutting timber.

The blacks who gravitated in increasing numbers to Southern cities moved into personal and domestic service, traditionally regarded as the province of the Negro. They found employment in urban districts throughout the South as waiters, saloonkeepers, bartenders, janitors, bellhops, barbers, laundresses, and housekeepers. The few who ventured North also found domestic work to be one of the few occupations open to the Negro, although there the black worker had to compete with foreign immigrants even for menial positions.

A small but growing segment of the black working force broke out of the traditional pattern of agricultural and domestic employment and gained entrance to manufacturing, mechanical, trade, transportation, and other industrial pursuits. From 1890 to 1910 there was a sizable increase of black workers in trade and transportation occupations. In 1890 the number of Negroes engaged in those two fields was 145,717; by 1910 the total had more than doubled.

Almost one-third of the black workers in trade and transportation were railroad workers. The large increase in black railroad workers resulted from the expanding network of railroad construction in the South. Companies engaged in these operations, always in need of a large labor force, looked upon the Negro as an important source of cheap labor for rough, heavy work. Only 4.1 per cent of the blacks in railroad work were classified as skilled employees; the vast majority were used in repairing and maintaining the road beds. Blacks who held skilled or responsible jobs on the railroads in the South were found primarily in such positions as locomotive engineers, firemen, brakemen, switchmen, and yard foremen. Most Negroes in railroad jobs in the North held positions in the Pullman Service as waiters or porters. As we have seen, the rise of the railroad brotherhoods, with their bitter animosity toward the Negro, caused a decrease in the number of blacks in skilled jobs after 1890. The determined assault of the brotherhoods against the skilled black worker had by the outbreak of World War I resulted in his exclusion from almost all responsible positions on the railroads.

The second largest group of blacks in trade and transportation were the Negro teamsters, draymen, hackmen, and chauffeurs, who more than doubled in number between 1890 and 1910. In the South nearly 100,000 blacks were employed in these positions, indicative of the region's custom of acknowledging certain low-level jobs as "Negro work." The scattered black workmen who held jobs of this nature in the North and West were able to obtain employment primarily because whites in those sections of the country preferred more remunerative factory work.

The remainder of the Negroes in trade and transportation held a wide variety of subordinate positions, such as porters, helpers, longshoremen, hostlers, clerks, copyists, and small merchants. The number of Negroes in trade or business was negligible. Race prejudice on the part of white employers and workers alike restricted all but the most gifted and fortunate Negro salesmen, bookkeepers, typists, and clerks to the Negro business world.

Some Negroes managed to gain clerical positions in federal and state governments by passing competitive examinations. But the pattern of segregation on the state level limited the number, and during the first year of Woodrow Wilson's administration, with the institution of segregated toilets, lunchroom facilities, and working areas in a number of federal departments, federal employment also became constricted for blacks.

The growing number of blacks in manufacturing and mechanical jobs between 1890 and 1910 indicated an industrial advance of the black worker. In 1910 there were more than 500,000 blacks in skilled and unskilled industrial jobs throughout the nation, a 165.1 per cent increase in black industrial workers over the preceding twenty-year period.

The heaviest concentration of Negroes in industry was in Southern lumber and mining establishments. In lumber manufacturing alone, rapid expansion saw the number of black workers increase fivefold from 1890 to 1910. The 122,216 Negroes at work in lumbering in 1910 represented almost one-fifth of all black workers in industry. Negro miners were to be found predominantly in the Deep South and the central Appalachian coal fields of West Virginia, Kentucky, and Virginia, but a growing number gained employment around the turn of the century in such Northern states as Ohio, Indiana, Illinois, and Iowa. Although he first gained admittance to the Northern mines as a strike-breaker, the Negro was soon an established quantity in the industry. Lumbering and mining involved hard, distasteful, and dangerous work at long hours for low wages, a fact that no doubt contributed to the Negro's substantial employment in these industries.[1]

Black workers in the iron and steel industry grew from 8,371 in 1890 to 36,646 in 1910, an increase of 325 per cent. Nearly all of the increase took place in the iron and steel factories of the South, where the black workman was a common sight, toiling at rugged, low-paying, unskilled tasks. North of the Mason-Dixon line, few Negroes were found in iron and steel work. Joseph Frazier Wall notes in his definitive biography of Andrew Carnegie that the iron and steel multimillionaire "made generous contributions to Hampton and Tuskegee Institutes" and "never entirely lost interest in the Blacks." However, there were few Negroes in Carnegie's plants, because, Wall explains, "almost none came North to work in his steel mills or mines." Yet prior to World War I the Carnegie Company regularly sent agents to recruit immigrants in Europe for work in the Homestead mills. It dispatched no recruiters South for black workers to work in the Carnegie mills. The contradiction between Carnegie's interest in industrial education for blacks and his preference for foreign labor in his mills puzzled the *Christian Recorder*, which could only surmise that Carnegie, "himself a foreigner, was in natural sympathy with that element and gave them preference."[2]

The preference for white immigrant labor in unskilled and semiskilled capacities extended throughout Northern industry. Most immigrants from Southeastern Europe arrived as unskilled peasants, so it could hardly be argued that they were more experienced as industrial workers than Negroes. But they obtained work when Negroes could not. Ironically, a few light-skinned Negroes did manage to get work in the basic industries by posing as foreigners and affecting an Italian or Slavic accent.

Only Cyrus McCormick's harvester plant in Chicago was willing to integrate blacks in its labor force. Robert Ozanne points out in his study of International Harvester's labor policies, however, that its black workers "were carefully selected so that the first Negroes working in any department were 'superior both in qualifications and personality' to the white workers in the department."[3] And this was hailed as equality for black workers!

Virtually the only means by which blacks could challenge the monopoly of foreign immigrants in the developing mass-production industries, even as unskilled workers, was by strike-breaking. Some were able to enter the iron and steel and meatpacking industries by this route.

Blacks registered few gains in such important light manufacturing pursuits as the garment, tobacco, and textile industries. They did not gain widespread employment in the textile mills despite the fact that textile manufacturing in the South was undergoing its greatest advances. For one thing, white mill employees flatly refused to work alongside Negroes. A strike at the Fulton Bag and Cotton Mill in Atlanta in 1897 was described by the Atlanta *Constitution* as a "spontaneous protest against the employment of twenty Negro women spinners, who were to work along with white women." The 1,400 strikers returned to work only after the manager agreed to the "discharge of all Negroes employed by the company except janitors and scrubbers." Another barrier was the mythology that black workers did not measure up to conditions in the textile mills. "A notion is abroad in the South," wrote James Dowd in *The Forum* of June, 1898, "that the Negro could not work in a cotton mill, because the hum of the looms would put him to sleep." But a Southern industrialist gave a more likely explanation: "It is a question of who will do the dirty work. In this country the white man won't. The Negro must." Then again, the legal system of white supremacy extended into the factory. South Carolina laws forbade Negroes and whites to work together in the same room in a textile factory and to use the same pay windows, or the same toilet and drinking facilities, or even "the same doors of entrance and exit at the time time . . . or . . . the same stairway or windows at the same time." It was obviously cheaper to operate a textile factory with poor whites, including white child labor, than with blacks and whites on the basis required by Jim Crow legislation. Black workers rebuffed by the cotton mills were somewhat more successful in finding employment in cottonseed-oil plants, fertilizer factories, brick- and tile-making plants, bakeries, and other small industries in the South.[4]

Although the black worker was increasingly employed in the heavy industries between 1890 and 1914, the Negro artisan and mechanic class experienced no improvement in employment opportunities. Instead, the skilled black craftsman declined in importance, even in the South. The black poet and novelist James Weldon Johnson, in his autobiography, recalls Negro artisans in Jacksonville and elsewhere in the South during the 1880's:

All the more interesting things that came under my observation were being done by colored men. They drove the horse and mule teams, they built the houses, they laid the bricks, they painted the buildings and fences, they loaded and unloaded the ships. When I was a child, I did not know that there existed such a thing as a white carpenter or bricklayer or plasterer or tinner. The thought that the white men might be able to load and unload the heavy drays of the big ships was too far removed from everyday life to enter my mind.[5]

By the mid-1890's, however, the Negro's advancement in the trades of the South was already being seriously checked. By 1899 the Virginia Commissioner of Labor reported that there were "fewer skilled Negro laborers in the state than there were before the Civil War." Substantially the same picture emerged from reports in other Southern states.

New machine processes were making the skills of many black craftsmen superfluous, just as they were the skills of white mechanics. Then, too, the black craftsman, often poorly trained, found it difficult to meet the standards of workmanship set by his white competitors even in the new industrial South. Industrial schools like Tuskegee and Hampton did little to improve the efficiency of the black skilled laboring force. In 1910 there were 119 schools in the country offering some type of industrial training for Negroes. Du Bois found that, as a general rule, the caliber of industrial training at them was abysmally low. "Negro youths," he protested, "are being taught the technique of a rapidly disappearing age of handicraft." He concluded that the primitive instruction given Negroes in such institutions perpetuated the black's status as an inferior craftsman and left him completely unequipped to gain a solid footing in the industrial life of the country.[6]

The trouble was that even blacks as good as or better than white workers had little chance to earn a living as skilled artisans. The Reverend C. S. Smith of Nashville, a critic of Booker T. Washington, wrote in 1899:

> How can the multiplication of Negro mechanics help to solve the so-called race problem, when those who are already skilled cannot obtain employment? In this city, to my personal knowledge, there are a score or more of skilled Negro mechanics who are subject to enforced idleness by reason of the colorphobia which dominates the trade-unions. Those who are disposed to advance the Negro's best interests can render him invaluable services by demanding, in tones of thunder loud and long, that the trade-unions shall cease to draw the color line, and that fitness and character shall be the only passport to their fellowship. When this barrier shall have been removed, the time for the multiplication of Negro mechanics, on anything like a large scale, will have become opportune, but not until then.[7]

The Reverend Smith's identification of trade-union exclusion of blacks as a key factor in the deteriorating condition of the black artisan was accurate. In the South, trade-union opposition to the black craftsman was the spearhead of a general drive by white workingmen to oust Negroes from skilled positions they had held since slavery. Beginning in the 1890's, white workers steadily eliminated black labor from jobs in the shipping, railroad, and building industries in the older Southern sea-

board cities. The jobs of electricians, plumbers, gasfitters and steamfitters, railroad engineers and firemen, stationary engineers, cranemen,
hoistmen, and machinists and hundreds of other skilled and semiskilled
occupations were labeled "for whites only." A severe blow was dealt to
the Negro in the building trades. Black electricians, plumbers, pipefitters, and carpenters had constituted a fair percentage of those crafts at
the turn of the century. A generation later, Negro building-trades work
had become "almost marginal," and by 1950 Negroes accounted for only
1 per cent of the electricians and 3.2 per cent of the carpenters. The figures on Negro participation in apprenticeship programs were even
bleaker: 1 per cent for plumbers and pipefitters, and 6 per cent for carpenters. In Atlanta the proportion of Negro carpenters decreased from
36.3 per cent in 1890 to 2.5 percent in 1920.

By 1898 John Stephens Durham, a black authority on the Negro
working class, was describing how, "as a result of the old guild idea of
exclusiveness" in many important crafts and industries in the South, the
Negro was being restricted to the lowest menial jobs. Writing in 1936,
George Sinclair Mitchell observed that "the Southern trade unionism
of the last thirty-odd years has been in good measure a protective device
for the march of white artisans in places held by Negroes." The white
worker and his trade union displaced black labor on street railways, in
firemen's jobs on railroads, in the jobs of switchmen and shopworkers,
in construction work and shipbuilding, and in hotel service and barber-
ing. Mitchell wrote that the "typical city central labor body of Mobile
or Savannah or Columbia or New Orleans or Richmond was a delegate
meeting of white men drawn from white locals, jealous of every skilled
place held by Negroes." Blacks who had spent years acquiring the skill
needed for craftsmen's work were denied membership in white unions,
which had signed closed-shop or union-shop agreements with employers,
and were forced into menial service at low wages.[8]

The few blacks in the cotton mills were excluded from the AF of L's
United Textile Workers and were left out as well of that organization's
limited schemes to advance the interests of workers in the industry. In
the tobacco factories of Virginia and North Carolina, where the machine jobs were reserved for white workers and the blacks were confined
to the least desirable and most unhealthy jobs, the Tobacco Workers'
International Union, affiliated to the AF of L, scarcely reached the
blacks in its feeble efforts to organize the industry. In November, 1903,
the Rucker and Witten Tobacco Company of Martinsville, Virginia,
eager to obtain the union label, asked the Tobacco Workers' International Union to organize its plant. The offer was rejected on the ground
that "nine-tenths of the labor employed is negroes, and this class cannot be successfully organized into a union."[9]

In his 1898 inquiry, Durham found the effects of the unions' black-
exclusion policy even "more manifest" in the North. His own city, Philadelphia, offered a convincing illustration. By the 1850's blacks had been
pushed out of the skilled trades they had once dominated by German
immigrants and out of unskilled work by the Irish. During the Civil

War, with increased demands for labor, job opportunities for blacks picked up, but they declined again in the postwar years. On July 12, 1888, the *Christian Recorder*, published in Philadelphia, lamented:

> Competency behind a black face, everything else being equal to the best, weighs very little when applying for a position in Wanamaker's store, or Sharpless's, or Strawbridge & Clothier's, or on the Philadelphia street-car lines, or even on the bricklayer's scaffold. Our chances are not equal. Color is too often pitted against color, rather than competency compared with competency.

Ten years later, Durham observed that "today one may safely declare that all the trades . . . are closed against the colored workman," and for this he blamed both the employers and the trade unions.

In his monumental study of the Philadelphia Negro, published in 1899, Du Bois summed up the job situation for blacks:

> No matter how well trained a Negro may be, or how fitted for work of any kind, he cannot in the course of competition hope to be much more than a menial servant. . . .
> He cannot become a mechanic except for small transient jobs, and he cannot join a trades union.
> A Negro woman has but three careers open to her in this city; domestic service, sewing, or married life.

When the Armstrong Association began in 1908 as a social experiment dedicated to the welfare of the black citizens of Philadelphia, it discovered that the situation described by Du Bois had not changed in the slightest. Negroes were still fixed in domestic service and as common laborers in trade and transportation. They were still unable to enter factory work in any numbers. They still could not join the city's unions. The Philadelphia *Public Ledger* of April 13, 1913, reported:

> The negroes in this section are practically shut out from all the skilled industries. The department stores may draw attention to the underpaid shop girl, but the few colored women who find employment in them receive less pay than the sales people. The colored waitress receives a child's pay. The other opportunities open to negroes in big stores are limited to portering and operating elevators. The great railway systems, too, discriminate against the negro, and here he is limited, no matter how high a degree of efficiency he may attain, to the menial and poorly paid tasks. Our street railways, with their thousands of workmen in the semi-skilled trades, completely bar the colored man. He is excluded from practically all the great industrial plants. This exclusion is especially striking in one great shop that at this minute employs more than 19,000 men daily, but carefully avoids the negro. In brief, the negro is denied the opportunity to earn an honest living in most of the big industries and commercial enterprises of this city.[10]

What was true of Philadelphia was true of much of the State of Pennsylvania. In the entire state, a study revealed in 1911, fewer than 200 blacks boasted skilled union status. And what was true of Pennsylvania was true of the entire North and West. Studies made of the

Negro in Saint Louis, Chicago, New York, Cleveland, San Francisco, and Portland, Oregon, reveal the futility of efforts to breach the barrier of employer and trade-union hostility.[11] Black workers were generally excluded from the trades and played no active part in the industrial life of those cities. "Manufacturers were not reconciled to hiring them; white workers were not reconciled to working with them," a study of the status of the black worker in Ohio concluded. There were few black members of the unions that dominated the trades of that state on the eve of World War I.

The restrictive membership policy of the trade unions in the North adversely affected immigrant and women workers as well as Negroes, but they hit the black artisan the hardest because he had to combat racism as well as the unions' practice of trying to limit the number of workers in the trades. In some Northern industrial districts unions were less restrictive toward foreign-born whites, but the pattern of union discrimination against blacks was followed in every city. Little wonder that the annual earnings of black workers in 1910 were just about one-third the earnings of white workers. Or that W. E. B. Du Bois could write sadly in 1913: "The net result of all this has been to convince the American Negro that his greatest enemy is not the employer who robs him, but his fellow white workingman."[12]

On the eve of World War I the black wage-earner had still to claim a place in America's developing industrial society. The millions of workers who toiled in the mines, packing houses, steel works, manufacturing plants, and transportation industries represented a bewildering variety of races and nationalities from the far corners of the globe. But it was rare to see among them one of those whose ancestors had first arrived in Virginia in 1619. Rarer still was a black face in the ranks of the nation's working elite, the trade unionists. The total Negro membership in the AF of L at that time is impossible to determine accurately, but a generous estimate would put it at about 55,000, only 3.6 per cent of the 1,526,000 workingmen in the federation.

Racism was still the main reason for the Negro's economic stagnation. Negro leaders insisted that fifty years of freedom had brought scant improvement in the black man's lot, and they despaired of the future. William L. Bulkley, one of the founders of the National Urban League, declared that "there seems to be a purpose to restrict the Negroes within the limits of unskilled labor, to reduce them to a state which, while not nineteenth-century slavery, may be twentieth-century peonage." A black minister stated forlornly: "The young colored men and girls who are graduating from the high schools, the normal schools, and the colleges don't want to be waiting maids and porters or elevator operators, and yet this is about the highest they can hope for in this country."[13]

In July, 1911, Ida Wells-Barnett, a militant black woman, wrote that the key problem facing the black worker, skilled and unskilled, was "the problem of unemployment. To him, especially, it comes with crushing force, for whatever obstacles handicap other working classes, no others of them suffer from the barrier of color. With all the others the question when seeking work is, What and how much work can you do? With him the primary question is, Have you negro blood in your veins?" She continued:

> The black man who has a trade at his fingers' ends finds all forces combined to prevent him from making a living thereby. First, the employer tells him that he has no prejudice against color, but that his employes will object and make his business suffer. If perchance the Negro gets by, is given a chance to make good, the employes in the office, factory and workshop combine to injure his work and to make life miserable for him. The unskilled laborer, who has little of such competition is a shade better off, because his work is usually done alone; but even there he finds that the neighbors of his employer have white servants and that neighbors and white servants look askance at a man who prefers Negro help.[14]

Just when the future seemed to hold out little hope of improvement in the status of the black worker, an important milestone occurred in Negro industrial history. The great migration of 1915–18 saw blacks leave the South by the hundreds of thousands for the job opportunities and freer life available in the North and West.

9 The Rise of the Black Industrial Working Class, 1915–18

Before 1915 the treatment of the Southern Negro caused a steady trickle northward. From 1916 through 1918 the trickle became a flood that brought hundreds of thousands of blacks to the North. Earlier migrations to Northern cities had come from the Upper South. Now blacks came in from all over Dixie, with the Deep South having the heaviest representation.

Many explanations have been advanced to account for the great migration of Negroes during World War I. Surely the general status of the Negro in the South, his lack of political rights, social subordination, economic peonage, poor educational facilities, intimidation, and segregation, contributed prominently. But the fundamental motivating force, as in the migration of any people, was economic—the great magnet of employment opportunities. In 1913–14 the country had been in a minor depression, but beginning in 1915 American industry—largely concentrated in the North—entered a period of great prosperity, stimulated by the demands of the war in Europe and, later on, by the war needs of the United States itself. A great demand for labor arose in such industries as steel, meat-packing, automobile manufacture, munitions, shipyards, mines, transportation enterprises, and many others that directly or indirectly played a role in war production.

In the past the immigrant masses had provided the industrial North with a cheap, readily available labor supply. But the war drastically curtailed the flow of immigrants: the volume declined from 1,218,480 in 1914 to 326,700 in 1915, 298,826 in 1916, 295,403 in 1917, and 110,618 in 1918. Moreover, 500,000 immigrants already in the United States left for Europe between 1915 and 1918 to serve in the armed forces of their native lands. With more than 4,000,000 men drafted into the armed services of the United States when war was declared on Germany in April, 1917, the need for workers to take the more skilled jobs of the draftees and to fill unskilled jobs became acute.

In the half-century between emancipation and the outbreak of World War I, blacks, with few exceptions, had been unable to get work in the North except in domestic and personal occupations. But now, with the nation's usual labor force enormously depleted, Northern industrialists eagerly turned to the Southern Negroes, women as well as men, the only untapped source of common labor remaining in the country.

An intensive campaign was launched to recruit Southern blacks. American firms had employed labor recruiters for work among European peasants for decades, but this was the first time agents went South to bring black peasants to the North. The agents, sent by railroad and steel companies, initiated the migration by promising high wages, offering transportation subsidies, and distributing leaflets like the following, scattered throughout Alabama:

> Are you happy with your pay envelope? Would you like to go North where the laboring man shares the profits with the Boss? Are you satisfied with your condition here? Has your family all the comforts they should have during these prosperous times or are you just making "Both Ends Meet" while the other fellow is growing rich on your labor? . . . Let's Go Back North. Where no trouble or labor exists, no strikes, no lock outs, large coal, good wages, fair treatment, two weeks pay, good houses. If you haven't got all these things you had better see us. Will send you where you can have all these things. All colored ministers can go free. Will advance you money if necessary. Go now. While you have the chance.[1]

In addition to the cost of transporting the worker, this particular agency offered to pay the fare for his family, the freight charges on his household goods, and a "reasonable amount" of what he owed in his present town.

Northern industries also asked the National Urban League's assistance in enlisting black labor as a replacement for the dwindling number of immigrant workers. The league helped to recruit blacks for Northern industry and aided them in their adjustment to life in the North.

The black press (more than 400 periodicals) also stimulated the trek of blacks northward. The Chicago *Defender* was the most influential voice, reaching thousands of Southern Negroes with blistering attacks on life in the South and glowing reports of the high wages and better social conditions in the "Negro Heaven" north of the Mason-Dixon line. Letters from blacks who had already moved North were especially influential. In some states the demand for labor had sent wages for the unskilled as high as thirty-six cents an hour, and even the eighteen to twenty cents hourly wage for unskilled workers on the railroads was considerably above what blacks commanded in the South. In Chicago, Saint Louis, East Saint Louis, Detroit, and Milwaukee, a black worker could make more money in a week than he could for a month's hard toil in the South, where farm laborers averaged fifty to eighty cents a day, and those who worked on cottonseed-oil mills, sawmills, and turpentine refineries received only slightly more. Further, the ravages of the boll weevil and the disastrous crop failure of 1916 had left thousands of agricultural laborers and sharecroppers without the means of subsistence. As landlords by the hundreds dismissed their tenants and laborers, the lure of a living wage in the North became irresistible.

With the improving economic situation after 1916, Southern landowners began to fear that the mass departure of Southern blacks would deplete their usual labor supply. "If the Negroes go," asked the Montgomery *Advertiser* in September, 1916, "where shall we get labor to take their places?"[2] Legislation was enacted on local and state levels to protect the cheap labor supply. Recruiters were charged prohibitive license fees and subjected to strict regulations, with heavy fines and imprisonment imposed for violators. To stop the migration, Du Bois notes, the South "mobilized all the machinery of modern oppression: taxes, city ordinances, licenses, state laws, municipal regulations, wholesale arrests, and, of course, the peculiar Southern method of the mob and lyncher."[3]

But such efforts came too late and were too easily circumvented to stem the northward tide of the blacks. Ray Stannard Baker wrote: "Trains were backed into Southern cities and hundreds of Negroes were gathered up in a day, loaded into cars and whirled away to the North. Instances are given showing that Negroes teamsters left their horses standing in the streets or deserted their jobs and went to the trains without notifying their employers or even going home."[4]

Black workers rushed to the mines of West Virginia, and the industries of New Jersey, Pennsylvania, New York, Ohio, and Illinois. Between 1910 and 1920 the black population in Chicago increased from 44,000 to 109,000; in New York from 92,000 to 152,000; in Detroit from 6,000 to 41,000; and in Philadelphia from 84,000 to 134,000. The labor-recruiting efforts of Chicago's packing houses and the Illinois Central Railroad, together with the appeals of the Chicago *Defender*, made that city a magnet for penniless sharecroppers in the South. Some moved along to Detroit, where the pressure of wartime needs forced open the automobile plants to Negroes. In April, 1917, a survey of twenty of the largest firms of Detroit, mostly manufacturers of automobiles and automobile accessories, showed a total of 2,874 black workers employed. Only two years before black employment in industrial Detroit had been practically nonexistent.

The decade 1910 to 1920 saw a net increase of 322,000 in the number of Southern-born blacks living in the North, exceeding the aggregate increase of the preceding forty years. Although the increase is less than the general estimates made at the height of the migration, it is still an impressive figure. Even more impressive is the fact that the booming wartime labor demands of rail lines, factories, foundries, mines, and packing houses, at a time when the normal supply of cheap labor was shut off, opened these industries for the first time to the black worker. Thus, with the outbreak of World War I and the great migration of 1915–18, the first black industrial working class in the United States came into existence.

In Chicago manufacturing industries in 1920 an average of 16 per cent of the working forces was black, with the percentage rising to 23 in the nonmanufacturing industries. The number of black workers in American industry nearly doubled from 1910 to 1920, from 551,825 to 901,181. The largest gain occurred in iron and steel, automotive, mining, shipbuilding, and meat-packing occupations. A smaller increase occurred in trade and transportation activities, mainly among railroad workers engaged in road repair and maintenance of way work. Negro longshoremen increased from 16,405 in 1910 to 27,400 in 1920, and there was also a rise in the number of black chauffeurs, hack drivers, and garage workers.

Between 1890 and 1920 the number of black workers in agriculture and in domestic and personal service increased by 552,634, or 20.5 per cent. During the same three decades, the number of Negroes engaged in manufacturing and mechanical work, trade, and transportation grew from 354,091 to 1,354,838, an increase of 282.5 per cent. In 1920 one-third of all gainfully employed Negroes were working in American industry.

The employment of blacks in occupations opened by the wartime demand helped, as Herbert J. Seligman put it, to "dispel the myth that the American Negro was at best an agricultural laborer and that complicated industrial processes overtaxed his abilities."[5] A contemporary government study of the migration, based on interviews with employment managers and higher executives in Northern industry, found them so worried by the acute labor shortage that they were in no mood for mythology. "The majority of executives interviewed were favorable to the experiment with Negro employment in the North, and were sympathetic to suggestions concerning selection, training, housing and recreation for the newcomers."[6]

The demand for black labor slackened when the war came to an end. The nation's war industries, which had depended heavily upon cheap, unskilled Negro labor, were dismantled and reconverted to peacetime production, resulting in mass discharge of black workers. In one week the American Steel Company in East Saint Louis, Illinois, reduced its work force from 1,282, to 25. Almost 700 of the discharged men were Negroes. As millions of whites returned to the ranks of industrial labor from the armed forces, employers did not hesitate to replace their black workers. Former Negro servicemen were not so lucky; in April, 1919, the Division of Negro Economics announced that 99 per cent of Chicago's black veterans were still unemployed, with little prospect of work in the immediate future. The same situation faced black ex-servicemen in other large industrial cities.

In Chicago, where as many as 10,000 black laborers were out of work, the local Association of Commerce wired to Southern Chambers of Commerce: "Are you in need of Negro labor? Large surplus here, both returned soldiers and civilian Negroes ready to work."[7] Actually, despite the demand for black labor in the South during the postwar months, very few blacks left the industrial centers of the Midwest and Northeast to take jobs offered by Southern employers.

The 1921 economic depression made the situation even more acute for black workers. In Detroit, black unemployment rates were five times as high as those of native white workers and twice as high as those of foreign-born whites. "Colored workers are the last to be hired, and first to be fired," the superintendent of the Colored Branch of the New York State Employment Bureau declared in February, 1921. "Always discriminated against by some employers, the present condition of unemployment is causing great suffering among the colored people."[8]

But the influx of Negro workers from the South did not cease. Economic recovery and the gradual elimination of foreign immigrant competition, due to the passage of restrictive immigration laws in 1921 and 1924, brought a second migration out of the South in the years 1922 to 1924. More than 500,000 Negroes took their scanty belongings and left for the North, most of them to stay. As William Graves told the Chicago Union League Club: "The Negro permanency in industry is no longer debatable."[9]

Yet the status of this work force was that of unskilled labor. "Everywhere," wrote Roger Baldwin in 1919, "the Negroes had the hardest and most disagreeable jobs."[10] Employers in both South and North agreed that the work whites usually shunned was reserved for blacks. The superintendent of a Kentucky plow factory expressed the Southern view: "Negroes do work white men won't do, such as common labor; heavy, hot, and dirty work; pouring crucibles; work in the grinding room; and so on. Negroes are employed because they are cheaper. . . . The negro does a different grade of work and makes about 10¢ an hour less."[11] A coke-works foreman in a Pennsylvania steel mill used almost the same language: "They are well fitted for this hot work, and we keep them because we appreciate this ability in them. . . . The door machines and the jam cutting are the most undesirable; it is hard to get white men to do this kind of work."[12] It was rare to find an industrialist who, like Henry Ford, in an effort to maintain influence with the black community, allowed a few blacks in his plants to be upgraded to skilled positions. The vast majority of black workers in the automobile industry, as in all industry, were confined to unskilled jobs.

This state of affairs was established during the war by employers and unions, often with government approval. The railroad lines and the railroad brotherhoods had worked out unwritten agreements confining blacks to low-level and menial occupations in railway work. When the federal government assumed control of the nation's rail network late in December, 1917, it simply sanctioned the informal agreements between railroad management and the unions by prohibiting the hiring or advancing of Negroes to positions they had not occupied in the past. Under the so-called Atlanta Agreement the Brotherhood of Railway Trainmen and the U.S. Railroad Administration—under the threat by the trainmen to tie up the Southern railroad network—agreed upon rules relating to seniority, job classification, and the composition of train crews that resulted in driving many blacks from positions they had long held on the railroads and relegating them to menial jobs.

In various shipyards around the country, employers and unions, again with government sanction, agreed not to give blacks positions above that of common laborer. Black carpenters, reamers, riveters, pipefitters, and drillers found it almost impossible to get work in the shipyards, even though men were badly needed in these occupations. Skilled blacks were forced to accept jobs as helpers to white craftsmen or as "fillers" in tasks demanding few or no skills. A skilled black shipyard worker complained to the federal government: "If . . . we are not fit to have a position as mechanics and officials then I contend we are not good enough to fight for the country."[13] A black riveter, unable to find employment at his trade in a California shipyard, wrote:

> We don't ask Social Equality, we only ask an Equal chance to take our part in the industrial world, to be given the right and opportunity to perform the work, which Almighty God saw fit to give us the brains and strength to do and for which hundreds of years in the most cruel school of slavery qualified and made us to do. . . .
>
> I beg of you to take up this matter at once, don't let the word be taken from the shipyards of America that . . . discrimination is being made in the matter of even Negro labor. What will our boys feel that they have to fight for, what hopes have they to look forward to when after the war they return and the work is done.[14]

Nothing was done during the war by employers, unions, or the federal government to eliminate the racial prejudice that prevented blacks from being hired as skilled workers. A survey published in August, 1917, found "Negro graduate engineers and electricians and experienced carpenters, painters and shipbuilders doing the work of porters, elevator men and janitors."[15] A year later, the situation was reported unchanged, and it continued after the war. A study published in 1921 by the Department of Labor, covering twenty-three establishments in five basic industries—foundries, slaughtering and meatpacking, coke ovens, iron and steel and their products, and glass manufacturing—disclosed that of eighty-five occupations in which five or more Negroes and five or more whites were employed, only eight of the occupations open to blacks were in skilled categories. Another observer of the Negro labor scene estimated in the mid-1920's that only 5 per cent of black industrial workers were in skilled jobs and 10 per cent in semiskilled positions.

While almost all black workers in industry were being kept at the level of unskilled occupations, the number of Negro artisans was declining. Between 1910 and 1920 the number of skilled blacks in the building trades increased by less than 4,000. Black plumbers, gasfitters, and steamfitters increased by only 1,000. During the same period, the number of black blacksmiths, forgemen and pressmen, builders and building contractors, millers, pressmen and plate printers, roofers and slaters, sawyers, stonemasons, and bricklayers decreased.

The decline of the Negro artisans was largely the result of factors that had been operating since the turn of the century. Most important was the hostile attitude of trade unions, which encouraged white workingmen to push the blacks out of skilled occupations and discourage black apprenticeships. In 1920 the total of white apprentices in all skilled trades was put at 144,177. The total of black apprentices was 2,067.

There is no doubt that the black worker had achieved a great industrial advance between World War I and the mid-1920's. Certainly, too, even work in the lowest industrial occupations was for many blacks an improvement over peonage in agriculture or domestic service. Even though an increased cost of living often wiped out a good part of the gains in wages, it was generally agreed that the black worker substantially improved his economic conditions by moving into Northern industry.

But the door to semiskilled and skilled occupations remained shut for the black worker. One reason for this was the racism of white employers.* Another important reason, as we shall now see, was the economic and racial prejudice of the white trade unions that dominated most of the occupations in question.

* On March 19, 1920, the New York *Call* carried an item on the New York Telephone Company's refusal to hire Negroes to meet a labor shortage. When a field secretary for the League for Democracy asked the assistant to the company's vice-president why he did not fill the 1,000 openings it claimed it had with black women, he replied that, while he "personally had no objection to colored employes, the white operators would leave en masse if they had to work side by side with colored girls." Informed that white girls were working with colored girls throughout the city, the executive stuck to his guns. "The sense of the interview with Mr. Schultz," the field secretary reported, "was that the telephone company would rather suffer complete demoralization than employ Negro girls as operators. In fact he stated as much."

10 The AF of L and the Black Worker During World War I

Many black leaders realized early in the "Great Migration" that active participation in the trade-union movement was vital to the economic future of the black working class, particularly if black workers were to rise above the unskilled level. Forward-looking labor leaders also saw that an explosive situation was developing and that the only way to prevent it from detonating, with disastrous consequences to both black and white workers, was through a change in organized labor's traditional approach to Negro labor. The *International Molders' Journal* warned: "So long as the Negroes remain unorganized they will continue to be exploited and used to break down the standard of living of not only their own race, but of all men who are forced to compete with them in the industrial field."[1] The Detroit *Labor News* asserted that the time had come for "the American Labor Movement to face squarely the fact that the Negro is a big factor in our industrial life and that he must be taken into account in the adjustment of our economic differences; never again can the Negro be ignored. Unionism must welcome the Negro to its ranks."[2]

The AF of L was slow to respond to the problems arising from the great migration. The first official reaction came at its 1916 convention. The Ohio State Federation of Labor and the Cleveland Labor Federation jointly sponsored a resolution asserting that blacks "are being brought north for the purpose of filling the places of union men demanding better conditions." Warning that the shortage of European labor guaranteed repetitions of the Ohio experience all over the North, the resolution called upon the Executive Council "to inaugurate a movement looking toward the organization of these men in the Southern states, to the end that they be instructed and educated along the lines of the trade union movement and thereby eliminate this menace to the workers of the Northern states."[3] The convention adopted the resolution and referred it to the Executive Council, which passed the matter on to Gompers. Some organizers were appointed, but they made no effort to reach black workers in either the South or the North. In the first year of the migration, some AF of L affiliates saw that their self-interest required bringing the message of unionism to blacks, but the federation did not take the matter seriously.

Before the next convention met, the urgent need for the action proposed by the Ohio labor federations was dramatically illustrated. A race riot erupted at East Saint Louis, Illinois, on July 2, 1917, less than three months after the United States declared war to save the world for democracy. Tension between whites and the black migrants over housing, transportation, and recreational facilities was a factor in the riot, but a more fundamental cause was the competition for jobs and wages. Blacks were imported to work at low wages—even though high by Southern standards—and the unskilled white workers found their own wage scales reduced as a consequence. When they organized a labor union affiliated with the AF of L and demanded higher wage scales, the employers threatened to replace them with black labor. The whites did not include blacks in their union, and so the employers were able to combat their organized efforts with Negro scabs. Organizing the blacks would have been difficult because of their suspicion of unions and their belief in employer paternalism, but because of the anti-Negro prejudice of the rank-and-file union members the effort was never even made in East Saint Louis. The number of blacks who acted as scabs was never large. But when, in April, 1917, a union-led strike against the Aluminum Ore Company was defeated with the aid of a few Negro strike-breakers, the infuriated trade unions of East Saint Louis launched a campaign not to organize the blacks but to bar further Negro migration to the city.

The unions won the support of the unorganized white unskilled workers by spreading the rumor that local manufacturers planned to bring in 10,000 to 15,000 more black laborers as part of an elaborate scheme to make East Saint Louis a Negro town. In a widely distributed letter issued on May 23, the Central Trades and Labor Union, a federation of AF of L craft unions, announced that its delegates would call upon the mayor and the city council demanding action to retard the "growing menace" created by "the influx of undesirable Negroes," and also to "devise a way to get rid of a certain portion of those who are already there."[4]

At a meeting of delegates with the mayor and the city council, the city officials were warned that if no official action was taken against the blacks, "violence" would be used to accomplish the objective. After the meeting small groups of whites attacked and beat up a half dozen blacks on the way home. The black community, fearing mob violence, began to arm in self-defense. On the night of July 1, a police car patrolling the black section of the city was mistaken for a carload of white vigilantes; rifle fire broke out, and two of the policemen in the car were shot dead. When news of the attack spread through the city the next morning, enraged mobs of white residents took to the streets and began shooting, lynching, and burning blacks wherever they found them, killing men, women, and children. For almost two days the rioting raged until order was finally restored. At least thirty-nine blacks and eight whites lost their lives in the riot, with a hundred or more injured and property damages running into the hundreds of thousands—making it one of the worst anti-Negro riots, in terms of lives lost, of the twentieth century.

Shortly after the riot, the Saint Louis *Post-Dispatch* quoted the president of the Central Trades and Labor Union of East Saint Louis as saying: "Before the tenseness of this situation is relieved these employers must convince the laboring whites that they will be given preference over imported blacks in applying for work." He and other labor leaders, including AF of L President Gompers, placed the blame for the outbreak squarely on the city's large industrial concerns, which they accused of importing Negroes from the South "to destroy organized labor, break down the standards of labor and create strife within the state."[5] Unless this practice ceased, "similar outbreaks would occur in Pittsburgh, Newark and a few other points where Southern Negroes have been induced to go in larger numbers than can be absorbed in the industries available to them."[6] Next to the industrialists, labor commentators blamed the blacks themselves for the riot, partly because they had allowed themselves to be used as strike-breakers but also because they had moved North without being ready for urban society. "There are exceptional negroes who will make good almost anywhere," wrote one commentator,

> but it is to be remembered that we are dealing with the one-tenth of the United States which for many generations to come will in some respects be inferior to the white race. Those who are constantly preaching equality of every sort to the negro race are not the real friends of the negro. While the negro should have equality of opportunity, it by no means follows that he is born with the same endowments of capabilities as the white man, and he is sure to suffer when he comes into competition with the white man in the city.[7]

After investigating the excuse offered by the unions for the riot, William English Walling, a socialist journalist, wired President Wilson: "The pretext of labor invasion from the South is invalid."[8] Black commentators agreed that employers were partly responsible for the riot by fostering competition for jobs and then standing back to watch blacks and whites kill each other. But they placed the blame chiefly on the racism of the white trade unions. Special investigators for the NAACP reported that "by all accounts of eye-witnesses, both white and black, the East St. Louis outrage was deliberately planned and executed."[9] Du Bois, however, concluded that the labor leaders in East Saint Louis had not purposely plotted the July riot or assumed direction of the massacre of Negroes; most of the whites who participated in the riot were unskilled, unorganized workers. But, he pointed out, the trade unions in East Saint Louis had excluded Negro workers from their ranks, were "antagonistic" to blacks, and had stirred up the white population against the Negroes through racist propaganda. "The result was the East St. Louis riots."[10] Ida Crouch-Hazlett wrote from East Saint Louis in the Socialist New York *Call* of July 22, 1917:

> The trouble in the East St. Louis massacre was that union men were fighting the wrong crowd. They should have been fighting the capitalists instead of their fellow workers. They should organize the blacks. This is where the American Federation of Labor has run against a snag. It has re-

sisted their organization, but the capitalists in their rush for profits are bound to bring them in. In lieu of organization, only force and barbarity are left to the union.

Stung by the criticism, the AF of L officially denied that any of its affiliates in East Saint Louis had been to blame for the riot. Yet there is little doubt that the accusation by black spokesmen that the AF of L was unwilling "to get rid of its color caste and industrial Junkerism"[11] caused consternation among the federation's leaders.

At the 1917 AF of L convention three resolutions were proposed relating to the Negro labor question. One, submitted by representatives of the black trade unions in Virginia directly affiliated with the AF of L, requested that black organizers be sent to industrial communities in cities where low wages were paid to Negroes to establish more local labor unions for black wage-earners. The second resolution, put forth by a delegate from a black railroad local, called for the appointment of a black organizer for the nearly 15,000 black laborers on the fifteen railroad lines operating in the Southeast. The third, introduced by a delegate from the San Francisco Labor Council, also called for the organization of black workers, but went on to list a number of offenses against the blacks, especially in the South, and noted that since black soldiers were fighting abroad under the slogan of democracy, it was reasonable for democracy to be extended to American blacks at home. The convention was asked to direct the Executive Council to influence the President and Congress "to the end that all of the political, civil and economic disabilities so offensive and destructive to the rights of negroes as human beings and American citizens be removed."[12]

The convention gave short shrift to the last resolution. Even the delegate who proposed it apologized for the resolution and acknowledged that the charges it contained were offensive to delegates from the South. He had simply introduced the resolution in behalf of the International Negro League out of appreciation for the support rendered his organization by black workers in a recent strike.* The Committee on Resolutions refused to approve the resolution and presented it to the convention with a special disclaimer of responsibility for any of its statements. But not even this satisfied the Southern trade unionists. Finally the delegates agreed to accept only that part of the resolution which referred to the organization of blacks.

---

* This was not the only occasion in that period when black workers rallied to the support of white labor. In the Port of Houston the Negro and white local of the International Longshoremen's Association had an agreement under which they divided the work equally. In 1914 the Southern Steamship Company offered work to Negro longshoremen only. Members of the Negro local refused to work unless members of the white local were allowed the same privilege, and they held to this demand for three years. The State Federation of Labor in 1917 adopted a resolution "endorsing the fight that the colored men have made for the white men." But at the 1917 AF of L convention the delegates of the State Federation of Labor refused to support the resolution calling for removal of "political, civil and economic disabilities" against blacks. Ruth Allen, *Chapters in the History of Organized Labor in Texas* (Austin, 1941), pp. 278–82.

The first two resolutions fared better. They were adopted by the convention and sent to the Executive Council with the recommendation that black organizers be appointed as soon as the finances of the federation permitted. The council in turn referred the resolutions to Gompers with the request that he draft a plan for organizing black workers on the Southeastern railroads. Gompers did not even bother with that request, and it was not until 1922 that the AF of L even concerned itself with organization of black railworkers in the Southeast.

Despite the fact that the delegates had in effect countenanced discrimination against blacks in America by rejecting the resolution proposed on behalf of the International Negro League, many black leaders cheered the events at the AF of L convention. The AF of L's consent to the further organization of black workers sufficed to produce a banner headline in the New York *Age* of November 22, 1917: "Negro Is Now Recognized by Federation of Labor." Many black spokesmen took the position that the AF of L had decided to strike down the color line. But there were others who were not swept off their feet. Both John R. Shilladay, Executive Secretary of the NAACP, and W. E. B. Du Bois, editor of its official organ, *The Crisis*, questioned the significance of the resolutions adopted by the delegates and doubted that even the promise to appoint black organizers would be kept. (The fact that four months after the convention not a single black organizer had been appointed lent substance to this skepticism.) In March, 1918, Du Bois wrote in *The Crisis*: "The most recent convention of the AF of L is no proof of any change of heart. Grudgingly, unwillingly, almost insultingly, this Federation yields to us inch by inch the status of half a man, denying and withholding every privilege it dares at all times."[13]

Between the 1917 and 1918 AF of L conventions, several meetings were held between a committee representing the National Urban League and a group of high-ranking federation leaders to discuss the initiation of a campaign to organize blacks in various trades, skilled and unskilled, North and South, government as well as civilian employees, and women as well as men. In the discussions, Gompers and other federation officials conceded that there were affiliates that refused to admit Negroes, but they repeatedly emphasized the AF of L position that working people must unite and organize "irrespective of creed, color, sex, nationality or politics" and that the federation welcomed "Negro workingmen to the ranks of organized labor" and would "like to see more of them join us."[14] They told the black delegation it was necessary to overcome the influence of black preachers, doctors, and heads of various fraternal societies who, with the encouragement of employers, had influenced black workers not to join unions. The black members of the Urban League committee promised to do their part to further the principles of unionism among black workers. Both parties agreed that the Negro delegation would prepare a suggested program to bring about the full participation of black workers in the organized labor movement, which would be submitted to the AF of L Executive Council for approval and then reported to the 1918 convention for action.

The memorandum was in fact submitted by Gompers to the 1918 convention in June. But the Executive Council did not call for any action on the proposal. It merely noted that the black leaders had agreed to call upon black workers to join both the regular and "Jim Crow" unions of the AF of L. Actually, the Urban League Committee, while reluctant to go as far as to urge the AF of L to include black workers in the unions already organized, had said nothing about separate unions for blacks.

The delegates at the 1918 convention referred the memorandum of the Urban League Committee to the Committee on Organization for official consideration. That body duly reported its appreciation of the black leaders' recognition of the need to organize blacks into unions affiliated with the AF of L and recommended that Gompers and the Executive Council give "special attention" to organizing Negro wage-earners in the future. Nothing was said to imply that the AF of L had not done its duty by black workers in the past, but the report conceded that with the cooperation "of leaders of the [Negro] race much better results can be accomplished."[15] The report was unanimously approved by the convention.

The Committee on Organization had said nothing about how the Negro leaders' program would be put into effect, but the Urban League committee was still optimistic. Its optimism soon vanished. After the 1918 convention, the committee made several attempts to learn what practical steps were being planned to carry out its recommendations, but not once did any federation official bother to respond.

By the time World War I came to an end on November 11, 1918, the AF of L had done nothing but discuss the problem created by the influx of black workers in industry, pat itself on the back for its past declarations, admit that more would be accomplished now that the Negro leaders saw the necessity of unionizing the black working class in affiliation with the federation, and adopt resolutions without creating effective machinery to put them in operation.

Nor was the record on the local level much better. Throughout the war evidence of discrimination by white trade unions mounted, even in federally controlled or supervised industries. In Key West, Florida, white union carpenters prevented black carpenters from working on the construction of army cantonments by charging that the blacks were not union men. The fact that the blacks had repeatedly petitioned for admittance or for separate charters and had been rejected carried no weight with the white trade union or the government. Even black union carpenters were shut out of government work because of the opposition of white unionists. In Petersburg, Virginia, thirty-six Negro carpenters, all union men, were dismissed from work at Camp Lee because white union carpenters refused to work with them.

During the war the national and local unions had grown rapidly, enrolling hundreds of thousands of new members, some even tripling in size. Few of the new members were black. Masses of Negroes had migrated to Pittsburgh; indeed, by mid-1917, the steel city's industrial life was said to be "partly dependent upon the Negro labor supply." But the unions, which grew rapidly in the Pittsburgh area during the war, with few exceptions continued to bar blacks. One union reported a growth of 100 per cent in a single year, but there were no blacks in the union. The union president claimed that efforts had been made to organize black workers, but a federal investigator found that prospective members were required to pledge "that I will not introduce for membership into this union anyone but a sober, industrious *white* person." The investigator found that in the entire city of Pittsburgh only two unions admitted Negroes to membership. They readily "became good unionists," he observed, "but the sentiment seems to be against their becoming members."[16]

The record was somewhat better in Chicago, but even there the traditional racism of the AF of L national unions and their members limited the unionization of black workers. Under the leadership of John Fitzpatrick, president of the Chicago Federation of Labor, and William Z. Foster, a former IWW member who by then was an organizer for the Railway Carmen's union, a campaign was launched to organize all stockyard workers into a semi-industrial union. In July, 1917, all the trade unions in the yards, with the exception of the Amalgamated Meat Cutters and Butcher Workmen, united to form the Stockyards Labor Council. Since between 10,000 and 12,000 of the stockyard workers were black—one-fourth of the total laboring force—the success of the organizing drive depended on the unionization of the black workers. It was necessary to overcome the resistance of the Negro to unionization, especially his fear that he would be betrayed once the organizing drive was successful. The campaign also had to overcome the efforts of Negro politicians and preachers, subsidized by the packers, to keep blacks from joining unions, and even the formation of a company union for Negroes only. But another major obstacle to the recruitment of black membership was presented by the racist provisions of the constitutions and rituals of the national unions in the yards. The Stockyard Labor Council appealed to Gompers for a solution, and he proposed that the AF of L award federal charters to all-black locals if no serious objections were raised by the nationals.

Despite the blacks' dislike for "Jim Crow" locals and the weakness of the federal labor-union structure, the Stockyards Labor Council succeeded in recruiting a substantial number of Negro packinghouse workers—estimates vary between 6,000 and 10,000. J. W. Johnstone, secretary of the council, repeatedly emphasized that "the non-union Negro is being brought into the yards by the Packers, he must be brought into the Union."[17] But many blacks were enlisted with the promise that they would be transferred later out of the federal labor unions to the locals of their respective crafts. When the AF of L unions refused to permit blacks to transfer, many of them simply dropped out of the federal unions.

Thus the stockyards organization drive, although temporarily successful, ended with only few more blacks in the yards organized than when it had begun. Foster and Fitzpatrick from the beginning had viewed the campaign as a gauge of the ability of the unions to organize blacks, but they seemed unaware of what the past two decades had already shown: that separate organization of blacks into "Jim Crow" unions was anything but satisfactory to the Negro. The unwillingness of the AF of L national unions to accept blacks as white workers were accepted only strengthened the hand of the employers and their agents, who could present black workers with real reasons for resisting unionization. "We know there are unions in the American Federation of Labor that have their feet in the 20th century and their heads in the 16th century."[18] Secretary Johnstone of the Stockyards Labor Council apologized to the black packinghouse workers for the necessity of organizing blacks into separate unions. But the blacks were tired of such explanations, which only confirmed their belief that white unionists would permit racist prejudices to stand in the way even of their own interests.

Viewing the record of the AF of L and its affiliated unions as World War I drew to a close, Du Bois commented sadly that, in his efforts to escape peonage, disfranchisement, segregation, the lack of a voice in local and state affairs, and extralegal violence, the black had at every stage met resistance "at the hands of his fellow laborers who have in reality a common cause with him."[19] A poem published in the Seattle *Union Record* at the end of the war expressed the same thought:

The Negro Worker

    . . . I can't get into
the UNION I belong to,
And have to manage by joining
a different union.
Yet the unions take in
All sort of FOREIGNERS,
Who never INTEND to be
American citizens.

And never were asked by any one
to COME HERE.
While I, whose fathers
were FORCED to come here—
I, who am of NECESSITY
And PERMANENTLY
A part of this nation—
Am BLACKMAILED.

I wonder why
They are so shortsighted,
As not to realize
That every time
They keep ANY WORKER,
Man or woman,
White, or yellow, or black,
OUT of a UNION,
They are forcing a worker
To be a SCAB,
To be used AGAINST THEM?[20]

11 Postwar Black Militancy

The period immediately following World War I witnessed the rise of militancy among organized workers, influenced partly by the revolutionary upheaval in Russia in 1917, mainly by a deterioration in living standards. By 1919 there were 4 million workers—longshoremen, stockyard workers, shipyard men, subway workers, shoe employees, carpenters, railroad shopmen, and steel workers—striking for higher wages to offset the mounting cost of living and for better working conditions.

In a number of struggles, past discrimination by organized labor bore fruit in the use of black strike-breakers. This was particularly important in the Great Steel Strike of 1919, during which many mills were operated with Negro workers, some already in the industry before the huge walkout but most brought North to break the strike. William Z. Foster, organizer of the strike, paid tribute to a Negro preacher who had forfeited a contribution of $2,500 from the steel corporations by urging the black workers in his congregation to support the strike. But Foster conceded such efforts were futile: "Race prejudice has everything to do with it. It lies at the bottom. . . . The white man has enslaved him, and they don't feel confidence in the trade union. . . . In the steel strike he lined up with the bosses."[1]

Roger Baldwin, who had worked in the steel mills and interviewed many of the black strike-breakers, reported that most were in favor of the union but "complained of union discrimination against the Negro [and] felt that they owed nothing to white men who had so long ignored and oppressed them."[2] According to the Interchurch Commission of Inquiry into the Steel Strike, "the great number of Negroes who flowed into the Chicago and Pittsburgh plants were conscious of strikebreaking. For this attitude, the steel strikers rightly blamed American organized labor. . . . Through many an experience Negroes came to believe that the only way they could break into a unionized industry was through strikebreaking."[3]

Discriminatory practices by labor unions and the consequent strike-breaking by Negroes were also factors in the terrible Chicago race riots of 1919, although clashes over the housing situation there contributed significantly to the bitter animosity between the races. Disgusted with the treatment they had received during the stockyards organizing campaign of 1918 and by the fact that the unions barred them from all but menial jobs, black workers frequently replaced striking whites in the stockyards during the summer of 1919. Black strike-breaking, in turn, "helped produce the bloody 1919 race riot."[4]*

Black strike-breaking was a major issue discussed at the 1919 convention of the National Urban League. In the belief that Negroes would benefit more by joining unions than by serving the interests of employers, the Urban League established a Department of Industrial Relations to facilitate "the organization and assistance of Negro mechanics." But black strike-breaking could not be halted by resolutions in favor of unionism. What was required was a determination on the part of the white unions to end the racist exclusion of black workers, and this was no nearer realization after the 1919 strikes than before.

An instance of how blacks were literally forced into strike-breaking by union racism occurred in Texas. Kept out of the Boilermakers' Union, Negro helpers of the Texas and Pacific Railway shops were organized by the Firemen and Oilers into Local No. 562. The Boilermakers vented their fury by ordering foremen not to hire any black helpers. Desperate, the blacks appealed to the 1920 convention of the State Federation of Labor for justice. In one of the most moving documents in labor history, they pleaded:

> We have been as loyal as the times demanded and our conditions would allow. We have bought Liberty Bonds, War Savings Stamps, and War Saving Certificates. We have contributed to the Red Cross, the War Work Activities, and whatever was for the advancement of the Nation and its people in the great struggle for the liberation of humanity. We have suffered with all others during the periods when the people of the country were called upon to deny themselves of the many comforts of, and necessities of life. Most of our "boys" have made the Supreme Sacrifice. We have helped the boys Over There. What more can we do? All of this and more have we done for the cause of the Nation and Democracy.
>
> Tell us please if it is the purpose of the Organized Labor Movement to organize the colored helpers so as to discriminate against them and force them out of jobs which they have held and are holding, and make scabs of them?
>
> We ask you, the State Federation of Labor of Texas, for assistance. We ask that we may but receive justice. Even-handed justice. We ask no more than a chance to work as we have always been known to do. Gentlemen, we implore you to assist us in seeing that we get justice. We ask no more! See that we get nothing less.

The plea was referred to the Executive Committee and promptly buried. In the next session of the State Federation of Labor, reports that unemployed black helpers had assisted in breaking strikes in the ma-

---

* In the South, too, white workers paid dearly during the postwar years for their insistence on "Jim Crow" unionism. Excluded from the white union at the Oscar Daniels shipyard in Tampa, Florida, blacks were offered a "negro union" but refused. "They demanded equal rights, with an open door for themselves." When this demand was rejected, Negroes helped break a strike at the shipyard in April, 1919, by refusing to honor the white union's walkout. Wayne Flint, "Florida Labor and Political Radicalism, 1919–1920," *Labor History* 9 (Winter, 1969): 86.

chine shops produced a chorus of denunciations of Negroes as "allies of the employers."[5]

Most blacks, however, were through with pleading for "even-handed justice." In both the steel strike and the Chicago race riot, a new mood was detected among the blacks. Roger Baldwin found radicalism widespread among the Negro strike-breakers, and not, as charged, as the result of "Bolshevik agents." "I found," he reported, "no trace of 'red' propaganda, but I found observations and conclusions expressed in as 'red' terms as I have ever heard from a soap-box agitator. It is obvious that conditions themselves produce radical thinking."[6] Similarly, during the Chicago race riot, the militant resistance of the Negroes to the white rioters and their readiness to use retaliatory violence, although attributed to a "Bolshevik plot," were actually an expression of a black radicalism that grew out of experience in white America.

The end of World War I coincided with profound changes among the Negro people. Some improvements had occurred in the conditions of life for hundreds of thousands who had migrated from the agricultural regions of the South to the industrial centers of the North. But these were not sufficient to compensate for the bitter experience of being herded into Northern ghettos with crowded, substandard houses, forced to pay exorbitant rents and high prices for food, and subjected to continuing discrimination on the job and in everyday life. The 1919 report of the Research Bureau of Associated Charities of Detroit told a typical story:

> There was not a single vacant house or tenement in the several Negro sections of this city. The majority of Negroes are living under such crowded conditions that three or four families in an apartment is the rule rather than the exception. Seventy-five percent of the Negro homes have so many lodgers that they are really hotels. Stables, garages and cellars have been converted into homes for Negroes. The pool rooms and gambling clubs are beginning to charge for the privilege of sleeping on pool tables overnight.[7]

With the heavy unemployment among black industrial workers caused by the slackening of demand for labor during postwar demobilization, black disillusionment and frustrations increased. Most blacks had patriotically supported the war "to make the world safe for democracy," and 400,000 blacks had served in the armed forces. They had met with discrimination and segregation while fighting for the nation, and when they came home they had to face Jim Crow and unemployment. Black veterans who were fortunate enough to find work were given only the most menial and lowest-paid jobs. Even Negro veterans with college degrees ended up as common laborers.

A new spirit of self-assertion began to develop in the Negro community. But when blacks protested the nation's failure to provide democracy for its Negro citizens, they were answered by a wave of lynchings and a string of race riots across the country, North and South. In Elaine, Arkansas, where black sharecroppers dared to form a union, employ a lawyer, and demand an accounting from landlords, one hundred of them were killed, and the courts sentenced twelve of the victims' fellow share-croppers to death and seventy-seven to long prison terms.

The rising hopes and the disappointments, the new spirit of self-assertion and the savage reprisals, contributed to the emergence of what was called the "New Negro" movement. Many blacks now rejected Booker T. Washington's answer to the discriminatory practices to whites-only unionism—an alliance with the employers against organized labor—in favor of organizing outside the AF of L and the railroad brotherhoods. The result was a rise of independent Negro unionism and a growth of radical, pro-IWW influence among black workers.

Independent Negro unions had existed before World War I but had enjoyed little success. The most important had been the National Association of Afro-American Steam and Gas Engineers and Skilled Laborers, founded in 1903 in Pittsburgh, where it had three locals. It had gained the recognition of the city's central labor body but, unable to achieve much in the way of benefits for its members, had soon disappeared.

The AF of L's indifference to black workers during the war had also given rise to independent Negro labor organizations. Many were local bodies, such as those of the sheet-metal workers in South Carolina; the plumbers, lathe operators, and electricians in Chicago; the hod carriers and waiters in Baltimore; the asphalt workers in Milwaukee; the elevator operators in New York; and the Pullman porters in Philadelphia. None of them was notably effective. They included at most only a few hundred workers and met with hostility from white trade unions, which, while unwilling to open their ranks to blacks, would not tolerate the operation of black unions within their jurisdictions. When the black unions were forced to strike to win their demands, they rarely received support from the white unions.

The one instance where independent Negro organization attained some effectiveness during the war was that of the railroad occupations where black labor predominated. There, unions were organized in protest against the exclusion of blacks by the railroad brotherhoods and the railway departments of the AF of L. In 1913 black workers in the railway mail service, excluded by the AF of L's Railway Mail Association, formed the National Alliance of Postal Employees. Two years later, a broader independent union of black railroad workers—the Railway Men's Benevolent Association—was established. Its purpose was to organize all Negro railway workers, regardless of craft or skill, into one big union. Prior to America's entry into the war it had fewer than a hundred members. But when the federal government took over the railroads and, in return for organized labor's support of the war effort, gave its backing to organization in the industry, the association grew rapidly. By 1920, at its peak, it claimed 15,000 members in 187 locals, and its president, R. L. Mays, asserted that the organization represented every grade of black worker on the roads. As a result of the association's protests to the U.S. Railroad Administration over discrimination in wages and treatment, black fire-men, trainmen, and switchmen were awarded the same wage rights as whites, and Pullman porters and dining-car employees received wage increases.

During the period of federal control of the railroads, the Brotherhood of Dining Car Employees—formed in 1920 through a merger between two groups of dining-car workers—won recognition on most of the important roads east of the Mississippi. By protesting to the U.S. Railroad Administration, the brotherhood won for all cooks and waiters in the railroad industry a long-sought raise to $240 a month, as well as overtime compensation.

The establishment of a black federation of labor was attempted in July, 1917, when the Colored Employees of America (CEA) was formed in New York City. In a booklet called "A Message From the North for Negroes," the new organization appealed to migrants from the South to join its ranks as a way to obtain information about the best employment opportunities available and as a basis for building unions of black workers. Branches of the CEA were to be established in all cities with a black population over 5,000, but the organization seems to have disappeared after August, 1917.

Meanwhile, two young black Socialists, A. Philip Randolph and Chandler Owen, had been busy organizing blacks in the hotels and apartment houses in New York City into the United Brotherhood of Elevator and Switchboard Operators. Within three weeks after they began, they had recruited 600 of the 10,000 Negro elevator operators in New York City. The group immediately put forth demands for an eight-hour day, weekly pay, and a minimum wage of $13. A strike was planned to attain these goals, but it never materialized. The union grew to 2,000, changed its name to the Elevator Operators and Starters Union, and received a federal charter from the AF of L. But it, too, shortly disappeared.

Randolph and Owen had been editors of a trade journal published by the Headwaiters and Sidewaiters Society of Greater New York. They were forced to resign because the headwaiter elements in the society objected to their tendency to comment critically on the sidewaiters' poor wages and unfavorable working conditions. Randolph and Owen then established their own journal, *The Messenger*, to promote labor unionism and Socialism among blacks. Assisting them was a group of leading black Socialists, writers, and agitators, including W. A. Domingo, editor of the weekly *Emancipator*, and William N. Colson, the Reverend George Frazier Miller, William Pickens, Richard B. Moore, and Cyril Briggs.

Briggs, a native of Saint Kitts, edited *The Crusader* and also headed the African Blood Brotherhood (ABB), founded in the fall of 1917 as a "revolutionary secret order" by Briggs, Richard B. Moore, Otto Hall, Otto Huiswood, and others, most of whom were West Indians who had been active in the Harlem Section of the Socialist Party but had left the party because they regarded its program in the struggle against colonialism and for Negro liberation as too moderate. ABB sought "absolute race equality—political, economic, social"—and "fellowship within the

darker masses and with the class-conscious revolutionary white workers."
Its platform called for armed resistance to lynching, unqualified franchise
rights for blacks, a struggle for equal rights and against all forms of discrimination, the organization of Negroes into established trade unions,
self-determination for Negroes in states where they constituted a majority—all as necessary prerequisites for the liberation of Africa from
colonial rule and the establishment of a "free Africa." At its peak in
1921, the ABB claimed 2,500 members in fifty-six posts throughout the
nation, including areas of strength among the black coal miners in West
Virginia. Through *The Crusader*, its monthly organ, the brotherhood
mounted campaigns against discrimination in industry and unions and
urged blacks, where they were banned by white unions, to organize into
separate Negro unions.[8]

The Messenger, published by Randolph and Owen, viewed the black
situation as the "great labor problem of America." Since 99 per cent of
blacks were working people, it advocated that they support the Socialist
Party, the only political organization that represented the American
working class, and through which black workers, like white workers,
would eventually establish a "co-operative commonwealth" in which the
ownership of the means of production would be in the hands of the people. But *The Messenger* did not scorn improvements under capitalism.
With the first issue in November, 1917, it launched a vigorous campaign
to educate the black working class to the importance of united labor
organization. Noting that capitalism drew no color line in exploiting the
working class, it concluded that the workers must, out of self-interest,
unite on the same basis to end exploitation. Meanwhile, it was useless to
argue that nonunion black workers should not allow themselves to be
used as scabs against unionized workers, when often the only way they
could find employment was by strike-breaking. The only solution was to
organize every worker in industry, black and white.

At first Randolph and Owen held out some hope for the black worker
in the AF of L. The 1917 convention was even applauded for having
displayed "considerable sanity in adopting a resolution calling for the
appointment of Negro delegates to organize locals to affiliate with the
AF of L, a necessary but a belated move."[9] But when negotiations between the leaders of the National Urban League and the AF of L ended
in 1918 without results, Randolph and Owen had had their fill of the
AF of L. Neither had really expected anything to come from the negotiations—it was hardly logical, after all, for an organization like the Urban
League, financed by open-shop millionaires like Rockefeller, Carnegie,
and Armour, to fight for the welfare of black workers—but the cold
shoulder the black leaders had received was the last straw. *The Messenger* did occasionally concede that there were members of the federation who believed in black-white unity. On November 22, 1919, four
white local officials of the AF of L were killed when they protected a
Negro organizer from a vigilante mob in Bogalusa, Louisiana.* *The*

* In 1919 the center of lumber operations in Louisiana was at Bogalusa, where the
Great Southern Lumber Company, reputed to be the largest lumber producer in the

Messenger commented: "All hail to the white workers of Bogalusa! You are learning! You are on the right road. Your enemy is the Southern white employing class, not the Negroes. Your only weapon is the solidarity of the working class, black and white."[10] But it still insisted that such acts were exceptional and that, in the main, the AF of L was too fossilized to hold any hope for black workers. According to *The Messenger*, the future of the black working class lay, rather, with the Industrial Workers of the World.

In 1915 the IWW, despite its many spectacular victories in strikes and free-speech fights, was about to collapse. Beginning in 1916, it launched determined campaigns to organize a number of industries and achieved a large measure of success in the Western lumber areas and among the agricultural workers of the Middle and Far West. Appealing for black support, Wobbly organizers posted notices throughout the West informing blacks that in the IWW there was "no color line." In 1917 the IWW initiated a drive to recruit members in the factories and mills of the East, especially the thousands of new black workers from the South. Their appeals were endorsed by *The Messenger*, which enthusiastically predicted that the IWW, augmented "with a million and a half or two million Negroes," would "fairly rival the American Federation of Labor."

The Messenger hailed the IWW as "the only labor union that has never, in theory or practice, since its beginning twelve years ago, barred the workers of any race or nation from its membership."[11] The IWW also merited black support because it dealt chiefly with the unskilled, and most black workers were unskilled. It advocated direct action, also an important point in its favor for the largely disfranchised Negro. With the ballot box closed to them, the only way blacks had of advancing was through industrial action. Moreover, the IWW, unlike nearly all other labor bodies, favored industrial over craft unionism. Industrial unionism alone was capable of encompassing the vast majority of black workers, who were unskilled, and it was furthermore the only effective labor instrument of class struggle. Time and again strikes had failed in the past because craft unions did not support each other and actually acted as strike-breakers against sister craft unions. The IWW's brand of unionism, *The Messenger* insisted, eliminated this fatal flaw by unifying all workers in the struggle against employers.

At the same time that they were urging black workers to join the IWW, Randolph and Owen favored the formation of an independent black labor movement. The postwar militancy of the Negro, they de-

---

United States, owned the lumber and paper mills. The International Timber Workers Union, AF of L, launched an organizing drive at Great Southern, and a local was established, three-fourths of whose members were black. Sol Dacus, a black native of Mississippi, was vice-president. The Self-Preservation and Loyalty League, established by the Great Southern, went through the town threatening to shoot blacks who remained in the union. Fearing for his life, Dacus fled to the swamps. When he emerged, he was protected by the white unionists, four of whom were killed by the vigilantes.

clared, indicated that the time was "ripe for a great mass movement among Negroes," which should take the form of "labor unions, farmer protective unions, cooperative business and socialism."[12] Hence, *The Messenger* welcomed the formation, in the spring of 1919, of the National Brotherhood Workers of America (NBWA). Delegates from twelve states and the District of Columbia, representing unions of carpenters, riveters, blacksmiths, caulkers, electricians, engravers, painters, longshoremen, janitors, jewelry workers, railroad firemen and other railroad workers, plasterers, moulders, hod carriers, plumbers, porters, and waiters, attended the founding session. T. J. Free and R. T. Sims, two radical black unionists (Sims was an early member of the IWW), were elected president and vice-president, respectively, and resolutions were adopted urging the organization of "every Negro worker into industrial labor or trade unions in all skilled or unskilled occupations," condemning "the unjust and inexcusable discrimination against Negro workers by the organized white labor unions," and calling upon Negroes wherever possible to "enter the unions side by side with their white brothers; but in the event of discrimination, we urge that Negroes, in any place, shall organize their own unions to exact justice from both the employer and the white labor unions."[13]

The initial strength of the NBWA came from black workers employed in the shipyards and on the docks at Newport, Norfolk, and Portsmouth, Virginia. The fact that many of these workers maintained their affiliation with AF of L locals gave the federation substantial influence in the councils of the Virginia State Federation of Labor. Shortly after its establishment, the new labor body was powerful enough to influence the selection of the president of the state federation and to obtain representation on its Executive Board. Moreover, these militant black AF of L unionists were to exercise an important influence at AF of L national conventions.

The new spirit of militancy among black workers, the move to establish independent Negro unions, and the growing appeal of the IWW for the black working class were all reflected at the 1919 and 1920 conventions of the AF of L. On the eve of the 1919 convention in Atlantic City, New Jersey, the Negro Workers' Advisory Committee, representing every black fraternal, welfare, religious, and labor body in Chicago, wired the AF of L to urge the removal of all restrictions against black workers by affiliated unions and to warn that otherwise black workers would move in increasing numbers into the IWW. The convention itself had a larger delegation of Negro unionists—twenty-three delegates from federal and local unions across the country—than had ever before been present at the annual assembly. Seated at one table in the convention hall, they told reporters of their disappointment that the methods of the AF of L had failed to achieve greater organization of Negro workers and their determination to fight hard to force the affiliated unions to "loosen up and give the black man of the South a chance to organize."[14] Several complained bitterly that black members of the AF of L were denied the rights and benefits enjoyed by the whites.

The convention witnessed a sharp confrontation between the protesting black unionists and AF of L officials when the black representatives introduced a series of resolutions reflecting their disappointment and anger. One resolution sought the services of two black organizers for the Southern District of Alabama. Another asked that a black organizer be appointed in every state of the union where needed, particularly in the South, where white organizers had had trouble in recruiting black workers, and also that a laboring man, preferably black, be appointed from each craft where separate black organizations existed to represent the black workers in any business concerning the affairs of the craft.

A third resolution protested the refusal of the International Union of Metal Trades to issue a charter to black craftsmen and boldly requested that the convention declare black unionists entitled to any charter according to their trade. Still another concerned a complaint on the part of organized black freight handlers, express and station employees that the Brotherhood of Railway Clerks, under whose jurisdiction they functioned, had given them little or no assistance in bargaining with the railroads over wages and grievances. The sponsors of this resolution asked the AF of L to organize the freight handlers into an organization for their mutual protection and benefit and to help them form a grievance committee to secure a working agreement with the railroads.

The fifth and final resolution called upon the convention either to grant an application to a representative group of black unionists for an International Union of Organized Colored Labor or to exert its influence on the international unions having jurisdiction over black workers to compel them to charter black labor bodies, thereby assuming responsibility for their welfare. Fourteen black delegates, representing federal and local unions from a variety of trades, signed the last resolution.

The Committee on Organization, to which the resolutions were referred, refused to endorse the demand for an international charter for black workers on the grounds that it would violate the jurisdictional rights of several unions affiliated with the AF of L. Passing over without comment the other four resolutions, the committee went on to maintain strenuously that many international unions within the AF of L admitted black members and granted them full protection of their rights and interests. In the cases of member bodies that did not accept blacks, the committee recommended organizing the affected workers under direct charters from the Executive Council. "We further recommend," it continued, "that the Executive Council give particular attention to the organization of colored workers everywhere and assign organizers for that purpose whenever possible."[15] The committee concluded by listing sixteen prominent AF of L affiliates that, it officially declared, admitted Negro workers.*

The chairman of the committee, Frank Duffy, then asked the dele-

---

* The unions listed were United Mine Workers; Mine, Mill, and Smelter Workers; Longshoremen; Carpenters; Textile Workers; Seamen; Cigarmakers; Teamsters; Plasterers; Bricklayers; Maintenance of Way Employees; Laundry Workers; Cooks and Waiters; Tailors; Brewery Workers; and Upholsterers.

gates if any other unions represented at the convention admitted blacks. John Lacey, a black union leader from Norfolk, Virginia, rose at that point and appealed to the convention to extend a hand of welcome to the black working class. "If you can take in immigrants who cannot speak the English language," he asked, "why can't you take in the Negro, who has been loyal to you from Washington to the battle-fields of France?" Lacey assured the delegates that he was not asking for social equality for the Negro: "We ask for the same chance to earn bread for our families at the same salary our white brothers are getting . . . equal rights the same as you have to earn bread for your families."[16]

Lacey's emotional plea broke the dam the Committee on Organization had constructed against black militancy. In an unprecedented demonstration for black-white unity, forty heads of international and national unions rose, one after another, to proclaim that their organizations would welcome black workers into their ranks. Even a Southern white delegate from the Brotherhood of Railway and Steamship Clerks stood up for equality of black and white labor. At the end of the speeches, the convention unanimously adopted the report of the Committee on Organization, which, though rejecting the request for an international charter for black workers and ignoring of the other four resolutions introduced by black delegates, called for special emphasis on organizing blacks within the AF of L.

The AF of L convention was said to herald a new era in labor relations. Not since the abolition of chattel slavery, declared the New York *Age*, had so important a step been taken toward the industrial freedom of the race. "If carried out towards its logical conclusion, it should mean the loosening of the shackles that have encouraged peonage and industrial dependency of all kinds."[17] The *New York Times* predicted that "all over the country the negro worker will have, as he has not had hitherto, a chance to enter all of the skilled, and therefore better-paid trades, and in them to be judged on his merits."[18] The convention had wiped out "the part of the color-line which most impeded the progress of the black race," according to the New York *World*.[19] The Boston *Guardian*, a militant black weekly, declared that the federation's action "opens the gateway to real American life for the first time within the last half century."[20] Eugene K. Jones, Executive Secretary of the National Urban League, hailed the "far-sightedness" the federation had shown: "The American Federation of Labor has sensed the absolute necessity for organizing negro workingmen along with white workingmen in order to face capital with a solid front in working out the serious problems of the new era."[21] Jones and other black commentators emphasized that there was now no need for an independent black labor movement or for blacks to join the IWW. The NAACP urged the Negro instead to accept the offer of "full and equal privileges" within the AF of L and "to follow it up and to go a hundred strong to the next meeting of the federation."[22] Gompers adjudged such an approach to be just what was needed to make the AF of L's stand a reality. "In the past it has been difficult to organize the colored man. Now, he shows a desire to be organized and we meet him more than half-way."[23] Typically, Gompers blamed the black workers, not the AF of L affiliates, for the paucity of Negroes in his federation.

W. E. B. Du Bois, on the other hand, was not so easily swept off his feet by the AF of L convention's declarations. Well acquainted with the difference between nonexclusion on paper and black membership in actuality, Du Bois cautioned in *The Crisis* that the convention might not have marked the beginning of a "square deal" for the black worker from the AF of L—it might mean a great deal or it might mean nothing:

> It will only mean a great deal provided that in every locality throughout this country the colored men and women come together and demand of the various labor locals recognition of Negro workingmen. It means that in Washington, there ought to be stationed men, who are big enough to see the importance of this decision on the part of organized labor; who will see that the internationals change their constitutions so as to admit Negro men; and to see that the international and the Executive Council pass on the final word to the locals in regard to this matter. Because, after all, it is entirely a local question as to whether a man will or will not be admitted when he is qualified. The internationals only decide as to policy, as to constitutional rights. Putting into execution is a matter of local concern.[24]

Du Bois, of course, touched on the key issue in the relationship between organized labor and the black worker since the days of Reconstruction. To what extent did the state and local unions of even those sixteen national affiliates originally listed as nondiscriminatory accept black members, and how many of those and other local unions would change their practices in light of the action taken at Atlantic City? To what lengths were the national officials, who had been so eloquent at the convention, willing to go in persuading their locals and members to open their doors to black workers? To Du Bois, history suggested that the answer in post–World War I America would be the same as it had been in post–Civil War America.

Even Du Bois overlooked another important fact: The report adopted unanimously by the convention did not call for full membership for black workers. Where national or international affiliates would not accept blacks, those in the affected occupations would be organized into separate federal and local labor unions chartered by the Executive Council. The federal and local labor bodies organized by the Executive Council before 1919 had already proved incapable of protecting their black members.

Events soon demonstrated that the AF of L was no more open to blacks than it had been before the 1919 convention. The AF of L could boast of a phenomenal growth in membership when it met in convention at Montreal in 1920. Its over-all membership stood at 4,078,748, nearly twice the number reported in 1916. The number of Negro members in 1920 was not announced, but it could not have exceeded by more than a few thousand the 60,000 generously estimated in 1916, and nearly all of the new black members were in separate local and federal unions. In fact, the number of AF of L affiliates denying admittance to black workers by constitutional provision or ritual had risen between 1910 and 1920 from eight to eleven.* Expectations that the great migration of black workers from the South would open wide the doors of the AF of L and the railroad brotherhoods had proved only a dream.†

It is not surprising, then, that the black unionists who had raised the issue of Negro membership at Atlantic City returned the following year angrier than ever and more determined to press their claims. A group of delegates from federal locals of the Railway Coach Cleaners initiated the battle early in the proceedings by demanding that the Brotherhood of Railway Carmen, which had jurisdiction over the coach cleaners, either drop its color ban or allow the coach cleaners to acquire an international charter of their own. Other black federal unions requested immediate AF of L action on the refusal of the machinists, the boilermakers, and the blacksmiths to admit Negroes. They also insisted that the federation use every means to have the words "white only" removed from the Brotherhood of Railway Clerks' constitution or else force the clerks to relinquish their jurisdiction over the freight handlers—mostly black and organized in separate federal unions—and permit them to establish their own national body.

For the first time, the black delegates had stopped talking in generalities and had hit directly at the AF of L leadership's refusal to do anything about racial restrictions of the affiliates. The far-reaching resolutions were once again referred to the Committee on Organization.

The committee said in its reports that the boilermakers and the machinists had "nothing in their constitutions prohibiting the admission of colored men of the trade"[25] and that the blacksmiths actually issued charters to black workers in the trade and also had no law denying them admission. This was an evasion, for it was well known that the boilermakers and the machinists accomplished the exclusion of blacks through their rituals. The blacksmiths admittedly chartered Negro unions, but they were auxiliary locals that had no voice in the affairs of the blacksmiths and existed only to prevent the blacks from organizing independently. Since the AF of L leadership had sanctioned and even counseled such methods for excluding blacks or accepting them with second-class status, the report of the Committee on Organization was an outrageous insult to the Negro delegation.

The committee acknowledged that the railway carmen barred Negroes from membership by constitutional provision but reported having re-

* During those ten years four new affiliates that specifically barred Negroes joined the AF of L: the Brotherhood of Railway Carmen, the Order of Sleeping Car Conductors, the National Organization of Masters, Mates, and Pilots of North America, and the Railway Mail Associates. One affiliate, the Brotherhood of Maintenance of Way Employees, voted at its 1917 convention to admit Negroes in allied or auxiliary lodges, which were placed under the control of its system division. This removed it from the list of affiliates that specifically barred Negroes.

† In addition to the railroad brotherhoods, eight unions unaffiliated with the AF of L limited membership to white workers through their constitutions or rituals in 1920. They were the Brotherhood of Dining Car Conductors; Order of Railway Expressmen; American Federation of Express Workers; American Federation of Railroad Workers; Brotherhood of Railroad Station Employees; the Train Dispatchers; the Railroad Yard Masters of America; and the Neptune Association.

ceived assurances from the president of the carmen that he would ask his organization at its next convention to admit black coach cleaners or, failing that, to surrender all claims to that class of work. In view of those assurances, the committee declared, it could "only recommend" that the carmen eliminate from the regulations all references to the admission of Negro workmen. At the same time, the Committee on Organization said it could not approve the coach cleaners' request to form an international of their own. "The American Federation of Labor," it stated, "does not organize workers of any trade or calling along racial lines." The committee conveniently ignored the existence of the United Hebrew Trades, an AF of L affiliate that had been very successful in promoting the interests of Jewish workers. The committee rejected the plea of the freight handlers, with the usual observation that the AF of L could not interfere with the autonomy of affiliated national and international unions. It held out to the black workers unable to join AF of L member bodies an opportunity to obtain membership in the separate unions chartered by the Executive Council. Thus far and no farther was the Committee on Organization willing to go.

The report sparked another debate, and this time it did not end in unanimous approval of the committee's recommendations. Robert Buford, a black delegate from Richmond, Virginia, who had originally submitted the freight handlers' proposal, pointed out that the refusal to take any action over the railway clerks' written exclusion of Negroes, in open violation of the AF of L's national charter, proved the hypocrisy of the federation's contention that it did not discriminate against Negroes. He complained that the freight handlers, forced to contribute to the expenses of the railway clerks' officials who were supposed to handle their grievances, were not even given representation in the national union and insisted that the clerks should be compelled to remove from the by-laws provision barring Negroes. If the federation refused to do so, it should give the freight handlers a charter of their own "that would enable them to have their own committee to handle their grievances."[26]

A debate followed between Frank Duffy, Chairman of the Committee on Organization, and delegate Buford. Duffy called the freight handlers' resolution illegal because it asked the convention to decide who was or was not eligible for admission as an AF of L affiliate, an authority that the national and international unions alone possessed. All the AF of L could do if affiliates refused to remove their prohibitions against Negroes was provide black workers with a charter. "What kind of charter?" asked Buford. "As freight handlers," Duffy replied. That was just what the freight handlers, who opposed separate organization outside the international union, wanted to avoid. "We don't want to be separated," Buford said vehemently. "We want the same kind of charters [as the whites]."[27]

While the AF of L leadership sat squirming on the platform, white delegates arose one after another to challenge the federation's readiness to draw the color line. A motion was made and seconded to amend the Committee on Organization's report with the recommendation that the convention formally request the railway clerks to delete the term "white only" from their constitution. Over the opposition of representatives of the clerks, the original recommendation of the Committee on Organization was rejected and the amendment passed.

Thus, for the first time since 1891, when AF of L delegates had endorsed Gompers's efforts to force the machinists to abandon their exclusion of blacks, an AF of L convention recommended that affiliated unions, in this case the railway clerks and the railway carmen, remove racial restrictions from their membership provisions.

Newspaper reporters covering the convention put special stress on the militancy of the black delegates. Men like David E. Grange, agent of the marine cooks and stewards in New York; Charles A. Sumner of the stereotypers and electrotypers; O. A. Anderson of the International Longshoremen's Association; D. D. Alesandre of the hod carriers and common laborers; and Cornelius Foley of the journeymen barbers, as well as Robert E. Buford, were widely applauded in the black press for speaking up boldly "for full industrial equality for the Negro workers."[28] They vehemently protested the repeated use of the word "nigger" by O. D. Gorham, delegate of the Order of Railroad Telegraphers, and they bluntly denounced as "taxation without representation" the AF of L practice of shunting blacks into federal and local unions that received no protection from the international affiliates but were assessed to pay the salaries of union grievance agents. Finally, they put it up squarely to the delegates to say once and for all if they stood for the equality of all workers. "Do not pussyfoot," David E. Grange shouted. "Stand for the democracy the American Federation of Labor is supposed to stand for. It did not offend the dignity of any man to send the Negro into the firing lines in France."[29]

The rejection of the Committee on Organization's report was generally regarded as the most significant AF of L action to date on black labor.* *Justice*, the official organ of the International Ladies' Garment Workers' Union, heaped praise upon the convention "for removing a degrading clause pertaining to negroes."[30] The Amalgamated Clothing Workers Union was not then affiliated with the federation, but its journal, *Advance*, hailed the news that "the American Federation of Labor was finally compelled to proclaim the identity of interests of the white and colored workers"[31] and predicted that a new era was opening for the black working class.

* In the excitement produced by the unusual action of the delegates in requesting an affiliated organization to remove the color ban from its constitution, little attention was paid to the rejection of other resolutions introduced by Negro delegates. These requested more effective representation of the interests of black federal and local unions; the launching of a program to increase Negro membership in the AF of L; the mounting of a campaign of education among both white and black workers to convince them of the necessity of bringing workers into the ranks of organized labor regardless of race, nationality, or color, and the appointment of a black worker in AF of L headquarters in Washington who would express the aspirations of the Negro working class to the federation. Only an emasculated version of the program to increase Negro membership was adopted. It simply called for the appointment of Negro organizers "where necessary" and referred the matter to the Executive Council for action if the funds of the federation should permit.

12 The AF of L and the Black Worker, 1921–29

A reporter who covered the 1920 AF of L convention wrote after the final vote on the report of the Committee on Organization that the decision to reject the report and order the railway clerks to remove the color ban from their constitution, like the stand in favor of black-white unity at the 1919 convention, was impelled, most delegates concluded, by "the threat that if the unions of the American Federation of Labor did not remove the color disability, the Negroes would join the IWW."[1] One newspaper ran the headline: "Negro Threat to Join IWW Impelled AF of L Action for Negro Equality."[2] Reporters for black papers attached more weight to the fear of an independent Negro labor movement. "The determination of Negro labor to have its own organization where it can be truly equal had a significant impact at the AF of L convention," was the way one black reporter put it.[3] *The Messenger* agreed that the unionized blacks' readiness to secede from the AF of L because of its indifference to the welfare of black workers and, with hundreds of thousands of unorganized Negro workers, to join the IWW or an independent black labor federation had hung like a "Sword of Damocles . . . over the head of the Federation of Labor."[4]

There was wide agreement that the rise of the independent black unions and, especially, the appeal of the IWW to black workers had prompted the AF of L's actions on the issue of Negro labor in the immediate postwar period. Unfortunately, it was soon unnecessary for the AF of L to carry out its pledges, for both of those threats to the federation soon disappeared.

The IWW campaign to recruit black workers got off to a promising start. In the summer of 1917 the Wobblies launched a massive effort to organize waterfront workers all along the Atlantic Coast on the basis of unity of black and white. They quickly recruited 2,000 members in Baltimore, among them hundreds of black stevedores, grain handlers, and metal handlers, who had long been dissatisfied with the ILA's policy of separate locals for blacks. But before labor solidarity on Baltimore's waterfront had a chance to materialize, the government put an end to IWW activities by arresting the chief organizers on a charge of interfering with the shipment of war supplies.

In 1918 the IWW campaign to organize the waterfront workers received a further setback when the leading black organizer, Ben Fletcher, was arrested for seditious activity. Along with 165 white Wobblies, Fletcher was indicted by a Chicago federal grand jury for having obstructed the war effort by sabotage and by speaking and writing against the war and the draft. Grand juries returned similar indictments against Wobblies in Fresno, Sacramento, Wichita, and Omaha. Ben Fletcher's indictment is hardly surprising, even though he had never spoken out against the war and the draft, having been too busy organizing the waterfront to become involved in any other issue of the day. The Philadelphia branch of the Marine Transport Workers Industrial Union, which he had been instrumental in building before the war, had been highly effective in nullifying the employers' traditional practice of playing Negro and white workers against each other. And now Fletcher was heading a drive to extend the gains won by the Philadelphia branch along the entire Atlantic Coast. Small wonder that big business, allied with the government against the IWW, decided he had to be stopped.

After a farcical trial, 101 Wobblies in Chicago were convicted, many receiving sentences of up to twenty years in prison and heavy fines. Fletcher was sentenced to ten years in the federal penitentiary at Leavenworth, Kansas, and fined $30,000. Condemning the trials of the IWW leaders as a deliberate effort to stem the drive to organize the unorganized, especially the black workers, *The Messenger*, joined by W. E. B. Du Bois launched a campaign to bring about Ben Fletcher's release. "We respect the Industrial Workers of the World," Du Bois wrote in *The Crisis* of June, 1919, "as one of the social and political movements in modern times that draws no color line."

At first the response to the campaign was not encouraging. This was the period of the great "Red Scare" and the Palmer Raids, and few black organizations were willing to speak up for a militant leader convicted of "conspiracy and violating the Espionage Act." But slowly the campaign for Fletcher mounted, and petitions and letters from black and white Americans urged President Harding to pardon the black Wobbly leader and release him from the federal penitentiary. In December, 1921, the Department of Justice, in its "Report on All Wartime Offenders Confined in Federal or State Penitentiaries," advised the Attorney General against recommending executive clemency for Ben Fletcher. The reason was stated quite bluntly:

> He was a negro who had great influence with the colored stevedores, dock workers, firemen, and sailors, and materially assisted in building up the Marine Transport Workers Union which at the time of the indictment had become so strong that it practically controlled all shipping on the Atlantic Coast.[5]

In 1923 President Harding commuted Ben Fletcher's sentence, and he was released from prison. (In 1933 President Franklin D. Roosevelt granted him a full pardon.) Fletcher remained in the IWW and continued to speak and write on industrial unionism and the need for labor solidarity. But by this time the IWW was only the shell of an organization. Wartime repression had all but destroyed the Wobblies, and what was left at the war's end was further weakened by a split in the ranks over attitudes toward the Soviet Union and the Communist International. One group supported the first Socialist state, and another refused its support because the Soviet Union had not based itself on the principles of syndicalism favored by the IWW. The one IWW union that still had a substantial number of black members was the Philadelphia local of the Marine Transport Workers Union (Local 8)—2,000 of its 3,500 members were black. Local 8 was the pride of those who believed that industrial unionism was the solution to racial problems. "Colored and White Workers Solving the Race Problem for Philadelphia" was the headline over an article about Local 8 in *The Messenger* of July, 1921.

But Local 8 was in constant battle with the national IWW on a wide variety of issues, and in 1923 the local severed relations with the IWW, charging the General Executive Board with a deliberate plot to dominate it and dictate its activities even against the best interests of the membership.

Harassed constantly by the government and further weakened by internal disputes, IWW could do little to take advantage of the vacuum created by AF of L indifference to the organization of black workers. To be sure, IWW journals in the postwar years agreed that there had never been a more favorable time "to organize colored men and women,"[6] but by 1921 even *The Messenger*, the fervent champion of the IWW in Negro circles, conceded that the organization was too weak to hold out hope for the black working class.

Even Fletcher realized as soon as he emerged from federal prison that the organization was too weak to fulfill its mission. He therefore called for the formation of a separate black labor federation. "There are fully 4,000,000 Negro men, women and children, ready to participate in such a Negro Labor Federation," he predicted.[7] Although it would promote the general welfare of the black working class, the federation's main purpose would be to compel the AF of L and the railroad brotherhoods to reverse their racist policies.

Fletcher's vision of an independent black labor movement never became a reality. The separate unions that might have served as the foundation for such a movement either disappeared, lost most of their members, or failed to grow. The National Alliance of Postal Employees—extended in 1923 to include all 22,000 black workers in U.S. Postal Service—never got off the ground because of its inability to win the official federal government recognition accorded to white unions. In 1926 the alliance claimed only 1,700 members.

The Railway Men's Benevolent Association received a fatal blow when its effort to have the so-called Atlanta Agreement declared null and void after the government relinquished control over the nation's rail system to private interests failed. This agreement, it will be recalled, was worked out between the Brotherhood of Railway Trainmen and federal railway officials during the war with the aim of driving blacks from positions they had long held on the roads. The four railroad brotherhoods made effective use of the Atlanta Agreement in the postwar years to oust black railwaymen from jobs acquired during the war. The Railway Men's Benevolent Association attempted in late 1921 to bring the various groups of black railway workers into one organization to prevent blacks from being forced out of the industry. When the effort failed, the association soon disappeared. The number of black workers in skilled and semiskilled occupations on the nation's railroads declined rapidly during the next decade. All black spokesmen could do was declare that, in their strikes, "the railroad unions richly deserved defeat."[8]

The National Brotherhood Workers of America, formed in 1919, collapsed after two years. Its initial strength had been among black dock workers in the Tidewater area of Virginia, but the International Longshoremen's Association, with financial support from the national AF of L, succeeded in recruiting those workers into its ranks. With the postwar reduction in shipyard workers, the brotherhood lost more of its base. Just before its dissolution, in the summer of 1921, the brotherhood announced its intention to unionize the black workers in the cotton fields as well as in every branch of industry. "How long are we to wait for justice at the white man's hands?"[9] it asked, denouncing the AF of L for its failure to organize the black working class. The brotherhood disappeared shortly thereafter with the question still unanswered.

The Messenger and the leaders of the brotherhood had split about a year before the latter's demise. Officials of the brotherhood had charged *The Messenger* editors were more interested in winning financial support for their magazine than in building up the new black labor movement. Randolph and Owen went their own way in 1920 to form first the Friends of Negro Freedom (FNF) and then the National Association for the Promotion of Labor Unionism Among Negroes. The FNF was to be an interracial organization, but control was to rest with Negroes, who knew the problems of the black workers. The program called for the establishment of committees for weekly educational assemblies, a labor committee to gain entrance for black workers into industry and unions, a boycott committee to wage campaigns against racist merchants, and a Tenants' League Committee to secure decent housing for blacks. Through boycotts, rent strikes, labor agitation, and general education, the FNF would mobilize blacks into a powerful direct-action group to win improvements as workers and consumers. Fourteen branches across the country were established, and the plan was to build an international organization, for it was "no more possible for Negroes in America to be indifferent to what takes place in Haiti, Egypt or Trinidad, than for New York Negroes to be indifferent to the fortunes of Negroes in Florida. The success of Negroes in one place encourages and emboldens Negroes in another. And the enslavement, the persecutors and oppressors in another."[10] But apart from the chapter in Philadelphia, which sponsored a weekly lecture series on important issues of the day, none of the branches amounted to much, and they soon disappeared, along with the national organization.

The National Association for the Promotion of Labor Unionism among Negroes was no more successful. With Owen as president and Randolph as secretary, it produced an impressive letterhead listing an advisory board of white leaders of the Socialist Party and of the needle-trades unions: Morris Hillquit of the party, Joseph Schlossberg of the Amalgamated Clothing Workers, and Rose Schneiderman and A. J. Shiplacoff of the ILGWU. With the assistance of the Socialist political and trade-union leaders, the association was to act as an educational and organizational force to bring all black workers into unions based on class lines and ultimately to unite black and white workers into a mighty class-conscious power capable of effectively challenging capitalist domination of American economic and political life.

But for all the praise and attention the association received from the Socialist press and in the journals of the needle-trades unions, for all the honors Randolph and Owen bestowed upon the ILGWU, the Amalgamated Clothing Workers, the International Fur Workers, and other unions for their support of *The Messenger*, nothing was accomplished. It was difficult for black workers to summon much enthusiasm for an organization endorsed by Socialist leaders when the party was doing very little in the struggle for black equality in American life, and when the Socialist needle-trades unions, whose officials were on the association's advisory board, did little to bring black workers into their trades or recruit them as members. These facts, however, did not interfere with *The Messenger*'s rhetoric in favor of the party and the unions.

In 1923 *The Messenger* issued a call for the formation of a United Negro Trades. Modeled after the United Hebrew Trades, it was to provide the machinery for bringing blacks into unions and to further the interests of those already within organized labor. But the United Negro Trades proved no more successful than the previous ventures launched by *The Messenger*. By then, the Negro monthly had alienated many black workers by its ceaseless attacks upon Marcus Garvey. The efforts of Randolph and Owen to have the black nationalist leader deported as an undesirable alien won them the approval of the Socialist political and trade-union press, but it antagonized the black masses, especially in the industrial centers of the North, who viewed Garvey as their champion and joined his Universal Negro Improvement Association by the hundreds of thousands.

In its controversy with Garvey, *The Messenger* lost the support of its contributing editor W. A. Domingo, a militant and articulate black spokesman for Socialism, who resigned from the magazine. As it became increasingly hostile to the Soviet Union and Communism, *The Messenger* lost young black militants like Cyril Briggs, Richard B. Moore, and others formerly associated with both it and the African Blood Brotherhood, who moved into the Communist camp.

Randolph and Owen continued to denounce "race prejudice within the unions" but conceded that little could be done about the situation, since "there is no machinery which can be set in motion either to get the Negroes in the unions . . . or to see that those who are in get justice both from the point of view of getting jobs in their trades and being elected officials in their unions."[11]

In 1924 *The Messenger* ceased to call itself the sole organ of "scientific radicalism" among Negroes the world over and adopted the subtitle "World's Greatest Negro Monthly." About the same time, Randolph abandoned his interest in promoting Socialism and a separate labor movement among blacks and devoted himself primarily to organizing the Pullman porters. Hoping to win an AF of L charter for the porters as an independent national union, Randolph kept *The Messenger* free of any criticism of the federation and its leadership for their indifference to the plight of the black worker, their rigid adherence to craft unionism, and their neglect of the unskilled and semiskilled of all races and nationalities. When Gompers died late in 1924, *The Messenger* paid tribute to him as a "dynamic and interesting" personality. It conceded that he had always been "diplomatically silent" on black labor but emphasized that the number of Negro trade unionists had increased under his regime.[12]

In 1925, as we shall see, the Brotherhood of Sleeping Car Porters was established with Randolph as general organizer, and *The Messenger* became the union's official organ. Randolph turned over the editorship of the once-radical magazine to George S. Schuyler, who produced its monthly issues until it ceased publication in the spring of 1928.

The battle against the trade-union philosophy and practices of the AF of L, abandoned by *The Messenger*, was carried forward in the early 1920's by a group of white and black left-wing members of the federation associated with the Trade Union Educational League. The TUEL was organized in November, 1920, by William Z. Foster to unite Communists, non-Communist radicals, and moderates within the AF of L and the railroad brotherhoods against the futile craft system of organization. The TUEL program called for amalgamation of existing craft unions into industrial unions, organization of the unorganized through industrial-type unions, independent political action by a party of workers and farmers, democratic unionism, a shop-steward system (much like the movement in England at the time), and recognition of and friendship with the Soviet Union.

The section on the Negro problem in the TUEL program, adopted in 1924, stated:

> The problem of the political and industrial disfranchised Negroes shall occupy the serious attention of the League. The League shall demand that the Negroes be given the same social, political and industrial rights as whites, including the right to work in all trades, equal wages, admission to all trade unions, abolition of Jim-Crow cars and restaurants.[13]

William Z. Foster's experience in the stockyards campaign of 1918 and the steel strike of 1919 had convinced him that no effective organization of the mass production industries was possible unless *special attention* was paid to the black workers. Yet he also knew from experience that opposition to white unions was strong among black workers, growing out of frequent betrayals and indifference to the blacks' needs. Hence, both as a Communist (he joined the Party in 1922), influenced by the Leninist approach to the special character of the black question, and as a practical trade-union organizer, he called upon all TUEL militants to join in a campaign "to open all unions to the Negro workers." It was necessary to this end to educate white unionists on the self-defeating effect of racism in organized labor and to impress upon black workers the need for joining with whites in a common struggle against the employers.

The *Labor Herald*, official organ of the TUEL, edited by Earl R. Browder, a member of the Communist Party, helped in the educational work with articles on the black worker and his problems. The issue of April, 1923, carried a story dealing with the black worker who had migrated from the cotton fields to the steel mills only to find that his rent, food, and clothing were costing more than he was making. He learned, too, that he was the last to be hired and the first to be fired. But, saddest of all,

> he learns to distrust the white workers, who will not take him into their unions, yet who call him scab because, as an unorganized worker, he must take whatever job is offered him. For years, various unions, while uttering official platitudes about no discrimination in the basis of nationality, color, creed, or politics, really followed the policy of Negro exclusion.

The article went on to point out that friction between black and white workers was "being nourished and developed by the employers for the purpose of dividing the workers and forcing upon them a fratricidal struggle." Unless the workers confronted the employing class with a united front regardless of race or color, they would never succeed. "All workers, Negro and white, foreign-born and native, skilled and unskilled, must organize industrially and politically, and thus present one front against the one enemy."[14] This was language reminiscent of the IWW's approach to the issue of black-white labor solidarity; indeed, quite a few former Wobblies were now active in the TUEL.

Even more pointed was an editorial in the *Labor Herald* of July, 1924, headed "Negroes and the Unions." It merits extensive quotation, for it was the most fully developed statement on the subject of black workers by the TUEL:

> Trade unions that neglect or discriminate against the negroes (and there are many such in this country) are following a narrow, short-sighted policy that will ultimately lead them to disaster unless it is changed.
> Leaving aside, for the moment, all questions of the interests of the negroes themselves (which are an essential part of the interests of the working class), and looking at the matter only from the selfish interests of the unions as now constituted, it is becoming plainer every day that if the labor movement is to be saved from the destruction at the hands of the "open shop" campaign . . . they must break down the prejudices instilled by capitalist institutions, they must accept the negroes on a basis of equality, they must organize them into complete solidarity with the white workers, native and foreign-born.
> It is no accident that in the industries dominated by the most militant

enemies of labor, the negroes are being brought in, in constantly increasing numbers. Because the unions are so short-sighted that they neglect the organization and education of our black brothers, they are thereby inflicting deep injury upon themselves. They are forcing the negroes into the position of strike-breakers. They are delivering a terrible weapon into the hands of the employers.

For the preservation of the unions, to defeat the "open shoppers," in order to build up working-class power—the negroes must be brought into the organized labor movement on a mass scale. All discrimination must be abolished. Every worker must be united in the unions without regard to race, creed, or color. It is time to put our high-sounding principles into effect if we would preserve the trade union movement.[15]

The leaders of the TUEL were not content to spout generalities about human brotherhood, which often were nothing but excuses for inactivity on the issue of Negro labor and a convenient mask for the prejudices of the trade unionists who spoke them. Instead, the TUEL leadership called upon the militants to work among the white sector of the trade-union movement, saturated with prejudice against the Negro, and win the support of the white unionists for a policy of opening all unions to the black worker and assuring him an equal opportunity to work on the same terms as the white worker.

James W. Ford, a black delegate to the Chicago Federation of Labor, described how the TUEL militants worked in the early 1920's. At one meeting of the federation, he charged the AF of L leadership with discrimination and "immoral trade-union conduct" toward Negro workers. As he had anticipated, several white delegates accused him of defending a class of workers who were mainly strike-breakers. To his utter surprise other white delegates came to his defense, although he was the lone Negro delegate. "They not only supported fully the charges I had lodged against the bureaucracy but succeeded in forcing it to permit me to continue my remarks." He later learned that these delegates were left-wingers and Communists, under the leadership of William Z. Foster, and that they were leading a fight in the TUEL for the rights of Negro workers. Ford immediately joined the league and later the Communist Party and became active in the battle against "race prejudice in the labor movement."[16]

The TUEL leaders were not generally successful in combating racism in the unions or in recruiting blacks. They grievously underestimated the resistance among white unionists to their program on the Negro question and often found them so blinded by race prejudice as "to prefer exploitation to cooperation with the colored man." The militants failed, too, to appreciate the resistance of the black working class to the white unions, instilled mainly by their experience with organized labor but deepened by the influence of the conservative Negro church and by the belief of many blacks employed in industry that their interests resided with the employing class rather than the white unionists. "The experiences of the Negro seeking work," commented *Opportunity*, the organ of the National Urban League, in October, 1924, "has forced him to believe that there is as much sacredness about the principles involved in his right to earn a living as were involved in the principles for which the white trade unionists stood."[17]

While thousands of workers rallied to the TUEL and conducted a series of strikes under its leadership, especially in the textile and needle-trades industries, in all these activities few black workers were involved. Few were touched by the great strikes in the needle trades, "since few of them," *The Crisis* noted, "are in the clothing-making industry."[18] All told, few blacks were recruited into the unions by the militants. A key issue for blacks was the written exclusion of blacks by federation affiliates, and the 1921 convention settled this matter decisively against the interests of black labor.* The battle began when Jordan W. Chambers, representing the Colored Coach Cleaners' Union in Saint Louis, aiming specifically at the Brotherhood of Railway Carmen, introduced a sweeping resolution requiring all member bodies to take the word "white" out of their constitutions, and every national or international union having jurisdiction over classes of work in which blacks were employed to admit workers regardless of creed, color, or nationality. This requirement was to be complied with before the AF of L's next annual convention. Should an affiliate fail to comply, the Executive Council was to revoke its charter.

Two other resolutions introduced by black delegates dealt with the same issue. One, by the union of Negro boilermakers from South Carolina, called for elimination of the term "white helpers" from the regulations defining certain classes of boilermakers' helpers' work. The other called for a conference at an early date of the Executive Council, the Brotherhood of Railway Clerks, and the Colored Freight Handlers to work out a plan for redressing the grievances of the freight handlers, particularly the refusal of the clerks to admit blacks or to appoint representatives to look after the freight handlers' interests in their dealings with the railroads. Any arrangement emerging from the conference was to be temporary, because it was taken for granted that the clerks at their next convention would accept the AF of L's 1920 recommendation to extend full membership to Negroes.

Only the resolution relating to the Brotherhood of Railway Clerks was approved by the Committee on Organization and later by the convention. On the other two resolutions, the committee would recommend

---

* The convention also delivered a setback to the efforts of the black delegates to present resolutions condemning the activities of the Ku Klux Klan in the South and urging the federal and state governments to take steps to crush the organization. The resolutions were not permitted to be presented. Condemning the action, the New York *Call* declared that "it was the duty of the convention not only to consider the resolutions of the Negro delegates, but to enlarge them to automatically exclude from membership any worker who holds membership in the Ku Klux Klan. It was an opportunity to draw the line on this matter, not alone in the interest of the Negro workers, but as a matter of self-protection for all the organized workers. Hutcheson of the carpenters is reported to have claimed the credit for objecting to any consideration of the resolutions. This shameless conduct will certainly have to be atoned for in the years to come. The membership and its interests have again been sacrificed by the reactionaries." (June 18, 1921.)

only that the grievances of the blacks be turned over to the Executive Council, which was to call meetings of the railway carmen and the boilermakers with the complaining Negroes within three months after the convention.

The black delegates refused to be bought off by this maneuver. Delegate Chambers pointed out that the carmen had done nothing in the year since the AF of L convention had told them to drop the term "white" from their bylaws. To call for another conference was an insult to the black members, and Chambers therefore moved that the committee's recommendation be rejected and his original resolution adopted. When Gompers declared Chambers's motion out of order, the delegate from the Colored Coach Cleaners appealed to the convention. For the first time in many years Gompers was overruled; the convention voted to recommit both resolutions, which the Committee on Organization had refused to endorse, to the Committee on Laws.

The AF of L bureaucracy rallied quickly from this defeat, and the Negro delegates received no better treatment from the Committee on Laws. Both proposals were again rejected with the observation that their adoption would commit the AF of L to interference with the trade autonomy of its national affiliates. The Committee on Laws, too, suggested conferences between the Executive Council and the interested parties.

Chambers still would not give up. To circumvent the objection that his resolution violated the principle of trade autonomy within the AF of L, he moved that action against the national affiliates that persisted in barring blacks be taken by the annual conventions rather than by the Executive Council. Gompers promptly sustained a motion that Chambers was out of order on the ground that he was merely resubmitting the motion that the Committee on Laws had turned down. A delegate from the Stereotypers International, a member of the TUEL, rose in Chambers's defense and bitterly charged the delegates with denying blacks the right to organize. "How can we hope for them to realize freedom in industry," he asked, "unless the American Federation of Labor gives them the same rights we enjoy?" He continued:

> I have discussed this with various individual delegates and they all agree with the principle, but they are sidestepping the issue, and I say to those in organized labor . . . the rights of the Negro have got to be considered, whether you like it or not. We are having the rights of international unions raised against this American principle the same as we have States rights against the rights of all the people of the country. The fight we make for industrial democracy, is the fight we make for political democracy, and we can no longer afford to deny equal rights [to] Negroes.[19]

A delegate from the laundry workers asked Gompers whether, if the convention decided to declare that AF of L affiliates must eliminate racial discrimination, it actually had the power to enforce its decision. Gompers replied that the convention could not enforce such a ruling if the affiliated bodies refused to abide by it. Daniel Tobin, Treasurer of the AF of L and Chairman of the Committee on Laws, supported Gompers by repeating the now familiar argument that the federation had no power to dictate to any international union the class of men they shall or shall not take in. That right, he declared, belonged to the unions themselves.

A move was made to suspend debate on the entire matter, and the delegates voted to accept the report of the Committee on Laws. The black delegates were left with the oft-repeated words of President Gompers that the AF of L had always declared it "the duty of all workers to organize regardless of sex, nationality, race, religion or political affiliation,"[20] and with the slim hope that the conferences to be held between black unionists and the railway carmen, the railway clerks, and the boilermakers would result in equal membership for blacks.

Only one of the three projected conferences was ever held, and it accomplished nothing to advance the interests of black unionists. The 1922 convention of the railway carmen provided for the admission of blacks in separate lodges, which were placed under the jurisdiction of the nearest white locals. Since the union would offer blacks nothing beyond auxiliary status, it saw no reason for a conference with representatives of the Colored Coach Cleaners. The AF of L Executive Council agreed, revoked the charters of the federal locals of the coach cleaners, turned them over to the carmen, and washed its hands of the matter. The boilermakers did not even bother to give black workers auxiliary status. They retained their constitutional bar against them and forgot about holding a conference with leaders of the Colored Boilermakers' Helpers Union. The AF of L Executive Council found this quite satisfactory.

Representatives of the Brotherhood of Railway Clerks and the Colored Freight Handlers did get together in the summer of 1921, and as a result the freight handlers obtained the right to form boards of adjustment on each rail line, which were to act in cooperation with representatives selected by the clerks' union to protect blacks in negotiations with railway management. The introduction at the 1922 railway clerks' convention of a resolution calling for elimination of the "whites only" clause in the constitution provoked such an uproar that it was immediately declared out of order. This, too, proved satisfactory to the AF of L, and no action was taken against the clerks for failing to live up to the federation's request to drop its written exclusion of Negroes. The matter was not even submitted by the Executive Council to the next annual convention, which, technically at least, had the power to expel any affiliate that violated its laws by a vote of two-thirds of the delegates assembled. The provision was being used to expel unions accused of being "Communist dominated," but there was no likelihood that two-thirds of the delegates to an AF of L convention would vote for expulsion of an affiliate to enforce the principle of equal membership for blacks.

Thus, by the time Samuel Gompers's lengthy tenure as president of the federation came to an end with his death in December, 1924, the only significant action for black labor taken by the organization he had headed—the recommendations at the 1920 and 1921 conventions to the railroad clerks, the railway carmen and the boilermakers—had produced absolutely no results. During this quarter-century, moreover, not only had black workers failed to register a significant increase in their membership in the AF of L, but also the number of federation affiliates denying admittance to black workers by constitutional provision or ritual had climbed from four to eleven.

"Jim-Crow unionism" had also increased, especially in the several black local and federal trade unions in the AF of L under the aegis of the Executive Council. In 1911 only eleven black unions held direct charters from the federation, but by 1919 this number had jumped to 161. Most of the new separate unions were made up of railway workers, and their organization was due not so much to the limited interest shown by the AF of L in recruiting blacks as to the government policy of dealing with employees only through organizations during the period of federal control of railroads.

By the time Gompers's presidency ended, the number of black locals had declined to fifty-one. The rapid decline was not explained by the international unions' absorption of the Negro locals. The freight handlers, who comprised the majority of the black locals, had been denied entrance into the Brotherhood of Railway Clerks by a constitutional ban, and the boilermakers and machinists, who also had jurisdiction over a fair number of segregated locals, continued to keep them out of the unions of their crafts in the same way. Other unions, such as the railway carmen and the blacksmiths, took in the black locals but gave them only second-class membership, under the supervision of white locals.

In short, ten years after the exodus of the black workers from Southern agriculture to Northern industry—a decade that had seen a phenomenal growth in the number of blacks employed as industrial workers, and at the end of which it was widely acknowledged that "Negro labor is a part of American industry, a spoke in the wheel of American production"[21]—black labor was no more able to gain large-scale admission to the AF of L than before the Great Migration.

When William Green succeeded Gompers as president of the AF of L in 1924, the hope arose among some blacks that he would lead a battle against the exclusionist practices of the federation's craft unions and the policy of limiting blacks, in the main, to segregated units. Green, after all, was a charter member of the United Mine Workers; he had served as a local union officer, subdistrict president, president of the Ohio district, and secretary-treasurer of the miners' union. It was reasonable to assume that his attitude toward black unionism would show some influence of the UMW's policy. Even Du Bois, skeptical though he was about white trade unionism in general and the AF of L in particular, entertained the hope that Green's background might cause him to combat the racial practices of organized labor.

Du Bois praised the UMW for having "organized the black miners without discrimination . . . throughout the country."[22] He appears to have been unaware that, by the time Green became AF of L president, the union's reputation for nondiscrimination was being seriously questioned. In Pittsburgh Abram L. Harris found that Negro members of the

UMW "seem quite happy in being affiliated with the organization," but, after investigating the status of the black miner for the West Virginia Bureau of Negro Welfare and Statistics, he reported that black miners who had quit the UMW had done so because, while the union was good for keeping up wages, "in many instances Negroes could not get jobs by which to earn the union wages" owing to the "Ku Klux spirit" in the union. Harris concluded his survey by warning the UMW that the Klan's power within the organization "must be checked or it will disrupt the labor solidarity among white and black workers at which the United Mine Workers aim."[23] Harris's evidence revealed that the "labor solidarity" had already been seriously disrupted.* Aside from that, the fact that William Green had never spoken out against violations of the union's professed policy of racial equality did not, to some black spokesmen, bode well for the relationship between the black worker and the AF of L under his leadership.

It was not long before the worst was known. An open letter from the NAACP to the 1924 AF of L convention, also addressed to other groups of organized labor, read in part:

> For many years the American Negro has been demanding admittance to the ranks of organized labor.
> For many years your organizations have made public profession of your interest in Negro labor, of your desire to have it unionized, and of your hatred of the black "scab."
> Notwithstanding this apparent surface agreement, Negro labor in the main is outside the ranks of organized labor, and the reason is first that white union labor does not want black labor and secondly, black labor has ceased to beg admittance to union ranks because of its increasing value and efficiency outside the unions.

Warning that the black worker had already broken the great steel strike and would soon be in a position to break any strike "where he can gain economic advantage for himself," even though this hurt both black and white labor, the NAACP insisted that it was essential for black and white labor to unite. "Is it not time for white unions to stop bluffing and for black laborers to stop cutting off their noses to spite their faces?" A proposal was advanced for formation of an Interracial Commission made up of the NAACP, the AF of L, the railroad brotherhoods, and other bodies agreed upon, which would seek: (1) to determine the exact attitude and practice of national labor bodies and local unions toward Negroes and that of black workers toward unions, and (2) to organize systematic propaganda against racial discrimination in local assemblies and unions. The NAACP stood ready to take part in such an effort and invited the cooperation of the entire labor movement. The appeal closed: "The Association hereby solemnly warns American laborers that unless

---

* In his study, "The Negro Miner in West Virginia" (unpublished Ph.D. thesis, Ohio State University, 1933), James T. Laing found that "the attitudes of union brothers who were also members of the Klan led some of the Negroes to withdraw from their locals" (p. 342).

some such step as this is taken and taken soon the position gained by organized labor in this country is threatened with irreparable loss."[24]

The NAACP plea for cooperation was acknowledged by the AF of L and then forgotten. Green's only sign of awareness of the black worker around that time was a warning he issued to blacks not to be enticed by the American Negro Labor Congress. The congress was sponsored by the Workers (Communist) Party, and two black Party functionaries, H. W. Phillips and Levett Fort-Whiteman, were instrumental in organizing the convention in October, 1925, at which the organization was born. The official call of the congress declared that its purposes were to accomplish the unionization of black workers and "the abolition of all discrimination, persecution and exploitation of the Negro race and working people generally; . . . to remove all bars and discrimination against Negroes and other races in the trade unions; . . . and to aid the general liberation of the darker races and the working people throughout all countries."

Thirty-two black delegates (men and women) and one Mexican-American, predominantly working class and representing a scattering of trade unions and farmer organizations, responded to the call and were present in Chicago. Greetings were sent to the congress by the TUEL, and William Z. Foster was a featured speaker. The congress declared that

> the failure of the American Federation of Labor officialdom, under the pressure of race prejudice benefiting only the capitalists of the North and South, to stamp out race-hatred in the unions, to organize Negro workers, and to build a solid front of the workers of both races against American Capitalism, is a crime against the whole working class. If the unions of the American Federation of Labor, through ignorance and prejudice, fail in this duty to the American workers in industry, we Negro workers must organize our own unions as a powerful weapon with which to fight our way into the existing labor movement on a basis of full equality.[25]

Preliminary to the founding of a separate black labor movement (which was never achieved) the congress favored the establishment of "local councils" in all centers of black population, which would form a united front with existing unions and other organizations. It called for the creation of "inter-racial labor committees" to "meet jointly for the purpose of bringing the Negro workers into the trade unions, preventing discrimination, undercutting of wages, the use of one race against the other in strikes, etc., and for bringing about the action of all workers, black and white, against lynching and race riots."[26] To help push the program, the congress started a newspaper, *Negro Champion*.

The Communist *Daily Worker* hailed the Negro Labor Congress and predicted that it would enable black workers to "become a power in the labor movement." The black press, however, was almost unanimously critical because of the Communist-inspired character of the congress. Du Bois was critical for the same reason, but he conceded that the congress's program was amazingly similar in objectives to the NAACP appeal to the AF of L. William Green, who had not bothered to comment publicly on that appeal, issued a public statement denouncing the Negro

Labor Congress as a Moscow-hatched plot "to convert the American
negro workingman to Bolshevism" and admonishing black workers not
to become "traitors to their Government." Green added that there was
no need for the congress: "The AF of L stands ready to give you the
protection of an organized movement."[27]

The American Negro Labor Congress, Ira De A. Reid points out,
"succeeded in arousing more public interest and editorial comment on
organizing Negro labor than has ever appeared in the public press."[28]
But the congress achieved relatively little to bring black workers into
the white trade unions.* The AF of L continued to warn blacks not to
be lured by "the Voice of Moscow" and to assure them that they had
no need for the Congress since the Federation offered them the "protection and experience of the Trade Union Movement."[29]

At the 1925 AF of L convention, a dispirited group of black delegates
who had been agitating since 1919 for wider recognition of their legitimate interests made their last effort. A delegate from a black federal
labor union introduced a lengthy resolution taking the AF of L to task
for its refusal to show an interest in the welfare of black workers. The
resolution singled out the policy of separate organization for Negroes,
condemning it as hardly better than no organization at all and as seriously undermining the doctrine of labor solidarity—a principle the AF
of L was so fond of proclaiming. The resolution urged the federation to
enter into negotiations with each affiliate for the purpose of eliminating
all traces of racial discrimination. Finally, the federation was asked to
proceed with "the greatest possible dispatch and energy" in launching
a drive to organize all black workers in the same unions with white
workers.[30]

The resolution fared no better than similar provisions submitted in
previous years. The 1925 convention, ignoring criticism of the federation's policy toward Negroes, boasted that all but a very few of the 110
member unions accepted black members. The AF of L practice of separate organization was overwhelmingly approved. Then, rubbing salt in
the wounds of the black delegates, the convention rejected a petition
from the Colored Coach Cleaners urging the Brotherhood of Railway
Carmen either to issue them a charter or to give them direct representation in both the union and the AF of L. (The petition noted that, by accepting limited membership in the carmen, the coach cleaners had
relinquished their right to govern themselves and with it their right to
send their own representatives to the AF of L's annual convention.) All
the convention offered the disenchanted black workers was help in arranging another meeting for the coach cleaners with the carmen, in the
slim hope that they could settle their differences.

From 1925 through 1927, no resolution relating to black labor was
even seriously discussed at an annual convention. Randolph, who attended the 1926 AF of L convention, complained that so far as black
workers were concerned "there was not a word on their problems, al-

---

* The American Negro Labor Congress lasted five years and was superseded in
1930 by the League of Struggle for Negro Rights.

though the American labor movement cannot reach its goal without them." The Pittsburgh *Courier* made the same point even more strongly:

> The American Federation of Labor, with its steadily declining member-ship, cannot afford to allow discrimination to continue within its ranks. . . . Otherwise it will become a means for destroying the organizations they have so laboriously built up. Some of the most loyal and militant workers in organized labor are Negroes. They have struck, walked the picket lines and starved in order that the right to bargain collectively with the employers might be established and maintained. The Negro worker demands the right to join every union, and having joined, he demands equal treatment with all other union workers regardless of race, creed, color or nationality. Otherwise organized labor cannot hope to retain his allegiance.[31]

But the AF of L was simply not interested in retaining the black work-ers' "allegiance." An attempt to have the Executive Council appoint a black adviser and organizer failed. "None of the international trade unions, which refused membership to Negroes, at the beginning of the year changed its policy," the National Urban League reported in its survey of the industrial and labor scene at the opening of 1927.[32] Mean-while, Negroes abandoned the separate federal and local unions in droves, so that by 1927 there were only twenty-one left in existence. As the resolution at the 1925 convention pointed out, black members had learned from bitter experience that such unionism was hardly better than no unionism at all.

On a state and city level, Negro labor was better represented, but how much better is difficult to measure. No one really knew just how many blacks were in unions, since few organizations kept membership statis-tics based on race. A survey made by Charles S. Johnson in 1928 esti-mated a black membership of nearly 200,000 in the trade unions, mostly in occupations where black labor was important—longshoremen, hod-carriers, and miners—or in independent black unions of railroad workers. But in 1930 the NAACP estimated the total at "no more than 50,000 colored members of national unions," and half of those were members of the black Brotherhood of Sleeping Car Porters.[33]

Often the presence of black unionists came to light only in strikes. Reports on the 1926 strike of the Paper Box Makers' Union in New York disclosed that "many Negroes are in the union." To allay any doubts, the union issued a special news release: "Our colored members who are on strike at the present time are just as vigilant as the rest of the workers in the strike. They have maintained their jobs and condi-tions in the past because they have found the Paper Box Makers' Union an upright and fearless body that will protect the rights of workers irrespective of color or creed."[34]

The fact that the presence of blacks in a union called for special mention indicates that black unionism was in a sorry state even in New York. So few blacks were in unions in the city that in December, 1924, the Central Trades and Labor Council of Greater New York called the presence of "tens of thousands of colored workers in New York as unorganized workers . . . a real menace to the higher standards of labor acquired at such a great sacrifice by the organized workers of New York." the council decided to give a helping hand to the Trade Union Committee for Organizing Negro Workers, an interracial Socialist group started by two blacks, Thomas J. Curtis and Frank L. Crosswaith. But not much was achieved. In January, 1926, the committee was reported to be encountering opposition from local unions in its efforts.[35]

The February, 1927, issue of *Opportunity* reported growing sentiment in favor of black membership on a local level. Even in the South, some unions were relaxing their rigid restrictions against black workers. By and large, however, "considerable prejudice still exists against Negro membership in trade unions." In too many cities, employers reported "willing to use Negroes, have been definitely prohibited by the unions." Too often, blacks who were admitted to unions found that, where hiring was through the organization, they ended up with no work.*

Two years later, in May, 1929, *Opportunity* found "no real advance in the attitude of organized labor toward the colored workers [and] sentiment in labor circles is still set against Negro participation."[36] As a consequence, all but a tiny percentage of the 1 million blacks in industry were still unorganized. The vast majority were still unskilled workers in steel plants, lumber and turpentine mills, slaughterhouses, and railroad construction. In automobile and rubber plants, textile mills, and box factories, blacks were still employed largely as janitors, truckers, and porters. Everywhere, North and South, they were mainly confined to laborious and unskilled tasks. Of the 1.5 million black women in gainful occupations, all but 80,000 were in agriculture, domestic and personal service, dressmaking, tobacco factories, or teaching. No other classification of women workers had as many as 10,000.

In April, 1928, Ira De A. Reid, a keen student of black labor, warned that black strike-breaking, which had declined since the 1919–21 period, would continue as long as the AF of L and its national affiliates remained indifferent to the black workers "despite their many resolutions and platitudes," international and local unions refused to admit black workers, and unions continued to discriminate against them after Negroes became members.[37] Writing in *The Nation*, John Davis, a young black, underscored Reid's point:

> I know a Negro bricklayer, a skilled workman, whose father was a bricklayer before him. He has no other vocation. He has spent his best years learning his trade. He has a family and the winter is coming. He would join a union gladly, but the white unions won't admit him. Our liberal white "friends" urge us not to irritate white unions by being scabs. They

* An investigation by the Federal Council of the Churches of Christ in America on Negroes in New Jersey unions noted many complaints from blacks that when they "join the union, the secretaries will discriminate against Negroes in favor of whites, so sometimes the Negro will be waiting for a job, having come first to the labor office, but the secretary will send out a white man who came in after him." *Toward Inter-Racial Cooperation: What Was Said and Done at the First National Inter-Racial Conference*, The Commission on Church and Race Relations, Federal Council of the Churches of Christ in America, Book Number 1 (1926), pp. 110–11.

tell us to wait until they can persuade the white unions to see the light. But who can wait when winter has come and there is no work, no feed?[38]

AF of L leaders continued to boast of their organization's support of labor solidarity and to blame Negroes for their nonunion status. In December, 1928, a National Interracial Conference was held in Washington at which John P. Frey of the Molders Union, a member of the federation's Executive Council, spoke for the AF of L. Frey—privately a notorious racist though publicly inclined to profess a sympathy for black workers—advanced the thesis that blacks suffered injustice in the labor world scarcely more than Jews, Poles, Italians, Russians, and even American workers. Racial prejudice had existed long before the formation of the AF of L, he insisted, and there was "no group in this country that I know of subject to more discrimination at the present time than the members of the American Federation of Labor." Frey stated flatly that "the American Federation of Labor and the great majority of the affiliated national unions not only organized the negro, but brought him into the white man's unions."[39] Restrictive membership policies in trade unions were largely legitimate efforts to avoid overloading the labor market, he claimed; with only few exceptions, the eagerness of trade unionists to recruit black workers outweighed the willingness of blacks to join. Negro leaders were especially to blame because they did not advise blacks to enter the trade unions even where they could do so, and Frey knew of no representatives of the race who had helped the AF of L to organize Negroes.

Frey's speech was sharply attacked in *The Nation* by NAACP leader Walter White. "The nature of his address," he wrote angrily, "can best be shown by considering his justification of exclusion of Negroes from labor unions on the ground that where the economic interests of white and Negro labor clashed the federation had considered the 'practical interest' of the federation and excluded the Negro." Regarding Frey's dictum that "unskilled labor must become skilled before it can gain rights," White commented: "Union labor keeps the Negro out of the skilled trades." How, in light of this and other obvious facts, could a spokesman for the AF of L stand before an intelligent audience and coolly justify "to his own satisfaction such a course?"[40]

William E. Walling, a Socialist active in the NAACP, in an effort to cool the controversy, told White (without convincing him) that public controversy could not lead to progress. He revealed his own feelings—shared by a number of other Socialists—in a letter to Frey in which he referred to Du Bois and other "nasty reds" among the NAACP leadership and reassured Frey that "labor's attitude on the color question is 100 per cent o.k. and it has nothing to be ashamed of."[41]

Frey concurred with this ridiculous evaluation in a reply to Walling and went on to blame the Negro worker for the low numbers of blacks in the unions. He again expressed the hope that "representative leaders of the negro race" would "assist the American trade union movement in organizing negroes by publicly advising them to become trade unionists."[42] Du Bois leveled a bitter blast at Frey in a *Crisis* editorial. Regarding Frey's charge that no leading black spokesman had joined the AF of L in attempting to organize Negroes, Du Bois quoted in full the NAACP appeal to the federation convention in 1924 and noted that, "besides perfunctory acknowledgements," no action had ever been taken on the plea. "This is a sufficient answer to Frey's awkward and insincere defense of the color line in the AF of L," Du Bois commented. His concluding observation summarizes the relationship of the AF of L to the black worker in the decade after the end of World War I: "The record of the American Federation of Labor toward the Negro is indefensible."[48]

13 The Brotherhood of Sleeping Car Porters

At the 1928 AF of L convention the white delegates were startled and somewhat shocked when a black union applied for an international charter. The application was presented by A. Philip Randolph, the dynamic Socialist who had left journalism to organize the Brotherhood of Sleeping Car Porters. At the time of the application, the Pullman porters had undergone three difficult years as an independent union.

Randolph and a few score of Pullman porters launched the brotherhood on August 25, 1925, in New York's Harlem. Its intention was to deal with the low wages, long hours, lack of adequate rest on trips, lack of bargaining power, and job insecurity in the porters' work. There were specific grievances as well: Porters were required to remain on call at sign-out offices for several hours a day without pay; porters-in-charge often had to perform conductors' work without adequate compensation for extra services; and the Pullman Employee Representation Plan did nothing to correct injustices.

When federal control of the railroads ended in 1920, the Pullman Company, eager to stifle the porters' efforts to organize, introduced the Employee Representation Plan, which, in the words of E. F. Carey, the company president, was "offered to our employees for the purpose of handling expeditiously and settling promptly and fairly all questions which arise as to wages, working conditions, and such matters as may be important to the welfare of the employees."[1] Basically, the plan was a company union. Like the antiunion schemes adopted by many other American companies during the postwar years, it included a promise not to discriminate against workers for membership in any union or fraternal order but insisted that "the right to hire and discharge shall be invested exclusively in the company." The workers' representatives could appeal a discharge as a grievance to the Bureau of Industrial Relations, whose decision was to be "final," but the bureau was simply the company's personnel department. Its chairman, who supervised the entire Employee Representation Plan, was appointed by the company, and the company controlled the operation of the plan by financing it and supervising the election of representatives.

It was not long before some of the porters' representatives under the

plan saw through it as merely a device to put a benevolent face on the
Pullman Company and discourage union consciousness. Some of the porters were ready to organize a real union but were deterred by a fear of
losing their jobs. In 1925, Ashley L. Totten, one of the militant employee representatives under the plan, heard A. Philip Randolph speak
and was impressed by the Socialist editor. He initiated a one-man campaign to sell the porters to Randolph and Randolph to the porters. At
the first meeting to launch the union movement, held privately in New
York, Randolph presided, read the motions he had drawn up in advance,
and then voted for approval himself, so that those present could not be
accused later by a company spy, certain to be there, of supporting a
union. A series of similar meetings followed, culminating in the establishment of a "National Committee to Organize Pullman Porters into
the Brotherhood of Sleeping Car Porters." Randolph was invited to become general organizer; W. H. Des Verney, who for thirty years had
been an operating porter, was chosen to assist Randolph; and Roy Lancaster, a former official of the Employee Representation Plan, became
secretary-treasurer.

From the beginning, *The Messenger* served as the spark for the brotherhood's organizational drive and the voice through which porters
(mostly anonymously) could express their grievances and desires. Porters operating between New York and Chicago risked discharge by serving as underground couriers, delivering bundles of *The Messenger* with
its descriptions of the porters' grievances and its presentation of the
brotherhood's program. They carried leaflets and confidential communi-
qués to the brotherhood nucleus already operating in Chicago.

It was not easy to win recruits for the brotherhood. Although unemployment had decreased by the mid-'twenties, blacks were still feeling
its effects. A large number of out-of-work blacks were eager to become
Pullman porters; indeed, it was often the only job a black college graduate could land. Those who were already porters were reluctant to risk
their jobs, and the company's welfare workers—ex-porters who paid visits
to porters and their families and usually received twice the salary of the
average porter—were quick to point out that Randolph, not being a Pullman porter and hence immune against the company's bitter hostility to
unions, had nothing to lose. Welfare workers, antiunion porters, and
company inspectors rode the trains on which union men worked and
invented charges of rule violations against them, which often led to their
discharge. To overcome the fear this practice created, the brotherhood
had to assure the porters that the membership list was carefully guarded.

Despite the stiff opposition of the Pullman Company, many porters
were convinced that they needed a real union to end the outrageous conditions under which they labored. There were 15,000 Pullman porters
traveling all over the country. Those assigned to regular runs began work
at $67.00 a month; if they remained in the service for fifteen years, they
would thereafter receive $94.50. Tips increased the actual earnings, but
the cost of uniform, shoe polish, meals, and so forth was deducted from
their wages. Their 11,000 miles of travel per month usually meant 400

hours, excluding preparatory time and time spent at the terminals. To aggravate the situation, porters often "doubled out" or ran "in charge" of a car, taking increased responsibility under unfavorable physical conditions for added pay at a diminishing rate. Many of the Pullman porters realized that only through collective bargaining could they hope for redress.

The rally publicly launching the brotherhood on August 25, 1925, in Harlem's Elk Hall, was hailed by the *Amsterdam News* as "the greatest labor mass meeting ever held of, for and by Negro working men." It drafted a set of demands and announced that the porters would settle for nothing less: (1) recognition of the brotherhood (which, of course, meant abolition of the Employee Representation Plan); (2) an increase in wages to $150 a month, with the abolition of tipping; (3) a 240-hour week and relief from unreasonable doubling out; and (4) pay for preparation time.

In August, 1936, Frank Crosswaith, a veteran black Socialist labor organizer who had been present at the meeting, eloquently declared:

The soldiers of labor's cause must never be permitted to forget that fateful August night eleven years ago, when enveloped by the suffocating heat of a summer's night and the stifling smoke from a hundred cigars, cigarettes and a few pipes, several hundred Pullman Porters defiantly threw down the gauntlet of battle to the nation's mightiest industrial monarch.

He went on to praise the porters for demonstrating "a courage hitherto unsuspected among Negroes in industrial warfare" and for awakening "the labor movement to the serious menace of the company union."[2] Though there were more than a few porters who did not dare to fight the company and face discharge, and though some were even spies for the powerful corporation, these black workers, in the main, merited Crosswaith's words of praise.

The brotherhood's first organizing drive in Chicago, headed by Milton P. Webster, a Republican leader in the city and a former Pullman porter himself, met with a magnificent response. But the majority of local black leaders were unenthusiastic. They argued that the porters could never successfully challenge the Pullman Company; that the company, because of its long record of hiring black workers, was a benefactor to the race and should be supported and not attacked; and that blacks should "not bite the hand that feeds you." The company made sure to distribute such statements by influential Negroes to rank-and-file porters, adding in its own releases that the brotherhood porter "nucleus" was made up of "derelicts who have been dismissed for incompetency," "traditional gripers," and "morons," and that Randolph was an "outsider," a "Communist agitator," and a "threat to our American way of life." Lancaster and Totten were fired, and Des Verney resigned before he could be dismissed.

Spearheading the attack for the Pullman Company was Perry Howard, a black Chicago attorney, Republican National Committeeman, and agent for the Department of Justice. Howard, an orator in the style of Booker T. Washington and an advocate of the expansion of segregation in government employment, challenged Randolph to a public debate in Chicago with the avowed purpose of "blasting and demolishing the Brotherhood and its leadership once and for all." The hall was packed with Negro workers, and Howard was lustily booed while Randolph received an ovation.

The debate occasioned not a single line in the Chicago papers, but word of mouth accounts among the porters gave the infant brotherhood much-needed publicity. This marked the beginning of a nation-wide offensive against the Employee Representation Plan. Ashley Totten drew on his wide experience and firsthand knowledge as a former official of the plan to blast its iniquities in *The Messenger*, leaflets, and speeches during an organizing tour across the country. Randolph and Totten swept victoriously through Saint Paul and Minneapolis, Seattle and Spokane, Portland (Oregon), Oakland, San Francisco, Los Angeles, Salt Lake City, Denver, Saint Louis, and Kansas City, leaving in their wake an ever increasing army of converts to the brotherhood. At the risk of their jobs, porters began assuming active roles in the union.

At first the Pullman Company did not take the brotherhood seriously, viewing it as just another of the many "fly-by-night" efforts of the porters to unionize. But as the brotherhood gained recruits, the company struck back viciously. Brotherhood stalwarts, several with decades of service as porters, were "dishonorably" discharged; thugs hired by the company struck down brotherhood organizers in broad daylight; and the black press was subsidized to launch an all-out offensive against the union. The Chicago *Whip* (which Randolph termed derisively the "Flip") and the *Defender* (which he called the "Surrender") not only advised porters to support the company union but urged members of the black community at large to "align themselves with the wealthier classes in America" as their only hope of salvation.[3] The *Argus* of Saint Louis, to that time a poorly financed publication, blossomed out in an increased size; its editorials flayed the brotherhood "reds," and it ran front-page stories presenting Pullman as the "benefactor of the Negro race." The Pullman Company placed half-page advertisements in the *Argus* and distributed copies free to porters. Following an investigation for *Labor Age*, Robert W. Dunn wrote that "praise of the company has come from negro papers all over the country in which advertising has been carefully purchased in return for a 'correct' editorial policy."[4*]

In the face of opposition from "respectable" black circles, the prompt firing of all who aided the organizing drive, and physical attacks on organizers, nuclei were established in several cities. Boston, Randolph acknowledged, was a "hard nut to crack" because porters there, like other New England workers, were steeped in conservatism and feared dire consequences for themselves from unionization, especially if it failed. But a nucleus appeared there as well.

With the Ku Klux Klan operating in high gear in the South, the

---

* There were a few exceptions, most notably, the New York *Amsterdam News*, the Chicago *Bee*, the Kansas City *Call*, and, for a time, the Pittsburgh *Courier*.

brotherhood restricted its organizational drives below the Mason-Dixon Line to a porter "underground," which made contact with the personnel of southbound trains and distributed literature explaining the union's program. When an organizer was finally dispatched to Jacksonville, the Pullman Company used its influence to hale him into court on a charge of preaching racial equality by distributing *The Messenger*. Given the choice of leaving Jacksonville within twenty-four hours or serving a term at a convict camp, he left at the advice of the brotherhood. Organization of the South would have to wait for some break in the hostile climate.

To counter the antiunionism of the black papers, ministers, and political leaders, the brotherhood sponsored labor institutes and Negro labor conferences in the larger cities throughout the country. The discussions centered on the grievances of the porters and the need for black workers in general to unionize. By the end of 1926, more than half the porters had pledged allegiance to the brotherhood. Pullman chose to ignore the fact and continued to deal with employees through its company union. However, it did step up its social-welfare program of summer picnics, parades, and Christmas parties. In order to deprive the brotherhood of one of its most effective organizing weapons—the porters' starvation wages—Pullman called a wage conference in 1926 and permitted the porters to elect delegates. At the conference, porters were granted an 8 per cent wage raise. Company officials were quick to point out that the Employee Representation Plan was responsible for the porters' pay rise. They neglected to mention that, in the election of delegates to the wage conference, the company had noted the name of every porter who failed to vote, and that these porters, assumed to be brotherhood members, were then threatened, suspended, or dismissed.

The company's concessions did not deter the brotherhood. In 1927 it pressed for the demands it had formulated two years before. But it was easier to formulate a series of demands than to win the porters' support for an all-out drive to realize them. Beset by company spies and detectives and subject to pro-company propaganda in much of the black press and most of their churches, many porters and their families dropped away. Only underground cells of solid, tried members continued to function, and their number was diminished whenever a cell was penetrated by a company spy and the identified cell members dismissed. To let the black porters know that they were not indispensable, the Pullman Company began hiring a few Chinese, Mexican, and Filipino porters. The brotherhood tried to reassure the black porters that U.S. immigration laws made this company threat meaningless, but the threat did have an effect.

With shrinking membership and a corresponding decline in dues, the brotherhood was forced to close many of its branch offices. It appeared that the efforts to unionize the black porters would have the same fate as Randolph's previous attempts to organize blacks into unions. But the brotherhood's long months of work and its courageous battles in the face of Pullman's vicious counteroffensive had won the admiration of many labor and liberal publications, which recalled Pullman's infamous record in the great strike of 1894 and urged support of the effort to curb the power of that long-time foe of unionism. The financial support came from a number of needle-trades unions and the Chicago Federation of Labor, whose president, John Fitzpatrick, spoke at public meetings and over the radio on behalf of the brotherhood. Soon other officials of the AF of L, including William Green, joined the supporting chorus. Worried about the influence of Communists in the Negro working class, they saw the brotherhood, whose leadership was bitterly anti-Communist, as a bastion against the American Negro Labor Congress.

Although most of the black papers continued to be hostile—the Pittsburgh *Courier*, formerly a champion of the brotherhood, did an about-face and declared that the company had properly refused to recognize the union because Randolph was a Socialist—*The Crisis*, the *New York Age*, the *Amsterdam News*, and other black journals rallied to the brotherhood's defense and sponsored benefits that netted funds much needed by the organization. The NAACP and locals of the National Urban League endorsed the brotherhood, and some black churches even permitted it to use their buildings for meetings. Most important of all, many black workers came to see the brotherhood both as a symbol of the Negro's claim to dignity, respect, and a decent livelihood and as a test of the ability of black workers to build and maintain an effective union. "The fight of the Pullman porters is the all absorbing topic wherever two or more Negroes gather in Harlem," one report said.[5] Many blacks knew the words of "The Marching Song of the Fighting Brotherhood," set to the tune of "My Old Kentucky Home":

> We will sing one song of the meek and humble slave
> 　　The horn-handed son of toil
> He's toiling hard from the cradle to the grave
> 　　But his masters reap the profit of his toil.
> Then we'll sing one song of our one Big Brotherhood
> 　　The hope of the Porters and Maids
> It's coming fast it is sweeping sea and wood
> 　　To the terror of the grafters and the slaves.

> (Chorus)

> Organize! Oh Porters come organize your might,
> 　　Then we'll sing one song of our one Big Brotherhood,
> Full of beauty, full of love and light.[6]

In its hour of distress, the brotherhood also had the support of the porters' wives and women relatives organized in the Colored Women's Economic Council. The council formed women's auxiliaries in various cities, which staged rallies, bazaars, picnics, boat rides, theater benefits, and other types of fund-raising socials. Of particular importance was the help the auxiliaries gave to porters' families who had suffered because of Pullman dismissals.

Encouraged by this support, the brotherhood moved against the Pullman Company on a government level. On May 20, 1926, the Railway

Labor Act had become law. It provided for "the prompt disposition" of all disputes between railroad carriers and their employees. In case of a dispute, the act called upon the two sides to meet in joint conference to "make and maintain agreements" on rates of pay, rules, and working conditions. Employee and employer representatives were to be designated without "interference, influence, or coercion," and any dispute that could not be resolved in conference was to be submitted to a federal board of mediation.

After trying vainly to get E. F. Carey, the president of the Pullman Company, to meet with the brotherhood as the "designated and authorized" bargaining agent of the porters, Randolph appealed on October 15, 1927, to the Railroad Mediation Board to settle the dispute between the company and the brotherhood. At the same time, the brotherhood invoked the quasi-judicial powers of the Interstate Commerce Commission against the system of tipping as a substitute for adequate wages, urging the ICC to compel the Pullman Company "to cease and desist from directly or indirectly informing or instructing applicants for positions as porters that they may expect increment to their wages from passengers" on the ground that this was a violation of the Interstate Commerce Act.[7]

The brotherhood met with failure in both appeals. In August, 1927, the Railroad Mediation Board announced that the parties had failed to reach agreement through mediation and recommended arbitration. But arbitration was voluntary, and the Pullman Company rejected the board's recommendation, which closed the first appeal.* Then, in March, 1928, the ICC ruled by a vote of four to three that it did not have jurisdiction in the dispute between the Pullman Company and the brotherhood.

Faced with dwindling membership, depleted funds, and a government clearly unwilling to stand up for the black workers, the brotherhood announced that it would strike the Pullman Company as the only way to compel recognition of the workers' right to collective bargaining. The strategy was to force President Calvin Coolidge to set up an emergency board under Section 10 of the Railroad Labor Act to investigate the dispute and report its findings to him, and then, confident that the findings would support the brotherhood, rally public opinion to induce the President to put them into effect.

The threatened strike made news in every paper the country over, and

* In reaching this decision, the Pullman Company seized upon Randolph's tactical blunder in sending it a fifteen-page letter in which he assured the company that it stood to benefit immensely from recognizing the brotherhood. "Under the influence of the Brotherhood," he emphasized, "discipline would flow from the principle of attraction, instead of coercion." Randolph conceded that the company had the right to require discipline from the porters and pledged that, if recognized, the brotherhood would do more for the company to maintain discipline than would any company union. In all, the brotherhood would cooperate to the full "to build a bigger and better Pullman industry to serve the nation." A. Philip Randolph to John R. Morron, June 4, 1927, Lowell M. Greenlaw Papers, Chicago Historical Society.

All Randolph accomplished by the toadying tone of his letter was to convince the company that the brotherhood was weak and its demand for recognition could be ignored.

denunciations of Pullman's system of tipping as a substitute for proper wages filled many columns. Heywood Broun, in the New York *Herald-Tribune,* called the Pullman Company "a panhandler. Some federal police officers should take away the tin can from the corporation and confiscate its pencils. . . . I'm tired of tipping the Pullman Company."[8]

But the brotherhood strategy came to naught. The Railroad Mediation Board ruled that Section 10 of the Railway Labor Act did not apply in the dispute between the union and the Pullman Company and that, "in the Board's judgment, an emergency as provided for in the said section does not exist in this case."[9] Many porters, fed up with the company's stalling and the government's do-nothing policy, urged the brotherhood to go ahead with the strike, indicating their willingness to risk the consequences. Randolph, in a newspaper interview, announced that "this is the first time we have threatened a strike and we intend to go through with it if our men favor doing so."[10] The brotherhood then took a strike vote, and the results were astounding, indicating how many porters were ready to prove that they were not "Uncle Toms." By a vote of 6,053 to 17 the strike was approved.

Then Randolph began to have second thoughts. The strike vote had indicated that the porters were willing to walk out if need be to secure their rights and win their demands, but "a strike vote doesn't mean that the porters will necessarily strike," he declared.[11] Randolph was aware that the company was building a huge mechanism to cope with a strike should one be called, but most influential in his decision to disregard the vote of the porters was the advice he received from William Green, who said that "a strike at this time would play into the hands of the Pullman Company" and counseled instead "a campaign of education and public enlightenment regarding the justice of your cause and the seriousness of your grievances."[12] On June 8, 1928, the brotherhood's leadership called off the strike.

Randolph's decision not to go forward after being empowered to do so by the membership was a serious blow to the morale of the porters. But the brotherhood's leader argued that the mere threat of a strike had brought the union a great gain, since it had "reversed the concept of the American public stereotype of a shuffling, tip-taking porter to an upstanding American worker, demanding his right to organize a union of his own, as well as a living wage." The Communists, who had long been critical of the "craft isolation" of the "present leadership of the Brotherhood of Sleeping Car Porters," claimed a sell-out and charged that it smacked of "typical AF of L and Railroad Brotherhood type of leadership." They called upon the porters to replace the leaders with "a militant, class conscious leadership."[13] For years to come, black Communists pointed to the calling off of the strike as a blow to the entire black working class. "The chances of success were very bright," *The Liberator,* a black Communist weekly, declared on July 20, 1931. "The rank and file of the porters were very militant. The Randolph leadership and the AF of L called the strike off, betraying Negro workers in the interest of the labor fakers."

Brailsford R. Brazeal, in his history of the union, agrees with the interpretation of the brotherhood leadership that the mere threat of a strike had produced gains for the union and adds that "this was the first time in the history of the United States that a large mass of Negroes, submarginal workers, conditioned as inferiors, threatened to project a strike on a national scale under Negro leadership."[14]

The sagging morale of the porters received a lift as a result of a court decree compelling the Texas and New Orleans Railroad to disband its company union. This ruling was the result of a petition by the Brotherhood of Railway Clerks charging that the Texas and New Orleans Railroad financed and otherwise controlled its employees' representation in violation of the Railway Labor Act of 1926. The Texas decision, which was finally upheld by the U.S. Supreme Court, encouraged the brotherhood leadership in the conviction that, despite losses in membership and funds, and although many long and bitter struggles and disappointments lay ahead, the battle against Pullman's company unionism would succeed. With this conviction, the brotherhood applied to the AF of L Executive Council for an international charter.

By 1925 Randolph had become as conciliatory toward the AF of L as he had once been critical. Already in 1923 he had attempted to mend his bridges with Gompers, whom he had condemned as the symbol of all that was evil in the federation, by inviting him to contribute articles to *The Messenger*. From the beginning of William Green's presidency in 1924, Randolph sought his advice, support, and practical know-how in building the brotherhood. As we have seen, Green, who was especially disturbed by Communist efforts to influence the black workers, regarded the success of the fledgling brotherhood and its affiliation with the AF of L as a way of assuring that, if blacks were to be organized, it would be under "wise leadership." The brotherhood's leadership, sorely in need of Green's financial assistance and moral support, and sharing much of his aversion toward the Communists, found it beneficial to cultivate harmonious relations. Most of the AF of L internationals did not share Green's enthusiasm for the brotherhood, recalling Randolph's earlier attacks on their unions and not forgetting that, while anti-Communist, he was still a Socialist. But since the porters' union did not threaten the segregated job structure or their monopoly, they were prepared to support the entry of the brotherhood within the "House of Labor."*

But the idea of admitting the Negro union as an equal was too much

---

* Even the railroad brotherhoods favored affiliation of the brotherhood with the AF of L, where it would be kept by jurisdictional rules from encroaching on railroad jobs set aside for whites only.

To a number of black papers and politicians, news of the prospective affiliation with the AF of L was enough to kick up another storm of criticism of the brotherhood. The Chicago *Defender* denounced the brotherhood for wanting to join the federation, which it called "paradoxically plutocratic and communistic." Through the Louisville *News*, a black politician urged the brotherhood to have nothing to do with the AF of L and, instead, "to seek to win the Pullman Company officials." Chicago *Defender*, August 20, 1927; Louisville *News*, December 26, 1925.

for the internationals to swallow. Consequently, when the Hotel and Restaurant Employees' International claimed jurisdiction over the brotherhood on the ground that the Pullman porters were hotel workers on wheels, the white internationals backed its claim. Randolph was already subject to sharp criticism for calling off the strike. He knew that if he consented to tie the brotherhood to an organization like the Hotel and Restaurant Employees' International, which had a constitutional provision establishing the inferior status of black workers, his leadership would be jeopardized. He rejected the "feasible solution" offered by the AF of L, and the porters gave him a resounding vote of confidence. At conferences before the Executive Council, Randolph made it clear that the brotherhood would never consent to be just another dues-paying "Jim-Crow auxiliary."[15] The AF of L international was equally firm in refusing to relinquish its jurisdictional claim. A compromise was finally reached under which Randolph, in order, as he put it, "to establish a beach-head,"[16] affiliated thirteen of the brotherhood's largest divisions as "federal unions" of the federation.

Some sections of the Negro press, along with certain black politicians and clergymen, denounced Randolph for having anything at all to do with the AF of L, citing its general exclusion for most black workers and Jim Crow status for the rest. But Randolph was criticized most of all for accepting "federal union" status when experience had proved it to be a type of unionism that completely hamstrung the efforts of black workers to improve their standards. The Communists termed Randolph's acquiescence another indication of the bankruptcy of the brotherhood leadership.

Randolph defended his decision as fundamentally sound. As the delegate of the New York division, he would gain entrance to AF of L conventions. Once there, he could study at close hand this "American version of the labor movement" and wage a battle to remove the stumbling blocks it placed in the way of unionizing black workers. Randolph saw the sleeping car porters as "the spearhead which will make possible the organization of Negro workers."[17] He was convinced that the brotherhood could best do so within the federation.

In 1929 the brotherhood called its first national convention in Chicago, at which it adopted a constitution and held its first election of officers. Randolph was elected president, Milton P. Webster first vice-president, and Roy Lancaster secretary-treasurer. The union was all but defunct at the time: The membership had declined to the vanishing point after the Pullman Company fired or suspended every porter found to have voted in favor of the strike. But Randolph was determined that the union of black workers must not fail. "We are making history for our race," he had emphasized in a letter to Webster. "We are sounding the tocsin for a new race freedom." In another letter to Webster, dated August 27, 1928, he gave this advice on how to recount the formation and early history of the brotherhood:

> One thing I would stress very fundamentally though, and that is that never again will Negroes permit white people to select their leaders for

them. I would make it very emphatic that upon that principle we shall not compromise, not only with respect to the Pullman porters but with any Negro movement. Negroes will no more permit white people to select their leaders than will white people permit Negroes to select theirs. I would emphasize the fact, too, that the Pullman porters organization is a Negro movement, and that it stands for the self-expression and interest of Negroes by Negroes for Negroes. I would also indicate . . . that it would not matter what the opposition would be, that the question of right of Negroes to choose their own leaders is as fundamental as the right of life itself.[18]

14 Black Workers During the Great Depression

"The depression brought everybody down a peg or two. And the Negroes had but few pegs to fall."[1] Thus did Langston Hughes, the great black poet, point up in his autobiography the stark fact that Negroes had never experienced anything but depression. The overwhelming majority of those who worked in the mines, the fields, and the factories, of course, white as well as black, never knew prosperity during the "golden years" of the 1920's. The black workers actually suffered severe privation. Consistently underpaid in relation to white workers; forced to accept the least desirable, most menial jobs; charged exorbitant rents to live in crowded black ghettos from which they could not escape, Negro wage-earners found themselves excluded, with few exceptions, from skilled and semiskilled, white-collar, and professional situations, and without exception from supervisory and managerial posts. E. Franklin Frazier, the noted black sociologist, summed up the situation in 1927: "There are two types of businesses in New York in terms of Negro hiring policy: those that employ Negroes in menial positions and those that employ no Negroes."[2] Black women were worse off than men. The U.S. Women's Bureau, in a survey of four states, reported that prior to 1929 Negro working women averaged less than $300 annually, or about six dollars a week.

The Negro in Southern agriculture during the so-called era of general prosperity was still ensnared in the system of enslavement known as peonage, despite federal antipeonage laws. Negro tenant farmers and sharecroppers, having no money, bought their goods on credit from plantation stores in return for the proceeds from crops. No accounts were kept, and when the season was over the Negro generally found that he owed the plantation owner money. Blacks who protested were kicked quietly outdoors and, in some cases, lynched.

The Great Depression of the 1930's had begun for the black workers by the end of 1926. "The last to be hired, the first to be fired," Negroes experienced widespread unemployment as early as 1927, as reported in the monthly bulletins of the Bureau of Labor Statistics. In the early months of 1929, with the economy supposedly flourishing as never before, 300,000 Negro industrial workers, about one-fifth of all blacks employed in industry, had already been thrown out of work.

Behind these statistics was the stark fact that areas traditionally open to blacks were shrinking. Since 1923 there had been a serious decline in cotton crop production, limiting work for agricultural labor and forcing migrations to cities and industrial areas. Simultaneously, the bituminous coal, iron and steel, and lumber industries, which had absorbed thousands of black workers, were suffering declining production and were laying off blacks. The substitution of machinery for hand labor and other technological changes were lessening the need for common labor, which Negroes traditionally provided. In May, 1929, Charles S. Johnson noted that the "numerical increase of Negroes in industry has been halted."[3]

The crisis of 1929–32 was a disaster for all American workers. From the stock market crash of October, 1929, which began the collapse, to its low point in 1933, the number of unemployed rose from 3 million to approximately 15 million (some placed it as high as 17 million). Wages dropped 45 per cent, and the percentage of the population living at or below the bare subsistence level rose from 40 per cent in 1929 (the year of greatest prosperity) to 75 per cent in 1932.

However much white workers suffered, blacks suffered even more. Soon after the Great Depression began, the position of the black workers became desperate. Many employers immediately fired their Negro workers, although a few discharged whites first because blacks worked for lower wages, often as much as one-third less. Soon it was the general practice to replace blacks with whites at "Negro" wages or lower. In the North white girls replaced Negro waiters, hotel workers, and elevator operators. The Pittsburgh *Courier* reported on June 27, 1931, that in one city alone 600 black janitors had lost their jobs to whites. White men in the South began building roads, digging ditches, waiting in hotels, and repairing railroad tracks—doing the type of work usually associated with Negro labor—and forcing employers to discharge Negro workers. When black firemen on the Louisiana division of the Illinois Central Railroad did not vacate their jobs, vigilante groups were organized to warn them that if they did not resign, they would not live to work again. Ten black railway employees were killed and eleven more were wounded. "Murder for the job" was the way *The Nation* described the bloody incident.[4]

When one realizes that almost 25 per cent of employed urban blacks on the eve of the Depression worked as household domestics and that their services were dispensed with as soon as the economic crisis began, that the largest concentrations of black industrial workers were in building construction (hod carriers and common laborers) and bituminous coal mining, which were among the first industries to feel the effects of the business slowdown and remained stagnant during the entire Depression, it is easy to understand that black workers felt the impact of the Great Depression earliest and bore its heaviest burdens.

Throughout the Depression years, the percentage of Negroes unemployed continued to be higher than that of either native or foreign-born whites. The U.S. Bureau of Census Special Unemployment Census showed the following unemployment percentage figures by race and nativity among male workers in thirteen U.S. cities for January, 1931: manufacturing and mechanical industries—white (native born) 31.7; white (foreign-born) 29.9; Negro 52.0. The figures for domestic and personal service (including female workers) were: white (native born) 17.7; white (foreign-born) 12.4; Negro 30.7. A National Urban League summary in 1931, based on reports from investigators in 106 cities, was that the proportion of Negroes unemployed was from 30 to 60 per cent greater than of whites, and that the percentage of Negroes among the unemployed ran sometimes four, five, or six times as high as their population percentage. In April, 1931, about one-seventh of the Negro males and one-twelfth of the Negro females in the North were unemployed; for whites, the proportions were one-twelfth of the males and one-twentieth of the females. In Detroit, however, about one-third of the white males and one-sixth of the white females were without jobs, whereas 60 per cent of the Negro males and three-fourths of the Negro females were unemployed. In Cleveland, where one-third of the white men and one-sixth of the white women were jobless, more than half the Negro men and women were unemployed. A few Southern cities showed the same pattern. In Houston, for example, the proportion of Negroes unemployed was twice that of whites.

As the Depression deepened, the differentials between white and Negro unemployed increased. In Cincinnati, 28 per cent of the white and 54.3 per cent of the Negro workers were unemployed in 1933. A survey in Pittsburgh revealed that in February, 1934, "48 per cent of the Negroes were entirely without employment . . . while only 31.1 per cent of the potential white workers were unemployed." A U.S. Department of Labor Study from 1928 to 1931 in Bridgeport, Buffalo, Syracuse, and Philadelphia pointed out that "the proportion of Negro women unemployed ordinarily was greater than their share in the total woman population or among those in gainful employment."[5]

Relief statistics tell much about the incidence of Negro unemployment. In 1933, in Chicago and Philadelphia, 34 per cent of the black families were on relief; in Pittsburgh and Cleveland the figure was 43 per cent; and in Akron, Ohio, 67 per cent. In Detroit the Negro population was only 4 per cent, but it supplied 25 per cent of the total relief cases; in Saint Louis only 9 per cent of the population and 60 per cent of the relief cases were Negroes; and in Englewood, New Jersey, with a 20 per cent Negro population, blacks accounted for more than 90 per cent of the relief cases. In addition to the relief families, thousands of unattached Negro men and women registered for relief between 1929 and 1935. Many had drifted from the drought-stricken areas of the Southwest to the cities, where, of course, they found no work.

In relief as on the job, the black received less than the white worker, especially in the South. In Jacksonville, Florida, the Negro received 20 cents an hour for the same relief work for which a white man was paid 30 cents. In Miami the black was paid $1.25 a day and a white unemployed worker $2.45. In one Southern city, where Negroes were 25 per cent of the population but 40 per cent of those unemployed, unemployed blacks received only 25 per cent of the relief funds. The nationwide average weekly grocery order allowed a Negro family on Home Relief was estimated in 1932 to be only $1.25.

Even these meager funds would not have been forthcoming from local and state governments had not black and white unemployed joined forces in a militant struggle for work and relief, mostly under the leadership of the Communist 'Party. The Communists set up Unemployed Councils with Negroes and whites on equal grounds to demand relief funds. They also sponsored hunger marches on state capitals and in Washington, D.C., demanding more relief and work and unemployment insurance.

Blacks not only participated on an equal footing in the various Unemployed Councils but often assumed leadership. Among the 1.25 million workers throughout the nation who responded to the call for a demonstration on National Unemployment Day, March 6, 1930, were thousands of blacks. Three thousand workers, two-thirds of them black, including a line of children, marched in Birmingham under the leadership of the Unemployed Council, demanding work or relief. The children were reported as singing:

> Empty is the cupboard, no pillow for the head,
> We are the hunger children who fight for milk and bread
> We are the workers' children who must, who must be fed.[6]

In Shreveport, Louisiana, unemployed blacks and whites demanded "work or feed" and battled police who tried to arrest them. Of 2,000 hunger marchers in the same city in 1931, 500 were blacks, and one was chosen to present a petition to Congress for unemployment insurance. The *New York Times* of April 2, 1931, reported that on the previous day more than fifty hunger marchers, of whom about forty were black, had entered the Maryland House of Delegates at Annapolis and demanded a hearing on petitions for aid to the unemployed. Three delegation spokesmen from Baltimore were permitted to address the House. "Colored men among them took papers from brief cases and recited the demands." These included the establishment of an unemployment insurance program and diversion of funds for a new penitentiary and state salaries above $2,000 into such a program. By the fall of 1931 it was a common sight to see blacks appearing at the heads of unemployed demonstrations at numerous state capitals. Two of the leaders of the national hunger march in December, 1932, were Negroes, and as many as one-fourth of the marchers were black. " 'No discrimination against Negro workers!' 'Equal relief for the Negro jobless.' These and similar slogans were displayed on banners carried by the marchers, both Negro and white."[7]

In Atlanta, Georgia, nineteen-year-old Angelo Herndon, a black Communist worker, veteran of the Birmingham hunger marches, was arrested for the crime of leading Negroes and whites in an unemployed demonstration. He was prosecuted under charges of violating a pre–Civil

War insurrection law revived for the occasion, and sentenced to life on the chain gang. In Atlanta in 1930 police broke up a meeting of blacks and whites under Communist sponsorship and arrested six organizers. The "Atlanta Six," as they were called, were charged with insurrection under a statute enacted during the Civil War against newly freed Negroes—a statute that carried the death penalty.

In 1931 a sharecroppers' union was formed at Camp Hill, Alabama, by two black Communist organizers and called "Society for the Advancement of Colored People" to conceal the fact that it was a union. Black sharecroppers joined and paid their initiation fee of five cents. Their trust in Communist leadership had been enhanced by the Party's role that year in the defense of the "Scottsboro Boys" in a trumped-up rape case* and by the educational work carried on by the *Southern Worker*, a Party paper published secretly in the South. The new union spread rapidly, gaining 800 members in a short time. It expressed the demands of sharecroppers as follows: continuation of the food allowance, which had been cut off in July when the crop was already cultivated, leaving the sharecropper to starve or beg until cotton-picking time in September; recognition of the sharecropper's right to sell his produce for cash where and when he pleased, rather than turn it over to the landlord for "division"; cash settlement for the season at cotton-picking time; a nine-month Negro school with free bus; and the right of the sharecropper to have his own garden. For agricultural laborers the demands were one dollar a day instead of 30 to 40 cents, and eight hours of work instead of work from sunup to sundown. For both sharecroppers and laborers the union demanded the right to vote and to serve on juries, equal education, and school facilities for their children. To its members, the union meant protection from the unlimited power of the landlord, merchant, and sheriff. "The union," Clyde Johnson, a black organizer, recalled, "represented hope and protection, it was their voice."[8]

A union meeting on July 16, 1931, near Camp Hill to protest the death sentence of eight of the nine Scottsboro Boys was interrupted by the Tallapoosa County sheriff and his deputies. Two officers were wounded, one Negro was killed, and more than thirty blacks were arrested, five of them charged with murder. Three hundred whites spread terror through the section. "Nigger hunts" were organized to kill or run out union men. Four of the sharecroppers who had been arrested "disappeared" from the Dadeville jail. The Birmingham *News* carried front-page headlines shrieking "Revolution" and "Communist Plot."[9] The historian Dan T. Carter points out, "any effort to give the Negro tenant a voice in the renting and sharecropping contract and a role in determining wages was essentially 'revolutionary.' "[10]

Nevertheless, the sharecroppers won the continuation of their food

* On March 25, 1931, the nine Scottsboro Boys were pulled from a train on which they had been traveling in quest of work and accused of raping two white girls riding the same train. The intervention of the International Labor Defense (ILD) halted the execution of the eight sentenced to death, and while the innocent victims remained in jail the defense movement, which reached international proportions, prevented their execution for many years.

allowance and the right to keep gardens rather than have to buy from the landlords. They forced the release of their imprisoned union brothers and compelled the landlords to let up on the terror. But not for long. A second race riot occurred in December, 1932. Three more Negroes were killed, and six were arrested for the wounding of four white officers. The ILD, the NAACP, the Commission for Interracial Cooperation, and the American Civil Liberties Union joined to defend the black unionists, but the sharecroppers' union was destroyed. The Communists also attempted to organize a Negro cotton-pickers' union in the same section of Alabama, but a strike for back pay was met with the arrest of seven Negro cotton-pickers, and the union was unable to function.

In 1928 the Communist Party issued a draft resolution "On the Negro Question in the United States." Most discussions of the resolution have focused on its declaration that the Black Belt of the South was an oppressed nation and its call for self-determination. This idea never met with much response from blacks and was short-lived. More lasting was the resolution's insistence that "the organization of the Negro in the trade unions must be recognized by the Party as one of its foremost tasks."[11] Acknowledging that the Trade Union Education League, despite its opportunities, had "neglected this important work," the Party called for the immediate launching of a "campaign to organize the Negro workers, in the existing unions, where possible, or in independent unions."[12] The task of carrying through this mission was undertaken by the Trade Union Unity League (TUUL), formed in 1929 with William Z. Foster as Secretary after attempts by the left-wing militants to work within the AF of L had resulted in nothing but expulsions and frustrations, leaving the mass of the workers still unorganized.

The TUEL had been a propagandist and educational organization, whereas its successor aimed at organizing outside the federation while continuing some boring from within. The TUUL sought to "create a trade union center of minority groups and individual militants" and to become the "organizer of the masses of unorganized workers, as well as to direct the work of the minorities in the reformist unions against the AF of L bureaucracy."[13] Of 20,000,000 organizable workers, only 3,000,-000 were organized in 1929, and these for the most part were skilled workers. Of the unorganized workers, Foster pointed out, the Negroes, being the "poorest of the poor . . . the lowest paid workers in the industries and in domestic service . . . the most bitterly and persecuted element of the whole population,"[14] were most in need of unionization. But the AF of L had long since demonstrated its unwillingness and inability to accomplish this. Hence "a primary duty" of the TUUL was to bring the black workers, "the most exploited and oppressed of the American working class," into the labor movement. "The Negro workers must be united with the white workers in the new unions; where necessary special unions must be built for that purpose; and the Negro masses brought organically into the trade union movement."[15]

The TUUL first set up independent unions in the coal and textile industries and the needle trades; later it entered the steel, automotive, and maritime industries. The unions established in these industries grew out of groups set up by the old TUEL, and all stated in their constitutions that they fought "for equality for the Negro worker both on and off the job."[16] Jim Crow unionism was outlawed, and blacks and whites were organized within the same locals, even in the South. In the great textile strike of 1931 at Gastonia, North Carolina, the TUUL's National Textile Workers' Union, with black Communist Otto Hall as chief organizer, organized black workers in the mills together with white workers. The mill owners, of course, accused the union of "breaking the color line," and even the AF of L's United Textile Workers' Union (which either ignored blacks or organized a few in separate unions) joined the chorus of white supremacists.* Handbills distributed among the white workers proclaimed: "You believe in White Supremacy. Would you belong to a union which opposes White Supremacy?"[17] The miserably paid, overworked white textile workers stood firm and endorsed the National Textile Workers' Union response that "unity between white and black workers" would be maintained despite terrorism against the strikers and their leaders.[18]

The abuses of the John L. Lewis administration in the United Mine Workers, climaxed by the catastrophic strike of 1927–28, led first to the "Save-the-Union-Committee" formed by the TUEL, followed in September, 1928, by formation of the National Miners' Union. The NMU appealed especially to the black miners, who were becoming increasingly dissatisfied with their status in the UMW. In its account of the founding convention, *The Coal Digger*, the official organ, pointed out: "No discrimination against Negro or foreign-born miners shall be the policy of the National Miners' Union, and the convention gave additional proof of its earnestness by electing William Boyce, a prominent Negro miner of Indiana, as National Vice-President."[19] Boyce immediately launched a campaign to recruit blacks into the NMW. He reminded them that, while the UMW's constitution prohibited discrimination because of creed, color, or nationality, every Negro miner knew from experience that "the words didn't amount to anything, not worth the paper they were printed on, for in deeds discrimination was rank everywhere." Black miners found it difficult to get work, and Negro members of the UMW "usually receive the worst place in the mine, dangerous and unfit to work in." If they complained, their grievances got "a merry-run-around" and were finally buried. The truth, he noted, was that the UMW did not really want Negro members.

---

* The AF of L had ignored the Southern textile industry, but when the textile workers in the South went out on strike against pay, long hours, and especially the "stretch-out" system, which required employees to do extra work with slight or no additional increase in pay, the United Textile Workers', fearing the success of the TUUL, stepped in and assured the employers that the AF of L union was "safe and sound and need not be feared. No representative of the United Textile Workers' has any connection or contact with these communists." UTWU President McMahon also assured employers that no charters would be issued for the organization of the Negro unless the leaders of the Southern white locals agreed and that, in any event, "no mixed unionization would be permitted."

But the National Miners Union wants the Negro miners. . . . To build the NMU means building a bulwark of defense to the Negro miners. . . . In the NMU the Negro is not a dues paying member, silent, bulldozed, discriminated, but an active, leading part of the directing councils of the organization itself.

Every Negro should join the National Union because it fights vigorously for full economic, political and social equality for them. It fights discrimination, segregation, Jim-Crowism and disfranchisement. In the NMU the Negro miners have a valiant defender.[20]

Early in 1930 Isaiah Hawkins, a Negro miner of Frederickstown, Pennsylvania, became full-time head of the NMU's Negro department. Working closely with NMU President Tom Myerscough, a white Communist miner and one of the founders of the NMU, Hawkins organized black miners in Pennsylvania and West Virginia. Blacks were among the most active members of the NMU in hard-fought strikes in the Pittsburgh area and West Virginia in 1931. The strike, under the leadership of the NMU, involved 42,000 coal miners, 6,000 of whom were blacks, and was the largest strike ever led by a left-wing union. That same year the NMU went into Kentucky and opened an organizing drive in Harlan and Bell counties. Although blacks were not numerous in the Kentucky mine fields, they were involved in the bloody strike at Harlan called by the NMU in February, 1931, and two black miners, Essley Philips and Gaines Eubanks, were among the most militant strikers. Both were framed by the operators on a murder charge. Although only about 300 or 400 Negro miners went out on strike, the NMU organizers insisted that blacks be treated as equals and eat in the same soup kitchens and sit at the same tables with the white miners. With the miners facing starvation and company gunmen as well as the charge that they and their union were Communists, the NMU drive failed. An NMU song written during the Harlan strike, "Which Side Are You On?", later became famous in the 1960's during the civil-rights movement when blacks changed the words to fit their struggles.

Although both the Pennsylvania and Kentucky strikes were failures, the Negro-white cooperation and interracial leadership that emerged during these struggles, as well as the courage and militancy of the black miners, aroused widespread and favorable comment in the black press. Arthur G. McDowell hailed the interracialism of the National Miners' Union and noted that, through the part he played in the radical union, the Negro miner "has proved his right to be regarded with full respect . . . worthy of the most experienced fighters in mine union ranks."[21] W. E. B. Du Bois remarked that the struggle of the blacks in the NMU should be enough to compel "colored thinkers and writers" to leap to the defense of trade unionism, especially when black workers were involved:

In the strikes among miners in Pennsylvania and Kentucky during the last year, many colored men have been involved. They have suffered with their white fellows. They have been starved, beaten, and killed; yet they have stood up staunchly for a living wage, for freedom. . . . They deserve the sympathy of all men.[22]

A number of blacks in the central and southern West Virginia coal fields formed a new movement, the Independent West Virginia Miners Union, at Charleston on March 19, 1931. Two of the seven members of the union's executive board were blacks. Aided by the TUUL, the union grew rapidly, reaching a membership of about 19,000 in the Kanawha field by the fall of 1931, making it the largest group of organized miners outside the UMW.

As the Depression deepened, the black and white miners were on the point of starvation. On March 11, 1931, the Charleston, Va. *Gazette* declared that conditions were so "pitiful" that they "cannot be exaggerated and relief must be given at once or many persons, particularly children, will die." It was largely thanks to the NMU that relief was forthcoming. Under its leadership, some 600 miners, black and white, staged a hunger march to the state capitol on May 21, demanding relief.

In the Birmingham, Alabama, steel workers' and coal miners' strikes against the Tennessee Coal and Iron Company in 1931, sponsored by the TUUL, black workers were among the most militant strikers. The Marine Transport Workers' Industrial Union led a strike in 1930 of hundreds of cargo handlers on the New Orleans docks, and black and white dock workers, members of the same local, fought side by side. This stood in sharp contrast to the unionism of the ILA, which established separate locals for black members.

On March 7, 1932, the TUUL Auto Workers Union, the Unemployed Councils, and the Communist Party jointly organized a march of 3,000 jobless workers, of whom 200 to 400 were blacks, to the gates of the Ford plant to demand work. About 90 per cent of Ford's employees were out of work, and a large number of the 3,000 marchers were jobless Ford workers. Many of the placards carried by the marchers called for an end to Jim Crow practices against Negro auto workers, and one of the fourteen demands to be presented to Ford was "no discrimination against Negroes as to jobs, relief, medical services, etc."[23]

The marchers never had a chance to present their demands. They were met by Dearborn police and firemen and Ford Service Company police. Shots were fired, tear gas was sprayed, hoses poured icy streams of water onto the marchers in the near-zero weather. When it was over, four workers were dead (Joe York, Joe Bussell, Joe Deblasio and Coleman Young), and Curtis Williams, a black former Ford worker, who was clubbed and gassed, died of wounds later. More than thirty marchers were wounded. The funeral procession on March 12, 1932, for the murdered workers, black and white, was the largest demonstration in Detroit up to that time.

Everywhere the TUUL unions faced bitter opposition from the employers, the AF of L bureaucracy, police, and vigilantes, and their growth was usually extremely slow. Except for the Miners' National Union (for a brief period) and the Needle Trades Workers' Industrial Union, not many workers, black or white, were organized into TUUL unions before 1933. Jack Meldon, Secretary of the Metal Workers' Industrial League, which included steel and metal workers, reported at the Plenum of the TUUL Executive Committee in September, 1931, that, while agitation among Negro steel workers had been persistent, the results were "entirely unsatisfactory." As for the Needle Trades Workers' Industrial Union, its secretary and leader of the militant Fur Workers' Division, Ben Gold, conceded in April, 1933, that the union "did not increase sufficiently the Negro membership during the last two years of successful struggles in spite of the fact that we gained thousands of white workers."[24] What made Gold's confession even more serious was that two and a half years earlier the radical-led needle-trades union had been the object of a sharp attack from Cyril Briggs, the leading black theoretician in the Communist Party. In September, 1929, Briggs noted that, while the needle-trades union "had scores of functionaries, with departments for Greek, Italian, Jewish, etc. workers, it has not a single Negro functionary and no department concerned even remotely with the organization of Negro workers," despite the fact that there were "several thousand" black workers in the New York needle trades.[25] Evidently little had been done to improve this situation since the formation of the Needle Trades Workers' Industrial Union.

However little the TUUL accomplished in unionizing black workers, its Unemployed Councils did unite many Negro and white workers in the fight for relief, jobs, and unemployment insurance. Moreover, while the Communists never succeeded in building a revolutionary alliance between white labor and black labor, they did manage, aided by the impact of the Great Depression, to create a greater willingness on the part of white labor to cooperate with blacks on the basis of mutual interest. Then, too, their activities forced the NAACP and the Urban League to turn their attention increasingly to the conditions of black workingmen. In a real sense, the Communist Party and the TUUL laid the foundation during the Depression years for the alliance of Negroes and the labor movement, on the basis of mutual interest, that was to flower in the middle and late 1930's. Du Bois admitted to having been convinced by the tireless activities of the radicals that unity of black and white labor was a possibility. "We believe," he wrote in 1935, "that colored workers should join the labor movement and affiliate with such trade unions as welcome them and treat them fairly."[26]

At the onset of the economic crisis, the AF of L seemed nearly moribund. It had the lowest membership since the end of World War I. From more than 4 million during and immediately after the war, it had declined to 3.2 million in 1923 and 2.9 million six years later. Of 30 million workers in America, less than one-tenth belonged to the main body of organized labor. The loss of membership during the 1920's occurred chiefly in the basic and mass production industries, where the AF of L had seen its greatest membership gains during the war. Despite a heavy loss of membership by the UMW in the 1927 strike, the miners remained the only source of federation strength in the basic industries.

Rubber, steel, and automotive manufacture remained unorganized, and textiles were only partially organized. *Opportunity* noted in November, 1929: "The American Federation of Labor not only has failed to unionize the black worker; it has failed to unionize the white worker."

Opportunity went on to say that the refusal of the AF of L to alter its traditional craft-union structure to accommodate industrial unionism especially injured black labor, which consisted for the most part of unskilled workers in the basic industries. This fact, added to the racial exclusionist practices of craft unions, meant that the federation held out little hope for blacks. The AF of L, frightened by the TUUL inroads among Southern textile workers, was indeed talking of "a mighty effort" to organize the South. But *Opportunity* saw little reason to believe that the campaign would aim for the black workers as well as whites, hence little possibility for its success.

William Green, the AF of L president, reacted with surprise that the official organ of the National Urban League should be hostile to the main spokesman of American workers. "An agency that has influence in formulating opinion among Negroes is assuming a very grave responsibility when it prejudices a group of workers against the American Federation of Labor." Green conceded that there were not many Negroes in the federation and that some affiliates refused to accept blacks as members. But, he triumphantly reminded *Opportunity*, "it is possible for the Negro workers to organize and secure a charter of direct affiliation with the American Federation of Labor." As for organizing the basic industries through industrial unions, history had demonstrated that the craft union was still the most effective type of union structure.

Opportunity was not impressed. Indeed, Green's letter only confirmed its original pessimistic outlook. If all the AF of L president could offer black workers was affiliation through the discredited federal labor union structure, what was there to hope for from the federation? "This expedient has offered an escape but not a solution; for it provides the badge but not the protection of unionism."

The next few years confirmed *Opportunity*'s gloom. The AF of L did join forces with the NAACP in 1930 to defeat Senate confirmation of Judge John J. Parker of North Carolina as Associate Justice of the Supreme Court. But Du Bois saw little evidence that such a joining of forces on a political issue, a judge offensive to white unionists because of his record as an injunction judge and to Negroes because of his racism, could be carried over into the economic field. Specifically, he did not expect it to affect the AF of L's restrictions against black workers or its reluctance to organize the unorganized in the basic industries. As usual, Du Bois's evaluation was accurate.

At the 1932 AF of L Convention, A. Philip Randolph urged abolition of the segregated "federal" unions for black workers. Randolph pointed out that the "federal" union was not on a par with the international. For example, the Brotherhood of Sleeping Car Porters, with thirteen "federals," could command only thirteen votes, whereas as an international, on the basis of its membership, it would have had forty votes in the federation. Since the thirteen "federals" were under the direct supervision of the Executive Council, they were subject to the pressures, prejudices, and whims of the internationals that Jim-Crowed or excluded black workers. Finally, the brotherhood was under a serious handicap because "federal" unions were not represented on the highly strategic National Railroad Adjustment Board, nor did it have recourse to the board for the settlement of grievances and claims. In short, AF of L "federal" affiliates had neither standing under the law nor recognition as equals within the family of labor.

As was to be expected, Randolph got nowhere. Delegate after delegate vigorously defended the institutional pattern of segregating black workers and reducing the effectiveness of their unions while preserving the job structure of the white craft unionists. Randolph's motion was overwhelmingly defeated.

At the 1933 convention, Randolph again gave battle to the white supremacists within the AF of L. This time he attacked the federation's failure to campaign for organization of the black workers. He pointed out that the Brotherhood of Sleeping Car Porters, with its 35,000 members, accounted for half the Negro workers in the AF of L. Yet, because a larger proportion of blacks worked for a living than of any other ethnic group in the country, blacks were a potential source for a considerable increase in union membership. The racial barriers of unions prevented them from tapping this source and at the same time weakened the unity and strength of those blacks who were already organized.

Specifically, Randolph asked the Federation to enlist black organizers to carry the message of unionism to black workers. He urged that his recommendation be put into effect at once, because it was clear that employers were pitting white against black in an attempt to weaken all organized labor. Section 7(A) of President Franklin D. Roosevelt's National Recovery Act (NRA) stipulated that workers were to be allowed to bargain collectively through representatives of their own choosing, which was certain to encourage the development of trade unions to protect the workers' interests. But employers could use racial prejudice to defeat the purposes of the NRA. To succeed, Randolph pleaded, labor had to "remove from the hands of the employing class the weapons of race prejudice." It could do so only by organizing black workers in large numbers.

Once again Randolph went down to defeat. Vice-President Frank Duffy declared that he was not basically opposed to Randolph's resolution. He then moved that it be referred to the Executive Council to be "put into effect if the cost will permit."[27] This was the AF of L leadership's usual method for squashing a resolution it did not wish to oppose openly. A resolution from the 1929 AF of L convention for an educational and organizational campaign among the blacks was still in the hands of the Executive Council, awaiting the propitious moment to carry it into effect. There was little prospect that Randolph's 1933 resolution would meet a better fate.

Still, Randolph had called attention to a new aspect of the old issue of the relationship between organized labor and the black worker. The new aspect was to increase in importance within the next two years and would play a significant role in uprooting the pervasive racism from the trade-union structure. Randolph had pointed out that the great opportunity for organizing labor under the NRA was seriously jeopardized by the traditional employer practice of exploiting racial prejudice to divide the workers. "The Negro worker," a contemporary student of the labor scene observed, "has good reason to feel that his government has betrayed him under the New Deal."[28] It did not take long for the black workers to discover this.

On June 13, 1933, the National Industrial Recovery Act became the law of the land. Speaking from the White House three days later, President Roosevelt hailed the act as "the most important and far-reaching legislation ever enacted by the American Congress." Henceforth, he said, American workers "would be guaranteed living wages. . . . By living wages I mean more than a bare subsistence living—I mean the wages of decent living."[29] The mechanism by which this was to be assured was the establishment of codes in every industry specifying minimum wages and maximum hours. It rapidly became clear that the code mechanism under the NRA was valueless for black workers; it merely legalized for all American industry the pattern of racial discrimination that had long been the practice of Southern employers. Conditions of blacks worsened under the NRA. Thousands were fired and replaced by white workers on jobs where blacks were being paid less than established minimum-wage scales; by August, 1933, blacks were calling it the "Negro Removal Act." NRA wage minimums were considered "too much money for Negroes."[30] Legal sanction was given to lower wage scales in Southern industry, especially for blacks. The cotton textile code, with a twelve-dollar minimum weekly wage and a forty-hour maximum week for the South, exempted outside workers, cleaners, and yardsmen, occupations in which most of the employees—12,000 out of 14,000 in the Southern textile industry—were blacks.

The steel code discriminated against black workers by providing a lower rate—25 cents an hour—in Southern districts. The lumber industry's code also stipulated a lower minimum in the South—23 cents an hour—where most of the workers were Negroes. Black sawmill employees received as much as $6.80 a week less than white workers on the same jobs. The bituminous coal industry established an hourly rate of 42.5 cents in Alabama, Georgia, and southern Tennessee, where many of the miners were black, as compared with 60 cents an hour in areas where most miners were white. The code for the laundry industry set wage rates for the seven Southern states as low as 14 cents an hour for a forty-five-hour week. The thousands of Negro women employed in the industry in these states earned as little as $6.30 for a full week's work.

In general, wage rates with differentials of up to 30 per cent were set in the South under NRA codes. Southern employers let it be known at code hearings that, if forced to pay higher rates, they would fire black workers and hire whites. When the codes provided for a minimum wage higher than that usually paid a Negro, violations abounded, and blacks who protested were threatened with replacement. The Scripto Company, manufacturer of pencils in Atlanta, Georgia, employed Negroes at from 6 to 13 cents an hour. In a message "To All Colored Employees," it warned them: "If the 'false friends' of the colored people do not stop their propaganda about paying the same wages to colored and white employees this company will be forced to move the factory to a section where the minimum wage scale will produce the greatest production. Stop your friends from talking you out of your job."[31]

Wage differentials in the South were professedly based on the presumed lower cost of living and lower efficiency of the Negro worker. However, Roy Wilkins, then an NAACP assistant secretary, put his finger on the real reason. Southerners, he wrote, "do not wish Negroes to have wages equal to whites." In acquiescing to the wage differential, the New Deal placed the government's stamp of approval on the principle of Negro inferiority. The wage differential allowed the black worker to keep his job, but it also divided the working class along the color line in the interests of the employer. Because employers considered minimum wages a ceiling as well as a floor, all blacks received the minimum Negro wage, which was lower than the minimum for whites. White workers soon discovered that they could not raise their own minimum as long as blacks received less for the same work. Any possibility of raising the standards of all workers was effectively destroyed, and so was the likelihood of uniting blacks and whites in a common front of protest.

As early as August, 1933, alarmed by the injection of the color line into the NRA codes, Wilkins wired President Roosevelt that the racial differentials would place the stigma of inferiority on Negroes, "which it would take years of suffering and misery to work off."[32] He urged the immediate appointment of blacks to the NRA Labor Advisory Board, to the research staff of the board, and to the post of deputy administrator. The only concession Roosevelt granted was the appointment of Mabel Byrd, a black scholar at the University of Chicago, to advise the NRA on Negro problems. Six months after her appointment, Miss Byrd denounced the NRA on four counts: (1) It had stepped up instead of slowed down displacement of Negroes by white labor, North and South, a process that had begun in 1929; (2) the fixed policy of sanctioning sectional wage differentials under the codes in practice meant racial discrimination against Negroes; (3) not a single black was serving anywhere in the country on enforcing agencies, which constantly tolerated discrimination against Negroes; and (4) discrimination against blacks was "the rule instead of the exception in New Deal work relief."[33]

The National Industrial Recovery Act, which granted workers the right to organize and bargain collectively through agents of their own choosing, spurred unionization among workers already aroused over drastically reduced wages and increased prices, but it provided few benefits for black workers. The Brotherhood of Sleeping Car Porters, the largest union of black workers, was excluded from its benefits because the porter was adjudged an employee of a carrier engaged in interstate transportation. Similarly, the porter was beyond the pale of the Emergency Transportation Act because the carrier for whom he worked was not a railroad.* It was estimated in October, 1933, that the AF of L had 4 million members, but few of them were blacks. Similarly, hardly any of the hundreds of AF of L organizers were black. Du Bois was so furious at the failure to accord to black workers the benefits of New Deal legislation that he condemned the NRA for having reinforced the "sinister power" of the AF of L, an organization, he wrote, that from the beginning had "stood up and lied brazenly about its attitude toward Negro labor. They have affirmed and still affirm that they wish to organize Negro labor, when this is a flat and proven falsehood. They do not wish to organize Negroes. They keep Negroes out of every single organization when they can."[34]

Negro leaders feared that the AF of L, in its organizing drives, would establish itself as the sole spokesman for labor and continue not only to exclude blacks from the unions but to freeze them out of jobs they already occupied. There was clear evidence that "rabid Negro haters" in many craft unions were belligerently "opposing an equal share to Negro workers of the various [New Deal] Recovery programs."[35] The building-trades unions of Saint Louis, to cite an example, kept blacks out of all skilled jobs supported from public funds. Refusing to admit black members to their locals, to set up Negro locals, or even to recognize union cards when presented by black carpenters, these unions would not even permit blacks to be employed in erecting a hospital for Negro patients. Everywhere, as AF of L craft unions signed agreements with employers, blacks found themselves outside the unions and very often out of jobs they had previously held.

Some Negro spokesmen advised black workers to join company unions, which were coming increasingly into existence. Others now welcomed the organizing efforts of the left-wing unions under the TUUL, in the belief that the radicals at least would prevent the blacks from being kept outside of organized labor and might force "more conservative groups to liberalize their own policies."[36]

The Communists, opposed to the NIRA from its inception, warned unorganized workers that its real purpose was to corrall them into company unions or place them under the domination of conservative AF of L unions, which often functioned as company unions. Hence, they argued, militant struggles to unite all workers regardless of skill, nationality, sex, or color and the selection of labor leaders in whom the rank and file would have confidence were urgently necessary.

In the steel, maritime, textile, and other industries, the TUUL began to build up national organizations. Everywhere special attention was paid to the black workers. Thousands of leaflets issued by the Steel and Metal Workers' Industrial Union listed the demands for which workers should organize and prepare to strike, among them "equal rights for

---

* In the summer of 1934 Congress amended the Railway Labor Act to bring the Pullman Company under its provisions along with the railroads, and thus compelled Pullman to enter into collective bargaining with its workers.

Negro workers."[37] At the same time, the Communists mobilized for "the fight for the rights of the Negro workers inside the AF of L unions and against discrimination against Negroes." A key demand of all left-wing groups in unions affiliated with the AF of L was "the right of Negroes to join all unions, and to work on all jobs, in all trades."[38] The only way to defeat the employers' strategy of company unionism, they said, was for the rank and file to destroy Jim Crow unionism. "The rank and file must at once put a stop to such discrimination. If the unions are to present a solid, united front against the employers, if their demands are to be won, this Jim-Crow policy must be wiped out."[39]

Black protests against AF of L racial policies, combined with the battles waged by the TUUL's industrial unions and its rank-and-file members in the federation, were to make their influence profoundly felt in the crucial years 1934–35.

15 The AF of L and the
Black Worker, 1934–35

The 1934 AF of L convention met in September in San Francisco, where, two months before, the laboring population had laid down their tools in a great general strike. Only about twenty Negroes were among the 3,000 who first struck the waterfront on May 9, 1934, but, as the strike of the longshoremen progressed, black-white unity blossomed despite the Jim Crow setup of the ILA locals.* For blacks the strikers' central demand—a hiring hall controlled by the union and democratically operated, with equality of job opportunity for all longshoremen—had special importance. It would bring not only the end of the "shape-up" and of favoritism and kickbacks,† but also the end of segregation on the docks and Jim Crow in employment.

Throughout the strike (in Seattle as well as San Francisco), Negro longshoremen took an active part. They worked on the relief committee collecting funds along with white longshoremen and manned the picket lines side by side with white strikers. "During those days," one Negro striker recalled, "men were not only fighting for their jobs; they were fighting for their lives. When you left home for the picket lines you were never sure of returning."[1] But the victory, ending discrimination in hiring

* Black workers played important roles in other strikes of 1934. Writing of the strike of Campbell Soup Company workers at Camden, New Jersey, Lester B. Granger noted that it "included 700 Negroes, men and women. . . . They walked out with the rest, picketed zealously, took active part in strike meetings and collaborated with the rest when the strike ended, and all returned to work under improved conditions." Similarly, writing of the strike of workers at Seabrook, New Jersey, Granger pointed out that blacks and Italians struck together, and the strike saw "Negro and white women and men battling shoulder to shoulder against police and sheriff's deputies armed with shotguns, clubs and tear gas bombs . . . in all defiance of South Jersey public attitude, in all defiance of Klan threats, in defiance of the traditional belief that Negroes will not strike and that Negroes and whites cannot organize together successfully." *Opportunity*, June, 1934, p. 190, and August, 1934, pp. 248–49.
† Under the "shape-up" system, men seeking employment on West Coast waterfronts and ships would gather on the wharf in groups from which workers would be selected by company representatives. Selection was often based on the amount of pay workers refunded to the selectors in the form of kickbacks. Black workers were continually discriminated against in hiring.

through abolition of the vicious shape-up, made the sacrifices worth while.

When the AF of L convention met in San Francisco, several of the militant black longshoremen joined local Negro leaders in picketing the convention hall with signs reading: "Labor Cannot Be Free While Black Labor Is Enslaved," and "White Unions Make Black Scabs." Left-wing AF of L rank-and-filers distributed leaflets to the delegates demanding abolition of the federal labor unions and the organization of the mass-production industries through industrial unionism on the basis of racial equality. A truck that circled the convention hall bore signs calling on the federation to admit Negroes as equals. One sign carried the message: "Unions should be color blind. White labor must smash the color line for its own interest."[2]

Two resolutions designed to end black exclusion and Jim Crow unionism were brought to the convention floor. One, introduced by James P. Dallas on behalf of a rank-and-file committee, was the most advanced resolution on Negro labor in the history of the AF of L. It denounced discrimination against black workers by many national and international unions and then called for

> the elimination of clauses in constitutions of any affiliated unions of the AF of L containing any suggestion of discrimination against Negro workers, and that all Jim-Crow locals be immediately merged with the existing locals to establish the closest unity of Negro and white workers [and] to rally the membership of organized labor against the provisions of the NRA codes which discriminate against Negro workers, and for a struggle to establish equal pay for equal work and equal opportunity for any jobs for Negro workers as well as to establish full equality with white workers in all other working conditions in the shop, and equal rights in the union, including the right to hold any office.[3]

So advanced a resolution—several of its proposals still have not been incorporated by the major unions—stood no chance of being adopted. The Committee on Organization rejected it with the brief comment that the AF of L was "without authority to interfere with the internal affairs and administration of affiliated unions," and the recommendation against its adoption was upheld by the delegates. At that point A. Philip Randolph ignited more fireworks on the racial issue with a resolution of his own. It noted that there was "widespread unrest . . . with the existing status of Negro workers in the American Federation of Labor, and with its policy toward the organization of Negro workers." Too often the grievances of blacks had been met with resolutions that, though splendidly phrased, did not effectively solve their problems.

Randolph's resolution charged that all the international and national unions of the Railway Department had either color clauses in their constitutions or racist pledges in their rituals, which it denounced as "unsound, defenseless, undemocratic, illegal, and unAmerican." It proposed that the convention go on record "for the elimination of the color clause and pledge from the constitution and rituals of all trade and industrial unions." Further, it asked for the expulsion of all trade and industrial unions that violated the AF of L constitution "by maintaining said color bar." Finally, Randolph proposed the appointment of a committee to "investigate the question of the status of Negro workers in the national and international unions, federal unions, and the general policy of the American Federation of Labor on the matter of organizing Negro workers, and report to the next convention its findings with recommendations to future policy in relation to Negro workers."[4]

Randolph's resolution was referred to the Committee on Organization, which again recommended nonconcurrence. To delegates who had been present at the conventions of 1919, 1920, 1921, and 1925, the report sounded like an old recording. Once again the claim was advanced that the AF of L, from its inception, had held all workers, irrespective of creed, color, nationality, or political views, eligible for membership. Again there was the argument that the AF of L could not "interfere with the autonomy of national and international unions" and could not "say who are eligible or who are not eligible to membership in national and international unions." These bodies had the right to restrict membership if they saw fit, a right of which unions "cannot be deprived." Finally, the report again pointed out that under the AF of L's constitution separate charters could be issued to black unions, so it could not be said that there was no room for black workers in the federation.

Randolph demolished this last argument. What good were declarations of principles in favor of labor solidarity when nothing had been done "to translate these declarations into concrete facts"? Everyone knew that color clauses and pledges still existed, and that "therefore no effort . . . is being made to organize the Negro workers." As long as the color bars continued nothing would be accomplished, since a "psychology is being created among white and black workers that makes effective organization more and more difficult." Since 1933, not only had nothing been done to organize blacks; there had not even been an effort to develop federal unions of Negro workers as part of the campaign to unionize the millions of unorganized. The time had come to stop reciting lofty declarations, to study the status of black workers affiliated with the AF of L, and to establish the machinery for organizing blacks. Randolph concluded: "If we go on from year to year and merely concur in the resolutions saying we are in favor of Negro workers' joining the unions and nothing is done to put the resolutions into effect we will not get very far."[5]

After Randolph's eloquent plea, the old-line craft-union leaders rallied to support the report of the Committee on Organization. The general tenor of their speeches was that the AF of L policy toward Negro labor was "fundamentally correct."[6] Still, it might be worth accepting Randolph's request for a committee to investigate the conditions of black workers, provided that the investigatory body be under the complete control of the Executive Council. The upshot was that the Committee on Organization accepted an amendment to its report authorizing the AF of L president to appoint such a committee.

Eight months passed after the convention before William Green even got around to appointing the committee, and all five members were white. Black spokesmen complained that the delay in naming the committee left little time for a full study, especially for regional hearings. Nevertheless, they attended the committee hearings, which opened and closed at the AF of L headquarters on July 12, 1935, armed with concrete evidence of union discrimination, including signed statements by blacks indicating specific acts of discrimination by many AF of L affiliates. Reginald Johnson, Atlanta Urban League representative, charged that the AF of L had "winked" at racism in its ranks for nearly fifty years.

The most impressive and complete presentation was made by John P. Davis, a young Harvard graduate and secretary of the Joint Committee on National Recovery, a coalition of twenty-two major Negro organizations established in May, 1935, to work for nondiscriminatory treatment of blacks under the New Deal. Davis attributed the disgraceful treatment of blacks to the AF of L leadership's policy of allowing local unions to "determine standards of admittance." "The crux of this situation lies right here in this building," Davis announced. He urged the national officials of the AF of L to carry out a six-point program: (1) ban constitutional color bars; (2) prohibit separate Jim Crow locals and insist that local unions abide by the prohibition; (3) abolish federal labor unions composed exclusively of the blacks excluded from trade unions; (4) urge that a black be placed on the Executive Council; (5) employ some black organizers "and a few Negro girl clerks here at headquarters where you have none"; (6) launch a nationwide educational campaign to show the entire membership that "there can be no American labor movement that's worth a tinker's damn until Negro and white workers are organized together."

Randolph, testifying before the committee, endorsed Davis's plan and counseled that the "educational campaign" should be "hitched up with practical concrete acts, such as public declarations of the Council and the Convention that no national or international will be permitted to remain in the Federation which persistently practices discrimination." "The country and the workers are ready" for this, Randolph insisted, as indicated by the willingness of black and white to unite in the integrated unions of sharecroppers in Arkansas and Alabama.*[7]

---

* The New Deal's Agricultural Adjustment Act of 1933 (AAA) worsened the distress of sharecroppers by tending to drive them from the land and making them even more dependent on landlords. Disenchanted with the New Deal, black and white sharecroppers in Arkansas, aided by Socialists, organized the first local of the Southern Tenant Farmers' Union in July, 1934. Several had been members of the Negro union wiped out in the Elaine massacre of 1919, and some of the whites had been former Ku Klux Klan members. But they united, black and white, and elected a white sharecropper as chairman and a Negro minister as vice chairman.

The interracial Sharecroppers' Union in Alabama was an offshoot of the all-Negro union formed by the Communists in 1931, which had been involved in the anti-Negro riot at Camp Hill.

There is some dispute among students over whether the STFU was really a labor union, but Donald H. Grubbs, in his *Cry from the Cotton: The Southern Tenant Farmers' Union and the New Deal* (Chapel Hill: University of North Carolina Press, 1971) has demonstrated that it functioned as a union throughout its history. His

Charles H. Houston, NAACP general counsel, also endorsed Davis's plan and urged the committee to hold additional hearings throughout the country, so that NAACP branches that had been "assembling data on discrimination against Negro workers in their cities" could present important evidence. But Green announced that no further hearings would be held. The Committee of Five recommended its own three-point plan: (1) All international unions that discriminated against black workers should take up the "Negro question at their next convention for the purpose of harmonizing constitutions, rules and practices to conform with the oft-repeated declarations of the AF of L conventions on equality of treatment of all races within the trade union movement"; (2) the AF of L should issue no more charters to unions practicing discrimination; and (3) the AF of L should begin an educational campaign "to get the white workers to see more completely the weakness of division and the necessity of unity between white and black workers to the end that all workers may be organized."[8]

The committee's plan was not so far-reaching as Davis's proposals, but it was more advanced than any previously brought before an AF of L convention. The committee had been specifically instructed to report to the 1935 convention, and, since the issue of craft *versus* industrial unionism was coming to a head at the same time, that convention could reasonably be expected to bring about some changes in AF of L policies. But it was not to be. An alternate report submitted by George Harrison, an Executive Council member and president of the lily-white Railway Clerks, recommended only "education" on the Negro question. Green and the Executive Council voted immediately not to release the plan of the five-member committee and to present only Harrison's recommendation to the AF of L convention.

Had the Committee of Five put up a fight for its three-point plan, the results might have been different. But John Brophy of the UMW was the only member really eager to put the AF of L on record in favor of outlawing racial discrimination and organizing Negro workers. The other members privately informed Green that they had gone along with Brophy only to achieve a "compromise," and that they favored maintaining the *status quo*. Jerry L. Hanks of the barbers assured Green that he personally opposed any action whatsoever on the black labor question, since racial discrimination predated the formation of the AF of L.

The fifty-fifth convention of the AF of L met in Atlantic City on October 7, 1935. Six years of devastating economic crisis had gone by. While many workers were better off under the New Deal than they had

---

book is especially valuable for its treatment of the STFU's biraciality, and he cites many examples of how oppressed whites and blacks worked together in their own organization as equals. The prospect that tenants and croppers of both colors might succeed in overcoming the racial hatred used by Southern planters for generations to play black and white against each other to the detriment of both frightened the Southern ruling class and guaranteed that the STFU would become the target of badge-wearing goon squads and night riders, and its members subjected to inhuman brutality.

been during the Hoover Administration, most blacks were still enduring terrible privation. Indeed, the winter and spring of 1935 were especially bleak for them. For example, "practically three out of every five Negroes in Allegheny County," Pittsburgh's county, were on the relief rolls, and in the Harlem area of New York City more than 43 per cent of the 56,157 Negro families were receiving relief. The New York *Post* summed up the New York situation for Negroes in 1935 in a single sentence: "One half are not working, the other half are existing on the crumbs from the table."[9] James W. Ford, secretary of the Harlem Section of the Communist Party, put it more strongly: "The masses live on the brink of starvation. Disease and pestilence stalk the community. Police brutality drives the people to the point of desperation."[10]

On March 19, 1935, the point of desperation was passed as Harlem exploded in a riot. Three blacks were killed by the police and 2 million dollars' worth of property destroyed. The press attributed the riot, known as the "Black Ides of March," to "Communist agitation." But it was clear that the outburst was the product of widespread unemployment, starvation, poor housing, and police brutality—in short, as the Mayor's Commission on Conditions in Harlem put it, "widespread discontent." "It was not a riot," Adam Clayton Powell, Jr., correctly noted, "it was an open, unorganized protest against empty stomachs, overcrowded tenements, filthy sanitation, rotten foodstuffs, chiseling landlords and merchants, discrimination in relief, disfranchisement, and against a disinterested administration."[11]

None of this, of course, was reflected in the opening remarks of William Green at the AF of L convention or in the report of the Executive Council. The main issue there was a split developing among the delegates, and even among the AF of L leadership, over industrial unionism. On the eighth day of the sessions, the Committee on Resolutions submitted majority and minority reports on the question. The majority report recommended that the federation leadership be delegated to grant industrial-union charters only where they did not expressly conflict with the existing or potential claims of the national and international unions. The minority report proposed *unrestricted* issuance of industrial union charters wherever workers were engaged in work that did "not fully qualify them for craft union leadership." In other words, the federation leadership was called upon to make possible the organization of millions of unorganized workers in the mass-production industries as well as all others engaged in unskilled and semi-skilled work.

After heated and protracted debate, highlighted by a famous fistfight between John L. Lewis and Bill Hutchinson of the carpenters, a champion of craft unionism, the convention defeated the minority resolution by a vote of 18,824 to 10,933, with 788 not voting.

On the last day of the convention, with the delegates exhausted and eager to adjourn, the Executive Council put before the convention a report by George Harrison of the railway clerks. The document, entitled "Supplemental Report on Colored Workers," did not even mention the Committee of Five. It pointed with pride to the fact that only a few national and international unions denied membership to blacks. In those few instances, "special provisions are made to organize the negroes into Federal Labor Unions directly chartered by the AF of L, and in other cases Negroes are placed in separate local unions with varying rights of membership." The Executive Council pointed out that because each union had complete autonomy the blacks' welfare would "be best served by a voluntary campaign of education" leading toward the "voluntary elimination of all restrictions."[12]

All this could have been said in 1900. The history of the black working class and of the labor movement since the turn of the century had produced not the slightest alteration in the attitude of the AF of L leadership.

Randolph, fresh from a great victory scored by the Brotherhood of Sleeping Car Porters (an overwhelming majority of the porters and maids employed by the Pullman Company voted for the union in an election supervised by the National Mediation Board), led the battle against the Executive Council's report. He denounced the report as "very inaccurate, fragmentary, and absolutely unsound." Despite the late hour, he insisted that the delegates discuss at length the whole issue of discrimination against black workers. After scoring the Executive Council report for its omission of the Committee of Five's recommendations, without which it was "merely a dignified, diplomatic camouflage," he read the Committee's three-point plan to the delegates. He then castigated those unions with color clauses in their constitutions and rituals and those that used more subtle ways to bar blacks. The federal unions, he said, were powerless under the law and were properly regarded by black workers as proof that the AF of L gave them "virtually no organization at all." Not one had negotiated a contract with employers; none had the power to represent its members before the federal labor boards; none could promote the interests of its black members or organize unorganized blacks.

Randolph termed the traditional "refuge of trade autonomy" an evasion of support for the principle of Negro organization—an evasion because the AF of L had overlooked autonomy when it wanted to punish affiliated unions for actions displeasing to the craft-union leadership. Why, he asked, should "an organization of labor which is interested in the welfare of workers . . . single out the Negro workers and attach to them the stigma of inferiority" by prohibiting them from joining its ranks and enjoying equal rights in the labor movement? Randolph closed by telling the AF of L, that it "will not be able to hold its head up and face the world as long as it permits any section of workers in America to be discriminated against because they happen to be black."[13]

The white supremacists in the labor movement rose to challenge Randolph. John P. Frey repeated his frequently quoted assertion that the trade-union movement had done more than any other American institution to break down racial prejudice, and he warned Randolph that it would "create prejudice instead of breaking it down if we make too strong an effort in that direction."[14] William Green emphasized the progress made by the AF of L in combating racial prejudice. To back up Frey's boast, he noted that 100 out of 105 unions in the American labor movement admitted Negroes to membership.* Personally opposed to the practice of the few unions that excluded blacks, he nevertheless held that the AF of L could not "say to an autonomous International union how it shall draft its laws." Revoking their charters, as Randolph proposed, was impossible. All the federation could do was hope that through education the racial problem would be entirely eliminated. Meanwhile, the needs of black workers who came under the jurisdiction of national and international unions that excluded them were being well provided for through the federal unions.

Harrison brought the debate to a close by repeating that the only way to end restrictions on black workers was by education. Federal labor unions for blacks were the logical way to provide for them until the white unionists were persuaded to grant full membership rights. He cited his own union in this connection. "We do not admit Negroes to our Brotherhood," he acknowledged. But because the railway clerks organized them into federal labor unions, blacks achieved "complete economic equality" in the brotherhood.[15] Harrison, of course, ignored the testimony of black railway clerks before the Committee of Five who had denied that the Jim Crow union structure of the brotherhood offered them any protection.

The 1935 convention came to a close with a rejection of Randolph's motion to adopt the three-point plan of the Committee of Five "as the spirit of this convention" and endorsement by voice vote of the Executive Council recommendation for "education" of the membership. Soon after the convention, John Brophy, secretary of the five-man committee, handed in his resignation to President Green. Brophy, evidently unaware that the other members of the committee themselves had sabotaged its recommendations, charged that the "maneuvering on the part of the Executive Council plainly indicated" that it wanted the special committee "to be merely a face-saving device for the American Federation of Labor, rather than an honest attempt to find a solution of the Negro problem in the American labor movement."[16]

The 1935 convention destroyed the last hope of effective changes from within the AF of L. The victory of the craft unionists on the question of industrial unionism convinced a number of far-sighted unionists that the AF of L leadership had no desire to "lead" the workers of the country. The Executive Council's suppression of the five-man committee report convinced many black spokesmen that nothing could be expected from the federation in furthering the cause of Negro labor. Walter White pointed out in a letter to John L. Lewis, "The recent hypocritical attitude of the American Federation of Labor in suppressing the report of the Committee . . . has destroyed the last vestige of confidence which

---

* This was a distortion of the facts. In 1934 twenty national and international unions, not five, completely excluded Negroes from membership. Eight of them were affiliated with the AF of L.

Negro workers ever had in the AF of L."[17] When young blacks, in an essay contest sponsored by *The Crisis* on "The Negro and Union Labor," proposed that Negro workers join AF of L unions and unite with whites "to overthrow the present AF of L bureaucracy," Du Bois reminded them that "this form of action . . . would be impossible" because numerous national and international unions barred blacks from membership, and the bureaucracy had successfully resisted every effort to change the situation.[18]

It had taken a long time to destroy the "last vestige of confidence" blacks had in the AF of L. Since 1918, black spokesmen had urged the federation to honor its commitment to organize workers irrespective of color. They had not even insisted that the federation throw its rolls open to Negroes overnight. The proposals they submitted were, in the main, designed to remove legal and procedural obstacles to the full membership of black workers in AF of L affiliates and to initiate a campaign to bring blacks into the labor movement. What they had sought was only a reasonable, achievable starting point and did not even go so far as some of the demands presented by the left-wing AF of L rank-and-file committees to the 1934 convention.

But at every stage the AF of L leadership and nearly all of the affiliated unions had stubbornly opposed even such cautious steps. Occasional convention resolutions had offered promises of future action, but by 1935 black workers had seen too many promises broken or ignored. That year, they abandoned all hope that the AF of L would end racism in its ranks.

In the past, such disillusionment would have all but ended any prospect that the black workers would become part of the American labor movement. Alternatives to the AF of L had existed in the form of independent black unions, the IWW, the TUEL, and the TUUL. They had managed to create some concern among the advocates of white supremacy and to produce new resolutions on Negro labor (never acted on) at AF of L conventions. But none had achieved the goal of organizing great numbers of blacks.

But in 1935 a situation existed that had no precedent in American labor history. The refusal of the AF of L's craft-union leadership to accede to the modest demands of the blacks coincided with its rejection of the demand that it alter the union structure to allow for the needs of the vast majority of workers in the mass-production industries. From the fifty-fifth convention came an organized movement for industrial unionism and organization of the unorganized, which was to encompass black as well as white workers. This was the Committee for Industrial Organization—the CIO—founded on November 9, 1935, the day after the AF of L convention adjourned. The CIO was composed of eight international unions: the United Mine Workers; the Amalgamated Clothing Workers Union; the International Ladies' Garment Workers' Union; the International Typographical Union; the Oil Field, Gas, Well, and Refinery Workers; the United Hatters, Cap, and Millinery Workers; and the International Mine, Mill, and Smelter Workers. Its purpose, as stated at its founding session, was

> to encourage and promote organization of the workers in the mass production and unorganized industries of the nation and affiliated with the AF of L. Its functions will be educational and advisory, and the committee and its representatives will co-operate for the recognition and acceptance of modern collective bargaining in such industries.[19]

Nothing in the statement referred specifically to black workers, and in fact some of the founders of the CIO were not noted for their concern with the problems of Negro labor. But it had long been clear that the success of industrial unionism depended on the unity of white and black in the mass-production industries. Without Negro participation there simply could be no viable and effective labor movement in such industries. Blacks averaged about 8.5 per cent of all iron and steel workers, approximately 17 per cent of all semiskilled and unskilled workers in the slaughter and packinghouse industry, 68 per cent of tobacco workers in North Carolina, Virginia, and Kentucky, and almost 9 per cent of all coal miners. But even those statistics do not reveal the true importance of the black worker to any move to organize the basic industries. Negro labor was concentrated in certain geographical areas, so that, for example, blacks accounted for almost 68 per cent of the workers in the basic iron and steel production industries in Alabama. Unionization along industrial lines, as advocated by the CIO, therefore required the cooperation and participation of black workers.

Almost simultaneously with the formation of the CIO came another unprecedented development that was to contribute immensely to changing the history of the black working class. More than 250 prominent blacks signed a call for a National Negro Congress. Among them were Lester Granger and Elmer Carter of the National Urban League; Dr. Alaine Locke and Dr. Ralph Bunche of Howard University; James W. Ford of the Communist Party; A. Philip Randolph, president of the Brotherhood of Sleeping Car Porters; Bishop James A. Bray; and the poet Langston Hughes. For the first time in the history of black Americans what Randolph called a "united front of all Negro organizations," from old-line Republican to Communist, had joined together, rejected Red-baiting, and stood ready to help in solving the urgent problems of the Negro people, among which the organization of black workers stood foremost.

At the opening session of the National Negro Congress on February 14, 1936, in Chicago, 817 delegates representing 585 organizations with an estimated combined membership of 1.2 million heard Randolph hail the new movement to organize the unorganized in industrial unions. Speaking from experience in the AF of L, he declared that "the craft union invariably has a color bar against the Negro worker, but the industrial union in structure renders race discrimination less possible, since it embraces all workers included in the industry, regardless of race, creed,

color or craft, skilled or unskilled."* Randolph gave the newly organized
National Negro Congress a special mission: to "seek to broaden and intensify the movement to draw Negro workers into labor organizations
and break down the color bar in the trade unions that now have it."[20]

As the delegates left Chicago, it could be said that, although black
workers had a history of relations with organized labor dating back to
Reconstruction, in a meaningful sense the history of trade unionism
among blacks was just beginning. For the first time, the possibility existed for a basic improvement in the black wage-earners' industrial status.

* Randolph, however, refused to bolt the AF of L and join the CIO. When asked
to do so by John L. Lewis at the Atlantic City AF of L convention, he inquired what
the new movement would do about equality for black workers. Assured that equality
would be a key feature of the CIO, Randolph told Lewis that in that case he had
better stay inside the AF of L and fight for equality for black workers in that organization. Interview with A. Philip Randolph, October 13, 1972.

16 The CIO and the
Black Worker, 1935–39

In 1935 Congress passed, and President Roosevelt signed, the National Labor Relations Act (the Wagner Act). It gave workers the right to vote for the union they wanted; outlawed certain unfair practices used by employers against unions; and created the National Labor Relations Board (NLRB) with power to enforce the act. Rigidly antiunion employers found ways to circumvent the law, but it did stimulate union growth by strengthening the labor organizations' hand in their campaign to unionize workers and secure contracts.

Black leaders had tried to have written into the Wagner Act a clause barring racial discrimination by unions. They feared that if the new law legalized the closed shop, requiring employers to hire only union members, the denial of union membership to blacks would be the same as denying them employment. In addition, the law compelled employers to rehire all strikers after a settlement was reached, which meant that Negroes who found strike-breaking the only way to gain employment would have that door closed to them.

The NAACP, the National Urban League, and leading black spokesmen insisted that inclusion of a clause denying the benefits of the act to any union that discriminated on the basis of race would prevent its use to sound "the doom of the Negro in American industry."[1] But the AF of L let it be known that, if the antidiscrimination clause were incorporated into the proposed bill, the federation would prefer to see the entire measure defeated. The Wagner Act was passed without the antidiscrimination clause.

The emerging industrial unions of the CIO had not opposed the antidiscrimination clause. Most of the AF of L unions that founded the CIO had already accepted the premise that there must be no race discrimination in the ranks of labor. Besides, the CIO could foresee that, in its rivalry with the AF of L in elections under the new act, it had a great advantage in the federation's unwillingness to organize thousands of black workers in the steel, auto, rubber, and meat-packing industries, which would form the backbone of the new labor movement. Indeed, blacks would hold the balance of power between the union and nonunion whites in union elections.

Beginning in 1936, the CIO conducted the most massive organizing campaign in American labor history. Unlike the traditional racial policies of the AF of L, the CIO policy from the first was to open its doors to all black workers on an equal basis. There were no constitutional bars, no segregation of blacks into separate locals, no Jim Crow rituals. Black organizers were employed in all the initial CIO campaigns as the most effective way to demonstrate that the policy of nondiscrimination was more than empty words and would be carried through. The CIO leader, John L. Lewis, knowingly hired members of the Communist Party to work as organizers, primarily because of their special interest in the unity of black and white labor and their achievement of such unity in the unions set up by the TUUL.*

Yet all the CIO efforts would have gained little had the traditional antiunion attitudes of Negro community leaders and many black workers continued unchanged. Because of their sad experience with white unions in the past, black workers were more than a little hesitant to join the CIO. The majority of Negro leaders encouraged their hesitance. In a bitter attack on the black middle class for its role in this period of labor's great upsurge, the black journalist George S. Schuyler accused it of deserting "the struggling Negro workers" in their hour of greatest need. Negro preachers, he charged, were the most vehement in denouncing the CIO unions as "radical" and were openly "siding with the employers," even to the point of recruiting strike-breakers "to take the jobs of black unionists." But most disheartening was "the indifference, hostility and open opposition of educated Negroes" who held positions of trust and leadership in their communities. "Their reactions to the labor drive seemed to range from sheer ignorance of the issues involved to active cooperation with the efforts of employers to halt the workers' bid for power and protection."[2]

While leaders of the NAACP and the Urban League realized that the formation of the CIO had brought into being a new, different, and probably powerful labor movement with which black workers might be able to ally themselves, they were still skeptical about the lengths to which the industrial unionists would go in combating racism among the rank and file. Speaking for the Urban League, Lester Granger warned black workers against "jubilantly rushing toward what they assume to be a new day for labor and a new organization to take the place of the AF of L."[3] The NAACP urged Negroes to wait for the proof of CIO sincerity before committing themselves to the new labor movement.

By the summer of 1936, the national NAACP had abandoned much of its skepticism, and *The Crisis* appealed to black workers not to be neutral in the emerging struggle to establish industrial unionism:

> In this struggle of labor to organize and win the right of collective bargaining, it is fitting that the Negro workers be represented in the front line trenches. . . . They have everything to gain and nothing to lose by

* In 1935 the Trade Union Unity League dissolved and militants were urged to merge with AF of L unions in their industries. In a number of basic industries the TUUL organizations were transformed into nuclei for the CIO organizing drive.

affiliation with the CIO and if they fight now, side by side with their fellow workers, when the time comes to divide the benefits they can demand their share.[4]

Unfortunately, the leaders of many local NAACP branches had formed close alliances with employers and were opposed to all unions, CIO as well as AF of L. The fact that the CIO included Communist organizers, cited in the press as proof that the new labor movement was financed by "Moscow Gold," was enough to turn conservative black spokesmen against it. At the 1936 NAACP convention in Detroit, several local black ministers who had had a long working relationship with Henry Ford and who received financial support from the Ford Motor Company vigorously opposed a motion to invite CIO representatives to address the convention. The delegates finally adopted a resolution reflecting a neutral position on organized labor. It suggested to black workers that they "go into no labor organization blindly but . . . instead appraise critically the motives and practices of all labor unions and . . . bear their full share of activity and responsibility in building a more just and more intelligent labor union."[5]

The Urban League urged Negroes to join unions and hailed the CIO as "a new champion to defend the rights of the underdog."[6] Still, it remained neutral in the rivalry between the AF of L and the CIO during the great organizing campaigns following 1935. Indeed, league officials assured the AF of L that open support of the CIO was contrary to the organization's policies.

Fortunately for the CIO, the National Negro Congress refused to be antiunion or neutral. John P. Davis had assured the labor movement in 1935: "At the very heart of the program of the National Negro Congress will be the question of organization of the hundreds of thousands of unorganized Negro workers. We feel the necessity of throwing the whole influence of the Negro population . . . solidly behind organized labor."[7] Although the founding convention of the congress had voted to support both the AF of L and the CIO, it was clear that its future, based in large measure on bringing black workers into the trade unions, was with the CIO. In the next few years, the National Negro Congress forged an alliance with the CIO that was crucial for the success of the industrial-union movement in a number of key mass-production industries where Negroes formed an important element. The Southern Negro Youth Congress, organized in February, 1937, at a convention in Richmond, Virginia, also aided the CIO in winning support among black workers, especially in the South. An important auxiliary force was the Workers' Alliance, a strong, militant organization that united unemployed groups, especially Negroes. It fought the use of the unemployed as scabs and provided the CIO with hundreds of volunteer and full-time organizers, blacks among them.

In 1936-37, under the personal leadership of John L. Lewis and with funds from the United Mine Workers, a series of great organizing campaigns took place in the steel, auto, and rubber industries; among packing-house and textile workers; in mining, woodworking, shipbuilding, and communications; and among seamen, warehouse workers, and many others. The CIO organizing campaigns provided crucial tests of the new movement's intentions toward black workers. The first and in some ways the most important one came in steel.

In June, 1936, the CIO took over the weak and ineffective Amalgamated Association of Iron and Steel and Tin Workers and established the Steel Workers' Organizing Committee (SWOC), with UMW Vice-President Philip Murray as chairman. William Mitch of the UMW was in charge of the Southern region. Mitch was a fortunate choice, for he had reorganized the UMW in Alabama from two locals with 225 members in June, 1933, to 23,000 in 1935, fully 60 per cent of whom were blacks. Mitch, denounced in the Alabama press as a "carpetbagger," had successfully fought the Klan's influence among white miners and had made considerable progress toward achieving unity between the races. Indeed, racists in the Alabama State Federation of Labor accused Mitch of "practicing what the Communists preach" because he introduced the "UMW formula" under which a local had a white president, secretary, and treasurer and a black vice president and black minor officers.

Mitch, determined to apply the UMW policy on racial issues in organizing steel, was one of 400 organizers sent by the SWOC into the steel towns of Pennsylvania, Ohio, Illinois, and Alabama to rally the more than 500,000 steel workers. The American Iron and Steel Institute met this challenge with a massive publicity campaign. Full-page ads in hundreds of leading newspapers accused the CIO of being a Communist organization and assured the nation that no "God-fearing, patriotic American worker" would sign up with "the emissaries from Moscow." The employers, for their part, "will oppose any attempt to compel its employees to join a union or to pay tribute for the right to work."[8] The future of the CIO and of organized labor in America was at stake in the colossal battle that was shaping up between the union and the steel industry for the loyalty of the steel workers.

Blacks occupied a crucial position in the emerging struggle. In 1936 there were 85,000 Negro steel workers, making up 20 per cent of the laborers and 6 per cent of the operators in the industry. Restricted to the worst jobs, they received the lowest wages, averaging between sixteen and twenty-two dollars a week for hazardous and degrading employment. The companies based wages on a differential pattern for whites and blacks, but they poured money into black churches and fraternal societies to buy their allegiance to the employers' cause. With their support, the companies were relatively certain that the black steel workers would remain loyal and, as in 1919–20, reject overtures from the unions.

But the leaders of the National Negro Congress were determined to write a different chapter this time in the history of the black steel workers and unionism. "There is no effort in which the National Negro Congress could possibly engage at this time more helpful to large numbers of Negro workers . . . than the organization of Negro steel workers. . . . 85,000 Negro steel workers with union cards will signal the beginning of the organization of all Negro workers," John P. Davis wrote early in

1936. It would "mark a start toward the liberation of hundreds of thousands of Negro sharecroppers, of hundreds of thousands of Negro women sweating away their lives as domestics." Davis saw the steel industry campaign as a chance to "write a Magna Carta for black labor," but he warned that the Negro organizations supporting the drive were "not writing the CIO a blank check." It was necessary to make certain that, once black workers were in the union, they were entitled to every office and every privilege granted other members. "We must see to it that Negro steel workers have a part in the formulation of all union demands and the making of all agreements, to the end that once and for all inequalities in jobs, labor conditions and wages will be abolished."[9] But the best guarantee of this was the solid organization of the nearly 85,000 Negro workers in the steel industry.

The SWOC welcomed the support of the National Negro Congress in a special statement issued in leaflet form, adding: "We are appealing to every Negro worker in the steel mills for the sake of his fellow men, his family and his country to join immediately with all others in the steel industry in building the union."

The National Negro Congress did more than issue endorsements of the CIO. In talks with John L. Lewis, Philip Murray, John Brophy, and SWOC regional directors, Davis recommended a dozen Negroes for appointment as organizers. Several were veteran organizers from the UMW; some were leaders of the congress's local councils; and a few were active Communists. James Hart, a UMW organizer for thirty-five years, was instrumental in convincing Negro steel workers in Gary, Indiana, that the CIO was a different union, one that "is not going to discriminate against blacks."[10] Benjamin Careathers, a black Communist who had led hunger marches that won public relief for the unemployed, personally enrolled nearly 2,000 steel workers in the Pittsburgh area, most of them blacks. He won public praise from Philip Murray for unionizing the Jones-Laughlin steel mill at Aliquippa, the biggest mill in the area.

Wherever local councils of the National Negro Congress existed in the steel areas, they contributed volunteer organizers and carried the campaign deep into the black community. The organizers would gather a corps of sympathizers who would then press local churches, clubs, and organizations to sponsor mass meetings encouraging blacks to join the steelworkers' union. The congress and its councils distributed more than a quarter of a million pro-union leaflets in black communities throughout the nation. A typical leaflet declared: "We colored workers must join hands with our white brothers . . . to establish an organization . . . which shall deliver us from the clutches of the steel barons. We appeal to all colored workers in the steel mills to join the union."[11]

The Congress widely distributed copies of Philip Murray's address to its 1937 convention in which the SWOC chairman declared:

> There is no other labor organization in this country that affords the Negro the same opportunity as do the great international and national unions affiliated with the CIO. I can conceive your situation—90 to 95 per cent

of our entire colored population poor. Thousands of them are undernourished and underprivileged. They have the same ideals and aspirations and the same hopes beating within their breasts that beat within the breast of a white man. Their wives and children have the same feelings and emotions and they are entitled by all the laws of nature itself to the same opportunity in the game of life as any white man.

We tell you your economic and political salvation lies in assisting the CIO in the course of its activities . . . and I beseech your support and the support of your officers . . . in this great undertaking which the CIO has now begun.[12]

The SWOC sponsored the formation of women's auxiliaries in the campaign to unionize steel, and the National Negro Congress helped recruit black women into the auxiliaries. The congress distributed the SWOC pamphlet *Women in Steel*, with its appeal: "Perhaps you are a Negro woman, driven to the worst part of town but paying the same high rent. . . . Your man is driven even harder than the white workers, but your man gets lower pay—hired the last and fired the first. . . . The remedy is to help the union. When it comes to exploitation, the mill owners draw no color line. They exploit the native white workers just as they do the Mexican, Polish and Negro workers." Black women responded enthusiastically to the appeal. "They are undaunted and have great moral strength with their persistence," one SWOC organizer recalled.[13]

On February 6, 1937, in cooperation with the SWOC, the National Negro Congress sponsored the National Conference of Negro Organizations in Pittsburgh. Attended by approximately 186 delegates from 100 Negro organizations and by 350 black union delegates, and addressed by leaders of the CIO, the conference dealt with methods of organizing black steel workers. Murray set the tone for the gathering by declaring that no industry exhibited greater racial discrimination than steel and affirming the CIO's determination that "there shall be no discrimination under any circumstances, regardless of creed, color or nationalities, in its unions." The resolutions adopted by the conference declared that the efforts of the SWOC to organize steel were "in the best interests of the Negro steel workers" and pledged to set up committees in every Negro community to help the organizers, and to make use of pulpit, press, and radio "to urge all Negro steel workers to join the union." The conference closed with an exhortation by Randolph to every delegate to "go out and engage in the business of contacting the steel worker himself."[14]

The National Negro Congress was by no means the only black organization supporting the SWOC. The Pittsburgh *Courier* and the Chicago *Defender* wholeheartedly endorsed the organizing campaign; the Urban League praised the attitude of the SWOC organizers; and the NAACP told black steel workers that they had "nothing to lose and everything to gain by affiliation with the CIO."[15] But the Urban League was too closely linked with management to do much for the campaign, and the NAACP, while enthusiastic in its support, did not commit organizers to the CIO. The National Negro Congress provided the SWOC with active, militant support, and its organizing work in conjunction with the CIO brought thousands of blacks into the SWOC. Indeed, in some areas of Pittsburgh and Chicago they signed up in greater proportions than the white steel workers. The pro-union campaign by the congress not only neutralized the influence of the steel companies among the black churches and societies but even redirected them to strong support for the CIO. Henry Johnson, a congress leader employed by the SWOC in Gary, reported that after his speech in a local black church, the minister arose and announced:

> I have always been against the AF of L and organized labor, but I am convinced that this CIO move is the only thing for my people. I want every steel worker of my church to sign up for this union. And . . . I want you . . . to sign up every steel worker you come into contact with in Chicago Heights. If anybody asks you what you are doing, tell them Rev. Pinkett told you to sign them up and he has God and the people with him.[16]

While recruiting continued in steel, the UAW-CIO in Detroit and Flint was engaged in a great struggle to organize the motor industry. Here, too, the National Negro Congress aided the organizing drive.

The automotive industry, like steel, had a history of discriminating against Negroes. Methods varied from plant to plant: Some would not hire blacks at all; others employed them only as sweepers or in jobs calling for the heaviest, dirtiest, most disagreeable work at the lowest pay. Outside the foundries they were barred almost everywhere from skilled and semiskilled jobs, or from anything that put them on the same footing as white workers. Black women were universally barred from employment. General Motors plants in Flint had a negligible number of Negro workers, exclusively in the most menial occupations. On the other hand, Henry Ford's River Rouge plant in Detroit had the largest black working force of all major automotive plants: Of the approximately 80,000 River Rouge workers, more than 11,000 were blacks. Some were even permitted to work in semiskilled, skilled, and technical capacities, but the overwhelming majority were employed in the foundries or in jobs traditionally considered "Negro work."

Still, Ford had gained the support of a substantial section of the Detroit black community, and even many Negro auto workers regarded him as one of the best friends they had. In addition to employing Negroes in large numbers, he had two black personnel officers. Whenever Dr. George Washington Carver, the black agricultural wizard and a close friend of Ford's, visited Detroit, he had full access to the Ford Company's laboratories. Finally, Ford had sponsored a city for blacks at Inkster, Michigan, and many of the Negro ministers in the Detroit area were on the company payroll.

The auto industry thus presented unusual problems for those intent on organizing black workers. The GM plant at Flint employed too few blacks to be a factor in a fight between the UAW and management. In Detroit, on the other hand, especially in the Ford plants, there were so many black auto workers that their response would influence the outcome of any struggle. But the Ford Motor Company, the chief target of the organizing drive in Detroit, had carefully developed a system of paternalism toward black workers that was designed to serve as a bulwark against labor organization. In addition, the UAW had to contend with widespread racism among the white auto workers. Many were poor whites from the South who had brought north with them the patterns of racial discrimination and segregation ingrained in their thinking from birth. In Detroit, anti-Negro organizations like the Ku Klux Klan and the Black Legion kept the old racial hostilities alive, and many white workers in the auto plants were members and even officers of these racist organizations.

Nevertheless, the UAW was determined to tackle the race question head-on in its unionizing campaign. Its constitution stated that one of its objectives was "to unite in one organization, regardless of religion, race, creed, color, political affiliation or nationality, all employees under the jurisdiction of the International Union."[17] Early in 1936 it began a series of educational programs to convince the white auto workers that they could never achieve better working conditions or rid themselves of the companies' notorious spy systems unless they threw overboard their traditional racial patterns. Blacks were invited to the sessions, and their comments made it clear that they too had to be convinced that the union would serve their interests.

A small shop in Detroit was organized into a UAW local by the fall of 1936. Although blacks made up about 25 per cent of the working force, the local had refused to allow them to become members, defying international union representatives who pointed out that they were in violation of the UAW constitution. Eventually it became clear that the only way the local could win its demands from management was through a strike. It dawned on the white members that no strike could succeed with one-fourth of the workers in the shop barred from union membership. A committee of black workers was invited to discuss the recruitment of Negroes into the local. The spokesman for the blacks put it on the line: "We represent most or all of the Negro workers in the plant. If we recommend that they join the union or participate in the strike, they will do so. We think we should be in the union and support the strike if one is necessary. We cannot recommend that unless we are guaranteed full membership privileges and equal consideration under the contract."

The response of the chairman of the meeting was immediate: "Anything you want, brothers, just get in here and help us win the strike." All the white auto workers present applauded the statement. Black workers came into the union and, a few weeks later, joined with the white members in the first of the auto workers' famous sitdown strikes. "Negro and white workers sat down together in the plant," an on-the-spot observer wrote, "marched the picket line outside the plant, shared the food from the strike kitchen, and when the strike was won they had a victory dance."[18] In a sharp break with precedent, the white workers did not desert their black union brothers after the victory. They kept their part of the bargain, and a truly interracial local union developed in the plant.

The few blacks in the Flint plants were involved in the greatest of the sitdown strikes—that at GM in 1936–37. Wyndham Mortimer, the left-wing UAW strike leader, directed special appeals to the blacks in the plants. At a small Negro meeting in a Spiritualist church, he vowed that the UAW would not be a Jim Crow union. The preacher rose to announce that Mortimer was an "emissary of God, and that the members must therefore join the union, which they all did," according to an account of the meeting.[19]

Had the black ministers in Detroit displayed the same attitude toward the UAW, the campaign to organize Ford in 1937 might have succeeded. But the clergy, together with black professionals and businessmen, sided against the union and openly favored Ford. The very same conservative black leaders who had condemned AF of L unions for its prejudice against Negroes now refused to endorse the nondiscriminatory UAW-CIO on the ground that it was "radical and communistic."[20] The Pittsburgh *Courier* correctly noted that the black conservative leaders in Detroit, being dependent on the Ford Motor Company, were "against any movement likely to jeopardize their position."[21] Several years were to pass before the UAW was able to make headway in its drive to organize Ford, and a change in the attitude of the Detroit Negro leadership had to come first.

Although the policy of accepting Negroes with full membership privileges was hardly ever questioned during the UAW's organizing campaigns of 1936–37, not many black auto workers were actually recruited, primarily because few were employed in the General Motors, Chrysler, and other plants where the union won recognition, while the Ford plants remained unorganized. However, a resolution passed at the 1937 UAW convention urged that "special efforts be made to bring the Negro auto workers into our ranks by hiring additional Negro organizers and clerical workers who are acquainted with the special problems of the Negro race, so that they may enjoy the benefits of organized labor."[22] In time this policy would bring a sharp increase in the UAW's black membership.

Few black workers benefited directly from the UAW's tremendous victory in the GM sitdown strike, but many did receive indirect benefits. The victory stimulated a rapid growth of unionism not only in the automobile industry but in mass-production industries in general, especially in the steel industry, where black workers were recruited along with whites. On March 1, 1937, the U.S. Steel Corporation, long the stronghold of the open shop in the industry, came to terms with the SWOC without a strike. The agreement negotiated between Myron C. Taylor, chairman of the corporation, and John L. Lewis made the CIO union the exclusive bargaining agent for "Big Steel's" workers. Two weeks later, wages were raised 10 per cent with certain differentials, and an eight-hour day and forty-hour week were established, with time and a half for overtime. A number of small steel companies followed suit, and by the end of 1937 the SWOC had signed with about 450 firms.

Although "Little Steel"—Bethlehem, Republic, Youngstown Sheet and Tube, and Inland—did not give in to industrial unionism until 1941, the coalition of the SWOC and the National Negro Congress and the impact of the great victory at General Motors had produced remarkable results. By the end of 1937, the SWOC was bargaining for 550,000 steel workers; it had raised wages by one-third, reduced working hours, and put an end to Jim Crow practices in parts of the steel industry. Blacks were now active in local SWOC lodges and even played leadership roles in several, including some in the South. The almost 85,000 Negro steel workers who were members of the SWOC constituted the largest group of black union workers in the United States. They continued to work under intense heat and amid noxious gases, but their wages and general situation had vastly improved.

The steel and auto campaigns were the most dramatic of the CIO's early drives to organize the mass-production industries. But the impact of the industrial-union movement was felt everywhere, especially after the great victories scored over General Motors and Big Steel. Many of these struggles did not involve blacks for the simple reason that the industries themselves excluded them. But blacks were brought into the labor movement in a number of important campaigns. One of the most remarkable advances for blacks in this period occurred in the tobacco industry. Tobacco employed a larger percentage of Negro workers than any other industry—stemmers, helpers, and laborers. The average wage in 1937 was a little over six dollars a week; some pay envelopes contained $4.45 for a week's wages, and even three dollars was not unusual.

The AF of L Tobacco Workers' International Union's constitution forbade discrimination because of race or color, but its half-hearted effort to organize blacks resulted in a few black members in segregated locals.* On May 6, 1937, 400 Negro women stemmers employed in the plant of I. N. Vaughan Company of Richmond walked out in a spontaneous protest against average wages of $3 a week and terrible working conditions—the first strike of Richmond TWIU members in thirty years—but when the strikers sought aid from the AF of L union, their representatives were told that black tobacco workers were unorganizable. The black women then turned to the Southern Negro Youth Congress, which joined forces with the National Negro Congress to help the black workers organize an independent union and formulate their demands. Within forty-eight hours the strikers secured wage increases, a forty-hour week, and union recognition. In eighteen months, several thousand black tobacco workers were organized into seven locals of the Tobacco Stemmers' and Laborers' Industrial Union, and contracts were negotiated bringing a total of $300,000 in wage increases, as well as increased pay for overtime and holiday work. The National Negro Congress and the Southern Negro Youth Congress turned the seven locals over to the CIO after a vote by the membership approving the proposal to affiliate with the industrial-union movement. "The successes of the tobacco unions," a reporter wrote, "have stirred other ranks in the Richmond community."[23]

On both the West and the East coasts, the maritime unions, assisted by the National Negro Congress, brought thousands of blacks into their ranks. During the great West Coast maritime strike of 1934, Harry

---

* In 1900 the union's convention recommended the appointment of a Negro organizer, but no action was taken to implement the resolution until 1913.

Bridges, the fiery left-wing, Australian-born leader of the strike, was elected president of the West Coast longshoremen. In 1937, most West Coast longshore locals withdrew from the AF of L's International Longshoremen's Association and joined the CIO as the International Longshoremen's and Warehousemen's Union (ILWU), with Bridges as president. The union's first object, declared its constitution, was "to unite in one organization, regardless of religion, race, creed, color, political affiliation or nationality, all workers within the jurisdiction of this International."[24] In keeping with this aim, the ILWU began a campaign against racial discrimination. Bridges announced that "Negro labor will never again find the doors of the San Francisco longshore locals closed." Special interracial antidiscrimination committees were organized to see that no worker would be discharged or intimidated because of race or color. Again and again the union announced its opposition to racial discrimination and segregation both within the union and outside. Spearheading the union's attack against Jim Crow was its official journal, the Dispatcher, which featured a series of articles on "The Economics of Prejudice": "Prejudice means profit for the Boss: Four and a half billion dollars every single year. For the worker—Black or white—it means lower living standards, humiliation, violence, often death."[25]

The ILWU's strongest ally on the waterfront was a maritime union with the best antidiscriminatory policy on the West Coast, the National Union of Marine Cooks and Stewards, CIO. Before 1934 black cooks and stewards were compelled to organize separately in the Colored Marine Employees Benevolent Association of the Pacific. But a few members of the union, led by Eugene Burke, for many years the union's highest official, campaigned vigorously for black-white unity. It was not, however, until the great general strike of 1934, when black and white maritime workers made common cause against the shipowners, that such unity began to materialize. As a reward for their help in winning the strike, the more than 500 blacks who had joined the picket lines were taken en masse into the National Union of Marine Cooks and Stewards, and the benevolent association disintegrated. The union's constitution was rewritten to include the statement that "race is no longer pitted against race in the struggle for jobs." One of the union's fundamental principles was set forth as "equality of opportunity for work and education and for the essential values of life to all people, regardless of race, nationality, religion or political opinion."

When several shipping lines tried to take punitive action against the black union members, the union held to its principles. It elected a committee of five, two of them Negroes, which studied the problem and recommended: (1) that equal rights to employment be established regardless of race for all members of the national union on all ships, and (2) that seniority rights be established, the oldest membership card to receive the first job regardless of race and regardless of the ship. As a result of the union's firm stand, "checkerboard crews"—mixed black and white—were established on all freighters and steam schooners as well as on the American President Lines.

In 1936 the ILWU and the Marine Cooks and Stewards struck together to maintain the system of hiring through the union (rather than allow hiring decisions to revert to the shipping concerns), for an eight-hour day for men aboard ships and for longshoremen, and for cash payment for overtime worked at sea instead of time off in port. Eight hundred Negro seamen and longshoremen employed on the Pacific Coast struck together with the white unionists. The maintenance of union-controlled hiring halls was of special importance to the black workers, for it prevented discrimination because of race. Fifteen blacks were on the longshoremen's strike committee, and blacks also served on the strike committees of the National Union of Marine Cooks and Stewards, the Miscellaneous Workers' Union, and the Bargemen's Union. The Joint Strike Committee, which controlled the actions of the smaller committees, included three blacks. With the victory in the 1936 strike, the black worker achieved a permanent position, including one of leadership, in nearly all the CIO maritime unions on the Pacific Coast. Revels Cayton summarized the achievement of black-white unity in the marine cooks and stewards: "All the time the struggle for integration was taking place, the general fight against the ship owners for better wages and conditions was also being intensified, thereby keeping the basis of Negro-white unity solid in the union."

Negro seamen on the East Coast had been the target of racism and discrimination under the AF of L's International Seamen's Union. Not only were black and white seamen organized in separate locals and segregated on different ships, but ships manned by Negroes often had their crews replaced by white seamen. With the formation of the CIO's National Maritime Union (NMU) in 1937, largely the work of Communist seamen, the situation soon changed. The constitution of the NMU guaranteed equal rights, privileges, and opportunities, to all its members regardless of color, creed, or political belief. In addition, it provided that all members must be hired through union halls on the principle of rotation. When a seaman left a ship for any reason, he had to register at the union hall at whatever port he might be. He received a number and was placed at the bottom of the list. Those who had registered earlier had the choice of accepting or refusing a job opening. The man at the bottom of the list gradually moved to the top, where he had first choice of available jobs.

Thus, the rotary system set forth in the union's constitution acted as a strict prohibition against job discrimination. But to put it into operation the union had to overcome the prejudice of white seamen. Although prepared to accept blacks as union members, a number of the white seamen refused to allow them on their ships as sailors, firemen, or stewards when the union hall sent them as replacements. As might have been expected, the shipowners worked hard to maintain racial divisions, hoping that it would weaken the rotary system and cause blacks to quit the union in disgust.

The NMU met the problem with an intensive educational campaign. The rotary system was discussed in the *Pilot*, the union paper, and at union meetings, and special committees were set up to deal with the issue. In the *Pilot* of August 20, 1938, Ferdinand C. Smith, a black Communist who was one of the founders of the NMU and its first secretary and vice-president, bluntly charged East Coast shipowners with attempting to use racial prejudice to break down the solidarity of black and white seamen in the union. Smith pointed out that absolute equality of treatment for all members, one of the basic principles of the NMU, "grew out of long and bitter struggle against the shipowners and their ISU allies." Unfortunately, the vestiges of prejudice were still present in the minds of some "misguided members," and the shipowners were quick to take advantage of this weakness:

> White crews are encouraged to reject Negro replacements and vice versa. Negro departments on some ships have been fired and all-white crews demanded by the companies. Shipping masters are constantly using discrimination in an attempt to break down the rotary system of hiring. . . .
> If the companies show preference for men of one race now, it is only for the time being. Once they get us divided, they will attack one race just as viciously as another. They know that race equality in a trade union is necessary to successful trade unionism—and successful trade unionism is the one thing they fear most.

Smith closed with an appeal: "White and Negro seamen! Let's not be taken in by these maneuvers of the shipowners. If we allow ourselves to be divided, the fight for better conditions will be long and hard. If we stand together, we can't be licked."[26]

The union expelled members who were openly racist and engaged in stirring up racial prejudice. In the face of employer-sponsored racist propaganda, the rotary system was maintained, and crews were required to accept Negro shipmates. Joseph Curran, NMU president, reported with pride to the 1939 convention on the success of the campaign to maintain equality in employment. Ferdinand C. Smith added:

> Within the National Maritime Union, at present, the Negro is entitled to all the benefits of membership, such as protection of wage, working and living conditions; he votes; he voices his opinion at meetings and in the union's paper, the *Pilot*, and he holds office. In the port of New York alone, seven Negroes are officers of the union; one as National Secretary; a second heads the Steward's Department. There are two Negro organizers, one in the New England area and another in the Middle Atlantic area.
> In two years the new union has boosted wages 36 per cent and improved conditions on the ships accordingly. Negro members got these benefits along with their white shipmates; there is only one scale and it holds for all members of the union. Negro delegates go aboard ships manned by white crews and help settle their complaints against company officials. Negro officials have had the unique privilege of serving on negotiating committees representing the entire union.[27]

A new day had indeed dawned for the black maritime worker.

In March, 1937, the AF of L expelled the CIO, which by then had grown to thirty-two international unions. On November 14, 1938, the CIO met in Pittsburgh for its first constitutional convention. Black del-

egates from newly formed industrial unions and organizing committees
came to Pittsburgh opposed to any organic unity with the AF of L and
in favor of a permanent existence for the CIO. Henry Johnson of Chicago, representing the Packing House Organizing Committee, reminded
the delegates how the group he represented had "suffered . . . by the
policies that are enunciated and practiced by the Executive Council of
the American Federation of Labor." He spoke from personal experience:
As a construction worker in Chicago he, along with other blacks in the
building trades, had tried unsuccessfully for over eighteen years to gain
admittance to the AF of L. When the CIO was organized, he and other
Negro workers had their "first opportunity . . . to join a union and
fight for collective bargaining."[28] Negroes made up 38 to 40 per cent of
the workers in the packing industry, Johnson pointed out, and they were
solidly behind the CIO. But they would quit the Packing House Organizing Committee if the convention voted to associate with the AF
of L.

The convention voted to continue the CIO. The name was changed
to Congress of Industrial Organizations, and John L. Lewis was elected
the first president. The constitution declared that its first objective was
"to bring about the effective organization of the working men and
women of America regardless of race, creed, color or nationality, and
to unite them for common action into labor unions for their mutual aid
and protection."[29] Regarding this provision, the CIO national office later
explained that many of the "old-line craft unions" discriminated against
Negroes and "failed to do anything for women workers and young people." The CIO, on the other hand, aimed "to organize all workers, Negro or white, skilled or unskilled, men or women, American or foreign-
born."[30]

The resolutions proposed at the convention and the discussions on
them* also showed how advanced the CIO was on issues relating to the
Negro people as compared with the old-line craft unions. On a resolution calling for abolition of the poll tax as a requirement for voting, introduced by the United Cannery, Agricultural, Packing and Allied
Workers (UCAPAW),† Delegate Linsley, a white unionist from Birmingham, Alabama, declared:

> We above all others must realize that if our movement is to go forward in
> the South, it cannot go forward without the aid and active support of the
> Negro people, and if we are to have this aid and support, if we are actu-

* A resolution endorsing a federal anti-lynch law and calling upon CIO officers to
push for the legislation in Congress passed unanimously without discussion.

† The UCAPAW was organized in July, 1937. Few black workers were employed
in canneries, but the union was important for Negroes because of its efforts to organize the agricultural workers, and its close association for two years with the Southern
Tenant Farmers' Union. The UCAPAW was interracial in composition, including
black agricultural workers and Filipinos, Mexican-Americans and Japanese-Americans.
In Alabama the Sharecroppers' Union and the State Industrial Union Council
(CIO) joined in demanding "immediate abolition of the poll tax . . . through
which democratic government is reduced by more than 80 per cent in Alabama."
Daily Worker, February, 1938.

ally to get anywhere in the South, we must re-establish the franchise of the Negro people, together with the white workers, most of whom are also disfranchised. This is going to be our only guarantee of the continued existence and progress of the CIO in the South and it is the job of the CIO throughout the whole nation to get behind this legislation and put it across.[31]

The resolution was unanimously adopted.

The discussion on a resolution calling for an intensive CIO Southern organizing campaign cited the experiences of various affiliates in that section. Southern delegates from the Textile Workers' Organizing Committee told of attacks on their members by vigilantes organized by local Chambers of Commerce and the Ku Klux Klan, with the cooperation of the AF of L, especially when they sought to organize blacks and whites together.[32] Sherman H. Dalrymple, president of the United Rubber Workers, described how he was severely beaten in Gadsden, Alabama, when he attempted to address a crowd of workers in the Goodyear plant. William Mitch of the UMW declared that unionization "on the basis of a black-and-white membership" was what Southern employers feared most; everywhere they were engaged in trying to break down the morale of white unionists by playing up "the racial problems." Some had believed it was futile to try to defeat the employer-sponsored campaign, but the success of the union drives in mining and steel had proved the contrary. Indeed, Mitch noted, the whole idea that black and white could not be organized together in the South was false:

> We don't fear the question of taking care of the labor problem from the standpoint of the blacks and whites, because, with all due credit to the Negro in the South, they join the labor organization where they are working even more readily than do the white men. We are getting fine support, we are making progress . . . regardless of all these things that have been said, and we expect to continue on until the South is reported properly by the CIO.[33]

Heywood Broun, president of the American Newspaper Guild and a foremost syndicated columnist, brought the discussion to a close by asserting "that in the labor movement all racial and religious prejudices must be wiped out, that if there is to be fraternity and efficiency in the labor movement these must be swept aside and we must all work together." The resolution in favor of a Southern organizing campaign was adopted, and although the CIO did not actually launch such a drive until a few years later, the principle that all racial issues had to be eliminated and prejudices overcome in organizing the South reflected the new way of thinking in the labor movement, as did the unanimous adoption of the significant resolution entitled "Unity of Negro and White Workers":

> *Whereas,* Employers constantly seek to split one group of workers from another, and thus to deprive them of their full economic strength, by arousing prejudices based on race, creed, color or nationality, and one of the most frequent weapons used by employers to accomplish this end is

to create false contests between Negro and white workers; now therefore be it

Resolved, That the CIO hereby pledges itself to uncompromising opposition to any form of discrimination, whether political or economic, based on race, color, creed or nationality.[34]

This policy was reiterated at the 1939 CIO convention. By then the CIO had demonstrated that white workers could be educated to rid themselves of prejudice. When the Georgia Ku Klux Klan declared war upon the Textile Workers' Organizing Committee in 1939, the NAACP commented: "It has often been said that you can tell a man by the kind of enemies he makes. If this is true of organizations also, then the CIO is certainly an unparalleled blessing in our land."[35]

The Ku Klux Klan was only one of many antilabor forces the CIO had to face in the South. Wilbur J. Cash has pointed out that the common equation applied by Southern employers and their agents to labor unions had long been "labor unions + strikers = communist + atheism + social equality with the Negro."[36] With Communists helping to build the CIO and with the organization's biracial policy, the equation was pushed for all it was worth.* In these circumstances, CIO organizers brought the industrial-union message to workers of the South at the risk of their lives. On March 26, 1938, the *CIO News* noted:

> Often an organizer dares not to enter a town in daylight; he relies upon a union-minded merchant or a handful of key men to keep in touch with those workers who are sympathetic to the union. Mass meetings are seldom held, except in large cities, and unionists in the same village many not even know their fellow union members. In many areas, mill workers provide union organizers with day and night body guards for there have been beatings and shootings by mill police, thugs, and vigilantes.

During a 1936 campaign to unionize the Florida citrus fruit workers, most of them blacks, a CIO organizer simply vanished, probably joining previous organizers whose bodies were in a nearby swamp. In the same state, the same year, the Klan flogged Joseph Shoemaker, a CIO organizer working among blacks, castrated him, covered him with tar and feathers, and dipped his legs into the boiling tar bucket. Shoemaker died a few days later. In Tampa, CIO organizers were attacked by an incredible alliance of the Klan, Catholic followers of Father Coughlin, leading state AF of L officials, and various criminal elements of the city. Hiram Evans, Imperial Wizard of the Klan, praised the AF of L for its anti-Communism. During the 1940 AF of L convention in Atlanta, the Klan showered delegates with leaflets urging them to join with the Klan in ridding the country of "CIO communists and nigger lovers."[37] While the national AF of L leadership never endorsed Klan violence, even against CIO organizers, it maintained a discreet silence and did noth-

---

* At times the CIO tried to offset the vicious propaganda by making some concessions to the traditional pattern of life in the South. In a strike against the Southern Bed Company of Atlanta in 1937, a local composed of both races sought recognition. The picketing was done by both blacks and whites, but the Negroes picketed one side of the plant and the whites the other.

ing to investigate frequent reports that hooded AF of L members participated in assaults on CIO organizers.

Despite vicious opposition, the CIO organized thousands of workers in the South—workers in mining, oil, textiles, tobacco, the pulp and paper industry, transportation, and automobile manufacturing. The fact that several Southern industries, especially textiles, the largest industry in the South, were white preserves kept down the number of blacks organized. Still, wherever they were employed, Negro workers, convinced that the organization meant what it said, streamed into the CIO. When Negro tobacco workers in Richmond went on strike in 1938 under the leadership of the CIO, they burst forth with the spiritual "We Will Not Be Moved," expressing the attitude of all black workers who now received the opportunity to join the labor movement through the CIO.[38] In Atlanta, every time the CIO Industrial Union Council held a meeting the Ku Klux Klan paraded around the union hall. But by 1940 the CIO had a strong organization in Georgia "with many of its most loyal unionist members of the Negro wage-earning population."[39]

All workers gained substantially from the organizing drives of the CIO, but black workers perhaps gained the most. Before the establishment of the CIO barely 100,000 blacks were members of American trade unions; by 1940, there were roughly 500,000. Before the rise of the CIO, the presence of a black union official at union events was a rare occurence; in 1939–40, it was commonplace. A body of militant black union officials had come into being. As spokesmen for hundreds of thousands of black union members, they occupied a strategic position in influencing union policies. On the East Coast and in the Midwest there were Ferdinand C. Smith of the NMU; William H. Gaulden of the State, County, and Municipal Workers; Manning Johnson of the Cafeteria Employees Union; Dora Jones of the Domestic Workers Union; Monte Garden of the Transport Workers Union, Floretta Andres of the New York Teachers Union; Lyndon Henry of the International Fur and Leather Workers Union;* C. A. Collins of the Hotel Service Employees Union; George Brown of the Dining Car Employees Union; Harold L. Green of the Building Service Employees Union; Henry Johnson, assistant national director of the Packinghouse Workers' Organizing Committee; Willard S. Townsend of the United Transport Service Employees of America; and, of course, longtime leaders like A. Philip Randolph and other officials of the Brotherhood of Sleeping Car Porters. On the West Coast there were Lem Geer, Joe White, and C. Richardson, officers of the Executive Committee and the Board of Trustees of the International Longshoremen's and Warehousemen's Union, Local 10; Revels Cayton, business agent of the National Union of Marine Cooks and Stewards and a trustee of the Marine Federation; Alex Forbes, busi-

---

* Lyndon Henry was elected organizer of Fur Dyers Union, Local 88, in 1935 by predominantly Italian membership. Since he had publicly denounced the invasion of Ethiopia by fascist Italy under Mussolini, a number of pro-fascist Italian newspapers had urged the Italian fur workers to defeat him. But Henry was elected by a two-to-one majority.

ness agent of the Musicians Union; Phil Slater, a member of the executive board of the Building Trades Laborers' Union; and Alex Walters, a dispatcher in the hiring hall of the ILWU.

The CIO cannot take sole credit for the increase in black union members and officials, but there is little doubt that, with the assistance especially of the National Negro Congress, it played the most prominent role. Nothing was more impressive to the black community than the leadership assignments given to Negroes in the CIO unions.

Assessing the status of black Americans in 1938, the Communist Party noted that many advances had been made in a few years. "Most important . . . has been the advance made in the economic field. The advent of the CIO and the great advance of militant trade unionism has doubtless been a prime factor in breaking down Jim Crow bars and practices in the trade unions, resulting in the participating en masse of Negro workers, on the basis of equality, in the trade union movement of the country."[40] Interviewed by the Pittsburgh *Courier* early in 1940, John L. Lewis asserted:

> I am sure you will agree with me when I say that Negroes as a group have made far more progress since the formation of the CIO than at any time before. This has been because of the uncompromising stand which the CIO has taken against any form of racial prejudice or racial discrimination.[41]

More convincing still is the observation of Joe Cook, black president of the Valley Mould (Illinois) Lodge of the SWOC. Early in 1940, he told the press:

> Has the CIO played fair with us Negro workers? Well, look at the new clothes our children wear; the homes that we are paying out since the SWOC enrolled us and showed us how to wage a successful fight for decent wages and better working conditions. See how the white and colored steel workers get along together since they started wearing the union buttons.[42]

Like the steel drive, the CIO's organizing campaigns in many industries brought higher incomes, better working conditions, and some measure of job security for hundreds of thousands of black workers. In four years, organized labor achieved more for black workers—with the participation of the black workers themselves—than it had in almost a century of previous existence.

For many black workers, the immediate effects of the CIO's early campaigns and strikes were necessarily slight. CIO unions, generally intent on winning union recognition and immediate improvements in wages and working conditions, paid little attention to the hiring practices of the companies. In none of the contracts signed by the unions, except in the maritime industry, were the unions given a voice in selecting new personnel. In 1940, three years after the UAW victory in the Flint sitdown strike, General Motors still followed a rigid Jim Crow policy ranging from the total exclusion of blacks at Fisher Body to the restriction of blacks to broom-pushers at Chevrolet or to foundry jobs at Buick.

So the early CIO victories were of immediate benefit only to blacks already working in the mass-production industries. Boycotts and picketing by such organizations as the Greater New York Coordinating Committee, a united-front movement formed in the late 1930's by Adam Clayton Powell, Jr., made some jobs available for middle-class and skilled working-class blacks in public utilities and other companies. But such militant activities made no real dent in Negro joblessness. Throughout the middle and late 1930's, unemployment was still more widespread among blacks than whites; by 1940 Negroes had not yet regained the ground lost during the Depression. The proportion of blacks in manufacturing had declined from 7.3 per cent in 1930 to 5.1 per cent in 1940.

The CIO also did little to break down the discriminatory lines in industries where blacks were employed, which made it impossible for Negroes to advance into better jobs. The first contracts signed by CIO unions in most cases froze the existing pattern of discrimination in industry. Seniority rules, considered necessary to protect job security, kept white workers ahead of blacks in line for skilled and semiskilled jobs, which were already a white monopoly. Consequently, in 1940, Negroes who had jobs were still chiefly in the unskilled and worst-paid sectors.

Still, in most industries with CIO contracts black workers, within the confines of the jobs to which they were restricted, received wage increases commensurate with those of white workers. Where wage differentials based on color had existed, they were usually wiped out. Through the CIO organizing drives, then, black workers did receive higher incomes and better working conditions, which improved their economic status sufficiently to guarantee that most of them would remain loyal to the new unions.

Their loyalty would have been even stronger had the CIO's nondiscriminatory policy been as effective in practice as it looked on paper. The constitutional provisions barring discrimination were sometimes circumvented, ignored, or, in the South, openly flouted. On paper, the SWOC in the South followed the "UMW formula" of integrated unions with black and white officers. But white steelworkers often refused to allow compliance with the formula. Consequently, black union steelworkers had no way to protest when they saw the best jobs going to white members. Horace Clayton and George Mitchell interviewed many newly recruited Negro members of the steel workers' union, who said that they fervently hoped the union might be able to open a path for them to more highly skilled jobs in the industry. Some, disgusted with their virtual exclusion from skilled jobs, even quit the union or voted against it in elections at their plants.

Opportunity acknowledged that complaints by black members of the CIO were justified. The unions had been so engrossed with the struggle to gain recognition and, once that was won, to gain some concessions from employers in wages and hours that they had seldom, if ever, attempted to negotiate regulations governing advancement in the industry. "If Negro trade unionists find that their hope in this respect for the time being is given but little attention by the newer unions, they should not be too deeply disappointed, nor should they blame the union for discrimination." At the same time, the organ of the Urban League urged the CIO unions not to ignore the issue of the advancement of their black members to more highly skilled jobs. Action on this issue "would do more than any other one thing to satisfy the aspirations and cement the loyalty of the Negro members."[43]

It was important advice. Many contemporary observers reported that Negroes willingly paid their dues if the union served them but that black membership would drop almost overnight if it did not. Blacks had experienced too many betrayals at the hands of unions to extend unqualified support even to the CIO.

With the growth of the CIO in the mass-production industries, with hundreds of thousands of blacks organized for the first time in steel, auto, rubber, maritime, and meat-packing plants, the black community expected that the AF of L would undertake a major revision of its craft-union tradition of racial exclusion and segregation. Some of its expectations were realized. In New York the Negro Labor Committee, formed in July, 1935, and headed by Frank Crosswaith, sponsored a series of conferences to organize black workers in industries under contract with AF of L unions. Advances were scored in the organization of Negro butchers by the Amalgamated Meat Cutters Union, with Conrad Kaye, a black organizer for the union, leading the drive. In the Painters' Union, Louis Weinstock, a white Communist rank-and-file leader and formerly an outstanding champion in the AF of L movement for unemployment insurance, was elected secretary-treasurer on a platform that included the call for "a special organizational drive in Harlem to organize the Negro painters without discrimination and to unionize the jobs."[44] Local 6, Hotel and Club Employees Union, and Local 302, the Cafeteria Employees Union, led a militant drive against discrimination in New York City, breaking down barriers to job opportunities for blacks in hotels, restaurants, and cafeterias. The struggle against discrimination in the Hotel and Restaurant Employees' International reached a climax at the 1938 convention in San Francisco. In response to a demand from left-wing and progressive delegates, the convention voted unanimously to leave the hotel chosen for their headquarters because it refused to accommodate black delegates. The following year, the convention voted to eliminate segregated locals and issued a call to all national and international unions "to remove any bars that may interfere with acceptance of Negro membership." *Catering Industry Employees*, official organ of the international, declared: "We fail to see the logic in unions barring their doors to Negro workers in their industry."[45]

But these advances by AF of L unions on the racial issue, influenced by the growth of the CIO, were the exceptions. The general practice in the building-trades unions was not to admit Negro bricklayers, plumbers, steamfitters, or carpenters and to prevent them from obtaining work. Since most building projects, including those financed by the Federal Housing Administration, used union labor, skilled black building-trades workers still found "little if any employment."[46]

In 1937 a Carolina local of the Tobacco Workers' International Union forcibly ejected Negroes from a meeting on orders from international headquarters. In 1939 the AF of L organized shipyard workers in the Tampa shipbuilding industry. Prior to unionization, some 600 semi-skilled and skilled blacks had worked in the Tampa yards. As soon as the International Brotherhood of Boilermakers was recognized as the bargaining agent, the black workers were forced out of their jobs by the union's exclusionist policy. President William Green made an ineffective gesture toward investigation, but the 600 blacks were still kept out of their old jobs, and *The Crisis* carried the headline, "Lily-White Unions Steal Negro Jobs."[47] The same thing happened soon afterward at the New Orleans shipyards and at the Boeing Aircraft Plant in Seattle, where the International Association of Machinists was empowered to bargain collectively.

New Orleans in 1937 was the scene of a bitter labor struggle during which the difference between the CIO and the AF of L on the racial question came into sharp focus. The CIO's ILWU, headed by Harry Bridges, was pitted against the AF of L's ILA, led by "King" Joe Ryan. The ILA had a long history of collaborating with employers in the Gulf ports and operated the "shape up" hiring system, which gave few longshoremen steady jobs but made corrupt union officials rich through kickbacks. Its practice of maintaining segregated locals was also in sharp contrast to the ILWU's egalitarian racial policies. As might be expected, the employers, racist politicians, and newspapers in New Orleans favored the AF of L, and federation officials joined them in a vicious reactionary campaign, denouncing the ILWU as "communistic" and, above all, as "a threat to white supremacy." The Alabama State Industrial Union Council, CIO, along with the black communities, supported the ILWU. The day before the election, William Mitch told an all-Negro audience: "The only social equality I ever heard a negro ask about is the same amount of money for the same amount of labor."[48]

The racist campaign, helped along by intimidation and terror, achieved an ILA election victory. The New Orleans press hailed the outcome as a victory for white supremacy. In 1940, addressing the Brotherhood of Sleeping Car Porters convention, William Green, who had remained silent during the battle in the Gulf ports, managed to assert without a blush, "So long as I can express myself, I shall fight against racial intolerance and hatred in America."[49]

Green had not expressed himself when eight prominent leaders of Negro unions and organizations had appealed to the national convention of the Railways Employees Department of the AF of L in April, 1938, for action to eliminate discriminatory clauses from the constitutions of affiliated unions. Nor did he use his influence in favor of the Negro redcaps when the Railway and Steamship Clerks Union barred them from membership while organizing the white redcaps. When the Brotherhood of Sleeping Car Porters applied to the AF of L for jurisdiction over the Negro redcaps, Green helped the Railway and Steamship Clerks Union in its successful effort to block its petition.

In August, 1936, the Brotherhood of Sleeping Car Porters celebrated its eleventh anniversary and the awarding of an international charter by the AF of L. On the front page of its official organ, *The Black Worker*, for that month were messages from President Roosevelt; President Green of the AF of L; President John L. Lewis of the UMW; Sir Walter Citrine, General Secretary of the British Trades' Union Congress; and George Lansbury, member of the House of Commons. The brotherhood, its shattered membership rebuilt under the impact of Section 7(A) of the NIRA, celebrated its twelfth anniversary with the greatest victory in its history. On August 25, 1937, exactly twelve years after the union was organized, the Pullman Company signed its first contract with the brotherhood, the first signed between a union of black workers and a major American corporation. The agreement called for the reduction in the work month from nearly 400 hours to 240 and a wage increase of $1.25 million. It also provided for job security and effective union representation. The NAACP hailed the victory:

> As important as is the lucrative contract, as a labor victory to the Pullman porters, it is even more important to the Negro race as a whole, from the point of view of the Negro's up-hill climb for respect, recognition and influence, and economic advancement. The porters' accomplishment undoubtedly marks the first time that an all-Negro union has signed a contract with one of America's largest industrial organizations; this is the first time that Negroes have contributed so much of their own pennies (some million and a half dollars) to push a fight for their economic betterment; stuck together so long in a struggle in which there were so many odds against them; this is the first time that so important a step forward has been made under entirely Negro leadership.[50]

By 1937, A. Philip Randolph, the brotherhood's president and president of the National Negro Congress, had emerged as the principal spokesman for black labor within the councils of the AF of L. From the 1934 convention on, Randolph had urged delegates to order "the elimination of the color clause and pledge from the constitution and rituals of the trade and industrial unions" and the expulsion of all unions that maintained "said color bar." In 1934 and again in 1935, the AF of L convention had rejected what came to be known as the "Randolph Resolution,"* despite the endorsement of the National Negro Congress, the Cleveland Metal Trades Council, the District Council of Painters, the Cleveland Federation of Labor, the Ohio Council, the Buffalo Central Labor Union, and the Maritime Federation of the Pacific Coast.

Finally, at the 1939 convention, the delegates adopted a weak resolution calling upon affiliated unions whose constitutions had discriminatory clauses to report on the question of the color bar and various forms of racial discrimination at the next convention.† By contrast, the 1939

---

* The 1935 convention also refused to endorse the Negro Labor Committee, which had been formed by representatives of 110 New York City unions to act as a center for organizing Negroes into AF of L unions.

† At the insistence of the Negro delegates, who pointed to such actions at the 1938 CIO convention, the 1939 AF of L convention endorsed a federal antilynching bill and called for the abolition of the poll tax and "lily-white" primaries.

convention of the CIO had unanimously resolved "that the CIO pledges itself to uncompromising opposition to any form of discrimination, whether political or economic, based on race, color, creed or nationality."

With all its limitations, then, the CIO marked a significant step forward for black as well as white workers. Whatever its shortcomings, the CIO was unquestionably the most important single development since the Civil War in the black worker's struggle for equality. The Pittsburgh *Courier* remarked on December 7, 1939: "The only real effort that has been made to let down the color bars since the days of the Knights of Labor is that of the Congress of Industrial Organizations." Thurgood Marshall, chief legal adviser to the NAACP, declared: "The program of the CIO has become a Bill of Rights for Negro labor in America."[51] Summing up the period between 1935 and 1939, Monroe Strickland wrote:

> To the American Negro the coming of the CIO has been the most important historical experience in 75 years of struggle for a chance to live and achieve. This is true also for millions of white industrial workers, but it is true in double measure for the forgotten black workers of American history.[52]

Perhaps the greatest tribute to the CIO came from the conservative leader of an AF of L union with a long history of exclusion of blacks. Frank Chinella, vice-president, International Brotherhood of Boilermakers, Iron Shipbuilders and Helpers of America, Local 104 (Seattle), told an interviewer in July, 1952: "The AF of L for years didn't care about taking Negroes in. It was only when the CIO came in that Negroes got into the unions."[53]

17 World War II

Of the nearly 13 million blacks in the United States, more than 5 million were in the labor force in 1940, but a disproportionate number of them, as compared with whites, were unemployed. The boom in industry as the defense build-up got under way seemed to hold out the prospect that the black worker's day had come at last. The demand for workers in the defense industries soon absorbed all the available white males in the labor supply; a cry arose from employers for more workers to man the expanding war industry. But the color ban remained. Although employers at aircraft factories were begging for workers, blacks who applied were informed that "the Negro will be considered only as janitors and in other similar capacities." Both Negro and white workers lacked the required skills for many of the defense jobs, and the government established training programs to remedy the lack. But the government-financed programs discriminated against Negro trainees, and blacks who received training found it did not assure them jobs. "While we are in complete sympathy for the Negro," the president of North American Aviation frankly declared, "it is against company policy to employ them as aircraft workers or mechanics . . . regardless of their training. . . . There will be some jobs as janitors for Negroes."[1]

Employment discrimination when the country was clamoring for labor, coupled with discrimination against blacks in the armed forces, aroused more anger in the black community than there had ever been before. If the Negro could not get work at such a time, it appeared that he was doomed forever to an inferior economic status. Black leaders protested heatedly to government officials, but nothing happened. Walter White wrote to John Temple Graves, the Southern journalist, that he had pleaded with Roosevelt to do something, but the President had refused, giving as his reason his belief that "the nation would rise up in protest."

In *An American Dilemma*, published in 1944, the sociologist Gunnar Myrdal stated that blacks made even less headway during the boom following the outbreak of World War II in Europe than during World War I. "In October, 1940, only 5.4 per cent of Employment Service placements in 20 selected defense industries were non-white, and this

238

proportion had by April, 1941, declined to 2.5 per cent. In September, 1941, it was ascertained that the great bulk of the war plants did not have any Negroes at all among their workers."[2] Of 282,254 prospective openings in defense industries in that month, more than half (51 per cent) were barred to Negroes, according to a survey by the Social Security Administration's Board of Employment Security. Of the war industries covered by the survey, shipbuilding was the outstanding exception; fewer than 28 per cent of the openings in shipbuilding were closed to blacks.

A vicious cycle operated. Many labor unions in the defense industries would not admit Negroes. Management that had closed-shop agreement with such unions would turn down black applicants for being non-union. Training schools would not accept Negro candidates either because they could not join labor unions or because they had no job offers. Management would not make offers to Negro job applicants because, without the training, they were not qualified. Little wonder that, while unemployment was declining among whites, among blacks it grew. As the Depression for white America was officially ended, the federal government drastically cut welfare appropriations, even though most blacks remained unemployed or underemployed.

Black protests brought action, but only on paper. The U.S. Office of Education announced a nondiscriminatory policy in the use of funds for vocational training in defense work. In 1940, Congress, appropriating funds for defense training, forbade discrimination because of sex, race, or color. Sidney Hillman, CIO vice-president and co-chairman, with William Knudsen of General Motors, of the Office of Production Management, issued special instructions calling for an end to discrimination in specific defense industries. But the various measures enacted were never enforced, and the orders were ignored.

It was painfully clear that the methods of the long-established Negro organizations were getting the black workers nowhere. The National Negro Congress was still functioning, but its effectiveness had been sharply reduced after a split at its 1940 convention between A. Philip Randolph and the CIO–Communist Party delegates. After the delegates voted overwhelmingly to affiliate with the CIO's Labor Non-Partisan League and to condemn American "involvement in this imperialistic war," Randolph resigned as National Negro Congress president, charging that the organization was white- and Communist-dominated.

It was Randolph who created the organization that continued the work of the early National Negro Congress—the March on Washington Movement (MOWM). However, it differed from the congress in that it excluded whites. In late 1940 and early 1941, the NAACP, the Committee for Participation of Negroes in the National Defense, and the Allied Committees for National Defense had held mass protest meetings, but the exclusion of blacks from defense industries continued. Walter White, Randolph, and other black leaders could not even get an appointment to see President Roosevelt to plead for government action. In January, 1941, a time of bitterness and frustration among black

Americans, Randolph published an article in the black press in which he noted that committees and individuals had failed to achieve a greater share for blacks in the defense effort and to eliminate discrimination in the armed forces. "Only power can effect the enforcement and adoption of a given policy," he concluded. "Power is the active principle of only the organized masses, the masses united for definite purpose."[3] To bring the power of the black masses into the picture, Randolph suggested that 10,000 Negroes march on Washington, D.C., under the slogan: "We loyal Negro-American Citizens demand the right to work and fight for our country." A postmarch rally would be held at the Lincoln Memorial to add emphasis to the demand.

Randolph's call for a march on Washington struck an immediate response in the black masses. By spring, Negro communities all over the North were seething, and the number to march on Washington, July 1, 1941, was increased to 50,000. Even then, so bitter were blacks that a minimum of 100,000 were preparing to march. By the end of May, march committees had opened headquarters at Harlem and Brooklyn in New York and in Washington, Pittsburgh, Detroit, Chicago, Saint Louis, and San Francisco. Financed and organized largely by the Brotherhood of Sleeping Car Porters, the movement spread to all the railway centers where local divisions of the brotherhood were located. Here, the organizing machinery merged with local units of the NAACP and the Urban League to form local march committees. The local black church, the Elks and Masonic halls, and even the city parks became the sites of mass rallies. The brotherhood's official journal, *The Black Worker*, became the March on Washington's organ. The May, 1941, issue carried the official call:

> We call upon you to fight for jobs in National Defense.
> We call upon you to struggle for the integration of Negroes in the armed forces . . . of the Nation.
> We call upon you to demonstrate for the abolition of Jim-Crowism in all Government departments and defense employment. . . .
> While billions of the taxpayers' money are being spent for war weapons, Negro workers are being turned away from the gates of factories, mines and mills—being flatly told, "NOTHING DOING." Some employers refuse to give Negroes jobs when they are without "union cards," and some unions refuse Negro workers union cards when they are "without jobs."

The call ended: "The Federal Government cannot with clear conscience call upon private industry and labor unions to abolish discrimination based upon race and color so long as it practices discrimination itself against Negro Americans."

Thousands of copies of the call were distributed by the members of the brotherhood, who also spread bulletins reporting on the progress of the movement and campaign literature explaining the purpose of the drive. In fact. the March on Washington movement represented the first occasion in American history when a black labor organization assumed leadership of the struggle of the Negro masses on a national scale and became the spokesman for all black Americans, conservative and radical alike. Even black newspapers, long hostile to unionism among black workers, acknowledged the leadership role of the union of Negro porters and urged the black masses to "converge on Washington in pursuit of jobs and justice."[4]

The militant challenge to the *status quo* represented by the march could not be ignored by Washington, even though the regular press carried little news about the forthcoming event. The powers-that-be tried to discourage the demonstration on the ground that it would do more harm than good. Even Eleanor Roosevelt enrolled in the campaign to stop the march; on June 10, she wrote to Randolph that she had discussed the entire situation with her husband and that "we feel very strongly that your group is making a very great mistake at this time to allow this march to take place." A few days later, at a conference called in New York City, Mayor La Guardia, who was handling defense problems for the President; Aubrey Williams; and Mrs. Roosevelt urged Randolph and Walter White to call off the march. Randolph insisted that the organizers "could not think of calling it off unless we have accomplished our definite aim, which is jobs and not promises."[5]

On June 12, in a further attempt to forestall the march, Roosevelt issued a memorandum to Knudsen and Hillman placing the support of his office behind letters Hillman had previously sent to defense contractors asking them not to discriminate—appeals that had been totally ignored. But the March on Washington Committee refused to consider half-measures and reiterated its demand for an executive order. On June 18, Randolph, Frank P. Crosswaith, Layle Lane, and Walter White met with the President. They were treated to a lecture on why the whole idea of the march was "bad and unintelligent." Following the conference Randolph announced, "The march will go on."[6]

But on June 24, after an all-day conference involving La Guardia, Randolph, Rayford Logan, Eugene Davidson, and Aubrey Williams, the march was called off. In exchange the MOWM obtained an executive order banning discrimination in defense industries. Roosevelt issued the order the following day, reaffirming the "policy of the United States that there shall be no discrimination in the employment of workers in defense industries or Government because of race, creed, color, or national origin" and declaring it "the duty of employers and of labor organizations, in furtherance of said policy, and of this order, to provide for the full and equitable participation of all workers in defense industries, without discrimination because of race, creed, color, or national origin; and it is hereby ordered as follows: All contracting agencies of the Government of the United States shall include in all defense contracts hereafter negotiated by them a provision obligating the contractor not to discriminate against any worker because of race, creed, color, or national origin."[7]

Thus was born the Fair Employment Practices Committee (FEPC). As Herbert Garfinkel notes, "The national press hailed the Executive Order as further demonstration of America's love for democracy, but continued to ignore the role of the 'march' in applying pressure on the administration."[8] On July 19, 1941, after considerable wrangling, Roosevelt appointed the first FEPC, which included Milton Webster of the Brotherhood of Sleeping Car Porters. The chairman was Mark Ethridge, publisher of the Louisville *Courier;* other members were William Green, Philip Murray, David Sarnoff, and Earl B. Dickerson.

Although the victory did not win most of the original MOWM demands—a law denying the benefits of the National Labor Relations Act to unions denying membership to blacks had been of special importance to black workers—and, although some criticized Randolph for having called off the march, comparing his action with his cancellation of the strike of Pullman porters in 1927 after the membership had voted overwhelmingly to walk out, the movement was truly a significant chapter in the modern history of black Americans. It was, for one thing, a black mass movement, the first since the decline of the Garvey movement, and, like its predecessor, it was entirely a black protest movement. For another, in its use of direct action, the MOWM foreshadowed the civil rights struggles of the postwar period. Finally, its major concern was the economic problems of blacks, and it projected on a national scale the entire decade's action for jobs on the local level through such movements as the Greater New York Coordinating Committee. The MOWM's activities—organizing local coalitions, soliciting thousands of endorsers, adopting resolutions, distributing hundreds of thousands of leaflets, releasing news stories to the black press—forced the issue of job discrimination to the center of the nation's life.

The President's Fair Employment Practices Committee began to function on July 18, 1941. Handicapped by inadequate funds and harassed by segregationist Congressmen, the FEPC held hearings in Los Angeles, Chicago, New York, and Birmingham. Its objective was twofold: (1) to put Negroes and workers from other minority groups into war industry, and (2) to raise the morale of those who suffered from discrimination. After the Japanese attack on Pearl Harbor and America's entrance into World War II, job openings for blacks increased only slowly. Labor shortages were reported in 102 industrial areas in December, 1942, and were anticipated in 77 others. Yet the National Urban League estimated that about 1 million Negroes were available for employment in those very areas. In the year 1941, some 118,000 Negroes were trained for industrial, professional, or clerical work. Of these more than 56,000 completed trades and industrial courses in technical schools. But only a small fraction of these trained, skilled Negro workers had been placed in war employment by the end of 1942.

The War Manpower Commission on December 7, 1942, recommended a firmer policy to eliminate barriers against the employment of qualified Negroes in war jobs. "Only by utilizing every possible source of untapped local labor—for example, women, handicapped workers, and minority groups—can a community classified as a labor shortage area be confident of discharging the war production commitments already entrusted to it."[9] The FEPC, now subordinate to the War Manpower Commission, tried to induce companies and unions to use black skilled workers. But the very companies that were loudly proclaiming the need for all Americans to pitch in and win the war refused to allow black Americans to make their contribution. In Houston, Galveston, Mobile, New Orleans, and Tampa, shipyard companies inserted advertisements in local papers begging white youths and white women to come in and be trained as welders. "Keep Our Boys from Dying," the ads appealed. When the FEPC suggested the hiring of skilled, trained black welders, the companies suddenly discovered that there was no real shortage of welders. Rather than hire blacks, the companies were willing to keep production down, and in this brazen affront to the war effort they had the connivance of the U.S. Employment Service in the South.

White Southern colleges received funds from the federal government to train manpower but excluded blacks, who had to travel far to get training in black colleges with inadequate equipment. Once trained, moreover, blacks had to look far afield for jobs in Southern war industries other than as menials. FEPC efforts to remedy the situation by holding public hearings encountered stiff opposition from Southern Congressmen and AF of L unions. The hearings were abruptly canceled.

In Mobile, the FEPC attempted to upgrade some Negro workers as welders in the yards of the Alabama Dry Dock and Shipbuilders Company. In response the company helped stir 20,000 white workers to walk off their jobs and riot for four days. Only the intervention of federal troops stopped the riot. The FEPC then backed down and agreed to let the *status quo* continue in the shipyards.

In its first report, the FEPC noted that in March, 1942, *two years after the start of the defense program*, Negro workers constituted only 2.5 to 3 per cent of all workers in war production; by November, 1944, the percentage had grown to over 8 per cent. In addition to almost 1 million Negroes serving in the armed forces during World War II—all in segregated sections of the services—more than 5,500,000 Negro civilian workers were employed in January, 1945. Between April, 1940, and April, 1944, the number of employed Negro workers had increased by more than 1 million, from 2,900,000 to 3,800,000 men and from 1,500,000 to 2,100,000 women. More would have been employed had the FEPC really received the backing of the federal government.

The economic horizons of the black workers were also enlarged during World War II as a result of FEPC rulings and especially court decisions affecting racial discrimination by trade unions, particularly the railroad brotherhoods and craft unions affiliated with the AF of L. All four of the railroad brotherhoods and many unions affiliated with the AF of L kept the color ban throughout the war years wherever they could; where they gave way, they did so grudgingly and under pressure.

Among the most important cases of discrimination brought before the FEPC during World War II were those of black railroad workers. The target of their complaint was the infamous "Washington Agreement" of 1941. In March, 1937, Negro trade union leaders and heads of Negro organizations met in New York's Harlem, under the sponsorship of the National Negro Congress, and mapped out a national campaign to break the color bar in railroad unions and in agreements between the brotherhoods and railroad management. "If these working agreements continue to be made and remain in force," declared John P. Davis, "it will be a matter of but a few years before practically no jobs exist in the railroad industry. Already as a result of these contracts the number of Negroes employed in the industry has seriously declined, leaving thousands of Negro workers and their families unemployed."[10] The campaign got nowhere, and it was not long before Davis's prediction was on its way to fulfillment.

In February, 1938, D. H. Robertson, head of the Brotherhood of Locomotive Firemen and Engineers, informed William Green that "in order that there may be no discrimination against white men, agreements have been negotiated to limit the seniority of colored firemen."[11] Two years later, purporting to act as bargaining agent for all railroad firemen, the brotherhood notified twenty-one Southern railroads that they must "exclude all Negro firemen from the service." Only white men were to be "employed as firemen or assigned to new runs or jobs or permanent vacancies in establishing runs or jobs." Only white firemen were to be eligible for promotion as engineers. As Robert C. Weaver points out, the introduction of the diesel engine on the railroads at that time gave the brotherhood the opportunity "to achieve an objective it had been seeking for over fifty years—namely, the perfection of a plan to eliminate Negro firemen."[12]

In February, 1941, with the assistance of the National Mediation Board, a compromise was reached between the Southeastern carriers and the brotherhood. The so-called Washington Agreement provided that "nonpromotable" firemen should not exceed 50 per cent in every class of the services. The Jim Crow aspect was embodied in the clause that read: "It is understood that promotable firemen, or helpers on other than steam power, are those in line for promotion, under the present rules and practices, to the position of locomotive engineers." Since Negroes were completely barred from such promotion, the process of eliminating black firemen from the roads began in earnest the moment the agreement was signed. Indeed, not even the 50 per cent ratio was maintained; in April, 1941, the brotherhood replaced *all* Negro firemen with white men.

The brotherhood was confident that it would get away with it. Under the Railway Labor Act the grievances of workers were to be handled by the National Railroad Adjustment Board (NRAB), on which workers were represented through their unions. But none of the unions of Negro railroad workers was represented on the NRAB.* Only the "Big

* These included the Association of Colored Railway Trainmen and Locomotive Firemen; Colored Trainmen of America; Dining Car and Food Workers' Union; International Association of Railway Employees; Southern Association of Colored Railway Trainmen and Firemen; Association of Train Porters, Brakemen, and Switchmen; Protective Order of Railway Trainmen; Interstate Order of Colored Locomotive Firemen, Engine Helpers, Yard and Train Service Employees, and Railroad Mechanics; and International Association of Railway Employees, Locomotive Firemen, Hostlers, and Hostler Helpers. The last-named operated on the Florida East Coast Railroad.

Four" brotherhoods were eligible. Obviously the Negro railroad worker had little chance before a board half of whose members represented the carriers and the other half the Jim Crow brotherhoods. Moreover, the courts had reinforced the position of the brotherhoods by ruling that the railroads could not bargain with black unions or individuals. Technically speaking, the Brotherhood of Locomotive Firemen and Enginemen, which barred black workers, was the bargaining agent for all firemen. Thus the black firemen were denied the services of the NRAB.

But the blacks were determined to fight. The black railway unions set up the Negro Railway Labor Executive Committee, which hired Charles H. Houston of Washington, D.C., a noted black attorney, to fight for their rights in the courts and before government bodies. When appeals failed to restore the black firemen to their jobs, Bester Williams Steele began a new struggle. Steele had been a fireman on the Louisville and Nashville Railroad since 1910 and had been discharged under the "Washington Agreement." He asked the Brotherhood of Locomotive Firemen and Enginemen to take his case to the NRAB, but the brotherhood refused. Steele then went to the FEPC in 1943, along with a number of other Negro railroad workers.

At the hearings the carriers were represented by Sidney Alderman of Greensboro, North Carolina, who declared: "Railroads must adapt their operations and employment practices to the social solutions of racial questions as worked out by the prevailing mores and legal systems of the states they serve."[13] In other words, while America was fighting the racism of Germany, the railroads, in collaboration with the brotherhoods, could continue racist practices at home, establishing what Charles Houston called "the Nordic closed shop" on American railroads.[14]

Steele testified that when he was hired on the Louisville and Nashville, 96 per cent of the firemen in his district were blacks, and that just before the "Washington Agreement" went into effect, the proportion was 80 per cent. By 1943, only 20 per cent had retained their jobs. The appeal of the Negro firemen was supported by Dr. Herbert R. Northrup, author of Organized Labor and the Negro, published soon afterward. "In no other industry," he testified, "has collective bargaining had such disastrous results for Negroes. Of the 29 national unions which exclude Negroes by explicit provision or by general practice, or which afford them only inferior status, 19 are found in the railroad industry." He noted the "anomalous position" of the Negro railroad worker, "denied a voice in the affairs of nearly all railroad labor organizations" at a time when "collective bargaining on the railroads has received wider acceptance than in almost every other industry."[15]

The FEPC found the "Washington Agreement" discriminatory and ordered the roads and unions to abandon it; it directed the Louisville and Nashville to adjust its employment policy and practices "so that all needed workers shall be hired and all company employees shall be promoted without regard to race, creed, color or national origin."[16] But the railroad brotherhoods remained firm in their anti-Negro practices and successfully defied the FEPC. Steele, represented by Charles Houston, brought suit against the Louisville and Nashville and the Brotherhood of Locomotive Firemen and Enginemen in the U.S. District Court at Alabama. Defeated there, he appealed to the U.S. Supreme Court.

In December, 1944, the Supreme Court reversed the lower court's verdict and ruled for Steele's petition, contending that it was the duty of a craft-union representative to defend the interests of all workers, regardless of race or color. In a vigorous concurring opinion, Justice Frank Murphy condemned "the economic discrimination practiced by the Brotherhood and the railroad under the color of Congressional authority" and added:

> The utter disregard for the dignity and the well-being of colored citizens shown by this record is so pronounced as to demand the invocation of constitutional condemnation. To decide the case and to analyze the statute solely on the basis of legal niceties while remaining mute and placid as to the obvious and oppressive deprivation of constitutional guarantees is to make the judicial function something less than it should be.[17]

On the same day the Supreme Court also handed down a decision in the case of *Thomas Tunstall v. Brotherhood of Locomotive Firemen of Norfolk, Virginia*. The facts in this case were similar to those in the Steele case, and the same decision was rendered. Both decisions held that, under the Railway Labor Act, contracts that arbitrarily discriminated against minority workers could be enjoined from enforcement. This was a victory for black railroad workers, but how great a victory has been a subject of some dispute. Professors Benjamin Aaron and Michael Komaroff pointed out, in the *Illinois Law Review* of September–October, 1949, that Chief Justice Stone's opinion in the Steele case implied that black workers could obtain equality of treatment in the railroad industry without full membership in the unions charged with responsibility to represent them—in short, through separate Negro unions or Jim Crow locals of the brotherhood, if they should be established. And Professor George D. Haller, in the *Labor Law Journal* of July, 1957, has argued that the Wisconsin Supreme Court inferred in a Milwaukee bricklayers' case (*Ross v. Ebert*) that the U.S. Supreme Court had actually recognized the right of a voluntary association to discriminate.

Regardless of the interpretation of the Steele decision, the number of Negro railroad firemen continued to diminish. Technological innovation caused part of the decrease, but the main cause was the continuance of discriminatory practices by both industry and the brotherhoods.

The miserable record of the railroad brotherhoods was duplicated during the war years by many AF of L unions. In June, 1942, *Fortune* magazine reported that nineteen international unions, ten of which were affiliated with the AF of L, practiced discrimination against black workers. Even when unions pledged nondiscrimination in their charters, they continued to employ subtle means to exclude Negroes, often using the initiation oath for the purpose. "In certain places and industries," *Fortune* reported, "the congestion of war orders has been so heavy that discriminating unions could not totally obstruct Negro employment without endangering production and their own jobs. In some of these instances a peculiar device is used: the Negro is not accepted as a member, but purchases from the union a working permit—an interesting hybrid of tenant feudalism and industrial democracy." Representative of the attitude in many AF of L unions was that of William Hutcheson of the carpenters' union, who retorted to charges of racial bias: "In our union we don't care whether you're an Irishman, a Jew, or a Nigger."[18]

Especially notorious during the war years were the Building and Metal Trades Councils, the machinist locals, and the International Brotherhood of Boilermakers, Iron Shipbuilders and Helpers of America. In general, their practice was to utilize closed-shop agreements to exclude Negroes and actively to oppose the employment and upgrading of blacks whenever possible. Whenever these unions could not keep blacks out, they gave them second-class status. When forced to permit blacks to join, the machinist local at the Boeing plant in Seattle gave them thirty-day renewable work permits. The blacks were charged higher initiation fees and dues than the regular members and received no membership rights in return.

The status of the Negro in the boilermakers' international reached the front pages of newspapers throughout the country as a result of two historic decisions in 1944, one on the West Coast and the other in Providence, Rhode Island. During the early period of the war emergency, Negroes were excluded from most skilled jobs in shipyards. However, the need for workers became so acute that the boilermakers, having failed to recruit a sufficient number of white workers, reluctantly allowed Negroes to take jobs. Jim Crow auxiliary locals were set up for them.

On the West Coast Negro workers, after paying their dues and initiation fees to the regular locals of the boilermakers, refused to be relegated to the status of second-class members in auxiliary locals. In Portland the NAACP branch filed formal complaints with the FEPC on behalf of the Negro boilermakers. While the committee was holding hearings in Portland, the boilermakers' international, on November 28, 1943, ordered the Marineship Corporation of San Francisco to discharge all nonmembers, including Negroes who had refused to join the Jim Crow auxiliary. The black workers, led by Joseph James, won a temporary injunction preventing the discharge of the men. When the case was dismissed, the black workers won a second temporary injunction from the local courts, and the issue went to the Supreme Court of California for a decision.

On December 9, 1943, while this case was pending, the FEPC ordered the boilermakers' union to "take such necessary steps and put in course of execution such required procedures as will effect elimination of the discriminatory policies and practices found to be in conflict with and in violation of Executive Order 9346."[19] But, like the brotherhoods, the boilermakers ignored the FEPC ruling. On January 13, 1944, Judge Alexander L. Churchill handed down a significant decision affecting the status of Negro members of the boilermakers in Providence, where the racial policy of the international was particularly vicious. In the Providence shipyards the boilermakers, anxious to win a union election in order to be designated the bargaining agent, had admitted all persons regardless of race or color and had even launched a special campaign to sign up Negroes. Prior to the election, blacks were admitted into the regular union, attended meetings, made motions, voted, and were treated like other members.

After the election was won by the boilermakers' international and the closed-shop agreement signed, officers of the international attempted to set up a Jim Crow auxiliary for blacks. Protests from Negroes were ignored, and even when a majority of the white members opposed the move, the international persisted and issued "auxiliary cards" to Negro members of the local. Blacks refused to accept the cards and attended meetings with whites as regular members. When the international replaced the officers of the local with men ready to segregate the blacks, the Negro boilermakers applied to the courts for an injunction to restrain the local from discriminating against blacks. Judge Churchill granted the injunction and stated that "the purpose and effect of the so-called 'auxiliary' was to segregate Negroes and persons of no other race and color, in a position less favorable in substantial matters than the position enjoyed by other members of Local 308." He ruled that the practice of segregating Negroes into an auxiliary local was "illegal and void."[20]

Nevertheless, the annual convention of the boilermakers in February, 1944, voted unanimously to keep its Jim Crow locals. The union made only one conciliatory gesture to black members: In the future, Negro auxiliaries would be permitted to elect delegates directly to national conventions and to affiliate directly with local metal trades councils and district lodges. The convention also directed the incoming Executive Council to secure insurance for Negro members on the same basis as for whites. But full-fledged membership for blacks was rejected.

On December 30, 1943, the Supreme Court of California rendered its decision in the case of *Joseph James v. Marineship Corporation*. James, it will be recalled, had brought action in behalf of approximately 1,000 other blacks in addition to himself, all skilled in the shipbuilding trade, charging the boilermakers' international with discriminatory practices. In its decision the court, holding that the Fourteenth and Fifteenth Amendments "evidence a definite national policy against discrimination because of race or color," found for the plaintiff James and, citing the recently decided Steele and Tunstall cases, held:

> Where a union excludes Negroes from membership therein but insists that they must, in order to work, join a Negro auxiliary which does not give its members privileges and protection substantially equal to those given members of the parent union, and which imposes unreasonable and discriminatory restrictions on Negroes who accept membership, such denial of union membership on terms of equality with other workers is the equivalent of a complete denial of union membership. Such discriminatory practices are contrary to the public policy of the United States and this state.[21]

Thus, by incessant appeals and expensive litigation, the black workers during World War II fought discrimination by AF of L unions. They received no support from Frank Fenton, William Green's alternate as AF of L representative on the FEPC. Fenton regularly opposed any action against union racial discrimination. When the Smith Committee, headed by Howard Smith, the segregationist, antilabor Congressman from Virginia, held hearings with the intent to discredit the FEPC, leaders of key AF of L unions readily appeared at witness to lodge complaints against being forced by the government agency to bring about social equality between black and white workers. At a Senate hearing on the issue of creating a permanent FEPC, W. C. Cushing, chairman of the AF of L national legislative committee, filed a statement opposing such legislation.

Meanwhile, at AF of L conventions during the war years, Randolph continued his efforts to end racial discrimination in the federation. At the 1940 convention, he cried out: "It won't do for the trade union movement, which ought to be the bulwark of democracy and which ought to maintain the traditions of democracy, to say 'no, you cannot participate in our organization, because you are not competent, because you are not worthwhile, because you are colored, because you are not white.' " But the delegates refused to listen, and the convention rejected a resolution introduced by Randolph and Milton P. Webster of the Brotherhood of Sleeping Car Porters calling for the creation of a committee to investigate the discriminatory practices of all AF of L unions. The convention was prepared to do no more than request national and international unions to consider policies to eliminate "any tendency to discriminate against working men because of race, color or creed"—a request that was totally ignored by the offending affiliates.[22]

When Randolph and Webster introduced their resolution again at the 1941 convention, a heated debate developed. Randolph took the floor to document the charges of discriminatory racial practices by AF of L unions and to attack the acquiescence of the federation in these racist acts. He told the delegates:

I want to cite a few cases. . . .

Negro painters in Omaha cannot get into the Painters' organization nor can they secure a charter.

Plasterers and cement finishers in Kansas City, Missouri, cannot get into the organization nor can they get a charter.

The AF of L unions in the shipbuilding yards in New Orleans refuse membership to Negro workers, although the company has expressed a willingness to employ them.

Recently, Metal Trades Department unions have secured at some yards, through a training formula, a monopoly on trainees who will be upgraded in these yards.

Stabilization pacts between the OPM and certain of the building trades have resulted in disqualifying qualified colored artisans from defense employment, and thereby retarding defense efforts.

In Saint Louis, Negro artisans cannot get work, but white workers come from outside of Saint Louis and are sent to work.

The most conspicuous and consistent denial of employment of Negroes which can be attributed almost directly to union influence is found at the

Boeing Aircraft Corporation in Seattle, Washington. From the beginning of the National defense program, the Boeing Company has given as its excuse for not employing Negroes the fact that it had a contract with the Aeronautical Mechanics Union, Local 751, International Association of Machinists, AF of L, and that the union accepts white members only.

Randolph went on listing case after case in which AF of L unions violated the rights of black workers, describing at length how such unions as the boilermakers and the International Association of Machinists and others had forced Negroes out of their jobs at shipyards and other defense installations. At the end of his lengthy indictment, Randolph challenged the leaders of the named unions to defend themselves. Several rose to reply, but their defense consisted of conceding that Randolph was essentially correct and then asserting that, because of the opposition of white members, they could do nothing to alter the situation. (These union officials failed to explain why, when locals of the machinists' and the boilermakers' unions, predominantly composed of white members, worked to eliminate racial restrictions against blacks, they were repudiated by the international leaders.) John P. Frey of the molders' union would not concede that there was justification for the mildest attack on AF of L racial practices; on the contrary, he said, "if there is any institution in these United States to whom the colored race owes more than to any other it is the American Federation of Labor." Matthew Woll and William Green concurred. They said that the issue facing the convention was not discrimination by affiliated unions but "how far this convention will want to intrude itself upon the rights of autonomous National and International unions." So holy were "rights" of the affiliates that protection of them—including the right to discriminate against Negroes—was more important than protection of the rights of black labor.

Randolph closed the debate by reiterating his frequent plea for action against discriminating unions and again charging that "the American Federation of Labor has not kept faith with the Negro workers."[23] But, as in 1940, the resolution calling for an investigating committee was soundly defeated. *The Crisis* commented: "There can be little surprise over failure of the annual convention of the AFL . . . to take any action against the flagrant racial discrimination of its member unions. The AFL has been ducking and dodging on racial discrimination these many decades."[24]

At the 1942 convention, Randolph again listed in detail the facts on discrimination against Negro workers in AF of L unions. But once again he failed to get action. The convention rejected the resolution for an investigating committee and also turned down a motion that workers "who are now in Uncle Sam's uniform . . . be given the freedom and eligibility to join any union affiliated with the AF of L at the end of the war without regard to race, color, religion, or nationality."[25] After this the delegates voted for labor to spare no efforts to secure the defeat of Nazi Germany!

The 1943 convention was again the scene of a heated debate on the

Negro labor issue. The Executive Committee's report touched on discrimination by affiliated unions but offered no proposal to achieve its eradication. Randolph attacked the reticence of the report, insisting that "racial discrimination should be abolished by every union affiliated with the AF of L, not only for the benefit of the Negro . . . but for the sake of the AF of L itself—to square its practices with its professions."

As at previous conventions, Randolph cited specific cases of racial discrimination. He cited Herbert Northrup's *Organized Labor and the Negro*, recently published, which said that thirty international and national unions excluded black workers by constitutional provision, union ritual, or tacit consent, or by arranging "representation" in unions that were segregated and had only auxiliary status. Randolph condemned auxiliary unions as equivalent to "colonies of colored people to the empire systems" and as groups of "economic, political, and social serfs" who possessed "none of the rights that the white population in the mother country enjoy, except the right to be taxed," and who, like the colonists, were used as cannon fodder "in defense of their oppressors when wars break out." The whole set-up was designed to reduce the black members to complete powerlessness and helplessness:

> The net effect of this scheme is to make it lawful for a white lodge and its business and other bargaining agents at their whim and caprice to permit Negroes to work on union jobs, reserving arbitrary control over their status, upgrading, and even their continuation in nominal good standing. All significant rights of union membership, including all participation in collective bargaining, are denied to the Negroes. In substance, he pays dues and gets in return only a work permit revocable at will. This travesty designed to sanction the inevitable temporary utilization of Negro workmen in these times without conferring any significant status upon them does not merit characterization as union membership.

The leaders of the AF of L unions under attack, as well as other top officials of the federation, united in denouncing Randolph as a "professional Negro" and a troublemaker at a time when unity in the ranks of labor was essential for victory over fascism. John P. Frey accused him of doing the greatest disservice to the Negro people by any man since the end of slavery. Frey voiced the opinion that the only real problem confronting black workers was caused by "men of their own race, who endeavor to stir up all the trouble possible."

Randolph refused to be intimidated. He pointed out that blaming Negro leaders who exposed the AF of L's racial practices was like "contending that a meteorologist that points out a storm is coming creates the storm." He told the AF of L it should stop praising itself for its policy statements on equality of all workers and accusing black leaders of ingratitude, and should develop the courage to say to international unions, even though they were autonomous: "Your policy is wrong and it is up to you to bring your policy in harmony and in conformity with the basic principles of the American Federation of Labor as expressed in the constitution."

William Green brought the discussion to an end with a gesture to Randolph. He could understand how the black leader was "moved by a deep sense of injustice," and he urged the delegates to be compassionate. But Randolph was wrong in trying to end injustice overnight. He, too, would like to see discrimination eliminated immediately from the entire federation. But he, unlike Randolph, understood that nothing could be gained through "forced methods or through the presentation of demands that groups . . . comply with said demands." Only education and time would solve the problem, and Negroes had to learn patience. True, auxiliary-union membership had its limitations, but it was, after all, union membership. Hence he urged black workers to learn from him: "I have found in life's experience that I don't have my way in a good many things, and many times I have to wait a good while before I can have my way, and sometimes I never get it."[26]

On this "promising" note, the debate between Randolph and the federation leadership ended, and the delegates moved promptly to endorse the Executive Council's innocuous statement on discrimination and to reject Randolph's by their familiar call for an investigation of racial discrimination in AF of L affiliates. The same outcome followed a repeat performance of the Randolph–AF of L leadership debate at the 1944 convention, with William Green again concluding the discussion by counseling black workers that "we can only win through patience . . . good judgment . . . and through relying upon the soundness of our position."[27] The 1944 convention turned down both the usual Randolph request for an investigation and a new proposal calling for the abolition of auxiliary unions.

At the beginning of World War II, the Council for Democracy published a pamphlet entitled *The Negro and Defense: A Test of Democracy.* It acknowledged that the AF of L had frequently set forth its desire to see all workers organized, irrespective of race, creed, color, or nationality. It added: "However, there is no evidence of any successful intervention by the Federation in the case of unions which, explicitly or by their practice, violate this principle of organization; constituent unions are left full autonomy in such matters and the process of discrimination in such matters continues unchecked."[28]

At the end of World War II, the exact same statement could have been published. The record of the federation was still one of exclusion and segregated unionism in the main. As Myrdal put it: "The fact that the American Federation of Labor as such is officially against racial discrimination does not mean much. The Federation has never done anything to check racial discrimination exercised by its member organizations."[29]

In a special pamphlet directed at black workers and distributed during the war years, the CIO declared: "The CIO welcomes you. It gives you strength to win justice and fair play. The CIO unites you with your fellow workers of all races and all creeds in the common struggle for freedom, for democracy, for a better life." The pamphlet listed the CIO's achievements in combating discrimination: fewer than 125,000 Negroes in the labor movement before the coming of the CIO, and in 1942 more than 500,000, "most of them in the CIO"; in every CIO union Negro workers had "the same democratic rights, with the same voice as all other members," and were elected to official positions by their fellow members; in every union affiliated with the CIO, the Negro worker had "the same chance to win a better life that the white worker has"; the CIO had organized the Negro along with the white worker in agriculture, the government, in the white-collar and professional field, in transport, in maritime and construction trades, "everywhere the CIO has gone," and had "brought new hope to the underpaid and sweated workers of the South . . . Negro and white alike." And all this had been accomplished not because the CIO was "a charity organization" but because its members and leaders understood that the only way "strong, industrial labor unions" could be built was by "organizing Negro and white workers alike." "For a union to practice discrimination is to hand over half its strength to the employer, who uses it to weaken and divide the workers." The appeal then concluded: "Negro workers, join the CIO union in your industry."[30]

The approach of the CIO to black workers was clearly in sharp contrast to that of the AF of L. The first and most important test of these claims after the war broke out in Europe came in the UAW-CIO. The danger of the use of Negro strike-breakers by the auto industry arose during the two-month strike of Dodge and Chrysler workers against a speed-up early in 1940. But only a few score blacks crossed the picket line manned by white and Negro strikers. Negro union and civic leaders, ministers, lawyers, social workers, and newspaper editors went to strike-breakers' meetings and urged the workers not to aid the auto industrialists, pointing up the CIO's record in the battle for the rights of Negro labor. Meanwhile, white union officials, through the use of leaflets and speeches, fought attempts to provoke the strikers into violence against blacks, emphasizing that such action would only help the employers to break the strike.

The strike was won, but UAW leaders and members saw more clearly than before that violent racial conflict was an ever present possibility in the automotive industry and that constant attention had to be paid to building solid relations between the union and the black community. Certainly if Ford, the last and biggest holdout in the unionization of the auto industry, was ever to be organized, the black workers at Ford would have to be convinced that the advantages of membership in the UAW outweighed any benefits arising out of Henry Ford's paternalism. Moreover, influential Negro citizens, who saw Ford as the friend of blacks and the CIO as a threat to the advantages their people were supposed to enjoy in his plants, had to be won over.

By the end of the summer of 1940, the UAW was ready to tackle Ford. Black organizers were transferred to the Ford Organizing Committee staff, and several black Ford workers, fired for union activities, were made full-time organizers. Black members of other local unions

became volunteer organizers, and an interracial committee was formed
that included Negro community leaders as well as union representatives.
Black union and volunteer organizers and the interracial committee
popularized the UAW's policy against discrimination through literature,
speeches, radio talks, and other methods. The Jim Crow set-up in the
Ford plants was exposed; the wages received by black Ford workers were
compared with those of black UAW members at General Motors and
Chrysler, and the Negroes themselves described the advantages they had
won through the union.

When the strike of Ford workers came on April 1, 1941, the union's
drive intensified. Perhaps the outstanding feature of the strike was the
campaign waged by black leaders to persuade the 17,000 black workers
at Ford not to permit themselves to be used as strike-breakers. While
Ford succeeded in pressuring black clergymen into condemning the
strike, the UAW, and unionism in general, the fact that only a few
black workers refused to stop working indicates that the clergymen's
influence was no longer decisive. For this the national NAACP and its
executive secretary, Walter White, and the National Negro Congress
and its secretary, John P. Davis, deserve special credit. White and Davis
flew to Detroit at the height of the strike to give direction to the local
branch organizations. There was no problem with the Detroit branch of
the National Negro Congress, but it was only after much pleading that
White persuaded the local NAACP chapters to endorse the UAW and
to urge about 1,500 black strike-breakers to leave the River Rouge plant
in Dearborn. White and the local NAACP leaders marched in UAW
picket lines and went to the River Rouge plant, spoke to the strike-
breakers over sound trucks, praising the union's racial policies, and
urged them to come out and join the picket line. And the workers did
indeed walk out.

Meanwhile, for their part, union officials had been speaking to white
Ford strikers, warning them that any racist actions or words could easily
defeat the strike. This proved successful in averting physical attacks
on Negro strike-breakers, which would have triggered an open racial
conflict from which only Ford would have benefited.

Defeated on all fronts, his notorious spy system as well as his paternalism toward Negroes no longer effective, Ford capitulated on April
11, 1941. The men were to return to work, and the CIO would be
recognized as the bargaining agent for its members in the plant prior
to an election ordered by the NLRB.

The strike victory at Ford was of tremendous importance to the
UAW. As long as Ford's plants remained unorganized, the union's organization in General Motors, Chrysler, and other corporations had
rested on weak foundations. Yet the victory would have been impossible
if the UAW had not succeeded, with the aid of its black members and
a good part of the Negro community, in convincing Negro workers at
Ford that the union's policy against discrimination was more than a
collection of hot air and cold print like that put out by the AF of L.
This became clear during the NLRB election following the strike. While

the AF of L, which had entered the picture during the strike, had Ford's blessings and those of many Detroit black ministers, the local units of the NAACP and the National Negro Congress made effective use of the federation's shameful record on racial issues in persuading the vast majority of Ford's Negro workers to vote for the UAW-CIO.

A month after the resounding UAW victory in the election, Ford signed the first union-shop contract in the industry. The contract gave Ford workers job security through a union shop, grievance machinery, and shorter hours of work. To the black workers the greatest victory was the clause that stated: "The provisions of this contract shall apply to all employees covered by this agreement, without discrimination on account of race, color, national origin or creed."[31]

Two other developments in the UAW prior to America's entrance into World War II further cemented the relationship between the auto union and the black community. In elections at the Ford plants, Negroes won positions of leadership, as white auto workers showed a willingness to accept and follow effective leaders without regard to race or color. Shelton Tappes, a militant black leader during the Ford strike, was elected recording secretary of Ford Local 600, whose members worked in the River Rouge plant. In the election at the Willow Run bomber plant (Local 50), two blacks were candidates. The slate on which they ran with white candidates was attacked by some workers as the "Nigger" slate. R. J. Thomas, UAW president, denounced those who were using race prejudice as a campaign weapon, and the two blacks were elected, although less than 5 per cent of the workers employed at Willow Run were Negroes.

In late 1941, 500 white workers at the Curtis-Wright aircraft plant in Columbus, Ohio, struck when a Negro was promoted to the tool and die department. Thomas immediately removed the local union official who had endorsed the strike and ordered the men back to work. This unequivocal action won praise from the NAACP, which issued a special release on November 21, 1941, calling the attention of the nation's black press to the event and citing it as proof of the CIO's ability to hold racial prejudice in check at the local level.*

Still, on the eve of Pearl Harbor the NAACP was hardly satisfied with the CIO's activities in industrial discrimination and civil rights. In December, 1941, The Crisis accused the CIO of being reluctant to deal with employment discrimination and of being deaf "to pleas for assistance in breaking down the barriers to the ballot box in the South."[32] The CIO claimed credit for the FEPC, which it said was created "as a

* The upgrading and transferring of black workers to more skilled departments in the auto plants continued to be an issue throughout the war. When Packard shifted two expert Negro metal finishers from work on automobiles to the polishing department of a new tank plant in 1943, 250 CIO members staged a forty-minute sit-down strike, holding up the work of 600 persons. The blacks were withdrawn, and for the next six months the government, the Executive Committee of the UAW, and the Packard Company were involved in a battle with white auto workers to bring about the transfer of the two blacks. Finally, the racist elements were told to work or to leave the plant, and the blacks were transferred.

result of CIO's campaign against discrimination and of CIO demands for all-out production,"[33] but it had actually played little part in the March on Washington Movement, which had prompted President Roosevelt to act against industrial discrimination. Stung by the criticism of the NAACP and the Urban League, early in 1942 Philip Murray, who succeeded John L. Lewis as CIO president, appointed a committee to investigate the problem of equal opportunity for Negro workers. This body evolved into the permanent Committee to Abolish Racial Discrimination. Its chairman was James B. Carey, CIO secretary-treasurer, and it included two black members, George L. P. Weaver and the committee secretary, Willard S. Townsend of the United Transport Service Employees of America. Townsend became the first Negro union leader on the national executive board when his union was chartered by the CIO in June, 1942. No Negro had ever served on the AF of L executive board in sixty-one years of the federation's history.

The CIO Committee to Abolish Discrimination conducted a vast educational campaign, which included frank discussions of racial discrimination and other issues. While placing the blame for exclusion of minority-group workers mainly on employers, it did not exonerate unions. "Where closed shop contracts exist and the union makes selections and referrals to employers, responsibility must be placed on the union unless the employer himself refuses to accept the worker because of race or color." Even CIO local unions were criticized for not resolutely supporting the national policy against discrimination. "When a decision to employ minority group workers is made, the union must be prepared to stand behind it." In similar fashion, the union had to make certain that seniority rights of minority workers were not violated, because "nothing destroys a worker's morale more completely than the knowledge that despite his proficiency, and his experience, he cannot be assigned to a more responsible job because of his race."[34]

The committee's literature also dwelt with certain stereotypes about Negroes that contributed to racism among white workers. Here is one sample:

THE SOCIAL-EQUALITY TABOO

Common use of eating facilities frequently creates conflict which unions can guard against. In communities where restaurants, cafes, and other public eating places do not serve Negro patrons, there may be strong sentiment in favor of providing separate eating facilities in or near industrial plants. . . .

The position of the union in this respect should be firmly taken. It is not enough to point out that thousands of white people every day eat and enjoy food prepared by Negroes and other racial groups. It must be emphasized that separation or segregation of workers in any form is undemocratic and unnecessary.

If segregation is tolerated by the union in one manner, it can be practiced by management without respect for the union's wishes in other matters. Shop stewards and committee members can do much to encourage the friendly association of workers during lunch periods through frank discussion of these and other related problems.[35]

Thus, while the AF of L annually proclaimed education the only way to eliminate racism among white members of the federation, and annually did nothing to educate its members, the CIO conducted a vast educational program to meet the issue. The literature distributed by the CIO's Committee to Abolish Discrimination was a milestone, and it alone is an indication of how far in advance of previous labor organizations the CIO was with respect to the racial issue.

In addition to the national Committee to Abolish Discrimination, ten CIO international and national unions established their own committees.* Many affiliates that did not do so adopted resolutions against racial and religious discrimination, pledged to cooperate with the national committee, and urged all locals to do likewise. The United Electrical, Radio, and Machine Workers (UE), which grew from 15,000 membership in 1936 to 435,000 in 1942 and claimed 570,000 members under 970 collective-bargaining agreements in 1943, pledged at its 1944 convention to continue all efforts to erase the economic factors "that are the fundamental bases of discrimination." It resolved to "call upon President Roosevelt as commander-in-chief of the armed forces to effect, by executive decree, an end to the racist army policy of segregation of Negro troops" and "to insure equal treatment of all Americans regardless of race or color, as the laws of the land properly guarantee."[36]

Under the direction of the national and local committees to abolish discrimination, the CIO's racial policies made significant advances. At its convention in November, 1941, the CIO condemned discriminatory hiring policies as a "direct attack against our nation's policy to build democracy in our fight against Hitlerism." A year later, the CIO convention denounced such practices as directly aiding the enemy "by creating division, dissension, and confusion." The 1942 convention declared that "such discrimination hampers production by depriving the nation of the use of available skills and manpower."[37]

Throughout the war the CIO and its Committee to Abolish Racial Discrimination joined black organizations in opposing reductions in funds for FEPC against the combined opposition of Southern Congressmen, employers, and AF of L unions. The all-out support of the CIO was undoubtedly a key factor accounting for the progress of the FEPC. *Opportunity*, which, along with *The Crisis*, had been critical of the CIO's activity against employment discrimination on the eve of Pearl Harbor, conceded that its contributions to employment opportunities for the black worker once the United States entered the war merited high praise. "Even the labor shortages of the war boom would not have opened the factory gates for him," it declared in September, 1942, "had he not had the protection of the pan-racial policy of the CIO."[38]

As the earlier barriers to Negro employment gradually gave way, black

* They included the American Newspaper Guild; International Mine, Mill, and Smelter Workers; National Maritime Union; Retail, Wholesale and Department Store Union; United Automobile, Aircraft, and Agricultural Implement Workers; United Farm Equipment and Metal Workers; United Gas, Coke and Chemical Workers; United Packinghouse Workers; United Public Workers; and United Office and Professional Workers.

migration to urban industrial communities grew. It was generally similar to the migration during World War I, but there were two new features. This time large numbers of blacks moved to urban industrial localities on the West Coast, and thousands of rural Negroes moved into Southern urban industrial centers. As in World War I, the influx into the cities created a serious housing shortage, which affected Negroes more severely than any other group. The CIO and its Committee to Abolish Racial Discrimination campaigned for more adequate public housing to help solve this problem. In Detroit, the UAW, after some early wavering, intervened in the Sojourner Truth Housing Project dispute in favor of integrated housing. Even though many white members of the union objected to the housing project for black workers adjacent to a white neighborhood (one UAW member was vice-president of the organization opposing black occupancy of the Sojourner Truth project), the union pressured the housing authority into ruling for Negro occupancy. The first blacks who attempted to move in were prevented physically from so doing, but the union refused to retreat. The firm stand taken by the UAW in favor of Negro occupancy was mainly responsible for victory that was finally won. Most of the blacks who became tenants in the project were UAW members, and the union's resoluteness in the dispute won their admiration as well as that of the local black leadership.

After the Sojourner Truth incident, the UAW led the fight for interracial housing in all housing projects in Detroit, advocating "a housing policy of first come, first served, regardless of color."[39] It condemned the proclamation of Detroit's Mayor Edward J. Jeffries, Jr., on April 29, 1943, in which he declared, with City Council approval, that "the Detroit Housing Commission will in no way change the racial characteristics of any neighborhood in Detroit through occupancy standards of housing projects under their jurisdiction."[40] The union called upon its members to join with local black organizations in opposing the Mayor's Jim Crow policy.

When the anti-Negro riot did come in Detroit on June 20, 1943, the UAW worked to keep its members off the streets, condemned those members who were leaders of the riot, and denounced police brutality against blacks. The UAW pointed with pride to the fact that even on Bloody Monday, when racist white mobs sought to exterminate the residents of the black ghetto, whose desperate resistance resulted in high casualties until federal troops took over, many white and Negro members of the union were working side by side in the war plants without conflict.

But the UAW did not really come to grips with the fact that its membership included men involved in the anti-Negro riots, former Klansmen from the South who had come to Detroit with their Jim Crow notions of the Negro intact, as well as followers of the pro-fascist Gerald L. K. Smith and Father Charles E. Coughlin. The influence of this element was strengthened by the vacillations of the union leadership on key issues involving its Negro membership. The 1943 UAW convention unanimously endorsed the union's role in the Sojourner Truth housing dispute, but it turned down, after an all-day debate, a proposal for the addition of an elective vice-presidency or an at-large board membership to be filled by a Negro. The Reuther brothers, Walter and Victor, opposed the proposal; Victor warned against "giving special privileges to special groups," and Walter took the stand that "any *special* position designated for a minority group" was "Jim Crow in reverse."[41] A number of Negro delegates supported the Reuther position, arguing that blacks opposed any "special" measures or "privileges"; others, joined by white delegates representing the left in the union, concluded that the argument of "Jim Crow in reverse" in practice meant that nothing would be done to bring Negroes into leadership.

In 1940 only 2 per cent of the workers in the aircraft industry were blacks; by the summer of 1944, there were 100,000 Negro aircraft workers, 6 per cent of the total labor force. The UAW was not alone responsible for this change, but in general the union drew praise from black leaders for breaking down old patterns of discrimination.

In an effort to gain equal employment opportunities for black workers, Local 8 of the United Packinghouse Workers voted unanimously in March, 1942, that black women should be given jobs in local meat-packing plants. Armour and Company responded by agreeing to employ Negro women in its Omaha division. In 1943, at the union's national convention, it wrote into its constitution the twofold objective: "the elimination of overt acts of discrimination and eventually of all prejudices."[42]

On January 2, 1942, the Swedish luxury liner *Kungsholm* lay in the port of New York ready to sail. She had been taken over by the U.S. Lines and converted into a troop ship. That afternoon the union hall of the National Maritime Union was called for 140 seamen to man the liner. The union dispatcher sent the men. One hundred and fifteen were accepted—all white. The assignment cards of the other twenty-five were marked "not acceptable." They were Negroes.

Although committed to an all-out effort to win the war, the National Maritime Union, with 10 per cent of its 50,000 members Negroes, was also committed to a policy of nondiscrimination. NMU President Joseph Curran wired President Roosevelt protesting the rejection of the twenty-five blacks. The next morning the company officials called the union hall and conveyed the information that the Negroes were now "acceptable." When the ship sailed, the twenty-five blacks were aboard.

The action by the NMU produced a letter from President Roosevelt that became a powerful weapon in the CIO union's fight against discrimination. Roosevelt wrote in part: "Questions of race, creed, and color have no place in determining who are to man our ships. The sole qualifications for a worker in the maritime industry, as well as in any other industry, should be his loyalty and his professional or technical ability or training." Three months later, the crew of the *Kungsholm*, returning home from their mission, having shared all of the ship's facilities together without any difficulty, unanimously adopted the following resolution:

It is only through unity of all people that we can successfully win the war, regardless of race, color, or creed, and

Our President has stated that discrimination is a threat to our national safety, and on this ship colored and white seamen have sailed together in perfect friendship and harmony,

Therefore be it resolved, that we go on record against any form of discrimination in our union or in any defense industry.[43]

In July, 1944, the NMU signed a contract with 125 ship companies that included an antidiscrimination clause. Largely as a result of the NMU's efforts, four ships with black captains and mixed crews were put into operation to bring troops and war materials to the fighting fronts. Most famous of them was the SS *Booker T. Washington*, with Captain Hugh Mulzac as master.

In one respect, both the Packinghouse Union and the NMU were ahead of most other CIO unions. The international vice-president of Packinghouse and head of the union's antidiscrimination department was a Negro, as was the vice-president of the NMU. Although there were many black officials in the local unions of the UAW, the 1943 convention, as we have seen, refused to make room for even one black member on the international executive board, a UAW pattern that was consistently maintained thereafter.

Even in the South, the CIO made progress during the war years. In 1945, Lucy Randolph Mason noted: "Today CIO unions are found in every Southern state and are growing steadily in the region's basic industries and their by-products. Among the many hundreds of thousands of CIO members there are a vast number of Negroes."[44] Before World War II the United Mine Workers and the International Union of Mine, Mill, and Smelter Workers had a fairly large black membership, but throughout the South union organization was generally limited to the skilled craft unions of the AF of L, which either excluded blacks or gave them only restricted membership. The picture changed considerably during the war. Southern manufacturing employment rose from 1,657,000 before the war to a high of 2,836,100 in November, 1943. With the aid of the War Labor Board, unionism boomed. While the AF of L, naturally preferred by employers, enjoyed the largest growth in union membership, the CIO also scored great gains. By 1943 steel unionism was well established in Birmingham, as the United Steel Workers (CIO) won elections and contracts at Tennessee Coal and Iron and other steel plants in Alabama. Iron-ore miners in Birmingham and vicinity also won a union contract under the leadership of the International Union of Mine, Mill, and Smelter Workers. The lumber and textile industries continued to be virtually unorganized, but the United Rubber Workers, the Oil Workers International Union, and the United Cannery, Agricultural, Packing, and Allied Workers (UCAPAW, changed to Food, Tobacco, Agricultural, and Allied Workers in 1944) scored membership gains and won agreements in the South.

In the early war years the CIO was hampered in the South by employer and community hostility to its racial policy. White workers hesitated to join a movement that admitted blacks, and blacks feared that they might lose out by entrusting their economic interests to a predominantly white organization. The blacks, however, eager for unionization and impressed by the CIO's reputation in the fight against racism, were quick to respond to appeals from organizers. The wartime "No Strike, No Lockout" pledge, in effect since December, 1941, made it easier for blacks to unionize than in the past, since they were not compelled to face white strike-breakers. In some instances, Negroes were the ones to start CIO local unions, with whites coming in afterward.

It did not take long for Southern white workers to learn that the black vote was crucial for victory in War Labor Board elections and that they, too, had to choose between a union with Negroes or no union at all. As one white worker in Georgia put it: "We left the colored people out when we first organized, and we lost two Labor Board elections. Then we asked them to join the union. We won the election with their votes. They have made good union members and we are mighty glad they are with us."[45]

The War Labor Board's policy of equal pay for equal work made it easier for CIO unions to insist on eliminating racial differentials in contracts, and FEPC rulings characterizing discrimination on account of race as "in line with the Nazi program" helped some CIO unions—particularly the Industrial Union of Marine and Shipbuilders of America—in reclassifying Negroes according to their skills, with the result that blacks were upgraded and paid at higher rates. But the WLB and FEPC orders were not always obeyed, and CIO unions often found themselves fighting the racist practices of Southern employers without much government assistance. The WLB was of help to the United Cannery, Agricultural, Packing, and Allied Workers in gaining contracts for blacks and Mexican-Americans—in many parts of the South the UCAPAW's membership was all Negro or Mexican-American—but the union was hampered because the WLB refused to extend its jurisdiction over agricultural labor.

The board was also of no help to the Negro workers at the R. J. Reynolds Tobacco Company in Winston-Salem, North Carolina. Tired of working for 40 cents an hour at back-breaking labor for long hours with inadequate sanitary facilities and other abuses, thousands of black workers listened to the urgings of organizers. Under the leadership of Robert Latham, Robert Black, Velma Hopkins, and Miranda Smith, all blacks, Local 22, Food, Tobacco, Agricultural and Allied Workers Union, CIO, was established. But Reynolds refused to recognize the organization, and the War Labor Board kept hands off. Meanwhile, militant black shop stewards were fighting workers' grievances against the white foremen and getting some improvements in conditions.

Recognition of the union came as a result of a strike, something the company believed the black workers would not dare to pull off because of the war. But on June 17, 1943, when a Negro worker died after the foreman had refused him permission to see the doctor following a series of dizzy spells, 11,000 Reynolds workers, white as well as black, went out on strike. When threats of government intervention failed to open the plants, the Reynolds management agreed to meet with the shop stewards as bargaining agents for more than 9,000 dues-paying members of Local 22. One of the first concessions was payment of $1,250,000 in retroactive pay for low-paid Negro workers. On April 24, 1944, the first contract was signed, and wages began a steady climb upward. The results of the strike were described by Louis E. Burnham, a leader of the Southern Negro Youth Conference, as "legendary in Winston-Salem."[46]

Despite community opposition, quite a few CIO unions in the South began to hold joint meetings of black and white workers. Negroes were also elected to union posts; the Alabama Industrial Union Council and the Louisiana Industrial Union Council both chose blacks 'for their executive boards, and Tennessee elected two to its board in June, 1942. Five Negro vice presidents were put on the Maryland–District of Columbia Industrial Union Council in December, 1942. Partly as a result of the presence of blacks on these bodies, the CIO Industrial Union Councils in the South took action in favor of expanding civil rights for Negroes—for the abolition of the poll tax and the "lily-white" primary and an increase in the inadequate appropriations for schools for Negro children. In 1943 the CIO director in Louisiana wrote:

> In the New Orleans area one of the most significant developments, since the organization of some forty-one local unions with a membership of some thirty-odd thousand, has been the improved understanding between the white and Negro workers. As a result of their working relationship, both in the shop and union, they have become better acquainted with each other's problems. The result has been that they are now in a position to approach their problems in the community on a basis of fact instead of prejudice, and understanding instead of misunderstanding.
>
> These workers have been instrumental in bringing to the attention of the leaders of the community in industry, government and civic affairs their needs and problems and, because of the manner in which both the Negro and white workers have presented their questions, for the first time the leaders of the community are beginning to have a better understanding of the workers' problems as such and the race problem as such.[47]

All this, of course, was a far cry from the activities of AF of L affiliates in the South. Still, nothing would be farther from the truth than to conclude that during World War II most CIO affiliates consistently fought to break down racial barriers. Some national CIO unions acceded to racist resistance from local unions and rank-and-file groups; others accommodated themselves to local racial prejudice and looked the other way while local unions ignored the welfare of black members in contracts negotiated with employers. Some even conspired with companies to maintain segregated facilities over the protests of the black membership. Few CIO unions in the South put up a fight to open the doors to Negro workers in occupations traditionally closed to them. Often, too, instead of appreciating that black workers "were more easily organized than whites," CIO organizers backed away, since "to organize the Negro workers first was to risk alienating the whites." Negro workers who played leading roles in the organization of a local union were shunted aside when it came to choosing leaders. The blacks were told by CIO district leaders that "to encourage white workers to join the union, we must elect a white president and a white chairman of the grievance committee."[48] Where the bulk of the industry was in the South, CIO unions too often averted their gaze from the racism in their Southern locals.

Taking Negroes for granted spelled disaster for some Southern CIO unions. Enjoying bargaining rights in the two Birmingham plants of the Ingalls Iron Works, the local steelworkers' CIO union did little to improve the situation of the black workers (about one-third of the personnel). Blacks complained to no avail that their job classifications were unfair, keeping them in a low-paid wage stratum regardless of the job done, and that the part they were allowed to play in union affairs was not commensurate with their numerical strength. Not even a threat by the blacks to bolt the CIO brought any improvement. When the AF of L assured the blacks of a new deal, they shifted their votes and the CIO lost jurisdiction at Ingalls.

When the SWOC became the United Steelworkers of America at a constitutional convention in Cleveland in 1942, black steelworkers were furious that not one black had been included in any position of importance in the international union. Fifty black delegates to the convention formed a caucus and protested that the international had made a mockery of its boasted principle—"There shall be no discrimination because of race, creed, color, or nationality." Specifically, the black caucus sought the election of a Negro to an international office. It rejected the union's argument that Negro organizers and field representatives spoke for all blacks in the union, for experience had demonstrated that these lower officials held no real power.

On the last day of the convention, Philip Murray, United Steelworkers of America president, met with the entire Negro delegation and promised to appoint a black as liaison officer to work out of the international office. The Negro delegation suggested Joe Cook of Chicago for the position, but Murray, ignoring the wishes of the blacks, appointed Boyd Wilson of Saint Louis as international field representative. To the Negro delegation the refusal to elect a black international officer and the appointment of a field representative who, they suspected, would do the bidding of the white leadership, was a "clear example of tokenism" and indicated how far the CIO union had yet to go before it practiced what it preached.[49]

In general, not too many CIO unions were prepared to take great risks for the principle of racial equality. Yet, for all its shortcomings, the CIO's record on the issue of racial equality during World War II was far in advance of the AF of L's. In a study of prejudice against Negroes among white merchant seamen during the closing months of the war, Ira N. Brophy found "a sharp prejudice differentiation . . . between those seamen who belonged to the industry's industrial union, Nation Maritime Union (CIO), and those who belonged to the various craft unions which are affiliated with the American Federation of Labor or

are independent. The NMU members showed noticeably less prejudice than did the craft union members." Brophy concluded that this
difference stemmed to no small extent from the fact that the NMU
was the only maritime union that "had an active program for the elimination of racism in the industry":

> It has an efficient educational and public relations department headed by
> an able labor historian, Mr. Leo Huberman, and this department has
> turned out many leaflets and booklets stressing industrial racial equality
> and pointing out the anti-social implications of "Jim Crow-ism." Supple-
> menting this, the union's leadership has carried on an active policy of
> forceful measures to enforce its non-discriminatory ideals. According to our
> information, no similar action has been taken by any other American sea-
> men's union. In fact, steps in the opposite direction have been taken, since
> the Negro is specifically excluded from membership in many unions.[50]

One can perhaps best see the difference between the AF of L and the
CIO on the question of Negro labor during the war in the cases of two
cities, Baltimore and Philadelphia. "Baltimore," Ira de A. Reid wrote in
1930, "is one of the areas in which the Negro was entirely excluded
from membership in the craft unions of the AF of L."[51] During World
War II, CIO unions broke the Jim Crow pattern of unionism in the
city through the activities of five of its affiliated unions: the Industrial
Union of Marine and Shipbuilders of America; the United Steel Workers; the United Automobile, Aircraft, and Agricultural Implement
Workers; the Amalgamated Clothing Workers; and the United Electrical, Radio, and Machine Workers. These five CIO unions organized about thirty plants in the area, representing approximately
55,000 workers, more than 50 per cent of the city's wage-earners. "The
Negro has participated [in] and profited from affiliation with the five
CIO unions," a student of the Baltimore labor scene during World War
II concluded, "and union locals of the CIO have sponsored his upgrading. The CIO unions have recognized the value of Negro leadership and
have placed capable Negroes in responsible positions. . . . In the CIO
union locals Negroes serve on committees and in the plants as shop
stewards."[52]

The Industrial Union of Marine and Shipbuilders led the way. Not
only did Local 43 organize blacks, but in October, 1942, Thomas Ayd-
lett, a Negro, was appointed a full-time salaried organizer. The following month, the local suspended six members for "race baiting and disruption." The local was largely responsible for obtaining employment for
blacks in the shipyards—in July, 1941, only 5 per cent of the 7,000 shipyard workers were black, but by June, 1943, there were about 8,000 Negro workers, about 20 per cent of the total work force—and the
IUMSWA put up a strong fight against the practice of giving Negroes
only common laborer jobs regardless of their competence and experience. In August, 1942, there were only fifty skilled black workers at the
Bethlehem Fairfield Shipyard as compared with 1,000 black laborers.
Through the efforts of Local 43, the Bethlehem Company finally permitted 150 eligible blacks to take welding-school training. The local's

officers and shop stewards made a list of those black workers with skills and demanded that they be assigned to work that "would permit them to contribute most toward winning the war."[53] After investigating the Baltimore shipyard situation, a Howard University study pointed out that Local 43, "in executing the anti-discrimination policy of its national body, has provided opportunities for Negroes to obtain skilled jobs in the shipyards."[54]

The UE entered the Baltimore area around the time of World War II and by 1944 had organized about 5,500 workers at six plants: Westinghouse, Alexander Millburn Co., Charles T. Brandt Co., Bendix Friez, Bendix Radio Timekeepers, and Ellicott Machine Workers. Before the UE's arrival, blacks were employed at these plants only in unskilled work at the lowest wage levels. Upon the UE's insistence, blacks were upgraded into more skilled positions and, with occupational seniority, were assured protection in those positions.

In July, 1943, an epidemic of "hate strikes" hit the Bethlehem shipyards at Sparrows Point. All three CIO unions involved—steel, electrical, and shipbuilding—acted resolutely to enforce a nondiscriminatory policy, and the racist instigators of the strikes met with no success. In December, 1943, a similar strike occurred at the Point Breeze plant of the Western Electric Company, which employed 1,750 blacks, over a demand by white workers for separate toilet facilities. The UE, with the endorsement of the CIO Industrial Union Council, urged the strikers to return to work and, when they refused, called upon President Roosevelt to intervene on the ground that the race issue was being exploited "in the interests of the nation's enemies."[55] Roosevelt ordered the army to take over the plant, and the strikers returned to work.

Eight months later the President was compelled to take similar action in Philadelphia against the worst "hate strike" of the war*—a wildcat strike staged on August 3, 1944, by white streetcar workers in Philadelphia protesting the assignment of eight blacks to jobs as motormen. For six days the city was without public transportation, and only after President Roosevelt issued an order placing the company under army control and sent 5,000 troops to restore normal operations did the strike end.

In 1940, according to a survey by the Armstrong Association (the Philadelphia branch of the National Urban League), only 15,000 blacks had industrial employment in Philadelphia.[56] The number increased considerably during the war, and trade union membership of blacks rose proportionately, especially in industries under contract with CIO unions. Blacks who were members of AF of L or independent unions frequently filed complaints with the Armstrong Association or the local branch of the NAACP protesting discrimination in employment, and none more so than those employed by the Philadelphia Transportation Company (PTC).

* According to Bureau of Labor Statistics, from March 1 to May 31, 1943, 101,955 man-days, or 2,466,920 man-hours, of war production were lost by hate strikes over the employment or upgrading of Negro workers.

Tradition had long ruled that Negroes could be employed only in menial positions in Philadephia's transportation system. Not even in World War I did blacks get the opportunity to work as other than porters or sweepers, nor did the situation change when World War II brought a significant shortage of transportation workers. The PTC advertised widely for white conductors and motormen but refused to upgrade any of its black employees, even though blacks in Detroit, New York, Los Angeles, and Chicago were driving trolley cars and buses efficiently and without friction with white fellow workers. The company claimed that a clause in its contract with the PTC Employees Union, labeled independent but actually a company union, prohibited any departure from "existing rules, regulations and customs . . . until changed by agreement between the parties." The Philadelphia branch of the NAACP petitioned the union leadership to initiate such a change, only to be told, on January 18, 1943, that the employment of blacks "is not a subject over which the union has any control."

In the fall of 1943, after mass protest meetings by Philadelphia blacks under NAACP leadership, the FEPC took jurisdiction over the case. On November 17, 1943, after hearings, it directed the company to "cease and desist" from discriminating against employees and applicants because of their race and color, and from so interpreting its contract with the union as to prohibit "the employment or upgrading . . . of qualified Negroes to positions as street car and motor coach operators, and conductors, motormen, guards, platform attendants, and station cashiers . . . or to any other job classification not presently held by Negroes."[57] A month later, the FEPC made its directive final. The union notified the committee that it would not comply and advised the company to do the same. While the FEPC directive was gathering dust, the PTC workers were confronted with an election to choose a bargaining agent from among the so-called independent union, the Amalgamated Street Car Workers Union (AF of L), and the Transport Workers Union (CIO). Both the AF of L and the "independent" union campaigned on the racist promise that, if they represented the workers, no upgrading of blacks would occur. The TWU, having already won a reputation as a champion of the upgrading of qualified black streetcar workers in other cities, announced that it would uphold the same principle in Philadelphia.

On March 14, 1944, to the surprise of many, the PTC workers elected the TWU. A few weeks later the company negotiated a new contract with representatives of the TWU and agreed, although not in writing, to employ black workers as operators.* Eight Negroes, upon completing their training for operators' jobs, were scheduled to make trial runs on August 1.

It soon transpired that the PTC, in league with elements of the old

---

* The black community was perturbed by the absence of a written provision in the contract, but the TWU negotiators took the position that, since the union's stand in favor of nondiscriminatory hiring and upgrading was a matter of public record, it was not necessary to insert a specific clause on the subject.

company union and with the cooperation of the AF of L's Amalgamated Street Car Workers, was plotting to stir up its white workers as a means of smashing the newly recognized TWU. Meetings to arrange a wildcat strike were held on company property and loyal CIO members were barred. Inflammatory handbills addressed to white operators were posted on company bulletin boards. One read: "Your buddies are in the Army fighting and dying to protect the life of you and your family and you are too yellow to protect their jobs until they return. Call a strike and refuse to teach the Negroes. The public is with you. The CIO sold you out."[58]

On the day the black trainees were to start their first run, all bus and trolley transportation workers reported ill, and the strike started—"a strictly black and white issue," a striking motorman put it.[59] To the surprise of the racists, the strike was immediately opposed by the people and press of the city and condemned by the Transport Workers Union and the Philadelphia CIO Industrial Union Council. TWU officials, accompanied by Army and Navy officers, toured the various work locations during the first afternoon of the strike and exhorted the operators, on patriotic as well as union grounds, to return to work. On the second day of the strike 200 TWU stewards voted unanimously for an all-out effort to persuade employees to end the strike, and for the next few days they acted strenuously on their vote. When their efforts proved fruitless, the TWU officials asked for army intervention. At the same time, the TWU, the CIO Committee to Abolish Discrimination, and the Philadelphia Industrial Union Council joined with organizations "of all races, creeds, and colors"—including the African Methodist Episcopal Church, the American Jewish Congress, the Catholic Interracial Council, the NAACP, the Baptist Ministers Conference of Philadelphia, and the Committee on Race Relations of the Society of Friends—in a full-page advertisement in the local press denouncing the strike as "treason against the American war effort," and "traitorous to the fundamental principles of American liberty and the right of all men to live and earn their living—without discrimination." The signers urged all citizens in the community not to retreat before the "unreasonable demands of the inciters of this strike."[60]

By August 7, with 5,000 troops in Philadelphia guarding the cars, all transit lines were again operating at full capacity.* Ten days later the transit system was turned back to the PTC, and the army withdrew from the city. The black trainees resumed instruction a few days after the strike was broken, and on August 15 they began regular operations.

On October 11, 1944, the TWU local held an election for officers. One of the four vice-presidents elected was a Negro.

Throughout the dispute, not a single AF of L union in Philadelphia condemned the company union or the Amalgamated Street Car Workers for their racist propaganda and practices. Not a single AF of L union

---

* A notice that those workers who did not return to their jobs would have their draft deferments canceled helped to break the strike, in addition to the military presence.

signed any of the advertisements condemning the strike, nor did the federation's City Central Labor Council. "The CIO stood firmly by the non-discrimination policy," *The Crisis* declared, noting the contrast with the indifference and inactivity of the AF of L.[61] The Philadelphia branch of the NAACP concluded that the future welfare of the city's black workers could be safeguarded only by unions affiliated with the Congress of Industrial Organizations.

Two years before, the national organization had already reached the same conclusion. In February, 1943, the *NAACP Bulletin* pointed out that "the CIO has proved that it stands for our people within the unions and outside the unions." By the time the war ended, nearly every Negro organization looked upon the CIO as "the black man's greatest hope for social and economic progress in the postwar world."[62]

18 The Economic Status of the Black Worker, 1945–55

On September 2, 1945, World War II came to an end. The dream that the war would bring a permanent improvement in the economic status of the black worker had ended even before that. As victory for the Allied Powers approached, war industries began cutbacks in production. Blacks, being among the most recent newcomers in many industries, were the first to lose their jobs. Progress had been made in upgrading blacks to semiskilled and skilled jobs during the war, but the vast majority of black workers had not risen above the unskilled categories; four out of every five employed black men were working at unskilled jobs in April, 1944, just as in April, 1940. The unskilled jobs were quickly eliminated as the war industries—shipbuilding, aircraft, munitions, and explosives—in which blacks had made their greatest employment gains, declined following V-J Day. Those industries had the least potential for reconversion to peacetime production. Throughout American industry in 1945, more than 93 per cent of the clerical and sales force and more than 95 per cent of the professional, managerial, and foremen groups were still white.

The decline of job opportunities for black workers right after World War II is evident from the final report of the FEPC: "Of the seven war centers studied by FEPC during reconversion, all but Chicago showed a heavier loss of jobs by Negro than by white workers, and a necessity on the part of Negro workers to accept the lowest paying jobs. . . . Whereas during the war many Negroes had risen into the skilled, professional, and managerial categories, by 1946 these openings for them had dwindled to a scant few. New York City was an exception."[1] In general, economists estimated that, as unemployment returned after World War II, black workers were "affected two and one-half times as severely as white workers."[2]

One reason for the declining employment opportunities for blacks in the period immediately after the war was that the FEPC itself was being reduced to impotence by President Harry S. Truman. The black attorney Charles R. Houston resigned from the committee when President Truman would not allow it to issue a decision ordering the Capital Transit Company to stop refusing to hire blacks on the streetcar lines of the nation's capital. Houston charged "a persistent course of conduct on the part of the Administration to give lip service to the matter of eliminating discrimination in employment on account of race, creed, or national origin since V-J Day, while doing nothing substantial to make the policy effective."[3]

When the FEPC ended in 1946, the employment of black workers on equal terms with whites no longer had even "lip service" support from the federal government. By 1953, seven states (Connecticut, Massachusetts, New Jersey, New York, Oregon, Rhode Island, and Washington) and four cities (Minneapolis, Chicago, Milwaukee, and Philadelphia) had enacted legislation barring discrimination in employment, which opened some doors for blacks to jobs previously held by whites only. But there was no such legislation in the South, where job discrimination against blacks was most widespread. The national picture five years after the war showed the effects of the demise of a federal FEPC. To be sure, the median income of nonwhite wage- and salary-earners had risen from 41 per cent of the white median in 1939 to 60 per cent in 1950; the percentage of male black workers in white-collar and professional jobs had risen from 5.6 in 1940 to 7.2 in 1950, and that of craftsmen and operatives from 16.6 per cent of the total in 1940 to 28.8 per cent in 1950. Economists and sociologists, surveying these statistics, were quick to point to the economic, political, and social gains made since World War II and insisted that the plight of the black working class was not as dismal as "preachers of discontent" among Negroes claimed it was. But, as Robert C. Weaver pointed out, most of the gains occurred between 1942 and 1945, and retrogression set in as soon as the war ended.

To Secure These Rights, the report of the fifteen-member committee appointed by President Truman in December, 1946, to study the nation's "shortcomings and mistakes" in the field of civil rights, noted that in all regions and all areas of employment the black man turned he had encountered job discrimination. Like the final FEPC report, it supplied clear evidence that blacks had dropped behind in the economic race since the close of World War II.

The 1950 Census report revealed that the median annual wage of a white worker in the United States was $2,481. For the black it was $1,295. The average black woman earned only $13 a week. One out of ten white families had an income of less than $1,000 a year, or $20 a week, whereas 28 per cent of the Negro families were at or below that pitiful level. *More than half* of the black families received less than $40 a week. Only one in ten Negro families earned more than $4,000 a year. Only three-tenths of 1 per cent of all black families received as much as $10,000 a year. Black families had an average income of $1,869, *only 54 per cent of the average income of white families*, despite the fact that in black families a large number of members generally worked. Victor Perlo pointed out:

> Since World War II there has been a sharp widening of the income differentials against Negro workers both in the North and in the South. By 1949, most of the wartime gains in the South had been lost, while the situation was no better than before World War II. Since World War II

the living standards of Negro people in cities have been reduced about one-fourth compared to a cut of about one-eighth for white urban working people.[4]

Nor did job opportunities for blacks develop either in number or in status, with the swelling labor rolls following the dispatch of armed forces to Korea in the middle of 1950. Many blacks who had worked in defense plants during World War II were not called for re-employment, while most white workers were. A study of discrimination in defense hiring by the National Urban League discovered that in almost all of the thirty key industrial cities investigated discriminatory policies and practices robbed blacks of the chance to earn a living; that in no area was there hiring without bias; that nowhere was there integration of blacks into the skilled or even semiskilled jobs; and that, although there was a trickle of employment of blacks, in most cases even those who had been employed during World War II were being bypassed in favor of new white recruits.* In its report "Discrimination in Defense Hiring," issued on February 4, 1952, the Urban League observed:

> Discrimination against Negroes follows a uniform pattern in plants located in Northern and Southern industrial centers. As the work force expands, a few Negroes have been added to the maintenance and common labor group of workers. Negroes are rarely accepted for in-plant training programs in any of the communities studied by League personnel. The employment of Negroes in white-collar, administrative, and technical jobs in these expanding industries is practically unheard of.[5]

Julius A. Thomas, director of the Urban League's industrial-relations department, warned, "Unless drastic steps are taken to curtail discriminatory practices in the majority of the nation's industries having defense contracts, there will be very few Negro workers in the manpower mobilization program."[6] To add to the black workers' difficulties, a technological revolution was under way in the areas of automation and cybernation, which meant systematic elimination of the menial, unskilled, and semiskilled jobs that had long been the main areas of black employment. Meanwhile, the introduction of technological innovations in Southern agriculture—tractors and herbicides right after the war, followed during the 1950's by mechanization of the harvest—was driving the tenants and sharecroppers out of the cotton fields.† Heavy unemployment in the countryside led to mass emigration of displaced blacks to the cities. Thus, while the need of basic industries for unskilled labor was declining, the

---

* A startling but not untypical example in the South, cited in the Urban League study, was the fact that in two Texas aircraft plants, only one black was found among a work force of 5,000.

† New Deal legislation had already displaced sharecroppers and tenants before World War II, since it subsidized reductions in acreage, the benefits of which went primarily to the landowners. By 1940 there were 650,000 fewer black farm operators and laborers than there had been a decade earlier—representing a one-third drop in the total.

influx of unskilled blacks from the agricultural regions of the South to Northern and Western cities was increasing. Between 1940 and 1950, some 608,000 black men and 125,000 black women left farm employment, and the percentage of blacks living in the South declined from 77 in 1940 to 68 per cent in 1950. In the same decade, the black population doubled in the states of Michigan and California and in some forty-five cities throughout the nation with populations of 50,000 or more. All but two of those cities (Baton Rouge, Louisiana, and Lubbock, Texas) were outside the South.

The migrants joined the labor force at the lowest rungs of the ladder, and the entire system of racial prejudices permitted only a small percentage to attain an occupational status at the level of the skilled categories. The racist pattern of wage and job-classification differentials in many occupational categories drove down the blacks' earnings further, with the result that a government study, "Average Median Annual Wage or Salary Income of Year-round, Full-time Workers by Color or Sex for 1955," found that white men earned $4,458 and black men $2,831, and that the average income for black workers was only 52 per cent of the average for white workers. The report also made it clear that the income gap and the unemployment gap between whites and blacks had been increasing since shortly after World War II.

The black worker, confined to the meanest jobs at the lowest pay, had to pay higher prices for food and overcrowded housing of inferior quality. In a 1941 report, the U.S. Housing Authority declared: "Most Negroes have been unable to rent or own decent, safe, and sanitary houses in which to live and bring up their children."[7] In a 1946 petition to the United Nations "on Behalf of 13 million oppressed Negro citizens of the United States of America," the National Negro Congress supplied details:

In the United States, in 1940, there were 3,293,406 dwelling units for Negroes. Of these over one million (1,082,128) "needed major repairs," and almost two million (1,908,100) had no running water. Over twice as many Negro homes as white (35.1% and 16.3%) needed major repairs, and almost three times as many Negro homes as whites (62% and 26.6%) had no running water. Twice as many white homes as Negro homes (82.9% and 43%) had electricity. All these figures, of course, are much worse in the South. . . . *Well over 70% of all Negro homes in that area have neither electricity nor running water.*[8]

The passing years brought little improvement in black housing. In *Forbidden Neighbors*, published in 1955, Charles Abrams estimated that, of the 9 million new homes built between 1935 and 1950, less than 1 per cent were open to nonwhites, and that only 50,000 out of some 3 million dwellings insured by the Federal Housing Authority were available to nonwhites. Yet, as James E. Jackson pointed out at the 1957 Communist Party Convention, "In the 14 largest metropolitan areas, where one-third of the total population lives, the Negro population increased as fast as the whites over the past 15 years."[9]

In 1952 the National Housing Agency reported: "At least 39 per cent of city housing in the United States is below standard for minimum health and safety regulations" with more than 16 per cent without running water and more than two-thirds without an inside private toilet. That same year a Kings County Grand Jury investigating a fire that killed seven blacks in Brooklyn found the trend increasing:

> Slums are being created much faster than they are being eliminated. Over-crowding is the germ of the slum disease. Occupancy of dark, damp, and filthy cellars that defy description, and families of six, seven, and more cooking, eating and sleeping in one room lacking proper toilet and bathing facilities, are spreading the slum blight.
>
> It is the poor who get the least, and not always at the lowest price.[10]

The vast majority of these "poor" were black workers and their families confronting in their daily lives ever new dimensions of grinding hardship, poverty, squalor, and misery. Much of the country seemed unaware of them. Sylvia Porter rhapsodized in the New York *Post* of January 7, 1953: "In my land, we have been traveling straight toward Karl Marx's dream. For America is closer to 'absolute equality' of income today than any other nation in the world. . . . We have virtually wiped out the very poor and poor classes."

Walter Reuther came closer to the truth in his presidential report to the UAW convention in March 1953, in which he noted that for most black workers the bright promise of World War II had turned into a nightmare, and that since the war, "in the absence of a federal FEPC and amidst increasing practices of discrimination at the hiring gate, minority workers were slowly but surely being pushed back to their prewar earnings and employment status."[11] It is tragic that the union Reuther headed and, in fact, the entire CIO did hardly anything to arrest the declining economic opportunities for blacks in the postwar period. In his study of the Negro in the United States, *An American Dilemma,* published as World War II was reaching its climax, Gunnar Myrdal had predicted that the labor movement in the postwar period would take the lead in efforts to promote better opportunities for blacks. Both Philip Murray and William Green, addressing the Negro people through the columns of *Opportunity,* assured the black workers that Myrdal's faith and optimism were justfied. Murray pledged that all the energies of the CIO would be directed toward seeing that the Negro worker, who had "given his efforts to production for Victory [would] be given the opportunity to produce for peace. His employment opportunities must not be tampered with because of his color." Green guaranteed that the AF of L would do its share to "assure the Negro access to the job" by fighting for nondiscrimination in hiring and job tenure and in the unions. "The doors to union membership for mutual aid and protection to them and to all workers must be opened to all qualified Negro wage earners willing and able to work."[12]

It came as no surprise to black workers that the AF of L's basically racist attitude persisted after the war. The 1946 convention defeated resolutions aimed at ending the system of "Jim Crow" auxiliary locals.

In 1949 a resolution endorsing federal Fair Employment Practices legislation passed only after delegates had deleted the words "and labor unions" from a motion calling for the "elimination of discrimination in industry and labor unions based upon race, color, religion, national origin, or ancestry."[18] What was surprising was that the CIO also forgot its pledge to the black workers. Testifying before a Senate Committee in 1947 about the serious employment problems of blacks, Walter Reuther said: "No single institution such as the CIO . . . can do more than fight a holding action until the community moves through law to guarantee basic freedoms."[14] Until the community acted, the CIO had more pressing duties. Among them, as we shall see, was the duty of joining the AF of L in support of the anti-Communist cold war policy of the Truman Administration and the expulsion of unions that dared to oppose that policy.

19 The Cold War Witch Hunts and the Black Worker

From the outset of its career, the CIO had had to face the charge of Communist conspiracy. In 1937–38 the National Association of Manufacturers distributed more than 2 million copies of *Join the CIO and Help Build a Soviet America*. Employers sought to defeat organizing drives by shouting that they were attempts to sovietize their industries. But the CIO refused to capitulate to the Red scare and follow the AF of L pattern of expelling militant Communists and left-wingers. Instead, it maintained its policy of organizing the unorganized without regard to political beliefs. Many of the early CIO organizers were Communists, often former members of the Trade Union Unity League, and their contributions were of great significance in the victories achieved in the mass-production industries. Saul Alinsky points out, "The Communists worked indefatigably, with no job being too menial or unimportant. They literally poured themselves completely into their assignments. The Communist Party gave its complete support to the CIO. The fact is that the Communist Party made a major contribution in the organization of the unorganized for the CIO."[1]

An important part of this contribution was the role of black and white Communists in forging the Negro-labor alliance, without which many of the basic industries, especially the steel, auto, and maritime industries, could never have been successfully organized. While traditional black leaders either joined in the Red scare against the CIO or remained neutral, awaiting proof of the new movement's equalitarian policy, the Communists and their left-wing allies, especially through the National Negro Congress, which they helped to found, made tremendous efforts to convince the black workers that only by joining the CIO could they begin to counteract their special oppression in American society. The previous struggles waged by the Communists and their allies against unemployment, for unemployment insurance, for work projects, against Jim Crow in general, and for the organization of black workers and for black rights in unions made them effective organizers for the new industrial union movement. Cayton and Mitchell reported the words of the white president of a SWOC women's auxiliary during the CIO campaign to organize steel: "The Communists think a Negro is just the same as they are.

They are very strong for that sort of stuff."[2] When published, this comment further increased the prestige of Communist organizers for the CIO.

After the new unions were established, the Communists and their left-wing allies fought to make certain that the principles of racial equality espoused by the CIO in organizing drives were put into effect. F. Ray Marshall points out in this connection that "Communists . . . were unquestionably a force for equalitarianism in the CIO. By raising the race issue to gain Negro support, the Communists forced white leaders to pay more attention to racial problems."[3]

The fact that the Communists were the most militant force in the great working-class uprising of the 1930's and in the fight for equal rights of the newly organized black workers has largely been ignored by historians of labor and of the black people. Another largely ignored fact is that many leaders of the CIO who were later distinguished for their anti-Communism recognized in the formative years of the industrial-union movement that the purpose of the Red-baiting attacks on the CIO was to destroy the "center-left" coalitions, which were achieving the organization of the unorganized. No one stated the case better than Walter Reuther did when he said that the purpose of the Red scare was to turn worker against worker. "So let's all be careful," he warned, "that we don't play the bosses' game by falling for the Red scare. Let's stand by our union and fellow unionists. No union man, worthy of the name, will play the bosses' game. Some may do so through ignorance. But those who peddle the Red scare and know what they are doing are dangerous enemies of the union."[4]

Yet it was Reuther himself who, with R. J. Thomas of the UAW, Emil Rieve of the textile workers, James B. Carey of the UE, and John Green of the Industrial Union of Marine and Shipbuilders, abetted by the House Un-American Activities Committee then headed by Martin Dies and the newly formed anti-Communist Association of Catholic Trade Unionists (ACTU), began the fight to break the alliance of center and left in the CIO, using Red-baiting as the chief weapon. Even during World War II, when the United States and the Soviet Union were allied against fascism, the cry was raised that the CIO had to dissociate itself from the Communists if it was to compete effectively with the AF of L in War Labor Board elections and maintain its wartime membership gains. Carey, with the aid of the ACTU, sought as early as 1942 to oust Communists from the UE, already one of the leading unions in the CIO as a result of its growth in the electrical and radio industries. Running for president that year on an anti-Communist platform, Carey lost at the convention to Albert J. Fitzgerald, one of the leading progressives in the union and a key figure in the organization of the huge GE plant.

Anti-Communism also reared its head during the war in the CIO's fight against racial discrimination. Several leaders of international unions attacked the Committee to Abolish Racial Discrimination as "Communist-inspired," even though Carey, its chairman, and Willard Townsend and George L. P. Weaver, its black members, were all vigorous anti-Communists and the committee "functioned in part as an organization to fight Communists in other organizations and in the Negro community."⁵ A close association between the fight against racial discrimination and the Communists in the minds of those leaders was grounds enough to oppose the committee, or at best to give it only token support.

Anti-Communism really began to flourish in the CIO once World War II was over and the tide of anti-Communist hysteria, held in check during the war, mounted under the impetus of the cold war policies of the Truman Administration. It was clearly evident during "Operation Dixie," which got under way in 1946.

Both the AF of L and the CIO launched campaigns after the war to organize workers in the South. The AF of L opened its drive in May, 1946, with announcements by William Green, George Meany, and other officials stressing that the CIO was "Communist-dominated." Green openly appealed to Southern industrialists to recognize AF of L unions, urge their workers to join them, and, in general, cooperate with the federation "or fight for your life against Communist forces." Meany declared that Southern workers faced a choice between the AF of L, which followed "the principle that you cannot be a good union man unless you are first a good American," and "an organization that has openly followed the Communist line and is following that line today."⁶

The AF of L, of course, had been voicing such charges since 1935. In the past, the CIO had in most cases succeeded in convincing unorganized workers that to swallow the anti-Communist line was to play into the hands of the bosses. This time the approach was different. The CIO threw tremendous resources into the Southern organizing campaign, which Philip Murray declared in 1946 was "the most important drive of its kind ever undertaken by any labor organization in the history of this country."⁷ But instead of moving into the South with the alliance of center-left forces that had made possible the great victories of the 1930's and early 1940's, the CIO now made it a practice from the outset to eliminate all Communists and Communist sympathizers from any connection with the drive. Van Bittner of the steelworkers, director of the CIO drive—whom *Fortune* called a "leading CIO right-winger"⁸—announced at the outset that no Communists would participate in the campaign and filled most of the organizing staff positions with implacable anti-Communists. He rejected offers from internationals associated with the left to send experienced organizers, black and white, to aid in the drive. Finally, he turned down volunteers from any organization with a left-wing tinge, depriving the campaign of forces that had been crucial in the earlier organizing drives of the CIO.

These actions may have started as a response to the AF of L–employer charge that the CIO was made up of "Communists," but actually the Southern organizing campaign was immediately exploited by anti-Communist forces in the CIO to eliminate Communists and their allies from the movement. The absence of the dedicated and tireless organizers of the left who had contributed to so many previous drives was particularly apparent in attempts to reach black workers in the South. To be sure, Communists in 1946 had less influence among black workers than ten years before, but that influence, particularly for the Communist and left-wing forces in the CIO unions, was still considerable.

The background of the left-wing appeal for blacks requires analysis. When the World War II began in 1939, the Communists labeled it the "Second Imperialist War" and launched a "The-Yanks-Are-Not-Coming" campaign. (The CIO took a similar position; it went on record at its 1940 convention as opposing "any foreign entanglements" by the United States "which may in any way drag us down the path of entering or becoming involved in foreign wars.") Slogans like "Yanks Are Not Coming," particularly "The Black Yanks Are Not Coming," won the support of many black Americans, who saw little distinction between German fascism and British colonialism and resented the call to defend democracy abroad when it was not a reality at home.[9] Although A. Philip Randolph quit the Socialist Party in 1940 because of its anti-war stand and became an active member of the Committee to Defend America by Aiding the Allies, many blacks agreed with the black columnist George S. Schuyler that "our war is not against Hitler in Europe, but against the Hitlers in America."[10]

But blacks also saw the enormous rise of government defense spending in 1940–41 as an opportunity for black employment; their objection was not so much that defense contracts were dragging the United States closer to war, but that everything was being done to reserve defense work for whites. Consequently, they joined the March on Washington Movement in the thousands to secure a place for blacks in the Arsenal of Democracy. But the Communists, adhering to the position that the defense industries were part of "imperialist war preparations," opposed any movement to increase the number of workers, black or white, in those industries. Moreover, since Randolph was now a leading advocate of American aid to the Allies, Communists viewed the MOWM as a plot to persuade blacks to support the war.

As the MOWM grew to a mass movement among blacks, the Communists adopted a less hostile attitude. Even though Randolph rejected Communist support, the *Daily Worker* began to feature news about the march and on June 19, 1941, called upon "all fair-minded citizens" who believed in "both peace and job equality" to "throw their full weight behind the Job March to Washington in July." Although their last-minute efforts probably helped build support for the march, the Communists undoubtedly lost prestige in the black community because of their earlier hostility to the MOWM and the time they took to come out in its favor.

On June 22, 1941, Nazi Germany attacked the Soviet Union, and the U.S.S.R. entered the war. From then until the end of World War II, the Communists and many left-wing leaders of CIO unions put the objective of winning the war first on the agenda. They continued to urge an end to Jim Crow practices and race discrimination in general in industry, labor organizations, and the army, but there was a tendency to frown upon any struggles that might interfere with the war effort. "We cannot temporarily stop the war until all questions of discrimination are ironed out," Ben Davis, a leading black Communist, explained, urging the "Negro people to be ready to sacrifice."[11] Of course, victory over fascism was most intimately related to the future welfare of all workers, black and white—a fact that many critics of the Communist position conveniently overlook—but it is also true that the Communist and left-wing union leaders were accused, not always unjustly, of putting the objective of winning the war ahead of the workers' interests in general and those of black workers in particular. It did not improve Communist prestige among blacks when the *Daily Worker* exhorted them to keep labor's "no-strike pledge" under all circumstances, lest they deliver a blow to the war effort. Nor did it help Communist prestige when that newspaper attacked the blacks involved in the Harlem riot of August, 1943, as "fifth columnists and pro-fascists"[12] who were not representative of the "good people" of Harlem—"good people" who would not allow their grievances to cripple the unity required to win the war. Frustrated blacks often failed to see how the Communists' approach was preferable to that of traditionally anti-Negro white forces.

It was to be exceedingly difficult for the Communists to overcome the resentment among blacks created by the Party's wartime policies. The Communists never completely erased the feeling in sections of the black community that they had placed the Soviet Union's survival above the battle for black equality. Veteran anti-Communist black leaders had a field day pointing this out. Frank Crosswaith, in a widely publicized article, wrote in November, 1943:

> To the average man of normal intellect with an ordinary sense of observation, the American Communists can be described literally as having their feet in America and their heads in Russia. As long as they continue to occupy this unrealistic posture, they will remain the outstanding force of destruction and confusion they have thus far been in the American labor movement, and will continue to hamper the progress of the Negro people toward ultimate equality and justice.[13]

Although the Communists defended their commitment to the war effort with the argument that, even as Crosswaith was writing, millions in the Soviet Union were sacrificing their lives to halt a threat to the rights and the very lives of all people, the argument was not very persuasive in the Negro community.

Communist prestige among blacks declined further when the Party in California failed to protest the government's unjust treatment of Japanese-Americans and when, at its twelfth convention in 1944, the Communist Party was dissolved and the Communist Political Association created in its stead. The dissolution of the Party ensued from General Secretary Earl Browder's insistence that the objective of continued national unity after the war required laying aside the idea of class struggle and cooperating with all sections of the population, including the monopoly capitalists, for the benefit of the nation as a whole. In such a postwar world of class harmony and peaceful relations between capitalist and socialist nations, Browder argued, there would be no need for the Communist Party as previously constituted. At the convention that dissolved the party, no resolution was adopted on the black question.

Despite the decline of the Communists' prestige among blacks, and despite their tendency to subordinate the grievances of black workers to the interests of winning the war, the left-wing unions had the best record in the fight against racial discrimination during World War II. As we have seen, such unions as the International Mine, Mill, and Smelter Workers, the NMU, the United Packinghouse Workers, the United Public Workers, and the United Office and Professional Workers were quick to form their own committees against racial discrimination. Leftist unions like the UE, the International Marine and Shipbuilders, the Packinghouse Workers, the International Fur and Leather Workers Union, the NMU, the National Union of Marine Cooks and Stewards, the ILWU, and the TWU fought most vigorously during the war to open jobs for blacks and to upgrade black workers. They also took a firm and unequivocal stand against "hate strikers." "It is significant," Ray Marshall observed, "that almost every organization that adopted special equalitarian racial machinery [during the war] either was Communist-dominated or had a strong Communist faction contending for leadership."[*][14] Early in 1942, a reporter asked Robert C. Lee, executive vice-president of the Moore-McCormack Lines, about the employment of black seamen together with white seamen on the company's ships. Lee answered that the company would employ blacks if the whites did not object. Confronted with evidence that white seamen, members of the NMU, did not object, Lee said he was not surprised: "They're all Commies."[15]

All this was well known to black Americans. Adam Clayton Powell, Jr., wrote in 1945, "There is no group in America, including the Christian church, that practices racial brotherhood one-tenth as much as the Communist Party."[16] The prestige of the CIO among black workers at the end of the war stemmed in no small degree from the record of the so-called Communist-dominated unions. But none of those unions was allowed to become involved in the CIO's Southern organizing drive launched after the war.

The CIO's generally more favorable record on Negro rights stood it in good stead in the early stage of the campaign, enabling it to win several NLRB elections in competition with the AF of L[†] where, as in

* Most studies of Communist and left-wing forces in the unions during the war emphasize the official Party position and ignore the record against discrimination chalked up by these unions. See, for example, Joel Seidman, "Labor Policy of the Communist Party during World War II," *Industrial and Labor Relations Review* 4 (October, 1950): 55–69. In the entire article there is not a single mention of black workers.

† An AF of L official frankly told an investigator that the CIO had "the advantage with Negroes of having a much better reputation on the race issue." William Kornhauser, "The Negro Union Official: A Study of Sponsorship and Control," *American Journal of Sociology*, March, 1952, p. 447.

the Masonite Corporation at Laurel, Mississippi, the Negro vote made the difference between victory and defeat. But, while the CIO thereafter rested on its reputation with the blacks, the AF of L, stung by its early defeats, began to pay special attention to black workers. The CIO rejected organizers from unions with a record of struggle for equal rights for blacks. It even refused to employ Miranda Smith, the dynamic leader of United Tobacco Workers, Local 22 of the Food, Tobacco, Agricultural, and Allied Workers Union (FTA), because she was a Communist. The AF of L on the other hand added seventeen Negro organizers and declared itself for "equal employment opportunities for the Negro worker and full participation in American Federation of Labor Unionism."[17] (To be sure, the 1946 AF of L convention was to reveal how little that posture actually meant.) The federation relied heavily on the anti-Communist theme in its appeals to black workers, claiming that twenty-one of thirty-six CIO unions were dominated by leaders who followed the Party line. But its major stress was that it could do more for the black worker than the CIO. *Pie in the Sky*, an AF of L pamphlet widely circulated among black workers during the Southern campaign, concluded: "The AF of L. offers you results now—not hot-air promises of pie in the sky by and by."[18] The very use of the words of Wobbly Joe Hill's famous song indicates that the AF of L was not afraid of a radical association in its appeal to blacks.* The CIO could have countered the pamphlet by telling black workers what had been accomplished for Negro members of CIO unions. But the most persuasive exponents of such an argument were Communists and left-wingers, and the CIO was taking the greatest pains to erase the impression that Communists exerted any influence in the organization.

Neither the AF of L nor the CIO, for all the resources they threw into the drive, accomplished what it had hoped for in the Southern campaign. The AF of L's campaign, which aimed at enrolling a million new members, ended on July 31, 1947, with a reported new enrollment of 425,000. The Taft-Hartley law, passed by Congress in June, 1947, "right-to-work" laws passed in several Southern states, and other anti-labor legislation made "a continued successful drive" impossible.[19] The CIO had even less to report in membership growth. It claimed 400,000 organized by January, 1948.

The CIO professed to be determined to continue the Southern drive "regardless of how long it takes."[20] But the bitter attacks launched by the CIO leadership against the left-wing unions overshadowed the drive. Indeed, the leadership devoted more attention after 1948 to destroying unions than to organizing the South,† and one of its earliest targets was the United Tobacco Workers, Local 22, affiliated with the left-wing Food, Tobacco, Agricultural, and Allied Workers Union.

---

* The pamphlet also claimed that the AF of L had 650,000 dues-paying Negro members, including 450,000 in the South. But the claim was wildly exaggerated and undocumented.

† The CIO Southern organizing drive was officially terminated in 1953, but long before that it had ceased to function effectively.

In the summer of 1947 Local 22 was engaged in a strike for a new agreement with R. J. Reynolds in Winston-Salem, employing 11,000 workers about equally divided between black and white. The House Un-American Activities Committee (the Dies Committee, later HUAC) began investigating the leaders of Local 22 on the ground that it was a "Communist-dominated union." The investigation made headlines in the Winston-Salem press, but the tobacco workers were not intimidated. On July 1 Paul Robeson, the militant black performer, spoke and sang at a mass meeting of 12,000 in Winston-Salem at which the theme was "full support for Local 22." The strike was won, and in the agreement between Reynolds and Local 22 wages were increased and working hours reduced. Shortly thereafter, as a result of Local 22's campaign to register its members to vote, Winston-Salem became the first Southern city in the twentieth century to send a black (the Reverend Kenneth Williams) to the City Council.

The CIO leadership picked up where the Dies Committee had left off. With funds provided by the CIO Executive Council, Willard Townsend, black President of the United Transport Service Employees, came into Winston-Salem in 1949 to challenge Local 22 in an NLRB election. At the same time, a campaign financed by the company was launched to persuade white members of Local 22 that they owed it to their country to quit a union dominated by Communists. The mayor of Winston-Salem went on the radio to read extracts from the report of the Dies Committee.[21]

The election went for no union by sixty votes. Townsend and his CIO staff of black organizers won over only a small number of black votes, but just enough, in combination with the white members influenced by the Red-baiting, to keep Local 22 from holding its majority. Local 22 continued to exist. (In 1949 its leader, Miranda Smith, became FTA Southern Regional Director and, as a member of the union's national executive board, occupied the highest position any black woman had held to that time in the labor movement.) But there was no longer a recognized bargaining agent for the workers at R. J. Reynolds, thanks to the CIO leadership's determination to smash the left-wing Local 22. Thus the black tobacco workers were the first to feel the sting of the CIO's Red-baiting drive.*

They were by no means the last. When the U.S.S.R.–U.S. alliance was erased by the cold war, the State Department and other government agencies called upon the trade-union movement to cooperate in advancing the new foreign policy. Within a few years the CIO had joined the AF of L in support of the cold war policy of the Truman Administration. It copied the AF of L by sending representatives on missions to split the trade unions in European countries, Latin America, Asia, and Africa and

---

* After the election, the Tobacco Workers International Union tried to replace the United Tobacco Workers at R. J. Reynolds. It won support among the white workers, but the Negro workers refused to back a union long associated with Jim Crow unionism. Hence Reynolds, one of the largest firms in the tobacco industry, remained unorganized.

to weaken the opposition abroad to U.S. foreign policy. The State Department appointed representatives of both the AF of L and the CIO to the staffs of various American embassies and foreign missions. Those "striped-pants" labor diplomats were considered essential for success in the cold war, for they had access to labor gatherings where regular diplomats would be unwelcome. Harry Bridges aptly termed this "American imperialism with a union label."

In 1949 the CIO withdrew from the World Federation of Trade Unions (WFTU), formed at the close of World War II by the trade-union centers of the Allied and liberated nations, because of the presence in the federation of the Soviet trade unions. Then, without consulting their own Executive Board, the CIO leaders joined with the AF of L to set up the International Confederation of Free Trade Unions (ICFTU) to split the WFTU. The sole guiding principle of the new international body was anti-Communism.

At the eleventh CIO convention in 1949, the process of tying the organization to the cold war was completed. The Constitution Committee proposed a catchall resolution that would bar from the Executive Board anyone who advocated "policies and activities" directed toward advancing the purpose of the Communist Party. Then came a resolution to expel the 50,000-member United Electrical, Radio, and Machine Workers of America because it did not support the Marshall Plan or the North Atlantic Pact and had endorsed Henry A. Wallace for President in 1948. Without a trial or hearing, the resolution to expel was passed. The charter of the electrical workers was handed to James B. Carey, the leading CIO cold war advocate and an acknowledged agent of the Association of Catholic Trade Unionists. The next day, the Union of Farm Equipment and Metal Workers was expelled and the union's jurisdiction turned over to the United Auto Workers. Expulsion of the Fur and Leather Workers Union; the International Mine, Mill, and Smelter Workers; the ILWU; the Food, Tobacco, Agricultural, and Allied Workers Union; the United Office and Professional Workers; the United Public Workers; the American Communications Association; the National Union of Marine Cooks and Stewards; and the International Fishermen and Allied Workers followed. In all, eleven progressive unions, with almost 1 million members, were expelled from the CIO as "Communist-dominated" (fourteen years earlier the CIO itself had been expelled from the AF of L).

While this dismal procedure was under way, Carey told the leaders of an American Legion–sponsored "anti-Communist" conference in New York: "In the last war we joined the Communists to fight the fascists; in another war we will join the fascists to fight the Communists."[22]

Among the unions expelled were several of the "pace-setters for the whole trade union movement" in terms of wage scales and conditions won and in terms of racial equality. They were the unions that had fought longest and hardest for black employment, black upgrading, black representation in trade-union offices. It can hardly be doubted that their fight had forced the more backward unions in the CIO toward an equali-

tarian position on the issue of black labor. But to the cold war warriors
in the CIO leadership that record was of no consequence.

A featured speaker at the 1950 CIO convention was the distinguished
black educator Dr. Mordecai Johnson, president of Howard University.
To the dismay of many delegates, Dr. Johnson warned the CIO not to
be taken in by the propaganda of the cold war. What, he asked, was the
"free world" that Truman, Churchill, Franco, Salazar, and other champions of the cold war professed to be defending against "Communist
aggression" inspired by the Soviet Union? It was made up of Britain,
France, Belgium, the Netherlands, Spain, Portugal, Germany, and the
United States—every last one of which had "been busy during the last
two hundred years securing and sustaining [its own] freedom by the
political domination, economic exploitation and social humiliation of
over half of the human race." The "free world," in other words, comprised "probably the most ruthless dominators and exploiters and humili-
ators of human life that ever spanned the pages of history"; instead of
bringing economic and political freedom to India, Africa, China, Ma-
laya, Indochina, and the Near East, they had used their power "to dominate them politically, to exploit their natural resources and their labor,
and to segregate and humiliate them upon the land upon which their
fathers have died and in the presence of the graves which hold the bodies
of their mothers." Dr. Johnson cited a case that would later erupt into
prominence:

> Now, suppose you were Indo-Chinese, wouldn't you be amazed at us? For
> over 100 years the French have been in Indo-China, dominating them
> politically, strangling them economically, and humiliating them in the
> land of their fathers.
> We [the United States] haven't ever sat down with the French and de-
> manded that they change that system. And in the defect of leadership on
> our part, they have turned to the Communists, and the Communists have
> given them leaders, they have trained their troops, and given them money
> and now it looks as though they can win, and as they are about to win
> their liberty we rush up to the scene and say, "Dear Brothers, what on
> earth are you getting ready to do? Are you going to throw yourselves into
> the hands of this diabolical conspiracy under the false notion they can
> bring you freedom? Why, they aren't free; we are the free people of the
> world, we have democratic institutions, we are your friends, we will send
> you leaders, we will send you ammunition, we will send you bread."
> And they look at us in amazement and they say, "Brother, where have
> you been? Why, if we'd a-known you was a-coming we'd have baked a
> cake."

Philip Murray praised the black educator's speech as an "inspirational
address that could only come from the soul of a man."[23] Yet only a year
before Murray had spearheaded the move for expulsion of eleven unions
for upholding a position practically identical to Dr. Johnson's. Having
paid his tribute to the black educator, Murray joined other leaders of the
CIO in intensifying the war against the expelled unions. Both the CIO

and the AF of L launched a series of raids to win over their membership.

At the same time, the U.S. Government was pushing its own offensive against progressive unions and unionists, invoking the anti-Communist provision of the Taft-Hartley law to indict left-wing union leaders for perjury. The first to be indicted was Hugh Bryson, president of the National Union of Marine Cooks and Stewards, who was brought to trial on the charge of falsification in signing the anti-Communist oath.* Other government weapons were deportation under the McCarren-Walter Act of left-wing union leaders who were not citizenst and imprisonment of militant trade unionists under the Smith Act's "teaching and advocating" provisions.

One victim of the deportation hysteria was Ferdinand C. Smith, a black NMU leader, who was branded an "undesirable alien" by the Truman Administration despite a long record of achievements for seamen and contributions to the struggle for Negro rights. Smith elected to leave the United States and return to Jamaica, his native land, in August, 1951. He told reporters: "I helped to build a union which enabled sailors to marry and have children and a home just like other workers, instead of being kicked around like bums. For this I earned the enmity of the shipowners and their agents, in and out of the government." He was confident that "the stormy night of reaction" would pass away, and that the American people would return their government "to the hands of the masses to whom it belongs."[24]

Scores of black and white members of the NMU gathered to bid Smith farewell, but Joseph Curran, NMU president, was not among them. He had joined the Red-baiters and was now one of the CIO's top anti-Communists. Curran had even sanctioned the Truman Administration's notorious "loyalty" screening program, which was depriving hundreds of progressive seamen, most of them Negro and Puerto Rican, of work. The program was launched at a conference in Washington, D.C., on July 24, 1950, attended by representatives of the Justice Department, various shipping interests, Curran of the NMU, representatives of "King" Joseph Ryan, lifetime president of the AF of L International Longshoremen's Association, and Allan Haywood, who had been deeply involved in the expulsion of the National Union of Marine Cooks and Stewards from the CIO. On July 31, 1950, the *New York Times* reported that "invitations to the conference pointedly exempted two unions, and in a definite sense these organizations are a target of the resolution. They are the dock union of Harry Bridges and the Marine Cooks and Stew-

---

* The Negro community of San Francisco came to Bryson's defense. A meeting sponsored by Negro leaders in the city passed resolutions praising him and his union for their "contribution to racial democracy." The Baptist Ministerial Alliance of San Francisco, representing Negro Baptist churches, also pledged full support to Bryson and his union. *Freedom*, January, 1954.

† Harry Bridges was the target of lengthy and unsuccessful deportation proceedings, which Supreme Court Associate Justice Frank Murphy characterized as a "monument to man's intolerance of man." "The Law and Harry Bridges," pamphlet, San Francisco, 1952, p. 1.

ards." Under the agreement worked out at the conference, which became government policy, maritime workers would not be permitted to
ship out if they were deemed poor security risks. The same provision was
soon extended to longshoremen, who were barred from working on military docks if they did not have the approval of the Coast Guard.

A reporter for the San Francisco *Sun-Reporter*, a black weekly, wrote
after an investigation: "Screening is an attempt to drive Negroes from
the waterfront and to undermine the unions that have fought for racial
equality. I have found that Negroes with key jobs have been the first to
be screened."[25] In April, 1952, *March of Labor* reported that "65 per
cent of the blacklisting are Negroes. In every union under a screening
program, Negroes have been disproportionately penalized."[26] The
ILWU *Dispatcher* declared that "sixty-five per cent of the longshoremen
screened off the waterfront are Negroes" and explained that "Negroes
are among the most militant ILWU members, because they have found
in our organization the sort of democracy and freedom from discrimination they seldom find elsewhere."[27] A study of the screening process on
the West Coast concluded that "approximately 70 per cent of the
screened members of the National Union of Marine Cooks and Stewards
have been Negroes."[28] In the "screening" process, as in the federal government's "loyalty" board hearing for government employees, any activity against Jim Crow was proof of a suspected person's disloyalty. Black
workers were asked: "Had you ever had dinner with a mixed group? Have
you ever danced with a white girl?" White workers were asked whether
they had ever entertained blacks in their homes. Witnesses were asked:
"Have you had any conversations that would lead you to believe [the
accused] is rather advanced in his thinking on racial matters?"[29]

Few unions were subjected to so many and such persistent attacks during this shameful period in American history as the National Union of
Marine Cooks and Stewards (MCS). When expulsion from the CIO
and the harassment of its president failed to destroy the union, the
NLRB directed the shipowners to cease recognition of the union "as the
sole bargaining representative for the stewards' department" aboard
Pacific Maritime Association vessels. The employers promptly recognized the "Marine Cooks and Stewards, AF of L, Anti-Communists,"
the brainchild of the segregationist Sailors Union of the Pacific, which
refused to admit blacks to membership. Few blacks were persuaded by
the AF of L's allegation that the militant MCS was controlled by "Commies." The vast majority remained loyal. Nor did they desert the union
when the National Maritime Union, at Curran's insistence, raided it.
"They supported MCS," declared Revels Cayton, "because of the
union's struggle against the shipowners, for democracy, for Negro-white
unity, for the fullest dignity for the Negro seamen." Hugh Bryson wrote
emotionally in *The Voice:* "The cornerstone of the very foundation of
our great union. . . . Negro-white unity has proved to be the most
effective weapon against the shipowners, against the raiders, and all our
enemies."[30] A black member of the union, born and reared in the South,
told an interviewer:

The union is my father and my mother and I am the son who will give my life for it. The union has put bread in the mouths of my children. It has given me a home, it has straightened my back so I do not bend to any man. It took me by the hand and said "Learn to read," and I learned to read. Big words, words they never had in those chicken coop schools. In the union I learned a trade. What would I be down in that country—an ignorant cotton picker? Wherever the union sees wrong, it points it out. It stands up and says, "That's wrong. Do right. Do like we do. Treat your brother right." I been in MC and S a long time, I lost my prejudices. I had them. But I met real brothers here. I met big men who mean what they say. If my brothers sleep in the foc'sles, I sleep with them. My white brothers, my black brothers, my brown brothers, all of them. We the children of the union, we all together.[31]

Expulsion from the CIO had no effect on the equalitarian policies of the expelled unions. A reading of the official journals of the UE; the International Fur and Leather Workers; the ILWU; the International Mine, Mill, and Smelter Workers; the Food, Tobacco, Agricultural, and Allied Workers; the United Office and Professional Workers; the MCS; and the other expelled unions reveals their continued interest in fighting anti-Negro discrimination and ensuring the civil rights of blacks and other minority groups. The same was true of the Distributive, Processing, and Office Workers Union, which took over many of the locals of the Food, Agricultural, and Allied Workers and the United Office and Professional Workers when those unions collapsed in the face of continuous government prosecution and CIO and AF of L raids. The union had emerged from District 65, which began life as an organization for Jewish dry goods workers on Manhattan's Lower East Side, participated in the great organizing drives of the 1930's, and, through mergers with other locals, such as the shoe workers, and organization of the city's textile workers, had increased its membership to about 10,000. With the appointment of Cleveland Robinson, a black worker, as organizer, later to become vice-president, District 65 began a drive to organize black workers in New York. It recruited a large black (and later Puerto Rican) membership. A militant left-wing union, it had a reputation for consistent support of the rights of black and had been involved, by the time the Distributive, Processing, and Office Workers Union was formed, in most of the key battles of the Negro people.

The Red-baiters dismissed any evidences of concern for the problems of black people with the claim that they were all devised "to further the program of the Communist Party" and that the blacks were being "used" for this sinister objective. One student who analyzed the problem in 1952 took issue: "If to 'use' is to advance the economic and social status of the Negroes, give them fuller citizenship rights, wage common struggle with them, and elect their representatives to high union offices, then the word has a meaning which the investigator cannot decipher."[32]

The evidence is clear that the CIO retreated on the struggle for black rights in the cold war era. Among other reasons, the expulsion of the left-wing unions removed a source of pressure to make equal rights for blacks a paramount issue. When conservative politicians and employers charged even the unions that had taken the lead in expelling the left-wing locals with being themselves "Communist-dominated," to champion the rights of black workers was to risk being accused of "subversive" activities. In fact, as the NLRB acknowledged, employers made effective use of the Red issue by branding CIO organizers from ordinarily conservative unions as Communists for seeking to include blacks in the same locals with whites.[33] Under such attacks, the CIO quickly retreated. The tendency was to maintain the *status quo* in collective-bargaining agreements; consequently it is not surprising that there was a slowdown in the fight to upgrade black workers.

In 1949 sections of the black press accused the CIO Committee to Abolish Racial Discrimination of doing "little or nothing to overcome discrimination against Negroes."[34] A writer charged in the Pittsburgh *Courier* that the committee was "serving no useful purpose to CIO union members and hasn't even proved itself to be of nominal nuisance value. It is nice window dressing for the organization . . . but in its present form is doing the unions and the liberal forces of this country a distinct disservice." He accused black members of the committee of holding their offices "on a 'puppet' basis" and described as "disgusting" their conduct at the 1949 UAW convention, where they supported Walter Reuther against the demand from black members for a black vice-president. "About the only thing missing from the show was a pair of handkerchiefs wrapped around each of the gentlemen's expansive brows."[35]

Even Willard Townsend conceded that in the black community the committee was "recognized not as a committee to do something, but more like a symbol." When it was proposed that the committee should publicize discriminatory practices by CIO unions, it was rejected because, as James B. Carey, the committee chairman, declared, the publicity "would injure all unions."[36] Some committee members supported revoking the charters of discriminatory CIO unions, only to be confronted with the hoary excuse, long advanced at AF of L conventions against A. Philip Randolph's similar demand, that such action would violate the autonomy of the member unions.

The Pittsburgh *Courier's* criticism of the black CIO officers at the 1949 UAW convention reflected a widespread feeling among black workers. A study of thirty-four unions in 1949 revealed that, although most of them were affiliated with the CIO, only seven had blacks on their national boards. Not even the United Mine Workers, long touted in the Negro press as well as by some white scholars for its equalitarianism, was among the seven. At the 1948 UMW convention, thirteen locals with a large black membership complained that a union with 100,000 Negro members had not had a single black on the Executive Board since Richard M. Davis's death in the late 1890's. "We think it is high time that the Negro membership . . . should have representation on the International Executive Board," they declared in a resolution put before the convention.[37] But the resolution was not even brought to a vote, and no Negro was elected to national office.

In the black press Walter Reuther was pictured as a devoted friend and champion of the Negro people, a faithful fighter for the civil and economic rights of black workers. Black members of the UAW were constantly being told how fortunate they were that the dynamic leader of the million-strong United Automobile Workers was an active board member of the NAACP. But many black workers in Detroit had a different opinion of Reuther's leadership. Since 1939 black members of the UAW had been raising the demand for the appointment of more blacks as organizers and representatives on the national staff, and especially for the creation of a special post for a Negro on the International Executive Board. At the 1943 UAW convention, it will be recalled, Reuther and his supporters had been able to defeat a resolution for a special Negro representative, introduced by left-wing delegates, with the argument that it was "racism in reverse." Quite a few black delegates at the convention agreed with this argument and voted with Reuther in defeating the resolution. But the passing years had produced a change in their thinking. By the end of World War II, the demand had the overwhelming support of the black membership. This is conceded even by Irving Howe and B. J. Widick, ardent admirers of Reuther's racial policies. "Negro members," they wrote in 1949 in an article curiously titled "The UAW Fights Race Prejudice," "seemed largely to favor this proposal, perhaps seeing in it a way to protect their status in the union."[38] That they might have needed such protection escaped the notice of the two scholars. The truth is that black members of the UAW were becoming increasingly bitter over the union leadership's unwillingness to push more forcefully for the upgrading of Negro auto workers, who, in the main, were forced to remain in the lowest-paid categories, working at the hardest jobs in an industry notorious for reducing the life-span of its workers. Since many blacks had come into the industry only during World War II, it was easy to justify inaction on this issue by referring to seniority. But this was unconvincing to the black membership, and even those who had bought the "racism in reverse" argument began to join the campaign for a Negro vice-president. The Reuther machine was too powerful, however, and the resolution invariably went down to defeat at UAW conventions.

In 1949 a bitter jurisdictional dispute erupted between the United Farm Equipment and Metal Workers (FE) and the UAW. Although the FE was still affiliated with the CIO, the union was under a mounting attack from the CIO leadership, with Reuther in the vanguard, for being "Communist-dominated," and the UAW leadership was only too willing to deal it a devastating blow by snatching the big McCormick Works of the International Harvester Company, with which the FE held a contract, from its sister union. In the spring of 1949, before an election to determine which union would be the bargaining agent of the workers at the plant, the UAW distributed leaflets in which it accused the FE of being "Communist-dominated." The FE countered the Red-baiting campaign with leaflets and advertisements in the Chicago edition of the Pittsburgh *Courier:*

Why hasn't the UAW ever elected a Negro to national office, to its international executive board or as a district director? At the recent national
convention of the FE, CIO, William Smith of Chicago, a worker in the
McCormick Works plant, was elected vice-president of the union.
. . . WALTER REUTHER'S MACHINE IN THE UAW DOESN'T
WANT NEGROES IN ITS LEADERSHIP. This union is currently trying to raid the FE-CIO at McCormick.[39]

The FE won the election, and an officer of the union commented,
"The Negro vote was solid for us." Even a UAW officer conceded that
the presence of William Smith on the FE Executive Board, a black
worker whom the Negroes in the plant knew had fought for their rights,
was the decisive factor in the victory. "This weapon proved very successful for FE," he told an investigator.[40]

Yet at the 1949 UAW convention, when black UAW members
pointed to the FE victory at McCormick as further reason for acceding
to requests for a Negro vice-president, they were confronted again with
the argument of "racism in reverse." The two Negro members of the
CIO Committee to Abolish Racial Discrimination, Willard Townsend
and George L. P. Weaver, were brought in to speak against the Negro
vice-president. The resolution was once more defeated.

Two studies, one in 1950 and the other in 1953, demonstrated that,
while many CIO unions had blacks on their staffs as national organizers
and as international representatives, they served too often either as
"window-dressing for the organization" or as "liaison men between white
union leaders and Negro workers,"[41] a one-way channel from the top
down, assigned to keep the black membership in line. One black union
leader admitted bitterly to an investigator: "Some unions have a Negro
on the staff, or a committee to deal with these matters [of race relations].
But they have no power! Their only function is to *take care* of the
Negroes, and they don't do that! Having a Negro on the staff is *just a
show* for most unions!"[42] It was an accusation of which not even the left-
wing unions were completely innocent, but their guilt was far less than
that of the unions that led the expulsion of the left. When black union
officials refused to play the assigned roles, they faced the charge of being
"Communists" or "Communist dupes." Some were threatened with
suspension from office unless they toed the mark, and in several instances
—the UAW was again a leader—were removed from office and expelled.

It is clear, then, that during the cold war era, the CIO position on
black labor began to move closer and closer to the stance long associated
with the AF of L, bringing with it "growing disenchantment with the
CIO in the Negro community." But, as long as disenchantment was the
price for supporting cold war policies in the labor movement, the CIO
leadership was prepared to pay it.

It is no coincidence that the one CIO union to continue its battle
for Negro rights following the expulsion of the left-wing unions was also
the union that opposed the cold war, opposed the expulsions, and never
stopped urging the CIO to end its "thinking and action" on the whole

question of "so-called Communist domination of unions" and its uncritical support of the cold war, and to begin a

> fearless defense of every constitutional right of every person, popular or unpopular, regardless of race, color, creed or political belief; against every form ·of attack whether by criminal prosecution or by economic or social prosecution, whether by threat of jail or by threat of discharge; there must be recognition that we need not fear free speech, even for Communists, but that we must fear suppression of speech even of Communists.[43]

That union was the United Packinghouse Workers of America, (UPWA), which even conservative historians concede was a "conspicuous exception to the usual practice" among CIO unions of doing nothing "to improve the job opportunities for their Negro members at the plant level."[44] While the CIO Committee to Abolish Discrimination became a mere figurehead, and while several of the international affiliates' civil rights committees ceased to function or functioned to no effect,* the UPWA Anti-Discrimination Department, formed in 1950, continued to be active and effective.

In 1949, following a nationwide strike during which employers were unable to defeat the union by dividing the workers on the racial issue, the UPWA decided "to discover the dimensions of the problem" and cooperated with Fisk University in a study of its membership directed by Professor John Hope, II. The preliminary findings† led, in 1950, to the creation of an Anti-Discrimination Department and a Convention Committee on Problems of Discrimination. The latter, in Professor Hope's subsequent judgment, soon became "a normal part of the convention machinery and has initiated far-reaching resolutions."[45] The Anti-Discrimination Department was empowered to do something unique in the labor movement—to lessen the gap between the national union's antidiscrimination professions and practices in the locals. It had the task of achieving the elimination of discrimination and segregation in all plants and from the union, and the inclusion of language in contracts that would forbid discriminatory hiring practice. The union announced that it would not approve or service any contracts by its locals that did not contain an antidiscrimination clause, and it enforced this policy even after a number of locals in the South disaffiliated.

By 1950 the UPWA was truly a "conspicuous exception" in the CIO. In the February 18, 1950, issue of the *Washington Afro-American*, columnist Ralph Matthews assailed "the new CIO policy which calls for conformity with America's traditional policy of segregation and Jim

---

* The committee set up by the United Steelworkers of America in 1948 to eliminate the "last remnants of injustice" in the steel industry refused to touch the major grievance of black steelworkers, the barriers to advancement in union contractual arrangements.

† Professor Hope found that one-tenth of UPWA's membership was located in the South; that the Negro and Mexican-American membership constituted a growing minority; and that, while progress had been made in placing Negroes in jobs and departments previously closed to them, minority workers were "conspicuously absent from the highly skilled mechanical jobs."

Crowism." Racial segregation was becoming so widespread at functions sponsored by CIO affiliates in the South that it was the practice to hold most meetings on a segregated basis, and in South Carolina, it was common knowledge, that "CIO union halls . . . have Jim Crow toilet facilities."[46] At a Birmingham steelworkers' meeting in 1952, not only was segregation strictly enforced, but when the crowd moved from the union hall into the street, "union officials gave policemen orders to maintain segregation in the street!"[47] When Len De Caux, CIO publicity director, objected, he was told, "You're talking like a Communist!"*[48]

Writing in *Labor History's* summer, 1973, issue, Ray Ginger observes: "We do not need any more trash about 'How the Communists Infiltrated the CIO.' Plain truth is they were a major force in building it."[49] They were also a "major force" in building the black-white unity that distinguished the early CIO, and when they and others who were erroneously accused of being Communists were expelled, much of the black-white unity also departed.

* The UPWA stirred up a storm within the CIO in 1953 when the union protested a segregated Political Action Committee banquet and dance in Birmingham.

20 The National Negro Labor Council, 1951–55

In 1950 there was no longer any organization in existence dedicated specifically to defending black workers and promoting their rights, even though black labor was facing increased discrimination in industry and the labor movement. The National Negro Congress had declined in membership during the war and passed out of existence shortly after. The Negro Labor Victory Committee, formed by Communists and their allies, had also disappeared. The March on Washington Movement, which at one time seemed to hold out the promise of becoming a permanent organization, had also declined rapidly in the postwar period; it held its last national conference on October 19, 1946, in Chicago and officially passed away late in 1947.

Of course, Randolph was still regarded as the spokesman for blacks in the AF of L, and at federation conventions he continued his attack on Jim Crow unionism, only to meet his annual rebuffs. At the 1950 convention, when he called for inclusion of "labor unions" in a resolution asking for federal legislation against discrimination, the delegates simply readopted the previous year's declaration, which had conspicuously left out the subject of Randolph's concern. All Randolph got was a convention recommendation that President Green consider a proposal for the establishment of a Department of Civil Rights.

The Brotherhood of Sleeping Car Porters itself was experiencing a loss in membership and influence. In the June, 1949, issue of *The Black Worker*, Vice-President Milton Webster with evident satisfaction claimed a brotherhood membership of 18,000, with established divisions in 117 U.S. and Canadian railroad centers and bargaining agreements with Pullman and thirty-nine "class A" railroads. But even these achievements and others soon to come* could not obscure the fact that since World

---

* In January, 1951, the Railway Labor Act, which had barred union-shop agreements, was amended to permit an employer to enter into an agreement with a union that represented a majority of the employees in a bargainable unit, such agreement requiring membership in the union as a condition of employment. This superseded state laws prohibiting union-shop contracts. On August 23, 1951, a union-shop clause covering the porters, attendants, maids, and bus boys of the Pullman Company became a part of the collective bargaining agreement with the brotherhood.

War II there had been a decline in the number of porters, attendants, maids, and busboys in the Pullman Company service as a result of economy drives and technological changes.

The NAACP had grown enormously during the war. For the first time in its history it had become a mass organization, with close to 450,000 members in 1946. But it was too absorbed in the cold war and anti-Communism and too uncritical of labor leaders with similar preoccupations to be of much help to the frustrated black workers. Much the same could be said of the National Urban League.

Thus, to fill an organizational void, more than 900 delegates, predominantly black but including some whites, met in Chicago in June, 1950, at the National Labor Conference for Negro Rights. Delegates told of black men and women who stood in lines at the gates of industrial plants to apply for jobs, only to be told that no help was wanted, while at the same time they could see white workers being hired. They told of black workers who had gained experience during World War II but were unable to find employment in defense plants. They complained that factories throughout the land denied blacks upgrading and better job opportunities while the unions stood by, arguing that their hands were tied by the seniority arrangements written into most basic industry contracts. All the delegates agreed that blacks were being closed out of apprenticeship training programs, either in industry or in government, in such fields as the building trades, machine tools, printing, and engraving,* and that racially segregated collective-bargaining agreements kept them from advancing to skilled and semiskilled jobs. Black firemen described the collusive agreements between railroad management and the brotherhoods to eliminate the opportunity for blacks to become engineers. Delegates from AF of L unions denounced the federation for its toleration of affiliates that excluded or segregated black workers, and a number from CIO affiliates reported that the congress was "running fast from the early position of the 'thirties when it really fought for Negro rights."[1] White labor leaders, noting that there were many more Negro workers in the labor movement than ever before in American history, apparently concluded that organized labor had fulfilled its duties to the black working class. But the delegates made it clear that black labor was not content with second-class membership even in unions that boasted of their equalitarianism. They pointed out also that millions of black workers were still to be unionized.

Paul Robeson, a long-time ally of Negro labor and editor of *Freedom*, the black monthly published in Harlem, delivered a powerful speech in which he denounced the cold war and the anti-Communist witch hunts for their adverse impact on the conditions of Negro Labor, condemned imperialist aims to continue domination of Africa, and called for a

---

* The 1950 census showed that in the building crafts Negroes constituted only 1 per cent of the electricians, 3.24 per cent of the plumbers and pipefitters, and 3.9 per cent of the carpenters. The figures on Negro apprenticeship programs, which were controlled to a large extent by the unions, were even bleaker. They showed 1 per cent for Negro electricians, .8 per cent for plumbers and pipefitters, and .6 per cent for carpenters.

return to peaceful relations between the United States and the socialist countries. Robeson predicted that black labor, supported by the whole Negro people together with progressive white working men and women, could "save the labor movement, CIO and AF of L," from the leaders who were betraying it.[2]

The Chicago conference adopted a "model FEPC clause" to be incorporated in every union contract* and established a Continuations Committee made up of three important black labor leaders: As provisional president, William R. Hood, serving his fourth term as recording secretary of Local 600, UAW-CIO; as vice-president, Cleveland Robinson, vice-president of the Distributive, Processing, and Office Workers Union (independent); and as executive secretary, Coleman Young of the Amalgamated Clothing Workers staff, veteran labor leader of Detroit and former director of organization of the Wayne County CIO Council. The committee was charged with the task of building chapters among black workers.

Within a year the Continuations Committee had established twenty-three Negro Labor Councils in major industrial centers and had launched a campaign to have the "model clause" incorporated into union contracts. The only success scored in the campaign was in the UE, which adopted the model clause as its official union policy and established a Fair Practices Committee to head a nationwide union drive for the full rights of its black and women members. As the committee's full-time national secretary, the UE hired Ernest "Big Train" Thompson, a militant black with long experience in the fight against racism in industry and unions.

The local Negro Labor Councils were active on a number of fronts. The Washington, D.C., council helped the United Public Workers (UPW) to win improvements in the conditions of black workers at the Bureau of Engraving. Half of the 6,000 workers in the bureau were black, but less than .5 per cent held any but menial, unskilled jobs. In addition, there were still separate toilet facilities and segregated areas in the bureau for black employees. In January, 1951, UPW's black secretary-treasurer, Ewart Guinier, a leader of the Greater New York Negro Labor Council, signed an agreement with the bureau; under it, segregated facilities were outlawed and seventeen blacks were hired to work as apprentice plate-printers. For the first time since the Bureau of Engraving was established during the Civil War, blacks were permitted to rise above the rank of unskilled laborer.

Most active of the local councils was the Detroit Negro Labor Council. Even in highly organized Detroit, the income of black families was far below that of white families.† Then again, Detroit, with a large

---

* "The Company agrees that it will not discriminate against any applicant for employment or any of the employees in their wages, training, upgrading, promotion, transfer, layoff, discipline, discharge, or otherwise because of race, creed, color, national origin, political affiliation, sex or marital status."

† According to a University of Michigan "Detroit Area Study," cited in the July 30, 1955, Detroit edition of the Pittsburgh *Courier*, the median annual income of Negro families in 1954 was $3,800, as compared with $5,700 for white families.

black population, still did not have a Negro councilman, whereas blacks had already been elected to the municipal legislatures of New York, Chicago, Cleveland, and other cities. Detroit also did not have a fair employment practices law (the Michigan Civil Rights law, known as the Diggs Act, was admittedly weak and practically useless). Finally, there was increasing resentment among black UAW members over the Reuther leadership's failure to push for the upgrading of black workers in the auto plants and over the continued absence of Negroes on the UAW's top policy-making body, the International Executive Board.

The Detroit Negro Labor Council, led by William R. Hood and including many black members of Local 600, brought all of these complaints into the open, causing an inevitable clash with the Reuther leadership. The clash was sharpest over the demand for a local FEPC ordinance. When the council began a petition drive for a citywide referendum on the ordinance, Reuther and seven other international officers issued a directive to local unions calling upon auto workers who had signed the petition to withdraw their names. The directive complained that "this irresponsible Communist-inspired approach to secure FEPC by referendum" had been launched without prior consultation "with the UAW-CIO . . . or other sincere advocates of FEPC in this community."[3] Since Reuther had already indicated that the CIO would not act on issues affecting black workers until it found the community ready to move, many blacks were of the opinion that it ill befitted the UAW top leadership—all white—to denounce a petition drive aimed at getting the community to move.

The petition campaign was not successful, but it managed to gather 40,000 signatures. The Detroit Negro Labor Council, attacked by the UAW leadership as "Communist-inspired" and "dual unionism," was nonetheless able, with twenty-two other councils, to initiate a convention held in Cincinnati, Ohio, on October 27, 1951, to found a National Negro Labor Council (NNLC). The delegates, overwhelmingly black and one-third women, came from mills, shops, offices, and even schools and colleges in Cleveland, Birmingham, San Francisco, Chicago, Houston, Bessemer (Alabama), New York, Detroit, Denver, Louisville, Winston-Salem, Pittsburgh, New Orleans, Seattle, Minneapolis, Buffalo, Jacksonville, Saint Louis, Philadelphia, and New York. They were continuing a tradition established more than a hundred years before in the National Negro Conventions of pre–Civil War America, and especially in the Colored National Labor Union, founded four years after the war.

On the eve of the opening session, three of the black delegates were interviewed by a reporter. Estelle Holloway, a tobacco worker from Winston-Salem, a shop steward of Local 22 (by then affiliated with the Distributive, Processing, and Office Workers Union), and an officer of the local branch of the NAACP, said that the members' wage, though only 78 cents an hour, was "twice as much as we used to make before we had a union." Joseph Oliver, president of the Watchco (Texas) leather workers' local of the International Fur and Leather Workers Union and president of the Watchco Methodist Men of the Church, told of increases in wages from 40 cents an hour in 1941, when the union stepped

in, to $1.09 ten years later. Asbury Howard, regional director of the In-
ternational Mine, Mill, and Smelter Workers, clerk of the Starlight Baptist Church in Bessemer, and President of the Bessemer branch of the
NAACP, told how his union and the Bessemer Voters League, of which
he was president, had put on a major drive to get blacks to register, pay
the poll tax, and vote. At the September, 1949, meeting of the CIO
Committee to Abolish Discrimination, Willard Townsend had expressed
alarm because blacks in the South were supporting the "Communist-
dominated Mine, Mill and Smelter Workers, in preference to the CIO
Steelworkers."[4] Howard's description of how his union in Bessemer had
transformed "the mines in that region from hell holes and death pits to
places where the worker had a fighting chance to stay alive and eke out a
living" and how it was mobilizing the power of the black community
against the "Klan-dominated" city government helped to explain that
"preference." Asked why he had come to Cincinnati, Howard answered:
"It's the lack of power, and not just the color of our skin, that is the
basic problem. The reason I'm sold on the NNLC is that it represents
power."[5]

All but one of the speakers at the convention were black. The exception was Maurice E. Travis, secretary-treasurer of the International
Mine, Mill, and Smelter Workers. Travis, who had lost an eye fighting in the South for unionization of white and black workers, told the
delegates:

> I didn't come here to tell the Negro workers of America or their leaders
> what to do. . . . What I've got to say is aimed at the white trade union-
> ists. . . . The white supremacists and their political stooges do not intend
> that the trigger, the lash and the noose shall be reserved for Negroes only.
> They intend that *all* workers shall feel the lash of reaction if they do not
> comply. The white workers who are here at this conference have . . . the
> job of going back to their homes, to the unions, and campaigning for
> Negro-white unity—not among the Negro workers—but among the white
> workers.[6]

"Jostling Joe" Johnson, port agent for the southern district of the National Union of Marine Cooks and Stewards, brought the delegates ap-
plauding to their feet as he struck back at critics in the black press and
the "establishment" Negro organizations who were already denouncing
the gathering as a "Communist plot." "We say to you . . . if you are
not going to join with us and help us—for God's sake get off our backs
so that we can go forward." He stormed on:

> Those who label us communistic every time we open our mouths to gain
> our rights don't know the difference between Communism and rheuma-
> tism and know little about either. The darker peoples of the world want
> to choose their own kind of government and their own leaders. It makes
> me mad as hell for our administration to give away millions to maintain
> the rulers of their choice in colonial and European countries and don't
> want to give me my unemployment insurance.[7]*

---

* The Truman Administration was attempting to deprive suspected Communist of
unemployment insurance.

Black men and women from the UE; the United Packinghouse Workers; the Food, Tobacco, Agricultural, and Allied Workers Union; the
International Mine, Mill, and Smelter Workers; and the International
Fur and Leather Workers denounced the raids on their unions by Red-
baiting leaders of the CIO and AF of L and the government witch
hunts. They emphasized that black workers were feeling the effects of
these attacks in the weakening of their hard-won rights in shops and factories, mines and mills. Several of the speakers had relatives in the South
facing long prison terms or execution on trumped-up charges. The delegates, moved to tears by accounts of the suffering these men and women
endured, voted to mount a nationwide campaign in their behalf.

William R. Hood was the keynote speaker. He began: "We come to
announce to all America and to the world that Uncle Tom is dead. 'Old
Massa' lies in the cold, cold grave. Something new is cooking on the
Freedom Train." He continued:

> We come here today because we are conscious at this hour of a confront-
> ing world crisis. We are here because many of our liberties are disappear-
> ing in the face of a powerful war economy and grave economic problems
> face working men and women everywhere. No meeting held anywhere in
> America at this mid-century point in world history can be more important
> nor hold more promise for the bright future toward which humanity
> strives than this convention of our National Negro Labor Council. For
> here we have gathered the basic forces of human progress, the proud black
> sons and daughters of labor and our democratic white brothers and sisters
> whose increasing concern for democracy, equality, and peace is America's
> bright hope for tomorrow.

Like Joe Johnson, Hood defied the whites who labeled the conference
"subversive" before the delegates had even gathered. He called them the
"common oppressors of both people, Negro and white," who advanced
the "false cry of 'subversive' to maintain and extend that condition of
common oppression." Blacks who had joined them, like Lester Granger
of the Urban League and George Schuyler of the Pittsburgh *Courier*,
were simply responding to orders from "the big white folks." Hood addressed them scornfully: "You have spent your lives growing fat on Jim
Crow, while your brothers and sisters cannot find jobs, are shot down in
cold blood, have their homes burned and bombed." He warned them
that their influence would soon pass, for "the day of the white-haired
'Uncle Toms' and the sleek 'Uncle Thomases' is at an end."

Regarding the charge of "dual unionism" leveled at the convention
by white trade-union leaders, Hood declared that convention's objective
was "to build a new type of organization—not an organization to compete with existing organizations of the Negro people already at work on
many civil rights struggles." The new organization would call upon
black people to support labor's fight and "will encourage Negroes to join
unions and urge unions to organize Negroes." Hood's reply came with
no apologies. On the contrary, he charged the white union leaders with
hypocrisy for criticizing blacks in their efforts to mobilize power to redress a host of grievances while they themselves failed to stand up for

the full rights of black workers and the black people as a whole. Where had the "great trade unions" of Illinois been when mobs in Cicero and Chicago violently prevented black families from exercising their basic right to live and raise their children in a decent environment? Resolutions and flowery speeches stressing equalitarian principles were standard features of union conventions, while blacks were "still barred from many trade unions in this country, denied apprenticeship training and upgrading, and refused jobs in many places." They were still "not represented in the policy-making bodies of most international unions."

> We say that we will no longer permit the denial of these basic rights in our country, and are pooling our strength for that purpose. We intend to do it on the basis of cooperation and unity, wherever possible with the organized labor movement.
>   *We wish to say further that the day has ended when white trade union leaders or white leaders in any organization may presume to tell Negroes on what basis they shall come together to fight for their rights. Three hundred years has been enough of that. We ask your cooperation—but we do not ask your permission!*
>   We believe it to be the solemn duty of trade unions everywhere, as a matter of vital self-interest, to support the Negro workers in their efforts to unite and to play a more powerful role in the fight of the Negro people for first-class citizenship based upon economic, political, and social equality. We believe, further, that it is the trade unions' duty and right to encourage the white workers to join with and support their Negro brothers and sisters in the achievement of these objectives.[8]

The convention adopted a Statement of Principles and a Program of Action. The statement asserted that the black people could attain first-class citizenship "based on economic and social equality" only if black workers, along with their white allies, united to protect black Americans "against those forces which continue to deny us full citizenship." The old forms of organization for winning Negro rights had been unable to bring about "full economic opportunity for the Negro worker in the factory, the mine, the mill, the office, and in government"; to stop brutal police killings and mob violence against blacks throughout the land; and to achieve for blacks in the South the right to vote and for all blacks "a full say in the political life of our country with proper representation in government on all levels," as well as the right to buy and rent homes or to use public transportation, restaurants, hotels, and recreation facilities everywhere. Consequently, there was a distinct need for the NNLC, "an organization which unites all Negro workers with other suffering minorities and our allies among white workers, and bases itself on rank and file control regardless of age, sex, creed, political beliefs, or union affiliation," an organization which, at all times, would "pursue . . . a militant struggle to improve our conditions." The statement pledged the NNLC "to work unitedly with the trade unions to bring about greater cooperation between all sections of the Negro people and the trade union movement; to bring the principles of trade unionism to the Negro workers everywhere; to aid the trade unions in the great unfinished work of organizing the South on the basis of fraternity, equality and unity; and to further unity between black and white workers everywhere."

The Program of Action included a fight for 100,000 new jobs for black workers in areas of employment then barred to them, with special emphasis on the right of black women to work anywhere and everywhere; a fight for a national Fair Employment Practices Committee and for a "model FEPC contract clause in every union, such as that already adopted by UE," which was credited with having achieved "marked positive results in building unity of Negro and white workers," and a fight for full freedom. The NNLC was prepared both to join hands with other organizations and to initiate campaigns on its own where necessary.

As its final act before adjourning the convention elected officers for the next year: William R. Hood, president; Coleman Young, executive secretary; Ernest Thompson, director of organization; and Octavia Hawkins of Chicago's Local 451 of the Amalgamated Clothing Workers, CIO, treasurer. Seven vice-presidents-at-large were elected. All but one of the officers were black; all but three were trade unionists, mostly officials. Four of the officers were members of unions affiliated with the AF of L, and six were with unions expelled by the CIO.

In speeches and articles by several of these officers in the months following the founding convention, the point was made that the NNLC had set two basic tasks for itself. One was to break the pattern of job discrimination against blacks in American industry. The other was to eliminate racism within the unions and to use the "trade union base to move the trade unions and our white allies within it into the liberation struggle for black people with a primary concentration on economic issues as the key." The writers did not envisage separate black unions, but they did assert the need of black workers to have their "own separate groupings, to plan and discuss their interests, and to define their interests." Hence the new organization was to be composed in the main of black workers. The founders conceded that white and black workers had common problems, but they insisted that black workers had "additional special problems." The trade-union movement had dealt with some of them, but "it cannot be a substitute for the independent movement of Negro workers fighting in all areas of equality." There was still no inherent conflict between the existing trade union movement and the NNLC. In fact, the council was viewed as "a necessary and vital organization to the trade union movement and vice versa. They complement each other in a parallel direction." In short, there was a "natural alliance" between the two—"if you could develop it."[9]

Developing it was far from easy in the early 1950's. The NNLC was launched at a time when the post–World War II witch hunt against Communists and all Americans of progressive thought was at its height. It was a time when most Americans, workers included, were fearful of joining any organization that might not have the approval of the government. There was little doubt that the NNLC was such an organization. To be sure, as the eminent black scholar Dr. W. E. B. Du Bois, himself a victim of McCarthyism, pointed out, "not all America has succumbed to this indefensible belief" that to favor the equality of all people was "subversive."[10] But most unions—and it was from labor that the NNLC was expecting to gain its greatest support—were among the first institutions to cooperate with the witch-hunters. Many unions that were themselves being attacked as "Communist-dominated" continued to capitulate before the Red-baiters or to remain silent.

At the 1951 CIO convention, immediately after the NNLC was born, several white spokesmen, led by James B. Carey, attacked the council as a tool of the Soviet Union.* Quick to act upon any such accusation, the House Committee on Un-American Activities (HUAC) undertook an investigation of the council in Detroit. The hearings, opening in February, 1952, and broadcast on radio, were marked by sharp exchanges between NNLC leaders and HUAC members. Coleman Young concluded his testimony with the statement:

> I am a part of the Negro people. I fought in the last war and I would unhesitatingly take up arms against anybody that attacks this country. In the same manner I am now in process of fighting against what I consider to be attacks and discrimination against my people. I am fighting against un-American activities such as lynchings and denial of the vote. I am dedicated to that fight, and I don't think I have to apologize or explain it to ·anybody, my position on that.[11]

The investigation proved nothing about a Communist connection with the NNLC. Nevertheless, the odds were overwhelming that the council would not survive long enough to hold a second convention. Yet it did survive until 1956, and, hampered though it was by intimidation, Red-baiting, and other kinds of political and economic pressure, it did conduct important struggles to realize the objectives set forth in its Program of Action.

The NNLC campaign included drives to win jobs for blacks in clerical and administrative positions in the vast Sears-Roebuck chain, among the office workers of the Ford Motor Company, in executive positions in hotels and banks, as motormen and conductors in San Francisco and other cities, as baseball players on the Detroit Tigers, on dairy trucks in New York, on the production line in Brooklyn breweries, and as pilots and stewardesses on airlines. Negro Labor Councils were joined in its campaigns on picket lines, in write-in drives, and on visiting committees by local unions, black educators and ministers, some branches of the NAACP and the Urban League, and sympathetic members of the white community. Their activities were publicized in the black press, in the organs of sympathetic or participating unions, and in the journals of such left-wing organizations as had been able to survive the McCarthy witch hunts.

During the second NNLC convention in Cleveland in November, 1952, some 1,200 delegates left the city's Public Auditorium and picketed

---

* Hood attacked Carey for saying nothing about "the all-white executive board of nearly every CIO international. He does not attack the leadership of the CIO Textile Workers Union for coddling Ku Kluxers. But he denounces the organization of the Negro people." *Proceedings*, CIO Convention, 1951, pp. 234-35.

the downtown offices of American Airlines. The marchers carried signs reading, "Negro Pilots Fly in Korea—Why Not in America?," "End Jim Crow in American Airlines," and "We Want Negro Stewardesses."[12] The demonstration received some attention in the Cleveland press, but no airlines were opened to black pilots and stewardesses.

Other campaigns brought better results. Early breakthroughs against job discrimination in Sears-Roebuck occurred in Cleveland and San Francisco. In the San Francisco the MCS and the ILWU backed the drive with funds, publicity, and recruits for the picket lines. Later, black women were hired as clerks and cashiers at Sears stores in Saint Louis, Newark, and Los Angeles. But in Chicago, Sears headquarters, it took a year of picketing and a widespread boycott, in which the United Packinghouse Workers lent substantial support, before Sears would capitulate.

In the Chicago Negro Labor Council's campaign to force the Drexel National Bank to hire its first black executive, mass picketing was supplemented by the withdrawal of accounts from the bank by businessmen, churches, and trade unionists. Community pressure finally forced the hiring of a black as assistant service manager of the savings department, and a few other Chicago banks bowed to similar pressure.

In November, 1952, the Greater New York Negro Labor Council began a campaign to end discriminatory hiring and upgrading practices in New York's hotel industry. In a radio broadcast and in leaflets, the council publicized the fact that, of the 14,000 employees hired by the "big sixteen" in the city, only 903, or 6.2 per cent, were black. None was an office worker, and fewer than 3 per cent were dining room workers. Of 800 bartenders in 94 downtown hotels, not one was a Negro. Few blacks were even waiters, a trade they had previously almost monopolized, and even fewer were waitresses and skilled kitchen help.

The Statler and Sherry Netherland hotels were selected as the focus of the campaign; black and white pickets surrounded the hotels, and the managements were flooded with postcards furnished by the council. Early in 1953, the drive received the support of Hugo Ernst, President of the Hotel and Restaurant Employees International Union, AF of L, who notified the council that "our local unions in New York will cooperate to the best of their ability to do away with discrimination wherever, whenever and as fast as possible, for it is one of our cardinal slogans—'no discrimination.'"[13] Blacks might well have asked why the union had done nothing to apply its slogan in dealing with New York's hotels until the Negro Labor Council initiated its campaign, but they welcomed the support nonetheless. The Statler and Sherry Netherland capitulated in the spring of 1953, and other hotels began to hire black waiters and waitresses and to upgrade black maintenance workers.

The most famous of the NNLC's campaigns for black jobs was the one in Louisville known as "Let Freedom Crash the Gateway to the South." A General Electric plant scheduled to open in Appliance Park in 1954 was expected to hire more than 16,000 workers. The Louisville Negro Labor Council and the UE Fair Practices Committee, headed by NNLC Director of Organization Ernest Thompson, began preparations right after the founding convention. They asked craftsmen in UE plants around the country to supply them with the requirements for most of the jobs contemplated for Appliance Park and to map out special courses of training for the different jobs. Then, with the assistance of the local NAACP, the Urban League, and black churches, the Louisville council exerted pressure on the Board of Education to set up day classes for students and night classes for adults in armature-winding, motor-wiring, and other skills in the electrical field. Another notable breakthrough was the agreement won from the Board of Education that courses not offered in the black high school would be made available to blacks in the white school. Thompson wrote later:

> For the first time in American history black workers were prepared when a plant opened. When GE said, "Well, we would hire you, but you're not prepared," they would say, "Wait a minute, Mr. Charlie, hold everything. These workers have been trained in the Louisville public schools according to GE specifications, testified to by our leaders in your plants." The most significant and satisfying aspect of the program was that it resulted in the hiring of Negro women as production workers, not merely maids.[14]

GE was not the only company in Louisville that was forced to change its hiring policy. Westinghouse and Reynolds also gave in to the broad community drive for black employment spearheaded by the Negro Labor Council, and another campaign, in which Local 600 of the UAW joined, compelled the Ford plant in the city to hire black production workers.

The Louisville campaign was actually the opening gun in the NNLC's "Operation Dixie," which aimed to open up factory production jobs to black men and women throughout the South and at the same time "force both the CIO and AF of L to deal with the question of organizing millions of unorganized Negro and white workers in the South."[15] After Louisville, the main areas of the Southern drive were to be Alabama, South Carolina, North Carolina, and Virginia. But Louisville was the only place where the campaign produced results. The council simply did not have the resources to do more in the other states than call attention to the fact that, as new industries moved South, they invariably adopted the rigid Jim Crow practices of the region, so that blacks continued to be excluded from new as well as old manufacturing industries or were employed only in the lowest-paid and most menial jobs.

The NNLC's campaign against discrimination in railroad employment, which the third annual National Negro Labor Council convention, held in Chicago in December, 1953, voted to make its main focus for 1954, fared hardly any better. Here, too, beyond adding to the by now voluminous information on discrimination against blacks in the railroad industry, especially through wide distribution of its pamphlet, "Let Freedom Ride the Rails," little was achieved. The NAACP, church organizations, groups of railroad workers, and the Urban League had all waged the same battle in the courts, before government committees, and at the bar of public opinion, with much the same results.

Without the resources available to these organizations, especially contributions from corporations, as in the case of the Urban League, the
NNLC was continually handicapped in its jobs-for-Negroes campaigns.
It depended primarily on community and local union support, which
was not always easy to obtain, especially as the Red-baiting attacks on
the council increased. But, even where the council did not accomplish
its aims, it helped to call public attention to the crucial issue of job discrimination. Moreover, it initiated struggles on a nationwide scale that
brought some important results immediately and were eventually to
bring others, even after the council had ceased to exist. Even critics of
the NNLC conceded that in a number of communities the efforts of the
national body and the local councils had placed black truck drivers,
streetcar motormen and conductors, hotel workers, bank officials, clerks
and salespeople, and industrial workers, including black women, in jobs
that were formerly lily white.

During the job-for-Negroes campaigns, a number of unions in which
the NNLC had members and sympathizers adopted the council's model
FEPC clause: the International Fur and Leather Workers; the International Mine, Mill, and Smelter Workers; the ILWU; the MCS; and the
United Packinghouse Workers. The UE, the first to adopt the clause,
achieved important gains, largely because of the work of its Fair Practices Committee and the cooperation its national secretary, Ernest
Thompson, received from the top union leadership. The committee
promoted nonwhites and women into leadership positions and developed training programs to prepare workers to advance to higher-paying
jobs. By 1953 the UE had three blacks and two women out of approximately twenty-five members of the National Executive Board, "an
achievement unparalleled by any other union in the country at that
time." The FPC also conducted training courses for women, with
classes on parliamentary procedure, grievances, discriminatory rates,
women's rights, and the history of women in the American labor movement. To overcome male chauvinism among members of the union, the
committee issued pamphlets pointing out the special problems facing
women workers—the need for a government program of day nurseries,
adequate maternity leave, health protection, and training for leadership
in the union—and why all members in their own interest had to join in
helping to solve these problems. In a pamphlet titled "UE Fights for
Women's Rights," the committee singled out the basic economic exploitation of women workers as the key to the oppression of women:

> It is no accident that big business all over the world fought the movement
> for votes and equal rights for women. For in their factories, the public ac-
> ceptance of women's equality would mean the loss of a huge source of
> labor they could segregate and exploit for extra profits, and as a means to
> hold down the wages of all workers.

The pamphlet pointed out the special situation of black women, who
were "barred from almost all jobs except low-paying domestic service in

private homes or menial outside jobs as janitresses and scrubwomen. In the basic sections of the electrical, radio and machine industry, as in industry generally, Negro women are not employed. In lamp plants and others where Negro women have been hired as a source of cheap labor, they suffer the exploitation of women working under discriminatory rates of pay because of their sex."[16]

Headed by a NNLC member, the United Packinghouse Workers' Committee to Abolish Discrimination, published in 1952, a pamphlet entitled "Action Against Jim Crow." The pamphlet emphasized, among other points, the tremendous stake white workers had in the fight for Negro rights. White workers had to see that racial slurs were "bigot-made blades handed to common people to use against each other and so sharp they'll never know they cut each other's throats, until—they try to put their heads together." The pamphlet took issue with union leaders who insisted that the battle for Negro representation in the highest decision-making bodies of their organizations was "Jim Crow in reverse." Mere membership for black workers in a union, it insisted, was no real solution to their problems.[17]

A year later, at the United Packinghouse Workers' first Annual Anti-Discrimination Conference, the union adopted the NNLC's model FEPC clause and set a target date for ridding its industry of discriminatory practices. Four hundred delegates, black and white, from shops in all parts of the country, unanimously resolved "that the UPWA set as a major goal the complete breaking-down by 1954 of all lily-white situations so that every UPWA plant employ minority group members without discrimination."[18] The goal was achieved.

Prodded by the packinghouse workers' action and by the activities of NNLC members in its ranks, the UAW held a fair employment practices conference in the fall of 1953, at which a drive to include a model antidiscrimination clause in all auto contracts was pledged. Unfortunately, not much was done to implement the pledge in subsequent negotiations in the auto industry.

Having made it clear at the outset that the NNLC was not a "dual union" but a potential ally of the trade unions, the council leaders were ready to lend their support to trade unions engaged in struggles in which black workers were involved—if, of course, the union leadership was prepared to accept such cooperation. The Chicago Negro Labor Council aided a strike led by the United Electrical–Farm Equipment Workers (UE–FE) against the International Harvester Company in the fall of 1952. The Chicago council mobilized community support for the strikers and successfully combated the company's efforts to persuade the 17,000 strikers (5,000 of them black) to return to work. It also played an important role in the defense of Harold Ward, black financial secretary of the United Electrical–Farm Equipment Workers and an NNLC member, charged with murdering a strike-breaker. At the 1952 NNLC convention, Ruth Ward told how her husband had long "been a thorn in McCormick's side because he fights for the rank and file," and the delegates voted to intensify the campaign in her husband's behalf.[19] In December, 1952, an all-white jury found Ward "not guilty," a verdict that was hailed in black papers, even those hostile to the NNLC, as a victory for both the labor movement and the black people.

When the International Fur and Leather Workers Union sought NNLC help in its campaign to organize the 15,000 workers in the menhaden-fishing industry (the menhaden is a fish caught mainly to supply oil for tanneries), Negro Labor Councils in Virginia, Florida, and Texas responded. All but 1,000 of the workers were black. The councils helped to rally the black communities, including the churches, behind the strikers.

In June, 1952, Local 266, United Furniture Workers of America, CIO, engaged in a strike against the Thomasville Chair Company in North Carolina (600 of its 1,500 workers were blacks), called on the NNLC for assistance. The council issued appeals to black communities to help the Thomasville strikers, who, black and white, were seeking "to bring to an end the system of poverty, Jim Crow and race hatred which is a halter on the progress of the nation."[20]

The NNLC was also involved in a militant strike of farm laborers on the Louisiana sugar plantations. In the spring of 1953, the AF of L's National Agricultural Workers' Union (NAWU), responding to an appeal from local Catholic priests, began organizing the workers in the sugar-cane fields of Southern Louisiana. (On the average the cane worker earned only from $700 to $1,200 in 1953 to sustain a family of six.) By the end of July, 2,000 had joined up, 80 per cent of them black, and the union tried to get the leading sugar planters to meet with its representatives. But having had a free hand since the organizing drives of the sugar workers under the Knights of Labor were violently crushed in 1887, the sugar barons were in no mood to negotiate an agreement with a union or to grant its modest demands of 75 cents an hour for unskilled workers and one dollar an hour for skilled tractor drivers and harvest-machine operators. Skilled and unskilled alike, the sugar workers, living in plantation housing, often buying in plantation stores, were almost "slaves" of the growers, who had dominated the politics of the parishes for generations.

After a strike vote had authorized a walkout if the employers continued to refuse to bargain, the union wrote to the employers asking for reconsideration. On October 10, 1953, the New Orleans *Times-Picayune* quoted G. J. Durbin, president of the American Sugar Cane League, as saying, "It is my firm conviction that no sugar grower will deal with the union under any circumstances." The league made it official by stating in an advertisement in the *Times-Picayune* that "the entire Louisiana sugar industry and the farmers will not deal with this particular 'union' IN ANY EVENT."[21]

On October 12, the field hands began walking out, and by the next day 1,600 union members, mostly blacks, were out on strike. A week later, the strike involved 2,000 farm laborers on seventy-five plantations. The strikers, facing eviction from company-owned houses, a cutoff of provisions by the company stores, and imported strike-breakers and gunmen, called for help. Along with the national AF of L and the Catholic Church, the NNLC responded, whereupon the American Sugar Cane League charged that the strikers were being helped by a "Communist front organization."[22] Council members in the sugar refineries under contract with the United Packinghouse Workers, CIO, helped organize firm solidarity between the packinghouse workers and the AF of L strikers. The packinghouse workers refused to cross the NAWU's picket lines despite the no-strike clause in their contract with the refineries.

Had the farm laborers been allowed to maintain their picket lines, they might have forced the sugar planters into bargaining. But the Louisiana courts issued sweeping injunctions that not only enjoined the strikers from picketing but also, as H. L. Mitchell, NAMU president, recounted, "prohibited meetings of the Union: prohibited distributions of relief—actually prohibited our attorney from advising us how to fight the injunctions."[23] Under such restrictions, the strikers were compelled to return to work at existing poverty wages.

Despite a record of assistance to unions in a number of key labor struggles, few of the establishment labor leaders were willing to accept NNLC offers of cooperation, and they continued to denounce the council for "dual unionism." Certainly the CIO could have benefited from the experienced and militant black members of the local councils in its "Operation Dixie." But Bittner refused to deal with the councils, and when Walter Reuther was elected CIO President after Philip Murray's death in 1952 the council lost all chances of cooperation with the national CIO on any level.*

William R. Hood, the NNLC president, had been a thorn in Reuther's side as recording secretary of Local 600 even before the National Negro Labor Council was formed. Local 600, with the largest black membership in the union, had long been in the forefront in urging the addition of a black vice-president on the International Executive Board. It had frequently criticized the Reuther leadership for indifference to the upgrading of black auto workers. (For example, although hundreds of tool and die shops operated in the Detroit area, and although the city's technical high schools were graduating a number of qualified blacks each year, not a single shop employed a Negro.) Hood had headed the Detroit Negro Labor Council, and Local 600 had actively supported it, before the national council was formed. The Detroit council fought a mounting battle with the top UAW leadership both before and after the NNLC came into being. In March, 1952, Reuther went so far as to appoint an administrator over Local 600, remove five of its most militant leaders from office, and deprive them of the right ever to run for re-election. The charge, as might be expected, was that they were "members of or subservient to" the Communist Party and were doing "irreparable harm" to the UAW. Two of the five, David Moore and Nelson Davis, were black. Both had been active in the organization of the Ford plant in the great drive of 1941. Moore had been vice-president of the

---

* Reuther liquidated the Southern Organizing Committee soon after he was elected.

Gear and Axle Plant of Local 600 prior to his removal, and Davis had been vice-president of the General Council.

Both had long been involved in fighting for the rights of black members of the UAW, and both were active in the NNLC and the Detroit Negro Labor Council. Defended by the two highest bodies of Local 600, the Executive Board and the General Council, and supported by the membership, the five deposed leaders appealed to the 1953 UAW convention for reinstatement. A joint statement on the eve of the convention by Moore and Davis said:

> If fighting against discriminatory policies of the Ford Motor Company and fighting for the rights of Negro men and women to be promoted to better jobs, if disagreeing with the International Union's lily-white executive board on issues affecting the good and welfare of members of Local 600 and the members of the UAW, constitute "membership or subservience to the Communist Party," then we say make the most of it.[24]

Three other black UAW leaders made statements on the eve of the convention. Hood, who had been investigated by both the House Un-American Committee and Reuther's administration, had refused to give up his office to an overseer appointed by Reuther, and had been overwhelmingly re-elected recording secretary of Local 600—a victory he interpreted as "an expression of support of the NNLC"[25]—urged the convention to have "the political stamina and moral fortitude" to elect a black to the International Executive Board. James Watts, Local 600's FEPC director, who had formerly been on Reuther's side in the issue, urged the convention to "face up to its responsibilities and elect a Negro to one of its vice-presidencies." Layman Walker, recording secretary of UAW Local 742, said:

> It is now a matter of history that where the successful fight has been waged to advance Negro workers, the whole union movement has benefitted and been strengthened. It is unfortunate that the example set by many locals in the matter of Negro participation in top union leadership has not so far been emulated by the International UAW-CIO. This is a fact which offers no credit to our International Union but presents itself as a definite chink in our armor and a weakness in the unity which our union must have in the critical period ahead.[26]

These urgings went for naught. As though nothing had happened since the 1943 convention, Reuther once again insisted that the proposal was fundamentally "racism in reverse," and his automatic majority defeated a resolution calling for the election of a black vice-president to the International Executive Board. Demands from the entire Local 600 delegation for reinstatement of the five members removed from office on the charge of being "subservient" to the Communist Party and for an end to the union's purging of militant members for their political beliefs were also rejected. Reuther made an impassioned attack on the proposal and on the NNLC, which he characterized as a "Communist-dominated, dual unionist organization which has as its sole objective the disruption and wrecking of the American labor movement."[27]

But the proposals defeated at the 1953 UAW Convention were not so easily brushed aside by Red-baiting. Nor did they die with the disappearance of the NNLC. The UAW leadership was to learn soon enough that black unionists were tired of having their grievances ignored.

From its first convention the NNLC had been the object of abuse, and that abuse grew steadily. The council was communistic, its foes declared, its leaders were "Party stooges and hacks," its demands were synonymous with Communism, and its real objective was to cause trouble for the true friends of blacks. In a pamphlet entitled "The American Negro in the Communist Party," issued in December, 1954, the House Committee on Un-American Activities cited, as an example of the council's pro-Communist ideology and its aim to weaken the true friends of black workers, the fact that "it has made charges of Negro discrimination against the United Auto Workers, CIO, which has done much to advance the cause of the Negro worker."[28]

It was inevitable, therefore, that in 1956 the NNLC would be called before the Subversive Activities Control Board to defend itself against being listed as a "Communist-front organization." Had the council not faced insuperable financial problems, it might have been able to make a successful defense, even though in those days hundreds of organizations, including trade unions, were being entered on the list by government fiat.* It would not be accurate to say that there were no Communists on the council or that the Communist press did not publicize its activities and lend it support (although its coverage sometimes conveyed hopes rather than facts). But the Communist Party had declined precipitously since the 1930's. Because of the weaknesses of its branches in 1956, its impecuniousness, and its difficult struggles for survival against government persecution under the Smith Act, the Party was simply not equipped to promote the kind of activities associated with the NNLC, even if the council had been under its domination. At any rate, the NNLC was composed overwhelmingly of black workers who, while opposed to witch-hunting and appreciative of the Communist Party's fight for Negro equality, made their own decisions on the basis of the needs of their people as they knew them from their own experience.

Confronted with defense costs estimated at $100,000, the NNLC leaders voted to dissolve the organization. A former supporter contributed $50 so that Ernest Thompson, then unemployed, might go to the hearing in Washington. He faced the government without a lawyer and told the board that the National Negro Labor Council was no more.

Despite gains scored here and there, the industrial scene in 1955 showed little in the way of improvement of black workers' conditions in the five years of NNLC activity. Although the gap between the annual wages of black families and white families had narrowed somewhat,

* The Subversive Activities Control Board, set up under the McCarren-Kilgore Act of 1950, was empowered to investigate unions seeking collective-bargaining rights and to determine if they were "Communist-dominated" or "Communist-infiltrated," in which case they would be permanently banned by the NLRB unless such a ruling was reversed by a regular federal court. A union was judged to be "Communist-infiltrated" if it had a single Communist Party member.

the annual earnings of black families in 1955 were still only 56 per cent
of white family income. In 1955 as in 1950, when the council was born,
the problems that had led to its birth—job discrimination and racism in
unions—were still unsolved. In 1955, only 7 per cent of all black workers were in skilled crafts as compared with 17 per cent of all white workers. On the railroads, nine out of every ten black workers were in service,
unskilled, and common-labor jobs; in the auto industry, at least 40 per
cent of the foundry workers were blacks and less than 3 per cent were in
the tool and die division; in the steel industry, almost all black workers
were in the eight lowest-paid of some thirty-two classifications. Only a
handful of black workers were employed in textiles, and in tobacco they
were still mainly in the low-paid stemming and drying plants. Six out of
every ten black women workers were in domestic and service jobs, and
only 20 per cent of black women held industrial, sales, and office jobs, as
compared to 59 per cent of white women workers.

To be sure, the picture was far better than it had been twenty years
before. Almost 2 million organized workers—11 per cent of all industrial
workers in the United States—were black. But few could be said to enjoy first-class membership. In the national CIO and in most of its international affiliates, blacks were still not included among the top national
officers or on policy-making executive boards. The situation in the AF
of L and its affiliates on this score was far worse. Although the number
of unions that practiced exclusion and segregation of blacks had diminished considerably, there were still powerful bodies, such as the AF of L
building trades unions and the railroad brotherhoods, that persisted in
barring blacks from membership or in maintaining Jim Crow locals.

Yet there was a distinct feeling among the NNLC leaders that "a new
wind was blowing in the labor movement, a good wind,"[29] and that the
council's position on many issues was gaining support even among the
entrenched labor leadership. The announcement of the merger of the AF
of L and CIO gave rise to hopes for a real breakthrough on some of the issues. Although black workers had long since learned to discount promises
from the big unions, there was an element in the statement of the AF
of L president on the eve of the merger that could not be lightly
dismissed. George Meany, who had become president upon William
Green's death in 1952, declared that

> the person who is unorganized because of a racial bar or discrimination of
> any kind is a threat to the conditions of those who are organized. Anyone
> who is underpaid, who has substandard conditions, threatens the situation
> of those in unions. . . . The merger would mean more effective means to
> attain a fair employment practices bill on a national scale, and in attempts
> to assure civil rights in other fields.[30]

Meany's statement was itself the product of changes in the labor
movement since the NNLC's birth. Partly it stemmed from the fact that
both the AF of L and the CIO had encountered increasing opposition
from employers and government—federal, state, and municipal antilabor
legislation was increasing rapidly—and resistance to organizing efforts by

unorganized firms was facing unions on every front. Labor leaders were beginning to understand NNLC President Hood's point that failure to form an effective alliance with the black working class "projects labor into its battle for life with an arm tied behind its back."[31] Some were even beginning to have doubt about the wisdom of labor's collaboration in the anti-Communist crusades with the very forces opposing it. They saw that by contributing to anti-Communist hysteria the unions had helped to create a set of circumstances that could easily be turned against them when they sought to launch new organizing drives. At the triennial convention of the Brotherhood of Sleeping Car Porters in Los Angeles in September, 1953, this argument helped in persuading the delegates to adopt a strong denunciation of McCarthyism.

Any consideration of the "new wind" in the labor movement must take into account the pressure of rank-and-file union members, shop fair employment committees, local antidiscrimination bodies, and the initiative of the black workers themselves in pushing the labor leadership to enter the fight for racial equality with some of the vigor that had characterized the early CIO. Some credit for the black initiative belongs to the National Urban League, which began a new campaign in 1953 for integration of blacks in industry, protection of the job security of blacks already in production jobs, and admission of blacks into many unions that still had limited black membership. Credit too belongs to the NAACP, which after 1954 began to apply pressure on the unions to join actively in its crusade for "freedom by '63." Twenty trade unions, both AF of L and CIO, sent fraternal delegates to the 1955 NAACP convention, and Herbert Hill, the association's labor secretary, announced that the union fraternal delegates would "participate in a discussion of organized labor and the NAACP, as well as a workshop panel on eliminating discrimination in the training and employment of Negro workers."[32] But much of the credit must go to the National Negro Labor Council. Despite all efforts to defame it, the Council was a prod to the established black organizations and to the labor leadership, forcing both to pay more attention to the key issue of eliminating racial discrimination in industry and organized labor.

Most studies of the so-called black revolution contend that it all began with the Supreme Court decision of May 17, 1954, declaring that "in the field of public education the doctrine of 'separate but equal' has no place. Separate educational facilities are inherently unequal." Others argue that it started in 1956 with the Montgomery bus boycott, led by Dr. Martin Luther King, Jr. Still others insist that it really began with World War II. Now and then there have been references to the activities of the Congress of Racial Equality in the early 1950's—sit-ins, freedom rides, and the like. No published studies, so far as I know, have pointed out that between 1950 and 1955 an organization manned and led predominantly by black workers was engaged in a struggle not only for the civil rights of the black people and an end to segregation but also for jobs for blacks and an end to racism in industry and organized labor. This was the National Negro Labor Council.[33]

21 The AFL-CIO and the Black Worker: The First Five Years

Walter Reuther listed four principles that the CIO would insist upon during merger negotiations with the AF of L. One was that all unions must enlist members without regard to race or color. But just what this meant was not made clear. Declarations of opposition to racial discrimination had been issued by the AF of L repeatedly since its formation, but the federation had only rarely expressed open condemnation of discriminatory policies and practices by affiliates, and it had not acted against an affiliate for discrimination since the 1890's. Moreover, the CIO's own Committee on Civil Rights had refused even to recommend disciplining affiliates that practiced discrimination.

It is not surprising, therefore, that black workers were unimpressed by Reuther's rhetoric. Randolph wrote in *The Black Worker* that the negotiating committee for the merger should make sure to provide in the new federation's constitution for sanctions against unions that practiced racial discrimination. However, Randolph was at first satisfied by the Merger Agreement's statement that the new federation "shall constitutionally recognize the rights of all workers without regard to race, creed or national origin to share in the full benefits of trade union organization in the merged federation. The merged federation shall establish appropriate internal machinery to bring about, at the earliest possible date, the effective implementation of this principle of non-discrimination."[1] Indeed, this provision so elated the CIO Committee on Civil Rights that its chairman, James B. Carey, and its black members joined in hailing it as even stronger on the question of racial discrimination than the CIO's own constitution. Carey proclaimed enthusiastically at the CIO merger convention: "The language is so clear, so forthright on the score that it banishes at once any qualms or misgivings that even the most timid could hold."[2]

But it did not banish the misgivings of the black press or of Michael J. Quill, a CIO vice-president and president of the Transport Workers Union. Quill criticized the statement as "weak and vague" rather than "clear and forthright." It was actually, he charged, a watered-down version of the position the CIO had originally advanced in the merger discussion. Quill urged delegates not to vote in favor of merger unless the statement was supplemented by an explicit guarantee of the timing of the "establishment of appropriate internal machinery" to effect non-discrimination. Reuther, on the other hand, echoed the position of the Civil Rights Committee. David McDonald, president of the United Steelworkers, said: "I defy anybody to write a stronger section on the subject of civil rights. These are not just words, these will be deeds."[3] Such assurances carried more weight than Quill's reservations, and the convention followed the lead of the AF of L in voting for the merger.

The black press and black union leaders welcomed the merger as "of great value and importance to the Negro workers" but took notice of Quill's arguments and cautioned vigilance. An editorial in the Oklahoma *Black Dispatch* on March 15, 1955, declared: "A unified labor will still need to be prodded to the recognition of the necessity of cleaning its house entirely of the virus of racial discrimination." The *Chicago Defender* was concerned that the AF of L, whose membership had soared in the ten years following World War II while the CIO's had declined, would dominate the merged federation, and it expressed the hope that "the CIO pattern regarding equal rights will be retained." Charles Hayes, director of District 1, United Packinghouse Workers, CIO, commented: "The Negro cannot sit back and feel secure that in the merger all his problems will be solved. . . . The Negro worker must become a union member and an active one." Even Willard Townsend declared that a "stronger and more alert Negro leadership" was essential if the merger was to mean anything to the 2 million organized black workers and the still greater numbers of unorganized workers.

The sharpest criticism, however, came from the National Negro Labor Council. In "An Open Letter to the AFL and CIO," it pointed out that "to encourage all workers regardless of race, creed, etc. 'to share in the full benefits of union organization' is a good deal short of, and different from, an ironclad constitution provision that all workers are to be guaranteed *full and equal membership in the new federation* and full and equal participation *in all union organizations and activities*." The open letter, of which many thousands of copies were distributed, concluded:

> The National Negro Labor Council publicly calls upon the leadership of the AFL and the CIO to correct the grievous error of their current constitutional provisions on the question of equal membership rights. In the highest interest of all the workers of America, white and Negro alike, we urge labor to stand fast by its highest concepts of democracy, to provide in their new constitution for an end to "lily-white" unions, and Negro auxiliaries, for an end to "second-class citizenship" in the labor movement, to guarantee Negro leadership on all union levels, and for the full support of the labor movement to the Negro people's fight for freedom and equality.[4]

It soon became clear, even to those who had hailed the provisions in the Merger Agreement, that there was little assurance that they would be backed by deeds. Speaking for the NAACP at a meeting of District 65 of the Retail, Wholesale, and Department Store Clerks Union (successor to the Distributive, Processing, and Office Workers Union), Dr.

Channing Tobias praised the merger but called upon the new organization to establish a firm policy against segregated locals, auxiliary colored locals, "lily-white" clauses in union constitutions, and wage differentials based on race in collective bargaining agreements. Randolph, too, had second thoughts about the Merger Agreement and advanced a series of proposals in *The Black Worker* designed to strengthen the new organization in the fight to eliminate discrimination, including the demand that it deny affiliation to unions that practiced racial or other discrimination. George Meany was at least frank when he told the press that "Randolph's request . . . is not likely to be granted."[5]

Randolph's response in the August, 1955, issue of *The Black Worker* summed up the attitude of black labor as the merger moved into its final stage. "The fight has just begun," he wrote. In Detroit a group of black trade unionists met and resolved to form a caucus to influence the final conventions of the AF of L and the CIO and the founding convention of the merged federation, scheduled to meet on December 5, 1955. The movement spread throughout Michigan, then through the Midwest, and, just before the December meeting, emerged as the Negro Trade Unionists Committee (NTUC). The committee issued a statement that appealed to the AF of L to "clear its house of remaining undemocratic, divisive, discriminating policies and practices" before entering the new federation.[6] Next, the NTUC called for a clear provision in the new federation's constitution guaranteeing equal rights and nonsegregation; Negro representation in the executive council; a campaign to organize the South on a nonsegregated basis; strong and adequately financed Fair Employment Practices Committees with authority to act effectively; and the expulsion of any union failing to eliminate discrimination after a fixed time limit.

At the founding convention itself, the small number of black delegates present tried to get these demands adopted. But they were successful only in achieving the election of two blacks among the twenty-seven vice-presidents named to the AFL-CIO Council—A. Philip Randolph and Willard S. Townsend. Another victory for the black delegates was said to be the appointment of James B. Carey as chairman of the AFL-CIO Committee on Civil Rights, but that could be interpreted as a doubtful triumph. As chairman of the CIO equal rights committee, Carey had not only opposed the expulsion of affiliates practicing discrimination but had even come out against publicizing their practices. Moreover, he had already expressed the view that the provision against discrimination in the Merger Agreement was so "clear" and "forthright" that it practically took care of the problem by itself.

The AFL-CIO constitution did indeed include the same language as the provision of the Merger Agreement. Article II stated that one of the objects of the federation was "to encourage all workers, without regard to race, creed, color, national origin or ancestry, to share equally in the full benefits of union organization." Article XIII, Section 1(b), directed the president to appoint a Committee on Civil Rights to be "vested with the duty and responsibility to assist the Executive Council to bring about at the earliest possible date the effective implementation of the principle stated in this Constitution of non-discrimination in accordance with the provisions of this Constitution." If those provisions met Carey's definition of "clear, forthright" language, then the words had lost their meaning. Indeed, defenders of the constitution found it necessary to explain to skeptics how the demand for the expulsion of any affiliate failing to eliminate discrimination after a fixed time limit was implied by the document. It was argued that the words "to share equally in the full benefits of union organization" meant that all affiliates adopting the Constitution would be compelled to end discrimination against black workers, including separate local unions, federal locals, and local councils made up of black workers exclusively. Moreover, the constitution assured implementation of the antidiscrimination policy even if it did not spell out the methods. A future Supreme Court Justice, Arthur J. Goldberg, a key figure in the negotiations leading to the merger, explained soon after the founding convention that the constitution embodied a code of "fair union practices" that affiliated unions committed themselves to uphold *and might not violate without facing expulsion from the merged federation.* "The autonomous rights of international unions within the federation," he wrote, "do not extend to the right of a union to be dominated by communists or controlled by racketeers, to impair the integrity of any other affiliate, or to discriminate against members or potential members on grounds of race, color or creed."[7]

Goldberg's tortured reasoning was quickly pointed out by a number of black commentators. Article VIII of the constitution, they noted, specifically empowered the Executive Council, after determining that an affiliate was "dominated, controlled or influenced in the conduct of its affairs" by "any and all corrupt influences and . . . undermining efforts of communist, fascist or other totalitarian agencies," to expel the affiliate, but the constitution gave no such authority to the council over affiliates that practiced racial discrimination. Their criticism of Goldberg's interpretation was reiterated in 1968 by Gus Tyler, ILGWU assistant president and a leading Socialist theoretician on labor. There appeared to be something "hypocritical," even inconsistent, in the AFL-CIO policy of quickly expelling affiliates "tainted by communism or 'corruption' " while remaining "most reluctant to expel national affiliates that are out of step with the Federation's policy on civil rights," Tyler argued. But he concurred with Meany's view that there was a "big difference" between unions "controlled by communists or crooks and those infected by racism." Communists and crooks are part of "an aggressive conspiracy with inner lines of communication" and, unless eliminated, "could threaten the very character of the total labor movement." But the segregationists in the labor movement "have no inner ties, no separate power structure," and hence pose no real threat to the house of labor. "At worst, the segregationists are vanishing relics, an annoying cultural lag."[8] Hence the AFL-CIO constitution reflected less urgency about expelling those "relics" than about dealing with Communists and crooks.

So much for Goldberg's assurance that there was no distinction in the constitutional power of the Executive Council to act against affiliates dominated by Communists and racketeers and against ones that discriminated against members or potential members. Had the Executive Council wanted to suspend or expel any affiliate for discriminatory practices, it could have based its action on Section 2 of Article VIII, which authorized it to "enforce the provisions contained in the Constitution . . . and to take such actions and to render such decisions [between conventions] as are necessary and appropriate to safeguard and promote the best interests of the Federation and its affiliated unions." But it is clear that the men who consummated the merger did not consider discriminatory practices by affiliates a highly objectionable wrong, like Communism.[9]

The AFL-CIO won respect in the black community early in its career, when the Executive Council called on President Eisenhower to comply with the Supreme Court's decision on school desegregation and deny school-construction funds to any state that defied the ruling. But it antagonized the community by remaining silent and refusing to join with the black people in their national Day of Prayer, March 28, 1956,* and by remaining completely aloof during the great Montgomery bus boycott in 1956. The boycott began when Mrs. Rosa Parks, a black woman, was arrested for refusing to give up her seat to a white passenger. In response, the whole black community, 40,000 strong, staged what one observer called "perhaps the greatest strike in the history of this country." For better than a year, they refused to patronize the city bus system until it was integrated. The courageous and militant blacks faced intimidation and repression, and the movement, led by Dr. Martin Luther King, Jr., was in constant need of funds and moral support. But the AFL-CIO gave neither. Only the Brotherhood of Sleeping Car Porters—the president of whose Montgomery local was a principal strategist of the boycott—the United Packinghouse Workers, District 65; Local 1199 in New York City, a small union of mainly Jewish drugstore clerks; and several locals of the UAW contributed to the boycott. (In the case of District 65 and Local 1199, the contributions came not from the union funds but from gifts solicited from the membership.) A white Southern writer on the staff of an AFL-CIO union criticized (under a pen name) the Executive Council and nearly all of the affiliated unions for having "defaulted" in the hour of the black people's greatest need.[10] No rebuke was forthcoming from the Executive Council when it was disclosed that on several occasions during the year-long bus boycott the Montgomery Building Trades Council and the Montgomery Bus Drivers Union had been involved in Ku Klux Klan attacks on the black community.

In 1957, Dr. King told a convention of the United Packinghouse Workers Union (from which he received a $11,000 check for the voter-registration campaign in the South conducted by the Southern Chris-

* The Day of Prayer was organized to render support to the struggles of Negroes in the South against segregation.

tian Leadership Conference) that "organized labor can be one of the most powerful instruments in putting an end to discrimination and segregation."[11] But the AFL-CIO leadership was not interested in assuming that role. Dramatic conflicts involving the Negro people's struggle for freedom broke out that year in Little Rock, Arkansas; Front Royal, Virginia; Tuscaloosa, Alabama; and other parts of the South. Once again the AFL-CIO "defaulted." The Executive Council passed a resolution approving President Eisenhower's sending of federal troops to Little Rock to guarantee the right of black children to enter Central High School, but it did little else to aid the embattled blacks.

The reason is not difficult to understand. The activities of the White Citizens' Councils and other segregationist groups in the South following the 1954 Supreme Court decision alarmed the leaders of many AFL-CIO affiliates, as it did the Executive Council, and made them extremely hesitant to be identified with the more militant struggles of the Negro people. When the Chattanooga Central Labor Union adopted a resolution on July 25, 1955, commending the local school board's plan to comply with the Supreme Court's decision, it came under sharp attack from union racists, egged on by the Ku Klux Klan and the White Citizens' Councils. Nine locals publicly disavowed the resolution, and several withdrew from the organization. The attacks included the charge that the Chattanooga Central Labor Union was headed by "alien Communist lovers" and was partly responsible "for the disgusting integration of Negro and white workers in the labor movement in Tennessee." The central union retreated, rescinded the resolution, and issued a statement that it would "henceforth refrain from involving itself on either side of this issue."[12]

Several attempts were made in 1956 to form Southern Klan-oriented labor organizations comprising members of AFL-CIO affiliates who opposed all efforts to "force integration upon the South." A few such organizations sought to work within the existing unions to make certain that they came out for segregationist policies. The organizations had in common a hatred of the NAACP, which they denounced as "Communist-influenced and dedicated to destroying our Southern civilization."[13] Because of inept leadership and the reluctance of even anti-Negro white workers to lose gains achieved by the unions, and despite employer financing, none of the Klan-unionist organizations achieved any success. Their threats to destroy existing locals through raids generally fizzled. But they did succeed in sending a scare wave through the union leadership of many AFL-CIO affiliates and forcing them and the Executive Council to maintain a stony silence throughout 1956 on events in the South. The federation's do-nothing policy made it easier for the White Citizens' Councils and the Ku Klux Klan to recruit extensively among white union members. Council and Klan forces, especially in Alabama and Mississippi, succeeded in moving in on many local unions "and made them, in effect, virtual extensions of segregationist organizations."[14]

The AFL-CIO might have launched an educational campaign to counter the segregationist propaganda flooding union halls in the South.

But it did not, and the educational programs carried on by most affiliates were concerned mainly with negotiations, grievance procedures, or in-tra-union policies. "Racial matters get a real soft-pedal," a Southern AFL-CIO official conceded, "becoming inaudible the further South you go."[15] Ray Marshall found that "many union educational directors [in the South] are afraid to discuss racial matters."[16] The Klan and the White Citizens' Councils, on the other hand, had no hesitation about discussing racial matters in the union halls from the most vicious seg-regationist point of view, without fear of being challenged.

While Southern white workers were not prepared, in most cases, to abandon unions accused of having antisegregationist racial policies, they either ignored the policies or altered them to suit the segregationists, usually without fear of disciplinary action from the national union lead-ership or the Southern representatives of the union. The most backward, pro-segregationist elements in affiliates of the AFL-CIO set the policies of the organization in the South. Union leaders feared that opposition to those elements would impede organizing efforts and alienate Southern members. As Carl Braden put it in 1957, after considerable experience in the South:

> [The trade union leaders] find it hard to believe that great strength will re-sult from unity of white and Negro workers. They are captives of the fears and prejudices of their members, and in some cases of their own back-wardness as well. They are falling right into the trap set for them by the new industrialists moving into the South.
>
> Some trade unions in the South are working hard to break down the myths that divide the people, but too many are afraid to speak out openly on this question. They fear to offend the prejudices of their more ignorant dues payers. As a result they hobble along when they could easily run.[17]

It is worth stressing that a forthright effort by the AFL-CIO to achieve racial equality in the South would probably not have had the catas-trophic results so many national union leaders and their Southern rep-resentatives feared. Although a few unions—the UAW, the United Packinghouse Workers, the letter carriers, and the American Federation of Teachers—lost some locals in the South because of their insistence on integration, the departed members often returned to the fold when they learned that the unions would not be intimidated into abandoning their policies.

A widely publicized incident occurred in 1957, when the International Union of Electrical, Radio, and Machine Workers (now the UE) was conducting an organizing campaign at the Vickers plant in Jackson, Mississippi, prior to an NLRB election. The owners of the company raised the cry that the UE was a "nigger-loving union" and that James Carey, the union president, was a "nigger-lover." As proof they distrib-uted copies of the *Jackson Daily News* showing Carey dancing with a black woman. The picture had been taken at a session of the Interna-tional Labor Organization in Geneva. Carey's dancing partner was a Nigerian delegate. The company warned the workers that they too would have to dance with black women if the UE won the election. But the union scored a victory. At the NAACP convention in 1957, Roy Wilkins, executive secretary, cited the experience at Vickers as evidence that racial issues could be overcome by effective education. He pointed out that a decisive argument used by the union was that wages in the Vickers plant in Indiana, where there was a union, were $2.12 an hour, while in Jackson, without a union, they were $1.26 an hour.

Ray Marshall concludes that, contrary to the common belief, equalitarian union policies "have not been important impediments to union organization in the South":

> Indeed, on balance it can probably be demonstrated that a forthright equalitarian racial position will cause the unions to gain more than they lose. For example, a Georgia teamsters' official whose local grew from 1,500 to 9,000 members between 1952 and 1964 listed the three main reasons: "First, we have plenty of free advertising. . . . Secondly . . . our union does not equivocate or pussyfoot on the race question. On the job and in the hall all members are union brothers. . . . Thirdly, we work harder."
>
> If the election is otherwise close, the race issue might be important, but workers who have become convinced that it is to their advantage to join unions will probably pay little attention to the issue. We noted that Negroes frequently constituted the balance of power throwing elections to unions.[18]

Despite this evidence to the contrary, most union leaders feared repercussions and avoided adopting a stand clearly in favor of equalitarian racial principles. The result was to alienate the black workers in the South from the new merged federation. It was scarcely surprising that blacks were not enthusiastic supporters of an organization whose local union halls in many parts of the South were also the meeting places of the Klan or the Citizens' Councils. Nor is it surprising that, in a number of key union certification elections in the South conducted by the NLRB where Negroes held the balance of power, blacks voted against the unions and accounted for the loss of elections. In general, it was the opinion of most observers that less than two years after the merger, blacks in the South were giving less support to unions than formerly, and that the unwillingness of the national AFL-CIO leadership and many of the affiliated unions to take a strong stand in favor of equalitarian racial policies was largely responsible for this.

With segregationist sentiment running high in the South, the AFL-CIO Executive Council backed away from the Southern organizing drive it had been expected to launch immediately after the merger. A successful drive, it was argued, would have to involve black workers on an integrated basis, and this would further alienate the Citizens' Councils and other segregationist groups. The decision was then made to assist international unions like the United Textile Workers Union and the Tobacco Workers International Union in their organizing campaigns, and if that succeeded to move ahead into other industries. But this effort produced few results, partly because of the contradictory policy in organizing whites and blacks.* The United Textile Workers launched

---

* The two unions had a long history of raiding each other, which had already used up much of their money and organizing strength. Their refusal to cease the practice during the Southern organizing drive was another reason for the meager results.

its campaign to organize 650,000 textile workers in the South by adopting a resolution urging "peaceful and orderly transition to an unsegregated school system" and denouncing the White Citizens' Councils as "enemies of law and order."[19] But black workers were not persuaded to rally to the union's support, because the union refused to take a stand in favor of employment of blacks as production workers in the mills, where they held mainly janitorial or other menial jobs. The Tobacco Workers International Union, for its part, had long ago alienated black workers by its policy of organizing blacks into separate units, signing agreements that discriminated against them in promotions and layoffs, and consistently backing away from efforts to desegregate plant facilities such as restrooms, water fountains, locker rooms, and cafeterias.

A successful Southern campaign would also have meant applying pressure on some AFL-CIO affiliates, especially those on the railroads and in the building trades, to organize their jurisdictions fully. Left to themselves they declined to do so, because it would have required them to accept black members. The Executive Council ignored the question.

To Michael Quill the collapse of the pre-merger expectations of a vast membership in the South came as no surprise. On August 11, 1957, he told the delegates to the New York State CIO convention, meeting to merge with the State Federation of Labor, that the failure to adopt a clear-cut, enforceable antidiscrimination policy in the AFL-CIO constitution, or even to implement what was adopted, had so antagonized black workers and the black community that no real growth of unionism in the South could be expected until the whole approach was reversed. "Since merger did we grow in the South?" Quill asked. "No. Who did? The Klansmen and the White Citizens' Council."[20] He asked why the national AFL-CIO could enact a code calling for the expulsion of union officers who invoked the Fifth Amendment—a code that he personally opposed—but could not establish one for the expulsion of union officers who were members of the Klan or the White Citizens' Councils.

Quill was sharply rebuked by several delegates for looking only at the negative side of the picture in the South. They reminded him of a survey made in that very year, 1957, which found that two-thirds of all local unions in the South were biracial, a substantial number of the biracial locals had at least one black officer, and approximately half had at least one Negro shop steward. All this indicated that there had been an extraordinary degree of progress toward integration under the leadership of AFL-CIO affiliates.

The facts were correct but had a misleading appearance. The unions generally accepted the racial patterns prevailing in a plant or industry, and in most Southern factories, including those that had only recently moved south from the North, the practice was to employ white workers in production jobs and blacks as janitors or in other unskilled and inferior capacities. Consequently, when the union organized all the workers in the plant in one local, both the majority of white production workers and the small number of Negroes in menial jobs were included.

The local could thus be listed as biracial or integrated, but for the black workers it left much to be desired. Local 12 of the United Rubber Workers of America, AFL-CIO, at the Goodyear Tire and Rubber Company plant in Gadsden, Alabama, had black members, but the local refused to process their grievances because, the NLRB reported, "they were filed by Negroes."[*21] It ignored appeals from black members to urge Goodyear to desegregate company facilities, such as restaurants, a cafeteria, and the company golf course, and it rebuffed their request to be paid for a period during which they were laid off while white workers with less seniority continued to work. Yet Local 12 was cited by the AFL-CIO as evidence that since the merger integrated unionism had advanced among affiliates in the South. "What we have in the South," one AFL-CIO official candidly admitted, "is segregation within the framework of integration."[22]

While blacks in the South were battling to break down the walls of segregation, a struggle was taking place in the nation's capital for the enactment of civil-rights legislation. Between 1953 and 1957, the House of Representatives had passed civil-rights bills several times, but none had ever come to a vote in the Senate, mainly because of filibustering tactics by a coalition of Southern Democrats and reactionary Republicans. On the eve of the merger in 1955, several CIO unions, most notably the United Packinghouse Workers and the UAW, had joined with black organizations to demand passage of a civil rights law "during the next session of Congress." In order to stave off a filibuster in the Senate, the founding convention of the AFL-CIO went on record as "strongly supporting" a change in Rule 22 "to permit a majority of Senators present and voting to limit and close debate" instead of the two-thirds of the total number of ninety-six, as was then required.[23] After the merger, the *AFL-CIO News* carried frequent reports of resolutions adopted by affiliated unions urging a curb on filibustering, specifically a change in Rule 22.

By the spring of 1957, the civil-rights action was helping to build a Negro-labor alliance, but it received a sharp setback when the AFL-CIO refused to endorse the Prayer Pilgrimage for Freedom, called by a group of black leaders headed by Martin Luther King, Jr., to be held in Washington, D.C., on May 17, 1967, to rally the nation's conscience for a meaningful civil-rights law. As might be expected, the packinghouse workers and UAW locals, District 65, and IUE sent members by car, train, and bus to Washington. But most AFL-CIO unions ignored the event, and trade unionists were conspicuous by their absence in the crowd of "Pilgrims," estimated at 27,000. Of the thirty people, mostly

---

* On December 18, 1964, the NLRB by a 3-to-2 decision ordered Local 12 to propose in its contract provisions prohibiting discrimination in terms and conditions of employment, and further to bargain in good faith to obtain them. The action, the first of this nature by the board, followed charges filed with the board in 1962 by eight black members of the local, aided by Robert L. Carter, general counsel for the NAACP. In its decision, the board noted that the local had a long history of "invalid interpretations of contracts" in a racially discriminatory way and a "continuing resistance to its duty of fair representation." *New York Times*, December 19, 1964.

religious and political figures, who sat on the platform before the Lincoln Memorial, the only trade-union leader was A. Philip Randolph, the meeting's chairman. Randolph criticized the AFL-CIO leadership and the leaders of many of the affiliated unions for their failure to understand labor's stake in the Pilgrimage and to realize sufficiently that the Negro people of the South, given the free vote and a right to be elected freely to legislatures and Congress, could become a decisive factor for repeal of "right-to-work" laws as well as for many other objectives of labor.

The 1957 Civil Rights Act, the first since 1875, shorn of the important feature empowering the attorney general to seek injunctive relief in the federal courts for persons whose constitutional rights had been violated, finally became law.* The AFL-CIO Executive Council expressed disappointment that "a meaningful civil rights bill" had not been enacted and pledged that "the AFL-CIO will continue, in the years ahead, to press for continued improvements until we reach the day when full civil rights are guaranteed for all our citizens."[24] The statement was widely published in the black press, and readers wrote in to ask if the "full civil rights" referred to by the Executive Council included rights as workers, whether the council was also willing to pledge a fight against discrimination within the AFL-CIO itself until the "full rights" of its black membership were guaranteed. What provoked such letters was a dismaying item of union news: At the very time the AFL-CIO Executive Council was making its pledge, it admitted the Brotherhood of Locomotive Firemen and Enginemen and the Brotherhood of Railway Trainmen to the merged federation, even though both still retained racial barriers in their constitutions. Reuther and Carey, to the chagrin of the Negro press, which had been hailing them as "true friends of the Negro people," joined with former CIO leaders on the Executive Council to admit the two champions of racism to the labor movement. To his credit, A. Philip Randolph recorded the sole dissenting vote.

It was indeed ironic that a union headed by a member of the AFL-CIO Civil Rights Committee and a federation vice-president, George M. Harrison, President of the Brotherhood of Railway Clerks, had to be told by the Supreme Court of the United States that it must represent all workers without discrimination. The brotherhood for decades had refused to admit Negroes, had evaded court orders against its discriminatory practices, or had formed "auxiliary units" for black members, and it continued to do so while its president served on the AFL-CIO Civil Rights Committee. In reading the Supreme Court's opinion, Justice Hugo Black stated that under the Railroad Labor Act a "bargaining

---

* The law authorized the federal government to bring civil suits in its own name to obtain injunctive relief in federal courts where any person sued because he was denied or threatened in his right to vote; elevated the Civil Rights Section of the Department of Justice to the status of a Division; and created the Commission on Civil Rights, with authority, among other duties, to investigate allegations of denials of the right to vote. The fact that the government had to wait for a suit seriously weakened the law.

unit is . . . obligated to represent all employes in the bargaining unit fairly and without discrimination because of race."[25]

With men like George M. Harrison on the AFL-CIO Civil Rights Committee, it is not difficult to understand why Victor Daly, Minority Group Consultant with the U.S. Employment Service called the committee "simply a waste of time."[26] The committee's main function after the merger was trying to persuade Cleveland and Milwaukee locals of the International Brotherhood of Electrical Workers and the Washington, D.C., local of the Bricklayers, Masons, and Plasterers Union to admit black applicants to membership. (The Washington local of the bricklayers would not even permit blacks to work on construction of the AFL-CIO headquarters in the nation's capital.) The committee succeeded in getting the Cleveland local to admit three black electricians, but only after months of argument and a threat by Meany to lift the local's charter. Endless meetings and wranglings before state commissions and before the AFL-CIO Civil Rights Committee were necessary before the Milwaukee local would admit four black electricians. The bricklayers' local in Washington simply ignored all requests that it discontinue its practices of racial discrimination, and there was nothing the Civil Rights Committee could do about it. Finally, in the summer of 1957, chairman James B. Carey and George L. P. Weaver, a black member, quit the Civil Rights Committee out of frustration.

A clear example of the contrast between words and deeds that was becoming characteristic of AFL-CIO policy on racial discrimination was the situation in the United Steelworkers. In the lead article in the January 23, 1957, issue of the AFL-CIO quarterly *Industrial Union Digest*, President David McDonald of the United Steelworkers told what the steel workers had learned: that the fight for civil rights could not "begin in the morning when a man enters the factory gate and end when he leaves at night. . . . The fight for freedom and equality must proceed simultaneously at all levels of our lives, since freedom itself is indivisible." The steel union, McDonald continued, had a fully integrated membership and would not sign an agreement permitting discrimination against any members. It was proud of its participation in official and private groups dedicated to ending discrimination. While there were still problems to be solved, McDonald concluded, the important thing was "that we recognize our problems and we are working actively to overcome any difficulties we may have."

There was no mention in McDonald's article or anywhere else in the AFL-CIO publication of a current situation in the Homestead, Pennsylvania, local of the United Steelworkers. Black members were complaining of discrimination in the local and of a definite union policy of keeping black workers in the labor pool of the three lowest of the thirty-two wage classifications. The January 19, 1957, issue of the Pittsburgh *Courier*, a black paper, carried the text of a resolution drawn up by the black workers in the giant Homestead mill of the U.S. Steel Corporation, who charged: "Whereas white workers have moved from labor gangs into electrical and machine shop departments with as little as one year's service, Negroes have been forced to remain in the labor gang with as much as 14 and 15 years' seniority."

The *Courier* also carried the news that black steel workers in the Pittsburgh area had formed an organization called the Fair Share Group of Steel Workers. They had announced their intention "to get their fair share of jobs and benefits" as members of the union and had written to McDonald and George Meany to complain of "the neglect of the Negro's problems and conditions throughout the industry. All we ask for is a fair share. Are we asking too much? In brief, we are tired of promises, and we want some concrete action." The *Courier* reported that the Fair Share Group was establishing similar groups in other locals of the steel union with black membership and was in contact with black auto workers who were beginning to air the same grievances in their union through the Trade Union Leadership Council, formed by a group of black unionists. None of these activities received attention in the white newspapers.

The protests of black unionists were, however, gaining listeners at the headquarters of the NAACP. The association enjoyed great prestige in the Negro community because of its role in the Supreme Court school desegregation decision of 1954—Thurgood Marshall, the NAACP counsel, had argued the school cases all the way to victory—but black workers still regarded it as a "black bourgeois" organization. In order to counteract their image of it, the NAACP was beginning to act on the complaints of black members of the AFL-CIO.

The NAACP announced six months after the merger that it would begin concentrating on the problems of Negro labor. Unless black wage-earners could improve their economic situation by overcoming job discrimination, it said, a civil-rights victory in Congress would be a "meaningless sham." It was prepared to give the new federation time to deal effectively with the problem. At the forty-seventh annual convention in June, 1956, Herbert Hill, the NAACP labor secretary, urged local branches to cooperate with the AFL-CIO's Civil Rights Committee to combat "anti-Negro employers" who practiced discrimination openly. It was the job of each branch, Hill advised, "to help the Negro worker to become more involved in the life and work of his union." He warned, too, that the use of black strike-breakers against the new federation, if successful, would weaken the Negro-labor political alliance that was essential to the struggle for civil-rights legislation. "The NAACP branch has the fundamental responsibility as a fundamental spokesman for Negro workers to keep Negro workers out of struck plants."[27]

At the forty-eighth NAACP convention, held in Detroit in June, 1957, Walter Reuther delivered a major address on "The International and Constitutional Implications of the Desegregation Crisis." Nothing at the convention indicated that relations between the NAACP and the AFL-CIO were anything but cordial. But a year later the association made it clear that its patience with the AFL-CIO on the issue of black labor was near exhaustion. Speaking at the convention of the United Packinghouse Workers in New York on May 21, 1958, Roy Wilkins, the NAACP executive secretary, praised the union's antidiscrimination fight in the South as well as the North and its success in combining the struggle for the civil rights of the Negro people with the battle against discrimination in its local unions and in the plants. But what made headlines the next day was Wilkins's attack on the AFL-CIO on two counts: (1) for admitting the two railroad brotherhoods—the trainmen and the firemen and enginemen—whose constitutions excluded blacks from membership, and (2) for permitting discrimination in varying degrees in locals of the steel, paper, and oil-chemical unions. "There are some unions," Wilkins observed sharply, "that pass resolutions for civil rights, hold conferences on civil rights, show movies on civil rights, but nevertheless stumble at the bargaining table and when it goes down to the local union."[28]

The speech produced only silence from the AFL-CIO. Six months later, in December, 1958, Wilkins addressed a letter to Meany pointing out that a Negro-labor alliance was a two-way street. He reminded the AFL-CIO president that NAACP branches had helped organized labor to beat back the attacks on the unions through "right-to-work" proposals in the November elections in such key states as Ohio and California. But in its efforts to eradicate Jim Crow practices within the labor movements, the NAACP had received mainly promises and declarations.

Wilkins's letter was followed by a public report by Herbert Hill, which stated that "all too often there is a significant disparity between the declared public policy of the national AFL-CIO and the day-to-day reality as experienced by the Negro wage-earner in the North as well as in the South." The report documented its charge and singled out specific unions and industries, especially in the railroad and construction fields. Hill mentioned that the admission of the trainmen and the firemen and enginemen to the AFL-CIO after the merger was in direct violation of the adopted constitution, and that when the Brotherhood of Locomotive Firemen, an AFL-CIO affiliate, had successfully defended its exclusion of Negroes from union membership in a 1958 suit brought by black firemen in Cincinnati, the AFL-CIO Executive Council had said not a word.

Hill's report noted that some AFL-CIO affiliates, including the railway clerks, continued to restrict black members to segregated locals, and that others circumvented their own constitutional provisions against discrimination by "tacit consent." Moreover, although there was no membership discrimination in auto and steel unions, most of their black members were restricted to unskilled jobs and did not enjoy the same rights as white workers when it came to promotion and seniority. Despite promises, the UAW had not included a Fair Employment Practices provision in its contracts, which left black workers particularly vulnerable as automation grew and created new unemployment. In many plants black workers had already been entirely eliminated—and at a time when there was already twice as much unemployment among blacks in the nation as among whites.

The NAACP report also dealt with the participation of some local unions and labor leaders in White Citizens' Councils in the South. It charged that, without fear of reprisal from the AFL-CIO, many shop stewards and business agents "openly solicit funds for the Council and the Klan." It said that the performance of the AFL-CIO's Civil Rights Committee and the Civil Rights Department showed that their main function was "to create a 'liberal' public relations image rather than to attack the broad pattern of anti-Negro practices within affiliated unions." Having no enforcement power against unfair practices of affiliated unions, they could do no more than use persuasion and conciliation, with results that were meager indeed. The AFL-CIO might boast that locals of the International Brotherhood of Electrical Workers in Cleveland and Milwaukee and of the Brotherhood of Railway Clerks in Minneapolis had been "persuaded" to admit blacks, but "the token admission of a few Negroes into an electrical workers union in Cleveland can no more be regarded as integration than can the token admission of two or three Negro children into a southern public school." Hill's report stated the key issue:

> As long as union membership remains a condition of employment in the building trades, on the railroads and elsewhere, and qualified Negroes are barred from union membership solely because of their color, then trade union discrimination is the decisive factor in determining whether Negro workers in a given industry shall have an opportunity to earn a living for themselves and their families.

The report concluded by noting that technological changes were eliminating unskilled jobs from the economy and that the "virtual exclusion" of blacks from apprenticeship and other training programs was concentrating them in the jobs being eliminated. Besides, many unions, especially in the building trades and the railroad brotherhoods, had long kept blacks out of better-paid work, and separate racial lines of seniority promotion had been written into collective-bargaining agreements, so it was no wonder that "Negroes constitute a permanently depressed economic group in American society."[29]

The NAACP report was widely publicized in the Negro and radical press but received little attention in the nation's mass media or in the labor press. Hill's comment that there was twice as much unemployment among blacks as among whites (14.4 per cent of the nonwhite work force was idle in March, 1958, as against 6.9 per cent of the white work force), and that Negroes were a "permanently depressed economic group" could hardly hope to arouse concern in a year when a leading bestseller was John Kenneth Galbraith's *The Affluent Society*. The Harvard economist boldly announced that poverty in this country was no longer "a massive affliction [but] more nearly an afterthought." In fact, mass poverty no longer existed in the United States. The poor had dwindled to two hard-core categories—victims of "insular poverty," who lived in the rural South or in depressed areas like West Virginia, and victims of "case poverty," which was "commonly and properly" associated with such individual characteristics as "mental deficiency, bad health, inability to adapt to the discipline of modern economic life, excessive procreation, alcohol, insufficient education." Such poverty was really due to individual defects, since "nearly everyone else has mastered his environment; this proves that it is not intractable."[30]

Many Americans accepted the Galbraith thesis as obvious truth. The facts in the NAACP report could be comfortably explained: Black workers who could not rise out of poverty were simply prey to their own inherent defects, unable to adapt to the discipline of modern economic life or to resist the allure of alcohol or sex. Discrimination in industry and racism in unions, if they existed—and it was commonly said that they were difficult to prove—were regarded as extraneous.

But black trade unionists knew better than to swallow the Galbraith thesis. They were determined to force the AFL-CIO to face the data presented in the NAACP report and to do something to rectify the evils it portrayed. In this they were joined by several white union leaders, including many from the United Packinghouse Workers and the UAW. Walter Reuther was under increasing pressure from black UAW members to do something in the AFL-CIO Executive Council, of which he was a member, about "discrimination within the unions on certain jobs, and in certain international unions which actually did not admit Negroes to their unions."[31] Randolph, too, came under increasing pressure from the Negro community to assume the gadfly role in the AFL-CIO conventions he had once played at AF of L annual gatherings. In August, 1959, Randolph and Reuther joined in an appeal to the AFL-CIO for greater emphasis on the elimination of racial discrimination. When this appeal brought no response, the stage was set for a showdown on the racial issue at the 1959 AFL-CIO convention.

Randolph and other delegates from the Brotherhood of Sleeping Car Porters came to the convention with a definite program and ready to do battle for it. They had prepared a resolution calling upon the convention to authorize adequate personnel for the Civil Rights Department to conduct a nationwide survey to determine the extent of discrimination and segregation in the affiliated unions. The Executive Council should then launch a campaign to persuade the guilty affiliates to reform or face stern measures. But the brotherhood delegates demanded action without waiting for the survey to abolish all segregated locals in the AFL-CIO and an ultimatum to the Brotherhood of Locomotive Firemen and Enginemen and the Brotherhood of Trainmen to eliminate the race barrier to membership within a specified time or be expelled. They were also prepared to blackball the International Longshoremen's Association from affiliation with the AFL-CIO on the basis of an Urban League report that it practiced discrimination.

Randolph, having opposed the admission of the firemen and enginemen and the trainmen in the Executive Council, had kept silent thus far because Meany had assured him in August, 1957, that he had received guarantees from the trainmen's officers that their next convention would remove the "whites only" clause from their constitution, and that the constitutional barrier to Negro membership was "being straightened out" with the firemen.[32] But the trainmen had done nothing since then, and the firemen had even gone to court to defeat a suit by blacks seeking membership in the brotherhood. The time had come to announce a time limit.

At the convention the brotherhood delegates introduced a resolution calling for the expulsion of the trainmen and the locomotive firemen unless they removed their racial barriers within six months. A debate got under way immediately after the report of the Resolutions Committee on the brotherhood's proposal. The committee conceded that the trainmen and the firemen had "failed to carry out their pledge to the AFL-CIO Executive Council made by them at the time of their admission to comply with the civil rights policy of the AFL-CIO." But instead of accepting the resolution's proposal for a time limit, the committee submitted the vague recommendation: "We authorize and request the AFL-CIO Executive Council to work with these organizations to obtain compliance at the earliest possible date."[33] Meany supported the report, arguing that a time limitation would only strengthen those within the raliroad unions who wanted to keep the color bars. Other white union leaders contended that discrimination in the railroad brotherhoods could be more easily eliminated if they were in, rather than out of, the AFL-CIO. The leaders of the firemen and the trainmen hid behind the argument that they had held no convention since the pledge to comply with the AFL-CIO's civil rights policy, not bothering to explain why they could not have called a special convention or why the Executive Council had not insisted they do so.

The sleeping car porters' delegates hit back with an array of facts and figures proving that the trainmen and the firemen had been, and were continuing to be, guilty of the most vicious type of discrimination against Negroes. They also argued that if the Executive Council could expel affiliates because of Communism and corruption, it should also do this with those guilty of racial discrimination. While the brotherhood received strong support from several delegates, including those from the United Packinghouse Workers, the Allied Industrial Workers, the Transport Service Employees, and the American Newspaper Guild, Walter Reuther was not among them. Arguments in favor of the brotherhood's resolution had no more effect at an AFL-CIO convention than Randolph's earlier pleas at AF of L conventions. The rebuttal to the comparison with Communism and corruption was that the race question differed from Communism and corruption in that they were mainly leadership and not membership problems, whereas the *officers* of the trainmen and the firemen (but not the members) favored compliance with the AFL-CIO's constitution. As an argument, this deserved a failing grade in a logic course, but the majority of white delegates apparently swallowed it, as they voted to approve the recommendation of the Resolutions Committee.

The brotherhood's delegates were also unsuccessful in opposing admission to the federation of the International Longshoremen's Association. Randolph challenged the resolution, pointing out that "of the 25,000 longshoremen on the New York waterfront, 6,000 were Negroes and Puerto Ricans, who are victims of racial discrimination fostered by the inherently corrupt shape-up system of hiring, gentlemen's agreements, and an apparent indifference on the part of permanent government agencies."[34] He recommended that the position of the longshoremen on racial discrimination be clarified positively before the union was officially accepted. His suggestion received the backing of all the black delegates and quite a few of the whites—enough, indeed, to compel Meany to take the floor to try to stop the trend. He began by accusing Randolph of distorting the facts. "I never knew of discrimination in the International Longshoremen's Association," he shouted. Meany said Randolph should have taken the matter up with the Executive Council or its special subcommittee on the ILA, implied that the black labor leader was seeking publicity, and told him it was time he "got on the team, joined the labor movement, and became part and parcel of the AFL-CIO."[35] A week before the convention the Urban League had sent an exhaustive report on waterfront discrimination to Meany, as well as to the members of the Executive Council and the members of the special subcommittee on the ILA, and several council members had acknowledged receiving the document, all of which Meany neglected to mention.

The heated debate—at one point Webster of the brotherhood called Meany a "weakling politician"[36]—reached its climax over a resolution introduced by Randolph requiring that segregated locals "be liquidated and eliminated." Delegates from internationals with segregated locals, including George N. Harrison of the Brotherhood of Railway Clerks, argued that blacks preferred the present arrangement and that the internationals could not abolish segregated locals against their will. But the internationals had opposed their segregated locals when they applied to government agencies to have themselves abolished and compel the international to operate as integrated unions. The brotherhood delegates argued that segregated locals usually deprived Negroes of equal opportunities and that to maintain Jim Crow unionism because the members of segregated unions might want them was no more defensible than it was to "maintain unions under Communist domination and corrupt influences on the ground the members of said unions desired to keep them." This produced a celebrated exchange between Meany and Randolph:

MEANY: Is this your idea of a democratic process, that you don't care what the Negro members think? You don't care if they want to maintain the union they have had for so many years? I would like an answer to that.
RANDOLPH: Yes.
MEANY (angrily): That's not my policy. I am for the democratic rights of the Negro members. Who in the hell appointed you as guardian of the Negro members in America? You talk about tolerance.[37]

Meany received a quick and fitting answer from Willie Baxter, vice-president and director of civil rights of the Trade Union Leadership Conference in Detroit:

> . . . to clear you up on the matter that seemed to be vexing you. . . . The mistake you made is that Brother Randolph was not appointed to this high position. Brother Randolph was accorded this position by the acclamation of the Negro people in recognition of his having devoted almost half a century of his life "in freedom's cause."[38]

All of the brotherhood's resolutions went down to defeat, but the militancy of the black delegates who supported them, also reflected in Baxter's letter to Meany, indicated that the AFL-CIO was being challenged by black labor leaders who, under pressure from the Negro community, were in no mood to function as did the Negro trade-union leaders in 1950 and 1952. The AFL-CIO was forced to produce something besides promises. In January, 1960, at its convention in Cleveland, the Brotherhood of Railway Trainmen voted to eliminate the "color bar" from its constitution. In November, 1960, the general policy committee of the firemen unanimously followed suit. (The union, however, refused to do so until 1964, and it did so, as Arthur M. Ross, Commissioner of Labor Statistics, observed, only "after the railroad 'work rules' arbitration had made it virtually certain that few, if any, additional firemen would ever be hired on American railroads."[39]) The Railway Labor Executives' Association also felt the impact of the militancy of the black union leadership and of the Negro community. At its November meeting in Washington, the association pledged to: (1) press with vigor to secure equal rights for all workers in the railroad industry, including employment in all crafts and promotions in accordance with the ability of the workers; (2) press to secure the full benefits of union organization for all workers without regard to race, creed, color, or national origin; (3) request all affiliates to take prompt and decisive action in their separate organizations to carry this into effect; (4) endorse and implement the resolutions on civil rights and civil liberties adopted at the AFL-CIO conventions. About the same time, sixteen civil rights specialists met with the AFL-CIO's Civil Rights Department and made the following recommendations: (1) that labor develop its own civil-rights training course for local union officers; (2) that more AFL-CIO affiliates establish civil-rights committees of their own, and that such committees be staffed full-time; (3) that each affiliate extend committee action from the national level to the local level, with the help of the local unions; and (4) that technical assistance and specific guidance be given to local unions in developing positive civil-rights programs of their own.

That was progress, although most of it was still in the form of words and hopes rather than deeds. It did not alter the fundamental characteristics of racial discrimination in the AFL-CIO. An Indiana University study of the federation's first five years concluded that, while racial discrimination through constitutional "and other obvious means" had diminished considerably, "less obvious means of discrimination against Negro workers"—exclusion by tacit consent, discrimination in job referrals, and the maintenance of separate lines of progression—still continued to be "evoked." Furthermore, it found that the unions making progress before the merger, mainly those affiliated with the CIO, were the ones that five years later had made "the most progress in the implementation of anti-discrimination policy." On the other hand, "those unions which possessed recorded histories of racial bias have not changed their positions noticeably" and, without the Executive Council's power to expel, might not change in the foreseeable future.[40] All this meant, of course, was that in the construction trades, the railroad industry, the metal craft industry, and other industries, unions affiliated with the AFL-CIO continued either to practice total exclusion of blacks or to restrict them to segregated or auxiliary locals. With few exceptions, such as the United Packinghouse Workers, the United Rubber Workers, and, to a certain extent, the United Automobile Workers, unions affiliated with the AFL-CIO continued to enforce separate racial seniority lines, which limited Negro employment to menial and unskilled classifications.

On January 3, 1961, the NAACP released a report on the first five years of the AFL-CIO. The report noted the removal of the color bar in the trainmen's constitution, the agreement by the International Brotherhood of Pulp, Sulphite, and Paper Mill Workers, following conferences with representatives of the NAACP, not to issue any new charters to segregated local unions and to merge segregated ones wherever possible; the merger of segregated locals by the American Federation of Musicians in some sixteen cities; and the fact that the ILGWU, with requested assistance from the NAACP, had merged separate black and white sections of the Atlanta local into one unit as signs of progress. But apart from these changes, everything that had appeared in the 1958 report could be reprinted without alteration. Hence the conclusion by the NAACP that racism was still a prominent feature of the AFL-CIO:

> Today, five years after the AFL-CIO merger, the national labor organization has failed to eliminate the broad pattern of racial discrimination and segregation in many important affiliated unions. Trade union activity in the civil rights field since the merger has not been marked by a systematic and coordinated effort by the national labor federation to eliminate discrimination and segregation within local unions. This is especially true of the craft unions in the building and construction trades where the traditional anti-Negro practices basically remain in effect.
>
> Efforts to eliminate discriminatory practices within trade unions have been piecemeal and inadequate and usually the result of protest by civil rights agencies acting on behalf of Negro workers. The national AFL-CIO has repeatedly refused to take action on its own initiative. In too many cases years have elapsed between the filing of a complaint by an aggrieved worker and acknowledgment and investigation by the Federation, if indeed there is any action at all.
>
> Discriminatory racial practices by trade unions are not simply isolated or occasional expressions of local bias against colored workers, but rather, as the record indicates, a continuation of the institutionalized pattern of anti-Negro employment practices that is traditional with large sections of organized labor and industrial management.[41]

22 The Negro-Labor Alliance, 1960-65

The NAACP report of the failure of the AFL-CIO, five years after the merger, to eliminate a wide variety of anti-Negro practices received considerable publicity and was immediately attacked by the federation's leadership, as well as by liberal and "radical" elements. They argued that the critical tone of the report was interfering with labor's organizing drives at a time of great difficulty, and that it would strengthen anti-Negro forces by rupturing the Negro-labor alliance, without which "precious little progress will be made toward full racial equality in this country."[1] They also said the report lacked objectivity and presented a distorted picture. What was needed was not exposure of weakness in implementing the AFL-CIO's constitutional ban against racial discrimination but more explication of what had been done and was being accomplished in the face of many difficulties.

At a conference of the Jewish Labor Committee at Unity House, the summer resort of the ILGWU, George Meany led the attack on the NAACP report, calling it "unnecessary and ill advised. There is no doubt that this sort of thing weakens the prestige of the labor movement and darkens our public image." He charged that the report was responsible for "the fact that labor has been unable to organize white collar workers and technicians, has lost the support of liberals and is generally looked on askance."[2] The reaction of the AFL-CIO president not only indicated an unwillingness on the part of the federation's leadership to search for new ways to meet the serious problems set forth in the document but also symbolized the organization's refusal to face up to the real reasons why, in the eyes of those who had previously been its champions, organized labor had become stagnant, a feeling that was to grow in intensity in the next few years.

Meany's choice of the Jewish Labor Committee conference to unleash the official AFL-CIO response to the NAACP report was not accidental. The JLC had been one of the shrillest critics of the report. Emanuel Muravchik, the committee's field secretary, criticized Herbert Hill, author of the report, for "inaccuracies and exaggerations," for "a distorted picture" of the labor movement's efforts "to obtain civil rights for our Negro minority," and for fabricating a "picture of extreme basic antagonisms between minorities and the labor movement."[3] Hill responded that his charge of racial discrimination in the AFL-CIO was based on "indisputable data" and suggested that the Jewish labor organizations "would do well if they ceased to apologize for the racists in the American labor movement and, instead of attempting to create a desirable public image for the AFL-CIO, joined with Negro workers and the NAACP in directly attacking the broad pattern of racial discrimination."[4]

Black trade-union leaders were not silent bystanders while spokesmen for the AFL-CIO attacked the NAACP report. By the time the report was made public, they had already formed their own organization to seek an end to the practices it documented. Their action was largely a response to rising discontent among black workers with the dominant modes of conduct adopted by the Negro trade-union leadership. There was also a growing feeling in black working-class circles that black union leaders were no more than "junior partners" in the Negro-Labor Alliance, having no role other than to voice approval of white leaders' public statements in favor of civil rights in the South and to refrain from raising questions about internal racial practices of organized labor. The widespread discontent among blacks in the civil-rights movement with the "go-slow policy" of the leaders and the influence of black nationalist feeling in Negro communities were also making inroads among black members of the trade unions. The established Negro trade-union leadership was increasingly aware that the black membership could no longer be satisfied with the labor movement's unionization of nearly 2 million Negroes when they could see that many unions had made barely a dent in trade-union racism. In 1957 the Trade Union Leadership Council, comprising Negro union officials in Detroit, was professedly organized in response to the black workers' feelings that they had received only hollow promises from the AFL-CIO and the UAW, that they could not "wait any longer," and that they expected black union leaders "to change the situation."[5] Similar pressure from black workers in other communities led to the organization of groups like the TULC in Youngstown, Saint Louis, Philadelphia, Pittsburgh, Buffalo, Milwaukee, Cleveland, Chicago, Gary, and New York.

It took the clash between Randolph and Meany at the AFL-CIO convention in the fall of 1959, along with the defeat of the resolutions introduced by the Brotherhood of Sleeping Car Porters delegates, to convert these local groups into a national movement. Black trade union leaders throughout the country were now determined to prove to the black membership and black workers in general that they were ready to assume a more militant role in the labor movement. A Philadelphia Negro union leader stated:

> We've got to stop Uncle Tomming it. The spotlight is on racial integration and we've got to move while we have the opportunity. If we have to hurt our friends then we will just have to hurt them. I consider myself to be one of the new breed of Negroes. I'm not begging at the back door for scraps, but knocking on the front door for my rights.[6]

In a speech to the 1959 NAACP convention Randolph had called for the formation of "a national Negro Labor Committee, comparable to the Jewish Labor Committee . . . to fight and work to implement the civil rights program of the AFL-CIO." The committee's purpose "should be both to secure membership of Negro workers in the unions and employment and promotion on the job as well as participation in the executive, administrative and staff areas of the unions."[7] On July 18–19, 1959, seventy-five black trade-unionists met in New York City at Randolph's invitation to discuss this proposal and to take concrete action to implement it. The "committee of seventy-five" called for a founding convention of the Negro American Labor Council in May, 1960, and declared:

> We resent Jim Crow locals; we deplore the freeze-out against Negroes in labor apprenticeship and training programs; we disclaim the lack of upgrading and promotional opportunities for Negroes; we repudiate the lockout against Negroes by some unions; we, above all, reject "tokenism," that thin veneer of acceptance masquerading as democracy. Since hundreds of thousands of Negroes are the victims of this hypocrisy, we ourselves must seek the cure, in terms of hundreds of thousands, in the dimensions of a mass organization.[8]

"We ourselves must seek the cure." While whites would not be barred constitutionally, the NALC at the outset would be made up and financed by Negroes only, "making it possible for them to take a position completely independent of white unionists." Randolph told the delegates to the founding convention:

> While the Negro American Labor Council rejects black nationalism as a doctrine and the practice of racial separation, it recognizes the fact that history has placed upon the Negro and the Negro alone the basic responsibility to complete the uncompleted civil war revolution through keeping the fires of freedom burning in the civil rights movement.[9]

The delegates elected Randolph president and Cleveland Robinson vice-president of the NALC. Although the organization was composed of black officials of existing unions, it made clear its intention to function as an independent and autonomous unit, exerting pressure from within the AFL-CIO for deeds, not words, in eliminating racism. One NALC founder declared:

> The leadership of the AFL-CIO, despite its good faith, good will, and splendid pronouncements against racial discrimination, cannot be expected to move voluntarily and seriously to take positive and affirmative action for the elimination of race discrimination unless they are stimulated, prodded, and pressured to do so, both from within and without.[10]

In June, 1961, Randolph told the NAACP convention that the NALC endorsed the association's criticism of the AFL-CIO's civil rights record since the merger in 1955:

> We in the Negro American Labor Council consider the report timely, necessary, and valuable. . . . Moreover, the Negro American Labor Coun-

cil can without reservation assert that the basic statements of the Report are true and sound, for the delegates of the Brotherhood of Sleeping Car Porters have presented these facts to convention after convention of the American Federation of Labor for a quarter of a century.[11]

That same month, on behalf of the NALC, Randolph presented to the AFL-CIO Executive Council detailed charges of anti-Negro practices in affiliated unions with specific recommendation "to eliminate segregation and discrimination within international and local organizations"— including, as a last resort, the expulsion of affiliates refusing to end their racial practices. The AFL-CIO leadership repeatedly postponed action on the proposals and finally, at its meeting in New York City on October 12, 1961, sharply rejected the recommendations. It went on officially to censure Randolph because, as Meany explained, the black labor leader was responsible for "the gap that has developed between organized labor and the Negro community" and because Randolph had "gotten close to those militant groups." The AFL-CIO president then released to the press a twenty-page subcommittee report critical of Randolph and, by implication, of groups like the NALC and the NAACP, which had dared to denounce AFL-CIO racial practices. Meany assured reporters that the report had his personal endorsement and that every member of the Executive Council, with the exception of the president of the Brotherhood of Sleeping Car Porters, had voted to censure Randolph and to accept the report. All had agreed that Randolph, the NALC, and civil-rights organizations like the NAACP, with their charges of discrimination in trade unions, were taking an antilabor position. Meany was asked why the demand of the black trade unionists for decisive action against affiliates found guilty of discrimination was any more antilabor than the expulsion of affiliates for corruption. His reply was curt: "I do not equate problems of racial discrimination with the problems of corruption any more than I equate Hungary with Little Rock."[12]

Randolph described the subcommittee report as "innocuous, sterile and barren" and warned that it would "create a sense of frustration and anger among Negro trade unionists, and in the Negro community as a whole." Many leaders of the Negro community, including Dr. Martin Luther King, Jr., of the Southern Christian Leadership Conference, protested the AFL-CIO's rebuke of the "dean of Negro labor," but Roy Wilkins made the sharpest attack in the name of the NAACP:

> The National Association for the Advancement of Colored People believes that the AFL-CIO's "censure" of A. Philip Randolph is an incredible cover-up. The so-called report made to the Federation's Executive Council by a three-man subcommittee is simply a refusal to recognize the unassailable facts of racial discrimination and segregation inside organized labor, as well as an evasion on the part of the AFL-CIO leadership of its own responsibility in fighting racism within affiliated unions.
>
> We reject the Federation's statement that A. Philip Randolph caused "the gap which has developed between organized labor and the Negro community." If such a "gap" exists it is because Mr. Meany and the AFL-

CIO Executive Council have not taken the required action to eliminate the broad national pattern of anti-Negro practices that continues to exist in many significant sections of the American labor movement, even after five and a half years of the merger and the endless promises to banish Jim Crow.

Wilkins pointed out that "the spokesman for the Executive Council's Subcommittee which rebuked Randolph was George M. Harrison, president of the Brotherhood of Railway Clerks, an international union which, for over half a century, has 'jim crowed' Negro railway workers into segregated locals."[13] (In addition to Harrison, the subcommittee consisted of John Walsh of the International Alliance of Theatrical State Employees and Jacob S. Potofsky of the Amalgamated Clothing Workers.)

Not surprisingly, the delegates to the second annual NALC convention, held in Chicago on November 10–12, 1961, were boiling mad. Their anger was directed primarily against the white "liberal" friends of the black workers in the labor movement, men who for so many years had been praised in the Negro press for their understanding of and sympathy for the oppressed black wage-earners. Richard Parish, national treasurer of the NALC, voiced the sentiments of the delegates when he asked: "Where was David Dubinsky, where was Walter Reuther, where was Joe Curran, where was Jim Carey? Where were all those liberals on the Council when the vote [to censure Randolph] was taken? This was a show of power to demonstrate to Negro union members that they represent nothing when it comes to setting policies in the labor movement even though they pay dues."[14]

Randolph himself dealt with his censure in his keynote address, which opened with a historical analysis. In mid-twentieth-century America, he said, black labor was "one hundred years behind white labor" in the skilled crafts, in workers' education, and in employment opportunities. The reason was not that white labor was "racially superior" or "more productive" but because, in the competition for a place in American industry, "black labor never had a chance." How could it be otherwise when Negro workers began as slaves while white workers started as either free men or virtually free men. Even after emancipation, black labor continued "a prisoner for a hundred years of a moneyless system of peonage, sharecropper-plantation-farm laborism, and a system which kept him a helpless and hopeless city-slum proletariat."

A major tragedy in American labor history, Randolph declared, was that black and white workers in the South fought each other, enabling their common enemy, "the feudalistic-capitalist class, to subject them to sharper and sharper exploitation and oppression." To compound the tragedy, black and white workers fought each other not because they hated each other but because they were made to fear each other, as "each was propagandized into believing that each was seeking to take the jobs of the others." The purpose of the propaganda was to exploit both black and white more effectively, and it succeeded:

By poisonous preachments by the press, pulpit and politician, the wages of
both black and white workers were kept low and working conditions bad,
since trade union organization was practically nonexistent. And even today, the South is virtually a "no man's land" for union labor. It is a matter of common knowledge that union organization campaigns, whether
under the auspices of the old American Federation of Labor, or the
younger Congress of Industrial Organizations, or the AFL-CIO, have
wound up as miserable failures.

There were plenty of easy explanations for these failures, all based on
the view that the Southern working class was so divided by race that a
successful organizing campaign was impossible. But the real reason was
that the AF of L, the CIO, and the AFL-CIO had each failed to build
its organization drives "upon the principle of the solidarity of the working class." They had accepted the fact that such solidarity was impossible
to achieve in the South and proceeded "to perpetuate this racial division," even though it was clear that segregated unionism was the antithesis of effective trade-union organization. "Thus, they sowed the winds of
the division of the workers upon the basis of race, and now they are
reaping the whirlwinds."

Randolph accused the leaders of organized labor of having never seriously challenged Jim Crow unionism in the South. Instead of rallying
the workers to fight institutional racism, the white leaders of the unions,
like those of the church, business, government, schools, and the press,
"marched together under the banner of white supremacy, in the Ku
Klux Klan, to put down and keep down by law or lawlessness the Negro."
The result was a disaster not only for the black workers, and not only for
the white workers in the South, but for the entire working class, North,
East, South, and West, which could not become, and was not, even in
1961, fully free. There was no principle "more obvious and universal
than the indivisibility of the freedom of the workers regardless of race,
color, religion, national origin or ancestry, being based, as it were, upon
the principle of least labor costs in a free labor market."

The unorganized state of Southern labor, Randolph continued, was
organized labor's fault, the direct result of the fact that neither the
AF of L, the CIO nor the AFL-CIO had "ever come to grips with the
racial problem in the South" but had always adopted "a policy of
appeasement, compromise and defeatism." To the anticipated response
that this was a "distortion of facts" typical of black labor leaders, Randolph asked if it could be denied that in the six years since its formation the AFL-CIO recognized and accepted (1) the Jim Crow union;
(2) the color bar in union constitutions and rituals or exclusionary racial
policies by tacit consent; (3) racially segregated seniority rosters and
lines of job progression; (4) racial sub-wage differentials; (5) indifferent
recognition, if not acceptance, of the concept and practice of a "white
man's job" and a "black man's job"; (6) racial barriers against Negro
participation in apprenticeship training programs; (7) failure to demand
Negro workers' participation in union democracy; (8) racially segregated

338   *Organized Labor and the Black Worker*

state conventions of the AFL-CIO in Southern cities; (9) racially segregated city central labor bodies of the AFL-CIO.

Was there anyone so "naive or cynical" as to believe that these forms
of racial bias were not organizationally and economically disadvan-
tageous to the black laboring masses? Not only had they confined Negro
workers to the lowest rungs of the occupational ladder, but they had
helped "to reinforce the accepted inferior hereditary position of black
labor, which drastically limits their economic mobility and viability."
But the most tragic aspect of this tragic development was that, even
though racial discrimination in unions affiliated with the AFL-CIO had
existed for almost a century, "no profound concern is now manifested
by the leadership about this dreadful evil." Rather than becoming
"aroused and disturbed about the existence of race bias in unions that
affect employment opportunities and the economic status of the Negro
worker, AFL-CIO leadership waves aside criticism of the movement's
racial policies as pure exaggeration unworthy of dispassionate examination."

Randolph then turned to the memorandum on race bias in the trade
unions that he had submitted, together with corrective proposals, to
George Meany and the Executive Council four months earlier. Instead
of giving the memorandum "a painstaking, rational analysis to determine
if it contained any meritorious suggestions," they used it as the occasion
for an attack on the man who had submitted it. Their reaction was both
proof that the AFL-CIO did not have "a single new, vital, creative
and constructive idea with which to grapple with the menace of race
segregation and discrimination," and a "distressingly vain effort to justify
a 'do little' civil rights record in the House of Labor."

Having opened his address with a discussion of the South, Randolph
closed with a brief analysis of the effects of race bias in unions and
industry in a key Northern city, New York City, a city considered to be
"relatively liberal." The two major industries were garment manufacturing and printing and publishing, both under the jurisdiction of unions
affiliated with the AFL-CIO. In both industries Negroes and Puerto
Ricans were concentrated in the low-paid, unskilled classifications. In
the building construction industry, under similar union jurisdiction,
little progress had been made in eliminating the traditional pattern of
Negro exclusion and discrimination. Negroes were members of the Hotel
and Restaurant Employees Union, AFL-CIO, but only a token number
were waiters and bellhops in hotels and restaurants, and one would need
the "proverbial microscope to discover a Negro bartender anywhere in
this city except in a Negro community." Then, too, there was the indisputable fact that in the "liberal" city of New York, black youths were
almost totally excluded from major apprenticeship programs jointly conducted by industrial management and labor unions. Black labor was still
confronted by the age-old dilemma. The only way a worker in many
occupations could qualify for employment was to complete the apprenticeship training program. Yet the unions that controlled the programs
and with it access to employment were precisely the ones that effectively

excluded Negroes. In New York, as throughout the nation, fewer than 1 per cent of the apprentices in the construction industry were blacks.

Was it any wonder, Randolph asked, that in New York City in 1961, nonwhite persons made up a very large part of those who lived in poverty—"a poverty that is frequently related to discriminatory racial practices that force Negroes into a marginal position in the economy, even though opportunities may increase for other groups within the community"? When blacks were unable to obtain employment in occupations at substantially higher incomes than those earned by unskilled workers, and when to this was added other income limitation, it was not in the least surprising that they constituted "a permanently depressed segment of American Society."

Randolph concluded his analysis on a note almost of despair. Despite the growth of black union membership, from scarcely half a million in the 1930's to more than 2 million, and despite the enormous upsurge in the nation's economy in those three decades, "the mass of Black Americans stand today in much the same economic position they occupied in the depths of the great depression."* Indeed, "the gap between Negro and white median income has widened in recent years."[15]

None of this, however, produced any greater impact upon the AFL-CIO than had Randolph's previous memorandum. Meany was now convinced that Randolph seemed "to be getting senile,"[16] and others felt that his description of the labor scene in the South as a union "no man's land" was entirely unrealistic, since a good deal of unionism did exist there, including unions with Negro membership.

The response to the second annual convention of the NALC ran the gamut from "that's not the way to go about it" to a rising chorus calling the NALC guilty of "dual unionism," a "racist caucus," and an exponent of "racism in reverse." Bayard Rustin, Randolph's assistant, answered the charges with the comment: "I am aware of no similar charge against any number of other ethnically centered groups, such as the Jewish Labor Committee. Under present conditions—i.e., general segregation and discrimination, and the unreliability of today's organized (or disorganized) liberalism—the Negro will find it necessary in many instances to organize independently."[17] But the reply did not stop the charges.

In 1960 the NALC claimed a membership of 10,000, with chapters in a number of industrial centers of the North—Chicago, New York,

---

* Official Labor Department figures bore out Randolph's conclusion. The statistics for winter of 1960–61 showed that the Negro unemployment rate was almost twice as high as the rate of white unemployment—13.8 per cent as against 7 per cent for white. An Urban League survey of unemployment among Negroes in fifty cities revealed that the "percentage of the Negro work force unemployed is frequently twice to three times that of the total unemployment rate." In Chicago, where the total unemployment rate was 5.7 per cent, the percentage of Negro jobless was 17.3; in Louisville, Kentucky, the total rate was 8.3 per cent, while the corresponding figure for Negroes was 39.8 per cent; in Pittsburgh, the figures were 11.6 per cent as against 24 per cent. In Gary, Indiana, 18,000 out of a total of 20,200 unemployed were black, and in Detroit, 112,000 out of a total of 185,000. *New York Times*, Dec. 12, 1960; Jan. 17, 1961.

Pittsburgh, Youngstown, and Detroit. The Detroit chapter, which was still called the Trade Union Leadership Council, with 2,000 members, was the largest. The Chicago chapter's membership was much less—700.

Between 1960 and 1962 NALC membership declined from 10,000 to 4,000. Randolph attributed the decline to a "lack of funds to carry on a nationwide systematic organizing campaign" and to pressure upon black unionists by white labor leaders to dissociate themselves from the organization.[18] A number of NALC members had informed the organization that they had found it impossible to retain official union positions and maintain their membership in the council.

In 1962 the *American Federationist*, official monthly magazine of the AFL-CIO, published a special feature headed "The Negro's Right to Vote." It opened with an editorial by George Meany that began: "The AFL-CIO is firmly determined to achieve full equality in all fields—education, employment, accommodations, housing and justice."[19] These words infuriated black labor leaders, coming as they did on the heels of repeated rejections of the NALC's proposals for ending racial practices in the federation; they informed Meany that they were prepared to picket the auditorium where the 1962 AFL-CIO convention was to be held if he continued to do nothing to implement labor's commitment in the House of Labor. A meeting was hastily arranged at which Meany would confer with a delegation from the NALC before the convention. Eighteen NALC members were selected to serve on the delegation, headed by Cleveland Robinson.

The night before the confrontation, some among the eighteen expressed the view that the group should be "docile and polite." Robinson dissuaded them from that approach, and the next day the eighteen presented Meany with a list of demands. Robinson later recalled:

> We pointed out the irrelevance of the labor movement to the oppressed workers. Instead of helping them, the unions and the employers, especially in the craft unions, are in a conspiracy to keep the blacks out. We told Meany he must change or the blacks would find a new home.[20]

Meany answered that, while he did not think there was a need for the NALC, he would take the demands seriously. The delegation invited the AFL-CIO president to speak at the NALC's third annual convention in 1962, and he accepted.

It had become clear that criticism by black organizations of AFL-CIO racial practices and their economic consequences for blacks could not be dismissed as "distortions" or "racism in reverse." On October 13, 1961, the day after the AFL-CIO's censure of Randolph, the U.S. Commission on Civil Rights, established by Congress in 1957, issued its *Report on Employment*, which not only documented the extent of discrimination in organized labor but also stated that "the efforts of the AFL-CIO have proved to be largely ineffective" in curbing racist practices. Discrimination by trade unions, especially in the skilled occupations, was singled out as a basic contributor to the concentration of blacks in menial, unskilled jobs in industry, their virtual exclusion from the construction and

machinist crafts, and their vulnerability to unemployment crises. Emphasizing that "existing federal law has little impact on the discriminatory
practices of labor organizations" and that organized labor appeared to
be unwilling or unable to take action on its own initiative, the commission called for new federal legislation to prohibit discrimination
by unions.[21]

A report of the New York City Youth Board, based on the 1960
Census, spelled out what the Civil Rights Commission's data meant to
black youth. The proportion of unemployed nonwhite youth in New
York City was more than twice that of unemployed whites. It also made
clear that, at a time of "increased demand for skilled and educated workers and a decrease in opportunities for the unskilled and uneducated,"*
black youth coming out of both general and vocational high schools
were untrained, unskilled, and ill prepared for anything but menial
work. Apprenticeship training was dismissed as a viable means to alleviate the acute unemployment among black youth. Of approximately
15,000 registered apprentices in New York State, fewer than 2 per cent
were blacks, and these were almost "all in New York City." In the city,
there were a few black apprentices in the building trades, especially in
electrical work, bricklaying, painting, and carpentry, but no blacks were
apprenticed as plumbers, steamfitters, sheet-metal workers, structural
and ornamental iron workers, plasterers, or mosaic and terrazo workers.
The number of black apprentices in printing was insignificant, except in
the Printing Pressman Assistants Union, and there were no blacks registered in the metal trades.[22]

It would have been a blow to the AFL-CIO's public image for its 1962
convention to be picketed by black union leaders with signs quoting
from the reports of the U.S. Civil Rights Commission and the New
York City Youth Board. Meany therefore seized the opportunity to
meet with the black unionists and came to the NALC convention in the
fall of 1962. He told the delegates that he still felt there was no need for
a special organization of black labor, "but I respect your motives and
share your objectives."[23] Most of the delegates were skeptical, but some
were convinced that Meany's presence meant that the agitation of blacks
within the ranks had finally produced results. In that very year, 1962, the
Trade Union Leadership Council in Detroit, the leading chapter in the
NALC, had finally succeeded, after twenty years of struggle by black
members and their white allies, in getting the first Negro elected to the
UAW Executive Board.

However, the NALC delegates were brought up short when Walter
Reuther addressed them. Speaking as an AFL-CIO Executive Council
member, Reuther urged the delegates to disassociate themselves from
the NAACP's attacks on the federation and its affiliates. Specifically, the
association's "unfair, unfounded, indiscriminate" attack on the International Ladies' Garment Workers' Union, he declared, would "help no

* The 1960 census disclosed that one of New York City's largest industries, the
apparel industry, which employed many Negro youths in unskilled capacities, had
70,000 fewer workers in 1960 than in 1950.

one."[24] The controversy he referred to, primarily between the NAACP and the ILGWU, had repercussions in the NALC.

In the early years of the ILGWU, the garment workers who founded and built the union, mainly Jewish immigrants from Eastern Europe along with a smaller number of Italians from Sicily, waged some of the most militant and bitter struggles in American labor history and helped to demolish the myth, put forth by the AF of L leadership, that immigrant workers from Southern or Southeastern Europe were incapable of being organized. Once the union was established, it gained the reputation of being a champion of black workers, especially during the 1920's when the ILGWU financially supported *The Messenger* and sponsored the Negro Labor Committee's efforts to instruct blacks in the principles of trade unionism. These activities received wide and favorable publicity in the black community. All black Socialists, especially Frank Crosswaith, pointed with pride to what they called the fine record of the Socialist-oriented garment workers' union in New York City.

There were others, however, who accused the ILGWU of not actively working to back up its equalitarian pretensions by organizing black workers. In its October, 1925, issue, *The Messenger*, which repeatedly praised the ILGWU and its Jewish members for racial equalitarianism, pointed out that, although there were blacks in the union, "there is not a single Negro in a paid position." Almost ten years later, an article in *Opportunity* of April, 1934, noted that "until last year Negro workers, in an organizational sense, had been distinctly on the outer side of the periphery in the great women's garment industry. . . . En mass [sic] . . . the Negroes in the garment trades were considered as poor organizable material."[25] The writer's references to "last year" alluded to the general garment workers' strike in the summer of 1933, in which Negroes for the first time participated in large numbers.

Few of the sons and daughters of Jewish immigrants followed their parents into the garment industry, whereas larger numbers of second-generation Italians did remain. By the late 1930's and into the 1940's, the mass of the workers were Negroes and Puerto Ricans in New York City, and Negroes, Cubans, and Mexican-Americans in other leading garment centers of the North. In the South the industry was manned mostly by American-born whites. The union's leadership, on the other hand, continued to reflect only the early composition of its membership; its practice of relegating blacks and Puerto Ricans to unskilled, low-paying jobs and its undemocratic election procedures were bound to cause objections. Unfortunately, the objections were often tainted with anti-Semitism, so the union leadership was able to fight off criticisms of its policies by contending that they furnished ammunition to anti-Semitic forces in the nation.

The controversy between the ILGWU and sections of the black community opened with a series of articles published in the Pittsburgh *Courier* in December, 1959. On December 12—under the front-page headline, "Will Negro, Jewish Labor Leaders Split Over Civil Rights?"—an article by Managing Editor Harold F. Keith began: "Negro and Jewish labor leaders are on the 'brink' of outright war between themselves with the civil rights issue spread out before them as a prospective field of battle." In that issue and the next four, Keith unfolded a summary of the difficulties that had been growing between the AFL-CIO and its Civil Rights Committee and the NAACP and black trade unionists over the federation's failure to act on discrimination practiced by its affiliates and to enforce civil rights within the trade unions. A special point was made of the failure of the AFL-CIO antidiscrimination department to act on the 1958 memorandum on discrimination by Herbert Hill, labor secretary of the NAACP. Keith argued that the conflict really boiled down to "warfare" between the Negro American Labor Council, then taking shape under A. Philip Randolph and Roy Wilkins, and the Jewish Labor Committee, chaired by Charles Zimmerman, a vice-president of the ILGWU and chairman of the AFL-CIO antidiscrimination committee. As Keith described it, the failure of the AFL-CIO to act against racism was due to pressure from the Jewish Labor Committee, because it "exerts more influence upon the AFL-CIO than any non-union group" and had "more say-so than the NAACP or the National Urban League." When it came to civil rights for blacks, he claimed, the ILGWU was long on talk but very short on action to remedy discrimination in its ranks. He charged that in the ILGWU "Negro members . . . don't fare so well in occupying staff positions."[26]

Randolph and Wilkins, in lengthy statements, denied that their conflict with the AFL-CIO was in reality a case of Jews versus Negroes. They charged that the articles in the *Courier* played into the hands of anti-Semitic forces and diverted attention from the "big offenders" against blacks. As Wilkins observed, those elements in American society that were mainly responsible for the Negro's degraded status "would like nothing better than to have the spotlight turned off them and onto a fake 'Jewish vs. Negro' fight. The *Courier* is allowing the big boys to get away while it whips up a 'Jewish vs. Negro' feeling." Herbert Hill's memorandum, which had sparked the controversy, had listed many unions that openly violated Negro rights, but the ILGWU was not among them, Wilkins pointed out, nor was a single union under the leadership of Jewish officers. Randolph enthusiastically endorsed Wilkins's praise of the ILGWU and asserted that its "anti-racial discrimination position cannot be questioned." Lester Granger of the National Urban League ventured the opinion that, if the American labor movement as a whole had had as good a record on racial issues as the members and leaders of the ILGWU over the past quarter-century, "there would be a labor movement today that could set an example in every area of American interest."[27]

This seemed to settle the complaints about the ILGWU for the time being. But in 1962 Herbert Hill, testifying before a subcommittee of the House Education and Labor Committee, charged the union with many forms of discrimination, including the virtual exclusion of blacks from higher-paid cutters' jobs, their relegation (and that of Puerto Ricans as well) to the lower-paid job categories, and the maintenance of an auxiliary local of blacks and Puerto Ricans under the domination of a smaller local of white pressers. The full statement was later circulated by the NAACP and published in *New Politics* under the headline, "The ILGWU Today—The Decay of a Labor Union."

Hill's charges received wide publicity and called forth indignant responses from the union and its defenders. Hill was accused of being anti-Semitic (although he himself is Jewish) and a Communist (an incredible charge in view of his previous writings). In *New Politics*, Gus Tyler, then ILGWU director of politics, charged Hill with distortion of facts, malicious interpretations, and "pure fabrications."[28] The so-called auxiliary local of blacks and Puerto Ricans, he maintained, in fact was open to all races and creeds, although most members were black or Puerto Rican. One local that Hill had charged with discrimination against blacks did not, in truth, admit blacks, but then neither did it admit Jews or Puerto Ricans, since it had been established specifically to help new Italian-speaking union members to become familiar with American unionism.

In rebuttal, Hill noted that Tyler had not answered the charges that blacks and Puerto Ricans were "concentrated in low-paid job classifications, with very little employment mobility," and that "there is a direct connection between the permanent condition of semi-poverty experienced by these workers and racial practices." Nor had Tyler refuted Hill's charge that blacks and Puerto Ricans were virtually excluded from the possibility of running for office by rules that limited candidacy to those already in full-time elected or appointed positions. Finally, Hill denied that he had accused the ILGWU leadership of a "conscious racial ideology." He did, however, contend that years before the union's officials had "made a fundamental decision to keep the industry in New York City on the basis of maintaining low wages and minimal standards for tens of thousands of unskilled workers, i.e., Negroes and Puerto Ricans."[29]

The NAACP defended Hill against the charge of anti-Semitism, and its board of directors urged the House subcommittee to "pursue a vigorous and thorough investigation of racial discrimination" within the ILGWU. "The union cannot live on its past glories," the board declared. "It must face the reality of its present practices and move to eradicate them."[30]

However, the ILGWU refused even to acknowledge that its policies and practices required a change, despite mounting evidence furnished by Hill and others that, while its "public image" was that of a progressive union concerned about the welfare of its increasing black and Puerto Rican membership, the reality was quite the opposite. Even a champion of the union, writing in a special issue of *Labor History* devoted in its entirety to praise of David Dubinsky, the ILGWU's long-time president, was compelled to comment that "it should be a source of concern that the twenty-three members of the general executive board, which consists of the two top executive officers and twenty-one vice-presidents, should contain only five non-Jews; that there should be, as yet, no Negroes and only one Puerto Rican in the group; and that, although four-fifths of the members are women, only one should be a woman."[31] Hill's charges against the ILGWU accomplished nothing, but relations between the union and the NAACP were soured for several years. At the 1962 NALC convention, Walter Reuther called Hill's charges "unfair" and "unfounded." This angered many delegates, who were familiar with the evidence produced by the NAACP as well as that furnished by black members of the union. They were further upset when Randolph refused to come to the NAACP's defense, even though in his keynote speech he had, without mentioning the ILGWU, cited a Harvard University study which concluded that in the New York garment industry Negroes and Puerto Ricans "were largely to be found in the less skilled, low-paid crafts and in shops making the lower priced lines, and in this industry their advancement to higher skills is not proceeding very rapidly."[32] But Randolph could not keep the delegates from adopting a resolution in support of the NAACP notifying the ILGWU and its defenders, including Reuther and Meany, that "this Convention views any attacks on the NAACP as ultimately attacks on all of us who support the NAACP program."[33]

However, because of Randolph's firm opposition one aspect of the "program" was not supported. In October, 1962, the NAACP petitioned the National Labor Relations Board for decertification of the Seafarers International Union of North America, Local 2401 of the United Steelworkers of America, and the Brotherhood of Railroad Trainmen, each an AFL-CIO affiliate, on charges of failing to uphold the "legal obligation of labor unions to represent their members fairly."[34] The seafarers were accused of openly practicing racial discrimination and thereby almost completely eliminating Negroes from maritime work along the West Coast. The steelworkers' local was charged with establishing separate job classifications and wage scales for black and white workers who did identical work and with providing in the collective-bargaining agreement for separate lines of promotion, which confined blacks to unskilled, low-paying jobs. The Railroad Trainmen, of course, were charged with a whole catalogue of discriminatory practices, including collusion with the companies to keep blacks in lower positions and to drive them out of the industry wherever possible.

Arguing that "when you decertify a union, brother, you are at the mercy of your employer,"[35] Randolph was successful in persuading a majority of the delegates not to support the NAACP's demand that the NLRB decertify unions for racial discrimination, and the resolution was defeated (the NLRB rejected the petition). Of course, blacks who continued to face racial discrimination in seeking jobs, apprenticeship training, and union membership were at the mercy of both the employers and the unions, but Randolph had neglected to mention that.

Although the delegates to the 1962 NALC convention may not have been fully aware of it at the time, they struck a spark at their gathering that was soon to burst into flames and greatly advance the civil-rights movement. Before adjourning, the convention took a historic step by

346 *Organized Labor and the Black Worker*

projecting a March on Washington for the late summer or fall of 1963 to demand jobs for blacks and an end to industry and union bias.

The year 1963 marked the climax of civil-rights activities. By the spring of that year, massive demonstrations were held in Birmingham, Alabama, led by Martin Luther King, Jr., to protest segregation and discrimination in every aspect of life in that city. The demonstrations captured the attention and aroused the indignation of millions of Americans, especially after they watched, horrified, the televised spectacle of Eugene "Bull" Connor's police dogs and high-pressure water hoses being turned against the marchers. During the week of May 18, forty-three major and minor demonstrations occurred in other cities (ten of them in the North). In the following month there were more demonstrations, especially after the slaying of Medgar Evers, leader of the Mississippi NAACP. From May to August 15 there were 978 demonstrations in 209 cities or towns in 36 states.

The culmination of these struggles was the March on Washington on August 28. In the late spring, Dr. King called on Randolph and Cleveland Robinson to expand the aims of the March to include pressure on Congress to pass the pending civil-rights legislation, which President John F. Kennedy, in a special message, had urged Congress to enact. In June, when the plans for a massive demonstration in Washington became public, the Kennedy Administration tried to have it called off, as the Roosevelt Administration had managed to do on a similar occasion. Top civil-rights leaders were summoned to Washington and asked to cancel the demonstration on the ground that it would be uncontrollable and that, despite the nonviolence of much of the civil-rights movement, there would be violence. But the request was rejected and, under the leadership of the NALC, assisted by the SCLC, CORE, the NAACP, and SNCC (Student Non-Violent Coordinating Committee), preparations for the March went ahead. Early in June, four weeks before the March was announced officially, the NALC hired Bayard Rustin to plan it. During these weeks, Rustin was paid out of District 65 funds. Cleveland Robinson of District 65 and the NALC was treasurer of the March. Thus the climax of the civil rights movement—the March on Washington for Jobs and Freedom—was initiated and planned largely by black trade unionists.

The demand for jobs and an end to industry and union bias, originally projected as the main themes for the March at the 1962 NALC convention, was also present in the civil rights demonstrations of the spring and summer of 1963. In Birmingham, Martin Luther King, devoting more attention than in the past to the desperate economic situation of the city's black community, demanded increased employment for blacks as well as an end to segregation. In New York, Philadelphia, and Newark, demonstrators led by the Joint Committee for Equal Employment Opportunity and including members of the NAACP, CORE, and the NALC sought more jobs for Negroes through direct action against employers, government, and unions, and they blocked tax-supported construction projects on which few or no blacks were employed. In New

York, in June, 1963, pickets disrupted work on a $23.5 million Harlem Hospital project, forced the president of the Building Trades Council to announce that qualified blacks would be put to work "right away," and pressed Mayor Robert F. Wagner to appoint an "action panel" to study the problem of increasing the employment of blacks in the building trades. In Philadelphia, demonstrators halted work on an $18-million building project, published the pictures of Negro workers who crossed their picket lines, threatened to have them "ostracized by the Negro community," and obtained agreement from contractors working on public projects to hire qualified black craftsmen. In Newark, pickets protesting building-trades discrimination halted a project and forced the mayor to order an investigation by the Newark Human Relations Council.[36]

In Detroit, 150,000 to 200,000 people, including members and leaders of the UAW, participated in a Freedom March on June 23, 1963, to honor Dr. King and show support for the Birmingham demonstrators and other struggles in the South. Following the march, the Trade Union Leadership Council threatened to picket Cobo Hall, the Detroit civic auditorium, unless the building trades opened up job opportunities for blacks. With the mayor acting as mediator in the dispute, the building trades unions took steps to open up their apprenticeship training programs to blacks.

At Howard University, in the nation's capital, black students discovered that only a few Negroes were working on the construction of their new gymnasium, and that the unions on the job either practiced total exclusion of blacks or accorded only token compliance to the requirement of racial equality where government contracts were involved. The students proceeded to stop further construction, which forced Secretary of Labor Willard Wirtz to call upon the unions to begin opening their ranks to blacks. The black students then asked the General Services Administration (the agency that lets government contracts) to inform all unions and contractors that unions having no Negro apprentices and contractors having employment agreements with such unions were ineligible for those projects.[37]

These and other demonstrations infuriated the discriminatory unions and employers and antagonized some "liberals" in the civil-rights movement, who frowned upon any methods but "passive resistance." But they did open some closed doors to blacks, and they produced a better understanding of the problems facing Negroes as they sought to escape poverty. So, too, did the publication in 1963 of Michael Harrington's *The Other America: Poverty in the United States*, which demolished the myth of *The Affluent Society* by demonstrating that mass poverty existed in this country and that blacks, suffering discrimination in job opportunities at the hands of industry and unions, were the largest group in the nation living in poverty. In July, 1963, the *American Federationist* conceded that Negroes were prevented by union-dominated apprenticeship training programs from becoming part of "the income elite of manual labor." About the same time, Herbert Hill called for renewed pressure to force a change in the situation. "Negroes," he observed, "may be slowly winning the broad legal and social struggles for full citizenship rights but are currently losing the battle for economic equality and job opportunity."[38]

Promises of change by the unions now came in fast and furious succession. In June, 1963, some 300 union leaders agreed to push forward against discrimination; the plumbers' local in New York vowed to increase its efforts to recruit apprentices from among blacks and Puerto Ricans; the New York Hotel Trades Council established a joint committee to survey the status of Negroes; and the presidents of eighteen building trades adopted a program to eliminate discrimination in apprenticeship training, membership, and referrals. In July the United Brotherhood of Carpenters and Joiners issued an order requiring locals to integrate and eliminate discrimination.

Fulfillment of all these promises was infrequent and slow. Late in July, Lyndon Johnson, then Vice-President, met with the leaders of forty building trades unions in New York and urged them to act immediately to end discrimination. The session, which lasted thirty-five hours, ended in total failure. "Nobody can move these people," Johnson reported. "They simply don't mean to do it."[39] How little they meant to do it was illustrated when Plumbers Local Union No. 2 in New York, the local from which Meany had advanced to his position of national labor leadership, struck the Bronx Terminal Market construction site when the contractor tried to comply with the state's fair employment laws by hiring a black and three Puerto Ricans who were not union members but who had tried in vain to gain entrance to the local. When Meany called the controversy a union-against-scab dispute, not a racial issue, and denied that the four men had ever applied for union membership, Morris Doswell, president of the New York NALC chapter, commented that his action "demonstrates that he is an outright prejudiced individual and cannot serve everyone in the American labor movement."[40]

Meany proposed giving tests to the Negro and the Puerto Rican workers to see if they qualified for membership in Local 2, assuring them of acceptance in the union if they passed. After some hesitation, the men took the test and failed. They appealed to the NLRB charging that such tests violated the National Labor Relations Act, which asserted that job competence may be determined only by the employer. The NLRB found Local 2 guilty of unfair labor practices, and the local lost its appeal in the courts.

In Cleveland, after months of mass picketing at the Municipal Hall construction site forced a sheet-metal subcontractor to hire one black worker, the all-white Sheet Metal Workers Local 65 walked off the job, refusing to work with a black man. Plumbers Local Union No. 55 reluctantly yielded to mass picketing at the Cleveland Municipal Hall construction site and signed an agreement with the city, the U.S. Department of Labor, and the United Freedom Movement under which blacks would be admitted to membership into the union-controlled apprenticeship training program. After four black journeymen employed by a black contractor were admitted, the local stopped admitting qualified black journeymen.

When the black students at Howard University succeeded in halting construction of the gymnasium unless blacks were allowed to become members of the union and work on the job, Thompson Powers, special counsel to the President's Committee on Equal Employment Opportunity, declared: "Once it becomes clear that unions who continue to exclude Negroes are placing themselves in a situation where their participation in federal projects is in jeopardy, they themselves will rectify this situation."[41] But he underestimated the strength of opposition to black participation and overestimated the government's willingness to support the demonstrators. For when the unions refused to bow to government pressure, it was the government, not the unions, that retreated. On July 17, 1963, the U.S. Department of Labor issued a directive entitled "Non-Discrimination in Apprenticeship Training," which would have provided for the selection of apprentices, under government supervision, on a nondiscriminatory basis. But the building trades unions immediately appealed to the Construction Industry Joint Conference, a national union-management group, to fight the directive. The conference, on behalf of the unions, lodged strenuous objections with Secretary of Labor Wirtz, who withdrew the original directive and issued revised regulations acceptable to the union-management group, eliminating any effective assurance that blacks would be selected as apprentices.

As August 28, 1963, the day for the March on Washington, approached, greater emphasis was placed on the employment issue by black leaders, who hoped to add a jobs-for-Negroes program to President Kennedy's civil-rights recommendations. But this ran into opposition from white trade-union leaders, who condemned the idea of "special preference" for Negroes in employment opportunities as "discrimination in reverse." Whitney Young, Urban League Executive Secretary, defended preferential treatment for blacks in a statement on August 11: "White people have had special preference all along, though they won't admit it. They've hired the white man though the Negro might have been as qualified or better qualified. It's time we instituted a program of special treatment for Negroes as compensation for generations of denial, at least for a while."[42] Furthermore, Cleveland Robinson explained on a TV program that same day, "We are not just fighting for jobs for Negroes. We're fighting for jobs for all Americans. I must say that it would be impossible for every Negro to be employed unless there is a program of full employment for all Americans."[43] But the opposition from white union leaders continued, and the jobs-for-Negroes program was played down in the March on Washington.

Nonetheless, the March on Washington was the high point in the history of the Negro-Labor Alliance up to that time. The AFL-CIO Executive Council under pressure from Meany, condemned the March by a majority vote. But the AFL-CIO Industrial Union Department, after Walter Reuther had denounced the action of the federation's leadership, defied the Executive Council and strongly supported the great demonstration. Of the 200,000 or more participants, blacks and whites, from all over the United States, an estimated total of 40,000 were union members, the largest mobilization of trade unionists in

American labor history. Two union leaders were among the ten-man leadership of the March: A. Philip Randolph and Walter Reuther.

After August 28 the Negro-Labor Alliance made its influence felt in the struggle to prevent Congressional attempts to dilute the civil-rights recommendations in Kennedy's special message. In February, 1964, responding to its pressure (as well as pressure from Lyndon B. Johnson, who became President on November 22, 1963, following the assassination of John F. Kennedy), the House of Representatives passed the civil-rights bill by a substantial majority. Once again the Dixiecrat-Republican coalition used the filibuster to prevent action in the Senate. The AFL-CIO Executive Council called upon all affiliates to join energetically in the fight to achieve passage by the Senate of the House-approved version of the civil-rights bill, and many responded. Most significant was the response in the South. The Alabama, Mississippi, Texas, and Oklahoma AFL-CIO councils defied segregationist forces within their affiliates and came out in favor of the House-approved version of the bill. Claude Ramsay, president of the Mississippi AFL-CIO human rights conference in the spring of 1964, said that because he had endorsed the civil-rights bill and stood up for the idea of a Negro-labor coalition in his state, he had been the target of attacks from the White Citizens' Councils and the Ku Klux Klan. He added that leaders of unions in his state had been physically attacked by Klansmen for taking the same position and standing up for equal rights for Negroes in their unions. Ramsay assured the delegates that neither he nor the other trade union leaders in Mississippi would be intimidated* and urged a strong campaign to assure that legislation was passed by Congress giving blacks in the South the right to vote. "Organized labor cannot reach its political goals until greater strides are made in granting Negro Mississippians the right to vote," he said.[44]

On June 7, 1964, the NALC fourth annual convention called for a national one-day work stoppage on August 28, the first anniversary of the March on Washington, if the civil-rights bill was not passed by that

---

* Ramsay was right. Otis Matthews, financial secretary and assistant business agent of the International Woodworkers of America, was abducted in Laurel, Mississippi, by hooded Klan mobsters, stripped, tied, and beaten with heavy straps. Sixteen officers of the local inserted an advertisement in the Laurel *Leader-Call* of November 22, 1964, reading in part: "Presumably Brother Matthews was kidnapped and attacked because the federal government has ordered the Masonite plant to treat the members of the Negro race exactly the same as members of the white race. We will not allow the fear of verbal denouncement, physical assault or even death to deter us from our following a reasonable, practical, sound course. Our members have been advised to arm themselves against future occurrence of violence."

At the 1963 convention of the State Council of Carpenters of Mississippi, the council president predicted that the locals in the state would have to accept Negroes as members and expressed the hope that the "various leaders in the locals of Mississippi will be big enough to educate their members and the public so they will accept the issue without incident." Clearly, members of the Laurel local of the International Woodworkers were educated to accept the issue. Donald Crumpton Mosley, "A History of Labor Unionism in Mississippi," unpublished Ph.D. thesis, University of Alabama, 1965, pp. 379–80.

date. But that same month the Senate, for the first time in the history of civil-rights legislation, voted cloture to break a filibuster, and the Civil Rights Act of 1964 became law. It was the most comprehensive civil-rights legislation ever enacted by Congress, and it was hailed as a victory for the Negro-Labor Alliance in both black and labor circles. The new law covered voting, public accommodations, public facilities, education, and fair employment practices. It established a federal Employment Opportunity Commission and extended the life of the Commission on Civil Rights to January, 1968. Title VII of the law prohibited unions and employers of more than 100 workers from discriminating in employment, membership, apprenticeship, or promotion "against any individual because of his race, color, religion, sex, or national origin."[45] Nevertheless, the law did not provide jobs, and the deadline for compliance with Title VII was extended to July, 1965. Moreover, the record of fair employment practices statutes already in operation in many states and cities had demonstrated that enforcement was a good deal more difficult than passage of the laws. Meanwhile, nonwhite unemployment continued to mount. A study of unemployment in Chicago concluded that "there are extensive areas within the ghetto in which unemployment is practically a way of life."[46] Over all, the rate of unemployment among blacks at the time the Civil Rights Act of 1964 was passed was placed at about 10 per cent; that of the white work force was about 5 per cent.

A major cause of black unemployment was still union discrimination. At the AFL-CIO convention in November, 1963, William Schnitzler, secretary-treasurer and chairman of the federation's Civil Rights Committee, delivered a lengthy report on the progress made toward eliminating discriminatory policies and practices in the affiliated unions. Although the cases cited were more numerous than in the past, they still consisted largely of instances in which one or two blacks broke through membership and apprenticeship bars. In New York's Plumbers Local Union No. 2 a massive protest movement had added four blacks to the membership of 4,100. Walter Reuther's comment was significant: "We have made progress, but progress is a relative thing. We are in the middle of a social revolution and when you are dealing with the dynamics of a revolution, people will not judge where we are or where we have come from, they will judge us based on how far we still must go."[47] The black people had a chance to pass judgment a few months later, when the leadership of the New York State AFL-CIO intervened to bring about the defeat of proposed legislation in Albany that would have helped to overcome discrimination against black and Puerto Ricans in apprenticeship programs on the part of employers and unions, especially those in the building trades.

The call for the NALC's fourth annual convention in Cleveland on June 2, 1964, featured the theme: "Fight for Freedom from Poverty Through Fair and Full Employment." It pointed out that the black unemployment rate was twice that of whites; that, although blacks constituted one-tenth of the population, they were one-fourth of the poverty-stricken; that 40 per cent of black teen-agers were unemployed, as against

16 per cent of white teenagers; and that each year automation abolished 2 million unskilled and semiskilled jobs, in which black workers had been and continued to be disproportionately concentrated. "Black and white workers are its victims," the call continued, "and neither group can solve the problem alone. Common sense indicates that a strong alliance between the Negro community and the labor movement must be developed and strengthened."[48] The call concluded with an appeal to the entire black community, organized labor, and white liberals in Cleveland to participate with the NALC in a one-hour "March for Freedom from Poverty Through Fair and Full Employment" in the downtown area. At the same time the call was issued, a Protestant Church study was published; it disclosed that 81 per cent of the 175,000 people living in poverty in the Cleveland area were black.

Randolph declared in his speech to the convention that, even if white liberals condemned the "jobs-for-Negroes" program as "racism in reverse," and even if union leaders pointed to "token" admission of blacks to union membership and apprenticeship programs as progress enough to satisfy blacks, the fight against industry and union bias would continue:

> We will continue our boycotts, sit-ins, and civil disobedience until our grievances are completely redressed. We will not slow down our pace because of a "backlash" reaction by our fair weather friends. We are in the midst of a full-dress revolution. We demand, we do not beg or plead, fundamental economic changes. Even Jesus Christ participated in civil disobedience. We have no alternative.[49]

Soon after the delegates left Cleveland, the *Wall Street Journal* carried on its front page an article that opened: "Northern civil rights groups, who last year carried on a broad campaign against discrimination in such areas as education, housing, and public accommodations, this summer are concentrating their efforts on what they consider the most important target of all: Jobs." For the next several months, NALC members joined with those from the NAACP and CORE to keep up the pressure on employers and unions through mass picketing, sit-ins, lie-ins, bank-ins, shop-ins, and boycotts from San Francisco to Chicago, from Philadelphia to Detroit—all with the single purpose of ending job discrimination. Much of the pressure was directed at employers, but unions, particularly in the building trades, were also the targets of demonstrations. In several cities pickets surrounded construction sites carrying signs demanding "Full Integration of the Building Trades Union," "Job Equality for ALL," and "Full Enforcement of Federal, State, and City Anti-Discrimination Laws—NOW!" When employers and unions protested that there were no blacks qualified to do the work, the civil-rights groups produced qualified blacks. At the same time the Woodlawn Organization in Chicago, a South Side civil-rights group, set up a program with government funds to train auto mechanics, clerk-typists, stenographers, and welders. In Philadelphia, the Reverend Leon Sullivan, head of the city's training effort, organized classes for unemployed

blacks in machine shop work, drafting, electronics and chemistry labora-
tory techniques, and restaurant skills. And in Cleveland the Urban
League began a program aimed at training Negroes to pass the apprenticeship examinations of a number of labor unions.

In the winter of 1965 the movement for jobs was pushed into the
background by events in Selma, Alabama, where a voter-registration
drive led by Martin Luther King, Jr., fresh from receiving the Nobel
Peace Prize for his civil-rights leadership, was under way. The opposition, under the direction of Sheriff Jim Clark, was especially fierce, with
the use of tear gas, whips, and clubs against demonstrators a daily occurrence. In February a black civil-rights worker was killed, and a few weeks
later the Reverend James Reeb, a young white minister from Boston,
was clubbed to death. The black community in the North, East, and
West responded with angry protests and was joined by organized labor.
The AFL-CIO international and state and local unions throughout the
nation denounced the official brutality against civil-rights workers in Alabama and demanded a federal investigation. Demonstrations were held
in Boston, New York, Detroit, and other cities to protest the brutality
in Selma, and union leaders marched with black ministers and public
figures. UAW shop stewards raised funds from auto workers in Detroit
for the Selma voter-registration movement. When Dr. King called for a
selective boycott of Alabama manufacturers, the ILWU voted not to
use or to handle Alabama-made products. Announcing the decision at a
union protest meeting against Selma brutalities in San Francisco, Harry
Bridges called on the entire labor movement to follow the ILWU's lead:
"It is time to quit talking, it's time for some action." William Chester,
ILWU regional director, drew applause from the protestors when he
suggested telling President Johnson that "the Marines in Vietnam could
be better used here at home to bring democracy to the deep South."[50]

At the famous Selma-to-Montgomery march in March, 1965, marred
by the murder of Mrs. Viola Liuzzo, wife of a Detroit teamsters' leader,
almost the entire American labor movement was officially represented,
with Cleveland Robinson of the NALC and Don Slaiman, director of
the AFL-CIO Civil Rights Department, among those who addressed the
huge turnout in Montgomery. This marked an even higher stage in the
Negro-Labor Alliance than the March on Washington in 1963, when
the AFL-CIO Executive Council refused to endorse the demonstration
and only a section of labor, mainly unions in the federation's Industrial
Union Department, participated.

Following the Montgomery demonstration, Walter Reuther, as head
of the "National Coalition of Conscience,"* and leaders of the 1963
March on Washington met to consider a Second Freedom March on

---

* The "National Coalition of Conscience" was initiated by Walter Reuther at the
1964 UAW convention, which authorized an expenditure of $1 million to launch it.
It had a national committee consisting of representatives of numerous labor, civil rights,
church, youth, farm, professional, and other organizations, with Reuther as chairman.
When UAW Local 34 in Atlanta protested the use of union funds for civil rights
causes, Reuther rebuked the local and said its stand was "ill-advised." *The Worker,*
May 16, 1955.

Washington to press for enactment of legislation to protect the rights of voters. The events in Selma had already forced President Johnson to propose such legislation after an address to a joint session of Congress in which he said: "The real hero of this struggle is the American Negro. His actions and protests, his courage to risk safety and even to risk his life, have awakened the conscience of this nation."[51] But a new March on Washington was not needed, so quickly did Congress pass the Voting Rights Act of 1965. The law provided for the assignment of federal examiners to conduct registration and observe voting in states and counties where patterns of discrimination existed and suspended all literacy tests and other disfranchising devices in states and counties where fewer than 50 per cent of the adults had voted in 1964.

There were celebrations in union halls in many cities after passage of the Voting Rights Act. Black civil-rights leaders and union officials toasted the power of the Negro-Labor Alliance. But one black NALC member told a reporter: "You left Alabama feeling the job was unfinished, and wondering if you'd be soon marching again, picketing some of these unions who were in Montgomery with us, demanding jobs for our people."[52]

23 The Negro-Labor Alliance, 1965-68

In the joint struggle for the civil-rights act of 1964 and the voting-rights act of 1965, the Negro-Labor Alliance had brought the black people's movement and organized labor closer together than ever before in American history. Yet even at the moment of its greatest triumph there were indications that the alliance rested on a shaky foundation.

Following the passage of the civil-rights act, a sharp rift developed between the more militant blacks in the movement and white liberal labor leaders over the drive to seat the Mississippi Freedom Democratic Party at the 1964 Democratic National Convention. Efforts by prominent white labor leaders to persuade SNNC and the Freedom Democratic Party to accept the compromise offered by President Johnson, which in effect meant acceptance of white racists as the official spokesmen for the party in Mississippi, convinced the black militants that the white liberal leaders were unreliable allies, more eager to appease the White House than to stand firmly for the basic rights of the black people.

A year later the Mississippi Freedom Democratic Party, under the leadership of Fannie Lou Hamer, organized the Mississippi Freedom Labor Union and began recruiting black sharecroppers in the state in a drive to end their desperate poverty. In May, 1965, after the planters had rejected a request from the union for $1.25 an hour and an eight-hour day, the sharecroppers in Leland, Mississippi, went on strike, the first such action by farmhands in the rich Delta area since an abortive uprising in the 1930's. Strikers were evicted from the ramshackle houses owned by the planters, and sheriff's deputies, with prisoners from the county jail in Greenville supplying the muscle, dumped their meager belongings on the highway. The Freedom Labor Union tried desperately to bring the plight of the strikers to the attention of the unions, which had sent large delegations to the Selma-Montgomery March, but, even though the June 7, 1965, *New York Times* carried a full-page story on the strike, the response of the unions was mainly indifference. The strikers were forced by starvation to abandon their drive.

In addition to the growing disillusionment among militant civil-rights activists with the behavior of the trade unions in legislative campaigns, there was growing opposition to the philosophy of nonviolence that had characterized the movement. To Martin Luther King, Jr., nonviolence was a great moral force that would overcome the brutal power of white supremacy through passive resistance. But to the militant black activists, especially the young, it was increasingly equated with broken heads, dead bodies, and bread-and-water diets in prison. When the activists came north to aid in the struggle for housing, education, and jobs, they met black people in the ghettos who knew from bitter experience that white racists in the police force laughed at nonviolence and respected only effective self-defense.

Such experiences lent considerable substance to the arguments that had been advanced during the civil-rights revolution by the eloquent Black Muslim spokesman Malcolm X. Malcolm had voiced scorn for the movement's nonviolent philosophy and what he considered its basic irrelevance to the fundamental needs of the black masses. He had repeatedly predicted that the white liberals, including the trade-union leaders, would be unreliable allies and urged blacks to develop their own sources of power so that they could determine their own destiny. Following his expulsion from the Black Muslims after the assassination of President Kennedy, Malcolm revised his view that all white people were, by nature of American racist society, implacable enemies of blacks, but he did emphasize that the "good white people" were only a small minority and that "most American white people seem not to have it in them . . . to do justice to the black man."[1] He now argued that it was the duty of the "sincere, well-meaning good white people" to stay out of black organizations and movements, leaving them under the control of blacks and work to eliminate racism among the white majority. Only when black people had developed sufficient power among themselves through their own solidarity, he argued, could there be any talk of black-white unity.

On February 21, 1965, while addressing an audience in Harlem, Malcolm X was assassinated. The white press and white liberals in general reacted to his death with a feeling of relief and "good riddance." Some prominent blacks shared this feeling: U.S. Information Agency Director Carl Rowan dismissed Malcolm as "an ex-convict, ex-dope peddler, who became a racial fanatic," who "preached segregation and race hatred," and whose viewpoint was rejected by all but "a tiny minority of the Negro population of America."[2] But this itself was quickly proved to be a minority viewpoint, for Malcolm X came to be regarded by black militants, especially the young, as the clearest ideologist in the black liberation movement. Soon his autobiography, published in 1965, became as well known to black militants as any other book by a black author. Together with Malcolm's posthumously published speeches, the book fueled a growing disillusionment with the civil-rights movement in important segments of the black community. The realities of life itself confirmed the feeling for growing numbers of black Americans.

Many American historians, sociologists, and economists were finding, slightly more than a decade after the 1954 Supreme Court decision, that the nation had embarked on nothing less than a "Second Reconstruction," which in a brief period had brought remarkable changes in the lives of black Americans. They conceded that social and racial problems were not at an end, but conditions for blacks had vastly improved. More blacks were going to college, using facilities and accommodations previously closed to them, moving to the suburbs, and entering the economic mainstream. From 1940 to 1960, the percentage of black males in professional, technical, and kindred occupations had more than doubled; their percentage among clerks, salespeople, and skilled workers had risen two and a half times. In 1960 there were nearly twenty times as many Negro engineers as in 1940, six times as many accountants and auditors, and twice as many lawyers and judges. From 1939 to 1964, the median wage of the black male worker rose more than sevenfold and that of the white only fivefold, reflecting the huge increase in black membership of trade unions. In Detroit black members of the UAW were among the city's elite. In 1960 more than 57 per cent of Detroit's blacks owned automobiles (11.4 per cent had two), and about 41 per cent owned their own homes. In short, as the historian Oscar Handlin of Harvard University argued, the changes since 1940, and particularly since the 1954 Supreme Court decision, offered convincing proof that Negroes were at last beginning to share the economic and social advances already made by white, foreign-born immigrant groups and that the country could look forward to an era of racial peace.

The riots in Watts, the black ghetto of Los Angeles, in August, 1965, punctured this euphoria. Why, bewildered white America asked, do the Negroes riot now, after so many gains?

The answer was clear. The Montgomery bus boycott of 1955–56, the lunch-counter sit-ins of the early 1960's, the March on Washington in 1963, the Civil Rights Act of 1964, and the Voting Rights Act of 1965, were all successes. But they were only dimly relevant to the lives of most Negroes in the North. As the *New York Times* put it after Watts: "The fact is that the new civil-rights laws—and the related anti-poverty program—have not greatly improved the lot of the teeming ghettos of the cities of the North."[3]

The obstacles still remaining in the black American's path to full participation in American life were underscored by the census figures of 1960 on the economic status of blacks in cities, released in November, 1964, through the National Urban League. They showed that 50 to 84 per cent of black wage-earners fell into three menial and unskilled categories: operative, household service, and laborer. (An operative is an unskilled mill or factory worker.) In New York City alone 63 per cent of black wage-earners were in those categories. In Detroit in 1940, some 75 per cent of black males were classified as factory operatives, service workers, or laborers. In 1960 the figure was still 70 per cent, as compared to 35 per cent of the white force. In New Orleans in 1960, 84 per cent of blacks were employed in menial tasks and as laborers, while in Miami the percentage was 83.

The figures disclosed that the percentages of Negro families with an annual income below the government "poverty line" of $3,000 were 23 in Los Angeles, 24 in Newark, 27 in Chicago and New York, 28 in Cleveland, 30 in Philadelphia, 32 in Baltimore, 36 in Pittsburgh, 35 in Kansas City, and 34 in Detroit.

Another set of telling statistics concerned the percentage of school dropouts among blacks twenty-five years of age or over. The figures were 88 per cent for Seattle and 68 for New York. In New York a total of 474,962 in a twenty-five-or-over group of 721,960 had not completed high school.

Unemployment figures were also revealing. In Detroit, where many blacks were said to be living in relative affluence, 16.8 per cent of the black labor force and 10.1 per cent of the whites were out of work in 1940. Comparable figures in 1960 were 17.4 and 7.1 per cent. Detroit unemployment, of course, varied with ups and downs in the sale of autos. When production in the plants dropped, black unemployment rose, since whites, having entered the industry earlier, had greater job security.

Unemployment rates in the inner cities rose after 1960 as the flight from the South to the Northern ghettos intensified. Conversely, the number of black farmers in the South declined; at the end of 1964, only 142,506 blacks were among the 718,900 farmers left in eight Southern states, and it was clear that farming was "becoming an all-white occupation in the South." The number of black sharecroppers also went down, as machines, chemical weed-killers, and flame cultivation took over work formerly done by black men, women, and children. Those who left for the North arrived at a time when the spread of automation was robbing the blacks already resident in the Northern ghettos of their traditional unskilled places in industry. Inferior education and other consequences of the long history of segregation were leaving the black behind in the race for better-paying jobs. It did no good to tell untrained, ill-educated men and women that there were many openings for computer programers or medical technicians.

By the summer of 1965, the mass of blacks living in the Northern ghettos were keenly aware that the civil-rights victories benefited primarily a very small percentage of middle-class blacks, while their own predicament remained the same or worsened. No one saw this more clearly than the man who had become the symbol of the civil-rights movement—Martin Luther King, Jr. While many black militants concluded that a Negro-Labor Alliance had no significance for blacks living in poverty and facing a permanent state of unemployment, King was convinced that the "invincible power" of the "grand alliance of organized labor and the Negro people," so important in the victories achieved in the civil-rights struggles, could be utilized to solve the problem the movement had failed to touch. Nor did he doubt that this "grand alliance" could be maintained and strengthened, even in the face of the rising tide of black separatism. For it was his firm belief that organized labor and the black people had many "mutual interests and concerns" that made the alliance essential to both groups. Both had an interest in organizing the unemployed and in waging the war on poverty, for the existence of large-scale joblessness among blacks, especially among black youth, was at once a threat to the living standards of the employed and a major underpinning for the continued existence of the slum ghetto. Both had an interest in the organization of the underpaid workers in hospitals, laundries, service industries, and the like, most of them black or members of other minority groups. In common, organized labor and the black people had to cope with the advent of automation, which threatened organized labor with disemployment for hundreds of thousands of its members and the black people with continued victimization by the technological revolution. Finally, in specific arenas, both faced the same opponents. Hence King urged a joint struggle by organized labor and the black people to open a new road for the whole nation that would lead to gains not encompassed in the civil-rights victories.

To Dr. King, endorsement of the Negro-Labor Alliance was not, as some charged, just an attempt to retain his hold on the black community. Since the 1955–56 Montgomery bus boycott, King had directed special attention to achieving such an alliance as part of the civil-rights revolution. He received financial and moral support from the unions in his crusade against segregation, but he also gave. When unions were attempting to organize black workers, he was ready to lend a hand. This was particularly true in the case of two relatively small unions, District 65 and the Drug and Hospital Employees Local 1199. King attended every District 65 convention after the Montgomery bus boycott and interrupted activities in the South to help in its organizing drives among blacks and Puerto Ricans. He once announced proudly that District 65 had made him an "honorary member" at the time of the bus boycott.

But the Drug and Hospital Employees Local 1199, affiliated, like District 65, to the Retail, Wholesale, and Department Store Clerks Union, AFL-CIO, was King's favorite union. He told a "Salute to Freedom" rally conducted by the union three weeks before his assassination: "You have provided concrete and visible proof that when black and white workers unite in a democratic organization like Local 1199 they can move mountains."[4] To King, Local 1199 was also "visible proof" of the importance of an alliance between the civil-rights and labor movements. Each had helped the other over the years, and each had benefited from the association.

Started by Jewish drug clerks in Harlem and the Bronx, Local 1199 undertook in 1958 the monumental task of organizing workers in the voluntary hospitals in the New York area. It was a field that many long-established unions said, apparently with good reason, was "unorganizable." The workers were nearly all uneducated blacks and Puerto Ricans whose wages ran as low as $28 for a forty-eight-hour week; many were so poor that they needed supplementary relief from the Welfare Department to feed, clothe, and house their families. They were barred by state law from collective bargaining, were not covered by laws guaranteeing minimum wages or unemployment compensation, and had neither Blue Cross nor sick-pay insurance. "It was a tragic joke in the hospitals that none of the nonprofessional employees could afford to be sick."[5] The philanthropists-businessmen who sat on the hospital boards all contributed to worthy causes, some even to civil rights, but their interest in the welfare of poor people stopped at the entrance to the hospitals. Unions, they claimed, were necessary neither for the hospital workers nor for the proper administration of the institutions. On the contrary, they would be a threat to the functioning of the hospitals, for in the event of strikes or walkouts, the lives of patients would be endangered.

Local 1199 thought otherwise. In 1959, a year after it had entered the hospital field, it won its first victory after a bitter forty-six-day strike. Again in 1962 it won a long strike. It had already organized over 15,000 hospital and nursing-home workers in the New York metropolitan area, raised their wages, reduced their working hours, and improved their working conditions.* Through all these struggles, the white, black, and Puerto Rican members of 1199 were in the forefront of unionists supporting the civil-rights struggles in the South with funds and volunteers to help man the demonstrations led by King and others. The union's organizing drives received support from a wide variety of sources, including Harry Van Arsdale, Jr., who, as president of the New York City Central Labor Council, defended Local 1199 before city and state authorities and persuaded construction workers to help man the picket lines in the strikes against the hospitals.

But it was the black community that gave the union its greatest support. Both the NAACP and the Urban League endorsed its drives; leading black performers, notably Ossie Davis and Ruby Dee, picketed alongside the black and Puerto Rican strikers; the National Negro Labor Council, and A. Philip Randolph, its president, lent support; and Malcolm X, in a speech shortly before his assassination, gave Local 1199 his stamp of approval, saying that he admired the union because its leaders were not "afraid of upsetting the applecart of those people who are running City Hall or sitting in Albany or sitting in the White House."[6] But it was Dr. King who became the union's patron saint. Disregarding the advice of some who accused the union of being "Communist-dominated" —a charge it repeatedly denied—and who warned that close association with its organizing drives would alienate wealthy contributors to the civil-rights movement, King announced that he was ready at any moment to help improve the condition of the black and Puerto Rican men and women who cooked and scrubbed and carried patients, who swept and hauled out the refuse in hospitals and nursing homes, achieve a life without poverty. When Local 1199 conducted a campaign in 1962 to win passage of a union-rights law in the New York State Legislature, King put through a personal call to Governor Nelson Rockefeller urging its enactment. When the union was organizing in Newark, New Jersey, in the fall of 1954, King was the featured speaker at a fund-raising "Rally for Freedom." "Your great organizing crusade," he told the hospital workers, "to win union and human rights for New Jersey hospital workers is part and parcel of the struggle we are conducting in the Deep

---

* The first two organizers assigned to the organizing campaign by Leon Davis, the union's president, were Elliott Godoff, a white druggist, and Ted Mitchell, a black organizer for Local 1199.

South. I want to congratulate your union for charting a road for all labor to follow—dedication to the cause of the underpaid and exploited workers in our nation."[7] Strikers carried signs reading, "Martin Luther King is an Honorary Member of Local 1199," and "Martin Luther King Supports Hospital Strikers." It was from a picket line of the Newark hospital strikers that King left for Oslo to receive the Nobel Peace Prize in 1964.

Before his departure for Norway, King had also appealed for support for 700 black women, members of a local of the Chemical Workers Union, AFL-CIO, who were on strike at the Scripto Pen Plant in Atlanta, Georgia, to upgrade the Negro women to higher-paid jobs held only by whites. Upon his return, he joined the picket line and issued a call for a boycott of Scripto products, helping to make the struggle a national issue. Speaking to the Scripto strikers in December, 1964, King indicated his understanding that civil rights alone were not the answer:

> Along with the struggle to desegregate, we must engage in the struggle for better jobs. The same system that exploits the Negro exploits the poor white man. The white power structure hollers nigger, nigger, nigger while exploiting both poor white and Negroes.
>
> We want our freedom and we want all of it now. It is all right to talk about milk and honey over there, but we need food down here. *What good does it do a man to have integrated lunch counters if he can't buy a hamburger?*[8]

King advanced his vision of a Negro-Labor Alliance to carry on where the civil-rights movement had left off in a speech to the sixth annual convention of the Negro American Labor Council in June, 1965 (he had also been the principal speaker at the 1961 NALC convention). He urged the council's cooperation in a new movement to achieve "a better distribution of wealth within this country for all of God's children." Randolph congratulated King on his understanding that "the civil-rights revolution, though indispensable to endow Negroes with full, first-class citizenship and with political potentiality to help shape and direct the course of the American government, is wholly inadequate successfully to grapple with the basic economic and social problems of black Americans." In the struggle to solve problems like unemployment and job bias, it was necessary for the Negro people to "fashion a new weapon." Like King, Randolph believed the weapon had to be an alliance of the Negro and labor and of the black poor and white poor. He pledged the support and cooperation of the NALC in strengthening an alliance of Negro and labor to "wage the war on poverty."[9]

With the aim of proving the value of the Negro-Labor Alliance to blacks in Northern ghettos (as well as the validity of nonviolence in solving the problems of the inner cities), King selected Chicago as a starting point. Chicago had a reputation as the most segregated Northern city. Of the ten largest cities, it had the greatest percentage of substandard housing except for Saint Louis; 41 per cent of all black families in the city lived in dilapidated dwellings; blacks paid $10 a month more than whites when buying houses and higher rates on mortgages. But

housing was only the beginning of a broad base of exploitation, for segregation in housing was bound up with inferior, segregated education
(even if *de facto* rather than *de jure*), health care, and cultural facilities.
At the base of it all were the higher rates of black unemployment and
concentration in low-paying jobs. Chicago, too, was governed by the
ruthless machine of Mayor Richard Daley, which ignored the needs of
the black community and openly catered to white racists who were determined to keep blacks hemmed in in the ghetto. Finally, Chicago had
the potential for an effective Negro-Labor Alliance. A strong section of
the labor movement had long been identified with the cause of civil
rights, and the leaders of those unions were eager to join with King in
proving the viability of the Negro-Labor Alliance at a time when blacks
were questioning the value of coalitions with any white organizations.
Moreover, those union leaders were under pressure from their black
members to do something about opening the opportunity for housing
outside the ghetto, since they had to travel long distances to plants increasingly being located on the outskirts of the city and in suburbs far
from the ghetto where they were forced to live.

In the fall of 1965 the Chicago Freedom Movement was formed under Dr. King's leadership. The CFM, a partnership of the Southern
Christian Leadership Conference and the Coordinating Committee of
Community Organizations, represented a coalition of Southern civil-
rights and Northern urban black movements. The Chicago chapter of
the NALC was an important element in the coalition and gave it a big
push with the publication in January, 1966, of a study entitled "The
Other Chicago: The City's Employed Poor." Presented with the endorsement of the Chicago branch of the AFL-CIO's Industrial Union
Department, the study intended to demolish the myth, accepted by
many white Chicagoans, that whatever poverty existed in the city was
created in Mississippi, Georgia, and Alabama and was no reflection of
the reality of life for those born in the city.

The study revealed that in 1964, when the U.S. Department of Labor
showed that it took $6,400 a year for a husband, wife, and two children
to live moderately well, more than 300,000 Chicago workers earned less
than $3,000, and 200,000 more an average wage of between $80 and $110
a week. "Thus, in the Greater Chicago area at least 515,000 are working
poor. Of these, at least 400,000 live in the city of Chicago, the overwhelming part in the slums and ghettos." The biggest proportion worked
in industries that were either totally or largely unorganized. Singling out
the hospital workers, mainly blacks, for special attention, the study
pointed out that 5,338 of them made less than $1.70 an hour, and
nearly 5,000 earned less than $1.50 an hour before deductions. More-
over, few were covered by medical insurance or had hospitalization protection and employer-provided life insurance, so that the health workers
themselves without health protection.

In the preface to the NALC study, Timuel Black, president of the
Chicago chapter, noted that its contents concerned every Chicagoan.
"None can escape the corroding effects of the deprivation and dire pov-

erty which, as the facts reveal, affect hundreds of thousands." He called for "an aroused community to join hands with organized labor" to bring an end to these conditions and help raise the income of slum and ghetto dwellers, "which, in turn, is the decisive condition for the elimination of slums, along with the fight for full employment."[10] The study was widely circulated by the Chicago Freedom Movement as well as by many trade unions in the city.

In February, 1966, seventy-eight Chicago labor leaders met with King at a luncheon sponsored by District 1 of the United Packinghouse Workers. (The building-trades union leaders were conspicuous by their absence.) In his speech, King conceded that the Civil Rights Movement had not done anything to "enlarge life" for the black ghetto-dweller and called upon the labor movement, whose techniques and methods as well as financial and membership support had been so crucial in the civil-rights victories, to join in the war against poverty and slums in Chicago. The job that had to be done was "bigger than just for Chicago,"[11] for a victory in this crusade would prove that the Negro-Labor Alliance could still be of value nationally in dealing with such problems as unemployment, poverty, and automation. The meeting resulted in pledges of moral and financial support for the Chicago Freedom Movement and the establishment of a steering committee of trade unionists to work with the CFM.

Then followed a series of mass meetings to mobilize the crusade to transform Chicago. In March a capacity audience of 14,000 greeted King at the Chicago Freedom Festival, held at the Amphitheatre. In the audience were top leaders of trade unions, including the United Packinghouse Workers, the UAW, and the meat cutters, and thousands of rank-and-file unionists, many identified by their union armbands. A banner emblazoned "United Steel Workers of America" was unfurled in one part of the hall. Never before, said King in his speech, had organized labor responded so overwhelmingly to appeals to deal with the problems of the ghetto black. "I am absolutely convinced that this evening will go down as one of the most significant events in the history of the civil-rights movement in the United States." Even reporters for the commercial press singled out the labor unions for "really making the rally a success."[12]

Dr. King took up residence in the Twenty-Fourth Ward of Chicago's West Side, an area of deep poverty, and the campaign of the Chicago Freedom Movement got under way. On July 15, 1966, the hottest day of the year, 50,000 packed Soldiers Field. Labor representation was indicated by the numerous union placards. "We are here today because we are tired," King told the audience. "We are tired of being seared in the flames of withering injustice. We are tired of paying more for less. We are tired of living in rat-infested slums. . . . We are tired of inferior, segregated, and overcrowded schools which are incapable of preparing our young people for leadership and security in this technological age. We are tired of discrimination in employment, which makes us the last hired and the first fired." The battle to end these conditions in Chicago would be won not through violence, but through the unity of the black people and organized labor. "Our power is in this unity. We must avoid the error of building a distrust for all white people. . . . Let us all, black and white alike, see that we are tied in a single garment of destiny. We need each other." After the meeting, about 5,000 joined Dr. King in a three-mile march to City Hall, where he posted on the city government's doors eight demands to make Chicago an open city: (1) that real estate agents refuse to handle property not available to all races and that banks and loan associations pledge nondiscrimination; (2) that public housing be constructed outside the ghetto; (3) that city purchases be restricted to firms with "full-scale" fair employment policies; (4) that business and local government publish racial employment statistics and that construction unions accept 400 black and Puerto Rican apprentices; (5) that the county public-aid department recognize unionized welfare recipients; (6) that a citizens' review board be established for the police department; (7) that the city immediately adopt a desegregation plan; and (8) that discriminatory businesses be boycotted.

Prominent among the marchers to City Hall were members of the United Packinghouse Workers, the UAW, the State, County, and Municipal Workers, the shoe workers, the United Steel Workers, and the meat cutters. The Industrial Union Department of the AFL-CIO was present, with a banner reading: "AFL-CIO Unions Support You." The marchers kept up the chant: "Jim Crow Must Go!" "Mayor Daley Must Go!"[13]

But neither Jim Crow nor Mayor Daley went. The Chicago Freedom Movement campaigned for more than a year, conducting weekly marches in Chicago and from Chicago to Cicero, many led by Dr. King, to protest discrimination in housing, education, and jobs. But week after week, the violence unleashed against the demonstrators mounted in intensity while the Chicago police looked on with approval. Mayor Daley issued statements denouncing King as an "outside agitator" who was trying to revive his sagging reputation by stirring up the contented black community of Chicago against its best interests. He reminded Chicagoans that in November, 1964, FBI Director J. Edgar Hoover had called King "the most notorious liar in the United States."[14] These statements, and the conduct of the Chicago police, long infamous for their brutality in defense of the *status quo*, could be expected. But what shook the demonstrators most was that racist mobs hurling stones and shouting foul epithets, especially during the violence-marred trek to Cicero, included not only many members of the building construction unions, but even white members of unions whose leaders were on the steering committee of the Chicago Freedom Movement. The liberal white union leaders had made a truly serious effort to prove that the Negro-Labor Alliance could break through the walls of prejudice in Chicago, but they were unable to speak for the racists in their own organizations. Black militants were shocked to find their efforts opposed not only by confirmed ultra-right racists but even by union members who had been with them in the freedom marches in the South. They had discovered what was already becoming clear in sociological surveys and public opinion polls—that many of the workers were themselves now living in lily-white suburbs and were as eager, as middle-class commuters, to preserve segregation.

Understandably, many of the black marchers concluded that many white unionists who supported civil-rights legislation were prepared to grant black people equality when it did not affect their own neighborhoods and did not require their own children to associate with black children. Malcolm X had been right, many followers of Dr. King now declared.

The bitter experiences during the protest marches tended to overshadow some real accomplishments of the Negro-Labor Alliance in Chicago. For example, AFL-CIO unions had sent organizers into the city's slums to form associations to bargain with landlords; the UAW alone sent 125 paid organizers for four days. Before the drive was over, nearly 10,000 ghetto tenants had been unionized, formally affiliated with the AFL-CIO, and recognized by the real-estate agents. This, one commentator notes, "was a considerable achievement and a step in the right direction of ghetto political and economic power."[15] But its potential lay in the future; Chicago's ghetto blacks still had received little benefit from the Freedom Movement Dr. King had led. On August 26, 1966, a "Summit Agreement" was reached in which the City Board of Realtors promised to "withdraw all opposition to the philosophy of open-occupancy legislation," and the Chicago Federation of Labor and the Industrial Union Council agreed that "their organizations have a major stake in working out the problems of fair housing and would do their utmost to promote this goal." Although this agreement was derided by black militants as "a lot of words," the Chicago Freedom Movement accepted it.

King departed for other battles, leaving behind in Chicago a black community increasingly disillusioned with his brand of struggle to solve its problems. When King returned in 1967 to launch Operation Breadbasket, a ghetto audience booed his reference to the "invincible power" of the Negro-Labor Alliance. When he criticized blacks who condemned alliances with whites, he was forced to leave the platform.*

The setback suffered by the Negro-Labor Alliance in Chicago was a

---

* The Negro-Labor Alliance in Chicago was revived by Operation Breadbasket under the leadership of the Reverend Jesse Jackson. In its campaign to increase employment for blacks, Operation Breadbasket received the support of a number of Chicago trade unions, and several officially endorsed its boycotts against a dairy, Country Delight; High-Low Foods, Inc., a grocery chain with fifty-four outlets in the black community; and its most spectacular, the sixteen-week campaign against the A & P food chain, which had some forty stores in Chicago's black community. Each of these firms finally agreed to hire scores of blacks. Later other companies, fearing they would be hit by boycotts, agreed to hire blacks.

Operation Breadbasket aided black hospital workers, teachers, and bus drivers during their strikes. Although critical of the unions, its ministers felt it important to join forces with organized labor. The Reverend Calvin Morris, in charge of Operation Breadbasket's trade-union work, told striking hospital workers: "Much of the labor movement is obese, fat, and tired. . . . Yet, the Lord never leaves us comfortless; even in the midst of fat-cat unions, we still see some light shining." Thomas R. Brooks, "Black Upsurge in the Unions," *Dissent*, March–April, 1970, p. 130.

severe blow to the Negro American Labor Council. But its prestige had been undermined still earlier. To the astonishment and dismay of black workers, newspapers in December, 1965, announced that at the AFL-CIO convention in San Francisco, A. Philip Randolph, president of the Brotherhood of Sleeping Car Porters and of the NALC, had given the labor federation a clean bill of health on discrimination. Although Randolph conceded that there were still vestiges of prejudice, enough progress had been made under the leadership of George Meany, he said, to justify his accolade. Reporters noted that Randolph delivered his tribute to a convention attended by only about fifteen blacks among 1,000 delegates.

In January, 1966, the NALC's accommodation to the AFL-CIO leadership continued. The council's Executive Board announced that it was sending a delegate to the AFL-CIO to cooperate in a drive to repeal Section 14-b of the Taft-Hartley Act, affecting "right-to-work" laws in nineteen states. No one interested in the welfare of black workers (especially in the South) could question this goal. But there were some who recalled that a year before Adam Clayton Powell, Jr., chairman of the House Education and Labor Committee, had threatened to hold up the bill for repeal "unless the trade unions eliminate some of the discriminating practices affecting hiring and apprenticeship for Negroes."[16] Powell had yielded to pressure from labor and Negro groups, but the conditions that had provoked his action had not changed markedly in a year. However, the NALC statement explaining its decision to cooperate with the AFL-CIO, written by Randolph, declared:

> The position was adopted to shift from its original strategy of attack upon the AFL-CIO on account of race bias to one of alliance and cooperation, because of its change in policy and program to wipe out racial discrimination in the House of Labor. While the business of eliminating racial discrimination has yet a long way to go, the Board acknowledged that some progress has been and is being made, through consistent and constant educational action campaigns in city central bodies, state federations, national and local unions under the leadership of George Meany and Walter Reuther.[17]

In June, 1966, at the sixth annual convention of the NALC, Randolph resigned as president. Although much remained to be done to eliminate racial restrictions in the AFL-CIO, he said, enough progress had already been made and enough evidence existed that the trend would continue unabated to warrant his turning over the leadership to others. He advised against making blanket attacks against the AFL-CIO "because some local union in New York or Georgia discriminates against Negro workers."[18] Randolph then introduced I. W. Abel, president of the United Steelworkers of America, as the type of leader who justified his confidence that remaining obstacles to full equality for black members of the AFL-CIO would soon be removed. At that precise moment, Local 379 of the United Steelworkers of America was one of eight AFL-CIO locals (along with five companies) charged with racial discrimination in a complaint filed by the NAACP with the Equal Employment Opportunity

Commission. Another was a local of the Plumbers Union in Pittsburgh, whose officers the Pittsburgh chapter of the NALC had asked Meany to remove after both the state and the city Human Rights Commissions and a city magistrate had found the local guilty of discrimination against two black plumbers. Roy Battles, president of the NALC Pittsburgh chapter, had written to Meany that the local's action was "a direct challenge, not only to the U.S. Constitution and Bill of Rights, but . . . also . . . to the declared policies and convention actions of the AFL-CIO and its affiliated unions, which time and again declared their commitment to the abolition of all discrimination within the ranks of Labor."[19] But Meany had ignored the complaint, and the Pittsburgh plumbers' local still did not have a single black member.

Had Randolph delivered his praise of the AFL-CIO in the fall of 1964 instead of in June, 1966, he would have been in the company of the NAACP. On September 2, 1964, at a meeting of 250 national, state, and local labor leaders, George Meany outlined the federation's stepped-up civil-rights program. He announced that labor could not wait until July 1, 1965, when Title VII, the section in the Civil Rights Act of 1964 barring job and union discrimination, took effect, and that all affiliates of the AFL-CIO should begin at once to comply voluntarily. Meany also asked all of the federation's 800 county central units that had not already done so to set up civil-rights committees to work with other community groups in carrying out desegregation of schools, hotels, restaurants, and other facilities. He further asked the county bodies and the fifty state central organizations to hold educational conferences to "counteract the misinformation"[20] circulating among union members about the Civil Rights Act, and he urged each national union to assign a top officer to be responsible for developing a fair employment practices program within the union. Finally, Meany declared that the federation would try to help nonunion workers to establish machinery to prepare complaints to the government when they encountered discrimination.

Meany's firm stand drew enthusiastic praise from Roy Wilkins, NAACP executive secretary, who was present and addressed the gathering. The New York Times called Wilkins's presence in itself "a sign that the AFL-CIO and the NAACP, which have been feuding over association charges of union discrimination that the federation regarded as unfair, have entered a period of cooperation."[21] It attributed this development to the organizations' common opposition to Barry Goldwater, Republican candidate for President.

Other commentators attributed Meany's strong civil-rights position to certain landmark decisions on the eve of the gathering. The first, on July 1, 1964, was the NLRB ruling in the Hughes Tool Company case, which for the first time since the Taft-Hartley Act was enacted in 1951 held discrimination by labor unions to be an unfair labor practice. "The principle set," wrote George Morris, veteran labor reporter for the Daily Worker, "will put many unions on warning that they risk the loss of certification as bargaining units if they discriminate," although he added that it "may have little more than moral influence in most of the building trades field. The unions in that area seldom depend on the NLRB's services, and many do not even register for certification under the Taft-Hartley Law."[22] Then, on August 25, 1964, New York State Supreme Court Justice Jacob L. Markowitz declared in a ruling against Local 28, Sheet Metal Workers, and the employers on the industry's Joint Apprenticeship Committee that the law and "the realities of today's society" require that unions abandon any apprenticeship plan that "could be used, directly or indirectly, to discriminate against any person on the basis of race, color, creed, or national origin."[23] Justice Markowitz's decision was directed against the father-son hiring tradition of the construction industry. The NAACP Labor Department urged Meany and the AFL-CIO Executive Council to utilize the decision at the conference in Washington to declare the ruling outlawing father-and-son unionism as "policy" for all construction unions, but the request was ignored.

Whatever the motivation for Meany's actions, they did win praise from the NAACP. While it continued to sponsor demonstrations against discrimination by the building trades unions, in late 1965 and early 1966 the NAACP lauded the activity of the AFL-CIO Civil Rights Department and the fact that an office had been set up in Atlanta to help Southern unions to comply with Title VII, as well as regional conferences held throughout the nation on implementation of the law. Perhaps, many in the NAACP now reasoned, the law would achieve what a decade of mass demonstrations, complaints filed with FEPC agencies, and repeated attempts to secure enforcements of federal antidiscrimination executive orders had failed to accomplish.

But a year after Title VII went into effect, the NAACP could report only negligible progress against discrimination in labor. Some unions with a long history of anti-Negro discrimination had been compelled to make "minimal strategic adjustment to the law." But over all, the action of the unions had been "a less than 'token' response to anti-discrimination demands and laws."[24] The disclosures in April, 1966, at hearings before the U.S. Commission on Civil Rights in Cleveland revealed that Local 38 of the International Brotherhood of Electrical Workers, with a total membership of 1,258, had no Negro members; Local 17 of the iron workers, with a total membership of 1,786, had no Negro members; Plumbers Local Union 55, with a total membership of 1,482, had three Negro members; Local 36 of the pipefitters, with a total membership of 1,319, had one Negro member; Local 65 of the sheet metal workers, with a total membership of 1,077, had forty-five Negro members. All together, the five craft locals had four black apprentices.

The same situation prevailed in Cincinnati, where six building-trades unions had not a single black member, and the only Negroes in the construction industry were eleven in the 3,600-member carpenters' local and "a small number" in the operating engineers and the roofers. In both instances, the blacks were limited to unskilled jobs. In Pittsburgh, too, eleven building trades unions had not a single black member, and five others had a total of sixty-two, again in unskilled jobs.

Title VII specifically prohibited discriminatory practices by labor unions but left a loophole: the use of qualifying tests, both written and oral, which many craft unions, the NAACP noted, had seized upon as "an effective means of excluding Negroes and circumventing the law." Complaints from black workers on this score were piling up in the NAACP office. The AFL-CIO's Civil Rights Department, for all its increased activity, took so long to process the complaints that blacks were compelled to turn to the Equal Opportunity Commission for redress. Complaints still pending with the commission a year after the law went into effect charged a number of AFL-CIO affiliates with negotiating separate racial seniority provisions of collective-bargaining agreements, maintaining segregated locals, excluding workers from membership because of race, and refusing to admit black workers into union-controlled training programs. Moreover, NLRB rulings against discriminatory employers in some instances were nullified by the unions, which would not allow the employers to stop discrimination. In San Francisco, for example, civil-rights organizations had won an agreement from the Hotel Employers Association that opened new job opportunities for black workers, only to have it invalidated by the Hotel, Restaurant, and Bartenders Union, "with the full support of the AFL-CIO Central Labor Council."[25] And although AFL-CIO affiliates like the Brotherhood of Railway and Steamship Clerks and the Brotherhood of Locomotive Firemen had been lauded for abolishing segregated lodges, they accomplished this by eliminating the jobs of the black workers.

Many industries that had collective-bargaining contracts with AFL-CIO affiliates showed a considerable amount of integration, but relatively few minority workers were in the better positions. A survey of the hotel industry in New York City in the fall of 1964 revealed that about 40 per cent of the 33,000 employees were either blacks or Puerto Ricans, but only a few were in building-maintenance positions or working as cashiers, auditors, typists, or switchboard operators.

The situation could not be remedied without eliminating discriminatory seniority provisions in union contracts. National attention was drawn to the problem in the fall of 1964 when the national chairman of CORE, Floyd B. McKissick, was retained by black union members at the Liggett & Myers Tobacco Company in Durham, North Carolina, to seek access there for blacks to jobs reserved for whites only. The plant had been organized in 1937 by the Tobacco Workers International Union, which created two all-Negro locals and one all-white. Locals 194 and 208 represented stemmers and workers in the product department; Local 176, the all-white unit, represented mostly machine operators in the manufacturing department. Promotions and layoffs were governed by separate seniority lists covering each local's jurisdiction, which restricted Negroes to the lowest-paid job categories. Under government pressure, Liggett & Myers had twenty blacks transferred to another jurisdiction where they could be promoted, but that was its last move against discrimination until 1962, when the President's Committee on Equal Employment Opportunities ordered the company to desegregate its rest

rooms, drinking fountains, locker rooms, and cafeteria; to stop dealing
with "racially identifiable" locals; and to clear away the barriers to the
hiring and advancement of blacks.

Desegregation of plant facilities took place without friction. The company's plan to deal with the seniority question was ratified by a plantwide vote in which the white employees commanded a majority. The
plan was to preserve seniority rights under the old lists for all people employed at the plant as of May 8, 1962, and to fill vacancies from inside
with blacks only at the level where no white worker was available. The
net effect was to place the Negro worker of longest standing at the end
of the white promotion list. The leaders of Local 208 accepted the majority vote at first, but unwillingly, and then hired McKissick to have it
vacated. They wanted instead a meshing of seniority lists on a plantwide
basis, so that any "white" job falling open would be filled by the most
senior qualified man, white or black. They also insisted that the blacks
slotted into the job hierarchy above whites should be able to bump them
into less desirable jobs in times of cutbacks.

Local 208's proposal ran into bitter opposition from the national
union's leadership and its white locals. It was a prime example of what
black militants had often complained about regarding labor's support of
civil rights: When it came down to equality and justice for black members of their unions, the labor leaders who paraded their records on civil
rights took sides against the blacks.

The Equal Employment Opportunity Commission indicated in the
spring of 1966 that it would act against segregated seniority provisions,
and the AFL-CIO promptly showed where it stood. On May 5, a committee representing several important affiliates and headed by Donald
Slaiman, director of the AFL-CIO Civil Rights Department, met with
the commission in Washington and urged its members to rule against
black workers who complained of discriminatory job classifications and
seniority provisions in union agreements.

Summing up the picture at its fifty-seventh annual convention in July,
1966, the NAACP declared that the largest industrial unions of the
AFL-CIO had shown continuing progress since the merger in 1955, although even there the situation "leaves much to be desired," that the
building craft unions were most guilty of discrimination, and that, in
general, after a decade of merger between the AF of L and the CIO, organized labor "has failed to eliminate anti-Negro practices by affiliated
unions in the North as well as in the South, and therefore has not fulfilled the public pledges made in 1955."[26]

How, in light of these conclusions, Randolph could argue that the
great progress made by the AFL-CIO justified the NALC's abandoning
its "original strategy of attack . . . on account of race bias" is impossible to explain, except through Randolph's demonstrated tendency to retreat from advanced positions if there was an advantage to be gained by
so doing. He had muted criticism of the AF of L in *The Messenger*
when he felt that the organizing efforts of the Brotherhood of Sleeping
Car Porters required him to do so, and it is not unlikely that his plan in
1965 to establish the A. Philip Randolph Institute had something to do

with his sudden awareness of a general trend in the AFL-CIO toward racial equalitarianism. After all, it might be difficult to obtain funds from the federation or its leading affiliates if he continued to denounce them for failing to live up to their pledges on issues affecting black workers. In any event, by the summer of 1966 Randolph's position on any aspect of the black struggle was far from advanced. The *Christian Science Monitor* correctly observed: "Mr. Randolph, who led militant Negro groups in World War I days and for decades afterward, is now considered a moderate."[27]

Cleveland Robinson, who succeeded Randolph as NALC President, was anything but a moderate. District 65, of which he was secretary-treasurer, and the Drug and Hospital Workers Local 1199 were the only two AFL-CIO affiliates to make large-scale efforts to organize the tens of thousands of blacks and Puerto Ricans who had entered the New York labor market since the mid-1950's. Under Robinson's direction, District 65 conducted a successful strike in 1965, involving more than 2,000 employees in the New York textile-converting industry, for the specific purpose of opening up new opportunities for black and Puerto Rican workers. Back in 1962 Robinson had told Meany during the interview the AFL-CIO president had granted an NALC delegation: "We belong to the house of labor, but when the house becomes so rotten and dilapidated that the walls crumble and the roof leaks and the floor sags, then it's time to get out and build a new, clean house." Whatever he might have felt as he saw the NALC, under Randolph's leadership, increasingly subordinate mass support to maneuvers with the AFL-CIO, Robinson had too much respect for Randolph and his long service in the labor and black people's movements to challenge the trend publicly. At the San Francisco AFL-CIO convention, however, where Randolph praised the federation for its progress under Meany's leadership in eliminating racial bias, Robinson sharply criticized unions and employers in the building trades for discrimination and accused the labor movement of neglecting the most impoverished workers. He also criticized the antipoverty programs of the Johnson Administration as an attempt to treat the "cancer in our society with aspirin tablets. . . . I say that something is radically wrong."[28] He was speaking in favor of a proposal introduced by Randolph for federally financed efforts to end massive unemployment among the poor.

At the 1966 NALC convention, where he was elected president to succeed Randolph, Robinson made clear his intention to continue pursuing the council's original aim of ending racism in the AFL-CIO and its affiliates. "We reject compromise and tokenism, and we will tear away the mask and expose the hypocrisy that still exists in too many places." That by itself was not enough, he said, and the NALC would now have to conduct a struggle "to insure widespread democratic reforms in the life and structure of the unions to the end that the Negroes will have a voice and a presence on bargaining committees as well as leadership councils where policy is determined."[29] It would have to push the unions to invest funds in the organization of the unorganized, particularly blacks, Puerto Ricans, Mexican-Americans, and other minority groups, who represented the most exploited section of the American working class.

In May, 1967, at a National Economic Conference under council auspices in Washington, the NALC showed the effects of its new leadership. The black delegates listened impatiently to Jack Conway of the Industrial Union Department, AFL-CIO, representing Walter Reuther, describe the progress made by the federation and express his confidence in its ability to solve whatever problems still faced black workers in the unions. "I have heard a number of similar speeches through the years," said Robinson, "and I am still waiting to see it happen." In his own address to the conference, he conceded that the efforts of the NALC so far had been no more effective in advancing the "basic human rights" of the black masses than had the civil rights movement.

The labor movement, Robinson charged, had failed to fulfill its mission. Fewer than 20 million workers were organized, while upwards of 50 million were unorganized, "and the unorganized are to be found, in the main, among the 70 per cent of the nation's work force who are not industrial workers but in service industries." The black workers particularly were to be found in laundries, hospitals, hotels and restaurants, stores, the fields, and the educational system. They performed services that were vital to the life of the nation, yet their jobs were often described as "menial," too insignificant for unions to bother with. It was a tragic fact that "except in rare instances the mainstream of labor has not seen fit to put forward the efforts necessary to organize in these areas."

Robinson proposed that the NALC take the initiative in convening conferences, especially in large urban communities, to map plans to organize the black workers into "unions that will be democratic institutions, unions whose program will respond to our needs, unions which will be a force to reckon with." He was convinced that the NALC would receive the support of "many fine unions now with the AFL-CIO, or even some independent unions," but it would be up to the people in the localities to decide with whom they wished to affiliate or whether or not to affiliate at all. Robinson acknowledged that many black workers were growing increasingly distrustful of all labor unions, but he believed that they should not judge all unions by those that discriminated against or exploited minority workers:

> It is up to us through such conferences as I have proposed in our localities and by other measures to bring home to the masses of our people the basic truth that unions are essential, and that in a large sense it is the people, the workers themselves, who really make the union; and that their physical participation in the life of the union is as necessary as their financial support.

Robinson did not shrink before the slogan "Black Power"; indeed, he denounced the mass media for creating the impression that it meant a commitment to violent means to achieve the objectives of blacks. In fact, the organization of black workers that he hoped the NALC might help bring into existence would "be the greatest manifestation of power ever to be realized by us. Power to demand—power to negotiate—power to decide. Power to make decisions, politically, economically, and socially." With such power at their command, black workers could give real meaning to the Negro-Labor Alliance and, together with progressive white unionists, could bring a change in national policy so that the "expenditure of countless billions for war in Vietnam" could be used instead to create jobs in urban areas by "building decent homes, hospitals, schools, and facilities for recreational and cultural activities. Certainly if this were done our building trades unionists would have no fear for jobs, since there could be enough jobs for everyone who wanted to enter these trades." In conclusion Robinson asked his people—today jobless, exploited, hungry, and angry—to learn from the history of the steel workers, the automobile workers, and the coal miners, all of whom had had to face repeated violence unleashed by "harsh, vicious, and unconscionable employers," but who were wise enough to stand and fight together and thereby win for themselves and their families dignity and self-respect, good wages, and security.[30]

In keeping with Robinson's plan, the NALC conference mapped steps to organize service workers throughout the nation. Theodore Mitchell, vice-president of Local 1199, urged the NALC to begin the drive immediately. "We are only a local union, and we cannot do this alone. The labor movement—and I accuse the AFL-CIO—is not doing anything about it. Yet this is where the majority of the Negro and Puerto Rican workers are." He emphasized the need to involve younger workers in the campaign, pointing out that most of the delegates, being over forty years of age could not communicate effectively with those masses in the service industries who were much younger. Robinson supported the suggestion and proposed that the NALC call upon young black workers "to be the organizers and directors of the drive."[31]

The NALC economic conference marked a new emphasis in the council's approach to the problems and needs of black workers. While still in favor of a Negro-Labor Alliance, it saw the need for more and better organization of the black masses before such an alliance could be really meaningful. Reflecting the influence of the rapidly emerging ideology of Black Power, it stressed that the black masses had to assume a greater leadership role in the alliance than in the past.

The NALC plan for conferences in urban communities to organize the service industries won the endorsement of Martin Luther King. Speaking at a meeting of Local 1199 a month later, King called for a closer union of labor and civil-rights forces to meet the "more difficult" task now before the Negro freedom movement, that of achieving genuine economic equality. The new phase, he predicted, would cost the movement some of its former allies, who were not ready to support the full dimensions of Negro rights. But it would attract new allies from among the great masses of black workers in the industries that unions like Local 1199 were seeking to organize. Those new allies, together with members of unions that practiced as well as preached equality, could become the base of a new and even more effective Negro-Labor Alliance.

Obviously King had learned from his experience in the Chicago Freedom Movement. He said in his speech that it was "much more difficult to eradicate a slum than it is to integrate a bus."[32] But it was also more difficult to overcome the growing hostility between unions and members of poverty-stricken black, Puerto Rican, and other minority groups in large urban centers than to make speeches about the urgency of organizing those masses. After the riots in Watts, when it became clear that federal and state funds would be made available for the reconstruction of the area, the black community, backed by prominent white sociologists, urged that black residents of Watts be admitted to the unions that would supply the workers, not only to lessen the enormous problem of unemployment but also to rebuild respect for organized labor. The all-white construction unions rejected the proposal. A headline in the Los Angeles *Times* of September 10, 1965, was "Unions Balk on Job Help for Watts Men." It and the story of the rejection of the proposal by the construction unions were reprinted in black papers around the country and did more to fix the public image of organized labor in the ghettos than did stories of the successful organization of hospital workers.

When the Detroit ghetto erupted in the "long, hot summer" of 1967, along with the ghettos of Newark, Cleveland, and a score of smaller cities, the first reaction of organized labor, including some of the black union leaders, was to denounce the "rioters." Nelson Jack Edwards, UAW International Executive Board member; Robert "Buddy" Battles III, UAW shop leader and president of the Trade Union Leadership Council; and Horace Sheffield, another TULC leader, issued a joint statement that revealed how little they understood what was involved in the uprising. The statement called the rioters "hoodlums and hatemongers" and declared: "One day of violence threatens to destroy years of effort to build a community Negroes and whites can be proud of. We have been far from satisfied with the conditions which have confronted Negroes generally in the community but none can deny that substantial progress was made." But, as one commentator noted, the progress had not "trickled down to the dispossessed in sufficient quantity and quality to prevent the social explosion of 1967."[33]

So bitter was the reaction of ghetto blacks to the union leaders' statement that even the popular black Congressman from Detroit, John Conyers, Jr., was booed by a black audience because he had formerly been a leader in the TULC. Dismayed by this reaction, the union leaders began to have second thoughts, and unions, led by auto workers, building trades, teamsters, and steel workers, organized a labor task force to help the residents of the smashed and fire-ridden 100-block area. Walter Reuther, addressing a meeting of community leaders, blamed social and economic conditions, not the black community, for the riots, and announced that his union was calling on President Johnson for federal funds to start building homes for the homeless in the burned-out areas. "Labor," he said, "has got to get into this and do something meaningful for the jobless youth living in the ghetto. The key to the situation is Negro-white unity to change things." Robert Holmes, Teamsters

Union international vice-president, warned organized labor that it had to move quickly to prove to the poor and disadvantaged in the urban ghettos that it was not their enemy:

> Labor has to use its great powers of pressure, independent political action, to change the conditions which cause these upheavals. Labor has to cleanse itself of this stigma of discrimination, of refusing to see what's happening to these Negro youngsters who can't get jobs, to the older workers, the unemployed and the Negro workers generally who earn less, have less work, whom employers toss into the scrap heap when they don't need them.[34]

"If Not Now . . . When?" the Amalgamated Meat Cutters asked in a pamphlet issued after the riot, noting that, while organized labor had contributed effectively to achieving passage of civil-rights laws, it had done little if anything "to root out evils which have been spreading for centuries in our society."[35] It was time now for organized labor to do what it should have done years before.

A White House report on the economic status of nonwhites in the United States released on November 2, 1967, showed how much had to be done. In all, it disclosed, 41 per cent of nonwhites were living in poverty and 14 per cent received welfare payments. Negro families with two or more jobholders still earned less than the average white family with one. The unemployment rate among nonwhites—7.3 per cent—was still roughly twice that of whites. Teen-age joblessness ran at 26.5 per cent among nonwhites and 10.6 per cent among whites. Nonwhites still made up only 6 per cent of the professional workers, 3 per cent of the managers and proprietors, and 6 per cent of craftsmen and foremen. They made up 25 per cent of laborers.

The proportion of nonwhite families living in city poverty areas had declined from 77 to 62 per cent from 1960 to 1966. But the percentage of the nonwhite slum families with incomes below the poverty level had remained constant at about 36 per cent. And in specific ghetto areas, conditions had either failed to improve or had worsened. In New York City the percentage of "poverty" families had increased from 28 to 35 per cent since 1960; in the Hough area of Cleveland, from 31 to 39 per cent. In the Watts area of Los Angeles, the percentage of poverty families was the same as it had been in 1960, 43 per cent. However, the report noted, "deteriorated housing increased from 14 to 21 per cent and rents were higher." "Worsening of the Slums" was the headline in the newspapers the next day.[36]

Even more revealing than the statistics was a report by Michigan's Governor George Romney after a visit to Watts in the fall of 1967. The *New York Times* ran this account:

> Governor Romney discovered that the discontent that touched off the first major race riot two summers ago was still burning in the grimy streets of Watts. Romney saw and heard detailed evidence that the people of Watts still rejected empty promises of equal opportunity and that many of them did not write off the possibility of renewed rioting. As one resident told the Governor; "We've prayed, we've voted, we've marched, we've rioted, we've done all we can. What else is there for us to do?"[37]

To Martin Luther King, as to many other Americans who read this message of despair, it was insufferable that the government could go on spending $50 billion a year and more in Vietnam while it complained of not having the wherewithal to solve the problems of Watts and other poverty-stricken areas. To be sure, both Randolph, now head of an institute bearing his name, and Bayard Rustin, its executive director, argued that the nation could have guns and butter and that the nation could pursue its course in Vietnam and still abolish poverty at home. But King knew that was nonsense.

Despite warnings from such black leaders as Roy Wilkins and Whitney Young that antiwar activity would hurt the cause of civil rights, King had for months vigorously opposed the war and marched in antiwar demonstrations. Early in 1968, he announced a two-pronged program: End the war in Vietnam and rearrange national priorities so that poverty could be abolished. To accomplish these objectives, he organized a Poor People's Campaign to be launched in the spring with a March on Washington. The campaign would demand that the nation allocate its resources not for destruction in Southeast Asia but to provide jobs for those able to work and a guaranteed annual income for those unable to work or unable to find work; for building 6 million decent new homes; for the development of jobs in rural areas; for schools to train jobless youths for skilled jobs; and for other measures designed to obliterate poverty. King's program and his plans to mobilize both black and white Americans made him a target for many of the same sources that had hailed his dramatic "I Have a Dream" speech in the March on Washington of 1963 and who had joined in the worldwide acclaim for the civil-rights leader when he received the Nobel Peace Prize.

The release in March, 1968, of the Kerner Commission's report on the causes of the riots of the previous summer gave substance to King's Poor People's Campaign. The report's most famous sentence was, "Our nation is moving toward two societies, one black, one white, separate but unequal." King himself had been saying much the same, and many of the commission's recommendations to prevent future ghetto uprisings had already been advanced in the Poor People's Campaign.

King hoped that the Poor People's Campaign would become a focal point in the Negro-Labor Alliance. However, he was under no illusion that the highest levels of the labor movement, conservative in outlook and committed to all-out support of the war, would embrace his plan for ending the war and rearranging national priorities. He was also aware, however, that an increasing number of labor leaders—though still a minority of the labor leadership—were becoming concerned over the public image of organized labor as having lost its fervor for broad social issues and having opted mainly for "a larger slice of the great American pie."

Addressing the convention of the Illinois AFL-CIO early in 1965, King accused much of the top labor leadership of betraying labor's "own fine traditions." As a consequence the trade unions, "as the historic ally of the underprivileged and oppressed," had lost much of their past "boldness."[38] He warned labor that if it continued on its path, it would alienate the youth of America and the poverty-stricken black, brown, and white masses.

The warning had no impact on most of the AFL-CIO leadership, but the accuracy of King's evaluation was underscored in a statement issued by the UAW to its members on December 22, 1966, suggesting that the AFL-CIO needed "revitalization," because it

> suffers from a sense of complacency and adherence to the status quo and is not fulfilling the basic aims and purposes which promoted the merger of the AFL and CIO. The AFL-CIO lacks the social vision, the dynamic thrust, the crusading spirit that should characterize the progressive, modern labor movement which it can and must be if it is to be equal to the new challenges and the new opportunities of our twentieth-century technological society.[39]

This step eventually led to a break with the AFL-CIO marked by the UAW's formal disaffiliation and suspension in July, 1968, followed some weeks later by the formation of the Alliance for Labor Action by the UAW and the International Brotherhood of Teamsters.

In view of this and other evidence of widespread dissatisfaction in the labor movement with the existing AFL-CIO policies, King was optimistic that the Poor People's Campaign would win the support of many union leaders. At the National Labor Leadership Assembly for Peace in Chicago on November 27, 1967, King, a featured speaker, criticized organized labor for supporting the war when "tens of thousands of Americans" opposed it and declared that resolutions in favor of programs designed to combat poverty were of little value as long as labor continued to give uncritical backing to the Administration's war policies.[40]

In the midst of preparations for the Poor People's March on Washington, King received an appeal from blacks and union leaders in Memphis, Tennessee, for help in a strike of 1,200 sanitation workers, all black. Before he left Atlanta for Memphis, King sent a message to be published in the journal to be issued in connection with the seventh annual convention of the Negro American Labor Council. He told the delegates, scheduled to meet in May, 1968, that the NALC represented "the embodiment of two great traditions in our nation's history: the best tradition of the organized labor movement and the finest tradition of the Negro Freedom Movement." He expressed admiration for the council's effort to continue the Negro-Labor Alliance and urged it to pursue in its endeavor to unite the black masses and organized labor in a campaign to help solve the "deteriorating economic and social condition of the Negro community . . . heavily burdened with both unemployment and underemployment, flagrant job discrimination, and the injustice of unequal educational opportunity." His message ended: "From the Deep South we grasp your hand in fellowship."[41] Martin Luther King, Jr., did not live to see his goal achieved, but in the next eighteen months the Negro-Labor Alliance, the relationship between the black communities and the labor movement he had sought to build, would produce great victories for black workers in Memphis and Charleston.

24 Memphis and Charleston: Triumph of the Negro-Labor Alliance

By the time Dr. King arrived in Memphis, on March 18, 1968, the sanitation workers had been on strike for five weeks. Although relatively few workers were involved in comparison with strikes in giant industries, it had already proved to be a titanic struggle between the forces of organized labor and the black community, on the one side, and the municipal authorities, the civic power structure, and powerful racist groups in the South, on the other. The strikers had defied a court injunction ordering their return to work and had braved police terror, which included the arrest of many strike leaders and the indiscriminate use of chemical mace, tear gas, and police clubs. Their ranks were still solid, and the support they were receiving from the Memphis black community and its labor movement was as firm as ever.

The strike had its roots in a long history of discrimination against and exploitation of the city's 1,300 black sanitation workers. Memphis was one of the Southern cities where the civil-rights movement had never really organized itself. There had been sit-ins in Memphis early in the freedom struggle, however, and the battles in Alabama, Mississippi, and Georgia had an impact on the black sanitation workers. Their grievances were many. There were no bathrooms, washrooms, or shower facilities for the men to clean up after work and no protective work clothing, which meant the workers had to go home in the same clothing they had worn while collecting garbage all day. There was no place for the men to eat lunch, which meant, in the words of one black worker, "having a sandwich in one hand and a garbage can in the other."[1] There were few opportunities for the black sanitation workers to advance; they were continually denied job promotions. They had no pension or retirement system, and since sanitation workers were not listed as regular city employees, did not qualify for workmen's compensation. Wages were exceedingly low: Hourly wages averaged $1.60 to $1.80, and in bad weather workers were often sent home after reporting to their jobs. The weekly wages, therefore, averaged $53–$60 a week after taxes, so that 40 per cent of the sanitation workers at the time of the strike qualified for supplementary welfare checks to support their families. Many were also in the food-stamp program.

In 1963 and in 1966 there had been attempts to organize; on both occasions, strikes were threatened unless working conditions were improved. But each time the city administration obtained an injunction against the impending strike, discharged the most militant workers, and threatened the same treatment for any worker who defied the injunction. Those threats had defeated the attempts to unionize. One of the black leaders fired by the city in 1963, after six years on the job, was T. O. Jones. A year later, the former sanitation worker was hired by the American Federation of State, County, and Municipal Employees to continue organizing among his former co-workers. It took almost four years before the sanitation workers were ready to challenge the powerful forces arrayed against them, but in 1967 Local 1773, with T. O. Jones as president, had 1,300 members, all but five of them black.

Two incidents helped spark the strike. Early in January, two men were crushed to death by a defective packer in their truck. Their families received $500 each from the city as a "gift" for "burial expenses" and one month's pay. Then, on a rainy day on February 11, a number of black workers were sent home while other blacks and all of the white sanitation workers were told to stand by the trucks. Later in the day the weather cleared, and those who had been told to stand by were able to earn a full day's pay. The workers sent home demanded that the city pay them for the lost time, but the administration refused to give more than two hours' compensation. That was the last straw. The following day, February 12, the black sanitation workers walked out on strike.

On the first day of the strike, Jones appeared with a union committee at the office of the city's director of public works to present a demand for a wage increase and improvements in working conditions. The answer was that the strike was illegal under the 1966 injunction and that the men would either return to work or else be jailed for violating the court order. Jones pulled out a brown paper bag, took off his business suit in the director's office, and changed into what he called his "jail clothes." He told the director that they could throw him in jail, but the strike would continue. The incident foreshadowed the militancy of the black sanitation workers throughout their long strike.

The following evening, Mayor Henry Loeb addressed a meeting of more than 800 strikers. This was not New York City, where the sanitation workers had just won a strike under the leadership of the same union, he told the men; in Memphis, "nothing will be gained by violating our laws." The strike posed a grave "health menace to the city," and the community would never support black workers who were responsible for this. But if the strikers returned to work immediately, the city would consent to meet with their committee and discuss their grievances.[2]

After the Mayor was booed off the platform, the meeting continued and drew up a series of specific demands. These included (1) recognition of the union as the sole bargaining agent for the workers and the granting of a dues checkoff; (2) an end to job discrimination against black workers; (3) a city-financed hospitalization, life insurance, and pension program; (4) additional sick leave and vacation time; (5) overtime pay after eight hours in any one day and a premium of ten cents an hour for night work; (6) a guarantee of a full work-week even in bad weather; (7) an increase in wages to $2.35 an hour; and (8) a written contract. The strikers began daily marches through downtown Memphis and nightly mass rallies to publicize their demands. But the Mayor still refused to deal with the strikers unless they returned to work. He was fully supported by the two daily Memphis papers, the *Commercial Appeal* and the *Press Scimitar*, both owned by the Scripps-Howard chain; by the business community; and by white-supremacist groups in the city, who saw the strike as a challenge to their domination of the community. The press blamed "outside agitators" for the strike and accused organizers from the State, County, and Municipal Employees, who were assisting the strikers, of inciting the blacks to "anarchy."[3]

Faced with such a combination of forces, the strikers by themselves could not have continued for long. But they soon won the support of the Memphis NAACP; the Unity League, another Negro organization; most of the city's black ministers; and the AFL-CIO Labor Council. A Committee of Concerned Citizens, uniting the black community (with some white liberals) behind the strikers, and a Citizens' Committee to Aid the Public Works Employees, composed of labor unions, black and white, were established. "The strike has united us as nothing has before," said the Reverend Harold Middlebrooks, a black minister. "I've lived here all my life and never seen anything like it. A movement has begun."[4] The slogan of the various groups behind the strikers was "Justice for the strikers—Jobs for all the people."

The support of the black community was especially important. Negro ministers helped raise funds for food and clothing for the strikers' families; an estimated total of $100,000 was contributed by the black community alone. Leaders of the black community formed committees to visit landlords, utility companies, loan companies, and retail stores, and succeeded in pressuring them, by threatening a boycott, into a promise that no evictions would take place for the duration of the strike and that a moratorium would be declared on the collection of all debts from the strikers.

With the plan to starve the strikers into submission defeated, the city administration began to recruit strike-breakers. It ran ads in the press promising high wages to those who would take the place of the men on strike. But here, too, the support the strikers received from the black community and organized labor was decisive in defeating the administration's new maneuver. A call went out for a boycott of the Memphis papers, endorsed by Negro ministers, black organizations, and the AFL-CIO Labor Council. It was respected by more than 80 per cent of the 200,000 black people who made up over 40 per cent of the city's population. Next the white trade unionists, black ministers and other leaders, and strikers formed joint committees to patrol the streets and guard against scabs. Men who took the place of the striking sanitation workers were photographed; if they were black, their homes were visited by black ministers and they were advised not to help defeat the strike. White union leaders did the same in cases of white strike-breakers. Meanwhile, the daily marches through the streets and the nightly meetings, some in black churches, others in halls contributed for the purpose by unions such as the United Rubber Workers and the teamsters, continued. Negro leaders from outside the city, including Roy Wilkins of the NAACP and Bayard Rustin of the A. Philip Randolph Institute, addressed the meetings.

The city administration tried a new strategy. State legislators from the Memphis area were urged by the business community as well as by the Mayor to introduce bills in the legislature that would have the effect of smashing the strike. Bills were actually introduced that would make it a felony punishable by up to five years to encourage strikes by public employees and would outlaw dues-checkoff for those employees. But this move was also defeated. The state AFL-CIO joined forces with the Shelby County Democratic Club to keep the bills bottled up in committee hearings throughout the strike, and they were never brought to a vote.

On February 22, the strikers interrupted a City Council meeting and appealed directly to Councilmen to bypass Mayor Loeb and meet the strikers' terms. At first the City Council was sufficiently impressed by the show of power to appoint a committee to negotiate with the strikers. But the following day the council reversed itself, endorsed the mayor's conduct during the strike, and granted him full authority to deal with the strikers as he saw fit. On that day, February 23, a parade of strikers through the downtown section was attacked by the police, demonstrators were clubbed and maced, and seven of the marchers, including T. O. Jones, were arrested and charged with "disorderly conduct" and "inciting to riot."

By then the strike was no longer a local struggle for the recognition of a union of government workers. The leadership of the American Federation of State, County, and Municipal Employees, considering victory crucial for further advances in the South, moved into Memphis in full force under the direction of Jerry Wurf, the international president. It was not long before they were the targets of the city administration. On February 24 authorities obtained an injunction that outlawed participating in, causing, authorizing, or inducing a strike against the city; made coercing of the city by picketing or other means to recognize a union illegal; and prohibited picketing of city property. Wurf, Jones, and other strike leaders were arrested for violating the injunction, found guilty, and sentenced to ten days in jail and a fine of $50 each. The union immediately appealed the sentence.

Instead of breaking the strike, as had been expected, the injunction solidified community and labor support for the strikers. A boycott of downtown stores was organized, and black ministers told their congregations, "No new clothes for Easter."[5] Daily marches through the downtown area grew in size. Students at the predominantly white Memphis State University organized support for the strike from the Black Student Organization and white radical students. Black high school students, defying threats of reprisals, cut classes to join the strikers, black citizens, and white and black trade unionists in the parades. They sang as they marched:

> Pork chops, pork chops, greasy, greasy
> We can beat Loeb, easy, easy
> Loeb shall, he shall, he shall be removed.
> Just like a can of garbage in the alley
> Loeb shall be removed.
> Freedom isn't free, freedom isn't free
> You've got to pay the price.
> You've got to sacrifice
> For your liberty.[6]

As the boycott caused a decline in retail sales of more than 40 per cent, the downtown store owners began to have second thoughts about supporting a fight to the finish. A group of businessmen formed a "Save Our City" committee to seek a settlement of the strike on terms acceptable to the strikers. At the same time, the AFL-CIO Central Labor Council began a recall drive to force Mayor Loeb to run for re-election two years before his term in office expired. The "Save Our City" group met with City Council leaders, and the council passed a resolution urging the mayor and the union to resume negotiations and named a mediator to intervene. This marked a breakthrough, for up to this time the entire city administration had taken the position that negotiations would begin only after the strikers returned to work.

Mayor Loeb was determined to make one last attempt to break the strike before yielding. Strike-breakers were now recruited from nearby rural areas in Arkansas and Mississippi and transported to Memphis at 4 A.M. back home at night in county penal-farm trucks. Police cars escorted the strike-breakers, and armed "auxiliary deputy sheriffs" from nearby counties were brought into Memphis to help the police cruise through the city's black neighborhoods. Mayor Loeb then made what he called his "final offer." It consisted of four points: (1) all sanitation workers would return to work immediately and unconditionally; (2) the sanitation workers would sign a "no strike" pledge; (3) the city administration and the workers would then negotiate a settlement of the issues; (4) all issues not agreed upon by both parties would be submitted to a city wide referendum in August, 1968. Under no circumstances would there be union recognition or a dues checkoff.

The strikers unanimously rejected the "final offer," and the black community supported the decision. It was now an issue of dignity for the Negro people that black workers should not be denied rights that white workers in Memphis enjoyed. At this point, black and union leaders called upon Dr. King to help the strikers. King, it was felt, could generate wider support for the sanitation workers by focusing national attention on Memphis.

King came to Memphis on March 18 and addressed a rally of 15,000 at which he called for all-out support for the strikers. He then left but announced that he would return four days later to lead a giant parade through downtown Memphis. Several SCLC staff members remained in the city to organize the parade. Black and trade-union leaders called upon Memphis workers to stay away from their jobs on the designated day and join the parade. But on March 22, a sixteen-inch snowstorm paralyzed the city and forced postponement of the parade until March 28.

On that day, 6,000 paraders left Clayborn Temple in the black community, with Dr. King in the lead. As the marchers entered the downtown section, some young black militants, disregarding King's advice to keep the demonstration nonviolent, pulled some placards off the sticks to which they were attached and began using the sticks against display windows. King called off the parade and left.

The incidents that disappointed King were just what the police had been waiting for. Policemen quickly put on gas masks and started shooting tear gas pellets into the ranks of the demonstrators. Most of the paraders retreated, but a few hundred young blacks did battle with fists, sticks, and stones. The forces were uneven and the youths were clubbed to the ground. Those who could do so ran back to the Clayborn Temple to join the thousands surging outside the building. Inside, the nave was jammed. The police continued shooting tear gas. As it seeped into the auditorium, those inside, choking and with tears streaming from their eyes, rushed to the street, where they faced clubbing.

Within hours there were 3,800 National Guardsmen in Memphis, mainly on occupation duty in the black sections. State police were rushed into the city, and the city police were placed on emergency status. President Johnson offered to send in federal troops if the city administration requested them. That night fires broke out in Memphis, martial law was declared, and a curfew was put into effect. For the next several days, the National Guardsmen continued their occupation.

Although King left, much of the SCLC staff came to Memphis for a final effort. With the leadership of the State, County, and Municipal Workers and local black and labor groups, they worked out details for King to return and lead another parade. At precisely this point, the Southern Regional Council released a prophetic report entitled "In Memphis: More than a Garbage Strike," which warned of "tragedy waiting in the wings."[7]

King returned to Memphis on April 4 to lead a second parade in support of the strikers. He told Jerry Wurf: "What is going on here in Memphis is important to every poor working man, black or white, in the South."[8] That evening, just before sunset, Martin Luther King, Jr., was shot down by a sniper. He died instantly.

In the wake of King's assassination, riots broke out in a hundred cities across the country. But while millions of Americans mourned and white racists rejoiced, the strike went on. On April 8, more than 40,000 were in line for the parade King was no longer able to lead. In his place was his widow, Coretta King, marching at the head of the line with Reverend Ralph Abernathy, King's close associate in the SCLC; Jerry Wurf and his staff; Walter Reuther, president of the United Automobile Workers;

Donald Slaiman, civil-rights director of the AFL-CIO; and of course, T. O. Jones and others representing the sanitation workers. Behind them marched representatives of Negro organizations and trade unions from coast to coast. It was both a demonstration of solidarity with the militant strikers and a memorial to the great black leader who had been struck down while helping some of the most exploited workers in the nation to seek, through union organization, a better life for themselves and their families.

In the speeches that day, black leaders and trade-union leaders vowed to continue Dr. King's effort to build the Negro-Labor Alliance. Cleveland Robinson, representing the Negro American Labor Alliance, pledged that the organization would redouble its efforts to organize the black workers in the service industry, among whom sanitation workers were an important element.

Even after King's death and the April 8 march, Mayor Loeb and racist groups working with him balked at an agreement that would include union recognition and a checkoff. But hundreds of dollars began pouring into the treasury of the striking sanitation men from the AFL-CIO, the UAW, the New York sanitation workers, and others; the lines of the strikers and community support in Memphis held firm; the boycott of the press and downtown stores continued; and, when President Johnson sent Under Secretary of Labor James J. Reynolds to Memphis with orders to settle the strike, Mayor Loeb was forced to capitulate. On Aprial 13, the Memphis *Commercial Appeal*, up to then a firm supporter of the mayor's position, called on him to surrender: "It is no longer a matter of 'hold the line at any cost.' The future of Memphis is at stake."

On April 16, 1968, the strike, which had lasted sixty-five days, ended. The black sanitation workers voted to accept a settlement proposed by the city administration. Entitled "A Memorandum of Understanding," it was to be in effect for fourteen months and, in addition to a "no-strike" clause, provided for (1) an end to discrimination against black workers; (2) no discrimination against any worker because of strike activities; (3) a grievance procedure; (4) voluntary dues checkoff to be channeled through the workers' credit union; (5) recognition of the union; and (6) a pay increase of ten cents per hour effective May 1, plus an additional increase of five cents per hour effective September 1, 1968.

This was not all the men had asked for, and the grievance procedure left ultimate authority in the hands of the mayor or his representative for adjustment of grievances of all laborers, drivers, and crew chiefs.* But since dues checkoff had been, as Wurf pointed out, "the key issue," and had been resisted to the very end, the settlement represented a clear victory. On April 17 the black sanitation men returned to work.

---

* A sanitation worker in Memphis told a *New York Times* reporter three years after King's assassination: "Yes, things are better, but they still ain't just right." Other sanitation men complained that they were bricklayers but had to work on garbage trucks because "whites won't let no Negroes into the union to do a day's work." *New York Times*, April 4, 1971.

"Monument to Dr. King," was the heading over the editorial in the *New York Times* on the settlement of the Memphis strike. "Out of this overdue advance for a single small group of exploited Southern workers," the editorial asserted, "can come a renewed effort to forge the kind of coalition between organized labor and the civil rights movement that was a constant goal of Dr. King." Editorials throughout the country, struck the same note. The victory in Memphis was viewed as a testimony to King and his vision of the "invincible power" of the "grand alliance of organized labor and the Negro people." Many saw the victory as evidence that the unorganized workers of the South could be organized despite powerful resistance from employers, local and state governments, and the press. Some urged the AFL-CIO to begin immediately a "drive to make the South a labor union citadel."[9]

Later that year, the SCLC came to the aid of sanitation workers in Saint Petersburg, Florida, and in Atlanta. Black garbage collectors in Saint Petersburg, organized by the State, County, and Municipal Employees, went on strike for a wage increase from $1.75 to $2.25 an hour. In May, 1968, the dismissal of 200 sanitation workers for union activity triggered a series of protest marches, supported by the local black community, and the SCLC entered the case. The Reverend A. D. King, the late Martin Luther King's brother, headed several of the marches. A "national march" organized by the local black community and the SCLC on August 3 was followed by settlement of the strike. The wage increase, reinstatement of the dismissed workers, and other gains were achieved.

In Atlanta, black garbage collectors struck for better wages and working conditions and against the all-white composition of their union's leadership, which had been completely indifferent to the needs of the black membership. The SCLC actively supported the strike from its beginning in September. A meeting of strikers and the black community at St. Joseph's church was addressed by SCLC officials and was followed by a mass picketing of City Hall. The next day Dr. Abernathy and his two top aides, the Reverend Andrew Young and the Reverend Hosea Williams, were arrested at a sanitation substation when they sat in the path of departing garbage trucks. In the face of an injunction from the Fulton County Superior Court prohibiting the strike and any acts to encourage it or to prevent emergency collections, the SCLC pledged to back the strikers "to the real finish." Its assistance, added to support from the black community and the State, County, and Municipal Employees, brought victory to the strikers. They won improvements in wages and working conditions, and their local union leadership was changed to include black leaders.

Thus, the fast-growing (with a membership nearing 400,000) American Federation of State, County, and Municipal Employees set the pace in organizing the South. It decided at its convention on June 4, 1968, to launch a nationwide campaign to bring state, county, and city employees under union agreements. Said Jerry Wurf: "If we can organize in Memphis, we can organize anywhere. We were supposed to get our brains beat out in Memphis, but we didn't. We intend to use the techniques learned there not only in the South, but throughout the country." During the ceremonies at the convention commemorating Dr. King, the Reverend Ralph D. Abernathy, King's successor as SCLC president, assured the federation and every other union that sought to improve the lot of "the garbage workers, the poor people, the people who pick up the slop, who take care of the waste, the people who are at the bottom rung of the ladder," that the SCLC would "be right in there to organize the community and stand with you 100 per cent to make the dream of Martin Luther King come true."[10]

Dr. Abernathy had come to Miami to address the convention from Washington, where the Poor People's Campaign was "making a witness" before the nation at its encampment in Resurrection City, calling attention to the existence of poverty. Soon after he returned to the nation's capital, the Johnson Administration gave its answer to the "witness" in the form of police and troops ordered to disperse the representatives of the poor. The Poor People's Campaign, it seemed, was a total failure. But on the first anniversary of the death of the man who had originated the campaign, a struggle was under way in Charleston, South Carolina, that soon became to the Poor People's Campaign what the Montgomery bus boycott had been to the civil-right movement. On April 21, 1969, the *New York Times* began an editorial on the strike in Charleston with these words: "The ghost of Martin Luther King marches the picket line outside two hospitals in Charleston, S.C."

Charleston was proud of its graceful mansions, its moss-hung trees, and its museum on the site of the old slave market. A booming tourist trade and convention business attested to the city's appeal. But behind the facade was a harsh life for the city's working class. Like Memphis, Charleston was one of the few large Southern cities that had not been touched by the civil-rights movement. But, unlike Memphis, it had also been largely bypassed by the upsurge in trade unionism since the 1930's. The waterfront workers who moved cargo from the docks to the warehouses, as distinct from those who unloaded the ships and placed the cargo on the docks, were not included in the ILA's collective-bargaining agreements. In February, 1969, 350 dock workers struck for union recognition. The state secured first a temporary and then a permanent injunction; a half dozen of the key strike leaders were fired, and the longshoremen went back to work without a contract.

When the dock workers could not win a union contract, it was taken for granted that black hospital workers would never succeed in organizing. The Charleston hospitals—one run by the state and the other by the county—paid most nonprofessional workers $1.30 an hour, thirty cents less than the federal minimum in private industry. The attitude of the hospital administration toward blacks could be illustrated by the findings of the Atlanta Compliance Office of the Health, Education, and Welfare Department's Civil Rights Division in mid-1968. The agency uncovered numerous examples of racially biased behavior, including refusal to permit any of the black doctors in Charleston to work in the hospital, which appeared to disqualify the hospitals for $12 million in federal contracts. The power of the state, already demonstrated in the dock workers' strike, could be brought into play quickly against any organizing drive to change these conditions.

Not even the capitulation of Memphis to the black sanitation workers shook the confidence of the power structure in Charleston in its ability to cope with any attempt to unionize the black hospital workers. Just as Mayor Loeb had arrogantly declared that Memphis was not New York, so the authorities in Charleston were convinced that their city was not Memphis. In a sense, this was correct. The leaders of the Negro community in Charleston—largely the black bourgeoisie, descended from the free blacks of the pre–Civil War era—were accustomed to working hand-in-glove with the white power structure. Even though blacks were politically powerless in Charleston—the suburbs had been incorporated into the city, enabling whites to outvote blacks on any issue—the black leaders were able to obtain prize patronage for themselves. They, too, were determined that Charleston should not become another Memphis. This also was the thinking of the AFL-CIO.

Charleston was thus an unlikely site for a major unionizing drive among black hospital workers. But local 1199 already had experience in conquering unlikely territory. By the spring of 1968, the union already had 34,000 members, mainly Negroes and Puerto Ricans, and mostly women, and had signed contracts with voluntary hospitals and nursing homes in New York City, New Jersey, upstate New York, and Connecticut. In the contract with the New York City voluntary hospitals that expired on June 30, 1968, the union had established minimum wages of $76 and a forty-hour week for workers who only ten years before earned as little as $28 a week for forty-eight hours. After a four-hour strike and within minutes of the expiration of that contract, the union had scored a major victory, winning a $100 weekly minimum in its new contract with New York's voluntary hospitals plus pensions and other improvements. A $12 raise was to go into effect on July 1, 1968, with another $12 the following July.

Soon after its victory, Local 1199 began preparations to form a national organizing committee of hospital workers and proposed to the SCLC that the two organizations cooperate in the campaign ahead. The union pointed out that the nearly 3 million hospital and nursing-home workers throughout the country were among the largest block of underpaid minority-group workers in the nation and, since most were desperately poor, a potential for realizing the main objective of the Poor People's Campaign. The SCLC responded favorably. When Local 1199 announced the formation in October, 1968, of the National Organizing Committee of Hospital and Nursing Home Employees, Coretta Scott King, Martin Luther King's widow, was its honorary chairman, and Abernathy and other SCLC leaders were committee members. Soon afterward, the union held sessions to train SCLC staff in the technique of union organizing. The SCLC members outlined the methods they had already used successfully in the strikes of the Scripto employees and the sanitation workers in Memphis, Saint Petersburg, and Atlanta. Events in Charleston provided an opportunity to test the developing working relationship between the union and the civil-rights organization.

Even before Local 1199 had set up the National Organizing Committee, the black workers in Charleston's hospitals, with the help of some groups in the black community, began holding meetings to organize. In September, 1968, the workers tried to talk with Dr. William McCord, president of the medical college and director of its hospital, about recognition of a union or, if that was not possible, the establishment of a grievance committee. They were denied an opportunity to meet. When Local 1199's National Organizing Committee began drives in several cities, the Charleston hospital workers got in touch with it, and several Local 1199 staff members came to meet with the workers and community leaders and pledged financial and organizing support. Finally, after several futile requests, Dr. McCord agreed to meet with a delegation representing Local 1199B, the local of hospital workers in Charleston, on March 17, 1969.

The meeting was never held. When the five hospital workers selected for the delegation arrived at the director's office, they were informed that he had called off the meeting. When they returned to their duties, they learned that they and seven union members had been fired for allegedly leaving their posts without permission. A union meeting was hastily called, and 400 nurses and nurse's aides, kitchen helpers, laundry workers, and orderlies walked off their jobs. A week later, ninety workers at the Charleston County Hospital walked out in sympathy. Dr. McCord vowed never to rehire the twelve who had been fired, but when the 400 workers walked out he was confronted not only with the demand that those workers be reinstated, but also with demands for union recognition, a wage increase, and a grievance procedure as well.

At first the hospital administration treated the demands with contempt. Dr. McCord, for example, offered to give the workers an additional holiday, the birthday of Robert E. Lee. Contempt was quickly replaced by force. An injunction handed down by the segregationist Judge Singletary limited picketing to "ten people . . . at a time—twenty yards apart," and no closer than eight blocks from the hospital. The black workers defied the injunction and conducted mass picketing around the hospital site. They were promptly arrested. By the end of the first week of the strike, 100 were in jail. The strikers, and particularly staff members of Local 1199, were also attacked by vigilantes. "It was really tough here these early weeks of the strike," recalled Henry Nicholas, assistant director of the National Organizing Committee, who had come in to assist the local organization.[11] His room had been firebombed, and the workers had to organize a security guard around the building as well as around their union hall.

With arrests piling up, SCLC and Local 1199 staff members arrived to direct the battle. Moe Foner, Local 1199 executive secretary, split his time between New York and Charleston, but NOC Director Elliott Godoff and Area Director David White joined Nicholas in spending full time in Charleston. Ralph Abernathy, Andrew Young, Carl Farris, James Orange, Stoney Cooks, and others of the SCLC field staff remained in Charleston. Together the SCLC and Local 1199 officers, over the initial opposition of some Negro leaders but with the enthusiastic support of the poor blacks in the community, made the nation aware that the strike of black hospital workers involved, in the words of a *New York Times* editorial, "values as fundamental as those in the original battles for school desegregation and equal employment opportunities."[12]

By the third week of April, Charleston had become the scene of mass meetings, daily marches, evening rallies in churches and union halls, and boycotts of stores and schools. It also became the scene of daily confrontations and mass arrests as the Charleston power structure, headed by J. P. Stevens, owner of twenty-three textile mills in South Carolina, struck back. Governor McNair quickly let it be known that the state would never recognize a public employees' union, and Dr. McCord emphasized the same point in his contemptuous remark to a *Business Week* reporter: "I am not about to turn over the administration of a 5-million dollar institution to people who never had a grammar school education."[13]

Governor McNair sent 600 state troopers and National Guardsmen into Charleston. Mass arrests were stepped up, and strikers and their local leaders, including Mary Ann Moultrie, president of Local 1199B, were jailed. The Charleston press applauded the governor for taking the only action the black strikers would understand. Ashley Cooper, a columnist of the Charleston *News and Courier*, wrote: "It seems—at least to me—that the only way the illegal uprising can be stopped is by force. That may have the ring of fascism—which I hate—but honestly, what other conclusion is there?"[14]

But the strikers were not intimidated. Thousands of Charleston's blacks turned out regularly for marches along routes lined with police, state troopers, and National Guardsmen with fixed bayonets. Standing at the ready in side streets were more troops, tanks, and other armed vehicles. Heavily armed National Guardsmen patrolled the streets. When Coretta King came to address a rally on April 29, a reporter just back from covering the war in Southeast Asia greeted her at the Charleston airport: "Mrs. King, welcome to Charleston, South Vietnam."[15] That night 7,500 people, nearly 30 per cent of Charleston's black population, packed the Morris Brown African Methodist-Episcopal Church and the Emmanuel Church to hear Mrs. King speak to both audiences in support of the strikers. The next day they joined her in a march around and through the inner city, ending up at the complex of five hospitals. Of course, a number of the marchers ended up in jail, joining strikers and black citizens already there. One of the strikers, Edrena Johnson, kept a diary during her nine-day stay in jail. On April 25, she recorded the following:

As I lie here in a cell at the Charleston County jail I feel the sympathy of all who are fighting for what is right. We, as black people in South Carolina, have awakened to the fact that we are no longer afraid of the white man and that we want to be recognized, not because of our race but because we are human beings and we have a right. A right which we shall fight and go to jail for. We the black people of South Carolina will no longer sit back and be counted. We're going to stand up for what is right because we're soul from our hearts, and soul power is where it's at.[16]

Two days later she wrote: "All of us in jail are very excited and we all feel wonderful to know that Charleston is finally getting the hell they wanted, and the more people they put in jail the more people go out to picket." Marie Moultrie, twenty-seven-year-old president of the union of black hospital workers in Charleston, said she had "a long time to think" during her eleven days in jail, and she thought "of the billions our government is spending to kill people on the other side of the world. I was thinking of the astronauts we are sending to the moon while children in Charleston go hungry."[17] One of the early leaflets issued by the strikers carried the heading: "Let Us End Poverty in Charleston (Our Own)."[18]

While the SCLC gave the strike its main support, it was not the only national black organization to back the black hospital workers. Late in April, the national heads of nine civil-rights organizations and five elected black officials issued a joint statement in support of the strike. It was the first time black leaders had come together on a single issue since King's death, they noted, and "the right of workers to be represented by a union is precisely the same issue that led to the tragedy in Memphis last year." But the struggle in Charleston was "more than a fight for union rights. It is part of the larger fight in our nation against discrimination and exploitation—against all forms of degradation that results from poverty and human misery."[19]

The signers were headed by Coretta King, and throughout the strike she gave herself entirely to the cause of the black hospital workers. Addressing a dinner in New York City in honor of A. Philip Randolph, Mrs. King said that the alliance Randolph had devoted a lifetime to building—"the alliance of civil rights groups and organized labor—is a reality today in Charleston." Apart from the tremendous support for the strikers in the black community, what impressed her the most about the struggle, she declared, was "the emergence of black women leaders as a new breed of union leaders." Such women as Mary Ann Moultrie, the dynamic president of Local 1199B; Emma Hardin, co-chairman of the Charleston County Hospital unit; and Rosetta Simmons "are following in the footsteps of Harriet Tubman and Sojourner Truth—of Rosa Parks and Daisy Bates and Fannie Lou Hamer. And they will be a source of great pride to the black people and to the entire labor movement."[20]

Mrs. King appealed to the guests at the dinner for the wide support desperately needed by the strikers. Part of the power structure's strategy was to bleed the strike to death financially. By the end of April close to 500 were in jail, including even high school students. With bail set at $1,000 per arrest, the union funds were exhausted. Black men and women at church rallies emptied their pockets for the strikers. And when Abernathy asked for volunteers for "jail-without-bail," 500 black people raised their hands.

On May 1, several newspapers, including the *New York Times*, carried a full-page advertisement with a picture of Mrs. King on one side and, on the other, the statement: "If my husband were alive today, he would be in Charleston, South Carolina." The text began: "Charleston, South Carolina, today is an armed camp." It then described the battle being waged there, the support the hospital strikers were receiving from the city's black community, the intransigence of the authorities, and the refusal of the trustees, supported by Governor McNair, to grant the right to have a union. Mrs. King appealed:

> The strikers and the black people of Charleston are poor. They are determined to assert their humanity, no matter how large the risks, no matter how many must suffer jailings. But they cannot win by themselves. They need your support—the support of all decent-minded Americans, white and black.

The appeal brought in much-needed funds, as did national television newscasts that brought Charleston's marching blacks, many with blue and white Local 1199 caps, courageously parading under the guns of armed Guardsmen, into millions of American homes. Unions across the country sent delegations to march with the strikers. Walter Reuther joined the demonstrations in person and gave a check for $10,000 to 1199B. George Meany also pledged support, and the AFL-CIO donated $25,000. Neither the South Carolina AFL-CIO nor the Central Trades and Labor Council in Charleston did much to back up Meany's pledge. However, a number of white women, members of a Spartanburg, South Carolina, ILGWU local, marched, went to jail, and, on their release, donated to the strike fund. The strikers also gained moral and financial support from Father William Joyce of St. Patrick's Catholic Church, who marched regularly with the strikers and the black citizens of Charleston.

Arrests continued. Heavily armed Guardsmen patrolled the streets; a 9 P.M. curfew was still in effect; and ugly rumors floated through the city that white racists were arming themselves, determined to repeat the tragedy that had marked the strike in Memphis, with Ralph D. Abernathy as the current target. Dr. Abernathy had enraged the racists by going on a six-day hunger strike after he was arrested during a demonstration and continuing to direct new marches from his prison cell. Leon Davis, president of Local 1199, also went to jail.

In late May, as the tension mounted, a split began to emerge in the opposition. Boycotts of stores and schools by blacks had slowed Charleston's normal activity to a trickle. A dozen scheduled conventions had been canceled. Business interests, concerned that a continuation of the strike might mean economic disaster, began to appeal for a settlement. But their appeals were ignored by more powerful forces. The men who dominated the power structure feared that a victory for the black hospital workers would pave the way for the organization of other black workers in Charleston. One told a Local 1199 organizer that even black domestic workers would demand better wages and conditions if the hospitals were organized. More important, it might bring unions to the powerful textile industry in South Carolina and to the military installations of the Charleston area, which had more than its fair share thanks to the influence of Representative L. Mendel Rivers, chairman of the House Armed Services Committee. *The Daily News Record*, the trade paper for the textile industry, frankly noted that South Carolina's "textile leaders" viewed "the Charleston hospital strike [as] a bombshell set to explode at the back door of the South Carolina textile industry" and were taking seriously the prediction of union leaders "that victory in the current struggle would lead ultimately to unionization of workers in government and industry throughout the state."[21]

On June 2, to pacify local businessmen who were eager to restore normalcy to the downtown area, Governor McNair moved the curfew from 10 P.M. to midnight and withdrew a large number of troops from the city. At the same time he made it clear that no concessions would be made to the strikers. Newspapers in various parts of the country began urging the Nixon Administration to intervene in Charleston as the Johnson Administration had done in Memphis. But President Nixon, for whom association with a militant union fighting for black workers would lose racist votes he had cultivated in the South, remained aloof.

However, the Department of Health, Education, and Welfare (HEW) did move into the picture. The hospital administration had by then exhausted the patience of HEW's Civil Rights Department, headed by Leon E. Panetta, by not moving to end the racially biased practices uncovered by the Atlanta office. On June 5, Hugh Brimm, Atlanta Compliance Chief, informed Dr. McCord that the Medical College was definitely "in noncompliance" with the antidiscriminatory provisions for federal contracts and that the hospital would have to adopt an affirmative program assuring equal employment "in order to continue as a government contractor."[22] As the first step toward proving its good faith, he suggested that the hospital rehire the twelve black workers fired in the spring—the action that had sparked the strike.

With $12 million in federal aid at stake, the hospital administration decided to listen to reason and agreed to rehire all strikers, along with the original twelve. At the same time, the state government, pressed by businessmen complaining that the marches, boycotts, and curfews were ruining both their trade and the tourist business in general, announced that it would raise the state minimum wage by thirty cents an hour, to $1.60.

On June 11, at a meeting between a committee representing the strikers and the hospital trustees, an agreement was reached and approved by Governor McNair that provided for reinstatement of all strikers, including the twelve. But the following day, hours before the agreement was to be signed and with negotiations still in progress on other issues, a negotiator for the union received word from Dr. McCord that "the offer to employ the 12 discharged workers" was withdrawn.[23] That same day the Charleston papers quoted South Carolina Senator Strom Thurmond and Representative Rivers as saying that HEW Secretary Robert Finch would intercede to forestall cancelation of the $12 million in federal aid. The hospital administration was relieved of a compelling incentive to settle. The union and the SCLC furiously accused President Nixon of "giving Senator Thurmond his political payoff for services rendered in the last [1968] election. A payoff whose real price is the suffering of black hospital workers."[24]

The publication in 1971 of *Bring Us Together: The Nixon Team and the Civil Rights Retreat*, by Panetta and Peter Gall, brought the full story of the last-minute switch by the hospital administration to the public. The agreement ending the strike, they wrote, had been undermined by "loud, clear signals out of Washington, extracted artfully by a Democratic Congressman [Rivers] and a Republican Senator [Thurmond], that HEW would at least stall any action. And the signals came directly from the Secretary of Health, Education, and Welfare."[25] About 7 A.M. on June 12, Finch had had breakfast with Rivers. The same day, Thurmond talked to Pat Gray, Finch's executive assistant. Both conversations dealt with the rehiring of the twelve hospital workers. By the end of the day, Rivers and Thurmond had Finch's agreement to review the requirement that the hospital rehire the strikers as evidence of its good faith in complying with antidiscriminatory policies. Immediately word was sent to South Carolina, and Dr. McCord withdrew the offer to rehire the twelve workers. As Panetta and Gall point out, McCord "had nothing to fear from HEW now."[26]

Local 1199 and the SCLC renewed demonstrations on a wider scale than ever before, and the black community, enraged by the double-cross, responded magnificently. The SCLC and Local 1199 also picketed the headquarters of textile companies operating in South Carolina, and in Washington pickets paraded in front of the HEW building demanding that Secretary Finch return from a vacation in the Bahamas and help end the strike. They carried signs reading: "Don't Fink Out, Finch"; "Rehire the Charleston 12"; and "Who Runs HEW, Finch or Thurmond?" Abernathy informed the press that the AFL-CIO director of organization was on his way to the longshoremen's convention in Miami with a recommendation that the port of Charleston—the main port outlet for South Carolina textiles—"be closed in support of the hospital workers."[27] The longshoremen's union confirmed its serious intention to tie up the port of Charleston unless a settlement was reached quickly.

The arrests continued. On June 21, Abernathy and Hosea Williams, director of the SCLC's voter registration drive, led a prayer meeting downtown. They were arrested on charges of rioting and "inciting to riot" and held on $50,000 bail each. That night a 9 P.M. curfew was reinstated, and troops were ordered to be ready to return in full force to Charleston. Leading newspapers, including the prestigious Washington *Post*, blamed Secretary Finch for the critical situation again shaping up in Charleston. Finch finally agreed to the issuance of a news release pledging that HEW would "fulfill its legal responsibility in the area of equal employment at Medical College of South Carolina."

John Veneman, Finch's secretary, sought White House permission to hand the HEW release to the press. John Erlichmann, President Nixon's adviser for domestic affairs, asked why it was necessary. "Well, for one thing," Veneman replied, "hundreds of blacks are already beginning to demonstrate, there's a potential of trouble, and it would help restore some needed confidence in the Administration that the law will be enforced." Ehrlichmann replied: "Well, haven't we got some pressure on this from Thurmond? You know, Jack, the blacks aren't where our votes are." Panetta and Gall later commented: "In one brief phrase, he had cut off over twenty million Americans from their Government because a political debt was not involved."[28] The HEW press release was not issued.

However, Secretary of Labor George Shultz, probably fearful that Charleston faced a repetition of what had happened in Memphis, did act. A federal mediator was sent to Charleston, and word was relayed to Dr. McCord from the White House that the strike had better be settled. The president of the hospital caved in. But, as Panetta and Gall note, because of the Nixon "Southern strategy," "weeks of additional turmoil, over eight hundred arrests, hundreds of demonstrations and rallies had taken place."

The front cover of the July, 1969, issue of 1199 *Drug & Hospital News* announced: "1199 Union Power Plus SCLC Soul Power Equals Victory in Charleston." The workers at the Medical College Hospital had won a $1.60 pay floor and pay boosts of 30 to 70 cents an hour. They also won the establishment of a credit union and a grievance procedure in which the union could represent them. All workers were to be reinstated, including the twelve whose firing had started the strike. It was a compromise settlement; the union did not win recognition as a bargaining agent, but the credit union and the grievance machinery were viewed as tantamount to union recognition. "The union's greatest gain in Charleston," the *Wall Street Journal* wrote several months later, "was credibility. When it talks about striking now, hospitals listen."[29]

On June 27, 1969, a victory rally took place at Zion Olivet Church to celebrate the settlement of the 100-day Medical College Hospital strike. The Reverend Ralph Abernathy was still in jail and vowed to remain there until County Hospital agreed to abandon its refusal to rehire all the striking workers. That came about on July 18, when a settlement was signed incorporating the terms of the Medical College Hospital agreement. The Reverend Andrew Young spoke for Abernathy, too, when he said: "We won this strike because of a wonderful marriage— the marriage of the SCLC and Local 1199. The first of many beautiful children of this marriage is Local 1199B here in Charleston, and there are going to be as many more children like 1199B as there are letters in the alphabet."[30]

It was not long before the second child was born. In August, again with strong support from the SCLC and the black community, Local 1199E won bargaining rights for 1,500 previously unorganized workers, mostly black, at Johns Hopkins Hospital in Baltimore. Workers in the lowest category, who had been earning $1.60 an hour, received a minimum wage of $100 per week plus fringe benefits that included health insurance and an increase in paid holidays. Within a year Local 1199E represented 6,000 hospital and nursing-home workers, making it one of the largest unions in Baltimore.

On October 6, 1969, at the AFL-CIO convention in Atlantic City, Mary Ann Moultrie, president of the Charleston black hospital workers' union, told the delegates that she had come to thank the labor movement for its support of the striking Local 1199B hospital workers in their struggle. "All of us are black. We fought so we could win the fight to be treated as human beings," she told a convention made up almost entirely of white delegates. She admitted that the workers had often felt that the power arrayed against them was too strong—the city administration, the state government, the National Guard, the state police, and above all "the textile companies who run the State of South Carolina." But Ralph Abernathy and Coretta King had kept reminding them that in Memphis, too, black workers had confronted powerful opposition, and yet the power of the Negro-Labor Alliance had proved to be even greater. And so it proved to be in Charleston. "The combination of union power and soul power won." The combination had not ended with the strike; the cooperation of Local 1199B, the SCLC, and the black community of Charleston had resulted in a drive to register black voters so that it might pay off politically as it had already paid off economically. The same combination, Mary Ann Moultrie pledged, would be maintained in future drives "to organize the hospital workers everywhere," and these efforts, she predicted, would end in victories equal to or even greater than those already achieved in Charleston. "We will overcome. Nobody, but nobody, will turn us back."[31]

On December 14, 1969, the *New York Times* carried the news that a national union of hospital and nursing-home workers, with Mrs. Coretta Scott King as honorary chairman, had been set up by the leaders of Local 1199. The new national union would represent employees of private hospitals and nursing homes. (Public hospital workers would be organized by the State, County, and Municipal Workers.) No one underestimated the difficulties that lay ahead for the National Union of Hospital and Nursing Home Employes. The army of kitchen helpers, orderlies, janitors, nurses' aides, secretaries, and other nonprofessional workers, mainly nonwhite, was 90 per cent unorganized, and the hospital and nursing-home administrators intended to keep it that way. They had in their favor the fact that the close to 2.5 million workers in the hospitals and nursing homes had been largely excluded from federal and state laws defining the rights of other workers to union representation. Thus there was neither NLRB machinery for conducting union elections nor legal definitions of fair and unfair labor practices. The exemptions meant also that hospitals were not legally required to recognize the union as official bargaining agent.

But the union had behind it the reputation of the great victory in Charleston and concrete evidence that it could effectively combine civil rights and union rights and enlist in the drive to organize the predominantly black and poor hospital workers the aid of local black leaders and the black community. Union power plus soul power was to prove effective in overcoming future obstacles as it had already done in Charleston.

As the decade of the 1960's drew to a close, a new movement was afoot to extend the principles of the Negro-Labor Alliance—the effective uniting of the labor and civil-rights movements—from Memphis and Charleston to the nation as a whole. And this movement was to be led by the two unions that had been associated with these two significant struggles in the history of black workers. Both Memphis and Charleston were strikes of previously unorganized, heavily exploited, poverty-level workers. Both were bitterly opposed by the power structure in the communities involved. Both were supported by the Southern Christian Leadership Conference, with the personal participation of its top leadership —Martin Luther King, Jr., in the case of Memphis, and the Reverend Ralph Abernathy and Dr. King's widow in the case of Charleston. Both had won the support of the black community in the form of marches, mass meetings, boycotts, and financial aid. Both had been backed by important unions, among them the United Auto Workers, the United Steelworkers of America, the meat cutters, the United Rubber Workers, and the Tobacco Workers' International Union. In the case of Memphis especially, the local and state AFL-CIO had given important assistance to the strikers, while in Charleston the longshoremen's union had played a key role in the final victory. Both strikes, however, had received only limited support from Southern white workers, most of whom failed to understand that the struggles in Memphis and Charleston were intimately linked to the improvement of living standards for all workers in the South, white as well as black.*

When the Charleston strike had ended in victory, Coretta Scott King revealed that her husband, on the eve of his death, had reached "a momentous conclusion about the struggle against poverty in the United States." In Memphis, Dr. King decided that "the key to battling poverty is winning jobs for workers with decent pay through unionism." And in Memphis and Charleston, she concluded, "this strategy came to life."[32]

---

* However, the black-white unity established in Memphis and Charleston did have an effect on Southern white workers. The Textile Workers Union campaign to organize the textile industry in the South during the summer of 1973 reflected this. As more black workers entered the textile industry, the union had made efforts to recruit them. "There is no formal or informal alliance between the union and civil-rights groups as yet," wrote Henry P. Leifermann in the *New York Times Sunday Magazine* of August 5, 1973, "but the strikers at Oneita Mills in Andrews, S.C., most of them black women, have asked Mrs. Coretta King, widow of Dr. Martin Luther King, to speak at a rally. The first union meeting . . . in Roanoke Rapids was in a black church, and there were about 10 whites and 70 blacks attending."

25 Black Power in the Unions

It has been estimated that of the almost 14 million members of the AFL-CIO in 1968, about 2 million were black, and that 500,000 to 750,000 blacks belonged to unions affiliated with the 3-million-member American Labor Alliance, founded that year by the UAW and the teamsters. Clearly, by 1968 only a few unions still had some form of racial membership bar. Practices commonly used in the past to keep out blacks had all but disappeared. But black representation in top leadership was not even at the token stage in most unions despite an influx of black workers into many industries and a rise in black union membership. Only about a dozen unions had so much as one Negro on their governing boards, and there were only two black union presidents—A. Philip Randolph of the Brotherhood of Sleeping Car Porters and Frederick O'Neil of Actors' Equity Association. In general, as one survey made clear, "black unionists are being held down to lower-echelon elective or appointive jobs in too many labor organizations."[1]

The demand to place blacks in union leadership was not simply a matter of "black pride." Even government agencies and the courts recognized that representation of blacks among union leaders affects the support of and response to the struggle for better economic and working conditions for black workers. Since blacks are excluded from most leadership positions in both craft and industrial unions and have a disproportionately small representation at the staff level, the grievances of black workers have been frequently neglected, despite no-discrimination clauses in union contracts. Many white union leaders and company officials, insensitive to the discriminatory treatment of blacks, have not stressed implementation of the clauses. Furthermore, as William B. Gould has persuasively argued, "normal arbitration procedures"—the major method by which grievances of workers are adjusted—"suffer from certain substantial shortcomings that render them totally incapable of dealing with the racial problems that beset the labor movement today."[2] This is because the union and the employer, who together select the arbitrator, are often precisely the parties who have participated in the discrimination. Where there is no black representation in the union at the decision-making level (workers themselves have no standing to intervene in the arbitration proceeding), the chances that the arbitration will serve the need of blacks are indeed slim.

This has been especially true in grievances involving discriminatory practices in hiring and promotion. Even in industries operating under agreements with unions that had a "liberal" reputation on racial issues, blacks have been consigned—and confined—to the lowest-paid jobs by employer-union–arranged seniority systems. Other consequences of black powerlessness are described in what is known as the HARYOU report on the situation in New York City in 1964:

> The status of Negroes in the power councils of organized labor in New York City is most tenuous, if not nonexistent. The persistent pattern of racial discrimination in various unions, including some which still enjoy the reputation of being liberal, reflects the essential powerlessness of Negroes to affect the conditions of their livelihood. HARYOU's difficulty in finding a suitable representative of labor for its Board of Directors highlighted the fact that there is no Negro who occupies a primary power position in organized labor in New York City. There are a few Negroes who are constantly referred to as representatives of labor, but upon careful examination it is found that these Negroes, for the most part, hold their positions at the pleasure of more powerful white bosses or leaders. Even in those unions where the bulk of all of the workers are Negroes and Puerto Ricans, the top overt or covert leadership is almost always white. There is evidence that under these circumstances the union leaders are not always above entering into sweetheart contracts, or other types of conspiracies with the bosses, to the disadvantage of the Negro and Puerto Rican workers.[3]

The situation, of course, was worse in the skilled occupations of the building trades and the railroads, where union officials openly collaborated to keep black workers out of good jobs. The relatively high percentage of blacks in the membership of unions involved in the hardest, dirtiest, and lowest-paying jobs reflects the segregated pattern. Thus black workers in 1968 accounted for only 1.8 per cent of the total membership in the largest construction union, the carpenters; 1.9 per cent among the electrical workers; 0.6 per cent in the plumbers; 0.3 per cent among sheet-metal workers—but 29.2 per cent of the construction laborers' union.

Discriminatory practices in hiring and promotion persisted even where unions had civil-rights departments, for black workers were deprived of adequate protection by under-representation in the leadership. Ironically, they were continually told that any constitutional change requiring that blacks be given better representation would violate the very principle blacks themselves had fought so hard to establish. "The election of any officer to this union on the basis of race or color," Joseph P. Molony, vice-president of the United Steelworkers of America, thundered righteously, "would be a contradiction in the basic theme of the civil rights movement that people should be judged, hired, or elected on the basis of their ability."[4]

The implication that lack of ability alone explained the absence of

Negro leadership in most unions was ridiculous in view of the obstacles erected against any changes in leadership. Many of the obstructions were originally conceived at a time when blacks could not even become members. But as the barriers against black members fell and, in some unions, they came to outnumber whites, the old devices proved extremely effective in keeping an all-white leadership in power. For example, the practice in many unions of giving pensioners, usually white, the right to vote on all issues—used effectively for decades in the United Mine Workers to maintain the existing leadership—helped perpetuate an all-white officialdom in power. In the United Steelworkers, district leaders are elected in each district and, with the three international officers, make up the General Executive Board. A black can be elected district director only if a substantial number of whites vote for him, so the issue of black representation ultimately depends on the white voters' choice of a black candidate over a white one.

Cleveland Robinson, black Secretary-Treasurer of District 65 in 1968, gave an effective answer to the "capability" argument:

> Generally, in the labor movement, they say they'd really like to have some blacks and Puerto Ricans in positions of leadership, but that they've got no one qualified for the job. . . . Now, when I was first with District 65 I was placed in charge of 10 or 15 organizers and every one of them knew more about organizing than I did. If they'd have waited for me to have experience I'd never have made it. It was the same when they made me secretary-treasurer. I was treasurer in name only after I was elected, but I worked in every department—as a bookkeeper, as a teller in the credit union —even if I was the secretary-treasurer, to make myself qualified. What I'm trying to say is that you can take a raw, dedicated guy and train him for the job if you really want to, and that's what has to be done. You can't wait for a person to be qualified because he never will be if he doesn't get the chance and the responsibility.[5]

The struggle against racism in the labor movement for a long time concentrated on opening membership to blacks, a struggle that continues today especially in such fields as the building trades. But since the rise of the CIO, the battle against racism has more and more taken the form of a struggle against discriminatory practices in hiring and promotion and for greater black representation in union leadership. The struggle, waged continually since the early years of the CIO, grew in intensity during the post–World War II era, when the CIO, as part of its general retreat on progressive issues, played down the fight to eliminate racism in its ranks. The short-lived National Negro Labor Council made efforts to change the situation, and they were continued, to some extent, by the Negro American Labor Council.

As the promise held out to blacks by the merger of the AF of L and the CIO remained largely unfulfilled in the late 1950's, the NAACP joined black union members in appeals to government agencies and the courts to end discriminatory practices by employers and unions. There have been, ever since World War II, black caucuses within the unions themselves to achieve equality for black members, like the "Fair Share" committees organized by black steel and auto workers.

These earlier movements accomplished little toward changing the general pattern in the trade unions, but they did serve to dramatize the emergence of new elements in the fight for equal rights for black workers. They indicated clearly that the black unionist was no longer satisfied with the right to be in a union and to be paid equally with whites for the same work. The Negro unionist now demanded an equal right to skilled jobs and skilled wages, not merely a symbolic right to skilled jobs in a few isolated spots, but a "fair share" of the opportunities. Finally, the Negro unionist was saying that he was no longer happy just to be tolerated by the white majority of union members. He now represented an important element in such unions as the UAW, the United Steelworkers, and the United Packinghouse Workers, which he wanted recognized clearly through Negro representation at all levels of union leadership.

But the major grievances of black workers remained unredressed thirteen years after the AFL-CIO merger. A number of the earlier pressure groups had been destroyed or emasculated by "the dual weapons of repression and cooptation." The National Negro Labor Council was largely destroyed by repression. A good example of cooptation occurred when the Reuther leadership of the UAW finally decided that there might be a black qualified to serve on the all-white International Executive Board. The man selected as member-at-large was Nelson Jack Edwards, a faithful supporter of Walter Reuther and the man who had denounced blacks involved in the 1967 uprising in the Detroit ghetto as "hoodlums and hatemongers."

In his keynote speech to the seventh annual NALC convention, held in Youngstown, Ohio, on May 24, 1968, NALC President Cleveland Robinson noted, "Our work and our activities are still not welcome in large sections of the labor movement." Established union leaders were ready to grant the black members "token" concessions, but the time for them had long since passed. "There is no place for tokenism in the labor movement. Negroes are a highly important part of it; they belong in the mainstream of the leadership. We want to share in the power of the labor movement by being properly represented in the policy-making councils of the unions."

To most white trade union leaders the chilling word in Robinson's speech was "power." It was a word being heard wherever black workers, indeed nearly all black Americans, gathered.

The slogan "Black Power" first came to national attention during the June, 1966, voters' march through Mississippi. The march had started as a one-man pilgrimage by James Meredith, the first black student at the University of Alabama, but had expanded into a mass demonstration after Meredith was wounded by a white sniper. At Jackson, Stokely Carmichael, the young chairman of SNNC, ended a fiery speech to the marchers with the words "Black Power." The crowd took up the chant, and the slogan was quickly given extensive publicity by the national press.

Civil-rights leaders, black and white, responded with hysteria. The slogan was denounced as "extremism" and "racism in reverse," a device to split the unity of black and white that had achieved so much in the civil-rights struggle. More conservative Negro leaders rushed to assure the white community that the black power advocates did not speak for the Negro people.

But to the black masses, especially those in the urban ghettos, "Black Power" was a clarion call. For almost a decade the cry had been "Freedom Now." But it was already clear that freedom was not about to come in 1966 or in the foreseeable future. The fact that the "Black Power" slogan struck fear into the white community proved to the black masses that it was more effective than "Freedom Now."

Throughout 1966 and 1967, as black militants moved to implement their ideas in such American institutions as the university, the church, business, and government, often through disruptive tactics, the trade unions were largely spared as a target for their activities. But by 1968 the labor movement too had begun to feel the impact of the black power ideology.

To most militants, black power in the unions meant a "sharing of the power of running the unions" for blacks, a "fair share" of positions on union executive boards, and a "fair share" of district directorships. On the other hand, some insisted that even "sharing" was not black power, that wherever union membership was "fundamentally black," the leadership should be black; wherever the membership was basically black and Puerto Rican, black and Puerto Rican workers "should hold the reins of leadership"; and that this principle applied not only to unions with a leadership hostile to the aspirations and needs of minority-group members but even to unions with a white leadership that had proved its concern for the welfare of its minority-group members. John Killens, an outstanding advocate of this concept of black power in the unions, put it succinctly: "Suffice to say, white leadership cannot serve the profounder aspirations of black membership. Period."[6]

Others argued that black power could be achieved only through unions made up solely of black workers, and still others maintained that the goal of the struggle of black workers was not only to end racism in the unions and in industry but also to convert the unions into "revolutionary" agencies that would become the "vanguard of the black revolution." Finally, there were those who insisted that black working-class power could never be realized through trade unions and advocated their destruction and replacement by some form of workers' councils in the plants and shops.

Black power in the unions has taken many forms—black caucuses, wildcat strikes in defiance of institutionalized union procedures, black unions organized outside the traditional AFL-CIO structure, and even black revolutionary union movements. But all such forms have had two things in common—the militancy of their demands and anger over the long lag in response to these demands by unions and management. The black power revolt in the unions most often took the form of a rank-and-file revolt against the top leadership.

To take these developments in order, let us turn to the summer of 1968.

The big labor news was the announcement in July by the United Automobile Workers and the International Brotherhood of Teamsters of the formation of the Alliance for Labor Action (ALA). In the joint document, the two unions pledged to apply their efforts and resources "affirmatively and constructively to the tasks of assisting in organizing the millions of unorganized, strengthening collective bargaining, and dealing with the critical political, social, and economic problems of the day." While organizing the unorganized was to be the ALA's major objective, it would also concern itself with the eradication of poverty and unemployment, the replacement of slums with decent housing, and removal of "the cancer of racism" in American society through elimination of "the economic barriers and all forms of discrimination that deny a child or youngster opportunity for maximum growth and development."[7]

But the July 9, 1968, issue of the *Christian Science Monitor* featured a labor story that reporter Ed Townsend called even more significant than the formation of the ALA. The article reported that Negro unionists were organizing into black caucuses and engaging in a "fight for a heftier union role." Townsend observed: "Negro pressures are beginning to build up for a more important role in the labor movement. . . . Negro workers contend that unions have not done all they can to eliminate prejudice in their ranks or to allow the Negro to take a deserved role in leadership ranks."

A few days before the article appeared, black bus drivers in Chicago had staged a wildcat strike. The action, soon to be duplicated in many unions, had been brewing for several months. Black members of Local 241, Amalgamated Transit Union, AFL-CIO, began early in 1968 to organize a caucus, which they called the Concerned Transit Workers (CTW), with the aim of ending the all-white union leadership of a local that was 60 per cent black. All the top officers and twenty-two of the executive board members were white, and they were able to stay in office while the Chicago Transit Authority hired more and more blacks by the constitutional provision allowing only pensioners—3,500 in number and all white—to vote. Wayman Benson, head of the CTW, pointed out: "This is nothing different than the old plantation system. Here you have a union with about 65–70 per cent blacks and the leadership is virtually all white. How long do you think we can stand for this?"[8]

The conflict came to a head on June 30, 1968, when the black caucus proposed a revision of the constitution to restrict the pensioners' voting privileges to matters that concerned them directly. When James J. Hill, the local's president, declared the proposal defeated by voice vote, the black caucus members demanded a standing vote or a secret ballot. Hill quickly adjourned the meeting. The following morning 900 black drivers refused to take their buses out. The number of strikers grew each day. Within a few days, about fifty bus lines were shut down entirely, and forty others were reduced to partial operation.

While the pensioners' voting power was at the heart of the problem, the black drivers also wanted other long-standing grievances remedied. They put forth five demands to the Chicago Transit Company and the union: (1) better scheduling of runs and working schedules to end the system of split shifts, whereby a driver might have to be out as long as thirteen hours to get eight hours' pay; (2) replacement of unsafe and unhealthy equipment on the buses, such as bald tires, broken heaters, and so forth, and compensation for time lost while assisting buses in refueling; (3) no reprisals against striking drivers and full pay for days lost in the strike; (4) elimination of pensioners' voting for union officials; and (5) representation of the rank-and-file in all dealings between the union and the Chicago Transit Authority.

The CTW made it clear that it was fighting for all bus drivers, and a number of white drivers, particularly the younger men, joined in support of the five demands. They too realized that the right of pensioners to vote in elections was a bar to younger men's rising to leadership, whether they were white or black. Wayman Benson greeted the white drivers with the comment: "This is one time that black men are leading white men. They know that what benefits us benefits them. The union isn't representing them any better than it is representing us."[9]

From the outset the Chicago press portrayed the strike as a "black power" plot and a blow at the "public interest." Scabs were brought in and police were assigned to ride the buses with them. On July 3 a number of strikers were arrested when they sat down at the barns to prevent strike-breakers from taking out the buses.

The black community supported the strike, and the offices of Operation Breadbasket became the strike headquarters. With a Shriners' convention in town and hotel reservations beginning to be canceled because of the strike, and with the Democratic national convention only a few weeks away, Mayor Richard Daley found it necessary to intervene. On July 6, five days after the strike had started, representatives of the strikers and the Chicago Transit Authority met in the mayor's office. Officials of Local 241 were not present, but the Chicago Federation of Labor attended. After seven and a half hours, Wayman Benson emerged from the meeting to announce that the men got "everything we asked for"[10] and would resume work immediately. All the demands of the black bus drivers had been accepted except for rank-and-file representation in future negotiations with the Transit Authority, and President Hill had agreed to meet with the CTW to discuss the black members' grievances.

However, once the men had returned to work, Hill repudiated his agreement and refused to meet with the black caucus. The CTW then took the issue to the circuit court and, at the same time, called on the union's international president to oust the local union leadership on the grounds that it was "no longer qualified to speak for its members."[11] When their plea was rejected, the black bus drivers walked out again. The second walkout began on August 28, the day before the Democratic convention, and continued until mid-September. Again Operation Breadbasket came to the strikers' aid, but an injunction finally broke the strike. At least 149 drivers were suspended and 42 were discharged. The injunction also kept the Concerned Rapid Transit Workers, a black caucus of elevated-line workers, from calling a sympathy strike.

The CTW still did not surrender. The black caucus decided to form an independent union. With the support of Operation Breadbasket, a drive was launched for signatures to a petition to the NLRB for an election in which pensioners would not have the right to vote. (Illinois had no state labor relations board.) The NLRB rejected the petition on the ground that it had no jurisdiction over local transportation systems.

In the face of the combined opposition of the Chicago Rapid Transit Authority, the courts, the NLRB, and, of course, the leaders of Local 241 and the international union, the CTW was forced to disband. But President Hill, in turn, was forced to name blacks as second vice-president, assistant recording secretary, and assistant financial secretary-treasurer, and to appoint four to Executive Board posts.

(In New York City, a Rank-and-File Committee for a Democratic Union was formed in 1969 within Local 100 of the Transport Workers Union with the aim of ousting a leadership thought to be unrepresentative of black and Puerto Rican members. It was estimated that 50 to 70 per cent of the Transit Authority's 28,000 employees were black and Puerto Rican. The committee collected about 7,000 signatures on a petition for a representative election in a challenge to the TWU's bargaining rights, and needed about 2,000 more signatures. The drive for decertification of the TWU, thus far unsuccessful, shows again what happens when the composition of a union's membership changes drastically and that of its leadership remains what it was when first organized. The New York Rank-and-File Committee, like Chicago's CTW, insists it is not fighting for black workers alone—in fact, unlike the CTW, it is not even seeking an independent black union. In a letter to the *New York Times*, published on March 12, 1969, Joseph S. Carnegie, a subway conductor and leader of the committee, wrote: "We welcome white participation both in leadership and membership in this struggle; we never opposed it. We are not a black separatist group, we seek change for all workers.")

The wildcat strikes of Chicago's black bus drivers gave the first signal that labor unions were no longer to be spared as targets of black power protests. They also gave publicity to the backward working conditions black union members were subjected to because of their exclusion from the leadership and demonstrated that the blacks' fight for decision-making roles could add impetus to the larger fight to improve the status of black and white workers alike.

"Negroes Picket as Steel Union Meets" was a headline in the Chicago *Sun-Times* of August 20, 1968. The story said members of the Ad Hoc Committee of the United Steelworkers were picketing the convention and planned to carry their fight to the convention floor in behalf of their demand for the appointment of blacks to the Executive Board.

It had taken twenty years for the UAW leadership finally to agree that the absence of a Negro vice-president on the International Executive Board was a justified grievance of its black membership. The United

Steelworkers of America had gone even longer without coming close to such an admission. Black steelworkers, always a substantial part of the membership, had long been complaining that their special problems had never been adequately tackled by the union. They were still mainly confined to unskilled, lower-paying grades, maneuvered out of promotions, frozen out of white collar and supervisory jobs, and hit hardest by the inroads of automation—all despite nondiscrimination clauses in contracts, a top-level union Civil Rights Committee, and fair employment committees at the local level.

At the 1963 convention a National Ad Hoc Committee representing more than 200,000 black workers in the steel union was organized. Walter Davis of Buffalo and Aaron H. Jackson of Detroit were elected president and secretary, respectively. Fifty Negro steelworkers, selected by the caucus, met with President David McDonald and presented him with three demands: (1) election of a Negro to the union's Executive Board; (2) total integration of staffs in the union, international and district, and hiring of black clerical help in the union's offices; and (3) reorganization of the union's Civil Rights Department, making one of the three top officers the chairman and a Negro steelworker director. McDonald refused to commit himself to the changes. Two years later, when I. W. Abel ran for president against McDonald, the black caucus of steelworkers asked him if he would, if elected, back the same three demands. When Abel agreed and incorporated the demands in his platform, the caucus, now representing black steelworkers in twelve states, announced its support for Abel.

Abel had already identified himself with the demand of black workers for wider recognition in the labor movement by his presence at the first (1960) convention of the NALC. McDonald had turned down an invitation to attend, and in 1965 his followers circulated these facts among white steelworkers, who bitterly opposed the push of the blacks in the union for wider recognition. At the same time, he made charges of racial discrimination against Abel, which his followers circulated widely among black steelworkers. The fact that John Nichols, a steelworker appointed by Governor Wallace as an assistant secretary of state in Alabama, endorsed Abel appeared to substantiate the charges. In the end, however, as a result of an intensive campaign by the Abel–black caucus forces, the black vote went for Abel. "We found," a survey of the vote stated, "that the Mexican-Americans and the Negroes in six locals voted for Brother Abel with the exception of one local at Bethlehem."[12]

There were some changes for the better for black steelworkers after Abel's victory. The union's Civil Rights Department was reorganized and headed by a black, Alex Fuller, and in some plants, particularly those of the U.S. Steel Corporation, more blacks were promoted from the labor pool to skilled jobs jobs than during McDonald's presidency. However, the steel union insisted on preserving the seniority system that confined most blacks to the lowest-paying and hardest jobs, and the major demand of the Ad Hoc Committee—a black vice-president—remained unmet.

On the eve of the steel union's 1968 convention, the Ad Hoc Committee of United Steelworkers, made up of eighty blacks from twelve steel union districts, met in Chicago and drew up three demands: (1) a black vice-president (2) more black staff members and (3) better jobs for Negroes. Their demands were forwarded to President Abel and other top union officials by Alex Fuller, with the message that the black caucus would meet again before the convention to hear the reply. "Their demands are taken seriously," a *Christian Science Monitor* reporter wrote on July 9, 1968. "Estimates of the Negro membership in the union vary from 17 to 25 per cent of 1.2 million members, a substantial-enough block to be embarrassing if not actually damaging to Steelworker officials." In fact, the reporter exaggerated the seriousness with which the officials took the demands, but black steelworkers demonstrated that *they* took them seriously just as the message went to the leaders of the steel union. The black caucus at the Inland Steel Local 1910 in East Chicago, Indiana, introduced a resolution at a membership meeting calling upon the huge local to withhold per capita dues from the AFL-CIO's Central Labor Council of Lake and Porter County and from the Indiana Federation of Labor "as long as they have affiliated unions that discriminate against minority groups." The local adopted the resolution, the first such step in the history of the United Steelworkers of America or even of the AFL-CIO.

In a preconvention conference, President Abel made it clear that he would not accede to the demands of the black caucus because he felt "there is no discrimination in the union." To ask the convention to adopt a constitutional amendment to open the way for the election of a black vice-president or to appoint a black district director, as the black caucus demanded, would be "special privilege."[13]

The black caucus picketed the steel union's convention in response. When AFL-CIO President George Meany arrived at the International Amphitheatre to address the convention, he was met outside the hall by thirty black steel union members carrying signs of protest against racial discrimination in their union. They distributed "An Open Letter to President I. W. Abel from a Black Steelworker," which noted: "Of more than 1,000 employees of the International, less than 100 are Negroes. Of 14 departments in the International, only two have Negro personnel. One of these two is the Civil Rights Department (obviously). Of more than 30 districts in the International, there are no Negro directors, and only one subdistrict director. Blacks were in the forefront during the formation of this union 24 years ago. Through the acceptance of crumbs down through the years, we now find ourselves hindmost."

The protesters also passed out literature demanding that Abel, as a member of the AFL-CIO Executive Council,

> secure the reorganization of the Civil Rights Department of the AFL-CIO. We insist that a Negro trade unionist be appointed Director of the Civil Rights Department. . . . The present Director of the AFL-CIO Civil Rights Department [Donald Slaiman] has no involvement with Negro workers and their problems. He does not represent us. He does not act in our interests. We believe we speak for many thousands of Negro workers

not only in the Steelworkers Union but in other AFL-CIO affiliates with large Negro memberships when we demand the replacement of a white paternalist with a black trade unionist who can honestly represent Negro workers and act on their behalf. . . . For years Negro workers have stopped filing complaints with the AFL-CIO Civil Rights Department because experience has taught us that the department is unable to function on our behalf. Most often it represents the discriminators in organized labor rather than the black workers who are the victims of white racism within the house of labor.[14]

On the third day of the steelworkers' convention, the Ad Hoc Committee proposed the creation of a second vice-presidency to be held by a black. The debate that followed was marked by the usual references on the part of the all-white leadership to "racism in reverse." Vice-President Joseph P. Molony, for example, said: "We are opposed to any procedure that would establish an office in our union based on race, national origin, religion, or color. That would be a form of Jim Crowism in reverse and contrary to our rigidly enforced policy of nondiscrimination." And President Abel declared: "I didn't hold office all these years as a Welshman, but as a steelworker elected to office." Both insisted, moreover, that a post such as the one advocated by the black caucus would be "appointive" rather than elective.

The blacks who defended the resolution urged the delegates to face realities. A black delegate from Duquesne, Pennsylvania, said, "We are some 20 per cent of the dues-paying membership, but it would be impossible to elect a Negro to a national office." Another from Pittsburgh declared, "It's all well and good to tell us to run for office, but you control the circle from which we have to run. In order to break this crust, there must be a place for us to run. We are asking you now to give us the second place on the ticket." A black shop steward from Sparrows Point in the Baltimore area insisted: "It is time now that we put a black man up there so my daughters and the daughters of all these Steelworkers . . . can say: 'Yes, now we are part—we are a real part. We are in the policy-making part of this union.'"

A member of the Ad Hoc Committee put it this way: "Sure it's best for a Negro to be elected, but there's not much chance of that. Since there isn't, one should be appointed." "Don't miss the tenor of these times," one black delegate urged. "Negro people are saying if we can't have our share of America, why have an America. If you're serious about combating white racism, then do something about this situation in our union." (The reference to "white racism" was an obvious thrust at President Abel, who had served on the Kerner Commission and only a few months before the convention had signed its report blaming "white racism" for the fact that black Americans did not enjoy equality.) Another member of the Ad Hoc Committee warned: "We believe that there will be an explosion situation in the United Steelworkers of America so long as Abel is unable to appoint and we are unable to elect a member to the board."

But neither appeals nor warnings prevailed. The black caucus's proposals were overwhelmingly defeated. After two decades of protest by black steelworkers of America, a major industrial union with a "liberal" reputation on the issue of race was still without a single Negro on its International Executive Board. The only consolation the Ad Hoc Committee had was the fact, noted by one labor reporter, that its week-long picket line and its floor fight at the convention had "spotlighted for the country that the Negro trade unionists are fighting for full top-to-bottom integration in labor."[15]

Some black steelworkers, frustrated by their inability to change conditions in their union, took the extreme step of forming an outside organization. At the Sparrows Point, Maryland, plant of the Bethlehem Steel Company, black union members who felt their local was not adequately concerned with their needs formed the Shipyard Workers for Job Equality. The group functioned as an independent black union, putting pressure on the government to end its multimillion-dollar contract with Bethlehem unless the steel company stopped discriminating in hiring and promotion. The group partially won its campaign for job equality and then dissolved, having achieved more in a short time by acting outside the union than the black caucus within the steelworkers' union had accomplished in nearly a decade.

Black power militants soon discovered, however, that independent black unions were difficult to establish in most areas. Philadelphia's black teachers, angered by the indifference of the Teachers' Union, an affiliate of the American Federation of Teachers, to their needs and the needs of the black community, sought to establish an independent union. They learned that, since AFT locals were in control as bargaining agents, an independent black union would have little to offer prospective members. Instead, they joined other black teachers in forming a black caucus inside the AFT, which has fought for community control of schools and for minority representation on the AFT staff and on the policy-making bodies of big-city locals.

The idea of independent black unions was also tried out in the building trades. Initially the Pittsburgh NAACP chapter formed an alliance of nearly all the black community organizations of that city, which was called the Black Construction Coalition. The coalition spread to Chicago, where sixty-one organizations, led by Operation Breadbasket, formed United Community Action. It then developed into a nationwide movement to bring blacks into the building-trades unions. The goals of the Pittsburgh coalition were a minimum of 1,130 jobs (not including common laborers) with union cards within two years; a minimum of 40 per cent black membership in each craft union; 20 per cent of the trainees to be recruited from among men with prison records; training programs limited to eight months; and qualifications for journeyman status to be determined by a committee including coalition representatives. United Community action in Chicago demanded that one-third of all construction jobs be held by blacks. An October, 1969, meeting of leaders of Black Construction Coalitions across the country adopted motions for a separate national black construction union. But the obstacles to creating such an organization proved so formidable that little came of the resolutions.

A few small independent black construction unions have emerged. The best known are the United Community Construction Workers of Boston (UCCW) and the Trades Union Local 124, in Detroit. Both were born (Local 124 in 1967 and the UCCW in 1968) out of disputes over black workers' right to work on federally subsidized construction jobs within the black community. In both instances, the white AFL-CIO unions had issued temporary permits to blacks, implicitly acknowledging that the workers had the skills to perform the jobs assigned to them. Approximately halfway through the projects, the assigned black workers were laid off. The abrupt layoffs led to the formation of the two all-black unions.

Leo Fletcher, formerly of the Boston Urban League, convinced the black construction workers in the Boston area that they needed a separate organization to represent the minority work force in the area. The group formed the UCCW and, in a "Black Construction Workers Manifesto," declared that it did not have faith in the commitment of the established union of construction workers or the political power structure "to secure and maintain the rights of minority group workers in the Roxbury, Dorchester, and South End Community, and that this organization will make policies and organize to enforce those policies." The UCCW pledged to move against "every contractor that practices racism and discrimination against our people and who is depriving us of our rights as Americans, depriving us of economic stability for ourselves and our families."[16]

In both instances the black unions won their initial battles, and the black workers were rehired. Local 124 succeeded through an NLRB ruling in gaining the right to represent its workers on the job site, although it could not recruit unskilled persons on the job as union members. The UCCW won the rehiring of all black workers previously laid off and the right to act as the bargaining representative for the black workers.

Each of the two black unions immediately realized the need to establish training programs and set up courses in industry crafts, including carpentry, brickmasonry, and electrical wiring. With the assistance of the Urban League, the UCCW also established several black contractor firms. Both Local 124 and the UCCW experienced "defections" by members who had the opportunity to join AFL-CIO unions, although in some instances such members continued to pay dues to the black unions and to support them. "We are not trying to undercut the union," Leo Fletcher of the UCCW declared.

> We want the same pay scale on industry jobs, though we work for what we call a "community wage" on houses owned by poor folks. But we want the jobs. Once we've got the jobs, if the union wants to go along and ask us to join, right on. If the unions refuse to cooperate, we have a standoff. We don't have the workforce to do the whole job—but we're not going to let them do it without us, either. I think the white workers themselves will

realize that the only reason they're not working is because they won't let some black folks work with them. Unions were started to fight management for better wages and working conditions. Now the construction unions are saying, "We got ours—now we're gonna forget the rest of you workers."[17]

While the influence of black construction unions, like that of other independent black unions, is limited, they have managed to keep the plight of black workers in the industry in the forefront for the black community.

Of all the developments since 1968 that have symbolized the emergence of black power in the unions, the most widely publicized is the "black worker insurgency in Detroit." To many young black militants (as to many white radicals), black power in the unions is summed up by the following poem in praise of the Dodge Revolutionary Union Movement (DRUM):

> Deep in the gloom of the fire-filled pit
> Where the Dodge rolls down the line,
> We challenge the doom while dying in shit
> While strangled by a swine. . . .
> For hours and years with sweated tears
> Trying to break our chain. . . .
> But we broke our backs and died in packs
> To find our manhood slain. . . .
> But now we stand for DRUM's at hand
> To lead our freedom fight,
> And now till then we'll unite like men
> For now we know our might. . . .
> And damn the plantations and the whole Dodge nation. . . .
> For DRUM has dried our tears. . . .
> And now as we die we have a different cry
> For now we hold our spears!
> UAW is scum. . . .
> OUR THING IS DRUM! ! ![18]

These pungent words, the theme of the revolutionary black union movement in the auto industry, were a shock to white liberal circles. After all, Walter Reuther, UAW president, was the foremost champion of equalitarianism among American labor leaders, a supporter of the NAACP, the SCLC, and Operation Breadbasket, and was even then conducting a struggle against the AFL-CIO over its lack of social vision. In a letter on December 29, 1966, to local unions, Reuther had called upon "the whole labor movement" to become more deeply committed "in the ongoing struggle for equal rights and equal opportunity not only at the opportunity level and through legislation but within the labor movement itself."[19] In the eyes of the NAACP's Labor Department, the UAW was "the best of the industrial unions on the issue of race."[20]

One of the plain lessons of the black revolt in the auto union is that, where equality of blacks in the labor movement is concerned, a public image as a champion of equal rights and integration is not enough. The disparity between UAW rhetoric and conditions in the union and on the job was what really mattered.*

In 1968 the UAW Fair Employment Practices Department revealed that of the Big Three auto manufacturers, Chrysler had 3 per cent blacks in its skilled trades, Ford had 3 per cent, and General Motors had 1.3 per cent. It is clear that despite UAW Model FEP Clauses in contracts, and despite federal and state legislation against discrimination, no significant changes in the status of black workers had taken place in the auto plants. They were still doing the hard press work in the foundries and other hard, dirty, dangerous jobs. The tool and die sections were still virtually lily-white. There was good reason for black UAW members to call the skilled trades department of the union the "Deep South of the UAW."

While conditions for black workers remained the same, their numbers in the Detroit auto plants kept increasing. To be sure, during the recessions of 1957–58 and 1960–61, few blacks were hired. However, after 1963, especially with the rapid economic growth during the escalation of the war in Vietnam after 1964, the number of black auto workers shot up enormously. In some plants, they comprised 60 to 75 per cent of the work force. Moreover, a large proportion were under thirty years of age, with little seniority. The UAW itself estimated in 1969 that nearly 36 per cent of its members at Chrysler were under 30, at General Motors 33 per cent, and at Ford nearly 30 per cent; the percentages of workers with less than five years' seniority were 51 at Chrysler, 41 at Ford, and 40 at General Motors.

Late in 1967 and in 1968, a new element was added to these young black workers—the hard-core unemployed, dropouts from the ghetto schools. The *New York Times* of August 13, 1967, reported that the heads of the big three auto companies and Walter Reuther were working with militant black nationalists and that "the purpose of the alliance is cooperation in . . . the prevention of another riot." One result of the Detroit power structure's sudden interest in the ghetto was the announcement by the auto companies that they would drop all "educational" qualifications for employment, train ghetto people with government financing, and bring them into the plants. Several thousand young blacks actually were hired. They moved into the hardest jobs, the foundries, assembly-line work, and press work. None went into the skilled trades.

It was not long before these young black workers were challenging

* A study of the attitude of white UAW members during an open-housing referendum held in September, 1967, in Toledo, Ohio, bears this out. The author concludes: "UAW members tend to accept the general view that Negroes should be treated more fairly in the acquisition of housing, but they reject the more immediate and specific resolution offered by this open housing ordinance. This case study is a good illustration of respondent's willingness to accept the more universalistic position on open housing rather than one more immediate and particularistic" (Norman Blume, "Union Worker Attitudes Toward Open Housing: The Case of the UAW in the Toledo Metropolitan Area," *Phylon*, XXXIV, March, 1973, p. 72).

conditions that other auto workers had learned to live with or had concluded, after many years of fruitless efforts, were impossible to change. They quickly learned that the union's grievance machinery simply was not geared to dealing with their problems. Before the auto corporations and the UAW leadership realized it, they were confronted with a new, and in some ways more basic, opposition.

What was to come was suggested in April, 1967, when 500 black workers shut down production at the Ford plant in Mahwah, New Jersey, for three days after a foreman called a production worker a "black bastard." The UAW urged the men to return to work, but they stayed out until the foreman was removed from the plant. After the wildcat strike, the United Black Brothers of Mahwah Ford, claiming to represent all 1,700 black workers at the plant, was organized, and a warning went out that the Black Brothers would keep up a campaign to eliminate all foremen "diseased with racial bigotry."[21]

By the time the UAW convention met in Atlantic City in May, 1968, the incident at Mahwah had already been forgotten, and the union's leadership proceeded to deal with the grievances of the black members in the usual fashion. Despite the increase in the number of black members, there were hardly a half-dozen Negro delegates at the convention. Walter Reuther's keynote address called for implementation of the Kerner Commission's recommendation that racism be eliminated in American society. But it made no mention of the demand presented to the convention by a "Detroit Black Caucus": election of a black second vice-president, black directors of the Ford and Chrysler departments, and a black director of Regions 1A and 1B, Detroit, where a great number of the union members were blacks. A leaflet distributed to the delegates by the black caucus pointed out that "only one Negro is now among the UAW's top 26 officers" and noted:

> The time has come to strengthen the solidarity, brotherhood and unity in our ranks in the face of mounting attacks of the company on our union and our working conditions.
> To assure this solidarity we must end the second class status and discrimination against our black brothers in this union. A real beginning can be made at this convention by elevating some of our black brothers to top policy-making positions in the international executive board.
> We must stand shoulder to shoulder—black and white as equals from top to bottom, to be really strong; to end the company policy of divide and rule.
> Black members have made big contributions at every stage of organizing, building, and defending this union. It is time they have a fair share of the leadership of the union they have helped to build.[22]

When the convention was over, none of the demands of the "Detroit Black Caucus" had been met. Nelson Jack Edwards was still the solitary Negro on the UAW International Executive Board. But while the union leadership was in Atlantic City an incident occurred at the Dodge Main plant in Hamtramck, an urban enclave entirely surrounded by Detroit, which in less than two years was to achieve more of what the "Detroit

Black Caucus" had hoped for than any number of appeals to the UAW leadership.

To understand what happened at Dodge Main it is necessary to know that a number of black workers at the plant were readers of the *Inner City Voice*, a newspaper founded in September, 1967, by a group of black revolutionaries headed by John Watson, Ken Cockrel, Mike Hamlin, General Baker, and John Williams. These men had been involved in civil-rights struggles led by SNNC and CORE; had been exposed to the ideas of Malcolm X, Marx, Lenin, Mao Tse-tung, Che Guevara, and Frantz Fanon; and were in close contact with the Black Panthers. Several had been working for years in the auto plants and were spending much of their time off in ghetto community activities. By the time of the Detroit riot of 1967, they had reached the conclusion that it was necessary to apply the revolutionary principles of Marxism-Leninism, as they understood them, to end what they saw as "black colonial oppression."[23]

The *Voice* group used the newspaper to establish a link with the black workers in the auto plants. It was distributed at the gate entrances, and soon nine assembly workers at the Dodge Main plant began meeting with *Voice* staff to discuss how to deal with conditions in the plant that black workers had been seeking to change through a variety of methods, including caucuses, without success. The grievances included discrimination in promotion to the skilled trades, racial slurs by white foremen, and an increasing speedup. Production at Dodge Main was up 63 per cent over the 1949–53 period even though the number of workers in the plant had declined from 14,500 to 6,500.

Tensions at the plant erupted on May 2, 1968, when a walkout occurred at the Dodge Main plant against the speedup. Within the previous week production had soared from forty-nine to fifty-eight units an hour, and workers, finding it impossible to keep up, simply walked off the job and set up picket lines outside the plant. They maintained their vigil through the afternoon shift into the first shift of the next morning.

When the workers returned to their jobs, the Dodge management fired seven of the leaders of the walkout, two white women and five black men. One of the men was General Baker, a member of the *Inner City Voice* group. Although white workers had participated in the outlaw strike, blacks took the brunt of the punishment. In addition to the five blacks fired outright, ten were suspended without pay for thirty days, and others from one to five days.

The reprisals triggered the formation of the Dodge Revolutionary Union Movement. DRUM started agitating for the return of the five black workers fired by management and distributed a mimeographed four-page weekly newsletter called *DRUM* outside the Dodge Main plant. The first issues consisted of articles and letters by workers in the plant complaining of management practices and accusing the UAW of failure to deal with their grievances. The ninth issue of *DRUM* called for fifteen demands, including fifty black foremen, ten black general foremen, black superintendents, a black plant manager, black doctors and nurses in the plant hospital, fifty black plant guards, a black chief of the Chrysler board, 50 per cent of all office personnel to be black, equal pay for equal work in all Chrysler plants and subsidiaries at home and abroad, and reinstatement of all black workers fired in the May walkout. In addition, the issue urged the black workers at Dodge Main not to pay union dues and to contribute two hours' pay to the black community in the battle for self-determination.

In support of these demands, DRUM led a march of black auto workers, black students, and unemployed youth from the ghetto streets to Chrysler headquarters in Highland Park, the offices of Dodge Local 3, and Solidarity House, the UAW headquarters. Inside the plant, meanwhile, there was agitation for another walkout. While most black auto workers were not favorably inclined toward the suggestion that they stop paying dues to the UAW, they were sympathetic to DRUM's fight against conditions in the plant, and they were in favor of blacks' taking over the leadership of a local union whose membership was 60 per cent black. Then, too, they were bitter over the UAW's failure to effect the reinstatement of the workers who had been fired for leading the walkout against speedup.

On July 8, 1968, nine weeks after DRUM was formed, its members, now considerably increased, established picket lines around the Dodge Main plant and at several of the entrance gates, manned by black students and the "street force"; DRUM members talked to workers one hundred yards from the picketers. Any closer action would have brought their arrest, since the Chrysler Corporation had obtained a court injunction prohibiting members of DRUM from initiating any struggle in the plant in violation of the union contract.

DRUM did not seek to prevent white workers from entering the plant; "in fact, we urged them to go in" Mike Hamlin emphasized.[24] But some white workers stayed out to show their solidarity, and about 70 per cent of the black workers walked out and stayed out. The two-day wildcat strike crippled Dodge production and forced the leaders of Local 3 to act on the cases of the workers who had been fired in May. However, the Local 3 leaders accepted a package deal offered by Chrysler in which five of the seven were to be rehired, but two, General Baker and Bonnie Tate, remained fired. Still, DRUM viewed the July walkout as a success, in that it was a test of what a radical, militant black organization could do, and because it brought the organization to the attention of black auto workers throughout the Detroit area.

Soon a second revolutionary group was formed, the Eldron Avenue Revolutionary Union Movement (ELRUM), to be followed by sister movements at Ford (FRUM), Jefferson Avenue (JARUM), Mack Avenue (MARUM), and General Motors (GRUM). In each case, the nucleus consisted of workers in the plants who had been at DRUM meetings, and in each a newsletter was distributed to the workers in the plants. In a few plants, too, there were brief strikes like the one at Dodge Main. Again, black students and youths from the streets manned the picket lines while the members of the caucus remained at a correct distance urging black workers to stay out. Generally the response was a shutdown varying in length from a day to three days, followed by a remedy of specific grievances. But in the case of the outlaw strike led by ELRUM, at Eldron, Chrysler's gear and axle plant, on January 27, 1969, the company discharged twenty-two of the black workers involved, and the group was not able to win their reinstatement.*

The setback at Eldron caused the revolutionary union movement to re-evaluate its strategy. It was clear that wildcat strikes by themselves were not going to achieve much, since they were difficult to maintain. While at first the workers gained a feeling of power from actually having shut down the plant, they began to waver when the company fired the leaders and threatened to fire others involved in the walkout, and when the union moved in to restore discipline. When the men returned to their jobs, the militants were subjected to further reprisals while the union washed its hands of the matter.

The revolutionary union movements decided, therefore, to concentrate on spreading their groups into other industries where black workers were an important element in the labor force and into the black community, with the purpose of advertising the struggle in the factories to the rising black-liberation movement throughout the nation. This led to the formation of the League of Revolutionary Black Workers, which sought to unite black workers, students, intellectuals, and the black street force. Its base was to be the black workers, who the militant founders of the league believed would be "the vanguard of the liberation struggle in this country."[25]

For all its vision, the League of Revolutionary Black Workers remained mainly a movement based on the caucuses in the Detroit auto plants. However, it did maintain relations with the Harvester Revolutionary Union Movement (HARUM) in Chicago; the United Black Brotherhood in Mahwah, New Jersey; and the Black Panther Caucus at the Fremont (California) General Motors plant. In Detroit the league functioned as an "umbrella group" and a working general staff for the various black caucuses; while it did not dictate policies, the central committee offered advice and technical assistance.[26]

Although the League of Revolutionary Black Workers viewed itself as an independent black workers' organization, it ran candidates in two UAW elections—in Eldron Gear and Axle Local 961 and Dodge Local 3. In both elections the league's candidates lost, although Ron Marsh, the DRUM candidate for trusteeship in Local 3 in the fall of 1968, won a preliminary election over a white candidate backed by Local 3's leadership—563 to 521. DRUM attributed Marsh's defeat in the runoff election to intimidation by the company, which threatened to

---

* Eventually all but two of the twenty-two were reinstated. Chrysler refused to reinstate Fred Holsey and another worker whom it accused of having been leaders of the strike. On December 1, 1971, the Michigan Civil Rights Commission upheld a finding by a hearing referee that the Chrysler Corporation was guilty of unlawful discrimination in discharging Fred Holsey. The commission voted to issue a cease and desist order against Chrysler.

move the plant out of Hamtramck to escape DRUM, to police interference, and to the votes of 1,300 retired white workers, who are allowed to vote in UAW elections even though no longer employed in the plants. In addition, DRUM charged that George Wallace supporters distributed leaflets asking white workers not "to let those niggers take over our union."[27]

The League of Revolutionary Black Workers took the election experience as proof of the futility of using the ballot box to change conditions for black workers in the unions; *south end*, a student paper at Wayne University, expressed the league's viewpoint:

> The election was still a significant victory for the black workers. It was their contention that the unions are inherently undemocratic, and that even with the overwhelming support of the workers, the union bureaucracy cannot be broken through peaceful, democratic methods. As a result, thousands of black workers have gained practical experience in a reform movement, they have seen that reform is impossible, and are therefore rapidly joining the revolutionary caucuses being set up by DRUM.[28]

How many were "joining the revolutionary caucuses" there is no way of knowing, but certainly enough did to cause concern among three groups in Detroit: the auto companies, the UAW officialdom, and blacks who had been in the leadership of the more traditional caucuses. To no one's surprise it was announced in September, 1968, that an Ad Hoc Committee of Concerned Negro Auto Workers, headed by Robert Battle III, vice-president of Local 600, had met with Walter Reuther to press for "full equity" for blacks within the union. The Negro group had warned the UAW president that, unless the problems facing black union members were solved and they received "full equity," "others" would stir action and "chaos would ensue." The "others," of course, were the revolutionary union movements. The Ad Hoc Committee reminded Reuther that Negroes made up one-fourth of the union's membership, but that only 75 out of 1,000 UAW international representatives, or 7.5 per cent, were black, and that only seven of more than 100 key staff jobs in the union were held by Negroes. Vital political decisions affecting Negroes were "determined and dictated by white union officers. This must be ended now." The group made it clear that Reuther's own integrity and commitment to racial equality were not at issue. "It is precisely because of our faith in your integrity and commitment that we seek to resolve these matters with you at the conference table, rather than, as many powerful voices have suggested, take the issue to the streets and the public press."[29]

Reuther was reportedly "unhappy with the complaints of the group"[30] and insisted that Negroes were already well represented in the union's life. Battle was quoted as having replied: "Brother Reuther, we feel certain that you understand our outrage over the continued restriction of Negroes to token participation in the life of the international union."[31] It was clear that, with even the "moderate union activists," as the Concerned Negro Auto Workers were described, beginning to see the need for more than "token" concessions lest the black revolutionaries grow in influence, Solidarity House would have to do something and do it quickly.

Suddenly the UAW leadership stopped the practice of mobilizing opposition to black candidates in local elections. Within a few months after the formation of the League of Black Revolutionary Workers, black workers were elected as presidents of Local 900 (Ford's Wayne plant), Local 47 (Chrysler Detroit Forge), Local 961 (Chrysler Eldron Gear), Local 7 (Chrysler), Local 51 (Plymouth), and even Local 1248 (Chrysler Mopar), where only 20 per cent of the plant's 989 workers were black. A black was elected for the first time as vice-president of Briggs Local 21, and in several plants black committeemen and shop stewards were chosen.

The UAW leadership, of course, pointed to these results, in well-publicized press releases, as proof of the union's vanguard position in the American labor movement on the issue of black representation in leadership and as proof of the ability of blacks to use the organization's democratic machinery to gain their goals. Brendon Sexton told labor historian Thomas R. Brooks: "I don't claim that black workers are equally represented at all levels in the union, but blacks have done better in the UAW than in any non-black national organization." Douglas A. Fraser, head of the Chrysler Department, also expressed the official view: "The most potent argument you can use against extremists is that the system works. The victories by Negro candidates show that the democratic way allows for change."[32]

But black members had worked for years through the union electoral process, putting their trust in the UAW's internal democracy, with the result that their militant leaders were expelled and the most aggressive local unions brought under administration control through a trusteeship. Perhaps it was not a question of electoral process but the simple fact that the UAW leadership was scared by the black revolutionaries. When Brooks asked William Gilbert, newly elected black president of Local 7, how he viewed the union leadership's attitude on the new black officials, he replied "rather sharply." "There was no publicity given to the fact that Negroes were kept out of the movement, in part due to caucuses backed by the International. If no coverage before, why now? Somebody must be feeling guilty." All the blacks in Local 7, Brooks discovered, felt the same way, and they also shared the view of Leon England, another black official, who declared: "It took seven years to get what we got."[33] He might have added that it also took the emergence of DRUM and its sister groups in the auto plants.

To the League of Revolutionary Black Workers, the election results in no way signified a change in the policies of "the racist UAW leadership . . . at the expense of the black community and the rank and file black union members." What was necessary to bring about change was set forth in the league's demands for the firing of Walter Reuther; the election of a black president, one black vice-president, and an international staff made up 50 per cent of blacks; the opening of skilled trades and ap-

prenticeships to any black worker who applied; and recognition of the
League of Revolutionary Black Workers and its affiliates "as the official
spokesman for black workers on the local and national level with the
power to negotiate black demands in the company and union and the
power to call officially sanctioned strikes." In addition, all UAW money
expended for political campaigns should be turned over to the league
"for black-controlled and directed political work." The league also demanded a cut in union dues; an end to the checkoff, which "today . . .
prevents workers from disciplining poor leadership"; the use of all UAW
investment funds "to finance economic development in the black community under programs of self-determination"; and the placing of all
union strike funds in black institutions instead of white banks. The
union's grievance procedure had to be "a completely new system" under
which grievances would be settled immediately on the job by the workers in the plant. At the same time, the union "must fight vigorously"
against speedups, force the companies to double the size of the work
force, and initiate a campaign for a five-hour day, a four-day week, and
"an immediate doubling of the wages of all production workers." The
final demand called on the UAW to use its political and strike powers to
call a general strike to achieve:

> an end to the Vietnam war and withdrawal of all American troops, an im-
> mediate end to all taxes imposed upon workers, increased profit and in-
> dustrial property taxes to make up the difference in federal funds, and re-
> allocation of all federal monies spent on defense to meet the pressing needs
> of the black and poor populations of America.[34]

To most auto workers these demands perfectly illustrated Eugene V.
Debs's classic remark: "There is a difference between class consciousness
and class craziness." The demands clearly implied that the union was a
greater enemy of the black auto workers than the companies. The league
insisted that only when the UAW was transformed along the lines of the
league's demands could black workers "proceed to move against the corporation with the might of the union behind us—and not in front of us."
Whether the union referred to would be a transformed UAW or a separate black union was never quite made clear. John Watson, a spokesman
for the league, insisted that it was "not concerned with institutions. We
are concerned with the working class and whatever ways we can get that
working class organized, that's the way we're going to move."[35]
If the League of Revolutionary Black Workers regarded the UAW as
the chief enemy of black workers, the UAW leadership just as plainly
viewed the league as the chief enemy of its membership. In an interview
in the Detroit *News* on March 16, 1969, Emil Mazey, UAW secretary-
treasurer, attacked the league and its contingent groups, especially
DRUM, as "a handful of fanatics, who are nothing but black fascists
. . . whose actions are an attempt to destroy this union," which, he
added, had done more for black workers than any other union. "We can
no longer tolerate the tactics of these young militants," he asserted. He
also called the "black peril" confronting the UAW greater than the "red

peril" of the 1930's. The entire interview contained not a word of criticism of the auto companies' practices that made the auto workers recep-
tive to the revolutionary groups' appeals, and not one reference to the
failure of the union's grievance machinery to end these practices.

A few UAW leaders understood what lay behind the black revolutionary upsurge. Douglas A. Fraser at least acknowledged that blacks in
the union suffered inequities and discrimination, and that the black revolutionaries' criticism of the grievance procedure was amply justified. A
reporter for the *Michigan Chronicle* asked Fraser, "What do you think
kicked off the DRUM organizations in the Chrysler shops?" He replied,
"anger, frustration, discrimination, the society did it to them, as it has
been doing for the last 300 years—and unsettled grievances." He conceded that the grievance procedure failed to deal with the major complaints of the blacks: "Some grievances could have whiskers on them."
And black representation in the union was totally inadequate. Fraser
went so far as to concede that the fifteen demands drawn up by DRUM
for the ninth issue of its shop paper were "in the main, valid demands."[36]

But none of this was reflected in the four-page letter the UAW Executive Board sent to 350,000 Detroit-area members on March 19, 1969.
Without mentioning any particular group, the letter managed to indict
the League of Revolutionary Black Workers and its black caucuses. "For
centuries the black man has suffered exploitation and discrimination
everywhere he has turned," the letter conceded. "He has been robbed of
his dignity as an individual. He has been denied his natural right to participate fully in the society in which he lives. Many times the hiring office was closed to him completely. When it was opened, he generally
was offered work that no one else would take, the hard, dirty, low-paying
job." But nowhere was there any recognition of the fact that discrimination exists not only because of century-old prejudices but also because it
is profitable, and that for decades the auto companies had saved billions
of dollars by shortchanging their black workers. Nor was there any ac-
knowledgment of the fact that the union had done very little to change
the situation. Now that many young black workers were not satisfied
with union rhetoric, the UAW leadership lashed out not at the conditions but at those who were seeking to change them. After the formal
recognition of racism in American society (but not in the union), the
letter was devoted entirely to a vehement denunciation of the revolutionary black workers' movements, which it charged with creating racial
conflict in the plants. "Fires have been started inside the plants . . . the
group of extremists and racial separatists have sought to spread terror
amongst both blacks and whites . . . incidents of violence, including
knifings and physical assaults, have occurred." The letter made it clear
that the league members would receive no protection from the UAW if
they were fired by the companies for resorting to "violence and intimidation with the conscious purpose of dividing our union along racist
lines."[37]

The League of Revolutionary Black Workers scoffed at the UAW letter. The Communist Party of Michigan remarked that it belonged

"alongside Meany's racist attack on A. Philip Randolph in the 1959 AFL-CIO convention." The Michigan CP claimed that the wildcat strikes, which the letter forcefully condemned, were "the result of 22 years in which the UAW leadership has done next to nothing about the unbearable racism of the profit-hungry corporations, and their snarled-up grievance procedure traps." If the UAW leadership was so concerned about "violence," why did it not do something to end the "violence" black auto workers faced because they were "confined in the main to the hardest, dirtiest jobs in the foundries, frame and engine-plants under killing speed-up pressures that ruin their health and shorten their lives," or the "violence" caused by their having "to drive to work long distances from their ghetto homes to plants located in lily-white suburbs where they dare not try to live because they cannot expect government or union protection from racist mobs"? To attack the victims of company violence instead of defending them was not unionism. "It is anti-union!"[38]

While the UAW leadership chose to ignore this attack, it could not adopt the same attitude toward a criticism of its letter by the Ad Hoc Committee of Concerned Negro Auto Workers, which represented many of the older black auto workers. The committee praised the union for having done much to improve working conditions, raise wages, shorten hours of work, and defend the interests of all UAW members. But it reminded UAW officials that the rise of revolutionary black caucuses was due primarily to the fact that "the UAW leadership is generally not responding to the special needs of black workers." Pointing to the Executive Board's insistence that "there can be no separate answers. No white answers. No black answers," the committee noted that this approach ignored the reality of life for the black auto workers, the fact that "because of racism, black workers are forced to perform the hardest, dirtiest, lowest-paying, hottest and heaviest jobs," and that because of company discrimination, they were kept "by and large out of white collar skilled trades and professional jobs." Instead of spending union funds on attacking black revolutionaries, the committee suggested that the UAW leadership make sure that in forthcoming negotiations with the auto companies the following demands be put forward:

(1) Workers in foundries and body shops be given premium pay for work on these jobs, more relief time for every eight hours, more paid absence allowance, more vacations with pay, more paid lunch, more wash time, and 25-year pension plans with full benefits.

(2) That inverse seniority be established for lay-offs, protecting the jobs of younger, newly hired workers—most of whom are black. Older workers can accept the voluntary lay-off to be paid full supplemental benefits.

(3) That the anti-discrimination clause be strengthened to read that any company representative or foreman guilty of discrimination against a worker because of his race, religion, sex, or political affiliation be fired.[39]

Shortly after the suggestion that it pay more attention to the special problems of black workers and less to attacking the black revolutionaries, the UAW leadership endorsed the "inverse" seniority concept, which would allow whites with greater seniority to take a layoff at their own option with supplemental unemployment compensation so that blacks would have a better chance and not be the first to be fired.

By the spring of 1970, the so-called black peril posed by the revolutionary union movement to the UAW leadership had largely subsided. It did so in part because the UAW leadership had finally realized that the best way to cope with the threat posed by the militant black caucuses was to open some staff jobs to "moderate black militants" and add another black to the International Executive Board. By then there were two blacks on the twenty-seven executive board, eighty black international representatives on a staff of 1,050, several black department heads, and more black officers in locals having large numbers of black members. About 400,000 of the 1.7 million UAW members, or about 25 per cent of the union membership, were black. Although the representation of blacks in union positions was hardly equal to the percentage of blacks who held UAW cards, it was a vast improvement over what had been the case only three years before and undoubtedly operated to reduce the influence of the revolutionary caucuses among black auto workers.

But what may have been even more important was the slump in car sales that started in July, 1969, and, except for a few brief upswings, accelerated through the rest of that year and into 1970. In January, 1970, auto sales were 16.5 per cent lower than in January, 1969. Having the least seniority, black auto workers felt the impact of the slump most severely, and the young black militants for whom the League of Revolutionary Black Workers had had the most appeal were among the first of the black workers to be laid off. Moreover, the most recently recruited young blacks, the hard-core unemployed from the ghetto, were laid off the moment production declined, and further recruiting soon came to a halt. A month later came the announcement that the Labor Department JOBS program contract with the Chrysler Corporation, under which the government agreed to pay the auto maker $13.8 million to hire and train 4,450 production workers in seven plants, had been canceled by "mutual" agreement. Chrysler had informed the government that "because of the auto-industry slump and widespread layoffs" it could not fulfill its contract obligations.[40] The Detroit press noted that while "financially pinched" Chrysler would miss the funds, there was a bright side to the cancelation of the contract, since it would reduce the pool from which DRUM and other revolutionary black caucuses in Chrysler plants recruited their membership.

The League of Revolutionary Workers was not, outwardly at least, dismayed by these developments. For one thing, the league had anticipated a protracted struggle, as indicated by its slogan: "Fight, Fail, Fight Again, Fail Again, Fight on to Final Victory." But by this time the league had all but disappeared as a force in the auto plants and was focusing on the battle against racism in the high schools and community colleges, devoting much of its attention to housing and welfare issues and to building a black movement to wrest control of Detroit's political life from the white power structure. In theory, the league claimed that it was still linking the struggle in the shops and in the UAW to the movement it was leading in the community, but there was no evidence to back the claim.

By 1970 most black auto workers were marching to a different drummer. They knew that the activities of DRUM and the other revolutionary black caucuses had been decisive in the appearance of more black officers and staff members in the UAW, but they were also convinced that the ideology and program of the League of Revolutionary Black Workers only weakened the struggle against the main enemy—the "Big Three" auto companies. To black auto workers, a UAW with inadequate representation for blacks in its leadership was far better than no UAW at all. The League of Revolutionary Black Workers had concluded that black workers must break away from existing "racist unions" and form their own rank-and-file unions based on the black workers in the plants and the unemployed in the black community. As the league saw it, the entire history of the American labor movement led logically and irresistibly to this conclusion. The white labor movement had functioned *at all times* to ensure a special place for the white working man at the expense of the black worker. In a series in the *Inner City Voice* on organized labor and its historical role where black workers were concerned, John Williams emphasized only one theme—that from its inception to the present day, and without exception, organized labor had worked hand-in-glove with institutionalized racism in the United States.

A corollary theme stressed by the league was that white workers in the United States had never been, were not now, and could not be in the foreseeable future sufficiently radicalized to be allies in any movement that would benefit black workers. To act otherwise would be impossible, for this would jeopardize the privilege that white workers, even the poorest, had always enjoyed in America's racist society. Mike Hamlin noted:

> Whites in America don't act like workers. They don't act like proletariat. They act like racists. And that is why I think that blacks have to continue to have black organizations independent of whites. In terms of the future it depends on whether or not whites can make that transition of giving up, you know, the privileges that they have; give up the material basis for their racism.[41]

Historical evidence as interpreted by the league, as well as the current experience of black workers as they viewed it, led to the conclusion that "the labor movement as represented by United Mine Workers, Steel Workers, UAW, AFL-CIO, etc., are all the antithesis of the freedom of black people, and that at this stage, white labor must be viewed as an enemy." But not all white workers, blacks know from experience, are "racist pigs," and they make a distinction between the majority of white labor leaders and most white rank-and-file workers, even though they are conscious of the racist prejudices still prevalent among the white rank and file. Moreover, they know that the struggle of black workers to end racist practices in the plants and unions is related to the problems of white workers. Certainly the struggle to achieve greater democracy in unions, such as the move to end voting by pensioners in union elections, has served the interests of white workers as well as blacks.

Even among the black auto workers, where the influence of the black revolutionary movement has been greatest, there is widespread recognition that their struggles are related to the welfare of white workers and that this is being understood increasingly by white auto workers. The editor of *The Stinger*, issued by black auto workers at the Mack Avenue Chrysler plant in Detroit, explained:

> It's true that we are fighting discrimination against black workers in the shop as one of the most important questions of our lives. But that isn't the only question. The reason many of the white workers in our shop also read—and even support—*The Stinger*, is that we are raising the question of the inhuman conditions of all workers in production. Automation speed-up and the inhumanity of the company and union bureaucrats is against workers as a whole. That is why *The Stinger* is fighting, and why white workers have told us they are glad we are distributing it.[42]

Similarly, when the United Black Brothers called a walkout at the Mahwah, New Jersey, Ford plant in late April, 1969, against racism in the plant, it appealed to all workers in the shop for support: The leaflet issued at the beginning of the wildcat walkout declared:

> Why Do We Ask Your Support?—Because the same thing can happen to you. The company has been laying off men by the dozens, but the lines have not slowed up a bit. You have been given more work, and if you can't do it, you lose your job or get time off. The supervisors are harassing the men and calling them all kinds of names such as "Dirty Guinea Bastard," "Black SOB," and "Stinking Spick," to name but a few. . . . We, the United Black Brothers, demand an end to this now and that those guilty of these charges be removed. . . . We ask all of you to stay out and support us in this fight![43]

It cannot be denied that the emergence of the revolutionary black union movement was inevitable. Sheldon Tappes, leader of the Trade Union Leadership Conference, is said to have told a group of black workers who had been fired for staging an outlaw strike at Chrysler's gear and axle plant and were picketing Solidarity House, the UAW's official home: "If the TULC had done what it was organized for there wouldn't be any such development as DRUM." One of the young black pickets is said to have answered, "And if Reuther and the other bureaucrats had done what the *union* was organized for, there wouldn't have been any need for TULC."[44] The quotations may or may not be accurate, but the sentiments expressed reflect the historical truth and sum up concisely why, beginning in 1968, the trade unions, like other American institutions in the two previous years, had begun to feel the impact of the black power movement.

Events since 1968 have demonstrated that sections of the long-entrenched white labor leadership will make concessions to the black membership when their domination is threatened or the union faces dislocation. By sheer numerical strength, black power in the unions has already brought more blacks into policy-making positions on both international and local levels. But in many sectors of the labor movement, it still has a distance to go. The largest unions—steel, carpenters, electrical, ladies' garment, clothing, plumbers, retail, miners, teamsters, structural iron, operating engineers, machinists—comprising at least half of the U.S. trade-union membership—still do not consider it a constitutional requirement to give black workers representation at the top board level. One thing, however, is certain. The labor movement will know no peace until all workers share power equitably regardless of race, color, or sex, and until there is an end to the category of "Negro jobs," in which the dirtiest, heaviest, most unsafe, and lowest-paying work is reserved for black men and women. The labor movement would do well to take seriously the "Declaration of Rights of Black and Minority Group Workers" proposed by the Black Labor Leadership Conference in Chicago in June, 1970, which proclaimed the right of black and other minority-group workers

to hold any job and position for which we are qualified or can be trained for; the right to that training; the right to promotion to higher skilled work. . . .

to hold any office, at any level of union leadership; the employment of special measures, wherever required, to insure that black trade unionists are represented at all levels of union leadership, especially policy-making bodies.[45]

26 The Black Worker, 1970-1981

In several ways the 1960s was a period of great promise for black workers. It was a period of comprehensive civil rights legislation, of the longest economic expansion in modern American history, and of gains for Afro-Americans unprecedented in their long suffering experience. These gains were the result of the economic pump-priming of the Vietnam War, special government programs funded by an expansionist economy, and intense, bitter, and often bloody struggles.

As a result of these developments, and particularly of struggles of black workers and their progressive white allies against the trade union bureaucracies, the American labor movement by the end of the 1960s had traveled a far distance from the days when most industries were entirely "lily-white" and when many unions excluded blacks from membership by either constitutional provision or initiation rituals, while others prohibited blacks by more subtle devices or permitted only token membership. By 1970, not only were there between 2,500,000 and 2,750,000 black trade unionists in America, but also the percentage of blacks in the unions was a good deal higher than the percentage of blacks in the total population—15 percent as compared with 11 percent.[1]

By 1970 about 9 million black men and women were part of the work force of the United States. In such industries as steel and metal fabricating, retail trade, food-processing and meat-packing, railroading, medical services, and communications, blacks numbered one-third to one-half of the basic blue-collar workers. All told, about 2,700,000 blacks were in basic industry. Carried away by such statistics, social science professors began predicting that the American labor force would soon be mainly darker in color, and younger. "By 1980," went one prediction, "the number of young black people entering the work force will be five times that of young white workers."[2]

Yet precisely at the time that was written in 1970, the black unemployment rate was still two to three times that of whites, and while black median family income was only 61 percent, black teen-age unemployment stood at the official figure of 29 percent that of whites.[3] Moreover, blacks remained grossly overrepresented in the low-skill, low-paying jobs and underrepresented in the highpaying jobs. Of the 9 million black workers, 2,004,000 were classified as "operatives," or, as it is generally defined, semi-skilled. Most of the others were in the two classifications below operatives—laborers and service workers. In most industries black workers made up a large proportion of these three categories. In the automobile industry, for example, blacks comprised 13.6 percent of the total work force but 21 percent of the three lowest categories; in steel, where 1.8 percent of the work force was black, the percentage in the lowest three categories was 21. In the electrical equipment industry, where blacks had 6.4 percent of the jobs, their percentages at various levels broke down as follows:

High-level managerial, professional, and sales jobs	0.7%
Clerical jobs	2.4%
Skilled blue-collar jobs	3.8%
Operatives	9.9%
Laborers	11.9%
Service jobs	18.5%

Thus, an increasing number of studies demonstrated that during the 1960s considerable economic gains were made by black workers, and that many industries once traditionally closed to blacks were forced to abandon their "lily-white" employment policies. Yet they also revealed that by 1970 blacks were still disproportionately concentrated in unskilled and semi-skilled work, earning the lowest wages, and were still in a precarious economic situation because, for the most part, they still occupied the lower rungs of seniority.[4] It was clear that any dramatic setbacks in the economy would have immediate impact for black workers, many of whom were only a pink slip away from unemployment.

Writing in The Black Scholar of May 1972, Carl Bloice saw a "triple threat" against black workers" "(1) the challenge ... presented by the rapidly expanding scientific and technological revolution; (2) the growing concentration of finance, the growth of multinational or transnational corporations, and the appearance of huge diversified conglomerates; (3) governmental policies designed to preserve a high profit financial system, which acts adversely on black people." Bloice envisaged an increase in the introduction of automated processes in industry, the export of capital and jobs by multinational corporations, and increasing government stimulus through tax credits to achieve more rationalization, automation, and mechanization of industry. He predicted that these developments would seriously reduce the demands for employees in the unskilled areas in which most black workers were concentrated. In short, the serious dislocations created for blacks by the mechanization of agriculture were already making themselves felt through this "triple threat" in steel, automobile, meatpacking, and other industries, and this tendency, Bloice contended, was bound to increase enormously.[5]

Yet even Bloice did not foresee the catastrophic developments facing black workers within a few years after his article was published. For one thing, to the "triple threat" to the future of black workers one had to add others. One was the fact that throughout the country industry was moving out of the cities to rural areas or suburban parks, diminishing employment opportunities for blacks, since they cannot in most cases move to the suburban areas. According to the 1970 census, half of all employment in the nation's 15 largest metropolitan areas is outside city limits. Indeed, one of the fastest expanding job markets, that of service and retail industries, is increasingly centered in the suburbs. "It's a nice atmosphere," said one white worker in a suburban plant. But as the National Committee Against Discrimination in Housing observed, this "nice atmosphere" was not for most inner-city black workers, who could not find housing in the suburbs. "They would have to own cars, or take several buses at high fares and long traveling times to get jobs that average from $2.50 to $3 an hour." [6]

In April 1977, Patricia Roberts Harris, Secretary of Housing and Urban Development in President Carter's Cabinet, made it known that she intended to use federal leverage to provide equal access to housing for poor and racial minorities in middle-class white suburbs. "When businesses are moving from the central city to the suburbs, it seems to me unjust to say to the black and the poor that you may not live near where you earn your living," she said. "Communities that say we will take the benefit of a good tax base but will not let people who might benefit from that employment live in this community ought to be required to think about the injustice of that." [7]

But talk opened no suburbs to black workers, and by September, 1977, the situation had grown even worse. A major new study prepared for the Department of Housing and Urban Development confirmed the continued economic drift of jobs to the suburbs which still continued to resist successfully housing for black workers.[8] "Troubled Town" was the heading of an article in the financial section of the *New York Times* of October 9, 1977. The town was New Stanton, Pennsylvania, chosen by Volkswagen for its plant in the United States to produce the *Rabbit*. What was troubling the inhabitants of New Stanton was that blacks from the Pittsburgh area would be seeking some of VW's 5,000 promised jobs and would simultaneously seek to find housing in the community. John Reagan, New Stanton's mayor, conceded that the community stood fast against blacks living in the town. "There's very, very few blacks around here and people worry about it. I always tell them, hey, they've got to live too but what can you do?" Volkswagen has met the problem by informing the NAACP in Pittsburgh that "35 miles is a logical commuting distance," not adding of course—for blacks only. Since the NAACP does not seem to be able to convince New Stanton to permit blacks to reside where they would work, it has come up with the proposal that Volkswagen "run shuttle buses into Pittsburgh beyond that 35-mile zone," buses which, of course, would be for blacks only. If adopted it would mean that while white worker who can live in New Stanton would have an eight-hour day, black workers who would be forced to commute between 35 and 50 miles each way would have at least a twelve hour day—for the same wages. The company's position, as reported to the *New York Times* by its vice president for personnel, F. J. Short, is that Volkswagen is "sincerely concerned" about the situation, but could think of no solution.

A *Wall Street Journal* headline read: "To Many Ghetto Blacks A Steady Job Becomes Only A Distant Hope." The article went on to point out that "companies and jobs are moving out of the cities to the suburbs and beyond, where most blacks can't reach them. The importance of this can't be measured. Black unemployment is going to be excessively high as long as present housing patterns continue." As the *Journal* article made clear, what can be measured is that race still plays a significant role, and that Professor William Wilson is not correct when he concludes in *The Declining Significance of Race* that "class has become more important than race in determining black life-chances in the modern industrial period."[9] Professor Wilson has failed to convince the black worker, for on August 24, 1981 the *New York Times* reported that the vast majority of black workers interviewed in a Times/CBS News survey, attribute the diminishing economic status of blacks in American society "to race."

The threats to the future of the black worker take on added significance when they are coupled with the serious blows black workers have suffered from the recession that got under way in the first quarter of 1974. Today unemployment in the black community is at depression levels. Officially, the unemployment rate for blacks in the last quarter of 1976 was put at 12.6 percent. The official rate, however, gives only a part of the real extent of joblessness among blacks. Blacks are more likely than whites to be numbered among those who are forced to accept part-time work when they want and need full-time jobs. Thus, just as the real level of overall U.S. unemployment is 10 percent, a more accurate measure would put the black rate at 20 percent or more.[10]

Black workers suffered a double blow from the recession and its aftermath. The recession hit black workers harder and the limited recovery has reached them to a lesser extent. Blacks, who held 10.9 percent of all jobs in September 1974, endured more than 21.7 percent of the recession-induced employment decline in just the next seven months. An Urban League report declared gloomily that "actual Black joblessness has remained at the depression level of one out of every four workers."[11]

As bleak as the unemployment picture is for black men, it is even worse for black women. In 1976, 13 percent of black women heading households were officially listed as unemployed; it is likely that the real figure was closer to 25 percent. Since about one-third of all black families were headed by women, it is clear that millions of black children were reared in families with unemployed heads. In fact, today about one-third of all black children under 18 are in families in which male or female heads are unemployed or not in the labor force.[12]

The unemployment problems of black youth are so severe that it has been stated again and again that a whole generation is growing up without the job experience that is vital for successful careers as adults. Black youth made almost no progress toward improving their relative economic position during the 1960's—in sharp contrast with white youth. Today the situation is much worse. Officially, two out of every five black teenagers actively seeking work in 1976 were unemployed. However, since unemployment among black youth often takes the form of low labor market participation, some experts judge the real black teenage unemployment rate to be close to 60 percent. (Even the Federal government conceded as early as February 1975 that 41.1 percent of all black teenagers in the country were out of work.) In New York City the unemployed percentage of black youth is officially placed at 86 percent!" [13]

Bernard E. Anderson of the University of Pennsylvania Wharton School of Economics, who has done considerable work in the field of unemployment among young blacks, declared pessimistically, "Nothing at the moment promises to reverse the 'permanence' of black joblessness." [14]

Mounting black unemployment makes a mockery of the last decade and a half of affirmative action programs designed to eliminate racial discrimination in the workplace. Indeed, the United States Commission on Civil Rights conceded the validity of these conclusions in its February 1977 report entitled, "Last Hired, First Fired—Layoffs and Civil Rights." The Commission's study brought to the fore a problem which most white unionists are unwilling even to face, let alone deal with. It stated that layoffs based solely on seniority in recession times threaten "to cripple the economic progress of minorities and women, and to erode affirmative-action plans." Again: "The continuing implementing of layoffs by seniority inevitably means the gutting of affirmative action efforts in employment . . .[15]

One does not have to be an expert in labor relations to understand that the seniority issue is a complex one. To the worker in the factory seniority is crucial. His standing on the seniority roster, which is determined by the date on which he was hired, governs whether, when layoffs come, he will be demoted or perhaps let go altogether. It also determines his prospects for advancement into more skilled and higher-paying jobs. Naturally, the worker can be expected to defend his seniority fiercely against any move to interfere with it. Still, it is difficult to escape the fact that the use of seniority promotes racial discrimination and black unemployment, since white workers, having obtained their positions in most cases before blacks, have the most jobs with senior status. As the events of the last years have painfully demonstrated, despite all the progress in the field of employment and union membership for black workers, the traditional slogan applied to the black working class since the founding of the nation—"Last Hired, First Fired"—is in full operation.

Of course, blacks who entered industries earlier and continued on the job also have seniority rights which they are anxious to protect. But even they confront the seniority issue when they try to move into better-paying categories.

The relation of seniority to black (and women) unemployment has been long recognized, but also long neglected, by the labor movement. Many union leaders argue that to modify the seniority provisions even slightly, especially in a period of unemployment, would be discrimination in reverse, in this case against white workers. To this, blacks answer that Negroes should be given some form of recompense, even at the expense of white workers in the same plant, for the discrimination they have endured in the past.

Perhaps the most vicious aspect of the complex seniority issue for black workers has been the maintenance by corporations, with union agreement, of separate lines of promotion and seniority for black and white workers. As a result of this, the black worker is virtually frozen into a dead-end position. This issue had been discussed for years in scholarly journals, but early in 1973 it was brought to the attention of many Americans who knew little of the problem when newspapers throughout the country carried headlines reading, "Bethlehem Steel Plant to Alter Seniority System to Aid Blacks." On January 15, 1973, Labor Secretary James D. Hodgson ordered the Bethlehem Steel Corporation to open job classifications formally restricted to whites only. The directive was issued under Executive Order 11246, which requires government contractors to follow nondiscriminatory employment practices and to take "affirmative action" to ensure that job applicants and employees are not discriminated against on the basis of race, color, religion, sex, or national origin. The executive order, in turn, is based on the Civil Rights Act of 1964.

The order followed by slightly more than two years a finding by a federally-appointed panel that Bethlehem practiced discrimination at Sparrows Point through its seniority system. It found that most blacks at the plant had been placed in inferior, dirty, low-paying jobs and that most whites had been placed in departments with more desirable, higher-paying jobs. For example, blacks were given refuse-disposal and coke-oven jobs, while whites worked as timekeepers and sheet-metal workers. The panel found that the company's seniority system "locked" blacks into their inferior positions and discouraged them from transferring to better units. The earnings of whites, the report noted, were higher than those of blacks. The average "job class" or pay rate of black workers at Sparrows Point was 5.71 while the average for whites was 9.62.

Blacks, in short, were assigned "to those departments, units, and jobs in which the working conditions were the least desirable, the pay lowest, and the opportunity for advancement smallest." Blacks were assigned to Construction Labor (100 percent black), Cinder and Refuse Disposal (99 percent), Blast Furnace (81 percent), and Coke Oven (75 percent). On the other hand, the more desirable departments or shops were entirely or predominantly white—Pipefitting (100 percent), Time-Keeping (100 Percent), Tin and Strip Mills (88 percent), Machine Shop (100 percent), Tin Mill Assorting—Female (98 percent).

When black workers at the plant had applied to the company for promotion to more skilled departments, their applications had been refused. When they took their case to their trade union, United Steelworkers Local 2610, requesting grievance papers to file a claim against the company, union officials refused to give them the papers and told them to take their case to the Equal Employment Opportunity Commission. Meanwhile, white workers with less seniority were promoted to the positions the blacks had applied for.

Pressured by the EEOC, Local 2610 finally prevailed upon Bethlehem to accept the application of one black worker, George Mercer, for promotion to crane operator. The company agreed, and Mercer was promoted. But he continued to be paid a laborer's wages while operating one of the company's huge cranes. After five years, on May 27, 1971, Mercer and four other black steelworkers who had had similar experiences brought suit charging Bethlehem Steel with racial discrimination. The suit named the United Steelworkers as a co-defendant!

The suit prodded the Labor Department into action. In his order, Secretary Hodgson called for the following measures to be taken. First, workers who have never transferred out of mostly black departments must be informed in writing of the opportunity to do so; second, transfers would be based on plantwide seniority, which meant that a worker in a "white" department with only three years' service would no longer be able to move to a better job before a black worker with more seniority who applied for the job; and finally, workers who transfer to better jobs would be "red-pencilled," which meant that they would keep the wage they reached through seniority in the "black" department even though the job in the "white" department paid less.[16]

A Labor Department lawyer described Hodgson's order as the "most far-reaching affirmative-action decision yet by the Federal Department."[17] He failed, however, to add that, although there had been several court rulings outlawing dual white and black seniority lines, the government had been slow to move to implement them. Indeed, one decision had been in the case of Bethlehem's Lackawanna, New York, plants, where the company and the steel union had again been defendants, charged with practicing the same type of discriminatory seniority and promotion lines that perpetually held blacks to low pay and undesirable jobs. Instead of penalizing Bethlehem by canceling government contracts, as the law requires, the government had refused to act.

Although Secretary Hodgson's order reversed that policy, insisting that the continued safe and efficient operation of the Sparrow Point plant did not require the maintenance of the existing dual seniority system, many black steelworkers at the plant voiced skepticism that their job opportunities would improve as a result of the order. The order, they pointed out to a New York Times reporter, required the company and the union to end discrimination through normal bargaining channels, and they viewed this as being "like telling the fox to help the chickens."[18]

The Bethlehem–United Steelworkers case pointed up sharply the fact that, even though barriers to union membership for black workers had been eliminated, they were basically second-class members who did not enjoy the same rights as white union members.

By the opening years of the 1970's many in the black community were convinced that—despite the burgeoning of rank-and-file groups of black workers, black caucuses, and black power activists seeking, among other objectives, the end of institutionalized racism on the job and in the unions[19]—the incumbent union bureaucracies were so entrenched that their hopes of success were slim. But one group of black workers had more confidence. This movement, known as the "Coalition of Black Trade Unionists," began at a conference in Chicago in September 1972, called by five black trade-union leaders: William Lucy, Secretary-Treasurer of the American Federation of State, County, and Municipal Employees; Charles Hayes, Vice-President of the Amalgamated Meat-cutters and Butcher Workmen of North America; Nelson Jack Edwards, Vice-President of the United Auto Workers; Cleveland Robinson, President of the Distributive Workers of America, and also of the National Afro-American Labor Congress; and William Simons, President of Local 6 of the American Federation of Teachers in Washington, D.C.

About 1,200 black unionists, both rank-and-filers and officials, from 37 unions attended the conference. While major attention was paid to the presidential campaign, the conference made it clear that it planned to go beyond it and deal with matters of particular concern to black workers. Among the issues stressed by many of the black workers and officials were the failure of the AFL–CIO to organize the unorganized and to bring substantial numbers of non-union black workers into the labor movement; the necessity for greater black representation in union leadership; the necessity for the organization of the poor in black communities; the importance of supporting actions in opposition to the Vietnam War; and the need to back legislation favorable to federal revenue-sharing programs that would bolster social services in the black community. It was also felt necessary for the Coalition of Black Trade Unionists to continue after the presidential election, regardless of who was elected, in order to provide a forum for blacks concerning their special problems within the unions as well as to act as a bridge between organized labor and the black community. "We must have a change," declared Charles Hayes, "and there will be no change without organization." [20]

Before adjourning, delegates from UAW locals, building trades and hospital workers unions, AFSCME, and dozens of other national unions decided to set up a continuing movement. A five-man steering committee was selected by the Chicago gathering to issue a statement of intent.

While the Chicago conference did not endorse George McGovern, the delegates voiced their determination to rally black voters in opposition to the re-election of Richard Nixon. The dismal showing McGovern made did not shatter the Coalition of Black Trade Unionists. The McGovern campaign, as William Lucy observed, had served merely as the "catalyst" for the new organization, and it would take concrete form at a constitutional convention to be held May 25–27, 1973, in the nation's capital.[21]

Barely had the news of the new organization been publicized when Bayard Rustin, black apologist for the white trade union bureaucracy, rushed into print with an attack on the media for their "extensive cover-

age devoted to the formation of a coalition of black trade unionists."
There was no need for the new movement. "Black trade unionists are
taking leadership positions in their unions, their communities, and in
the political world with increasing frequency," Rustin assured all Americans. The A. Philip Randolph Institute, which Rustin headed, would
solve whatever problems still faced black workers. "And we are happy
to have the support of the labor movement in general and (AFL–CIO
President) George Meany in particular in this effort."[22]

Asked to comment on the statement, William Lucy observed that
Rustin's reaction to the coalition was "apparently in accord with the
viewpoint of the AFL–CIO leadership." While the A. Philip Randolph
Institute did important educational work, it "was in danger of becoming
counterproductive because of its unqualified defense of the status quo
in the unions."[23]

Some 1,141 delegates from 33 international and other unions attended
the second annual convention of the Coalition of Black Trade Unionists
in Washington, D.C., May 25–27, 1973. Most were from unions affiliated with the AFL–CIO, and 35 to 40 percent were black women.
In general, the delegates represented basic industry, government, and
service workers. A number of white delegates attended.

The Coalition of Black Trade Unionists was formally established by
this convention, it was to meet at annual national conventions, and
between conventions the Executive Council would be the governing
body.[24]

A separate statement on "The Need for a Coalition of Black Trade
Unionists," signed by William Lucy, Nelson Jack Edwards, Charles
Hayes, Cleveland Robinson, and Bill Simons, made the point that the
nearly three million black workers in organized labor constituted "the
single largest organization of blacks in the nation." It then pointed
out that

> As black trade unionists, it is our challenge to make the labor move-
> ment more relevant to the needs and aspirations of black and poor workers.
> The CBTU will insist that black union officials become full partners in
> the leadership and decision-making of the American labor movement.[25]

"The sleeping giant is awakening," is the way a black unionist
described the Coalition of Black Trade Unionists at its founding
convention.[26]

In his 1977 study *Black Workers in White Unions: Job Discrimination in the United States*, Yale University professor William B. Gould
presented a frightening and angry picture of the roles which powerful
unions have played in maintaining job deprivation and discrimination.
Gould identifies six practices that have been utilized by unions in order
to retain the system of racial imbalance: (1) the restriction of admis-
sions to apprenticeship programs jointly administered by employers
and industrial and craft unions; (2) the denial of journeymen cards to
qualified black non-unionists; (3) the refusal of union admission to
membership despite constitutional prohibitions; (4) the creation of

segregated auxiliary locals for blacks; (5) the maintenance of separate lines of progression and seniority which prohibits or discourages transfers by black members into better paying and more desirable jobs; and (6) the absence of blacks and other minorities from policy-making positions, both selected and appointed, inside the unions.[27]

Prodded by a rank-and-file revolt of black and white steelworkers, the United Steelworkers, all-white at the top and in regional offices since its formation, finally added a black vice-president to its roster of union officials in 1976. In general, however, blacks in unions still have an infinitesimal percentage of top and middle-level union leadership positions. Most major unions, representing the overwhelming majority of union members, still do not have blacks in leadership beyond the local union level (and very inadequate even there).

In William B. Gould's opinion the primary issue around which the struggle against discriminatory practices continues is "how to reconcile equal employment opportunity today with seniority expectations based on yesterday's built-in discrimination."[28]

Over the opposition of the AFL–CIO, black workers, supported by the NAACP, have challenged the traditional seniority provisions as discriminatory. At first they were eminently successful. On March 24, 1976, by a vote of 5 to 3, the Supreme Court ruled that blacks who were denied jobs in violation of Title 7 of the Civil Rights Act of 1964 (prohibiting discrimination in employment because of race, religion, sex, or national origin) must be awarded retroactive seniority once they succeeded in getting those jobs. Blacks must be given the same seniority they would have had if they had been hired initially, the Court said, with all the accompanying rights, including pension benefits and, in the event of layoffs, better job security than that possessed by workers with less seniority. (The ruling on the rights of blacks in jobs appeared to assure the same rights to women who were discriminated against on the basis of sex.) The ruling did not mean that every minority member or woman who is newly hired by a company that once discriminated could get retroactive seniority. The person must prove in federal court that he or she was denied the job because of unlawful discrimination after Title 7 went into effect. The decision also left unanswered the question whether retroactive seniority is to be awarded to a person who was denied a job on the basis of race or sex before the enactment of Title 7, or to a person who did not initially apply for a job because it was well known in the community that the employer did not hire blacks or women.

Despite weaknesses, the ruling considerably strengthened Title 7's provision for affirmative action as a remedy in discrimination cases. It established the principle, in the Court's words, "that whites must share with blacks the burden of the past discrimination" in employment as they already must do in schools. Jack Greenberg, director of the NAACP Legal Defense and Educational Fund, which argued the winning side of the case, told a *New York Times* reporter that the ruling "assures the black victims of racial discrimination will be put in the rightful place."[29]

Greenberg was vastly over-optimistic. Despite the loss of newly won jobs by blacks (and women) in the recession years under the last-hired-first-fired principle, the AFL–CIO leadership would brook not the slightest interference with the seniority principle. The organization mounted a vigorous campaign against the Supreme Court's 1976 decision. On June 1, 1977, the campaign paid off. The Court retreated from its previous ruling, and declared 7 to 2 that seniority systems that perpetuate the effects of past racial discrimination, placing blacks at a disadvantage in the competition for better jobs and other benefits, are not necessarily illegal. The gist of the ruling was that unless a seniority plan intentionally discriminates against the workers it covers it is not illegal. The burden of proof of proving intent—an almost impossible task—is on the worker who claims he or she was discriminated against.

The Court thus made it clear that seniority systems can legally perpetuate favored employment for white males if the systems were in operation before the Civil Rights Act took effect in July 1965. Further, the Court placed more stringent requirements for proof of individual discrimination against complainants in cases after 1965. It thus became clear that changes in seniority systems in such landmark settlements as the ones between black workers and steel companies (such as the one in Bethlehem Steel discussed above), which have given wider opportunity to blacks trapped in the least disirable, lower-paying jobs, will be more difficult to achieve in the future. Indeed, the Court's dissenters, Justices Thurgood Marshall and William J. Brennan, Jr., declared the Court's ruling would mean that equal employment for a full generation of minority workers would remain a "distant dream." [30]

But William Pollard, civil rights director for the AFL–CIO, which had fought for the decision, hailed the ruling, and smugly told black workers that "the problem is economic downturn, and not seniority." [31] The argument that the real answer to black unemployment is full employment is raised whenever existing racist practices in the unions are challenged, and is a frequent theme among black apologists for the trade union bureaucracy. But it has rarely been coupled since the recession hit hard in 1974 with meaningful trade union action on behalf of full employment. The AFL–CIO leadership, and especially George Meany, only reluctantly endorsed a mass rally in Washington, D.C., on April 26, 1975, sponsored by the AFL–CIO's own Industrial Union Department, calling upon the government "to put America to work." The New York Coalition to Support the Rally took a full-page ad in the New York Times, urging:

> We've got to go to Washington. We've got to stage a peaceful, orderly rally where hundreds of thousands of Americans will tell President Ford and all our elected officers: We want action! We want Jobs!

When the rally broke up into a series of bitter outbursts against the trade union leadership and establishment political leaders, the AFL–CIO leaders let it be known that the era of mass demonstrations for jobs was over.[32] This was one pledge the AFL–CIO kept.

Meanwhile, the prestige of the labor movement in the black community, already seriously damaged by the battle over seniority, sank to a new low. This loss of prestige is also being reflected in other areas of American life. In May 1977 the Roper organization found that public confidence in labor leaders had slipped from 50 percent in 1975 to 48 percent, and that among union members 51 percent had confidence in the "system of organized labor"—down 13 percentage points from a poll in mid-1974! [33] Undoubtedly, the failure of the trade union leadership to mount an effective campaign to alleviate the rising problems of unemployment helped explain the downward trend.[34]

Early in 1978 the Martin Luther King Jr. Center for Social Change granted its Social Responsibility Award to AFL–CIO President George Meany. In accepting the award—the justice of which I leave for future generations to assess—Meany emphasized that "full employment is absolutely essential if civil rights are ever to be fully enjoyed and exercised by every American." Later he observed, "Thanks to Arthur Burns and the Nixon–Ford Administration there is a new segregation in America. A segregation as bitter and brutal as the one outlawed by the Civil Rights Act. It is a segregation based on whether or not an individual has a job—those always working and those always jobless. Like segregation based on race, this new segregation must go." Still later, he noted that "black workers ... are union members in greater percentage than their percentage in the work force generally ..." [35]

Not a word did Meany utter about the fact that these black workers are meagerly represented in AFL–CIO conventions, on the AFL–CIO Executive Council, and in the leadership of the unions affiliated with the Federation. Not a word about the fact that for black workers there is no such thing as "a new segregation in America," since black workers have faced this so-called "new segregation" throughout the history of this country. Finally, we are supposed to believe that until "full employment"—certainly a worthy goal—is achieved the problems facing black workers must remain problems; that nothing need be done about the troublesome issues of seniority, the increasing trend of industry to move to suburbs where blacks cannot live, and the failure of so many unions to deal adequately with the legitimate grievances of their black members. This is a position which progressives cannot and must not accept.

However, when asked what his view was on the issue very close to the black population in the United States—the suit of Allan Bakke against the right of the University of California to set aside a segment of each medical school class for blacks and other "approved minorities" as part of a proper plan of affirmative action—Meany hedged. The AFL–CIO President replied, "I don't know what the Supreme Court's going to do. Some of our unions take a pro-Bakke position and some oppose." Blacks were hardly assured by this seeming neutrality, or by the fact that Meany did not instantly endorse the position of the American Federation of Teachers, whose president, Albert Shanker, bitterly opposes meaningful affirmative action, and which had filed an amicus curiae brief on the side of Allan Bakke. The fact that the AFL–CIO itself was silent on Bakke, Ken Bode points out, "should not mask its underlying sentiment. Most of the unions of the federation hierarchy line up with Albert Shanker and Allan Bakke." [36]

To their credit, five unions signed a common amicus brief defending the University of California. The five include the United Mine Workers, the United Electrical Workers, the American Federation of State, County and Municipal Employees, the United Farmworkers, and the United Auto Workers.

The Supreme Court ruling in the Weber case in June, 1979 has been ranked in importance with the 1954 ruling in school desegregation. To the black (and women) workers the decision dealt a tremendous blow to the main ideological weapon used against affirmative action programs—"reverse discrimination." If the court had ruled in Weber's favor, the only kind of affirmative action programs which would have been "legal" would be ones where prior discrimination was proven, and it would have been illegal for trade unions to compel employers to negotiate affirmative action programs.

The story begins in 1973. Congress had recently tightened up Title VII of the 1964 Civil Rights Act, barring discrimination in employment. The Kaiser Aluminum Company faced numerous Title VII suits with potentially huge back pay liabilities. In the area surrounding Kaiser's Gramercy, Louisiana plant where the Weber case originated, 39 percent of the work force was black, but there were just five blacks among the plant's 273 craft workers.

In early 1974, Kaiser and the United Steelworkers of America, AFL–CIO, negotiated a collective bargaining agreement for fifteen Kaiser plants throughout the country. The agreement created a craft training program patterned on a nationwide steel industry plan approved by the courts. Fifty percent of those selected for the program were to be minority, and the trainees were to be selected on the basis of relative seniority within their racial groups.

Brian Weber, working as a lab technician at Kaiser since 1968, applied in 1974 for one of the nine new craft training positions and was turned down because some thirty-five whites had higher seniority. But low as he was on the white list, Weber still had more seniority than two of the five blacks selected from the minority list. He promptly sued both Kaiser and the Steelworkers, charging "reverse discrimination" against all white workers.

A federal district court and the Fifth Circuit Court of Appeals ruled in Weber's favor. The courts held that Kaiser could create a racial quota only if it had discriminated against blacks in the past. And even then, Kaiser could grant a preference only to the specific blacks who had themselves been discriminated against in craft hiring. The "affirmative action" plan was therefore illegal. Employers cannot be forced to make up for general "societal discrimination," the court declared.

Kaiser, the union, and the Government applied for and obtained Supreme Court review.

One of the most significant aspects of the Weber case is that the official labor movement took a forthright, unequivocal position against Weber's opposition to "affirmative action" and "reverse discrimination" argument. Rarely, indeed, in recent years, has such significant sections of the labor movement joined together in support of the demand for "affirmative action," a demand which can lead to an improvement in the condition of minority workers. Moreover, a significant role was played by the women's movement, and especially women workers, who emerged as a leading force in struggle for "afirmative action." Yet it was primarily the black workers, in conjunction with the black community organizations, who advanced the struggle by leading the fight in the trade union movement to force the official leadership to move.

They were joined, in important centers, moreover, by white workers. In Gary, Indiana, for example, over 600 steelworkers, about 40 percent white, turned out in a mass meeting on the Weber issue. But the important point in the Weber case is that the trade unions did move, and they moved in conjunction with the civil rights forces. Representatives of more than 25 major labor, civil rights and women's groups met in Washington, January 12, 1979, and formed a common front in defense of affirmative action programs. Representatives were present from the United Steelworkers, International Association of Machinists, United Auto Workers, International Union of Electrical, Radio, Machine Workers, United Electrical and Machine Workers, American Federation of State, County and Municipal Employees, United Mine Workers, National Education Association, and Local 1199 of the Drug and Hospital Workers. Also participants at the meeting were the NAACP, Mexican American League Defense Fund, the American Civil Liberties Union, National Conference of Black Lawyers, National Lawyers Guild, Lawyers Committee for Civil Rights Under Law, and the Affirmative Action Coordinating Center.[37]

The United Steelworkers of America took up the struggle against Weber, and it joined eleven other international unions and the AFL–CIO to file friend of the court briefs before the Supreme Court. The Washington Teamster, organ of Joint Council No.20 of the Teamsters Union, declared: "In the interest of labor in the long run, both white and black, the court should rule in favor of the union and the company." [38]

By a 5–2 decision, the Supreme Court rejected the "reverse discrimination" charge. Justice William Brennan, writing for the majority, found that Congress had "left employers and unions in the private sector free to take ... race-conscious steps to eliminate manifest racial imbalance in traditionally job categories." Since the agreement does not involve state action and was adopted voluntarily, said Brennan, the only issue before the court was whether Title VII of the Civil Rights Act—the fair employment provision—forbids such a plan. It does not, the court majority concluded, and "it would be ironic indeed if a law triggered by a nation's concern over centuries of racial injustice" were used to prevent voluntary, private measures to overcome inequities.

"Labor Hails Ruling As Total Victory," read the headline on the first page of the *AFL–CIO News* after the decision was made public.[39] "We are delighted with the decision," said the AFL–CIO president. "It allows unions and employers to use the collective bargaining process to speed up elimination of the vestiges of centuries of racial injustice." [40]

We have traveled a far distance from the days when most industries were entirely "lily-white" and many unions excluded blacks from membership by either constitutional provision or initiation ritual, while others prohibited blacks by more subtle devices or permitted only token membership. But we also have a long way to travel before we can say that racism is no longer an important influence in organized labor. Discussing "Racial Discrimination and White Gain" in June 1976, Albert Szymanski concludes from a study of considerable evidence that white workers often lose from economic discrimination against blacks, since the entire trade-union struggle to achieve better conditions even for the white working class is seriously weakened. Racism, he argues, is a divisive force which undermines the economic and political strength of working people and acts to worsen the economic position of white workers as well as that of the black working class. The answer, he insists, is the total elimination of racism from the labor movement.[41]

The need to follow this path is more urgent than ever. Following a meeting with President Reagan at the White House on February 4, 1981, the 18-member Congressional Black Caucus (CBC) warned the Administration they will fight economic and budget policies that victimize minorities, working people, and the poor. All 18 members of the Caucus were present for the session at the White House informing President Reagan that he should slash military spending while preserving vital human need programs. They called on the President to preserve and strengthen affirmative action programs to overcome three hundred years of racial inequalities.

"The goal of affirmative action is to increase black participation in all areas of American economic life. We, ourselves, have not been totally satisfied with the various equal opportunity enforcement mechanisms of the federal government. But until new or revised mechanisms are put in place to address the goals of equal opportunity, it is critical that current mechanisms be left intact." [42]

As the Reagan Administration ends its first year, the time is indeed ripe for a new labor-black coalition to preserve the gains of the past and advance to new victories for both white and black workers. An important step in this direction is represented by the September 19, 1981 Solidarity Day Mass demonstration against Reganomics in Washington, D.C., where, in response to a call issued by the AFL–CIO Executive Council, white and black workers from all over the United States were joined by delegations from the National Association for the Advancement of Colored People, the National Urban League and other concerned citizens in what did prove to be the greatest labor-black alliance in American history. The resolution adopted by the NAACP's 5,000 delegates to the 72nd annual convention of the nation's oldest civil rights organization, welcomed the initiative taken by the AFL-CIO and the federation's invitation to the NAACP and other concerned organizations to take part in the AFL-CIO Solidarity Day Rally, September 19, 1981 on the National Mall, Washington, D.C., "for Jobs. Justice. Human Rights. Social Progress." "We are heartened," said Lane Kirkland, AFL-CIO president, "to know that the NAACP is at our side." [43] Black workers everywhere in the United States were heartened to see as the symbol of Solidarity Day the hands of a black and a white worker firmly grasped in a demonstration of labor solidarity.

By mid-afternoon on September 19, 1981, Solidarity Day, the official count from the mayor's office in Washington had passed the 400,000 mark, including hundreds of thousands of union members and tens of thousands of participants from the coalition of organizations that responded to the AFL-CIO's call. Black Americans were present in large numbers either as members of the union delegations or of the coalition of organizations that cooperated with the labor movement.

The historic rally in Washington, the massive demonstration, and the unity that was revealed between the labor movement and nationally oppressed peoples, cannot be an end in itself. It must become the foundation for the realization of goals which progressive forces in the American labor movement have long fought to achieve. The powerful monopoly forces in the United States who, through the Reagan administration, are trying to turn back the clock and wipe out all that has been achieved in a half century, must and can be defeated by the combined efforts of the people led by organized labor. Benjamin Hooks, NAACP Executive Director, made this clear when he told the Centennial Convention of the AFL-CIO that the NAACP had brought thousands of civil rights activists to Washington to march with labor on Solidarity Day because it believed that "the labor movement is now in the forefront of leadership in America. The torch has been thrown to you. . . We stand ready to help you. We stand ready to march with you," he told the delegates in November, 1981. "We stand ready to demonstrate with you. We stand ready to vote with you."

But Hooks reminded the AFL-CIO that with leadership came responsibilities and obligations. With leadership, he urged, labor has "an obligation to forthrightly perform . . . in civil rights, human rights, rights for women in the workplace." [44]

Notes

CHAPTER 1. FROM SLAVERY TO FREEDOM

1. Winthrop D. Jordan, *White over Black: American Atttiudes Toward the Negro, 1550–1812* (Chapel Hill: University of North Carolina Press, 1968), p. 27.
2. Carl Bridenbaugh, *Cities in the Wilderness: The First Century of Urban Life in America, 1625–1742* (New York: Knopf, 1938), p. 201.
3. Philip Taft, *Organized Labor in American History* (New York: Harper & Row, 1964), p. 664.
4. *Statuten des Kommunisten-Klubs in New York,* manuscript copy in Wisconsin State Historical Society, Labor Collection, Political Parties, Box 25.
5. *Frederick Douglass' Paper,* March 4, 1853, reprinted in Philip S. Foner, *The Life and Writings of Frederick Douglass* (New York: International Publishing Co., 1943), 2:224.
6. Carter G. Woodson and Lorenzo J. Greene, *The Negro Wage Earner* (Washington, D.C., 1930; reprint, New York: Russell & Russell, 1969), p. 213.
7. Leon F. Litwack, *North of Slavery: The Negro in the Free States, 1790–1860* (Chicago: University of Chicago Press, 1961).
8. Leonard L. Richards, *Gentlemen of Property and Standing: Abolition Mobs in Jacksonian America* (New York and London: Oxford University Press, 1970), p. 7.
9. Foner, *Life and Writings of Frederick Douglass* (note 5 *supra*), 2:226.
10. Richard B. Morris, "Labor Militancy in the Old South," *Labor and Nation,* May–June, 1948, pp. 34–35, and Robert S. Starobin, *Industrial Slavery in the Old South* (New York and London: Oxford University Press, 1970).
11. *The Life and Times of Frederick Douglass* (Hartford, Conn., 1883; reprint New York: Collier-Macmillan, 1962), p. 284.
12. Quoted in Litwack, *North of Slavery* (note 7 *supra*), p. 114.
13. *Ibid.,* p. 133.
14. John Campbell, *Negromania* (Philadelphia, 1851), p. 32.
15. U.S., 27th Cong., 3d Sess., House of Representatives, "Free Colored Seamen—Majority and Minority Reports, Jan. 20, 1843," *Report No. 80,* pp. 3, 7, 38.
16. Karl Marx, *Capital,* edited by Frederick Engels (New York: Modern Library, 1939) 1:287.
17. Herbert Aptheker, ed., *A Documentary History of the Negro People in the United States* (New York, 1951), p. 112.
18. *Charleston Mercury,* quoted in Philip S. Foner, *History of the Labor Movement in the United States* (New York: Internationl Publishing Co., 1947), 1:280.
19. Quoted in *ibid.,* 1:294.
20. *The Liberator,* December 13, 1860.
21. Quoted in Willis H. Lofton, "Northern Labor and the Negro During the Civil War," *Journal of Negro History* 34 (July, 1949):259–60.

442 *Notes*

22. Quoted in Albion P. Mann, Jr., "Labor Competition and the New York Draft Riots of 1863," *Journal of Negro History* 36 (October, 1951):387.
23. *Christian Recorder*, September 12, 1863.
24. Sidney Kaplan, "The American Seamen's Protective Union Association of 1863: A Pioneer Organization of Negro Seamen in the Port of New York," *Science and Society* 21 (Spring, 1962):154–59.
25. *Boston Daily Evening Voice*, November 3, 1865.
26. *Documents of the First International: The General Council of the First International, 1864–1866* (Moscow: Foreign Languages Publishing House, n.d.), pp. 310–12.

CHAPTER 2. THE RECONSTRUCTION PERIOD

1. J. T. Trowbridge, *The South: A Tour of Its Battlefields and Ruined Cities, etc.* (Hartford, Conn., 1866), p. 205.
2. New Orleans *Tribune*, April 22, 1866; reprinted in *Boston Daily Evening Voice*, May 7, 1866.
3. See issues of the *Boston Daily Evening Voice* for December 13 and 28, 1865; January 12, 13, 19, and 24; February 2; March 7, 15, and 29; April 19; May 11, 14, 21, and 29; August 16 and 22; October 25; and November 22, 1866.
4. Quoted in David Montgomery, *Beyond Equality: Labor and the Radical Republicans, 1862–1872* (New York: Knopf, 1967), p. 273.
5. *The Address of the National Labor Congress to the Workingmen of the United States*, Chicago, 1867.
6. *Workingman's Advocate*, August 24, 1867.
7. *Ibid.*, August 31, 1867.
8. *Boston Daily Evening Voice*, August 7, 1867.
9. *Workingman's Advocate*, October 10, 1868.
10. *Christian Recorder*, November 28, 1868.
11. *Workingman's Advocate*, August 31, 1867; James C. Sylvis, *The Life, Speeches, Labors and Essays of William H. Sylvis* (Philadelphia, 1872; reprint, Clifton, N.J.: Kelley, 1968), pp. 233–35, 333–34, 339, 342–43.
12. *Baltimore Sun*, July 20, 1869.
13. Philip S. Foner, ed., *The Voice of Black America: Major Speeches of Negroes in the United States, 1797–1972* (New York: Simon & Schuster, 1972), pp. 367–70.
14. *Workingman's Advocate*, September 4 and 11, 1869.
15. *Ibid.*, September 11, 1869; *American Workman* (Boston), October 2, 1869.
16. *Christian Recorder*, October 9, 1869.
17. *New York Times*, March 2, 1869.
18. *Workingman's Advocate*, October 2 and 21, 1869.
19. New York *Tribune*, September 17, 1869; *Workingman's Advocate*, October 2, 1869.
20. *Workingman's Advocate*, June 26 and July 3, 1869.
21. *New York Times*, August 8, 1869.
22. Reprinted in *Proceedings of the International Typographical Union for 1870* (Philadelphia, 1870), p. 31.
23. Reprinted in *National Anti-Slavery Standard*, July 17, 1869.
24. *Christian Recorder*, October 9 and November 20 and 27, 1869; *New York Herald*, November 17, 1869; *New York Times*, October 29 and November 12, 1869; and *Baltimore American*, November 8, 1869.

CHAPTER 3. THE COLORED NATIONAL LABOR UNION

1. *Proceedings of the Colored National Labor Convention Held in Washington, D.C., on December 6, 7, 8, 9, 10, 1869*, Washington, D.C., 1870; New York

Tribune, December 8 and 9, 1869; and *New National Era*, January 13 and April 4, 1870.

2. W. E. B. Du Bois, *Black Reconstruction in America, 1860–1880* (New York, 1935; reprint, New York: Atheneum, 1969), p. 362.

3. U.S., 41st Cong., 2d Sess., *Senate Miscellaneous Document No. 3*; reprinted in Aptheker, ed., *Documentary History of Negro People* (see note 17 for Chapter 1), pp. 633–36.

4. *New National Era*, January 13 and April 4, 1870.

5. *Ibid.*, April 21˙and 28, 1870.

6. *Ibid.*, April 28, 1870.

7. New York *Tribune* and New York *Times*, August 26, 1870.

8. *Workingman's Advocate*, August 13, 1870.

9. *Ibid.*, October 21 and 28, 1869.

10. *New National Era*, November 17, 1870, and January 12 and 17, 1871.

11. *National Anti-Slavery Standard*, May 29, 1869.

12. *New National Era*, January 12, 17, and 19, 1871, and *Washington Daily Morning Chronicle*, January 14, 1871.

13. *New National Era*, May 11, 1871.

14. *Report of the Joint Committee on the Condition of Affairs in the Late Insurrectionary States* (Washington, D.C., 1872), 4:496 and 695, and 7:689.

15. *New National Era*, January 19, 1871.

16. *Proceedings of the Southern States Convention of Colored Men* (Columbia, S.C., 1871), p. 3.

17. *Ibid.*, p. 24.

18. *New National Era*, January 12, 1871.

19. *Workingman's Advocate*, October 8, 1870.

20. *Ibid.*, November 25, 1870, and January 22, 1871.

CHAPTER 4. THE KNIGHTS OF LABOR AND THE BLACK WORKER

1. Jno. R. Ray to Terence V. Powderly, June 22, 1885, Terence V. Powderly Papers, Catholic University of America, Washington, D.C.

2. Sidney H. Kessler, "The Negro in the Knights of Labor" (unpublished M.A. thesis, Columbia University, New York, 1950), pp. 48–49.

3. Cleveland *Gazette*, July 17, 1886.

4. Foner, *History of Labor Movement* (see note 18 for Chapter 1), 2:70.

5. Cleveland *Gazette*, May 8, 1886; *John Swinton's Paper*, February 13, 1886, and January 2, 1887.

6. Detroit *Plain Dealer*, reprinted in the Huntsville (Ala.) *Gazette*, April 10, 1886.

7. North Carolina Bureau of Labor Statistics, *2nd Annual Report*, 1888, p. 82, and New York *Freeman*, May 15, 1886.

8. New York *Freeman*, March 13 and 20 and May 15, 1886.

9. *Ibid.*, April 17 and December 18, 1886, and *John Swinton's Paper*, February 13, 1886, and January 2, 1887.

10. Washington *Bee*, July 2, 1887; Indianapolis *Freeman*, February 8, 1890; *Journal of United Labor*, September 25, 1886; and George Talmadge Starnes and John Edwin Hamm, *Some Phases of Labor Relations in the South* (New York, 1934), p. 74.

11. New York *Times*, September 28, 1886.

12. Knights of Labor, General Assembly, *Proceedings*, 1886, pp. 7–8 and 12; Terence V. Powderly, *Thirty Years of Labor* (Columbus, Ohio, 1889), pp. 652–53.

13. "Knights of Labor and the Color Line," *Public Opinion*, October 16, 1886.

14. New York *Freeman*, October 9, 1886.

15. Powderly, *Thirty Years of Labor* (note 12 *supra*), 656–59.
16. Knights of Labor, General Assembly, *Proceedings*, 1886, pp. 194, 238–40, and 254.
17. New York *Tribune*, October 10, 1886, and Louisville *Labor Record*, reprinted in *Knights of Labor*, December 23, 1886.
18. New York *Freeman*, October 23 and 30, 1886.
19. Cleveland *Gazette*, October 23, 1886.
20. Louisville *Labor Record*, reprinted in *Knights of Labor*, December 23, 1886.
21. New Orleans *Weekly Pelican*, July 30, 1887, and New York *Age*, June 16, 1886.
22. Memphis *Watchman*, reprinted in New York *Freeman*, January 15, 1887, and in Cleveland *Gazette*, January 22, 1887.
23. Richmond *Planet*, reprinted in New York *Freeman*, August 14, 1886.
24. Knights of Labor, General Assembly, *Proceedings*, 1888, p. 50.
25. New York *Freeman*, December 25, 1886; Detroit *Labor Leaf*, December 22, 1886; Denver *Labor Enquirer*, January 1, 1887; and Huntsville (Ala.) *Gazette*, February 25, 1887.
26. *John Swinton's Paper*, June 19, 1887; New Orleans *Weekly Pelican*, July 2, 1887; Detroit *Advance and Labor Leaf*, February 19, July 23, and August 27, 1887; Knights of Labor, General Assembly, *Proceedings*, 1887, p. 1283.
27. George Brown Tindall, *South Carolina Negroes, 1877–1900* (Baton Rouge: Louisiana State University Press, 1966), pp. 114–17.
28. New Orleans *Times-Democrat*, October 27 and November 7, 1887; New Orleans *Weekly Pelican*, November 5 and 19, 1887.
29. Sidney H. Kessler, "The Negro in Labor Strikes," *Midwest Journal*, Summer, 1954, pp. 32–34; New Orleans *Weekly Pelican*, November 19 and 26, 1887, and Covington Hall, "Labor Struggles in the Deep South" (unpublished manuscript, Howard-Tilton Library, Tulane University, New Orleans), Section II, Chapter 6, "The Knights Sugar Strike," pp. 30–35.
30. B. W. Scott to Powderly, December 8, 1887, and Powderly to Scott, January 6, 1888, in Philip S. Foner, ed. "The Knights of Labor," *Journal of Negro History* 53 (1968):73–74.
31. Knights of Labor, General Assembly, *Proceedings*, 1888, p. 115, and 1889, p. 3.
32. *Journal of the Knights of Labor*, January 16, 1890, and Knights of Labor, General Assembly, *Proceedings*, 1893, p. 34.
33. *Christian Recorder*, December 12, 1893.
34. *New York Times*, February 26, and Philadelphia *Press*, June 3, 1894.
35. *Northwestern Christian Advocate*, reprinted in the *Christian Recorder*, March 15, 1894.
36. *Christian Recorder*, April 12, 1894.
37. Chicago *Interocean*, June 2, 1894.
38. Robert R. Jockaway, *The Great Labor Question, or the Noble Mission of the Knights of Labor* (Savannah, Ga., 1886), p. 23; *Globe and Lance*, reprinted in *Knights of Labor*, December 23, 1886.
39. Foner, *Life and Writings of Frederick Douglass* (*see* note 5 for Chapter 1), 4:382.

CHAPTER 5. THE AF OF L AND THE BLACK WORKER, 1881–1915

1. *Proceedings of the American Federation of Labor*, 1881–1888, p. 14.
2. *Ibid.*, pp. 15–16.
3. *Proceedings*, AF of L Convention, 1890, pp. 31 and 54–56, and 1891, p. 12; Samuel Gompers to T. N. Talbot, April 15, 1890, and Harry E. Eaton, National Association of Machinists, to Gompers, April 26, 1891, in *American Federation of Labor Incoming Correspondence* (hereafter *AFL Corr.*); and Gompers to

Martin Fox, May 11, 1892, in *Samuel Gompers Letter-Books* (hereafter *GLB*).
4. Gompers to James H. White, September 14, 1889; to H. M. Ives, November 10, 1892; to Charles E. Archer, June 1, 1894; and to Frank L. Rist, April 30, 1890, in *GLB*.
5. Roger W. Shugg, "The New Orleans General Strike of 1892," *Louisiana Historical Quarterly* 21 (April, 1938): 547–56; Foner, *History of Labor Movement* (see note 18 for Chapter 1), 3:200–203; New Orleans *Times-Democrat*, October 23, 24, and 28 and November 1–14, 1892; and New Orleans *Daily Picayune*, November 10–14, 1892.
6. New Orleans *Times-Democrat*, November 4, 1892.
7. John M. Callahan to Gompers, November 7, 1892, in *AFL Corr.*
8. New Orleans *Times-Democrat*, November 11, 1892, and B. Sherer to Gompers, November 8, 1892, in *AFL Corr.*
9. Gompers to Callahan, November 21, 1892, in *GLB*.
10. Circular issued by AF of L national office, December 12, 1892, in *AFL Corr.*
11. New York Colored Mission, *Annual Report for 1893* (New York, 1894), pp. 14–17.
12. Arthur Raymond Pearce, "The Rise and Decline of Labor in New Orleans" (unpublished M.A. thesis, Tulane University, New Orleans, 1938), pp. 31–37; New Orleans *Daily Picayune*, October 27 through November 7, 1894, and March 15, 1895.
13. James Duncan to W. S. Davis, April 1, 1895, quoted in Philip Taft, *The AF of L in the Time of Gompers* (New York, 1957; reprint, New York: Octagon, 1970), pp. 309–10.
14. James O'Connell to John McBride, March 25, 1895; to Gompers, February 26, 1896; and to Frank Morrison, March 20, 1903, in *AFL Corr.*
15. W. E. B. Du Bois, *The Negro Artisan* (Atlanta, 1902; reprint, New York: Kraus, n.d.), p. 157.
16. W. S. Carter to Gompers, May 10, 1897, and to Frank Morrison, May 12, 1897, in *AFL Corr.*; Gompers to Frank P. Sargent, August 17, 1896; to George W. Perkins, October 27, 1896; and to W. D. Lewis, April 9, 1897, in *GLB*; and *Proceedings*, AF of L Convention, 1896, p. 19.
17. Samuel Gompers, "Why Affiliate with the Federation, *American Federationist* 7 (February, 1900): 34–35.
18. Gompers to James E. Porter, May 19 and June 15, 1900; to James Leonard, March 9 and June 7 and 23, 1900; and to Henry M. Walker, November 8, 1899, in *GLB*; Porter to Gompers, March 4 and 13, April 20, May 19, and June 15, 1900; Walker to Gompers, November 4, 1899; and William W. Davis to Gompers, January 1, 1901, in *AFL Corr.*; *Proceedings*, AF of L Convention, 1900, pp. 12–13, 22–23, 112–29, and 263; and New York *Tribune*, December 13, 1901.
19. F. L. McGruder to Gompers, March 17 and 24, April 22, May 26, and October 4, 1899; Prince W. Greene to Gompers, September 18 and November 19, 1899; and Samuel Mitchell to Gompers, October 18, 1900, in *AFL Corr.*
20. Samuel Gompers, *Seventy Years of Life and Labor* (New York: Kelley, 1925), 2:160; Samuel Gompers and Herman Gutstadt, *Meat vs. Rice: American Manhood Against Asian Coolieism—Which Shall Survive?* (San Francisco, 1908); Samuel Gompers, "Three of the Others," *American Federationist* 7 (May, 1904): 282–84; and Gompers to D. L. Sullivan, June 24, 1904, in *AFL Corr.*
21. *Proceedings*, AF of L Convention, 1895, pp. 41 and 45, and *American Federationist* 10 (October, 1902): 706–7, 709.
22. Gompers to H. N. Randle (*sic*), March 19, 1903, in *GLB*; Gompers's testimony in *Report of the Industrial Commission* (Washington, D.C., 1900–1902), pp.

647–48; and *American Federationist* 9 (April, 1901): 118–20, 13 (September, 1905): 636, and 14 (August, 1906): 534.
23. Foner, *History of Labor Movement* (see note 18 for Chapter 1), 2:347–48.
24. *The Colored American*, October 8 and November 5, 1898, and *Christian Recorder*, September 8 and October 20, 1898.
25. *Christian Recorder*, October 20, 1898.
26. Indianapolis *Freeman*, October 8 and 15, 1898, and *Recorder*, October 22, 1898.
27. Indianapolis *News*, reprinted in the *Recorder*, November 22, 1898.
28. *The American*, March 1, 1899.
29. Andrew F. Hillyer, chairman of Committee for the Hampton Conference, to Gompers, April 21, 1899, in AFL *Corr.*
30. Booker T. Washington, "The Negro and the Labor Unions," *Atlantic Monthly*, June, 1913, pp. 756–58; *idem, The Negro in Business* (Boston, 1907), p. 317; and Samuel R. Spencer, *Booker T. Washington and the Negro's Place in American Life* (Boston: Little, 1955), pp. 756–68.
31. *The Colored American Magazine*, February, 1904, and July, 1908; and *Christian Recorder*, July 5, 1900.
32. *American Federationist* 8 (April, 1901) 118–19.
33. Du Bois, *Negro Artisan* (note 15 *supra*), pp. 7–8, and Philip S. Foner, ed., *W. E. B. Du Bois Speaks: Speeches and Addresses, 1901–1919* (New York: Pathfinder Press, 1970), pp. 68, 156, 165, 166–68, 190–92, 262–63.
34. *The Negro in the South: Booker T. Washington and W. E. B. Du Bois*, introduction by Herbert Aptheker (New York: Metro Books, AMS Press, 1970), p. 116.

CHAPTER 6. THE AF OF L AND THE BLACK WORKER, 1881–1915 (CONT.)

1. Gompers to F. D. Hornlin, May 6, 1890, and to the delegates to the International Labor Congress, August 4, 1891, in GLB.
2. United Mine Workers of America, *Constitution of the International Union*, Article II, p. 3.
3. Paul B. Worthman, "Black Workers and Labor Unions in Birmingham, Alabama, 1897–1904," in Milton Cantor, ed., *Black Labor in America* (Westport, Conn.: Greenwood Press, Negro Universities Press, 1969), p. 68.
4. Du Bois, *Negro Artisan* (see note 15 for Chapter 5), pp. 158, 160–61.
5. E. Franklin Frazier, "A Negro Industrial Group," *Howard Review* 1 (June, 1924): 140–44.
6. R. R. Wright, "The Negro in Chicago," *Charities* 15 (October 7, 1905): 69–73.
7. Indianapolis *Record*, December 8, 1900.
8. Mary E. McDowell, "Woman's Union in Packing House," Folder 15, Mary E. McDowell Papers, Chicago Historical Society.
9. Foner, *History of the Labor Movement* (see note 18 for Chapter 1), 2:356–58.
10. Melton Alonza McLaurin, *Paternalism and Protest: Southern Mill Workers and Organized Labor, 1875–1905* (Westport, Conn.: Greenwood Press, 1971), p. 65.
11. *The Carpenter*, September, 1903, quoted by Herbert Gutman, "The Negro and the United Mine Workers of America," in Julius Jacobsen, ed., *The Negro and the American Labor Movement* (Garden City, N.Y.: Anchor Books, Doubleday, 1968), p. 120.
12. *Ibid.*, pp. 119–20.

Notes

13. Worthman, "Black Workers and Unions in Birmingham" (note 3 *supra*), pp. 63–64.
14. Tindall, *South Carolina Negroes* (see note 27 for Chapter 4), pp. 139–40.
15. Worthman, "Black Workers and Unions in Birmingham" (note 3 *supra*), pp. 77–79.
16. Du Bois, *Negro Artisan* (see note 15 for Chapter 5), pp. 111–12, 177.
17. *United Mine Workers Journal*, March 5, 1903.
18. Oscar Ameringer, *If You Don't Weaken: The Autobiography of Oscar Ameringer* (New York, 1940), pp. 197–99.
19. New Orleans *Daily Picayune*, November 17, 1902.
20. *Ibid.*, October 5, 18, 19, and 30 and November 1, 2, 3, 9, and 21, 1907.
21. Foner, *History of Labor Movement* (see note 18 for Chapter 1), 3:196–97.
22. Ruth Allen, *Chapters in the History of Organized Labor in Texas* (Austin, Tex., 1941), p. 112.
23. Woodson and Greene, *Negro Wage Earner* (see note 6 for Chapter 1), p. 280.
24. Du Bois, *Negro Artisan*, pp. 111–12, 177.
25. Paul B. Worthman, ed., "A Black Worker and the Bricklayers and Masons Union, 1903," *Journal of Negro History* 55 (October, 1969): 398–404.
26. Richard E. Wright, Jr., *The Negro in Pennsylvania: A Study in Economic History* (Philadelphia, 1911), pp. 94–95.
27. The letters quoted here are in the file of the *United Mine Workers Journal* in the library of the U.S. Department of Labor, Washington, D.C. Richard L. Davis's letters are in the issues of December 24, 1891; January 14 and 28, April 18, July 21 and 28, August 4, September 15 and 22, and October 6 and 20, 1892; June 1 and August 22, 1893; October 3, 1895; April 30 and December 3, 1896; and October 13 and December 8, 1898. "Old Dog's" letter appeared in the issue of May 12, 1898; those of "Willing Hands" in the issues of March 24, 1892, and March 30, 1893; and that of Lewis Coleman in the issue of September 21, 1893.
    The proceedings of the Illinois State Miners Convention of 1900 are in the *Journal* of March 8, 1900; those of the 1906 convention in the issue of February, 8, 1906; and those of the 1909 convention in the issue of January 28, 1909.
28. Washington *Bee*, April 22, 1899, and Worthman, "Black Worker and Unions in Birmingham" (note 3 *supra*), p. 69.
29. Herbert R. Northrup, "The Negro and the United Mine Workers of America," *Southern Economic Journal*, April, 1943, p. 321.
30. Chicago *Daily Socialist*, May 1, 1912.
31. *The Crisis*, July, 1912, p. 131, and May, 1913, pp. 31–33.
32. *Proceedings*, AF of L Convention, 1910, p. 237, and Samuel Gompers, "The Negro in the AF of L," *American Federationist* 17 (January, 1911): 34–36.
33. Brotherhood of Railway Carmen, *Convention Proceedings*, 1905, p. 9; *Railway Carmen's Journal*, 1907, pp. 189, 211; and *Proceedings*, AF of L Convention, 1910, pp. 96–98, and 1911, pp. 323–25, 334.
34. Taft, *AF of L in Time of Gompers* (see note 13 for Chapter 5), pp. 311–14.
35. Frank E. Wolfe, Admission to Trade Unions (Baltimore, 1920), pp. 120–25.

CHAPTER 7. THE RAILROAD BROTHERHOODS AND THE IWW, 1890–1915

1. Ray Ginger, *The Bending Cross: A Biography of Eugene V. Debs* (New Brunswick, N.J., 1949; reprint, New York: Russell & Russell, 1969), pp. 42–43, 68, 93, 116, and Foner, *History of Labor Movement* (see note 18 for Chapter 1), 2:247–49.
2. Philadelphia *Press*, reprinted in *Christian Recorder*, July 12, 1894.

3. Ginger, *Bending Cross*, pp. 92–93.
4. Cleveland *Gazette*, July 10, and *Christian Recorder*, July 12, 1894.
5. Eugene V. Debs, *The Negro Worker* (New York, 1923), pp. 6–7.
6. *Literary Digest*, December 24, 1898, p. 740.
7. *Locomotive Firemen's Magazine*, 21 (September, 1896): 248–49; 22 (April, 1897): 264; 26 (January, 1899): 133; 27 (November, 1899): 593–94; and 33 (September, 1902): 427–35.
8. Atlanta *Constitution*, May 16 through 20, 1909; *The Public*, June 4, 1909; *Literary Digest*, June 5 and July 10, 1909; and New York *Age*, June 11, 18, and 25, 1909.
9. George James Stevenson, "The Brotherhood of Locomotive Engineers and Its Leaders" (unpublished Ph.D. thesis, Vanderbilt University, 1954), p. 232.
10. Mary White Ovington, "The Status of the Negro in the United States," *New Review*, September, 1913, pp. 747–48.
11. Foner, *History of Labor Movement* (see note 18 for Chapter 1) 4:5–16, and *Proceedings of the First Convention of the Industrial Workers of the World* (New York, 1905), pp. 18, 154, 298–99.
12. "Justice for the Negro—How Can He Get It," and "To Colored Workingmen and Workingwomen," leaflets in Wisconsin State Historical Society, Elizabeth Gurley Flynn Collection; *Voice of the People*, December 14, 1912, and February 12 and November 26, 1914; *Solidarity*, May 28 and June 24, 1911, June 8, July 27, and August 2, 1912, and September 13, 1913; *Industrial Worker*, August 1 and 15, 1914, February 3, 1917, and September 19, 1919; Justus Ebert, *The IWW in Theory and Practice* (Chicago, 1920); and Foner, *History of Labor Movement*, 4:35–40.
13. Sterling D. Spero and Abram L. Harris, *The Black Worker: The Negro and the Labor Movement* (New York, 1931), p. 331, and Donald H. Barnes, "The Ideology of the Industrial Workers of the World" (unpublished Ph.D. thesis, Washington University, 1962), p. 21.
14. Chicago *Defender*, August 30, 1913.
15. *The Longshoreman* (Erie, Pa.), 4 (August, 1913): 2; *Solidarity*, June 7 and October 14, 1913, and February 28, May 16 and 30, November 28, and December 19, 1914; *Industrial Worker*, February 3, 1917, and July 28, 1945; Philadelphia *North American*, May 14 through 30, 1913; Philadelphia *Public Ledger*, May 19 and 20 and June 16 through 19, 1913, and Fred W. Thompson, *The IWW: Its First Fifty Years* (New York, 1955), p. 67.
16. Covington Hall in *Industrial Worker*, July 7, 1945.
17. Ruth A. Allen, *East Texas Lumber Workers: An Economic and Social Picture, 1870–1950* (Austin: University of Texas Press, 1961), pp. 54, 58, and Vernon H. Jensen, *Lumber and Labor* (New York, 1945), p. 6.
18. Charles H. McCord, "A Brief Survey of the Brotherhood of Timber Workers" (unpublished M.A. thesis, University of Texas, 1959), pp. 19–20, 27, 47–48; New Orleans *Times-Democrat*, July 20 and August 8, 1911; *National Rip-Saw*, June, 1912; and *Voice of the People*, December 25, 1913.
19. *Bill Haywood's Book* (New York, 1929), pp. 241–42; Hall, "Labor Struggles in Deep South" (see note 29 for Chapter 4), p. 138; McCord, "Brief Survey of Timber Workers" (note 18 *supra*), pp. 51–52; *Solidarity*, May 25 and September 28, 1912; and *Industrial Worker*, May 30, 1912.
20. *The Rebel*, November 16, 1912; *Lumberjack*, January 9 and February 27, 1913; *Industrial Worker*, December 26, 1912, and February 27 and March 6, 1913; *Voice of the People*, July 17 and November 7, 1913, and January 1 and March 5, 1914; Hall, "Labor Struggles in Deep South" (see note 29 for Chapter 4), p. 149; Allan A. Holland, Jr., "The Negro and the Industrial Workers of the World" (unpublished paper in Labadie Collection, University of Michigan Li-

brary), p. 13; Phineas Eastman, "The Southern Negro and the One Big Union," *International Socialist Review*, 13 (June, 1913): 890–91; and Merl E. Reed, "The IWW and Individual Freedom in Western Louisiana," *Louisiana History*, Winter, 1969, pp. 62–70.

21. Ovington, "Status of Negro" (note 10 *supra*), pp. 747–48.
22. Selig Perlman and Philip Taft, *History of Labor in the United States, 1896–1932* (New York, 1935), p. 247.

CHAPTER 8. THE BLACK WORKER ON THE EVE OF WORLD WAR I

1. United States Bureau of the Census, *Negro Population, 1790–1915* (Washington, D.C., 1915), pp. 25, 526–27; Charles H. Wesley, *Negro Labor in the United States, 1850–1925: A Study in American Economic History* (New York, 1927; reprint, New York, Russell & Russell, 1967), p. 250; Woodson and Greene, *Negro Wage Earner* (see note 6 for Chapter 1), pp. 59–60, 115, 133; Ray Stannard Baker, *Following the Color Line: American Negro Citizenship in the Progressive Era* (New York: Harper & Row, 1964), Chapter IV; and Robert D. Ward and William W. Rogers, *Labor Revolt in Alabama: The Great Strike of 1894* (University of Alabama Press, 1965), pp. 21–22, 44–47.
2. Joseph Frazier Wall, *Andrew Carnegie* (New York and London: Oxford University Press, 1970), pp. 147, 167, 972–77, and *Christian Recorder*, March 24, 1893.
3. Robert Ozanne, *A Century of Labor-Management Relations at McCormick and International Harvester* (Madison: University of Wisconsin Press, 1967), pp. 188–89.
4. Broadus Mitchell, *Rise of the Cotton Mills of the South* (Baltimore, 1921; reprint, New York: Da Capo, 1968), pp. 220–21; Jerome Dowd, "Textile War Between the North and the South," *The Forum*, June 1898, pp. 442–43; Atlanta *Constitution*, August 5 through 8, 1897; and Claude H. Nolen, *The Negro's Image in the South: The Anatomy of White Supremacy* (Lexington: University of Kentucky Press, 1967), p. 190.
5. James Weldon Johnson, *Along This Way* (New York, 1933; paperback, New York: Viking, 1968), p. 31.
6. Du Bois, *Negro Artisan* (see note 15 for Chapter 5), pp. 180–85.
7. Foner, ed., *Voice of Black America* (see note 13 for Chapter 2), p. 608.
8. John Stephens Durham, "The Labor Unions and the Negro," *Atlantic Monthly*, February, 1898, pp. 222–31, and George Sinclair Mitchell, "The Negro in Southern Trade Unionism," *Southern Economic Journal* 2 (January, 1936): 27–38.
9. Foner, *History of Labor Movement* (see note 18 for Chapter 1) 3:239–41, and Richmond *Planet*, October 21, 1899.
10. W. E. B. Du Bois, *The Philadelphia Negro: A Social Study* (Philadelphia, 1899), p. 323, and Wright, *Negro in Pennsylvania* (see note 26 for Chapter 6), pp. 94–99.
11. W. A. Crosslands, *Negroes in St. Louis* (Saint Louis, 1910), p. 82; Lillian Brandt, "The Negroes of St. Louis," *American Statistical Association* 8 (March, 1903): 233–40; Seth M. Scheiner, *Negro Mecca: A History of the Negro in New York City, 1865–1920* (New York: NYU Press, 1965), pp. 45–85; John Gilmer Speed, "The Negro in New York," *Harper's Weekly* 44 (December 22, 1900): 1249–50; Mary White Ovington, "Negroes in the Trade Unions of New York," *Annals* of the American Academy of Political and Social Science 28 (May, 1906): 89–96; Kelly Miller, "The Economic Handicap of the Negro in the North," *Annals* 28:84; and Leslie H. Fishel, Jr., "The Negro's Welcome to the Western Reserve," *Midwest Journal* 2 (Winter, 1949): 50–53.
12. *New Review*, January 1, 1913, pp. 139–40.

13. Foner, ed., *Voice of Black America* (see note 13 for Chapter 2), pp. 692–93, 745–57.
14. Ida Welles Barnett, "The Negro's Quest for Work," Chicago *Daily News*, reprinted in New York *Call*, July 23, 1911.

CHAPTER 9. THE RISE OF THE BLACK INDUSTRIAL WORKING CLASS, 1915–18

1. Handbills of Jones-Maddox Labor Agency, Bessemer, Alabama, Record Group 174, Files of the Secretary of Labor, National Archives; also quoted in John D. Finney, Jr., "A Study of Negro Labor During and After World War I" (unpublished Ph.D. dissertation, Georgetown University, 1957), p. 81.
2. Montgomery *Advertiser*, reprinted in *Literary Digest*, October 7, 1916.
3. W. E. B. Du Bois, *Darkwater* (New York, 1919), p. 43.
4. Ray Stannard Baker, "The Negro Goes North," *World's Work* 34 (July, 1917): 315.
5. Herbert J. Seligman, "The Negro in Industry," *Socialist Review* 8 (February, 1920): 169.
6. U.S. Department of Labor, *Negro Migration in 1916–1917* (Washington, D.C., 1919), p. 124.
7. William M. Tuttle, Jr., *Race Riot: Chicago in the Red Summer of 1919* (New York: Atheneum, 1970), pp. 130–32.
8. New York *Call*, February 14, 1921.
9. Quoted in Harold M. Baron, "The Demand for Negro Labor: Historical Notes on the Political Economy of Racism," *Radical America* 5 (March–April, 1971): 21–22.
10. Roger Baldwin, quoted in Seligman, "Negro in Industry" (note 5 *supra*), p. 170.
11. Spero and Harris, *Black Worker* (see note 13 for Chapter 7), p. 169.
12. Horace R. Cayton and George S. Mitchell, *Black Workers and the New Unions* (Chapel Hill: University of North Carolina Press, 1939), p. 31.
13. George Carmody to Charles Schwab, September 18, 1918, Records of U.S. Shipping Board, Record Group 32, National Archives.
14. S. L. Mash to L. C. Marshall, August 30, 1918, Records of U.S. Shipping Board, *loc cit*.
15. New York *Call*, August 9, 1917.

CHAPTER 10. THE AF OF L AND THE BLACK WORKER DURING WORLD WAR I

1. *International Molders' Journal*, reprinted in New York *Call*, July 1, 1919.
2. Quoted in Wesley, *Negro Labor in United States* (see note 1 for Chapter 8), pp. 65–66.
3. *Proceedings*, AF of L Convention, 1916, p. 148.
4. U.S. Department of Labor, *Negro Migration, 1916–1917* (see note 6 for Chapter 9), p. 131.
5. J. H. Walker to William B. Wilson, July 5, 1917, Files of the Secretary of Labor, National Archives.
6. William B. Wilson to Commissioner of Labor Statistics, July 16, 1917, *ibid*.
7. *Literary Digest*, September 22, 1917, p. 32.
8. Finney, "Study of Negro Labor" (see note 1 for Chapter 9), p. 120.
9. *Ibid.*, p. 122.
10. *Intercollegiate Socialist* 6 (December, 1916–January, 1917): 25.
11. Foner, ed., *Voice of Black America* (see note 13 for Chapter 2), p. 624.
12. *Proceedings*, AF of L Convention, 1917, pp. 249–50.

13. *The Crisis,* March, 1918, p. 41.
14. New York *Age,* April 17 and May 4, 1918.
15. *Proceedings,* AF of L Convention, 1918, pp. 198–99.
16. *New Appeal,* April 20, 1918.
17. Earl Browder, "Some Experiences in Organizing Negro Workers," *Communist* 9 (1930): 38.
18. Quoted in William J. Tuttle, Jr., "Labor Conflict and Racial Violence: The Black Worker in Chicago, 1894–1919," *Labor History* 10 (Summer, 1969): 425; Carl Sandburg, *The Chicago Race Riots* (New York, 1919), p. 48.
19. Foner, ed., *Du Bois Speaks* (see note 33 for Chapter 5), p. 271.
20. "The Negro Worker," by Anise, Seattle *Union Record,* reprinted in *The Messenger,* July 1919, p. 8.

CHAPTER 11. POSTWAR BLACK MILITANCY

1. Chicago Commission on Race Relations, *The Negro in Chicago: A Study of Race Relations and a Race Riot* (Chicago, 1922; reprint, New York: Arno Press, 1968), pp. 428–29.
2. Quoted in Seligman, "Negro in Industry" (see note 5 for Chapter 9), p. 170.
3. Interchurch World Movement Commission Inquiry, *Report on the Steel Strike of 1919* (New York, 1920), pp. 177–78.
4. Tuttle, *Race Riot* (see note 7 for Chapter 9), p. 156.
5. Allen, *Organized Labor in Texas* (see note 22 for Chapter 6), pp. 292–94.
6. Quoted in Seligman, "Negro in Industry," p. 171.
7. Quoted in Kenneth G. Weinberg, *A Man's Home, a Man's Castle* (New York: Saturday Review Press, 1971), p. 5.
8. "Cyril Briggs and the African Blood Brotherhood," WPA Writers' Project No. 1, reporter: Carl Offord, Schomberg Collection, New York Public Library, and Mark I. Solomon, "Red and Black: Negroes and Communism, 1929–1932" (unpublished Ph.D. dissertation, Harvard University, 1972), pp. 79–84.
9. *The Messenger,* November, 1917, p. 3.
10. *Ibid.,* December, 1919, p. 4.
11. *Ibid.,* July, 1919, p. 8.
12. *Ibid.,* May–June, 1918, p. 8.
13. *Ibid.,* December, 1919, p. 17.
14. New York *Call,* June 14, 1919.
15. *Proceedings,* AF of L Convention, 1919, p. 305.
16. *New York Times,* June 14, 1919, and *Literary Digest,* June 28, 1919, p. 12.
17. New York *Age,* June 21, 1919.
18. Reprinted in *Literary Digest,* June 28, 1919, p. 12.
19. Reprinted in *ibid.*
20. Quoted in *ibid.*
21. Quoted in *ibid.*
22. New York *Age,* June 21, 1919.
23. Quoted in *Literary Digest,* June 28, 1919, p. 12.
24. *The Crisis,* September, 1919, pp. 239–41.
25. *Proceedings,* AF of L Convention, 1920, pp. 351–52.
26. *Ibid.*
27. *Ibid.,* p. 309.
28. New York *Call,* June 11, 1920.
29. *Ibid.*
30. *Justice,* June 18, 1920.
31. *Advance,* July 23, 1920.

CHAPTER 12. THE AF OF L AND THE BLACK WORKER, 1921–29

1. New York *Call*, June 11, 1920.
2. *Ibid.*, and Chicago *Daily News*, June 12, 1920.
3. New York *Amsterdam News*, June 15, 1920.
4. *The Messenger*, August, 1919, p. 20.
5. Miscellaneous Political Records, Political Prisoners, U.S. Department of Justice Files, December 20, 1921, TAF/G2C1, National Archives.
6. *New Solidarity*, September 27, 1919.
7. *The Messenger*, July, 1923, pp. 759–60.
8. *The Crisis*, September, 1921, p. 200.
9. *National Brotherhood Worker*, May, 1921, quoted in Spero and Harris, *Black Worker* (see note 13 for Chapter 7), p. 119.
10. *The Messenger*, April–May, 1920, pp. 3–4.
11. *Ibid.*, December, 1924, p. 12.
12. *Ibid.*, December, 1924, p. 12.
13. *Labor Herald*, July, 1924, p. 152.
14. *Ibid.*, April, 1923, p. 14.
15. *Ibid.*, July, 1924, p. 156.
16. James W. Ford, "Foster and Negro-Labor Unity," *Masses and Mainstream*, March, 1951, pp. 21–22.
17. *Opportunity*, October, 1924, p. 300.
18. *The Crisis*, December, 1921, p. 104.
19. *Proceedings*, AF of L Convention, 1921, p. 432.
20. *Ibid.*, p. 433.
21. Preston News Service, Pittsburgh, quoted in *Opportunity*, May, 1924, p. 137.
22. *The Crisis*, July, 1922, p. 132.
23. Abram L. Harris, Jr., "The Negro Worker in Pittsburgh" (unpublished M.A. thesis, University of Pittsburgh, 1924), and *Opportunity*, July, 1925, p. 195.
24. *The Crisis*, August, 1924, pp. 53–54.
25. *Constitution and Program of the American Negro Congress* (Chicago, n.d.), p. 9.
26. *Workers Monthly*, December, 1925, pp. 65–74.
27. Reprinted in *Literary Digest*, November 21, 1925, p. 14.
28. Ira de A. Reid, *Negro Membership in American Labor Unions* (New York, 1930), p. 127.
29. *American Federationist* 30 (October, 1925): 162.
30. *Proceedings*, AF of L Convention, 1925, pp. 323–24.
31. *The Messenger*, November, 1926, p. 12, and *Pittsburgh Courier*, reprinted in *Daily Worker*, November 10, 1926.
32. *Daily Worker*, February 5, 1927.
33. Raymond Wolters, *Negroes and the Great Depression: The Problem of Economic Recovery* (Westport, Conn.: Negro Universities Press, Greenwood Press, 1970), p. 172.
34. *The Crisis*, January, 1927, p. 131.
35. Letter of Trade Union Committee for Organizing Negro Workers to Joint Board, Furriers Union, December 19, 1924 (original in author's possession).
36. *Opportunity*, February, 1927, p. 52, and May, 1929, pp. 144–45.
37. New York *Call*, April 21, 1928.
38. *The Nation*, January 9, 1929, p. 45.
39. *American Federationist*, March, 1929, pp. 296–305.
40. *The Nation*, January 9, 1929, p. 42.
41. William E. Walling to John P. Frey, January 8, 1929, John P. Frey Papers, Library of Congress.

42. John P. Frey to William E. Walling, January 10, 1929, William E. Walling Papers, Wisconsin State Historical Society.
43. *The Crisis*, July, 1929, p. 241.

CHAPTER 13. THE BROTHERHOOD OF SLEEPING CAR PORTERS

1. *Labor Age* 15 (March, 1926): 2.
2. *Black Worker*, August, 1936.
3. Chicago *Whip*, May 15, 1926.
4. Robert Dunn, "Pullman 'Company Union' Slavery," *Labor Age* 15:3.
5. *New Leader*, January 16, 1926.
6. *The Messenger*, August, 1926, p. 223.
7. *Railway Age*, March 17, 1928, p. 28.
8. Quoted in A. Philip Randolph, "Story of the Porter," Silver Jubilee Anniversary Folder (Chicago, 1950), p. 9.
9. *Ibid.*, pp. 9–10.
10. New York *Evening Journal*, March 15, 1928.
11. *The Messenger*, April, 1928, p. 90.
12. Chicago *Defender*, June 16, 1928.
13. Communist Leaflet, quoted in *New Leader*, June 16, 1928.
14. Brailsford R. Brazeal, *The Brotherhood of Sleeping Car Porters* (New York, 1946), p. 87.
15. Brotherhood of Sleeping Car Porters, *Executive Council Minutes*, New York Headquarters, 1929.
16. *Proceedings*, AF of L Convention, 1928, pp. 137–39.
17. *Ibid.*, pp. 384–85.
18. A. Philip Randolph to M. P. Webster, August 3, 1926, and August 27, 1928, Brotherhood of Sleeping Car Porters Papers, Chicago Historical Society.

CHAPTER 14. BLACK WORKERS DURING THE GREAT DEPRESSION

1. Langston Hughes, *The Big Sea* (New York: Hill & Wang, 1967), p. 247.
2. Quoted in Gilbert Osofsky, *Harlem: The Making of a Ghetto* (New York, 1936), p. 136.
3. Charles S. Johnson, "Present Trends in the Employment of Negro Labor," *Opportunity*, May, 1929, p. 146.
4. *The Nation*, September 17, 1933.
5. *New Leader*, December 5, 1931; Philip Klein, A Social Study of Pittsburgh: Community Problems and Social Services of Allegheny County (New York, 1938), p. 279; and Mary Elizabeth Pidgeon, *Employment Fluctuations and Unemployment of Women: Certain Indications from Various Sources, 1928–31* (Washington, D.C., 1933), p. 43.
6. Angelo Herndon, *Let Me Live* (New York, 1937), p. 93.
7. Elizabeth Lawson, *The Jobless Negro* (New York, 1933), p. 93.
8. Quoted in Dale Rosen, "The Alabama Share Croppers Union" (unpublished B.A. honors paper, Radcliffe College, March, 1969), p. 39.
9. Birmingham *News*, July 18, 1931.
10. Dan T. Carter, *Scottsboro: A Tragedy of the American South* (Baton Rouge: Louisiana State University Press, 1969), pp. 128–29.
11. Otto Huiswood, "The Negro and the Trade Unions," *The Communist* 7 (1928): 775.
12. *Ibid.*
13. *American Labor Year Book* (New York, 1930), p. 96.
14. William Z. Foster, *Toward Soviet America* (New York, 1932), p. 224.
15. *The Coal Digger*, April 1, 1929.

16. Cayton and Mitchell, *Black Workers and New Unions* (see note 12 for Chapter 9), p. 84.
17. *The Liberator*, June 13, 1931.
18. *Southern Worker*, February 7, 1931.
19. *The Coal Digger*, September, 1928.
20. *Ibid.*, January 10, 1929.
21. *Opportunity*, August, 1931, p. 236.
22. *The Crisis*, March, 1931, p. 94.
23. *New York Times*, March 8, 1932.
24. *The Liberator*, October 10, 1931, and *Daily Worker*, April 6, 1933.
25. Cyril Briggs, "Our Negro Work," *The Communist* 8 (September, 1929): 498.
26. Baltimore *Afro-American*, September 21, 1935.
27. *Proceedings*, AF of L Convention, 1933, pp. 268–69.
28. T. C. Hill in *Journal of Negro Education* 4 (1936): 41.
29. *New York Times*, June 17, 1933.
30. *Ibid.*, September 10, 1933, and *Opportunity*, September, 1933, p. 311.
31. Wolters, *Negroes and Great Depression* (see note 33 for Chapter 12), p. 106.
32. *New Leader*, August 25, 1933.
33. *Daily Worker*, December 2, 1933.
34. *The Crisis*, December, 1933, p. 292.
35. T. C. Hill, *op. cit.* (note 28 *supra*), p. 42.
36. *Ibid.*
37. *Daily Worker*, May 22, 1934.
38. *Ibid.*, March 1, 1934.
39. *Ibid.*, April 13, 1934.

CHAPTER 15. THE AF OF L AND THE BLACK WORKER, 1934–35

1. *Opportunity*, May 5, 1939, p. 22.
2. *New York Times*, October 12, 1934.
3. *Proceedings*, AF of L Convention, 1934, pp. 331–32.
4. *Ibid.*, pp. 330–31.
5. *Ibid.*, pp. 331–32.
6. *Ibid.*, p. 333.
7. *Daily Worker*, July 22, 1935.
8. Philip Taft, *The A.F. of L. from the Death of Gompers to the Merger* (New York, 1959; reprint, New York: Octagon, 1969), p. 443.
9. *New York Post*, March 25, 1935.
10. James W. Ford, *Hunger and Terror in Harlem* (New York, 1935), p. 3.
11. *New York Post*, March 25, 1935.
12. Taft, *A.F. of L. to Merger* (note 8 *supra*), pp. 443–44.
13. *Proceedings*, AF of L Convention, 1935, pp. 807–14.
14. *Ibid.*, pp. 815–16.
15. *Ibid.*, pp. 818–19.
16. Taft, *A.F. of L. to Merger* (note 8 *supra*), p. 443.
17. Wolters, *Negroes and Great Depression* (see note 33 for Chapter 12), p. 181.
18. *The Crisis*, June 1935, p. 183.
19. *The CIO: What It Is and How It Came to Be* (Washington, D.C., 1937), pp. 11–12.
20. *Daily Worker*, March 1, 1936.

CHAPTER 16. THE CIO AND THE BLACK WORKER, 1935–39

1. Norfolk *Journal and Guide*, March 31, 1934, and *Opportunity*, April, 1934, pp. 120–21.

2. George S. Schuyler, "Reflections on Negro Leadership," *The Crisis*, November, 1937, p. 328.
3. *Opportunity*, January, 1936, p. 29.
4. *The Crisis*, July, 1936, p. 209.
5. *Ibid.*, August, 1937, p. 246.
6. "New Trade Union Movement of the Negro," *Workers' Council Bulletin* No. 18.
7. Lawrence Wittner, "The National Negro Congress: A Reassessment," *American Quarterly* 22 (Winter, 1970): 891.
8. *Daily Worker*, March 5, 1937.
9. *The Crisis*, September, 1936, pp. 262–63, 276; Cayton and Mitchell, *Black Workers and New Unions* (see note 12 for Chapter 9), pp. 17–42; and Wittner, "National Negro Congress" (note 7 *supra*), p. 892.
10. *Daily Worker*, December 20, 1936.
11. Wittner, "National Negro Congress," p. 893.
12. *Proceedings*, Second Convention, National Negro Congress, 1937, p. 45.
13. *The Crisis*, February, 1938, p. 54.
14. *Daily Worker*, February 8 and 28, 1937.
15. *The Crisis*, July, 1937, p. 209.
16. Wittner, "National Negro Congress" (note 7 *supra*), p. 894.
17. *Proceedings of the First Annual Convention, International Union of United Auto Workers*, 1936, p. 12.
18. Frank Winn, "Labor Tackles the Race Question," *Antioch Review* 3 (Fall, 1943): 346–47.
19. Sidney Fine, *Sit-Down: The General Motors Strike of 1936–1937* (Ann Arbor: University of Michigan Press, 1970), p. 110.
20. Cayton and Mitchell, *Black Workers and New Unions* (see note 12 for Chapter 9), p. 382.
21. *Pittsburgh Courier*, September 2, 1937.
22. *Proceedings of the Second Annual Convention of the International Union, United Automobile Workers of America, August 23 to 29, 1937*, p. 151.
23. Augusta V. Jackson, "A New Deal for Tobacco Workers," *The Crisis*, October, 1938, p. 323.
24. *Constitution of the International Longshoremen's and Warehousemen's Union* (San Francisco, 1951), p. 3.
25. *Dispatcher*, February 15, 1938.
26. *Pilot*, August 20, 1938.
27. *Opportunity*, April, 1940, p. 114.
28. *Proceedings of the First Constitutional Convention of the Congress of Industrial Organizations, Pittsburgh, Pa., November 14–18, 1938*, pp. 110–11.
29. *Ibid.*, pp. 123–24.
30. *The CIO* (see note 19 for Chapter 15), 1941 edition, pp. 57–58.
31. *Proceedings of First Constitutional Convention* (note 28 *supra*), pp. 167–68.
32. *Ibid.*, p. 174.
33. *Ibid.*, pp. 177–79.
34. *Ibid.*, pp. 179–80.
35. *The Crisis*, January, 1939, p. 19.
36. Wilbur J. Cash, *The Mind of the South* (New York, 1941), p. 362.
37. Billy Hall Wyche, "Southern Attitudes Toward Industrial Unions, 1933–1941" (unpublished Ph.D. dissertation, University of Georgia, 1969), pp. 159–69; *New York Times*, March 21, 1936, and October 31, 1937; "The Klan in Florida," *New Republic*, June 9, 1937, p. 118; and David W. Chalmers, *Hooded Americanism: The First Century of the Ku Klux Klan, 1865–1965* (New York: Doubleday, 1965), pp. 320–21.

38. Jackson, "New Deal for Tobacco Workers" (note 23 *supra*), p. 322, and Herbert Northrup, "Tobacco Workers International Union," *Quarterly Journal of Economics* 56 (August, 1942): 643.
39. Edward Aaron Gaston, Jr., "A History of the Negro Earner in Georgia, 1890–1940" (unpublished Ph.D. disssertation, Emory University, 1951), p. 345.
40. *Is Japan the Champion of the Colored Races?*, issued by the Negro Commission, National Committee, Communist Party, U.S.A., August, 1938, pp. 144–45.
41. Pittsburgh *Courier*, January 25, and *Daily Worker*, February 1, 1940.
42. *Daily Worker*, January 28, 1940.
43. *Opportunity*, February, 1939, pp. 318–19.
44. *Daily Worker*, February 17, 1936.
45. *Catering Industry Employee*, December, 1939.
46. *The Crisis*, February, 1938, p. 51.
47. *Ibid.*, September, 1939, p. 273.
48. F. Ray Marshall, *Labor in the South* (Cambridge, Mass.: Harvard University Press, 1967), p. 207.
49. Herbert Hill, "Labor Unions and the Negro," *Commentary*, December, 1959, p. 483.
50. *The Crisis*, November, 1937, p. 333.
51. Quoted in F. Ray Marshall, *The Negro and Organized Labor* (New York: John Wiley, 1965), p. 41.
52. Monroe Sweetland, "The CIO and the Negro American," *Opportunity*, September, 1942, p. 292.
53. Quoted in Robert Friedman, "The Attitudes of West Coast Maritime Unions in Seattle Toward Negroes in the Maritime Industry" (unpublished M.A. thesis, State College of Washington, 1952), p. 63.

CHAPTER 17. WORLD WAR II

1. Howard Sitkoff, "Racial Militancy and Interracial Violence in the Second World War," *Journal of American History* 58 (December, 1971): 665.
2. Gunnar Myrdal, *An American Dilemma* (New York, 1944), p. 475.
3. A. Philip Randolph, "Why I Would Not Stand for Reelection as President of the National Negro Congress," *American Federationist* 48 (July, 1940): 24–25.
4. Herbert Garfinkel, *When Negroes March* (Glencoe, Ill.: Free Press, 1959), p. 85.
5. New York *Amsterdam News*, June 16, 1941.
6. *Ibid.*, June 23, 1941.
7. *New York Times*, June 26, 1941.
8. Garfinkel, *When Negroes March* (note 4 *supra*), p. 60.
9. *Labor and the War: Labor Fact Book 6* (New York, 1943), p. 140.
10. *Daily Worker*, March 12, 1937.
11. Taft, *A.F. of L. to the Merger* (see note 8 for Chapter 15), p. 445.
12. Robert C. Weaver, *Negro Labor—A National Problem* (New York, 1940), p. 105.
13. John H. Jones, "The Steele Case," *Freedom*, October, 1953.
14. *The Crisis*, October, 1949, p. 269.
15. *Phylon* 5 (1944): 159–64.
16. Jones, "Steele Case" (note 13 *supra*).
17. *Bester William Steele v. The Louisville and Nashville Company, Brotherhood of Locomotive Firemen and Engineers*, 65 S.C. Reporter, 228.
18. *Fortune*, June, 1942, p. 73.
19. *The Crisis*, March, 1944, p. 78.
20. *Ibid.*

21. *Ibid.* p. 58.
22. *Proceedings*, AF of L Convention, 1940, pp. 507–10.
23. *Proceedings*, AF of L Convention, 1941, pp. 475–92.
24. *The Crisis*, January, 1942, p. 7.
25. *Proceedings*, AF of L Convention, 1942, p. 321.
26. *Proceedings*, AF of L Convention, 1943, pp. 416–25, 426–45.
27. *Proceedings*, AF of L Convention, 1944, pp. 491–507.
28. Council for Democracy, *The Negro and Defense: A Test of Democracy* (Washington, D.C., 1941), pp. 19–20.
29. Myrdal, *American Dilemma* (note 2 *supra*), p. 402.
30. *The CIO and the Negro Worker: Together for Victory* (Washington, D.C., 1942), pp. 2, 4–7, 11.
31. Louis Emmanuel Martin, "The Ford Contract: An Opportunity," *The Crisis*, September, 1941, p. 285.
32. *The Crisis*, September, 1941, p. 285, and December, 1941, p. 556.
33. *CIO and Negro Worker* (note 30 *supra*), p. 9.
34. CIO Committee to Abolish Racial Discrimination, *Working and Fighting Together: Regardless of Race, Creed, or National Origin* (Washington, D., 1943), pp. 5–7.
35. *Ibid.*, pp. 14–16.
36. United Electrical, Radio, and Machine Workers of America, *Resolutions and Statements* (New York, 1944), pp. 53–54.
37. *CIO and Negro Worker* (note 30 *supra*), pp. 2, 11.
38. *Opportunity*, December 1943, p. 432.
39. Winn, "Labor Tackles Race Problem" (see note 18 for Chapter 16), p. 357.
40. *The Crisis*, January, 1944, p. 8.
41. *Proceedings of the Eighth Constitutional Convention of the International Union of United Automobile, Aircraft, and Agricultural Implement Workers of America*, 1943, pp. 370–91.
42. John Hope II, *Equality of Opportunity* (Washington, D.C., 1956), p. 2.
43. Ferdinand C. Smith, "National Maritime Union Fights Discrimination," *Opportunity*, January, 1943, p. 197.
44. Lucy Randolph Mason, "The CIO and the Negro in the South," *Journal of Negro Education* 14 (1945): 555.
45. *Ibid.*
46. *Freedom*, March, 1951.
47. Mason, "CIO and Negro in South" (note 44 *supra*), p. 557.
48. Henry O. Mayfield, "Memoirs of a Birmingham Coal Miner," *Freedomways*, First Quarter, 1964, p. 54.
49. "Short History—Ad Hoc Committee, United Steel Workers of America," four-page leaflet labeled "Program of National Ad Hoc Committee Conference, July 12, 13, 1969" (copy in author's possession), and Pittsburgh *Courier*, May 30, 1942.
50. Ira N. Brophy, "The Luxury of Anti-Negro Prejudice," *Public Opinion Quarterly*, Winter, 1945–46, pp. 463–64.
51. Reid, *Negro Membership in Labor Unions* (see note 28 for Chapter 12), p. 139.
52. John Jay Holmes, "The CIO and the Negro Worker in the Baltimore Area: A Study of Five CIO Unions" (unpublished M.A. thesis, Howard University, 1946), pp. 119, 121.
53. *CIO News*, November 9, 1942, p. 1.
54. Holmes, "CIO and Negro Worker in Baltimore Area," p. 48.
55. *CIO News*, December 8, 1943, p. 1.
56. James A. Goss, "Negro Labor and the Industrial Department of the Armstrong

Association, the Philadelphia National Urban League" (unpublished M.B.A. thesis, Temple University, 1957) p. 67.

57. *The Crisis*, September, 1944, p. 282.
58. American Council on Race Relations, *Negro Platform Workers* (Chicago, 1944), p. 12.
59. Allan M. Winkler, "The Philadelphia Transit Strike of 1944," *Journal of American History* 59 (July, 1972): 81.
60. Philadelphia *Evening Bulletin*, August 5, 1944.
61. *The Crisis*, September, 1944, p. 280.
62. James S. Olson, "Organized Black Leadership and Industrial Unionism: The Racial Response, 1936–1945," *Labor History*, Summer, 1969, p. 486.

CHAPTER 18. THE ECONOMIC STATUS OF THE
BLACK WORKER, 1945–55

1. Quoted in E. Franklin Frazier, *The Negro in the United States* (New York, 1949), p. 619.
2. Victor Perlo, "Trends in the Economic Status of the Negro People," *Science and Society* 16 (Spring, 1950): 132.
3. *Freedom*, September, 1953.
4. Perlo, "Economic Status of Negro People," pp. 132–34.
5. National Urban League, 'Discrimination in Defense Hiring," news release, New York, February 4, 1952.
6. *Ibid.*
7. U.S. Public Housing Authority, *Public Housing and the Negro* (Washington, D.C., 1941), p. 1.
8. National Negro Congress, *A Petition to the United Nations on Behalf of 13 Million Oppressed Negro Citizens of the United States of America* (New York, 1946), p. 10.
9. James E. Jackson, "Basic Data on the Negro People," *Political Affairs*, January, 1958, p. 61.
10. Quoted in Leo Huberman, "The 'High' American Standard of Living: The Great Capitalist Hoax," *Monthly Review*, October, 1953, p. 238.
11. *Proceedings*, 1953 Convention, United Automobile, Aircraft, and Farm Equipment Workers, p. 31.
12. *Opportunity*, August, 1945, p. 80.
13. Herbert Hill, "Labor Unions and the Negro," *Commentary*, December, 1959, p. 483.
14. Irving Howe and B. J. Widick, *The UAW and Walter Reuther* (New York, 1949), p. 226.

CHAPTER 19. THE COLD WAR WITCH HUNTS AND
THE BLACK WORKER

1. Saul Alinsky, *John L. Lewis: An Unauthorized Biography* (New York, 1949), p. 214.
2. Cayton and Mitchell, *Black Workers and New Unions* (see note 12 for Chapter 9), p. 221.
3. Marshall, *Negro and Organized Labor* (see note 51 for Chapter 16), p. 36.
4. Quoted in Richard O. Boyer and Herbert M. Morais, *Labor's Untold Story* (New York, 1955), p. 326.
5. F. Ray Marshall, "Unions and the Negro Community," *Industrial and Labor Relations Review* 22 (January, 1964): 185.
6. Marshall, *Labor in the South* (see note 48 for Chapter 16), p. 247.
7. *Ibid.*, p. 254.

8. "Labor Drives South," *Fortune*, November, 1946, p. 139.
9. *Proceedings*, CIO Convention, 1940, pp. 111–12, and John Henry Williams, *The Negro Looks at War* (New York, 1940), p. 31.
10. Pittsburgh *Courier*, September 9, 1939.
11. *Daily Worker*, September 16, 1941.
12. Quoted in Harold Orlansky, "The Harlem Riot: A Study in Race Frustration," *Social Analysis—Report No.* 1, p. 4.
13. Frank R. Crosswaith, "Communists and the Negro," leaflet reprinted from article published in *Interracial Review*, November, 1943.
14. Marshall, "Unions and Negro Community" (note 5 *supra*), p. 187n.
15. PM, January 17, 1942.
16. Adam Clayton Powell, Jr., *Marching Blacks* (New York, 1945), p. 69.
17. Marshall, "Unions and Negro Community" (note 5 *supra*), pp. 183–84.
18. Marshall, *Labor in the South* (see note 48 for Chapter 16), p. 249.
19. *Ibid.*, p. 253.
20. *Ibid.*, p. 254.
21. F. Ray Marshall, "Union Racial Problems in the South, *Industrial Relations*, May, 1962, p. 118.
22. New York *Herald Tribune*, January 29 and March 24, 1950, and New York *Compass*, February 1, 1950.
23. *Proceedings*, CIO Convention, 1950, pp. 24–28.
24. *Freedom*, September, 1951.
25. *The Story of Screening* (San Francisco, n.d.), p. 2.
26. *March of Labor*, April, 1952, p. 22.
27. Quoted in *Union Busting: New Model* (San Francisco, 1952), p. 18.
28. Friedman, "Attitude of Maritime Unions in Seattle" (see note 53 'or Chap. 16), p. 181.
29. *The Voice*, May 11, 1951.
30. *Ibid.*, April 20, 1951.
31. Friedman, "Attitude of Maritime Unions in Seattle," p. 155.
32. *Ibid.*, p. 206.
33. Rudolf Sachs, "The Racial Issue as Anti-Union Tool and the National Labor Relations Board" (unpublished M.A. thesis, New School for Social Research), n. c.
34. Marshall, "Unions and Negro Community" (note 5 *supra*), p. 185.
35. Pittsburgh *Courier*, July 9 and 16, 1949.
36. Marshall, "Unions and Negro Community," p. 186.
37. *Proceedings*, United Mine Workers of America Convention, 1948, pp. 134–.
38. Irving Howe and B. J. Widick, "The UAW Fights Race Prejudice," Co mentary, September, 1949, p. 265.
39. Pittsburgh *Courier*, Chcago edition, April 16, 1949.
40. William Kornhauser, "The Negro Union Official: A Study of Sponsorship an. Control," *American Journal of Sociology*, March, 1952, p. 446.
41. William Kornhauser, "Labor Unions and Race Relations: A Study of Unio. Tactics" (unpublished M.A. thesis, University of Chicago, 1950), and Scott Greer, "Situational Pressure and Functional Role of the Ethnic Labor Leader," *Social Forces*, October, 1953, pp. 41–45.
42. Kornhauser, "Negro Union Official" (note 40 *supra*), p. 450.
43. *The Road Ahead*, pamphlet issued by Executive Board, United Packinghouse Workers of America, Chicago, 1953.
44. Marshall, "Unions and Negro Community" (note 5 *supra*), p. 184.
45. Hope, *Equality of Opportunity* (see note 42 for Chapter 17), pp. 2, 120.
46. *Washington Afro-American*, February 18, 1950.
47. Marshall, "Unions and Negro Community," p. 184.

48. Len De Caux, *Labor Radical: From the Wobblies to the CIO* (Boston: Beacon Press, 1970), p. 365.
49. *Labor History*, Summer, 1973, p. 427.

CHAPTER 20. THE NATIONAL NEGRO LABOR COUNCIL, 1951–55

1. *Daily Worker*, June 15, 1950.
2. Paul Robeson, *Forge Negro-Labor Unity for Peace and Jobs* (New York, 1950), p. 15.
3. *Freedom*, August, 1951.
4. Marshall, "Unions and Negro Community" (see note 5 for Chapter 19), p. 186.
5. *Freedom*, November, 1951.
6. Ernest Thompson, "Autobiography" (unpublished manuscript; I am indebted to Mindy Thompson for the opportunity to study the "Autobiography").
7. *Freedom*, November, 1951.
8. *Uncle Tom Is Dead!: Full Text of Address of William R. Hood, Delivered at the Founding Convention of the National Negro Labor Council at Cincinnati, Ohio, October 27, 1951* (Detroit, 1951), and Mindy Thompson, "A History of the National Negro Labor Council, 1951–1956" (unpublished honors paper, Bryn Mawr College, May, 1971), pp. 28–41.
9. Vicki Garvin in *Freedom*, October, 1951; Coleman Young and Jack Burch quoted in Mindy Thompson, "As Valid as Today's Struggles," *Daily World*, January 16, 1971.
10. Foner, ed., *Du Bois Speaks* (see note 33 for Chapter 5), p. 241.
11. House Un-American Activities Committee, *Hearings on Communism in Detroit*, 1:2879–92.
12. Cleveland *Plain Dealer*, November 22 through 24, 1952.
13. *Freedom*, March, 1953.
14. Ernest Thompson, "Autobiography" (note 6 *supra*).
15. *Freedom*, April, 1953.
16. UE Fair Employment Practices Committee, "UE Fights for Women's Rights," New York, 1953.
17. Anti-Discrimination Department, United Packinghouse Workers of America, "Action Against Jim Crow," Chicago, 1952.
18. *Freedom*, October, 1953.
19. *Ibid.*, December, 1952.
20. *Ibid.*, June, 1952.
21. New Orleans *Times-Picayune*, October 27, 1953.
22. *Ibid.*, November 2, 1953.
23. Marshall, *Labor in the South* (see note 48 for Chapter 16), p. 293.
24. *Freedom*, March, 1953.
25. *Ibid.*, October, 1952.
26. *Ibid.*, March, 1953.
27. *Proceedings, Fourteenth Constitutional Convention, United Automobile, Aircraft, and Farm Equipment Workers, CIO, March 20–23, 1953*, p. 264.
28. University Research Corporation, *Communism: A Menace to the American Negro* (Chicago, n.d.), pp. 12–13, and U.S. Congress, House Committee on Un-American Activities, "The American Negro in the Communist Party," Washington, D.C., 1954, pp. 11–12.
29. *Freedom*, September, 1953.
30. *Ibid.*, March, 1955.
31. *Ibid.*
32. *Ibid.*, May–June, 1955.

33. Mindy Thompson, "History of National Negro Labor Council" (note 8 *supra*), pp. 136–40.

CHAPTER 21. THE AFL-CIO AND THE BLACK WORKER: THE FIRST FIVE YEARS

1. *Freedom*, March, 1955.
2. Baltimore *Afro-American*, May 21, 1955.
3. *Proceedings*, CIO Convention, 1955, pp. 305–8.
4. *Freedom*, March, 1955, and "The Only Road to Labor Unity Is Equality and Democracy for All!" NNLC leaflet, 1955.
5. New York *Herald Tribune* and *New York Times*, August 13, 1955.
6. Art Preis, *Labor's Giant Step: Twenty Years of the CIO* (New York: Pathfinder Press, n.d.), p. 518.
7. Arthur J. Goldberg, *AFL-CIO United* (New York, 1956), pp. 147–48.
8. Gus Tyler, "Contemporary Attitudes Toward the Negro," in Jacobsen, ed., *Negro and American Labor Movement* (see note 11 for Chapter 6), pp. 364–65.
9. N. F. Davis, "Trade Unions' Practices and the Negro Worker: The Establishment and Implementation of AFL-CIO Anti-Discrimination Policy" (unpublished Ph.D. dissertation, Indiana University, 1960), p. 61.
10. Shubel Morgan, "The Negro and the Union: A Dialogue," *American Socialist*, July–August, 1958, p. 38.
11. *Daily Worker*, October 4, 1957.
12. Ray Marshall, "Union Racial Problems in the South," *Industrial Relations*, May, 1962, pp. 119–20.
13. *Ibid.*, pp. 121–25.
14. Herbert Hill, "Racism Within Organized Labor: A Report of Five Years of the AFL-CIO," issued by Labor Department of NAACP, New York, 1960, p. 3; and reprinted in *Journal of Negro Education* 30 (Spring, 1961): 109–18.
15. Morgan, "Negro and Union" (note 10 *supra*), p. 58.
16. Marshall, "Union Racial Problems in South" (note ·2 *supra*), p. 128.
17. *American Socialist*, February, 1957, p. 11.
18. Marshall, *Labor in the South* (see note 48 for Chapter 16), p. 336.
19. *Reporter*, May 1, 1958, p. 29.
20. *Daily Worker*, August 12, 1957.
21. *New York Times*, December 19, 1964.
22. *Reporter*, May 1, 1958.
23. *Proceedings*, AFL-CIO Convention, 1955, p. 122.
24. *Daily Worker*, August 14, 1957.
25. *New York Times*, November 18, 1957.
26. Davis, "Unions' Practices and Negro Worker" (note 9 *supra*), p. 84.
27. *Daily Worker*, July 2, 1956.
28. *New York Times*, May 22, 1958, and United Packinghouse Workers of America, *Eleventh Annual Convention, Proceedings, New York City, 1958*, pp. 124–25.
29. Memo from Herbert Hill to Boris Shishkin, December 4, 1958, and Herbert Hill, "The Racial Practices of Organized Labor: The Contemporary Record," in Jacobsen, ed., *Negro and American Labor Movement* (see note 11 for Chapter 6), p. 292.
30. John Kenneth Galbraith, *The Affluent Society* (Boston: Houghton-Mifflin, 1958), pp. 12, 34, 48, 76.
31. "Trade Union Leadership Council: Experiment in Community Action," *New University Thought*, September–October, 1963, pp. 34–35.
32. *Daily Worker*, August 16, 1957.
33. *Proceedings*, AFL-CIO Convention, 1959, pp. 47–48.

34. *Ibid.*, p. 422.
35. *Ibid.*, pp. 429–30.
36. *Ibid.*, p. 488.
37. Marshall, "Unions and Negro Community" (see note 5 for Chapter 19), p. 190.
38. *Ibid.*, p. 191.
39. Arthur M. Ross, "The Negro in the American Economy," in Arthur M. Ross and Robert Hill, eds., *Employment, Race and Poverty* (New York: Harcourt Brace Jovanovich, 1967), p. 8.
40. Davis, "Unions' Practices and Negro Worker" (note 9 *supra*), pp. 201–3.
41. Hill, "Racism Within Organized Labor" (note 14 *supra*), pp. 109–18.

CHAPTER 22. THE NEGRO-LABOR ALLIANCE, 1960–65

1. Tom Kahn, "The 'New Negro' and the New Moderation," *New Politics*, Fall, 1961, pp. 72–73.
2. New York *Herald Tribune*, May 27, 1961.
3. *Commentary*, February, 1960, p. 12.
4. *Ibid.*, March, 1960, p. 8.
5. Interview with TULC officers in *New University Thought*, September–October, 1953, p. 3.
6. *Greater Philadelphia Magazine*, February, 1963.
7. A. Philip Randolph, "The Civil Rights Revolution and Labor," address at the NAACP Convention, New York, July 15, 1959, NAACP Papers, Library of Congress, Manuscripts Division.
8. New Politics, Fall, 1961, p. 67, and Tom Brooks, "Negro Militants, Jewish Liberals, and the Unions," *Commentary*, September, 1961, pp. 209–10.
9. Marshall, "Unions and Negro Community" (see note 5 for Chapter 19), p. 192.
10. U.S. Commission on Civil Rights, *Employment Report 3* (Washington, D.C., 1961), p. 142.
11. Herbert Hill, "Organized Labor and the Negro Wage Earner," *New Politics*, Winter, 1962, p. 17.
12. *New York Times*, October 13, 1961.
13. Hill, "Organized Labor and Negro Wage Earner," p. 18.
14. Hill, "Racial Practices of Organized Labor" (see note 29 for Chapter 21), p. 288n.
15. A. Philip Randolph, "The Struggle for the Liberation of the Black Laboring Masses in This Age of a Revolution of Human Rights," keynote address delivered at second annual convention of NALC, Chicago, November 10–12, 1961.
16. Gene Grove, "Something New in the House of Labor," *Tuesday Magazine*, March, 1970, p. 21.
17. *New America*, November, 1961, p. 12.
18. Brooks, "Negro Militants, Jewish Liberals, and Unions" (note 8 *supra*), pp. 213–14.
19. *American Federationist*, July, 1962.
20. Grove, "Something New" (note 16 *supra*), p. 21.
21. U.S. Commission on Civil Rights, *Employment Report 3* (note 10 *supra*), p. 61.
22. *New York Times*, December 12, 1961.
23. Marshall, "Unions and Negro Community" (see note 5 for Chapter 19), p. 192.
24. *New York Times*, November 12, 1962.
25. Edith Kine, "The Garment Union Comes to the Negro Worker," *Opportunity*, April, 1934, pp. 107–8.
26. Pittsburgh *Courier*, December 12, 19, and 26, 1959, and January 3 and 10, 1960.
27. *Ibid.*, December 17, and *Amsterdam News*, December 19, 1959.

28. Gus Tyler, "The Truth About the ILGWU," *New Politics* 2, No. 1:6–17.
29. Herbert Hill, "The ILGWU Today–The Decay of a Labor Union," *New Politics* 1, No. 4:6–17, and *idem*, "The ILGWU–Fact and Fiction: A Reply to Gus Tyler," *New Politics* 2, No. 2:7–27.
30. Hill, "ILGWU–Fact and Fiction," p. 27.
31. *Labor History*, Summer, 1968, pp. 63–64.
32. Randolph, "Struggle for Liberation" (note 15 *supra*).
33. *New York Times*, November 12, 1962.
34. *Ibid.*, October 17, 1962.
35. *Ibid.*, November 12, 1962.
36. *Ibid.*, May 30; June 22, 23, and 30; and July 3, 1963.
37. *The Hilltop*, Howard University, April 26, 1963.
38. Herbert Hill, "The Economic Status of the Negro," *Freedomways*, Spring, 1963, p. 158.
39. *New York Times*, April 13, 1964.
40. Hill, "Racial Practices of Organized Labor" (see note 29 for Chapter 21), p. 310.
41. *The Hilltop*, Howard University, April 26, 1963.
42. *New York Times*, August 12, 1963.
43. *New York Post*, August 12, 1963.
44. *Daily Worker*, June 21, 1964.
45. Albert P. Blaustein and Robert L. Zagrando, eds., *Civil Rights and the American Negro: A Documentary History* (New York: Simon & Schuster, 1968), pp. 537–40.
46. Harold Baron, Negro Unemployment: A Case Study," *New University Thought*, October, 1963, p. 46.
47. *Proceedings*, AFL-CIO Convention, 1963, pp. 192–93.
48. *Daily Worker*, May 19, 1964.
49. *Ibid.*, June 7, 1964.
50. *Ibid.*, March 16 and April 18, 1965.
51. Blaustein and Zagrando, eds., *Civil Rights and American Negro* (note 45 *supra*), p. 566.
52. *Daily Worker*, March 20, 1965.

CHAPTER 23. THE NEGRO-LABOR ALLIANCE, 1965-68

1. Malcolm X, *The Autobiography of Malcolm X*, edited by Alex Haley (New York: Grove Press, 1965), pp. 223–25, and George Breitman, ed., *Malcolm X Speaks: Selected Speeches and Statements* (New York: Grove Press, 1965), pp. 13–16.
2. *New York Times*, February 24, 1965.
3. *Ibid.*, August 25, 1965.
4. *1199 Drug & Hospital News*, "We Remember Martin Luther King, Jr.: A Commemorative Issue," May, 1968.
5. A. H. Raskin, "A Union with 'Soul,'" *New York Times Magazine*, March 22, 1970.
6. *Ibid.*
7. *1199 Drug & Hospital News*, November, 1964; RDWSU *Record*, October 18, 1964; and Victor Riesel, "Hospital Union in Move Across the Nation," New York *Journal-American*, November 14, 1964.
8. *The Worker*, December 22, 1964.
9. *New York Times*, May 29, and *The Worker*, June 6, 1965.
10. Negro American Labor Council, Chicago Chapter, "The Other Chicago: The City's Employed Poor," Chicago, 1966.
11. Chicago *Sun-Times*, February 24, and *The Worker*, February 27, 1966.

12. Chicago *Sun-Times*, March 8, 1966.
13. *Ibid.*, July 16, and *The Worker*, July 17, 1966.
14. Mike Royko, *Boss: Richard J. Daley of Chicago* (New York: Dutton, 1971), pp. 274–76.
15. David L. Lewis, *King: A Critical Biography* (New York: Praeger, 1970), p. 351.
16. *The Worker*, June 15, 1965.
17. *Ibid.*, January 12, 1966.
18. *Ibid.*, June 5, 1966.
19. *Ibid.*, July 14, 1964.
20. *New York Times*, September 3, 1964.
21. *Ibid.*
22. George Morris in *The Worker*, July 12, 1964.
23. *New York Herald Tribune*, August 25, 1964.
24. *The Worker*, July 17, 1966.
25. *New York Times*, December 13, 1964.
26. *The Worker*, July 17, 1966.
27. *Christian Science Monitor*, March 4, 1968.
28. *Proceedings*, AFL-CIO Convention, 1965, pp. 65, 112–16.
29. *The Worker*, June 5, 1966.
30. *Ibid.*, June 11, 1967.
31. *Ibid.*, June 11 and 25, 1967.
32. *1199 Drug & Hospital News*, July, 1967, and *The Worker*, June 20, 1967.
33. B. J. Widick, "Motown Blues," *The Nation*, August 14, 1967, p. 103.
34. Detroit *Free Press*, July 28, and *The Worker*, August 1, 1967.
35. "If Not Now . . . When?" Pamphlet of Amalgamated Meat Cutters and Butcher Workmen of North America, AFL-CIO (undated).
36. *New York Times*, November 3, 1967.
37. *Ibid.*, September 27, 1967.
38. Chicago *Sun-Times*, February 14, 1965.
39. *New York Times*, December 30, 1966.
40. Philip S. Foner, *American Labor and the Indochina War: The Growth of Union Opposition* (New York: International Publishers, 1971), p. 7.
41. *The Worker*, June 2, 1968.

CHAPTER 24. MEMPHIS AND CHARLESTON: TRIUMPH OF THE NEGRO-LABOR ALLIANCE

1. Fred Lacey, "Union Battle Won in Memphis," *The Movement*, June, 1968, p. 9.
2. Memphis *Press Scimitar*, February 13, 1968.
3. *Ibid.*, February 15, and Memphis *Commercial Appeal*, February 17, 1968.
4. *The Worker*, March 3, 1968.
5. *Ibid.*, March 10, 1968.
6. Lacey, "Battle Won in Memphis" (note 1 *supra*), p. 14.
7. Southern Regional Council, "In Memphis: More than a Garbage Strike," Atlanta, 1968.
8. *New York Times*, April 17, 1968.
9. *The Worker*, April 21, and Memphis *Press Scimitar*, April 22, 1968.
10. *The Worker*, June 16 and 23, 1968.
11. *1199 Drug & Hospital News*, April, 1969.
12. *New York Times*, April 18, 1969.
13. Quoted in Arthur Elias, "The Charleston Strike," *New Politics* 8 (Summer, 1969): 22.

14. Charleston *News & Courier*, April 26, 1969.
15. Speech of Mrs. Coretta Scott King at dinner honoring A. Philip Randolph, New York, May 8, 1969 (copy in Local 1199 archives).
16. *1199 Drug & Hospital News*, May, 1969.
17. *Daily World*, April 25, 1969.
18. J. H. Odell, "Charleston's Legacy to the Poor People's Campaign," *Freedomways*, Fall, 1969, p. 208.
19. *Daily World*, April 22, 1969.
20. Mrs. King's speech at Randolph dinner (note 15 *supra*).
21. Odell, "Charleston's Legacy" (note 18 *supra*), p. 208.
22. Leon Panetta and Peter Gall, *Bring Us Together: The Nixon Team and the Civil Rights Retreat* (Philadelphia: Lippincott, 1971), p. 141.
23. *Ibid.*, p. 142.
24. *1199 Drug & Hospital News*, June 1969.
25. Panetta and Gall, *Bring Us Together*, p. 144.
26. *Ibid.*, p. 145.
27. Odell, "Charleston's Legacy" (note 18 *supra*), p. 209.
28. Panetta and Gall, *Bring Us Together*, p. 146.
29. *Wall Street Journal*, March 3, 1970.
30. Charleston *News & Courier*, July 19, 1968.
31. *Proceedings*, AFL-CIO Convention, 1969, pp. 232–35, and *Daily World*, October 7, 1969.
32. *Daily World*, July 12, 1969.

CHAPTER 25. BLACK POWER IN THE UNIONS

1. *Christian Science Monitor*, July 9, 1968.
2. William B. Gould, "Labor Arbitration of Grievances Involving Racial Discrimination," *University of Pennsylvania Law Review* 40 (1969): 118.
3. "Youth in the Ghetto: A Study of the Consequences of Powerlessness," HARYOU-ACT, New York, 1964, pp. 78–79.
4. B. J. Widick, "Minority Power Through the Unions," *The Nation*, September 8, 1969, p. 204.
5. *Tuesday Magazine*, March, 1970, p. 21.
6. *The Black Scholar*, October, 1970, p. 37.
7. *New York Times*, July 2, 1968.
8. Noel Ignatin, "Wildcats in Chicago," *The Movement*, September, 1968, p. 6.
9. *Daily World*, August 24, 1968.
10. Ignatin, "Wildcats in Chicago," p. 6.
11. *Daily World*, July 16, 1968.
12. John Herling, *The Right to Challenge: People and Power in the Steelworkers Union* (New York: Harper & Row, 1972), p. 266.
13. *Daily World*, June 16 and August 22, 1968.
14. Quoted in Herbert Hill, "Black Dissent in Organized Labor," in Joseph Boskin and Robert A. Rosenstone, eds., *Seasons of Rebellion: Protest and Radicalism in Recent America* (New York: Free Press, 1972), p. 61.
15. Brooks, "Negro Militants, Jewish Liberals, and Unions" (see note 8 for Chapter 22), pp. 126–27; Widick, "Minority Power" (note 4 *supra*), p. 205; *Daily World*, August 24 and 27; and Herling, *Right to Challenge* (note 12 *supra*), pp. 357–59.
16. Interview with Fletcher, president of United Community Construction Workers, in *Black Panther*, May 22, 1971, pp. 2–3, and "Manifesto, Black Construction Workers" (copy in author's possession).

17. "History of Racism in Construction Unions," two-page leaflet of United Community Construction Workers of Boston (copy in author's possession).
18. "Our Thing Is DRUM," *Leviathan*, June 1970, p. 9.
19. *New York Times*, December 30, 1966.
20. Letter from Herbert Hill in *New York Times Magazine*, October 11, 1970.
21. *New York Times*, April 26, 1967.
22. *Daily World*, May 7, 1968.
23. "Black Editor: An Interview," *Radical America*, July–August, 1968, p. 31.
24. "Our Thing Is DRUM" (note 18 supra), p. 9.
25. *Ibid.*, p. 6.
26. Robert Rudnick, "Black Workers in Revolt," A Guardian pamphlet, New York, 1969, p. 5.
27. *New York Times*, September 22, 1968.
28. Quoted in Thomas R. Brooks, "DRUMbeats in Detroit," *Dissent*, January–February, 1970, p. 21.
29. *New York Times*, October 1, 1968.
30. *Ibid.*
31. *Daily World*, October 3, 1968.
32. Brooks, "DRUMbeats in Detroit" (note 28 supra), pp. 18n, 20.
33. *Ibid.*, p. 20.
34. Four-page leaflet issued by League of Revolutionary Black Workers (copy in author's possession).
35. Brooks, "DRUMbeats in Detroit," pp. 23–24.
36. *Michigan Chronicle*, January 15, 1968.
37. *Daily World*, March 20, 1969.
38. *Ibid.*, April 10, 1969.
39. *Detroit Free Press*, March 21, 1969.
40. *Wall Street Journal*, February 16 and March 3, 1970.
41. "Our Thing Is DRUM" (note 18 supra), p. 34.
42. Quoted in Charles Denby, "Black Caucuses in the Union," *New Politics* 7 (Summer, 1968): 14.
43. Quoted in *Ibid.*, p. 15.
44. *Ibid.*, pp. 12–13.
45. *Labor Today* 9 (July–September, 1970): 28–29.

CHAPTER 26: THE BLACK WORKER 1970–1981

1. Bayard Rustin, "The Blacks and Unions," *Harper's Magazine*, May, 1971, p. 76.
2. *American Sociological Review*, June, 1970, p. 32.
3. Lester Thurow, "Not Making It in America: The Economic Progress of Minority Groups," *Social Policy*, March-April, 1976, pp. 5–8.
4. Among these studies the most interesting are the volumes published by the University of Pennsylvania Press under the direction of Herbert R. Northrup and Richard L. Rowan and carrying the general title, *The Racial Policies of American Industry*. In all, thirty-two volumes will be published.
5. Carl Bloice, "The Future of Black Workers Under American Capitalism," *Black Scholar*, May, 1972, pp. 14–16.
6. *New York Times*, December 5, 1972; *Census of the Population: 1970 General Population Characteristics, U.S. Summary*, Washington, D.C., 1973.
7. *New York Times*, April 8, 1977.
8. *Ibid.*, September 18, 1977.
9. *Wall Street Journal*, November 15, 1976. William Wilson, *The Declining Significance of Race: Blacks and Changing Institutions*, Chicago, 1978, p. 150.
10. *AFL–CIO American Federationist*, May, 1977, p. 6.
11. *New York Times*, January 18, 1976.
12. *Ibid.*, August 3, 1976.
13. *Philadelphia Sunday Bulletin*, February 23, 1975; "The American Underclass:

Destitute and Desperate in the Land of Plenty," *Time*, August 29, 1977, pp. 14-27.

14. *New York Times*, July 12, 1976.
15. *Last Hired First Fired—Layoffs and Civil Rights*. A Report of the United States Commission on Civil Rights, February, 1977, p. 61. For a brief but excellent analysis of seniority and its relations to the freezing of racial status quo, see Herbert Hill, "The Equal Employment Opportunity Acts of 1964 and 1972: A Critical Analysis of the Legislative History and Administration of the Law," *Industrial Relations Law Review*, Vol. II, Spring, 1977, pp. 18-24.
16. *New York Times*, January 15, 16, 1973.
17. *Ibid.*, January 17, 1973.
18. *Ibid.*, February 10, 1973.
19. *Dissent*, pp. 397-424.
20. *Labor Today*, September, 1972.
21. *Ibid.*; *Daily World*, September 12, 23, 26, 1972; *New York Times*, October 3, 1972; and Stanley Plastrik, "Coalition of Black Trade Unionists," *Dissent*, Winter, 1972, p. 12; Conference Report, Coalition of Black Trade Unionists, Chicago, Illinois, September 13–14, 1972, pamphlet.
22. "Letter to the Editor," *New York Times*, October 20, 1972.
23. Plastrik, "Coalition of Black Trade Unionists," p. 13.
24. *Labor Today*, May, 1973.
25. *Daily World*, June 1–4, 1973.
26. *New York Times*, October 3, 1972. See also William Lucy, "The Black Partners," *Nation*, September 7, 1974, p. 180.
27. William B. Gould, *Black Workers in White Unions: Job Discrimination In the United States* (Ithaca, N.Y., 1977), pp. 15, 19.
28. Proceedings, AFL–CIO Convention, 1973, p. 242; *New York Times*, March 25, 1976; Gould, *op cit.*, p. 424.
29. *New York Times*, March 25, 1976.
30. *Ibid.*, June 2, 1977.
31. *New York Times*, April 3, 1975.
32. *Ibid.*, April 27-29, 1975.
33. *Wall Street Journal*, May 3, 1977.
34. *New York Times*, August 30, 31, September 5, 1977.
35. *AFL–CIO News*, January 27, 1978.
36. Ken Bode, "Unions Divided," *New Republic*, October 15, 1977, p. 20.
37. *AFL–CIO News*, January 27, 1978.
38. *New York Times*, January 13, 1979; Philip S. Foner, *Women and the American Labor Movement* (New York, 1980), pp. 490, 543–45; William H. Harris, *The Harder We Run* (New York, 1982), p. 187.
39. *AFL–CIO News*, June 30, 1979.
40. *Ibid.*
41. Albert Szymanski, "Race Discrimination and White Gains," *American Sociological Review*, Vol. LXI, June 1976, pp. 403–13.
42. *Daily World*, February 5, 1981.
43. *Ibid.*, July 1, 1981.
44. *AFL–CIO News*, November 28, 1981.

Selected Bibliography

BOOKS DEALING SPECIFICALLY WITH ORGANIZED
LABOR AND THE BLACK WORKER

Anderson, Jervis. A. Philip Randolph: A Biographical Portrait. New York, 1973.

Brazeal, Brailsford R. The Brotherhood of Sleeping Car Porters. New York, 1946.

Cantor, Milton, ed. Black Labor in America. Westport, Conn., 1969.

Cayton, Horace R., and George S. Mitchell. The Negro Worker and the New Unions. Chapel Hill, N.C., 1939.

Du Bois, W. E. B. The Negro Artisan. Atlanta, 1902.

Franklin, Charles H. Negro Labor Unionist of New York. New York, 1936.

Hope, John, II. Equality of Opportunity: A Union Approach to Fair Employment. Washington, D.C., 1956.

Jacobson, Julius, ed. The Negro and the American Labor Movement. New York, 1968.

Mandel, Bernard. Labor: Free and Slave. New York, 1955.

Marshall, F. Ray. The Negro and Organized Labor. New York, 1965.

Northrup, Herbert R. Organized Labor and the Negro. New York, 1944.

Reid, Ira DeA. Negro Membership in American Labor Unions. New York, 1930.

Ross, Arthur M., and Herbert Hill, eds. Employment, Race, and Poverty, New York, 1967.

Ruchames, Louis. Race, Jobs and Politics: The Story of FEPC. New York, 1953.

Rudwick, Elliot M. Race Riot at East St. Louis. Carbondale, Ill., 1964.

Schleuter, Hermann. Lincoln, Labor and Slavery. New York, 1913.

Spero, Sterling D., and Abram L. Harris. The Black Worker. New York, 1931.

Weaver, Robert C. Negro Labor: A National Problem. New York, 1946.

Wesley, Charles H. Negro Labor in the United States, 1850–1925. New York, 1927.

BOOKS DEALING WITH ORGANIZED LABOR
AND THE BLACK WORKER IN OTHER CONTEXTS

Angle, Paul. Bloody Williamson: A Chapter in American Lawlessness. New York, 1952.

Aptheker, Herbert, ed. A Documentary History of the Negro People in the United States. New York, 1951, New York, 1973.

Barnes, Charles B. *The Longshoremen*. New York, 1915.
Bernstein, Irving. *The Lean Years: A History of the American Worker, 1920–1933*. Los Angeles, 1960.
Brody, David. *Steel Workers in America: The Non-Union Era*. Cambridge, Mass., 1960.
Cochran, Bert, ed. *American Labor in Midpassage*. New York, 1959.
Commons, John R., and Associates. *History of Labor in the United States*, vols. I-II. New York, 1918.
Derber, Milton, and Edwin Young, eds. *Labor and the New Deal*. New York, 1957.
Du Bois, W. E. B. *Black Reconstruction in America*. New York, 1935.
————. *Economic Co-operation Among Negro Americans*. Atlanta, 1907.
————. *The Philadelphia Negro*. Philadelphia, 1899.
Ernst, Robert. *Immigrant Life in New York City, 1825–1863*. New York, 1949.
Fitzhugh, George. *Cannibals All: or Slaves Without Masters*. Richmond, 1857.
Foner, Philip S. *History of the Labor Movement in the United States*, vols. I–IV. New York: 1947–65.
Foner, Philip S., ed. *The Autobiographies of the Haymarket Martyrs*. New York, 1969.
Fortune, T. Thomas. *Black and White: Land and Labor in the South*. New York, 1884.
Foster, William Z. *The Negro People in American History*. New York, 1954.
Galeson, Walter. *The CIO Challenge to the AFL: A History of the American Labor Movement, 1935–1941*. New York, 1960.
Ginger, Ray. *The Bending Cross: A Biography of Eugene V. Debs*. New Brunswick, N.J., 1949.
Grob, Gerald N. *Workers and Utopia: A Study of the Ideological Conflict in the American Labor Movement, 1865–1900*. New York, 1960.
Grossman, Jonathan. *William Sylvis, Pioneer of American Labor*. New York, 1945.
Harrington, Michael. *The Other America*. New York, 1963.
Herreshoff, David. *American Disciples of Marx: From the Age of Jackson to the Progessive Era*. Detroit, Mich., 1967.
Kipnis, Ira. *American Socialist Movement, 1897–1912*. New York, 1952.
Litwack, Leon F. *North of Slavery: The Negro in the Free States, 1790–1860*. Chicago, 1961.
Logan, Rayford W. *The Negro in American Life and Thought: The Nadir, 1877–1901*. New York, 1954.
Mandel, Bernard. *Samuel Gompers*. Yellow Springs, Ohio, 1963.
Marshall, F. Ray. *Labor in the South*. Cambridge, Mass., 1967.
Mason, Lucy. *To Win These Rights*. New York, 1952.
Meier, August. *Negro Thought in America, 1880–1915: Racial Ideologies in the Age of Booker T. Washington*. Ann Arbor, Mich., 1963.
Minton, Bruce, and John Stuart. *The Fat Years and the Lean*. New York, 1940.
Montgomery, David. *Beyond Equality: Labor and the Radical Republicans, 1862–1872*. New York, 1967.
Morris, James O. *Conflict Within the A.F. L.: A Study of Craft Versus Industrial Unionism*. Ithaca, N.Y., 1958.

Morgan, H. Wayne, ed. *American Socialism, 1900–1960.* Englewood Cliffs, N.J., 1964.
Oberman, Karl. *Joseph Weydemeyer, Pioneer of American Socialism.* New York, 1947.
Osofsky, Gilbert. *Harlem: The Making of a Ghetto.* New York, 1963.
Ovington, Mary White. *Half a Man: The Negro in New York.* New York, 1910.
Perlman, Selig, and Philip Taft. *History of Labor in the United States* (vol. III of John F. Commons and Associates, above). New York, 1935.
Preis, Art. *Labor's Giant Step: Twenty Years of the CIO.* New York, 1964.
Rayback, Joseph G. *A History of American Labor.* New York, 1966.
Shannon, David A. *The Socialist Party of America: A History.* New York, 1955.
Scheiner, Seth M. *Negro Mecca: A History of the Negro in New York City, 1865–1920.* New York, 1965.
Shugg, Roger W. *Origins of Class Struggle in Louisiana.* Baton Rouge, La., 1939.
Taft, Philip. *The A.F. of L. from the Death of Gompers to the Merger.* New York, 1959.
———. *The A. F. of L. in the Time of Gompers.* New York, 1957.
———. *Organized Labor in American History.* New York, 1964.
Ward, Robert D., and William W. Rogers. *Labor Revolt in Alabama. The Great Strike of 1894.* University of Alabama, 1965.
Washington, Booker T. *The Future of the American Negro.* Boston, 1899.
———. *My Larger Education.* New York, 1911.
Wolfe, Frank E. *Admission to American Trade Unions.* Baltimore, 1912.
Wood, Forrest G. *Black Scare: The Racist Response to Emancipation and Reconstruction.* Berkeley, Calif., 1968.
Wright, Richard R., Jr. *The Negro in Pennsylvania.* Philadelphia, 1911.

ARTICLES

Baron, Harold. "Negro Unemployment," *New University Thought,* October, 1963.
Bloch, Herman D. "Craft Unions and the Negro in Historical Perspective," *Journal of Negro History,* January, 1958.
———. "Craft Unions as a Link in the Circle of Negro Discrimination," *Phylon,* Fourth Quarter, 1958.
———. "Labor and the Negro, 1866–1910," *Journal of Negro History,* July, 1965.
Foner, Philip S. "The IWW and the Black Worker," *Journal of Negro History,* Spring, 1970.
———. "The Knights of Labor," *Journal of Negro History,* Spring, 1968.
Ginger, Ray. "Were Negroes Strikebreakers?" *Negro History Bulletin,* January, 1952.
Gutman, Herbert. "Peter H. Clark, Pioneer Negro Socialist, 1877," *Journal of Negro Education.* Fall, 1965.
Haynes, George E. "The Opportunity of Negro Labor," *Crisis,* September, 1919.
Henderson, Donald. "The Negro Migration of 1916–1918," *Journal of Negro History,* October, 1921.

Hicken, Victor. "The Virden and Pana Wars," *Journal of the Illinois State Historical Society*, Spring, 1959.

Hill, Herbert. "In the Age of Gompers and After, Racial Practices of Organized Labor," *New Politics*, Spring, 1965.

————. "Labor and Segregation," *New Leader*, October 19, 1959.

————. "Labor Unions and the Negro," *Commentary*, December, 1959.

————. "Patterns of Employment Discrimination," *Crisis*, March, 1962.

————. "Racial Inequality in Employment: The Patterns of Discrimination," *Annals of the American Academy of Political and Social Science*, January, 1965.

————. "Racism Within Organized Labor: A Report of Five Years of the AFL-CIO," *Journal of Negro Education*, Spring, 1961.

Houston, Charles H. "The Elimination of Negro Firemen on the American Railways," *Lawyers Guild Review*, Spring, 1944.

————. "Foul Employment Practices on the Rails," *Crisis*, October, 1949.

Kessler, Sidney. "The Organization of Negroes in the Knights of Labor," *Journal of Negro History*, July, 1952.

Levine, Daniel. "Gompers and Racism: A Strategy of Limited Objectives," *Mid-America*, April, 1961.

Lofton, Willston H. "Northern Labor and the Negro During the Civil War," *Journal of Negro History*, July, 1948.

Mandel, Bernard. "Samuel Gompers and the Negro workers, 1886–1914," *Journal of Negro History*, January, 1955.

Mann, Albon J., Jr. "Labor Competition and the New York Draft Riots of 1863," *Journal of Negro History*, October, 1951.

Marshall, F. Ray. "Union Racial Problems in the South," *Industrial Relations*, May, 1962.

————. "Unions and the Negro Community," *Industrial and Labor Relations Review*, January, 1964.

Matison, Sumner P. "The Labor Movement and the Negro During Reconstruction," *Journal of Negro History*, Spring, 1948.

Mitchell, George. "The Negro in Southern Trade Unionism," *Southern Economic Journal*, January, 1936.

Morris, Richard B. "Labor Militancy in the Old South," *Labor and the Nation*, May–June, 1948.

Northrup, Herbert R. "The Negro and the United Mine Workers of America," *Southern Economic Journal*, April, 1943.

————. "Organized Labor and the Negro Workers," *Journal of Political Economy*, June, 1943.

Ovington, Mary White. "The Negro in the Trade Unions in New York," *Annals of the American Academy of Political and Social Science*, June, 1906.

Slaiman, Donald. "Discrimination and Low Incomes," *American Federationist*, January, 1961.

Washington, Booker T. "The Negro and the Labor Unions," *Atlantic Monthly*, June, 1913.

Index

A. Philip Randolph Institute, 370–71,
381, 431, 434
Aaron, Benjamin, 246
Abel, I. W., 366, 405, 406, 407
Abernathy, Ralph, 385, 386, 391, 393,
394, 395
Abrams, Charles, 272
"Action Against Jim Crow," 305
Actors' Equity Association, 397
Ad Hoc Committee of Concerned Auto
Workers, 416–17, 420
Adger, Robert M., 24
Advance, 157
Affluent Society, The, 326–27, 347
AFL-CIO Council (Memphis), 380
AFL-CIO News, 321
Africa, 32, 63, 67
African Blood Brotherhood, 148–49, 162
African Methodist Episcopal Church,
113, 267, 389
Africans, 3–4
Afro-American Labor and Protective
Association of Birmingham, 77
Agricultural Adjustment Act (AAA),
207n.
Alabama, 96, 120
Alabama Labor Union, 43–44n.
Alabama State Federation of Labor, 88,
218
Alderman, Sidney, 245
Alinsky, Saul, 275
Allen, Robert, 118
Alliance for Labor Action (ALA), 377,
402
Allied Committees for National Defense,
239
Allied Industrial Workers, 328
Amalgamated Association of Iron, Steel,
and Tin Workers, 218
Amalgamated Clothing Workers, 157,
162, 212, 264, 295, 300, 336, 375
Amalgamated Meat Cutters and Butcher
Workmen of North America, 85–86,
142, 234, 363, 396

Amalgamated Street Car Workers Union,
266–67
Amalgamated Transit Union, 402
American Anti-Slavery Society, 40
American Civil Liberties Union, 193
American Communications Association,
283
American Dilemma, An, 238–39, 273
American Federation of Express Workers,
155n.
American Federation of Labor (AF of L):
abandons early progressive approach to
black workers, 70-81; accused of being
reactionary, 150; accused of racist discrimination against blacks, 108; affiliates cooperate with Klan, 230; anti-
Negro practices during World War II,
252; appeals to blacks in South, 281;
attitude toward black workers blamed
for East Saint Louis riot, 139; black
membership, 102, 127; black spokesmen fear will dominate under New
Deal, 202; black-white unity in, 80–
81; calls on affiliates to report on color
bar, 236; champions craft unionism,
92-93; committee to investigate conditions of black workers, 206-7; Communists fight Jim Crow unionism in,
203; cooperates with government in
anti-Communist hysteria, 284-85; craft
unionism in, 82; craft union outlook
adversely affects black workers, 92-93;
debates at conventions on anti-Negro
practices, 248-52; defended on record
toward black workers, 175; discriminatory practices defended, 101; discriminatory record during World War II,
246-52; dispute with United Brewery
Workers, 92-93; Du Bois attacks on
record toward black workers, 175-76;
during World War I, 136-43; early
progressive attitude toward black workers, 64-70; employs racism in combating CIO, 235; exclusion of blacks from,

About Haymarket Books

Haymarket Books is a radical, independent, nonprofit book publisher based in Chicago.

Our mission is to publish books that contribute to struggles for social and economic justice. We strive to make our books a vibrant and organic part of social movements and the education and development of a critical, engaged, international left.

We take inspiration and courage from our namesakes, the Haymarket martyrs, who gave their lives fighting for a better world. Their 1886 struggle for the eight-hour day—which gave us May Day, the international workers' holiday—reminds workers around the world that ordinary people can organize and struggle for their own liberation. These struggles continue today across the globe—struggles against oppression, exploitation, poverty, and war.

Since our founding in 2001, Haymarket Books has published more than five hundred titles. Radically independent, we seek to drive a wedge into the risk-averse world of corporate book publishing. Our authors include Noam Chomsky, Arundhati Roy, Rebecca Solnit, Angela Y. Davis, Howard Zinn, Amy Goodman, Wallace Shawn, Mike Davis, Winona LaDuke, Ilan Pappé, Richard Wolff, Dave Zirin, Keeanga-Yamahtta Taylor, Nick Turse, Dahr Jamail, David Barsamian, Elizabeth Laird, Amira Hass, Mark Steel, Avi Lewis, Naomi Klein, and Neil Davidson. We are also the trade publishers of the acclaimed Historical Materialism Book Series and of Dispatch Books.

Also Available from Haymarket Books

Black Panthers Speak
Edited by Philip S. Foner
Introduction by Clayborne Carson
Foreword by Barbara Ransby

The Letters of Joe Hill
Centenary Edition
by Joe Hill
Edited by Alexis Buss and Philip S. Foner
Foreword by Tom Morello

CPSIA information can be obtained
at www.ICGtesting.com
Printed in the USA
JSHW040200280822
29804JS00004B/1